# CLASSICS IN PSYCHOLOGY

# CLASSICS IN PSYCHOLOGY

## A NOTE ABOUT EDWARD L. THORNDIKE

EDWARD L. THORNDIKE, America's most productive psychologist, was born in Williamsburg, Massachusetts, in 1874. He studied several disciplines during his undergraduate years at Wesleyan, then became interested in psychology as a student of William James' at Harvard. He received his Ph. D. under James Cattell at Columbia. His doctoral dissertation, *Animal Intelligence* (1898) was published and immediately became one of the most important works in all of psychology.

Thorndike achieved eminence at an early age and remained an important figure in American scientific circles until his death in 1949. His work did much to give psychology its behavioral and functional cast during the early years of the century. Even his critics agreed that any discussion of education and learning had to come to grips with Thorndike's contributions. During the last years of his life, while still at Columbia, he became involved in studies of the place of social science in American society which culminated in *Human Nature and the Social Order,* published in 1940.

# THE MEASUREMENT OF INTELLIGENCE

By

EDWARD L. THORNDIKE, E. O. BREGMAN, M. V. COBB,
ELLA WOODYARD, and the Staff of the Division of Psychology of the Institute of Educational Research of Teachers College, Columbia University

**ARNO PRESS**
A New York Times Company
New York ★ 1973

Reprint Edition 1973 by Arno Press Inc.

Reprinted from a copy in
The University of Illinois Library

Classics in Psychology
ISBN for complete set: 0-405-05130-1
See last pages of this volume for titles.

Manufactured in the United States of America

————◆————

**Library of Congress Cataloging in Publication Data**

Thorndike, Edward Lee, 1874-1949.
    The measurement of intelligence.

    (Classics in psychology)
    Reprint of the ed. published by Bureau of Publica-
tions, Teachers College, Columbia University, New York.
    Bibliography: p.
    1. Mental tests.    I. Title.    II. Series.
[DNLM:    BF431 M484 1927F]
BF431.T45  1973              153.9'3              73-2993
ISBN 0-405-05165-4

# THE MEASUREMENT OF INTELLIGENCE

# THE MEASUREMENT OF INTELLIGENCE

By

EDWARD L. THORNDIKE, E. O. BREGMAN, M. V. COBB,
ELLA WOODYARD, and the Staff of the Division of Psychology of the Institute of Educational Research of Teachers College, Columbia University

The investigations and results reported
in this volume were made possible by
a grant from the Carnegie Corporation

Bureau of Publications
TEACHERS COLLEGE, COLUMBIA UNIVERSITY
NEW YORK

# PREFACE

This volume represents the fruits of three years of investigation (from July 1, 1922, to July 1, 1925) by the Division of Psychology of the Institute of Educational Research. It attempts to answer the essential questions concerning the nature and meaning of the measurement of a mental fact in the sample case of intelligence, or rather of a defined segment thereof. Its conclusions, in so far as they are warranted, should become the basis of sound practice in the construction and calibration of scales for use in mental measurement. According to them, the present theory and practice of measurement of mental abilities are justified to a remarkable degree in certain respects, but in others should be almost recreated.

Some of the most important of these conclusions were reached only in the last six months of the inquiry and are consequently presented with less adequate evidential support than is desirable. The concept of area of intellect in particular needs more experimentation to make it clear, and still more to demonstrate its soundness and worth.

We had intended to add a long chapter reviewing the literature on the topics dealt with in this volume, but it seemed more important to exemplify and apply the results of our conclusions in a concrete series of tasks selected and scaled according to the principles described; and there was not time to do both. We hope to be able to publish such a review later, and in particular to do justice to the notable contribution of Kelley ('23a), which deserves most careful study by everyone who is concerned with the general logic of mental measurements.

We had intended also to include full treatment of the method of obtaining a group of approximately known forms of distribution in respect of a mental trait measured in truly equal units, by taking the members of an array in that trait who have identical scores in a second trait correlated with the trait in question. This method was abandoned in favor of a better one, but nearly a third of our time and effort was spent in exploring its possibilities. The results should be made known, both because of their intrinsic interest, and because otherwise someone will surely be tempted to do again what has already been done by us. The material is, however, highly technical and elaborate; and it seemed best not to include it in this volume.

The general responsibility for the work rests upon the senior author, who planned and directed the various inquiries, organized the results, and wrote this book, with the exception of Appendix III. It would, however, have been utterly impossible for him to have carried the work through without the financial assistance of the Carnegie Corporation and the Trustees of Teachers College, and without the loyal cooperation of the staff of the Division of Psychology of the Institute of Educational Research, and many scientific workers in all parts of the country. Dr. Bregman collected and organized most of the facts which are used in Chapter VII and Appendix III, and some of those used in Chapter VIII. Miss Cobb devised many of the tasks of levels A, B, C, D, E, and F, and, with the aid of Dr. Murdoch, Dr. Tilton and Miss Robinson, measured 180 imbeciles of mental age 3 to 5 and 100 of mental age 6. Dr. Woodyard has arranged and supervised most of the testing and scoring in grades 4 to 9, and has shared in the evaluation of the difficulty of the thousands of tasks which have been used in our experiments. Dr. Murdoch made all the tests with the fifty feeble-minded at Polk. Mrs. Miner has computed most of the correlations. Miss Robinson, Dr. Hunsicker, Dr. Tilton, and Mr. Upshall have given expert and painstaking service in testing and scoring.

Dr. Toops and Mrs. Ruger worked up the data which provided the first set of tasks graded in difficulty from which the final scale eventually developed. Miss Hanson, Mrs. Work and Miss Wilcox have had a large share in the arrangement and tabulation of the results.

We are indebted, for most courteous and efficient cooperation, to all the psychologists on the staff of Teachers College, to fifty members of the American Psychological Association who made various ratings for us, to Dr. Raymond Franzen and Dr. Grace A. Taylor who supplied valuable records, to Miss Elizabeth E. Farrell, Inspector of Ungraded Classes, New York City, Mr. George Melcher, Assistant Superintendent of Schools, Kansas City, Missouri, Dr. E. H. Nifernecker, Director of the Bureau of Educational Research of New York City, Dr. Howard W. Potter, Clinical Director of Letchworth Village, Dr. Louise M. Poull, Psychologist at the Randall's Island Institution, Mr. Lionel J. Simmons, Superintendent of the Hebrew Orphan Asylum of New York City, and to the many principals and teachers who have facilitated our experimentation.

# CONTENTS

## CHAPTER I.—*The Present Status.*

## CHAPTER II.—*The Measurement of Difficulty.*

## CHAPTER III.—*The Measurement of the Intellectual Difficulty of Tasks and of Level of Intellect: More Rigorous and Exact Methods.*

# LIST OF TABLES

1, 3, 8, 15, 22

38, 41, 55, 96, 97,

106f 433, 439, 475,

495, 572f, 576

405ff

Corporation

## STANFORD-BINET INTEL-
## LIGENCE SCALE: FORM L-M
*Lewis M. Terman and Maud A. Merrill*

all ages

**Purpose:** Measures an individual's mental abilities. Used to substantiate questionable scores from group tests and when the subject has physical, language, or personality disorders which rule out group testing.

**Description:** 142 item verbal and nonverbal IQ test assessing the following factors: language, memory, conceptual thinking, reasoning, numerical reasoning, visual motor, and social reasoning. Measures IQ through individual assessment from ages two years through adulthood. In most cases, only 18-24 test items need be administered to a given subject. The basal age is established (year level at which all items are passed), and testing continues until the ceiling age is reached (year level at which all items are failed). Responses are then scored according to established procedures to yield mental age and IQ. Results identify children and adults who would benefit from specialized learning environments. Administered only by professionally trained, certified examiners. Examiner required. Not for group use.

**Timed:** 45-90 minutes

**Range:** Ages 2 and older

**Scoring:** Examiner evaluated

**Cost:** Examiner's kit, form L-M (includes manual, large and small printed card material, miniaturized objects) $123.75; 35 record
$14.01.25

---

years 3 months

**Scoring:** Hand key; examiner evaluated

**Cost:** Complete specimen (includes Pattern Completion, Rubberboard, Subtest 7, 8, 9 Form Board B, manual, vulvalite case, 2 sheets of cellophane paper and 2 general answer sheets (orders from outside The RSA will be dealt with on merit).

**Publisher:** Human Sciences Research Council

## THE STANDARD PROGRES-
## SIVE MATRICES (SPM-1938)
*J.C. Raven*

all ages

**Purpose:** Measures an individual's mental ability through assessment of nonverbal abstract reasoning tasks. Used for school and vocational counseling and placement

**Description:** 60 item paper-pencil nonverbal test in five sets of 12 problems each. In each problem, the subject is presented with a pattern or figure design which has a part missing. The subject then selects one of six possible parts as the correct one. The patterns are arrayed from simple to complex. The test is often used with the Mill Hill Vocabulary Scale. Examiner required. Suitable for group use. Standardized in Great Britain.

BRITISH PUBLISHER

**Untimed:** 45 minutes

**Range:** Ages 8-65

**Scoring:** Hand key; machine scored

**Cost:** Specimen set (includes book of tests, 5 matrices and Mill Hill Vocabulary record forms, sample machine scorable record form) £9.70 plus

# CHAPTER I

## The Present Status[1]

Existing instruments for measuring intellect[2] developed from three roots, the interview, the school examination, and the 'tests' of sensory acuity, memory, attention, and the like, devised during the early history of psychology. The Stanford Binet, for example, is an improved, systematized and standardized interview. The Army Alpha is in part an improved school examination and in part an improved battery of tests like those used before 1900 by Galton, Ebbinghaus, Cattell, Jastrow, and others.

Existing instruments represent enormous improvements over what was available twenty years ago, but three fundamental defects remain. Just what they measure is not known; how far it is proper to add, subtract, multiply, divide, and compute ratios with the measures obtained is not known; just what the measures obtained signify concerning intellect is not known. We may refer to these defects in order as ambiguity in content, arbitrariness in units, and ambiguity in significance.

### AMBIGUITY IN CONTENT

If we examine any of the best existing instruments, say the Stanford Binet, the Army Alpha or the National Intelligence Test, we find a series of varied tasks. Some concern words, some concern numbers, some concern space relations, some concern pictures, some concern facts of home life. Some seem merely informational; some are puzzle-like. Some concern mental activities which will be entirely familiar to almost all of the individuals to be tested; some con-

[1] This chapter is reprinted with some alterations from the *Psychological Review*, Vol. 31, pp. 219 to 252.

[2] We shall use 'intellect' and 'intelligence' as synonyms throughout this book.

cern novelties. Some are irrespective of speed; in some speed is a large element in success. In particular, as we shall see later, the score attained is a composite in variable proportions whereby A is rated as more intelligent than B —first, if he can do certain hard tasks with which B fails, second, if he can do a greater number than B can of tasks of equal difficulty, and third, if he can do more rapidly than B tasks at which both succeed. The only sure statement of what abilities the Army Alpha measures is to show the test itself and its scoring plan.

To this it may be retorted that this variety is not really an ambiguity, that one of these tests is a representative sampling of tasks for intellect, and that the scoring plan is one which weights each response according to its importance as a symptom of intellect. Unfortunately this is not true. We may cherish the hope that these tests approximate to such representativeness of sampling and suitability of weights. In fact, however, nobody has ever made an inventory of tasks, determined the correlation of each with intellect, selected an adequate battery of them, and found the proper weight to attach to each of these. Such a procedure was carried· out in part by the Committee responsible for the construction of the National Intelligence Test, but limitations of time and funds restricted it to a very small fraction of what would be adequate. If anybody did this wisely, a large fraction of his labor would be precisely to find out what abilities our best present instruments did measure, and how these abilities were related to intellect; or to find out what abilities constituted intellect, and how these abilities were measured by our present instruments.[3]

One of the main lines of work in the improvement of instruments for measuring intellect is then to find out what abilities our best present instruments do measure.

[3] The balance of his labor might be expended upon experimentation with tasks that seemed promising as symptoms, even though we did not know what abilities they required.

## ARBITRARINESS OF UNITS

The score obtained by using the instrument to measure an intellect is in present practice either a number representing a summation of credits and penalties or, more rarely, a number representing the grade of difficulty of the tasks which the person can respond to with some assigned percentage of correct responses. Thus in Army Alpha he may score by summation from 0 to 212; in the first suggestion of Binet he could score 5 or 6, or 7, or 8, or 9, according as he was able to do correctly all but one of the tasks set as 5-year tasks, 6-year tasks, 7-year tasks and so on.[4]

In neither case (even supposing the measurement to be a perfect representation of the person's abilities) can the numbers be taken at their face value. If A scores 50 on Alpha, B, 75, and C, 100, we do not know that the difference between A and B in the abilities tested by Alpha is the same as the difference between B and C, nor that C has twice as much of these abilities as A. If D scores mental age 4, E mental age 6, and F mental age 8 by the Binet, we do not know that, in the abilities tested by the Binet, F excels E as much as E excels D, or that F has one and one third times as much of these abilities as E has. The numbers, 1, 2, 3, 4, etc., designating the scores made by individuals, do not represent a series of amounts of intellect progressing by equal steps. The difference in intellect between Army Alpha 10 and Army Alpha 20 may indeed conceivably be as great as the difference between Alpha 100 and Alpha 150. From Stanford Binet 40 months to 60 months may be as great a difference in intellect as from 140 months to 180 months. The value of what is called a difference of 1 on the scale is not known, and its value may fluctuate greatly as we move along the scale.

[4] This suggestion was, however, abandoned in favor of a procedure which mixes two sorts of measure. The procedure is, ''Take for point of departure the age at which all tests are passed; and beyond this age count as many fifths of a year as there are tests passed.'' ['The Development of Intelligence,' Eng. trans. of Kite, 1916, p. 278.]

We have then no right to add, subtract, multiply, or divide with these scores of A, B, C, D, E, and F in the way that we do with their heights or weights. Suppose that A scores 100; B, 110; C, 90; and D, 120. We cannot say that the average intellect of A and B equals the average intellect of C and D. If E changes from 60 to 70, while F changes from 70 to 80, we cannot say that they have made equal gross gains.

The numbers designating the scores made by individuals are usually not even approximately related to any true zero point.[5] Consequently, even if the scores 1, 2, 3, 4, did represent an equal-interval series of amounts or degrees of the ability in question, they would properly be treated as $x + 1$, $x + 2$, $x + 3$, $x + 4$. The 'times as' or ratio judgment is thus not surely applicable and the relations of the scores to anything else are thus undetermined. For example, we cannot say whether the intellect of the average twelve-year-old is one and a quarter times that of the average six-year-old or twice it, or ten times it.

The second main problem in improving measurements of intellect is thus to attach fuller and more definite meanings to these credit summations and difficulty levels, and if possible to find their equivalents on absolute scales on which zero will represent just not any of the ability in question, and 1, 2, 3, 4 and so on will represent amounts increasing by a constant difference.

We have to estimate equivalents of this sort somehow before we can make much use of ratings by either credit summations or difficulty levels; before, for example, we can conveniently compare individuals or groups, or the changes made by individuals or by groups, or the effects of different environments. The commonest method at present is to take as the equivalent for any score by any instrument, the age whose average achievement is that score, and to assume that

[5] Attempts have been made to define 'zero' or 'just not any' ability and to assign scores in relation to zero in the case of knowledge of English words, ability to understand sentences, handwriting, drawing, and English composition.

the increments in average ability are equal for equal differences in age up to some limit such as 192 months, and are zero thereafter. This of course is purely hypothetical in general and is almost certainly in error for the ages near the point where the age change suddenly turns from its full amount to zero. The curve of ability in relation to age is almost always smooth as in the continuous line of Fig.

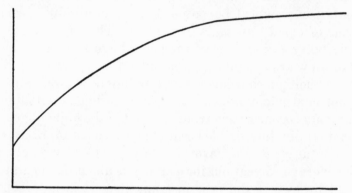

FIG. 1a. The probable form of the curve of intellect in relation to age.

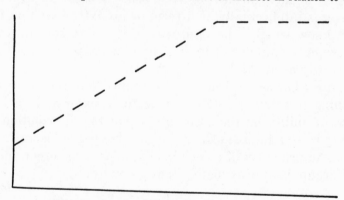

FIG. 1b. The form of the curve of intellect in relation to age, if annual gains are equal up to some stated age, and are zero thereafter.

1a, but not with a sharp turn as in the dash-line of Fig. 1b. The competent thinkers who use the method know this and are cautious in inferences based upon its application to the higher ages; but they use it rather freely for the lower ages, because some method must be used, because it is easy to understand and apply, and because we do not know what method is really right.

It may be objected that equality of units is an unnecessary refinement, for present practical purposes, since the mental age defines the status of an individual sufficiently, 'as able as the average ten-year-old,' 'as able as the average twelve-year-old.' These, it may be said, are better measurements for practical purposes than some absolute scale in terms of equal 'mentaces' or 'intels.' The convenience, intelligibility and realism of the mental age scale up to about 12 or 13 years are indeed great advantages, but after 13 or 14 it is neither convenient nor intelligible nor realistic. It is not convenient because the computation of intelligence quotients becomes very troublesome for the higher ages. It is not readily intelligible because mental ages 14, 15, 16, etc., are *not* 'as good as the average' 14-year old, 15-year old, etc. The average 25-year old for example is about the mental age of 14 by one of the best instruments. It is not realistic because we have no clear or vivid sense of what the average person is intellectually at fifteen, or at sixteen, and do not even know whether he improves in the next two or three years. A mental age of 15 or 16 or 17 is in fact as arbitrary a quantity as an Alpha ability of 123.

A rarer but more promising procedure than that of transforming test scores into 'ages' is to transform them into units of ability on the assumption that the distribution of ability in all adults 21–30, or in all twelve-year-olds, or in all pupils in grade six of a certain city, or in some other specified group, is approximately that given by

$$y = \frac{1}{\sigma\sqrt{2\pi}} e^{\frac{-x^2}{2\sigma^2}}$$

For example, the Alpha scores from 0 to 212 were not used in the army at their face value, which would give a distribution of the form shown in Fig. 2, but were transmuted into seven letter measures by the following scheme, which assumed an approximately 'normal' distribution for a random sampling of 128,747 of the literate white draft:

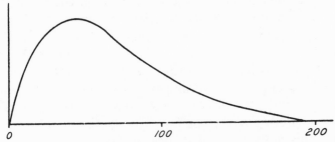

FIG. 2. The form of distribution of the literate white draft if Army Alpha are taken at their face value.

$$135\text{–}212 = A$$
$$105\text{–}134 = B$$
$$75\text{–}104 = C +$$
$$45\text{–}\ 74 = C$$
$$25\text{–}\ 44 = C\text{—}$$
$$15\text{–}\ 24 = D$$
$$0\text{–}\ 14 = D\text{—}$$

The score used in the Thorndike-McCall test of paragraph reading is not the number of correct answers, but a transmutation on the assumption that the real ability concerned is distributed 'normally' amongst twelve-year-olds in American cities.

We know very little concerning the permissibility of the assumption of the so-called normal distribution for adults or for an age, or for a school grade. The search for evidence pro and con is one important feature of the attempt to obtain units of mental ability which shall be at least approximately equal.

### AMBIGUITY IN SIGNIFICANCE

The test score measures directly only the measurer's impression from the subject's performance, or the summation in a more or less capricious fashion, of credits and penalties for the subject's responses to the different elements of the tests, or a combination of these. What this

3

score signifies about the subject's intellect depends upon the intuition of the measurer, or upon the correlation between the summation and intellect, or upon both. When we assert that a child is found by measurement with the Stanford Binet to have the intellect of a child 10½ years, all that is really asserted is that the child does as well in that particular standardized interview as did the average of the children of 10½ years of age tested by Terman in making his standards. We do not know what the average intellect of these children was, nor how closely the Stanford Binet score represents or parallels or signifies it.

When we assert that a man is found by measurement with the Army Alpha to have the intellect of an average recruit in the draft, all that is really asserted is that he does as well in that particular battery of tests scored and summated in a particular way, as the average recruit did. Just what the intellects of recruits were and how closely their Alpha scores paralleled their intellects, we do not know. The measurement is one thing, the inference to intellect is a different thing.

This is of course true of many measurements. The amount of silver deposited in one second by an electric current is not the amount of current. The dividend rate on stock during any one year is not the worth of the stock. The amount of silver is, under proper conditions, of perfect significance as an indicator of the amount of current, since the correlation between it and a perfect criterion of amount of current is perfect. The dividend rate is of very imperfect significance, since the correlation between it and a perfect criterion of the worth of the stock is far from perfect.

We do not know how closely the rating or score in the Stanford Binet or the Army Alpha or any other instrument correlates with a perfect criterion of intellect, because we do not know what such a criterion is, much less its correlations with these tests. One great task of the measurement of intellect is to obtain such a criterion, or a closer approximation to it than we now have, and to use it to improve the selection and weighting of the elements of our testing instruments.

The present status of such instruments as the Binet or Army or National tests is roughly as follows: We have chosen tests where the judgment of sensible people in general is that correct response or speed of correct response is characteristic of intellect. Such is the case with directions tests, arithmetical problems, common sense questions (as in Alpha 3), and the like. We have chosen tests using the judgment of psychologists in the same way. Such is the case with the completion tests devised by Ebbinghaus, the mixed relations or analogies test devised by Woodworth, and the like. We have tried these or other tests with children secluded in institutions because of imputed intellectual inferiority and with children of like age who are in ordinary schools (as by Norsworthy), with adult males of good health and morals who were found in a Salvation Army home, glad to work for a dollar a day, and with adults of the professional classes (as by Simpson), with children in general of different ages (as by Binet and Terman), with various groups of children ranked for imputed intelligence by teachers, fellow pupils, school advancement, and other symptoms (as by Spearman, Burt, Terman, Whipple, Yerkes, and others), with children of alleged superior intelligence in comparison with others (as by Whipple and Terman), with soldiers in the National Guard and regular army in connection with ratings for intelligence given by their officers (as by the Psychology Committee of the National Research Council), with students whose success in high school and college studies was also measured (as by Colvin, Wood, and many others), with individuals who were tested with a very long series of tests (as by Terman and Chamberlain, Stenquist, and others), and in other ways.

As a general result we know that certain systematized interviews and batteries of tests measure somewhat the same trait, since they correlate somewhat one with an-

other; and that this trait has to some extent the same constitution as the trait which sensible people, psychologists,
and teachers rate as intellect.

The failure of perfect correlation between the amount
of intellect a person has, as revealed by the criterion, and
the amount indicated by the instrument is due, as has been
said, partly to the imperfection of the criterion, but partly
also to the imperfection of the instruments. They (at
least all but one of them) are demonstrably imperfect, since
no two of them correspond perfectly in their findings for
the same intellects. Since it is extremely unlikely that,
out of a dozen instruments devised with about equal care
by a dozen individuals or committees at about the same
date one should be very much superior to all the others,
we may assume, until there appears proof to the contrary,
that all are imperfect.

The imperfection may be of two sorts. First, the responses measured by the instrument may not be representative of the whole intellect and nothing but intellect; the
score obtained may not give enough weight to certain factors or elements of intellect and may give weight to others
which really deserve less or even zero weight. The instrument is then like a wattmeter which gives only half weight
to the voltage of the current or adds two watts for every
time that the current is turned on or turned off. Second,
the same person may receive a different score when re-
measured by the instrument. In so far as such differences
are due to the 'accidental' ups and downs in the person's
achievements, they are taken care of by measuring him at
enough different times; but in so far as they are due to acquaintance with the instrument itself or with instruments
like it, they are a very serious imperfection. For example,
a given score with Army Alpha represents a very different
status according as it is from a first, a second, or a third
trial. The case here is as if a thermometer tended after
subjection to a temperature of 200° once to register 220°
when 200° was next encountered. The provision of means

for distinguishing between that part of the score due to certain general characteristics of the person measured and that part of the score which is due to certain special training that he has had with the tasks of the tests, or with tasks like them, is thus an important part of the work of making the measurements more fully and exactly significant of intellect.

In general, all our measurements assume that the individual in question tries as hard as he can to make as high a score as possible. None of them can guarantee that the scores would correspond at all with a perfect criterion if the individuals measured tried to appear as dull as they could. The correlation would indeed then probably be inverse, the more intelligent persons being more successful in their efforts to appear dull! It is theoretically possible to arrange a system of incentives such that each person measured by an instrument would put forth approximately his maximum effort, and in scientific testing of the instruments this can often be done. In general practice, however, we rarely know the relation of any person's effort to his possible maximum effort. Since, however, the disturbances due to differences in effort on the part of those tested require in study and treatment procedures which have little or nothing to do with the procedures by which the instruments are made to give better measurements of those who do try their best, we shall disregard the former and shall limit our inquiry to the latter sort of procedures.

### MEASUREMENTS OF INTELLIGENCE ARE MEASURES OF INTELLECTUAL PRODUCTS

All scientific measurements of intelligence that we have at present are measures of some product produced by the person or animal in question, or of the way in which some product is produced. A is rated as more intelligent than B because he produces a better product, essay written, answer found, choice made, completion supplied or the like, or produces an equally good product in a better way, more quickly or by inference rather than by rote memory, or by more ingenious use of the material at hand.

We can conceive of states of affairs such that a man's intellect could be measured without consideration of the products he produces or the ways in which he produces them.   Intellect might be exactly proportionate to the activity of the thyroid gland, or to the proportion of the brain weight to body weight, or to the number of associative neurones in the frontal lobes or to the complexity of the fibrillary action of certain neurones, or to the intensity of a certain chemical process, and hence be measurable by observations of the thyroid's action, or estimates of the brain's volume, or by a count or measurement of neurones, or by a chemical analysis.

Psychologists would of course assume that differences in intelligence are due to differences histological or physiological, or both, and would expect these physical bases of intelligence to be measurable.  At present, however, we know so little of the neural correlates of intellect that if twenty college freshmen were immolated to this inquiry, ten being the most intellectual of a hundred, and ten being the least intellectual of the hundred, and their brains were studied in every way by our best neurologists, these could probably not locate sixteen out of the twenty correctly as at top or bottom.   Moreover, what we do know of neural correlates is of little avail during life, the living neurones being extremely inaccessible to present methods of observation.

Even if one aimed at discovering the physiological basis of intellect and measuring it in physiological units, one would have to begin by measuring the intellectual products produced by it.   For our only means of discovering physiological bases is search for the physiological factors which correspond to intellectual production.

MEASUREMENTS OF INTELLIGENCE IMPLY VALUATION

Our present measurements of intelligence rest on human judgments of value, judgments that product A is 'better' or 'truer' or 'more correct' than product B, that method C is 'preferable' to method D, or that C is 'right' while D is 'wrong,' and the like.

In some cases this is so clear that everyone must admit it. Thus in three of our best tests of intelligence, giving the opposites of words, completing sentences by supplying omitted words, and answering questions about a paragraph read, we make elaborate keys assigning credits to the different responses.[6] These keys are obviously made by human judgments of the value of each response.

The credits given may represent valuations by the truthfulness or wisdom of the answers or sentences, by their grammatical form, by their rhetorical excellence, by their originality, by the rate of producing them, or by a subtle sense of their significance as evidence of intelligence.

[6] For example, the task being to complete,

'God made . . . and . . . let him pass for a man,' we find among the responses of high-school graduates:

| | |
|---|---|
| him | therefore |
| him | so |
| him | then |
| him | will |
| him | they |
| him | he |
| him | I |
| him | let |
| man | always |
| man | then |
| man | God |
| man | has |
| man | he |
| man | therefore |
| man | please |
| Adam | then |
| Adam | Eve |
| Adam | he |
| animal | wouldn't |
| Eve | God |
| us | we |
| heaven | earth |

and must assign some value to each, or make a dividing line between full value and no value somewhere.

In some cases the value is assigned so easily (as a simple deduction from, or following of, a general rule) that we may thoughtlessly assume that the response indicates intelligence regardless of any process of valuation. For example, we may consider that in a test in arithmetical computation or problem solving, the right answers are signs of intelligence, regardless of what anybody thinks. A little thought will convince us, however, that in such tests the human judgment acts as truly as in a completion or paragraph-reading test. The main difference is that, having once for all decided that right answers are better than wrong answers, we do not raise the issue about any particular answer. We simply assume or make a general rule of valuation. The valuation becomes obvious if we collect all the responses made to an arithmetical task and ask whether all the different 'rights' are equally good or right, and whether all the different 'wrongs' are equally undesirable.[7]

One criterion of value, *truth,* is so widely used in framing, keying, and scoring tests of intelligence that it deserves comment, especially since there may be in the case of truth an objective criterion, power in prediction, by which our judgments of value are or should be determined. Two other criteria of value also need comment because they have been suggested explicitly or implicitly as direct criteria for intelligence. They are *development with age and ability to learn.*

### TRUTH

Probably over half of our present tests of intelligence are tests where the response is given credit as a symptom of intelligence in proportion to its truthfulness. Such is the case, for example, with eight out of ten tests of the Otis

---

[7] In the special case where we arrange for *Yes* and *No* answers valuation is doubly active. We arrange so that a Yes or a No will be 'good' as a response. Then, since some of the correct 'Yeses' or 'Noes' may be due to chance, and since chance answers are deemed of no value, we plan our scoring so as to give the chance 'Yeses' and 'Noes' zero value.

Advanced; and with Army Alpha, 2, part of 3, 4, 6, 7, and 8. It is more or less the case with Stanford Binet III, 5; IV, 1, 2, 3; V, 1, 2, 3, 4; VI, 1, 2, 3, 5; VII, 1, 2, 5; VIII, 4, 5, 6; IX, 1, 2, 3; X, 1, 2; XII, 1, 2, 8; XIV, 1, 2, 3, 5, 6; and with National Intelligence A, 1, 3, 4, and B, 1, 2, 3, and 5.

One could make an attractive theory of intelligence and its measurement somewhat as follows: Intellect is concerned with facts, being the ability to see and learn the truth, to get true knowledge and use it to the best advantage. Truth is insight into the real world, the evidence that knowledge is true is its predictive power. Measures of intelligence are then ultimately measures of a man's mastery of prediction, that 2 and 2 will be 4, or that it will be profitable to buy such and such a stock, or that a planet will be found having such and such a path. More immediately, they are measures of certain abilities which contribute to, or accompany, or indicate the existence of, the ability to get and use the truth.

By this theory we should rest our valuations of truth all on the ultimate test of power of prediction. One truth would be better than another in proportion as it predicted more facts, or more important facts, or predicted the same facts more acccurately, or helped more in the acquisition of other truths. Our valuations of abilities as evidences of intellect would rest on their significance as symptoms of ability to get and use truth.

It seems sure, however, that people in general, psychologists, and framers of intelligence tests, alike mean by intellect something more than ability in truth-getting to improve prediction. They mean what Pericles and Washington and Gladstone had as well as what Aristotle and Pasteur and Darwin had. In the oral interview of the business man or physician to test intelligence, in such tests as Ebbinghaus' completions, and in such a battery of tests as Army Beta, there is little obvious reference to prediction or truth getting. In the first case, the aim is rather to see how the person fits his thoughts and acts to little problems or emergencies; in the second, it was rather to give him a chance to use all the so-called higher mental powers; in the third, many tasks were selected in which people who were regarded as intelligent could do better than people regarded as dull, and those of them which most conveniently distinguished the alleged bright from the alleged dull were kept as the final choice. If these instruments do really measure ability at truth getting, it is only indirectly and more by accident than by design.

It may be that truth-getting is what we unwittingly do measure by our intelligence tests, or what we ought to try to measure, but very few of those who devise or apply the tests think so. And it is surely wise to find out what we do measure before deciding that it is or ought to be truth-getting.

### DEVELOPMENT WITH AGE

Binet had it in mind to discover those intellectual abilities which six-year-olds had that five-year-olds did not have, those which seven-year-olds had that five-year-olds and six-year-olds did not have, and so on. It might seem that, except for the one judgment that abilities were 'better' or represented 'greater intelligence' the later they came in this series of normal chronological process, the Binet measurement would be free from valuation.

However, valuation came in from the start because Binet tried only abilities which he valued as intellectual. He did not take *all* the psychological features of five-, six-, and seven-year-olds and choose as his series of tests those which separated the ages most distinctly. In revising Binet's series Terman and others have paid less and less attention to lateness of development and more and more to significance as valued symptoms of intelligence in their choice of tasks.

This is well. For if Binet or they had collected a series of tasks such as showed the least overlapping of one chronological age on the next, the resulting series would be inferior as a measure of intellect to the series as it stands. For example, quality of handwriting, rate of tapping, and ability in checking A's on a mixed sheet of capitals would probably show less overlapping with age than vocabulary, rate of reading, and ability in completing sentences. But they would be far less effective in diagnosing amount of intelligence.

Development with age would be a poor and partial criterion for intellect of any sort or degree, and for the higher ranges of intellect, say those above the 70-percentile intellect of the average of the white draft, or above the average ninth-grade pupil, it would be well-nigh worthless. It has never been so used. The Terman mental ages above 14, for example, are not functions of development with age, but of differences between individuals, regardless of age.

ABILITY TO LEARN

An obvious hypothesis, often advanced, is that intellect is the ability to learn, and that our estimates of it are or should be estimates of ability to learn. To be able to learn harder things or to be able to learn the same thing more quickly would then be the single basis of valuation. Success in solving arithmetical problems, or defining words, or completing sentences would then be good, simply and solely because it signified that the person had greater ability to learn.

If greater ability to learn means in part ability to learn harder things, we have excluded the vague general valuation of certain products and ways of producing only to include it again. For we shall find ourselves selecting or defining A as harder to learn than B on the ground that only the more intellectual persons can do it, or on the ground that it requires a higher type of intellect, and shall find ourselves using those vague general valuations to pick the persons or describe the type of intellect required.

If greater ability to learn means only the ability to learn more things or to learn the same things more quickly, we have a view that has certain advantages of clearness and approximate fitness to many facts. Even less than in the case of truth-getting, however, do our present actual instruments for measuring intelligence measure directly a person's ability to learn more things than another person can, or to learn the same things more quickly. The substitution test included in Army Beta, in the National Intelligence Examination and in some others, is about the only test of speed of learning that is used; and it is more than a learning test.

Much evidence will therefore be required before we can wisely replace our present multifarious empirical valuations by the formula that intellect is the ability to learn more things or to learn the same things more quickly.

The reduction of all valuations of response to valuation as symptoms of ability to learn more and more quickly thus seems too narrow a view. It has other defects. Were it true, we ought, other things being equal, to get better correlations with a criterion of intellect from tests in learning something new and from tests deliberately framed to measure how much one has learned in life so far, than from the existing batteries of miscellaneous tasks.

This does not seem to be the case. Quantitative data concerning individual differences in learning under experimental conditions are rather scanty, and their correlations with a criterion of intellect are scantier still; but what facts we have been able to gather do not show that, per hour of time spent, tests in learning predict the criterion as well as do the tests now in use. Tests framed to measure how much one has learned in life so far, such as vocabulary tests, information tests, or such Binet elements as 'Knows whether he is a boy or a girl,' and the like, are valuable, but not, so far as we can determine, more valuable than a composite containing also tests primarily of selective, relational, generalizing, and organizing abilities.

### OTHER ATTEMPTED SIMPLIFICATIONS OF THE PROCESS OF VALUATION

#### Response to Novelty

In one way allied to the doctrine just described and in one way sharply contrasted with it, is the doctrine that a person's intellect is measured by his ability to respond well to new situations, to do 'originals.' The importance of some such ability as this will, of course, be admitted. However, in view of the great difficulty of deciding just what situations are 'new' for any given individual; in view of the fact that 'to respond well' is likely to bring in many or all of our vague general valuations again; in view of the fact that distinctions among novel situations as 'harder' (that is, making greater demands on intellect) will have the same effect; and in view of the fact that our most approved present instruments include many tasks which seem as fittingly called responses to the familiar as to the new— in view of all this it seems best at present not to try to narrow our valuations to fit this theory.

## Relational Thinking

Spearman has argued that intellect equals the apprehension of experience, the eduction of relations and the eduction of correlates. The two processes are defined as follows: "The mentally presenting of any two or more characters (simple or complex) tends to evoke immediately a knowing of relation between them." [23, p. 63.] "The presenting of any character together with any relation tends to evoke immediately a knowing of the correlative character." [23, p. 91.]

There is no doubt that the appreciation and management of relations is a very important feature of intellect, by any reasonable definition thereof. Yet it seems hazardous and undesirable to assume that the perception and use of relations is all of intellect. In practice, tests in paragraph reading, in information, and in range of vocabulary, seem to signify intellect almost as well as the opposites and mixed relations tests. In theory, analysis (thinking things into their elements), selection (choosing the suitable elements or aspects or relations), and organizing (managing many associative trends so that each is given due weight in view of the purpose of one's thought), seem to be as deserving of consideration as the perception and use of relations. Moreover, I fear that, in all four cases, we need other valuations to decide which are the *better* relations or *more abstract* relations, or the *more essential* elements, or the *more sagacious* selection, or the *more consistent* organization, or the *more desirable* balance of weights, and the like.

However this may be, our present tests of intelligence are not merely instruments to measure how little stimulus is required to produce a perception of a relation, or how many relations will be perceived from a given constant stimulus, or how quickly. And we may best study them as they are before dismissing the valuations on which they are based, in favor of any simpler and more objective system.

We shall then accept for the present the status of measurements of intellect as measures of different products produced by human beings or of different ways taken by them to produce the same product, each of these products and ways having value attached to it as an indication of intellect by a somewhat vague body of opinion whether popular or scientific.

### THE CONTENT OR DATA OF TESTS OF INTELLECT

Presumably a man can use intellect and display the amount of it which he possesses in operations with any sort of material object, any living plant or animal, including himself, any quality or relation that exists in reality or in imagination, any idea or emotion or act. Our tests might draw upon anything for their material.

They have, in fact, greatly favored words, numbers, space-forms, and pictures, neglecting three-dimensional objects and situations containing other human beings. How far this has been due to convenience, and how far intellect is really best measured by its operations with words, numbers, space-forms, and pictures, is a matter that obviously deserves investigation. Our choices of test material have certainly been somewhat determined by convenience. They have also favored ideas, general notions, abstractions, symbols and relations, to the relative neglect of percepts and particulars. This has been in the main deliberate, our general scheme of valuation attaching on the whole more intellectual worth to operations with generals and facts in relations than to particulars and facts in isolation.

The nature and extent of the specialization of intellect, according to the content or material operated on, has been and still is a matter of dispute; and the difference of opinion carries over into the practice of measurement. Some psychologists would be fairly well satisfied to measure intellect by a series of mazes alone; or by a series of sentence completions alone. Others, the great majority, attach much more confidence to a battery of tests including surely both words and numbers, probably also some space-forms and perhaps some more concrete pictorial material.

### THE FORM OF TESTS OF INTELLECT

Whether we consider the external appearance of the tasks or the internal nature of the processes in the person doing them, there is a great variety in respect to form, that is, to the operations performed with the words, numbers, pictures, and other content. Externally, there appear questions to be answered, sentences or pictures to be completed, errors to be found and corrected, definitions to be given and to be chosen, items to be matched, directions to be followed, disarranged parts to be put together, disarranged events to be put in proper sequence, keys or codes to be learned, true statements to be distinguished from false, items to be checked as fit by various criteria, items to be crossed out as unfit, and so on.

Internally, the individual finds himself striving to attend to certain matters, to fix others in memory, to recall what he knows about others, to select from many things or ideas the one which best satisfies certain requirements, to define the relation between two terms, to discover an element common to three or four given facts, to hold in mind many different facts and use them to some specified purpose, and to inhibit customary habits in view of some rule. He also finds himself in some cases (such as many elements of information tests, vocabulary tests, and arithmetical computations) utilizing a wide range of knowledge and skills.

Any system of units of measurement that is to be adequate must then apparently be flexible enough to apply to a wide variety of operations such as we may call attention, retention, recall, recognition, selective and relational thinking, abstraction, generalization, organization, inductive and deductive reasoning, together with learning and knowledge in general.

### SCORING THE PRODUCTS OF INTELLECT

In the great majority of instruments for measuring intellect the score or rating is determined in part by the degree of difficulty of the tasks the individual can do successfully. Thus 'There are three main differences between a president and a king; what are they?' (Stanford Binet XIV, 3) is harder than 'Are you a little boy or a little girl?' (Stanford Binet, III, 4). To complete 3 6 8 16 18 36 . . . . (Alpha 6, 20) is harder than to complete 10 15 20 25 30 35 . . . . (Alpha 6, 2). Psychologists and scientific and sensible people in general readily rank tasks as easy or hard for intellect and would accept the principle that, *Other things being equal, the harder the tasks a person can master, the greater is his intelligence.* The concept of hardness or difficulty in intellectual tasks, as now used, is somewhat vague and variable. Its outstanding characteristic is that among a large group of persons varying in intelligence, the harder the task, the fewer will be the persons who can do it, and the more intelligent they will be. Sometimes, however, tasks are called hard which really are only recondite, familiar to few; and sometimes tasks are called hard which really are only long.

We shall presently define this concept of the intellectual difficulty of a task, so as to make it more useful in science, but for the present we may leave it vague, the principle stated above being true for any reasonable definitions of 'difficulty,' and 'intelligence.'

In many of the instruments for measuring intellect there are tasks which are of equal difficulty (or at least tasks so nearly equal that which of them is hardest is not certain). In the Binet series the tasks for any one year of age were supposed to be equally hard. In Alpha 7 only by statistical inquiry could one decide which of these is hardest, which next hardest and so on.

| | | |
|---|---|---|
| 6 | love—hatred :: friend—*lover mother need enemy* | 6 |
| 7 | wrist—bracelet :: neck—*collar leg foot giraffe* | 7 |
| 8 | sailor—navy :: soldier—*gun private army fight* | 8 |
| 9 | carpenter—house :: shoemaker—*hatmaker wax shoe leather* | 9 |
| 10 | shoestring—shoe :: button—*coat catch bell hook* | 10 |
| 11 | quinine—bitter :: sugar—*cane sweet salt beets* | 11 |
| 12 | tiger—wild :: cat—*dog mouse tame pig* | 12 |
| 13 | legs—man :: wheels—*spokes carriage go tire* | 13 |
| 14 | north—south :: east—*north west south east* | 14 |
| 15 | feather—float :: rock—*ages hill sink break* | 15 |
| 16 | grass—cattle :: bread—*man butter water bones* | 16 |
| 17 | fin—fish :: wing—*feather air bird sail* | 17 |
| 18 | paper—wall :: carpet—*tack grass sweep floor* | 18 |
| 19 | food—man :: fuel—*engine burn coal wood* | 19 |
| 20 | sled—runner :: buggy—*horse carriage harness wheel* | 20 |
| 21 | poison—death :: food—*eat bird life bad* | 21 |
| 22 | Japanese—Japan :: Chinese—*Russia China Japanese pigtail* | 22 |
| 23 | angels—heaven :: men—*earth woman boys Paradise* | 23 |
| 24 | Washington—Adams :: first—*contrast best second last* | 24 |
| 25 | prince—princess :: king—*palace queen president kingdom* | 25 |

Now if a test includes a dozen tasks absolutely equal in difficulty for people in general, any one person who gets some right will by no means always get them all right, and any one person who gets some wrong will by no means always get them all wrong. So a person's score is partly determined by the number of tasks of equal difficulty that

4

he does. We must then consider as a possible principle *'Other things being equal, the greater number of tasks of equal difficulty that a person masters, the greater is his intelligence.'* This principle would not be accepted so readily as the principle about greater difficulty, and perhaps would not be accepted at all unanimously. 'Knowing more things than someone else, and being able to do more things than someone else' is not so clearly and surely having more intelligence as 'being able to do harder things than some one else can do.'

The two things have been somewhat confused in general discussions and in the construction of measuring instruments because, by and large, a person increases the number of things he can do in large part by adding on harder ones, and also because the person who can do the harder can on the average learn those which the duller person can learn more quickly than he, and so learns more of them. Consequently what we may call the *level* or *height* or *altitude* of intellect and what we may call its *extent* or *range* or *area at the same level* are correlated and either one is an indicator of the other. It will be best, however, to keep them separate in our thinking.

In many of the instruments for measuring intellect a person's score is determined partly by the speed with which he can do the tasks. Even in batteries of tests where all candidates attempt all the tasks, speed may count, since the persons who do the easier tasks more quickly may have time to review some of the tasks and perfect their work. If speed deserves any weight in determining the measures of intellect it is by virtue of the principle that, *'Other things being equal, the more quickly a person produces the correct response, the greater is his intelligence.'* Giving much weight to speed arouses decided objections in the laity and among some psychologists, and the principle just stated certainly would not be accepted as axiomatic. By and large, however, if A can do harder things than B can, A will do those things which B can do more quickly than B can.

A certain moderate weight attached to speed will not then much decrease a test's significance; and, per hour of time spent on testing and scoring, an even greater significance may perhaps be obtained by giving a liberal weight for speed than by giving none.

For the practical purposes of estimating intellect, a battery of tests in which *level, extent,* and *speed* combine in unknown amounts to produce the score may be very useful. For rigorous measurements, however, it seems desirable to treat these three factors separately, and to know the exact amount of weight given to each when we combine them.

We shall try to make the concepts of intellectual product, difficulty of producing an intellectual product, range of products produced, and speed of producing a product, more definite and precise, but without so altering them as to lose the elements which have given them practical value in the best current practice in measurement, or to weaken in any way their usefulness in measuring intellects as we actually find them by the tests which we have so far developed.

We shall start with certain first approximations. For a first approximation, let intellect be defined as that quality of mind (or brain or behavior if one prefers) in respect to which Aristotle, Plato, Thucydides, and the like, differed most from Athenian idiots of their day, or in respect to which the lawyers, physicians, scientists, scholars, and editors of reputed greatest ability at constant age, say a dozen of each, differ most from idiots of that age in our asylums.

Let an intellectual product, *i.e.,* a product or response requiring, or depending on, intellect for its production, be defined as a product or response which, given the same external situation, the intellects in the half toward Aristotle are more likely to make than the intellects in the half toward the idiot. For example, if, when all Athenians of age forty were confronted by the question 'Is a straight line the shortest distance between two points?' the growth of the white blood corpuscles was equal for the Aristotelian and the idiotic halves, whereas the answer *Yes* was more prevalent in the Aristotelian half, we should rate the latter as a product depending on intellect, and the former as a product not depending on intellect.

Let the intellectual difficulty of producing a given intellectual product in response to a given external situation be defined as follows: Enough time being allowed for production so that an increase in time would not increase the number producing it, the difficulty for Athenians of forty is approximately greater the smaller the number of them who produce it, provided that the ranking of those who do produce it differs from the ranking of those who do not by greater nearness to the Aristotelian end. We could be much more rigid here by supposing a population to vary from the idiots to the Aristotles in amount of intellect only, being identical in all else. Then, if all conceivable productions of intellectual products in response to given external situations were ranked for difficulty, the order would be very closely that of rarity and of the nearness to Aristotle of those who achieved it. We could omit the 'approximately,' and the 'provided that.' Our definition has deliberately been left loose, since we do not know exactly what it is in which Aristotle differs most from the idiot, much less can we know in the case of any group of actual individuals that they are identical in all else than it.

The range of products produced at any one level, *i.e.* of products which are equally hard to produce, is defined simply by their number. What we may call the relative range at any level may be defined as the percent or fraction of the products at that level which can be produced by the intellect in question. The speed of producing any given product is defined, of course, by the time required.

It will be convenient to use the word *task* to mean the production of a given product in response to a given external situation, and to speak of the difficulty of tasks, the number of tasks of a given difficulty that can be done, and the speed of doing a given task.

We now have *intellect* defined by a ranking of men whose differences therein are roughly appreciated as we appreciate the differences of the world's varied objects in volume (only much more roughly.) We have *intellectual tasks and products* defined in a catholic way that would, for instance, probably include every task in all the stock instruments in use by psychologists to-day. We have *difficulty* defined objectively so that a series of tasks could be approximately ranked as to their respective amounts of difficulty for any specified group.

If we list all tasks, find the difficulty of each, apply an intellect to them, observe which it can do, and how long it requires to do each, we have measured how hard tasks it can do, how many it can do at each level, and how quickly it can do them. If we use in place of a complete list of tasks a fair sampling from them, we have attained the same end, subject to the error of our sampling.

The new problems of theory and technique in the measurement of intellect, that is, the problems not soluble by the general methods of measurement in any science, concern the measurement of difficulty of task. Extent and speed are measurable in two of the most perfect units there are—number and time. In the case of difficulty, however, we have so far provided only for an inventory of intellectual tasks and their arrangement in an *order* of difficulty.

Their differences in *amount* of difficulty and the differences between the amount of difficulty of any one of them and some zero point of difficulty (some task which is just below a task of infinitesimal difficulty), are not determined. To find ways of determining these will be our main work.

Before attempting it, however, we may best consider certain further facts about difficulty, extent and speed in the production of intellectual products, and certain consequences of our analysis of a measurement of intellect into this three-fold determination.

### FURTHER FACTS CONCERNING DIFFICULTY

We have defined intellectual difficulty in relation to a defined group of individuals. How far the rank order for difficulty obtained in the case of one human group will hold for others, or for a group of dogs or of chickens, is a matter better ascertained by experiment than prejudged. Difficulty in our treatment is always difficulty for some specified group of intellects, such as our Athenians aged forty. We can, if we wish, specify the group as all human beings of all ages, or all animals, and so get measurements of something which we might call *difficulty in general*. The value of such a measure will, however, depend largely on the closeness of correspondence between the rank orders for the same series of tasks at different ages, in different civilizations, and so forth. If these are very low, the measurement of such difficulty in general may be of very little use.

Many cases of grouping, as by age, by amounts of general education, by amounts of special education, or by city and country environment, are of great importance. Two may be considered briefly now as samples, namely, grouping of those of equal chronological age by amounts of intellect, and grouping of those of equal intellect by chronological age. If certain tasks are of difficulty $k$, $k + a$, $k + a + b$, $k + a + b + c$, etc., for 12-year-olds of low or small intellects, say the bottom tenth of twelve-year-olds, how far will they retain the same relations in respect of difficulty in the case of the top tenth? If certain tasks are of difficulty $k_1$, $k_1 + a$, $k_1 + a + b$, etc., for the eight-year-olds of a certain degree of intellect, how far will they retain the same difficulty relations for sixteen-year-olds of the same degree of intellect?

We have eliminated speed entirely from influence upon the measurement of difficulty, by our condition that such a time allowance be given for the task that no further increase in time would alter the production. In practice, this would only be approximated. Obviously we must not make the time so long that during it the intellect in question changes appreciably by growth or training. We should not leave individuals to strive for ten hours to complete: 'The body _____gives light_____the_____is the sun,' because once in ten thousand times, some child who failed during nine hours succeeded in the tenth. This would be a valuable experiment, but we have far more valuable ways of using ten hours of his time.

What we are really concerned about is to avoid rating one task as harder than another merely because it is longer, so that the poorer intellects do it less quickly than the others, and so, within a too short time limit, show a spuriously greater percentage of failures.

We have made the requirement that the intellectual ranking of those who do produce the response shall be higher than that of those who fail. Usually this requirement is unnecessary. It can, that is, usually be assumed that the good or correct response will be obtained by the better intellects more often than by the poorer. It is inserted to provide against cases where the better intellects are subject to some constant error so that they give fewer correct responses than the dull do, or where other factors than intellect distort the percent of rights from what it would be if everything but intellect were equalized. For example, it is conceivable that, if ($a$) and ($b$) below were given to a random sampling of intellects,

Underline the right answers:

($a$) $4^{-1}$ equals $\frac{1}{4}$  3  5  41

($b$) $4^{\frac{1}{2}}$ equals 2  $3\frac{1}{2}$  8  412

ratings for difficulty by the percents correct would be very much in error. The percent for ($a$) would probably be lower than for ($b$) because, lacking knowledge of exponents, the more intelligent one was, the more likely one would be to report 3 for ($a$), (valid if $4^{-1}$ means $4-1$), and to report 2 (valid if $4\frac{1}{2}$ means 4 halves or $4 \times \frac{1}{2}$) for ($b$).

We have treated the task as being to produce a certain product. It is scored, consequently, as done or not done, success or failure, right or wrong. Now when any task for intellect is set there are often many different responses varying in 'goodness' or correctness. In such cases, our method requires that in determining the difficulty of the task, a dividing line be set somewhere.[8] Our method will not, however, prevent us from later using different credit values in a scoring plan for such a task and taking full advantage of whatever added value these more detailed credit values may have in estimating an individual's intellect.

It may be noted further that a task may consist of various combinations and complications of other tasks. Thus the task may be to get the right answer to $8 + 3$, or to get the right answer to $11 + 7$, or to get the right answers to both $8 + 3$ and $11 + 7$, or to get the right answers to $8 + 3$ and $11 + 7$ and also $18 + 4$, or to get the right answer to:

Find the sum

9
4
7
3
8
—

which ordinarily involves the above, plus knowledge of $22 + 9$, of certain words and procedures, and control over certain habits, such as holding numbers in mind, and adding a seen to a thought-of number.

We are now in a position to state one theorem of the measurement of intellect. Let difficulty be defined as above, then:

*Theorem I:* Other things being equal, if intellect A can do correctly all the tasks that intellect B can do save one and in place of that one can do one that is harder than it intellect A has the higher level.

One is tempted to go further and assume that, other things being equal, if A and B can do correctly the same number of tasks, A has the higher level, if the average diffi-

---

[8] What seems to be one task to the person tested may be used as two or more tasks by scoring it first with the dividing line at one place, and second with the dividing line at another.

culty of the tasks he can do is greater than the average difficulty of the tasks B can do. This cannot, as yet, be wisely assumed first because we do not know that we have any right to average measures of difficulty,[9] and secondly, because, even if we could, it is not safe to assume that as much intellect is required to do 10 tests each of difficulty 20 as to do one task of difficulty 200.

On the other hand one is tempted to suggest the measurement of an intellect by the hardest things it can do, assuming that since it can do these, it could do all easier, as we assume that one who can jump over a bar 6 feet high could surely jump over bars at 5 ft. 10 in., 5 ft. 8 in., and so on. The possible variety and specialization of intellectual tasks makes this uncertain.

### WIDTH OR EXTENT OR RANGE

Our definition of greater difficulty enables us also to define equal difficulty and so to make a fairly rigorous definition of width or extent or range by making it separately at each level of difficulty. For any specific group $G$ and any specific time $t$ those tasks are equally difficult which are done correctly by equal percentages of intellects.

Consider then all the tasks which are of a certain difficulty $D$. Some intellects will fail with all of them. Among the intellects which succeed with some of them we may make comparisons according to the number succeeded with. Such a statement as '$N$ tasks, of equal difficulty $D$, being given, with $t$ time allowed per task, A did $0.1N$ while B did $0.2N$ and C did $0.3N$,' is clear and useful. We can say that B did twice as many as A, that C exceeded B in the number done as much as B exceeded A, and that the average for A and C was the same quantity as the score for B. Where the problem concerns the extent of an ability, as in the number of certain facts that are known in history or science or the

---

[9] We have provided for determinations of which one of two or more tasks is the more difficult, but not, as yet, for determinations of how much more difficult it is.

number of certain procedures that are mastered in arithmetic or carpentry, it is often, perhaps usually, desirable to free the measurement from differences in difficulty by making the tasks equal in difficulty and measuring extent at that level.[10]

In the measurement of intellect, measurements of extent at each level are obviously instructive for many purposes. The inventory of what intellect A can do is improved by being classified into Tasks 1, 2, and 4 at level $D_1$, 16, 19, 27, and 28 at level $D_2$, 37, 43, 48, 49, and 56 at level $D_3$, and so on.

We can set down as *Theorem II:* Other things being equal, if intellect A can do correctly all the tasks that intellect B can do, and can also do one more task at the level of any of the others, intellect A has a greater range than intellect B has. We could also safely say that A is a better or more useful intellect; whether we can rightly say that it is *a greater* than B is more doubtful. The latter seems to imply that superiority in extent can be made commensurate with, weighed in the balance against, superiority in level. For the present let us leave the question open.

SPEED

There is of course no essential difficulty in measuring the time required for intellect A to produce a certain product. Number and time figure in mental measurements as they do in physical measurements. The units of number and time are indeed so much more convenient and intelligible than units of difficulty that there is a strong natural tendency in those who devise instruments for measuring intellect to let their measurement depend largely upon the

---

[10] It should be noted that a number of tasks of equal difficulty may be given in a test instrument, not with any intention of measuring extent of intellect at that level for its own sake, but simply in order to obtain a more accurate measure of the level itself. For example suppose that in instrument $x$ we have tasks at ten levels $D_1 D_2 D_3 \ldots D_{10}$, one at each. Suppose that in instrument $y$ we have ten at each level. Then by whatever convention we determine how hard a task a person can do, we shall determine it much more exactly by instrument $y$ than by instrument $x$.

number of correct responses and the speed of producing them.

In the instruments that are actually used, it is customary to have the time a mixture of (1) the time spent in doing some tasks correctly, (2) the time spent in doing other tasks incorrectly and (3) the time spent in inspecting other tasks and deciding not to attempt them. This confusion may be permissible, or even advantageous, in the practical work of obtaining a rough measure of intellect at a small expense of time and labor and skill, but for theory at present and for possible improvement of practice in the future we need to separate the speed of successes from the speed of failures.

To the number of tasks correctely done at each level we may add a record of the time for each or of the average time for all at that level.

Since to save time in intellectual production is a 'good,' we may frame *Theorem III* as follows: *Other things being equal, if intellect A can do at each level the same number of tasks as intellect B, but in a less time, intellect A is better.* To avoid any appearance of assuming that speed is commensurate with level or with extent, we may replace 'better' by 'quicker.'

### THE RELATIVE IMPORTANCE OF ALTITUDE, EXTENT, AND QUICKNESS OF INTELLECT

Each of these three factors is essential. If it required an infinite time per task, an intellect would produce no product at any level no matter how high its potentialities as to altitude and extent might be. If it had zero extent at all levels, it would not matter how high its potentialities as to altitude or how quickly it could do nothing. In the ordinary sense of the word, however, altitude or level is by far the most important. The chief evidence for this is that it alone is indispensable, irreplaceable by anything save itself. If the best available intellect can do only things of level $D_{19}$, we cannot get things of level $D_{20}$ done at all. If the best available intellect can do only 72 things at level $D_6$ and we need to get 144 things at that level done, we need only to get other intellects at work, say one that can do 45 of the balance and another that can do the remaining 27. If the best available intellect can do only 10 tasks per minute at

$L_{20}$

| | | | | | | | | | | | | | | | |
|---|---|---|---|---|---|---|---|---|---|---|---|---|---|---|---|
| 470 | 810 | 330 | | | | | | | | | | | | | |
| 460 | 410 | 480 | 320 | 630 | 190 | 770 | 320 | 340 | | | | | | | |
| 450 | 180 | 300 | 400 | 320 | 570 | 310 | 340 | 360 | 220 | 250 | | | | | |
| 307 | 252 | 240 | 231 | 263 | 318 | 245 | 175 | 168 | 252 | 242 | | | | | |
| 179 | 288 | 205 | 304 | 146 | 285 | 216 | 234 | 196 | 223 | 227 | 211 | | | | |
| 170 | 192 | 98 | 155 | 164 | 203 | 165 | 127 | 158 | 186 | 160 | 230 | 147 | | | |
| 127 | 88 | 109 | 92 | 123 | 73 | 147 | 81 | 124 | 162 | 135 | 64 | 116 | | | |
| 96 | 111 | 48 | 98 | 91 | 100 | 113 | 109 | 102 | 115 | 58 | 65 | 104 | 72 | | |
| 81 | 123 | 98 | 80 | 67 | 85 | 59 | 96 | 38 | 83 | 108 | 70 | 72 | 110 | 86 | |
| 28 | 66 | 102 | 45 | 30 | 63 | 51 | 71 | 62 | 58 | 70 | 34 | 68 | 91 | 81 | 70 |
| 55 | 43 | 52 | 47 | 28 | 71 | 52 | 45 | 36 | 31 | 56 | 57 | 39 | 55 | 64 | 60 |
| 41 | 52 | 29 | 38 | 40 | 34 | 21 | 50 | 39 | 55 | 38 | 50 | 32 | 38 | 25 | 54 |
| 27 | 36 | 50 | 20 | 29 | 26 | 18 | 15 | 27 | 29 | 40 | 35 | 28 | 23 | 34 | 25 |
| 21 | 19 | 15 | 20 | 18 | 19 | 16 | 18 | 20 | 24 | 16 | 18 | 15 | 11 | 23 | 26 |
| 12 | 14 | 10 | 11 | 12 | 9 | 14 | 7 | 8 | 15 | 6 | 6 | 11 | 12 | 10 | 12 |
| 8 | 8 | 6 | 8 | 10 | 12 | 8 | 10 | 6 | 9 | 7 | 6 | 8 | 5 | 7 | 9 |
| 4 | 5 | 3 | 4 | 4 | 3 | 5 | 2 | 4 | 4 | 6 | 5 | 4 | 3 | 2 | 4 |

($L_5$, $L_4$, $L_3$, $L_2$, $L_1$ mark the last five rows)

FIG. 3. The measure of a superior intellect.

level $D_3$ and we need to get 20 done per minute, we can hire five common people who can do two a minute to help. Indeed, we shall be wise to hire ten common people to do two a minute each, and leave the best available intellect to put its time on tasks far above level $D_3$.

Common sense recognizes the greater importance of altititude. It rates a Pasteur far above the most widely competent general practitioner. It does not ask how quickly Milton could give opposites, or turn out doggerel rhymes. Probably Pasteur was very much above the average in extent of intellect; probably Milton could have written as good poetry as A can write and much faster than B can. But common sense considers extent and quickness as unimportant in comparison with reaching a level far above the average.

From the economic and philanthropic points of view, altitude is enormously more important. If an intellect could be hired from Mars of so high level that it could learn how to prevent war as easily as Jenner learned how to prevent smallpox, a million dollars a day would be a cheap wage for the earth to pay him.

Our analysis of the measurement of intelligence may be represented by space and number as follows:

Let one sixteenth of a square inch represent one intellectual task. Let those equal in difficulty be placed in the same row across the page; let the order of the rows from the bottom to the top of the page be the increasing order of difficulty; let the square be shaded if the individual in question cannot do it; if he can do it, let it bear a number representing the time he requires to do it. For illustration, we have assumed that there are 320 tasks and that they are of 20 levels of difficulty, 16 at each level.

Figures 3 and 4 then represent the measurements or inventories of two specimens of intellect. Such measurements or inventories may be abbreviated by using a random sampling of tasks at each level, or by using only every other level or every third or every fourth level, or in other ways. Only one thing is needed to make such measurements submissible to the arithmetic and calculus of science in general. That is the expression of the altitude of each level (now merely a rank) as an amount of difference from the altitude of the others and from some group of tasks which require intellect, but so little of it that they border on a true zero of difficulty which may be set as their lower limit. This is the fundamental problem of mental measurements.

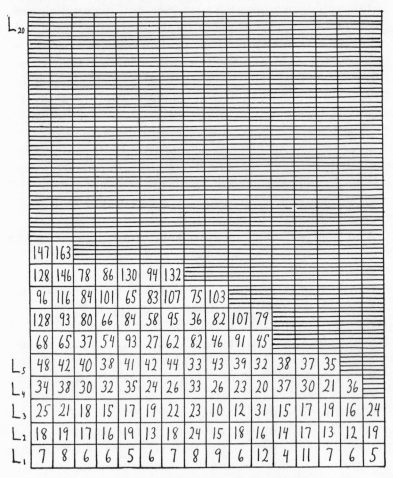

FIG. 4. The measure of an inferior intellect.

# CHAPTER II

## THE MEASUREMENT OF DIFFICULTY

### THE PRESENT STATUS

If the members of a group are tested with each of a number of intellectual tasks, these can be put into an approximate rank order for intellectual difficulty for that group by the percentages of successes. For example, tasks A to G below are arranged by steps in an approximate order of intellectual difficulty for the group, "persons at the time of graduation from Grade 8 in City A in 1924."

The same sort of validity that attaches to the statement that G exceeds A in intellectual difficulty for that group, attaches also to the statement that G so exceeds F, that F so exceeds E, and so on.

Write words on the dotted lines so as to make the whole sentence true and sensible. Write one word on each inch of dots.

A. A strong man...................................lift a heavy box.

B. The rose is a favorite...................................because of ...................................fragrance and................................... .

C. A body of...................................entirely surrounded by ...................................is called an................................... .

D. It may...................................effort and a long................................... but the result is sure.

E. You may safely conclude that you...................................in yourself the means of...................................at the truth.

F. He believed in ................................... h a r d  t h i n g s ...................................because...................................  ...................................hard.

G. Judicial decisions are of...................................or less authority as precedents...................................to circumstances.

The same sort of evidence and argument which decides that G has more intellectual difficulty than A, was used to place B, C, D, E, and F in order between A and G. The

37

evidence is the number and nature, in respect of intellect, of those who succeed with each task. The harder the task, the fewer the persons who succeed at it, and the more intellect they have. The argument implicitly involved is (1) that whether a person succeeds or fails in such tasks is determined largely by the amount of intellect which he possesses, and not greatly by anything other than intellect, and (2) that in the hardest tasks which a person masters, he uses in general nearly all the intellect which he has.

The argument is sound enough to justify such a rank order as the A, B, C . . . G order shown above, or the order of a series made of Stanford Binet tests for Mental Age 10, Mental Age 12, Mental Age 14, Mental Age Adult, and Mental Age Superior Adult, but we shall find trouble if we try to make a very close ordering, or to use the percentages of successes for other than approximate rankings.

The exact determination of a rank order of test elements for intellectual difficulty requires that the individuals in the group be tested with each of the tasks under similar conditions, including interest and effort, which is a matter of general scientific care that needs no further discussion here. It requires also that each of the tasks in the series shall be 'intellectual;' and this requirement will eventually need very elaborate discussion. We shall, indeed, find that it is desirable to define an intellectual task as one in which the person tested uses all the intellect he then has; and in which he differs from other persons in nothing save the amount of intellect used.

If, however, we applied any such rigorous definition now, we should be unable to deal with any elements of any tests ever used in measuring intellect, since not a single one of them is a task which depends on intellect in its entirety, and differentiates individuals with no disturbance by anything other than intellect. A test element which did so would correlate 1.00 with a perfect criterion. In order to maintain continuity with previous work, we shall first treat each test element as if correct response to it was caused by intellect intact and uncontaminated by aught else.

Two methods have been used to measure the difficulty of intellectual tasks. The first has used the judgments of teachers, psychologists, and other judges of presumable competence, relying on some assumptions such as that if K percent of competent judges rate A as harder than B, and B as harder than C, the differences in difficulty, A–B and B–C, are equal. We shall report our investigations of this method later; for the present, it may be disregarded.

The second has used the percentages of some defined group of individuals who succeed with each task, relying on some assumptions about the form of distribution (in that group) of the ability involved in doing such tasks.

For example, suppose that we knew that ten thousand individuals were, in respect to levels of intellect, distributed as follows:

| At level x | 10 |
|---|---|
| " " x + k | 100 |
| " " x + 2k | 1000 |
| " " x + 3k | 1190 |
| " " x + 4k | 1000 |
| " " x + 5k | 1000 |
| " " x + 6k | 2000 |
| " " x + 7k | 2000 |
| " " x + 8k | 1000 |
| " " x + 9k | 500 |
| " " x + 10k or higher | 200 |

and suppose that the ten thousand were tested with various intellectual tasks with the following result:

| 10000 had Task No. 6 right |
|---|
| 9990 " " " 18 right |
| 9990 " " " 19 right |
| 8890 " " " 15 right |
| 8890 " " " 20 right |
| 6700 " " " 22 right |
| 3700 " " " 28 right |
| 1700 " " " 29 right |
| 700 " " " 30 right |
| 200 " " " 31 right |
| 200 " " " 33 right |

Using these results at their face value, we should conclude that within this group No. 6 can be done by intellects of level x, and perhaps of lower levels; Nos. 18 and 19 require level x + k; Nos. 15 and 20 require level x + 2k; No. 22 requires level x + 5k; No. 28 requires level x + 7k; No. 29 requires level x + 8k; No. 30 requires level x + 9k; Nos. 31 and 33 require level x + 10k or higher.   Nos. 31 and 33 are thus 1k harder than 30, which in turn is 1k harder than 29, which in turn is 1k harder than 28, which in turn is 2k harder than 22, which is 3k harder than 15 or 20, and so on.

## THE MEASUREMENT OF DIFFERENCES IN DIFFICULTY BY WAY OF KNOWLEDGE OF THE FORM OF DISTRIBUTION OF THE VARIATIONS OF AN INDIVIDUAL IN LEVEL OF INTELLECT[1]

An individual does not display the same level of intellect at all times and seasons.  He varies around his average status.  If we know the real form of distribution of his variations in level, we can use it to compare the differences of tasks in real difficulty, just as we use knowledge of the form of distribution of a group.

[1] We began our search for means of measuring differences in difficulty by inquiring whether the real form of distribution of the real abilities of the individuals represented *in a single array in a correlation table*, might not be determined with greater certainty than the form of distribution of the group as a whole.  This is indeed often the case; and the use of a group sorted into arrays has much to recommend it.  The consideration of the factors which do influence the form of distribution of the real ability of the individuals in an array, led us to a broader view of the means of scaling difficulty of task and level of intellect.

The form of distribution of the real abilities in an array is determined by three causes: (1) The form of distribution of an individual's variations around his own average; (2) the relation of an individual's variability to his amount of ability, and (3) the form of distribution of the entire group from which the array is sorted out by its correlation.

It will be shown that if we can determine the facts for any one of these, we can transmute certain differences in rank into differences in amount.  The transmutations by (1) and (2) are almost, if not quite, independent of those by (3) in respect of facts and assumptions, and so provide a check of great value.  The use of an array instead of a total group utilizes all three methods together in a way that has many advantages.  We shall not, however, make use of this method in the main body of our work.

Suppose, for example, that an adult is measured with a hundred examinations, each consisting of 100 tasks, each of ten levels, $l_1$, $l_2$, $l_3$, $l_4$, etc., of increasing difficulty. Suppose that the highest level at which he attains 50 percent correct[2] is level $l_3$ in 27 cases, level $l_4$ in 50 cases, and level $l_5$ in 23 cases. Then, if we know the form of distribution of his variability, we can compare $l_5$–$l_4$ with $l_4$–$l_3$ in terms of amount. We could thus put into comparison the differences between any two levels between his upper and lower limits.

This method will be very useful as a check upon estimates of difficulty *via* the form of distribution of a perfectly measured group, because it is so independent thereof. The forces which make one individual vary from one time to another are probably almost, if not quite, different from the forces which make one individual vary from other individuals when all are perfectly measured.

We have therefore studied the variability of an individual in repeated tests of intelligence and other mental abilities at some length, trying to discover the form which its distribution would have if the ability in question were measured by a scale of truly equal units, instead of the arbitrary scales which we have. The results, which appear in Appendix I, are substantially unanimous in fitting the hypothesis that, omitting such extreme conditions (for example, being asleep or being seriously ill) as prevent an individual from being tested at all, depressing conditions are neither more frequent nor greater in their effects than elevating conditions, the real variability being symmetrical.

For example, 60 pupils in Grades 4, 5, and 6 were tested with Stanford Binet, National A, National B, Otis advanced,[3] Myers Mental Measure, Haggerty Delta 2, Illinois, and certain parts of Dearborn. Each score was first turned into a deviation from the median for the group in that test,

2 Or 60%, or 90%, or whatever percent we are using as a measure in our experiments.

3 Some had the Otis Primary instead. For these, estimated scores in the Otis Advanced were computed.

in terms of the variability of the group in the test in question. Then it was expressed as a deviation from the average of the eight such deviation-scores for the individual in question. These last deviations represent the variability of an individual around his average ability in intelligence tests. Their distribution is as follows:

| Deviations | Frequencies |
|---|---|
| − 165 to − 194 | 0 |
| − 135 to − 164 | 2 |
| − 105 to − 134 | 1 |
| − 75 to − 104 | 9 |
| − 45 to − 74 | 40 |
| − 15 to − 44 | 124 |
| − 14 to + 14 | 137 |
| + 15 to + 44 | 86 |
| + 45 to + 74 | 41 |
| + 75 to + 104 | 10 |
| + 105 to + 134 | 3 |
| + 135 to + 164 | 2 |
| + 165 to + 194 | 1 |

65 pupils in grades 8 to 12 were tested with Alpha Form 5, Alpha Form 8, Terman Group Test Form A, Terman Group Test Form B, and half of Part I of the Thorndike Examination for High-School Graduates. These five scores for each pupil were treated just as the eight scores described in the previous paragraph, except that the final deviations are deviations from the individual's median instead of from his average.

The resulting distribution was as follows (including the 65 zero deviations of the medians themselves):

| Deviations | Frequencies |
|---|---|
| − 110 to − 129 | 1 |
| − 90 to − 109 | 2 |
| − 70 to − 89 | 10 |
| − 50 to − 69 | 10 |
| − 30 to − 49 | 34 |
| − 10 to − 29 | 47 |
| − 9 to + 9 | 117 |
| + 10 to + 29 | 55 |
| + 30 to + 49 | 27 |
| + 50 to + 69 | 15 |
| + 70 to + 89 | 5 |
| + 90 to + 109 | 2 |
| + 110 to + 129 | 0 |

We can then use the method to compare amounts of difficulty up and down from an individual's average level. Our results also seem to fit the hypothesis that the real variability of an individual, under the conditions stated above, fits a probability surface limited at about $+$ and $-3$ S.D. better than it fits any other one surface. They are not, however, such as justify a rigorous quantitative treatment of fit.

### THE RELATION OF THE VARIABILITY OF AN INDIVIDUAL TO HIS AMOUNT OF ABILITY

The facts of the previous section enable us to compare and equate differences in difficulty for an individual of average level $l_k$, using of course many such individuals to gain exactitude, or general reference, or both. These differences will be restricted in range to levels not very far below or above $l_k$. If we wish to compare and equate them with differences outside that range, we must use individuals of average level higher than $l_k$ and individuals of average level lower than $l_k$. To use them we must know how much less or greater their real variability is than that of our starting group with average at $l_k$.

We have, therefore, made very extensive investigations of the relation of an individual's amount of variability to his amount of ability. These are reported in Appendix II. Only their general nature and results will be stated in this section. Here as elsewhere we distinguish sharply between (a) the apparent, or face-value, relation observed between the variability of an individual's separate *scores* and his average *score,* and (b) the real relation that would be observed if these scores were transmuted into measures such that 1, 2, 3, 4, 5, 6, 7, etc., represented a real arithmetical progression of amounts of the ability. For example, we find that twenty individuals each of whom took (after two preliminary trials, to eliminate the practice effect) from eleven to thirteen forms of Part I of the Thorndike Intelligence Examination for High School Graduates, showed the results of Table 1. If the scores are taken at their face value, it appears that the variability of an individual whose median score is about 105 (from 100 to 113) is very nearly the same as the variability of an individual whose median score is about 128 (125 to 132). If, however, the units of the scoring scale from 90 to 120 really represent smaller increments of ability than the units from 120 to 145, the real variability of an individual of ability 105 is less than the real variability of an individual of ability 128, and conversely, if the units of the scoring scale from 90 to 120 really represent larger increments of ability than the units from 120 to 145.

We thus record the face-value-score results for many different sorts of tests of intelligence,[4] noting in each case any facts about the construction of the tests which concern the probability that its units progressively swell or shrink in 'real' value over any considerable fraction of the range we are concerned with. We note especially the results in those cases where there is no reason to expect swelling more than shrinking. The average relations between variability and ability found in these cases may be taken to represent approximately the real relation, until some one produces evidence that, in all or nearly all tests for the ability in question, there are forces leading psychologists, quite without intention, to devise scoring plans which make for progressive swelling or shrinking of units.

The general drift of the facts is shown in Table 2 which gives the variability (in face-value-score units) of an individual from day to day in intellect as a percent of the variability of a person whose amount of intellect is that represented by an Army Alpha first-trial score of about 100.

---

[4] We have secured extensive data concerning Army Alpha, Examination A, Army Beta, Stanford Mental Age, the National Intelligence Test, the Otis Advanced Test, the Haggerty Delta 2, the Myers Mental Measure, the Kelley-Trabue, the Stanford Binet, the Terman Group Test, the I.E.R. Test of Selective and Relational Thinking, the I.E.R. Test of Generalization and Organization, the Thorndike Non-Verbal Test, the Thorndike Examination for High School Graduates, series of 1919 to 1930, and the Toops Clerical Test. See Appendix II.

## TABLE 1

VARIATIONS OF THE SCORES OF THIRTEEN (OR FEWER) 30-MINUTE TRIALS WITH PART I OF THE THORNDIKE INTELLIGENCE EXAMINATION FOR HIGH SCHOOL GRADUATES FROM THE MEDIAN SCORE FOR THE INDIVIDUAL IN ALL THIRTEEN TRIALS. 20 GIFTED PUPILS, A, C, D, E, . . . U. 13 DIFFERENT DAYS.

| Individual Median. | j 87 | s 95 | d 96 | i 99 | o 99 | j to o 87 to 99 | a, c, e, f, g, h, k, n, q, t 100 to 113 | u 125 | p 125 | l 128 | m 128 | r 132 | u to r 125 to 132 |
|---|---|---|---|---|---|---|---|---|---|---|---|---|---|
| −11, −12, −13 | 1 | | | 1 | 2 | 1 | 1 | 1 | 3 | 2 | 1 | 1 | 2 |
| − 8, − 9, −10 | 4 | 1 | | 2 | 2 | 5 | 8 | 1 | 2 | 0 | 1 | 0 | 4 |
| − 5, − 6, − 7 | 3 | 0 | 2 | 0 | 1 | 5 | 10 | 2 | 3 | 3 | 0 | 1 | 5 |
| − 2, − 3, − 4 | 0 | 4 | 2 | 0 | 2 | 11 | 20 | 3 | 1 | 2 | 2 | 2 | 11 |
| − 1, 0, + 1 | 4 | 3 | 5 | 5 | 1 | 18 | 32 | 1 | 1 | 2 | 3 | 2 | 13 |
| + 2, + 3, + 4 | 1 | 1 | 2 | 2 | 2 | 6 | 9 | 4 | 2 | 1 | 1 | 3 | 8 |
| + 5, + 6, + 7 | | 1 | 2 | 1 | 1 | 10 | 20 | 1 | 1 | 1 | 3 | 2 | 11 |
| + 8, + 9, +10 | | 1 | | 2 | 2 | 5 | 12 | | | 3 | 1 | 1 | 8 |
| +11, +12, +13 | | | | | | 2 | 3 | | | | 1 | | 2 |
| +14, +15, +16 | | | | | | | 4 | | | | | | |
| ......... | | | | | | | | | | | | | |
| +24, +25, +26 | | | | | | | 1 | | | | | | |
| n | | | | | | 63 | 120 | | | | | | 64 |
| Average Variation | | | | | | 4.2 | 4.8 | | | | | | 4.8 |

It appears from Table 2, and still more clearly from the consideration of the detailed facts in Appendix II which Table 2 barely summarizes, that if we had scales for intellect whose units were really equal, the variability of an individual from day to day would be the same, regardless of whether the average amount of intellect possessed by him was that of a 'low grade ten-year-old' or of a 'superior adult,' that of an Army Alpha score of 25 or that of a score of 175.

This result is so important, if true, that we have sought for facts and probabilities in real or apparent opposition to it.

First, there are the obvious opposing facts of range of variability in intellectual or similar production. Keats may have written *"On Reading Chapman's 'Homer' "* in one hour, and have written nothing in some other hour when he tried as hard, whereas an average twelve-year-old varies at the most from nothing up to a composition scoring 50 on the Hillegas scale. A gifted stock-exchange trader who in transactions of 10,000 shares a day, averages $100 profit, may vary from a profit of $25 to one of $2,500, whereas a less gifted trader who averages $10 a day on 100 shares in the same market, it is said, varies over a much narrower range.

Such apparently opposing facts as these are, however, not so simple as they seem. If we had a full record of all of Keats' hours of equal effort, the production called zero might turn out to be far above zero. The ideas he had then might rank in poetic value far above those of the best hours of the average man. The less gifted trader may vary over just as wide a range. For example, a still less gifted trader *losing* $100 on the average, may lose in two days the $25 and the $2500 that the gifted trader gains. Furthermore, we have to consider the alleged common observation that as one increases his expertness in acting, music, dancing, or athletic feats, he seems to reduce his variability. Thus a sprinter who can on the average run 95 yards in 10 seconds almost never runs less than 90 yards or more than 98 yards

TABLE 2

THE RELATION OF THE VARIABILITY OF AN INDIVIDUAL TO HIS AMOUNT OF ABILITY IN FIFTEEN TESTS OR AMALGAMATIONS OF TESTS, USING EIGHT LEVELS OF ABILITY

| | Low Level Fourth or Below Alpha 15–29 | Fourth Grade Alpha 30–49 | Sixth Grade Alpha 50–69 | Grade Seven Eight Alpha 70–89 | Ninth Grade Alpha 90–109 | Upper High School Alpha 110–129 | College Freshmen Alpha 130–149 | Upper College Alpha 150 or + |
|---|---|---|---|---|---|---|---|---|
| Alpha | 67 | 97 | 109 | 108 | 100 | 107 | 101 | 88 |
| Exam. A | 90 | 88 | 88 | 98 | 100 | 104 | 83 | 79 |
| Thorndike I | 85½ | 77 | 94 | 101 | 100 | 92 | 92 | 84 |
| Otis Adv. | | | 106½ | 98 | 100 | 85 | 86 | 62 |
| Terman Group | 138 | | | 85 | 100 | 116 | 94 | 89 |
| St. Mental Age | | 115 | 116 | 117 | 100 | 116 | | |
| National | | 139 | 153 | 119 | 100 | 109 | | |
| Haggerty, Myers | | 100 | 120 | 106 | 100 | | | |
| Beta+Picture | 81½ | 103 | 103 | 118 | 100 | 106 | 81 | |
| Toops | | | 98 | 110 | 100 | | | |
| Thorndike, New I | | | 66 | 53 | 100 | 107 | 129 | |
| Thorndike, II | | | | 87 | 100 | 105 | 96 | 87 |
| Thorndike, III | | | | | 100 | 111 | 123 | 114½ |
| Thorndike Total | | | | 61 | 100 | 92 | 83 | 75 |
| Median | 85½ | 100 | 105 | 101 | 100 | 106½ | 93 | 85 |
| Average (equal weights) | 92 | 103 | 106 | 97 | 100 | 104 | 97 | 85½ |
| Average (half weight to entries whose sum of weights <10) | 93 | 103 | 108 | 99 | 100 | 104 | 96 | 85 |

in that time, whereas the heavy-footed youth whose average is 50 yards in 10 seconds may reach 60 and fall below 40. On the whole, what facts there are concerning the relation of variability to amount of ability in mental traits in the world at large, seem to favor a slope down about as much as a slope up.

Certain hypotheses concerning the constitution of increases in amount in the case of mental traits are in opposition to our result. One such hypothesis is that there are certain factors producing intellect all of which act positively and by addition. For simplicity's sake, we will assume that each factor contributes as much to intellect as any other. Then the average amount of intellect that an individual displays depends on the number of these factors that he possesses, and his variability from time to time depends on how many of them are then active. Assume that each of them has the same probability of acting as any other and that the number of them that will be active at any one time is a result of the probabilities of their several combinations. In such a case the variability increases as the square root of the average amount of the ability. For example, if there are five, ten, fifteen, and twenty factors in individuals A, B, C, and D, respectively, the status of A, B, C, and D at a thousand points taken at random in their lives, will be as shown in Table 3, and the variability of D will be twice that of A. If intellect is caused in any such way as this, the number of factors is probably very large so that we may better change our illustration from 5 and 20, to say 1,000,000 and 1,500,-000. The variabilities are then (mean square deviations) $\sqrt{250,000}$ and $\sqrt{375,000}$.[5] The ability which is 500,000 greater, or $1\frac{1}{2}$ times as great, has a variability which is only 1.2 times as great.[5]

---

[5] These are for points of time. The variabilities in tests covering thirty minutes or so are the variabilities of averages of many such points, and may be represented as $\dfrac{\sqrt{250,000}}{\sqrt{n}}$ and $\dfrac{\sqrt{375,000}}{\sqrt{n}}$ where n is relatively large, say 1,000; this, however, does not change the relation of variability to amount of ability.

Such hypotheses as this can be nearly reconciled with our results if the difference between the intellect of the level of Alpha 25 and Alpha 175 is due to an increase in the number of factors which is large absolutely, but small in comparison with the number involved in Alpha 25. Thus if the difference is 500,000, but an ability of Alpha 25 involves 5,000,000 then the variabilities around levels of 25 and 125 will be as $\sqrt{1,250,000}$ and $\sqrt{1,350,000}$, or as 1118 and 1162, the second being only 4 percent greater. The reasonableness of this depends upon the location of the absolute zero of intellect. If that is ten times as far below Alpha 25 as Alpha 25 is below Alpha 175, it is perfectly reasonable.

Another way out of the difficulty is to deny the validity of the theory that intellect is constituted by the addition of positive factors only. If the factors in the above illustrations were inhibitive against some maximum amount of

TABLE 3

THE VARIABILITY OF FOUR INDIVIDUALS IN INTELLECT ACCORDING TO A CERTAIN ADDITIVE COMBINATION OF FACTORS ALL POSITIVE

| Amount of Intellect | Frequencies at 1000 Random Periods | | | |
|---|---|---|---|---|
| | A | B | C | D |
| 0 | 31 | 1 | | |
| 1 | 156 | 10 | | |
| 2 | 313 | 44 | 3 | |
| 3 | 313 | 117 | 14 | 1 |
| 4 | 156 | 205 | 42 | 5 |
| 5 | 31 | 246 | 92 | 15 |
| 6 | | 205 | 153 | 37 |
| 7 | | 117 | 197 | 74 |
| 8 | | 44 | 197 | 120 |
| 9 | | 10 | 153 | 160 |
| 10 | | 1 | 92 | 176 |
| 11 | | | 42 | 160 |
| 12 | | | 14 | 120 |
| 13 | | | 3 | 74 |
| 14 | | | | 37 |
| 15 | | | | 15 |
| 16 | | | | 5 |
| 17 | | | | 1 |
| Average | 2.5 | 5.0 | 7.5 | 10.0 |

intellect that would otherwise act, so that the more of them that acted the less intellect there would be, the relation between amount and variability would be reversed, the variability of a man's intellect being as the square root of the amount by which the man was *below* the maximum intellect! There may be, and probably is, some combination of additive and inhibitive factors making the average intellects of men vary up and down from an amount typical of the human species; and this may result in equal variability for A, who is much below the average, and B, who is much above it. For example, suppose there are 6 factors, a, b, c, d, e, and f, each contributing — 1, and 6 factors, A, B, C, D, E, and F, each contributing + 1; and that every intellect is constituted by 6 factors chosen from the 12; and that the momentary conditions of each intellect represent the chance combinations of its six factors. Then we have intellects whose averages range from — 3 to + 3, according to whether they are constituted by six minus causes, or by 5 minus and 1 plus, or by 4 minus and 2 plus, or by 3 minus and 3 plus, and so on. All will have the same variability, however, the frequencies being in the proportions 1, 6, 15, 20, 15, 6, 1, with a mean square deviation of 1.2247.

A consideration of the relative probabilities of various types of constitution of intellect out of positive and negative factors would be interesting, but is too speculative to be profitable for our present purpose. The attainment of greater intellect by the lack or suppression of negative factors as well as by the possession and use of positive factors is at least a possibility; and will seem highly probable to many.

On the whole, then, we do not need to be especially skeptical of the experimental findings that the variability in tests of a half hour from time to time is approximately equal over the range from, say, the ten-percentile adult intellect to the ninety-five percentile adult intellect.

MEASUREMENT BY WAY OF THE FORM OF DISTRIBUTION OF
INTELLECT IN SOME DEFINED GROUP

If $T_1$, $T_2$, $T_3$, and $T_4$, etc., are intellectual tasks with which $\dfrac{K}{n}$, $\dfrac{K+a}{n}$, $\dfrac{K+a+b}{n}$, $\dfrac{K+a+b+c}{n}$, etc., individuals of a group of individuals succeed respectively (K, a, b, c, etc., all being positive, K being greater than 0 and the largest percentage being under 100), we can measure the differences in difficulty for intellect between $T_1$, $T_2$, $T_3$, $T_4$,

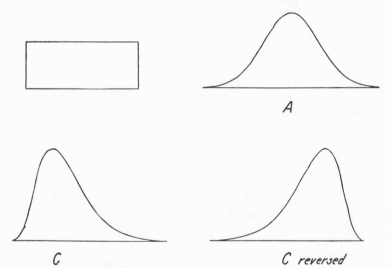

FIG. 5. Four surfaces of frequency: A rectangle, Form A, Form C, and Form C reversed.

etc., in terms of amount, if we know the form of distribution of intellect in the group.[6] If, for example, n is 100, K is 5, and a, b, c, d, and e are each 10, the differences in difficulty will be in the proportions shown in Table 5, according as the form of distribution of the group is a rectangle, a surface like A, a surface like C, or a surface like C reversed, shown in Table 4 and Figure 5.

[6] Our measures will approximate perfection in proportion as $T_1$, $T_2$, $T_3$, $T_4$, etc., depend upon all of intellect and nothing but intellect. As has been noted, we are assuming this for the present, reserving for full treatment later the influence of failures of certain tasks to utilize intellect fully, and the influence of admixture of other factors than intellect.

We have estimated the form of distribution for certain groups, using the following procedure. Choose some group which is caused by forces that can be studied and which, so

TABLE 4

FOUR FORMS OF DISTRIBUTION

| Quantity | | | Frequency | |
|---|---|---|---|---|
| | Rectangle | Form A | Form C | Form C (reversed) |
| K + | $8\frac{1}{3}$ | $\frac{1}{2}$ | 0 | $\frac{1}{2}$ |
| K + 1 | $8\frac{1}{3}$ | $1\frac{1}{2}$ | 1 | 1 |
| K + 2 | $8\frac{1}{3}$ | $4\frac{1}{2}$ | $11\frac{1}{2}$ | $1\frac{1}{2}$ |
| K + 3 | $8\frac{1}{3}$ | 9 | $22\frac{1}{2}$ | $3\frac{1}{2}$ |
| K + 4 | $8\frac{1}{3}$ | 15 | 23 | $6\frac{1}{2}$ |
| K + 5 | $8\frac{1}{3}$ | $19\frac{1}{2}$ | $17\frac{1}{2}$ | $11\frac{1}{2}$ |
| K + 6 | $8\frac{1}{3}$ | $19\frac{1}{2}$ | $11\frac{1}{2}$ | $17\frac{1}{2}$ |
| K + 7 | $8\frac{1}{3}$ | 15 | $6\frac{1}{2}$ | 23 |
| K + 8 | $8\frac{1}{3}$ | 9 | $3\frac{1}{2}$ | $22\frac{1}{2}$ |
| K + 9 | $8\frac{1}{3}$ | $4\frac{1}{2}$ | $1\frac{1}{2}$ | $11\frac{1}{2}$ |
| K + 10 | $8\frac{1}{3}$ | $1\frac{1}{2}$ | 1 | 1 |
| K + 11 | $8\frac{1}{2}$ | $\frac{1}{2}$ | $\frac{1}{2}$ | 0 |

far as can be ascertained, represents a clustering around one amount of intellect with divergences therefrom due to a large number of causes each small in amount of influence.

TABLE 5

APPROXIMATE PERCENTAGES WHICH THE DIFFERENCES IN DIFFICULTY BETWEEN TASK $T_1$, TASK $T_2$, TASK $T_3$, ETC., ARE OF THE DIFFERENCE BETWEEN $T_5$ AND $T_6$, ACCORDING TO THE FORM OF DISTRIBUTION OF THE GROUP

| | For a Rectangle | For Form A | For Form C | For Form C, reversed |
|---|---|---|---|---|
| $T_1$ to $T_2$ | 100 | 244 | 141 | 355 |
| $T_2$ to $T_3$ | 100 | 148 | 105 | 186 |
| $T_3$ to $T_4$ | 100 | 112 | 91 | 136 |
| $T_4$ to $T_5$ | 100 | 104 | 96 | 109 |
| $T_5$ to $T_6$ | 100 | 100 | 100 | 100 |

Choose many instruments for measuring intellect (such as the Otis Advanced, Army Alpha, National and Terman tests), each of which (1) is known to correlate fairly well

with any reasonable criterion of intellect; (2) is different
from the others; (3) was constructed without any depend-
ence of the selection of elements or of the scoring system,
upon the assumption that the distribution of intellect in the
group in question approximates Form A. Find by each test
by actual experiment the form of distribution for the group,
using the scoring system for each test at its face value.
Find the form of distribution which best fits all these varying forms. Observe the effect (upon the form of distribution) of reducing the chance error in the scores by obtaining
the form of distribution for the group when two or more
trials with the same instrument are combined for each individual. If the best fit distribution is of Form A, and if the
reduction of the chance error does not produce divergence
from this form, we may conclude that Form A represents
closely the form of distribution of the real ability in the
group, as measured by a scale of equal units of difference
in that ability. The general argument is that nothing in the
instruments themselves or their scoring favors this form of
distribution for this group, and that it can not be due to the
chance error, since reducing that leaves it unimpaired.

The details of the argument and the evidence are presented in Appendix III. They demonstrate that for Grades
from 6 to 12, and probably for freshmen in colleges of equal
standards of admission, the form of distribution of the population of a grade, when perfectly measured in respect of
the ability required for success with standard types of intelligence tests, in truly equal units, will be unimodal, symmetrical, and very closely of Form A, the 'normal' probability surface, the equation of whose bounding curve is the
exponential curve $y = \dfrac{1}{\sigma\sqrt{2\pi}} e^{\frac{-x^2}{\sigma^2}}$ where $\sigma$ is the mean
square deviation.

The critical reader should examine Appendix III with
especial care. The method of measuring the intellectual
difficulty of tasks which we adopted for our actual scale construction is based on it. It also provides support for certain

features of previous work which up till now has been taken on faith. Appendices I and II are perhaps of greater theoretical importance, but Appendix III is fundamental for present and future practice in mental measurement.

We can then measure the difficulty of any intellectual task for pupils in any one of these grades by the percent of the group succeeding with it, as shown in the illustration that follows:

3190 pupils in grade 9 were tested with four tasks in completing sentences. The percentages succeeding were respectively 60, 30.5, 46.1, and 37.1. We assume that these are intellectual tasks, that is, that success with each depends upon intellect.

The form of distribution of the intellects of the group being Form A, a percentage correct of 60 corresponds to a division of the group at — .25330, that is, at — .25330 of the mean square deviation of the group (in the ability measured in truly equal units by that task) below the average or median of the group (in the ability measured by that task).

.51010, + .09790, and + .32920 have similar meanings for the difficulties of tasks 21, 22, and 23.

The differences in difficulty between the tasks are 21–20 = .7643, 21–22 = .4122, and so on, in truly equal units, unity being taken arbitrarily as the mean square deviation of the group in intellect.

MEASUREMENT BY WAY OF THE FORM OF DISTRIBUTION OF AN ARRAY IN A CORRELATION TABLE

The fourth method of attacking our problem uses, as the group whose form of distribution is to be determined, the population comprising one array in a correlation table of the sort shown in Table 6, where the individuals are arrayed under their scores in some examination symptomatic of intellect. Each array consists of two compartments representing the two scores (Failure and Success) attainable in the intellectual task whose difficulty we wish to measure.

For example, we might have data concerning success with the task in question from 1000 persons each scoring 30 in Army Alpha, from 1000 persons each scoring 35 in Army Alpha, from 1000 persons each scoring 40 in Army Alpha, and so on. Or we might have data concerning success with the task in question from 1000 persons scoring Mental Age 8.0 in the Stanford Binet, from 1000 scoring Mental Age 8.5 in the Stanford Binet, and so on.

If both the total score and success in the task depend upon intellect, and nothing but intellect, the latter being one of the varying manifestations of intellect of which the former represents the average condition, the form of distribution of the intellects measured in an array in such a

TABLE 6

THE CORRELATION OF SUCCESS IN TASK 281 WITH AVERAGE SCORE IN A
TOTAL SERIES OF INTELLECTUAL TASKS.[7]

| Score in task 281 | Score in the total series | | | | | | | | | | | | | | |
|---|---|---|---|---|---|---|---|---|---|---|---|---|---|---|---|
| | 17 | 18 | 19 | 20 | 21 | 22 | 23 | 24 | 25 | 26 | 27 | 28 | 29 | 30 | 31 |
| Wrong | 14 | 44 | 72 | 94 | 151 | 213 | 259 | 274 | 281 | 187 | 75 | 55 | 6 | 5 | 1 |
| Right | 2 | 4 | 14 | 19 | 38 | 60 | 111 | 203 | 265 | 302 | 223 | 260 | 90 | 39 | 12 |

correlation table, measured in truly equal units, will be symmetrical and approximately 'normal.' For they are a random sampling from the combined distribution of certain individuals closely alike in average intellect, when all the variations of each individual from time to time are taken; and we have shown that each of these individual's distributions is symmetrical and approximately "normal."

The use of such an array[8] is in fact a convenient means of applying our knowledge of the form of distribution of the variations of an individual in intellect. It is impracticable to obtain a hundred trials of an individual with an

---

[7] The entries of Table 6 are genuine, but the total series is not a series representing all of intellect, nor is the score in it an average of many trials. Such data are not available. The "Score in the total series" in Table 6 is in fact the score in one trial of one-half hour test of certain features of intellect.

[8] We shall later see uses of other sorts of arrays.

intellectual task; and even if we did, the results would be hard to interpret because of possible effects of practice. It is possible to find a hundred individuals who are substantially identical in their average performance at intellectual tasks, and test them all once with any given task.

The measurements of the difficulty of one intellectual task in terms of the distance + or — from the average of one such array, expressed as a multiple of the variability of that array, can be made approximately commensurate with measurements of the difficulty of another intellectual task in terms of the distance + or — from the average of the corresponding array, expressed as a multiple of its variability. For we have shown that the variability of an individual (and so of such an array) in intellect is approximately the same regardless of his average amount of intellect. Consequently the two multiples are of approximately the same unit and the distance between the two averages of overlapping arrays can be measured in terms of this same unit. If two arrays do not overlap, we can bridge the gap by inserting data from intermediate arrays which do form a series of overlapping arrays.

### THE DEFECTS OF THE MEASUREMENTS SO FAR DESCRIBED

We have determined the approximate form of distribution of a grade population, from Grade 6 to Grade 12, in respect of level of intellect at one time, if that were measured in truly equal units. We have done the same for a population (an array) characterized by identity in average of intellect measured by a random selection of times. By an extension and refinement of the methods which we have used, this could be done with greater precision.

If all that we require for the measurement of the intellectual difficulty of tasks is to secure a group of known form of distribution in intellect when measured in truly equal units, whose members we may test with the tasks in question, the problem is solved. Unfortunately more is required. The chief defect in our procedures is that the difficulty which we measure by the percentages of our group which succeed is not pure intellectual difficulty. Any such task as solving an arithmetical problem or completing a sentence or obeying a command is deficient by not involving all of intellect, and often also by involving other factors than intellect. From the percentage of a group of known distribution in respect of intellect, which succeed with it, we can derive a close measure of its difficulty, but not of its *intellectual* difficulty. Although this has not been understood in the past, it can easily be realized by considering cases like the following: A group of known distribution in respect of intellectual level measured in truly equal units, is tested with (a) leaping over a certain hurdle, (b) distinguishing a certain pitch from one higher, (c) spelling a certain word, (d) giving the opposite of a certain word, and (e) giving the opposite of a certain other word. The percent of success is equal for a, b, c, d, and e, being, let us say, 40, so that each of the five tasks is $+ .2533$ S.D. The five are not equal in intellectual difficulty, however. Common sense tells us this; and the verdict of common sense is a crude intimation of the scientific fact that for (a) the $+ .2533$ S.D. means .2533 times the S.D. of the group in ability to leap that hurdle above the mean of the group in ability to leap that hurdle, whereas for (d), the $+ .2533$ S.D. means .2533 times the S.D. of the group in ability to think of the first opposite above the mean of the group's ability to think of that opposite. Ability to think of the second opposite may conceivably differ from ability to think of the first opposite by involving much more of intellect, or much less of non-intellect, or both, in the same way that the ability to think of the first opposite differs from the ability to leap a hurdle. If we take the tasks chosen as intellectual tasks and put in any of the stock intelligence examinations, they will so differ. This has been abundantly proven by investigations which will be reported in Chapter IV. Moreover, no one of them will measure all of intellect and nothing but intellect.

In fact, no one short task does or can involve all of intellect and nothing but intellect. Any one short task measures only a fraction of intellect and is influenced by other forces than intellect. That is, any one short task measures intellect plus an error. The nature and amount of this error must be considered in connection with any procedure for estimating the intellectual difficulty of a task from the percentage of individuals who succeed with it.[9]

There are other hidden assumptions and weak or even missing links in the argument by which we proceed from knowledge of who and how many can do a task, to a measure of its intellectual difficulty. In the next chapter we shall expose these, subject the entire argument to a much more rigorous treatment, and seek to remedy the defect noted above and such others as are found.

[9] The exposure of this defect should not diminish our use of the general procedure of inferring degree of difficulty from percentage of failures in a distribution of known form. On the contrary, now that we are aware of the defect, we can make much better use of the procedure than when we were ignorant of it. As we shall elsewhere show in detail, if we replace a single task by a composite of forty tasks, and use twenty or more right as our mark of ''success,'' we can use the procedure with better results than have ever been obtained hitherto.

# CHAPTER III

## THE MEASUREMENTS OF THE INTELLECTUAL DIFFICULTY OF TASKS AND OF LEVEL OF INTELLECT: MORE RIGOROUS AND EXACT METHODS

In the two previous chapters we have operated with provisional and somewhat vague definitions and inexact assumptions, largely in order to maintain continuity with what has been done to date in the measurement of intellect. It is now necessary to treat the whole matter of intellectual difficulty and level of intellect more rigorously.

We have assumed (1) that there is such a quality or characteristic of man as altitude or level of intellect; (2) whose amount or degree is measured by the height at which it can attain success with a series of intellectual tasks ranked for difficulty; (3) that the same individual differs in the amount or degree of it which he has available from time to time; and (4) that different individuals differ in the amounts or degrees of it which they have available on the average. (5) We have defined intellectual tasks only loosely and vaguely as those in which men esteemed very intelligent differ most from men esteemed very unintelligent. (6) We have defined intellectual difficulty only loosely and vaguely as that characteristic of a task, an increase in which reduces the number of intellects who can succeed with it, eliminating those esteemed unintelligent more rapidly than those esteemed intelligent.

Since we are treating intellect as the ability to perform intellectual tasks, our primary need is a clearer and more exact notion of intellectual tasks. We can reach this in either of two ways. The first is by assuming that certain abilities, such as to understand directions, or to know facts, or to use relations of likeness, part and whole, actor and acted upon, genus and species, and the like, or to use facts

59

together, and certain tasks which represent them, are *as a whole* intellectual. We must then describe these tasks, and the credit or weight to be attached to each, precisely, and put them in a total series in such form that an individual intellect can attempt them all.

The second is by assuming that the ranking of individuals in an order from idiots to Aristotles for amount of intellect[1] by some defined consensus of opinion is valid. We must then describe this consensus and the method of its operation.

If we take the former way, we may attach the term "intellectual task" to *any selection from the total series which, when treated in the same way, gives measures for individuals which correlate + 1.00 with measures from the total series.* This task would be just as intellectual as the total series, would involve just the same abilities as it involved and no others. Everything would be rigorous and precise after the selection of the tasks and arrangement for scoring them. In practice a selection which gave a correlation slightly under 1.00 might be accepted as substantially an intellectual task.

Further, if any selection from the total series, when treated in the same way as the total series, correlates as closely with the total series as its own self correlation permits, that selection is an intellectual task.[2] Its failure of

1 Amount of intellect means here the average amount which the individual has available over a period long enough to be representative of him.

2 Let the group be measured a number of times by the total series i and by the task t. Let $r_{i_1 i_2}$ be the correlation between any two measures by i and let $r_{t_1 t_2}$ be the correlation between any two measures by t. Let $r_{t_1 i_1}$ be the correlation between any measure by t and any measure by i. Let $r_{t_\infty i_\infty}$ be the correlation between the average measure by t repeated indefinitely, and i repeated indefinitely.

Then by the well-known attenuation formula,

$$r_{t_\infty i_\infty} = \frac{r_{t_1 i_1}}{\sqrt{r_{t_1 t_2} r_{i_1 i_2}}}$$

and if $r_{t_1 i_1}$ is no less than the geometric mean of $r_{t_1 t_2}$ and $r_{i_1 i_2}$, $r_{t_\infty i_\infty}$ will be 1.00 or perfect correlation. Since $r_{i_1 i_2}$ in a group of wide range in intellect will approximate unity, we may set as the requirement that, in a group of wide range in intellect, $r_{t_1 i_1}$ should be little if any less than $\sqrt{r_{t_1 t_2}}$.

perfect correlation is due entirely to the fact that the intellect of the same individual varies from time to time, not to any intrinsic inadequacy or irrelevance.

If we take the latter way, we may attach the term "intellectual task" to any task or collection of tasks, the score in which correlates $+1.00$ with the ranking of individuals in an order for intellect by the consensus, or correlates as closely with that ranking as its own self-correlation permits. By collecting such tasks we may obtain a total series which may then be used as a criterion in the same manner as a series derived by the other method.

These two procedures are more definite and systematic and rigorous forms of what has been done in test construction. Psychologists have on the one hand taken tasks which they assumed to be intellectual and have put samplings of them into teams of tasks. On the other hand they have assumed that a certain validity attached to rankings by teachers, by the sifting process of advancement in school, or by other forms of consensus, and have selected those collections of tasks which showed high correlations with such a criterion.

What abilities and tasks shall be treated as intellectual is essentially a matter of arbitrary assumption or choice at the outset, either directly, of the abilities or tasks themselves, or indirectly, of the consensus which provides the criterion. After the first choice is made, tasks not included in it, and even not known, may be found to correlate perfectly with the adopted total, and so to be "intellectual"; but their intellectualness is tested by and depends on the first arbitrary choice. Had a different first choice been made, they might not be intellectual. This arbitrariness is a sign of weakness, but it is at present unavoidable. We have to define intellectual tasks as best we can, and trust that future scientific uses of the definition will improve it. We shall see later that the arbitrariness is greatly tempered by certain guiding principles and facts, and that a total series of intellectual tasks can be defined so as to represent a fairly clear, unified, coherent feature of human life, suitable for theoretical treatment and of great practical importance.

## INTELLECTUAL DIFFICULTY

We are now in a position to make the concept of intellectual difficulty more rigorous and exact. Having, by either method, derived a series of tasks (N in number) which as a whole are intellectual, we define the group in respect of whose members the difficulty of the task is to be determined, (for example, as *ten thousand taken at random from all living human beings twenty years of age*), test each individual of the group with each of the N tasks, rank the tasks in order by the percents succeeding with each, and divide them into $x$ sub-series[3] (called $D_1$, $D_2$, $D_3$, etc.) in accord with the ranking, $D_1$ containing the "easiest," $D_2$ the next "easiest," and so on.

If the score in each of these sub-series of tasks gives correlations of 1.00 (or as high as its self-correlation permits) with the total series, we can define intellectual difficulty as that feature, which $D_1$, $D_2$, $D_3$, etc., have in increasing amounts. They differ in nothing else of consequence to our inquiry, the score in each being determined by all of the intellect defined by our total series and nothing but that intellect.

The attainment of such sub-series may conceivably be an impossibility. It may be that, no matter how large N (and consequently N/$x$) is, the sub-series of tasks at some points in the success-frequency ranking may fail of perfect correlation with the total series. The kind of tasks chosen as intellectual may, for example, vary in such manner that all of even a "small" intellect can not be utilized without tasks from the very hard end; or in such manner that non-intellectual factors can not be eliminated or equalized for all twenty-year-old individuals without tasks at widely sep-

[3] For convenience of exposition we will assume that the number of tasks in each sub-series is the same, though the argument will hold regardless of the size of the sub-series.

arated points of the success-frequency ranking. This is a matter for experimental determination after the total series has been chosen and the group of intellects in respect of which difficulty has been defined has been chosen. The results of such experiments are of great significance, informing us of the degree to which amounts of intellect as defined by the total series do represent increases in the same kind of thing, and are amounts of some unified, coherent fact in nature which can properly be isolated in thought from non-intellectual factors. Our experiments on this matter will be reported elsewhere,[4] but we may note now that they indicate that intellect has a rather high degree of unity and consistency and independence of non-intellectual factors; and consequently permits a fairly close approximation to sub-series of tasks which, as total sub-series, do approximate to perfect "intellectualness," while differing enormously in difficulty. We proceeded by an approximation to the first method, and later checked our choice by an approximation to the second method. In our choice we were guided by the following considerations:

(1) Of psychological theory:—(a) that responding to parts or elements or aspects of situations is more "intellectual" than responding to gross total situations; (b) that responding to parts or elements or aspects which do not present themselves separately to sense but must be abstracted is more intellectual than responding to those which do; (c) that responding to relations between objects is more intellectual than responding to objects; (d) that, in particular, responding to so-called subjective or logical relations, such as likeness and difference, is more intellectual than responding to the so-called objective relations of space and time; (e) that organizing several mental connections or habits to secure a certain result, "thinking things together," as James put it, is more intellectual than using one habit

4 In Appendix IV and Appendix V.

at a time; (f) that responses to novel situations are likely to be more "intellectual" than responses to familiar situations.

(2) Of the theory of measurement:—(a) that the tasks representing any one ability should be capable of very fine gradation from very easy to very hard; (b) that they should be capable of very wide extension by alternates at any degree of difficulty; (c) that, so far as possible, any one ability should represent in some real and useful sense something varying only in amount, so that the different degrees of it might properly be represented by numbers.

(3) Of common sense:—(a) that the tasks should be from among those which had high standing on the basis of correlations with reasonable criteria; (b) that they should be convenient for use in the actual measurement of intellect; (c) that they should be tasks concerning which subjects for experiment were obtainable.

Over and above the narrowness due to these considerations, our choice is also deliberately narrow. We have not included any tasks involving responses to actual human beings or to material objects present to sense—tasks of what has been called social intelligence and mechanical intelligence. Our tasks all concern responses to ideas and symbols, especially words and numbers. The reasons for this need not detain us here. Also we limit ourselves to tasks which are intellectual for a group of persons bred in the United States and aged twelve or over.[5] The reasons for this narrowness may also in general be omitted.[6]

[5] The tasks will very probably serve to measure intellect for younger ages even more accurately than tasks now in use, but we have not demonstrated this to be so.

[6] The chief reason was that the measurement of intellect in children up to twelve or fourteen and the definition of the measurement by an age-scale are in a far more satisfactory condition than the measurement of intellect at older ages and at higher levels.

INTELLECT CAVD

In view of these elaborate and arbitrary restrictions, the intellectualness of our total inventory of tasks, and the intellect whose level or altitude, range or width, and facility or quickness it measures, will be called hereafter Intellectualness CAVD and Intellect CAVD (the symbol CAVD refers to the four series of tasks which constitute it—completions, arithmetical problems, vocabulary and directions). The total series of tasks concerns four lines of ability:[7]

C. To supply words so as to make a statement true and sensible.
A. To solve arithmetical problems.
V. To understand single words.
D. To understand connected discourse as in oral directions or paragraph reading.

The arrangement of scoring is such as to attach equal weight to each of these four varieties of tasks.

The whole series is put into a rough approximate order of intellectual difficulty by the methods described on pages 39 to 56 of the previous chapter. Consequently all the single tasks or task elements of any one sub-series are of somewhere nearly equal intellectual difficulty.

Each single task is scored 1 (right) or 0 (wrong or omitted). The number right at each level, that is in each sub-series, is recorded. The time required for each task may be recorded, if desired. Selections of forty single-task elements from each of certain sub-series of the total series are shown below, making composite tasks A, B, C, D, N, O, P, and Q.

[7] We shall sometimes use also Intellect CAVDI, which is constituted by including a fifth sort of task—to understand and answer questions which require information about such facts as are considered by the world to-day worthy of study in school and of record in encyclopedias; plus organization thereof and sagacious inference therefrom.

## SUB-SERIES A

### SENTENCE COMPLETION, ORAL A

1. You are sitting on a ................................
2. We take a ride on the ................................
3. At night you sleep in ................................
4. You like to drink ................................
5. We get up in the ................................
6. Mary has a ring on her ................................
7. You wear gloves on your ................................
8. The snow is on the ................................
9. We go to church on ................................
10. You wear a ................................ on your head.

### ARITHMETIC, ORAL A

11. Counts 2 pennies. (Binet procedure, but credit for success 2 of 3 trials.)
12. Counts 3 pennies. (Credit if successful in 2 of 3 trials.)
13. "Show me 2 pennies." (Credit if successful in 2 of 3 trials.)
14. "Show me 2 pennies." (Credit if successful in 3 of 3 trials.)
15. Recognizes 2 fingers. (Credit if successful in 3 of 5 trials.)
16. "Show me the littlest pencil; show me the littlest one of all," showing 3. (Credit if successful in 2 of 3 trials.)
17. "Show me the littlest square; show me the littlest one of all," showing 3. (Credit if successful in 2 of 3 trials.)
18. "Show me the biggest square; show me the biggest one of all," showing 3.
19. Adds unseen, 1 plus 1.[8] (Credit if successful in 2 of 3 trials.)
20. Subtracts unseen, 2 minus 1.[8] (Credit if successful in 2 of 3 trials.)

[8] In adding unseen, as 2 plus 1, for instance, the procedure is as follows: 2 pennies are shown, the subject answers (rightly or wrongly) the question,

## VOCABULARY A

(A row of 5 small pictures like those shown in Figure 6 is put before the person who is being measured. He is told to "Show me the horse," or "Put your finger on the horse.") The words in A are:

| | |
|---|---|
| 21. pitcher | 26. baseball |
| 22. man | 27. girl |
| 23. string | 28. train |
| 24. apple | 29. socks |
| 25. violin | 30. dog |

## DIRECTIONS, ORAL A

31. "Make a ring, like this," showing act.
31. "Make a line, like this," showing act.
33. "Make a cross, like this," showing act.
34. "You can write, can't you? Show me how you can write." (Credit if S imitates effect of writing.)
35. "Put the cover on the box." (Credit if S attempts to do so, turning cover to correct axis.)
36. "Turn the box upside down."
37. "Put the pennies in the box and then shake the box." (Have 4 pennies; credit even if cover is not put on, if box is shaken.)
38. "Stand on that paper." (A sheet of paper is left on the floor.)
39. "Put your hands behind you." (Give while S is standing.)
40. "Make a ring." (If S fails, show again, but do not credit.)

---

"How many?" and the 2 pennies are slipped under the card. Another penny is shown. "How many?" is answered (rightly or wrongly); this penny also is slipped under the card, and he is asked, "How many are under here *now*?" In subtracting, as for instance 2 minus 1, proceed as follows: The 2 pennies are shown and the subject answers to "How many?" The pennies are then slipped under the card. One is then taken out as he watches, and the question asked, "How many under here *now*?" It is necessary to make sure that he watches what is done.

## SUB-SERIES B

### SENTENCE COMPLETION, ORAL B

1. We put stamps on a ........................................
2. We cut meat with a ........................................
3. When we are sick, we call the ........................................
4. We go to ........................ at night.
5. I can ........................ with a pencil.
6. The rug is on the ........................................
7. One and one make ........................ ........................
8. A dog has four ........................................
9. Apples are to ........................................
10. Chairs are made of ........................................

### ARITHMETIC, ORAL B

11. Counts 2 pennies. (Credit if successful in 3 of 3 trials.)
12. Counts 4 pennies. (Credit if successful in 2 of 3 trials.)
12. "One and one make ............." Add "what?" if necessary.
14. "Which is the biggest pile?" showing 13 and 2 pennies. (Credit if successful in 3 of 3 trials.)
15. Recognizes 2 fingers. (Credit if successful in 4 of 5 trials.)
16. "Which is the longest of these three lines?" (Credit if successful in 3 of 3 trials.)
17. "Which is the biggest, a baby or a man?" (Credit if successful in 2 of 3 trials.)
18. Adds unseen, 1 plus 2. (Credit if successful in 2 of 3 trials.)
19. Subtracts unseen, 3 minus 2. (Credit if successful in 2 of 3 trials.)
20. Subtracts unseen, 3 minus 1. (Credit if successful in 2 of 3 trials.)

## VOCABULARY B

(The method is as in A above.) The words are:

| | |
|---|---|
| 21. soup | 26. comb |
| 22. bag | 27. locomotive |
| 23. window | 28. door |
| 24. wings | 29. cradle |
| 25. envelope | 30. sun |

## DIRECTIONS, ORAL B

### Set 1. (with paper and pencil)

(Unless otherwise specified, the tasks of Directions Oral B
are those of set 1.)

31. "Make a line." (If S fails, show again, but do not credit.)
32. "Make a cross." (If S fails, show again, but do not credit.)
33. "Turn the paper over and make a ring on the other side."
34. "Turn the paper back again, and make a line on the other side."
35. "Make two rings down here," pointing.
36. "See the lines? Make one more line." (Credit if one or two lines are drawn anywhere.)
37. "Make two crosses, like these two. Make one here and one here," pointing.
38. "Make the other arm on this man," pointing.
39. "Make the other leg on this man," pointing.
40. "Make 2 lines, like these two," pointing.

Fig. 7 shows the pictures used in connection with tasks 37, 38, and 39, reduced to half size. For task 36, three parallel lines two inches long and half an inch apart one from another, drawn parallel to the side of the sheet, are shown in the lower left-hand corner of a letter-size sheet. For task 40, two such parallel lines are shown, at the top of a sheet otherwise blank.

FIG. 6.   Six rows of pictures such as were used in the Picture Vocabulary tests: reduced to three-fourths of the original dimensions.

## SUB-SERIES C

### SENTENCE COMPLETION, ORAL C

1. Clouds are in the ............................... .
2. We send children to school, because they must ............................... .
3. We burn ............................... in the stove.
4. The ............................... is barking at the cat.
5. We wash clothes with ............................... and water.
6. Grass is ............................... .
7. ............................... is sweet.
8. We see with our ............................... .
9. Roses and daisies are ............................... .
10. The ............................... eats the mouse.

X  X

FIG. 7. The pictures used with Directions Oral B, 37, 38 and 39: reduced to one-half the original dimensions.

## ARITHMETIC, ORAL C

11. Counts 5 pennies. (Credit if successful in 3 of 3 trials.)
12. Counts 10 pennies. (Credit if successful in 2 of 3 trials.)
13. "Show me 3 pennies." (Credit if successful in 2 of 3 trials.)
14. "Which is the biggest pile?" showing 10 and 5 pennies. (Credit if successful in 3 of 3 trials.)
15. "Two and one make _____." (Add "what?" if necessary.
16. Recognizes 3 fingers. (Credit if successful in 4 of 5 trials.)
17. "Which is the biggest, a chair or a cup?" (Credit if successful in 2 of 3 trials.)
18. Subtracts unseen, 5 minus 4. (Credit if successful in 2 of 3 trials.)
19. Subtracts unseen, 3 minus 3. (Credit if successful in 2 of 3 trials.)
20. Subtracts unseen, 2 minus 2. (Credit if successful in 2 of 3 trials.)

## VOCABULARY C

The method is as before. The words used are:

| | |
|---|---|
| 21. camera | 26. pistol |
| 22. stationery | 27. vase |
| 23. hole | 28. stamps |
| 24. corn | 29. tiger |
| 25. puppy | 30. kennel |

Three of the rows of pictures used in this type of test are shown in Figures 8, 9 and 10. It will be observed that the task sometimes involves a considerable degree of ability in interpreting the pictures.

FIG. 8.   Picture used with "lamp."

Fig. 9. Picture used with "pond."

Fig. 10. Picture used with "cork."

## Directions, Oral C

In the actual tasks the drawings have twice the dimensions of those shown here:

31. "See the square?" (A 1½ inch square is shown at the top of a sheet 11 by 8½.)
    "Make a ring in the square."
32. "Now make another ring in the square."
33. "See the ring? Make a cross in the ring." (A circle 2 inches in diameter is shown near the middle of the sheet.)
34. "See the cup. Draw a line around the cup." (Fig. 11 is shown at the bottom of the sheet.)
35. "Make a ring and a cross up here," pointing.
36. "Make a cross where the line is." (A line 2½ inches long is shown, parallel with the bottom of the sheet.)
37. "Draw a line to finish the square." (A half-inch square with the left-hand side omitted is shown.)
38. "Make a cross in here," pointing to a triangle which is printed with a square on one side of it and a circle on the other. The square is 1½ in.; the triangle has a base of 1½ in.; the circle has a diameter of 1½ in.
39. "Make a cross $\times$ in the square." (Fig. 12 is shown.)

40. "Make two squares out of these." (Two $\frac{5}{8}$ in. squares are shown, one with the right-hand side lacking, the other with the lower side lacking.)

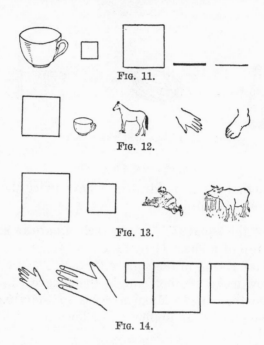

FIG. 11.

FIG. 12.

FIG. 13.

FIG. 14.

## SUB-SERIES D

### SENTENCE COMPLETION, ORAL D

There being only eight tasks, each is counted as 1¼.

1. Boys ........................... baseball.
   ("Playing" and "play ball" are called wrong.)
2. The stars and the ........................... will shine tonight.
3. Two and one make ............................
4. A boy has ........................... and legs.
5. The bird sings; the ........................... barks.
6. Men are ........................... than boys.
7. The ........................... pulls the cart.
8. Horses are big and ............................

## Arithmetic, Oral D

11. Counts 15 pennies. (Credit if successful in 3 of 3 trials.)
12. Recognizes 4 fingers. (Credit if successful in 3 of 5 trials.)
13. "Show me 4 pennies." (Credit if successful in 3 of 3 trials.)
14. "How many fingers have you on one hand?"
15. Recognizes 3 fingers. (Credit if successful in 5 of 5 trials.)
16. Recognizes 5 fingers. (Credit if successful in 5 of 5 trials.)
17. "Which is biggest, 3 or 1?" (Credit if successful in 2 of 3 trials.)
18. Adds unseen, 2 plus 2. (Credit if successful in 2 of 3 trials.)
19. Adds unseen, 3 plus 2. (Credit if successful in 2 of 3 trials.)
20. Subtracts unseen, 5 minus 3. (Credit if successful in 2 of 3 trials.)

## Vocabulary D

The method is as heretofore. The words are:

21. tools
22. fuel
23. screw
24. angel
25. cartridge
26. trumpet
27. cube
28. cork
29. blade
30. arrow

## Directions, Oral D

The illustrations shown here all have dimensions half those used in the actual tasks. Each row is also in the actual tasks separated from the one above and from the one below it by from 1 to 3 inches.

31. "Make a cross inside the little square." (Fig. 13 is shown.)

32. "Draw a line to make this a cross," pointing. (A thick line ¾ in. long, parallel to the side of the sheet is shown.)

33. "Make a ring on the cup." (Fig. 11 is shown.)

34. "See the ring. Make 2 crosses in the ring." (A circle 2 inches in diameter is shown.)

35. "Make a cross on top of the boy's head." (Fig. 13 is shown, on a new sheet.)

36. "Draw a line around the big hand." (Fig. 14 is shown.)

37. "Make a cross on the horse." (Fig. 12 is shown, on a new sheet.)

38. "Make a cross outside the big square." (A second copy of Fig. 13 is shown.)

39. "Make this a circle," pointing. (An incomplete circle with a diameter of ¾ inch, lacking the right-hand quarter, is shown.)

40. "Make a line outside the ring." (A circle 2 inches in diameter is shown.)

The sub-series N, O, P, and Q which follow presuppose ability to read in the individuals measured by them.

## SUB-SERIES N

### SENTENCE COMPLETION

*Write words on the dotted lines so as to make the whole sentence true and sensible. Write one word on each inch of dots.*

1. At ............................ time was progress ............................ rapid ............................ during the last half of the nineteenth ............................ .

2. He will come to the m e e t i n g ............................ ............................ ............................ the fact............................ he ............................ rather stay quietly at home.

3. His friends, ............................ wished to dissuade him from this undertaking, asserted that ............................ he followed their advice ............................ would withdraw their support.

4. It would _____ several pages _____ to contain the list.

5. Standing beside the grave_____ _____ great Englishman _____ _____ enough for us to know _____ _____ lived and died, and made the _____ his heirs.

6. You may safely conclude that you _____ in yourself the means of _____ at the truth.

7. _____ the fact that you disagree with me, I shall continue to aid you.

8. At ancient banquets the _____ of the day seems _____ have _____ the chief _____ of conversation.

9. As _____ the treasure he had come to seek, probably it existed _____ in his own _____.

10. The Declaration _____ _____ affirms that the Creator _____ all men with certain inalienable _____.

## ARITHMETIC

11. A camp has food enough to last 300 men 4 months. How long will it last 200 men?

12. A watch was set correct at noon Wednesday. At 6 P. M. on Thursday it was 15 seconds fast. At that rate how much will it gain in half an hour?

13. Five sixths equal how many thirds?

14. How many quarters of a quarter equal half of a half?

15. How long will it take a man to walk 14 miles at the rate of 3 miles an hour while walking, if he makes three stops of an average length of 10 minutes each?

| | | | | | |
|---|---|---|---|---|---|
| A | 2 for 5c. | E | 6 for 5c. | I | 8 for $1.00. |
| B | 3 for 5c. | F | 4 for 10c. | J | 4 for 25c. |
| C | 4 for 5c. | G | 40c. per lb. | K | 1¼c. each |
| D | 3 for 25c. | H | 10c. each. | L | 3¼c. each. |

*A, B, C, D, etc., are articles costing as shown above. 1A means 1 of A, 2A means 2 of A, 3A means 3 of A, etc. Sup-*

*ply the missing numbers in lines 16 to 20 as shown in lines I, II, and III. Use the bottom of the page or another sheet of paper to figure on.*

I. 3 E cost   $\frac{1}{2}$   as much as 3 B.

II. 3 D cost  *just*  as much as 4 J.

III. 1 H cost 4 *times* as much as 1 A.

| | | | | | |
|---|---|---|---|---|---|
| 16. | 3 I | costs | .............. | as much as | 2 J. |
| 17. | 1 J | " | .............. | " | 1 D. |
| 18. | 6 F | " | .............. | " | 8 A. |
| 19. | 2 B | " | .............. | " | 4 C. |
| 20. | 5 oz. G | " | .............. | " | 2 F |

## VOCABULARY

Look at the first word in line 21. Find the other word in the line which means the same or most nearly the same. Write its number on the line at the right side of the page. Do the same in lines 22, 23, 24, etc. Lines *A, B, C,* and *D* show the way to do it. Do all the lines you can. Write only one number for each line.

*A.* beast     1 afraid.....2 words.....3 large.....4 animal.....5 bird      4

*B.* baby     1 cradle.....2 mother.....3 little child.....4 youth.....5 girl      3

*C.* raise     1 lift up.....2 drag.....3 sun.....4 bread.....5 deluge      1

*D.* blind     1 man.....2 cannot see.....3 game.....4 unhappy.....5 eyes      2

21. sexton     1 cube.....2 janitor.....3 compass.....4 archbishop.....5 six singers

22. buckler     1 keel.....2 servant.....3 stag.....4 shield.....5 scraper

23. animosity     1 hatred.....2 animation.....3 disobedience.....4 diversity.....5 friendship

24. conflagration     1 carnival.....2 celebration.....3 decoration with flags.....4 contagion.....5 fire

25. confidential     1 respectable.....2 secure.....3 sensitive.....4 secret.....5 confident

26. scrivener     1 searcher.....2 forger.....3 chaplain.....4 clerk.....5 sceptic

27. beaker     1 cup.....2 binnacle.....3 beak.....4 slanderer.....5 bottle

28. emanate     1 populate.....2 free.....3 prominent.....4 rival.....5 come

29. landau     1 pier.....2 coach.....3 postern.....4 gable.....5 headdress

30. amaranthine     1 jubilant.....2 bitter.....3 maritime.....4 ungracious.....5 purple

## DIRECTIONS AND COMPREHENSION OF SENTENCES AND PARAGRAPHS

*In each set of sentences, check the two which mean most nearly the same as the sentence printed in heavy type.*

31. Show me the man you honor. I know by that symptom, better than any other, what you are yourself.—(Carlyle.)

...............A man is known by the company he keeps.

...............Tell me what you've done and I will tell you what you are.

...............A man is known by his idols.

...............Show me your chips and I will tell you whether you are a good woodsman.

32. It is one thing to see that a line is crooked and another thing to be able to draw a straight one.

...............It is one thing to see the mote in our neighbor's eye and another to see the beam in our own.

...............Those who see mistakes cannot always correct them.

...............As the eye is trained to accuracy the hand develops skill.

...............We may recognize faults that we are unable to overcome.

33. If we agree that morality is what is social and immorality, anti-social, we shall be led to inquire of any course of action how it affects the welfare of society.—(Pearson.)

...............To judge whether an action is good, we must investigate its results on society.

...............An act is moral or immoral regardless of its effects.

...............We must judge a man's deeds by his motives.

...............Acts which are socially harmful are immoral.

34. There was a painter became a physician, whereupon a citizen said to him: "You have done well; for before the faults of your work were seen but now they are unseen."—(Bacon.)

...............The citizen indicates that long training is necessary to appreciate true art.

...............He implies that science is more exacting than art.

...............He means to make sport of the medical profession.

...............He implies that doctors may make mistakes
which remain undetected.

35. **It is easy to be virtuous when one's own convenience is not affected.**—(Stevenson.)

...............Virtue is its own reward.

...............It is easier to preach virtue than to practice it.

...............It is difficult to do right when it conflicts with
our inclinations.

...............We would all be virtuous if virtue were merely
a matter of doing what we enjoy.

36. **Don't cross the bridge before you come to it.**

...............Look before you leap.

...............Don't borrow trouble.

...............Don't lock the barn after the horse is gone.

...............Take care of today and tomorrow will take care
of itself.

*Read this and then write the answer. Read it again if
you need to.*

There is an old saying, "As harmless as a fly;" and
until recently the fly has been regarded only as an unpleasant but harmless nuisance. Had our forefathers known as
much about flies as we now know, they might have made the
proverb, "As dangerous as the fly." His origin and his
habits are of the worst sort.

37. Copy the words which mean the same as proverb.

-------------------------------------------------------------------------------------

*Read this and then write the answer. Read it again if
you need to.*

## EVERY HOME NEEDS A GARDEN

A MAGAZINE published to promote real gardening.
Most people do not think much about their gardens at this
time of the year, but if more people did, there would be
more good gardens. If you live in the city where space is
at a premium, we provide pleasure for you by suggesting
how to grow flowers indoors. If you live in the country
and have a garden and do not experience the satisfaction of
seeing things grow as a result of your own efforts—then
you need the X.Y.Z. magazine.

38. At what time of year do you think this advertisement appeared? ................................................................

*Read this and then write the answers. Read it again if you need to.*

However certain it may seem to be that men work only because they must, and would avoid labor except for the food, clothing and luxuries that are its rewards, the facts may well be to the contrary. It can hardly be the case that men dislike work because they wish to be utterly idle. For mere rest, mere inactivity, is not commonly enjoyed. To have nothing to do is not what men seek. Were that so, we should envy the prisoner shut up in his cell. If men had to choose between a life spent at eight hours of work daily in a factory and a life spent at eight hours of sitting on a throne without moving hand or foot, many of them would, after trying both, choose the former. Activity of body or mind, at which a man can succeed, is, in and of itself, rather enjoyed than disliked.

39. What, according to the paragraph, has no appeal *per se?*................................................................

40. What is it the author of the paragraph suspects men might choose unless they had tried it?................................

## SUB-SERIES O

### COMPLETIONS

1. India is rich in ........................... of scenery and climate, ........................... the ........................... mountains to vast ........................... deltas raised ........................... a few ........................... above sea ........................... .

2. Undue consciousness often ........................... the flow of expression ........................... diffuseness is detrimental to a clear and ........................... exposition of our ideas.

3. Knighthood and Chivalry are ........................... words ........................... are n e a r l y ........................... not ........................... synonymous.

4. Throughout the river plains of northern India, two harvests, and, ........................... some provinces, ...........................are ........................... each ........................... .

5. _____ a man _____ time sufficient for all laudable pursuits, and _____ sufficient for all generous purposes, he is free _____ _____ shadow of blame or reproach.

6. Maize contains _____ small a proportion of nutritious matter _____ it _____ not _____ for horses _____ which fast work is _____.

7. The drafting _____ a measure depends _____ the pains _____ and skill exerted by its _____.

8. _____ is natural that being dissatisfied with the _____, we should f o r m a t o o _____ estimate of the past.

9. He believed in _____ hard things _____ because _____ _____ hard.

10. Not _____ do living things grow themselves, they _____ produce _____ life like _____.

### Arithmetic

11. A factory earns $70 a day for its owner when it is working full capacity and $15 a day when it is working to half capacity. In how many days will it earn $1,000 if two days out of every three are only half capacity?

12. A company marched 120 miles in 5 days. How many times as fast must they march to cover 90 miles in three days?

13. A man started with $12,500 and doubled his capital every year for five years. How much had he at the end of the fifth year?

14. An airplane went 60 mi. at the rate of 90 mi. per hour. It made a stop of 30 minutes. On the return trip it went half the distance at 100 mi. and half the distance at 80 mi. per hour. How long was the total time?

15. If the dividend were multiplied by 4, and the divisor divided by 2, the quotient would be 40. What is the quotient?

16. How long will enough food for 400 men for 120 days last 250 men?

17. How many times as big an area has a circle with radius of 9 as a circle with radius of 3?

18. At an average rate of 12 miles per hour for the first half of the time spent and 10 miles per hour for the last half of the time spent, how long will it take a truck to cover 110 miles?

19. Three fourths equals how many thirds?

20. A push-cart man buys eggs at 15c. per dozen and sells them at 15 for 25c. How many eggs must he sell to gain $1.80?

## Vocabulary

The directions and samples are the same as in Sub-Series N.

21. gainsay    1 persuade.....2 beshrew.....3 deny.....4 profit.....5 imprint
22. eclogue    1 obituary.....2 a poem.....3 carousal.....4 epigram.....5 portrait
23. cloistered    1 miniature.....2 bunched.....3 arched.....4 malady.....5 secluded
24. reciprocal    1 saturnine.....2 mutual.....3 receptive.....4 morose.....5 careless
25. accolade    1 salutation.....2 anchovy.....3 procession.....4 bivouac.....5 acolyte
26. benighted    1 fraudulent.....2 weary.....3 insuperable.....4 ignorant.....5 venal
27. madrigal    1 song.....2 montebank.....3 lunatic.....4 ribald.....5 sycophant
28. pinnace    1 a boat.....2 doublet.....3 pinnacle.....4 hold fast.....5 forfeiture
29. broach    1 dodge.....2 clasp.....3 open.....4 top.....5 edify
30. nectarine    1 bouillon.....2 a fruit.....3 a jewel.....4 a drink.....5 diurnal

## Directions and Comprehension of Sentences and Paragraphs

There are only six tasks in place of the usual ten. So each is counted as 1⅔.

*In each set of sentences, check the two which mean most nearly the same as the sentence printed in heavy type.*

31. **Better be a big frog in a little puddle than a tadpole in a lake.**

...............Better the head of an ass than the tail of a horse.

...............I had rather be a door-keeper in the house of my God than to dwell in the tents of wickedness.

.............Better to reign in hell than serve in heaven.

.............Better to be a beggar in Rome than a prince
in a village.

32.   **Don't cross the bridge before you come to it.**

.............Look before you leap.

.............Don't borrow trouble.

.............Don't lock the barn after the horse is gone.

.............Take care of today and tomorrow will take
care of itself.

The paragraph for questions 33 and 34 is the last paragraph in Sub-Series N.

33.   What choice is described as an argument that work, merely as such, is not always avoided?.............

34.   In what respect is a prisoner in his cell like a man with a million dollars?.............

*Read this and then write the answers. Read it again if you need to.*

## THE AMERICAN STATE

He who looks at a map of the Union will be struck by the fact that so many of the boundary lines of the States are straight lines. Those lines tell the same tale as the geometrical plans of cities like Leningrad or Washington, where every street runs at the same angle to every other. The States are not areas set off by nature. Their boundaries are for the most part not natural boundaries fixed by mountain ranges, nor even historical boundaries due to a series of events, but boundaries, purely artificial, determined by an authority which carved the national territory into strips of convenient size, as a building company lays out its suburban lots. Of the States subsequent to the original thirteen, California is the only one with a genuine natural frontier, finding it in the chain of the Sierra Nevada on the east and the Pacific Ocean on the west. No one of these later States can be regarded as a naturally developed political organism. They are as trees planted by the forester, not self-grown with the help of the seed-scattering wind.

35.   What action is likened to scientific forestation?.............

36. To what may we attribute the similarity between the plans of certain cities and the arrangement of the States? ............................................................................................

## SUB-SERIES P

### COMPLETIONS

1. The monuments of P e r s e p o l i s ............................
................................ the u s e ................................ incense
................................ as ................................ in ancient Persia
as ................................ Babylonia.

2. Ever since the hearing before him ................................ the governor ................................ ................................ g i v i n g ................................ spare moment ................................ a ................................ of the case.

3. So far ................................ ................................ the displeasure of the people by ................................ the will of their representatives, a President generally gains................................ by the bold use of his veto power. It conveys the ................................ ................................ firmness; it shows ................................ ................................ has a view and does ................................ ................................ to give effect to it.

4. The ................................ of character is its ability to ................................ liberty ................................ from license.

5. Judicial decisions are of ................................ or less authority as precedents ................................ to circumstances.

6. The deepest difference, practically, in the moral ................................ of ................................ is the difference ................................ the easy-going and the ................................ mood.

7. Ibsen's whole problem ................................ it has well been stated, is the ................................ of the individual to his social and personal ................................ .

8. In the sixteenth century, ................................ was not more decidedly the land of the fine arts, ................................ was not more ................................ the land of bold theological speculation, ................................ Spain was the ................................ of statesmen and soldiers.

9. The human race may be ............................ as parcelled
   ............................ into a ............................ of distinct
   g r o u p s ............................ societies, ............................
   greatly in size and circumstances.

10. Farmers brought up in the traditions of the
   ............................ of New England, on going where close
   association and cooperation were ............................ to
   carry on irrigated agriculture, found that it took a
   long ............................ and involved ............................
   ............................ waste to learn ............................ to act
   .............................

## ARITHMETIC

*Write the numbers and signs in each line below in the
proper order, so that they make a true equation as shown
in the three sample lines. Use the bottom of the page to
figure on if you need to.*

Sample lines
$\begin{cases} 3 \ 3 \ 6 = + & 3 + 3 = 6 \\ 4 \ 7 \ 8 \ 20 = + \times & 7 \times 4 = 20 + 8 \\ 2 \ 3 \ 3 \ 7 \ 18 = + - \times ( ) & 7 + 2 = 18 - (3 \times 3) \end{cases}$

11.  1  3  3  3  3   21 $= + - \times \div ( )$
12.  $\frac{1}{3}$  2  3  5   33 $= + \times \times ( )$
13.  $1\frac{1}{3}$  2  2  2  8   12 $= + \times \times \times ( )$
14.  2  2  5  10   70 $= + \times \div ( )$
15.  $\frac{3}{4}$  1  4  4   20 $= - \times \times ( )$

A  2 for 5c.          E  3 for 10c.          J  3 for 25c.
B  3¼c. per lb.       F  4 for 10c.          K  4 for 25c.
C  4½c. per lb.       G  50c. per lb.        L  6 for 25c.
D  3 for $1.00.       H  2½c. each.          M  6 for $1.00.

*A, B, C, D, etc., are articles costing as shown above. 1A
means 1 of A, 2A means 2 of A, 3A means 3 of A, etc. Supply the missing numbers in lines 16 to 20 as shown in lines
I, III, and III. Use the bottom of the page or another sheet
of paper to figure on.*

I.  2 A cost   $\frac{1}{2}$   as much as 3 E.
II.  1 E costs  $1\frac{1}{3}$   as much as 1 F.
III.  3 D cost  *just*  as much as 12 J.

16. 3 F      costs  ................  as much as 2 J.
17. 3 K       "        ................      "       5 L.
18. 2 K       "        ................      "       1 dozen H.
19. 2 J + 1 M "        ................      "       10 H.
20. 3 A       "        ................      "       1 K.

## VOCABULARY
### Directions and Samples as in Sub-Series N.

21. monomania 1 flying machine......2 conceit.....3 one-colored.....4 endogen......5 aberration
22. saturnalian 1 reptilian......2 impertinent......3 gloomy......4 impregnated......5 riotous
23. pristine      1 flashing......2 earlier......3 primeval......4 bound......5 green
24. quaternion 1 officer......2 fourfold system......3 four-line stanza......4 tremolo......5 geologic age
25. predatory    1 hasty......2 ante-dated......3 rapacious......4 foretold......5 four-footed
26. persiflage    1 camouflage......2 wit......3 banter......4 vivacity......5 metaphor
27. encomium    1 repetition......2 friend......3 panegyric......4 abrasion......5 expulsion
28. abattoir      1 usurpation......2 cessation......3 legal desertion......4 slaughterhouse......5 nuisance
29. meticulous   1 partial......2 spacious......3 finical......4 melodic......5 tiny
30. largess       1 enormity......2 present......3 monstrosity......4 amiability......5 size

## DIRECTIONS AND COMPREHENSION OF SENTENCES
### AND PARAGRAPHS

Only six are included instead of the usual ten, so each one is counted as 1⅔.

*Read this paragraph. Then read the questions. Make a (∨) check before the best answer to each question. Read the paragraph again as much as is necessary.*

War ship and merchant ship alike clung to the coast— or if they ventured out to sea, they did so for a voyage to be counted by the hour, as, for example, from the southwest of Sicily to the opposite coast of Africa—or they relied on regular trade winds, like the seamen who sailed from the Red Sea to the coast of Malabar going and coming with the monsoons. In spite of exceptions, more apparent perhaps than real, such as the voyages of Irish anchorites to Iceland, and of the Norsemen to that island, and to Greenland, seamanship continued to be the art of the coaster till the close of the middle ages. Chaucer's sailor has hardly lost sight of the coast. Such treatises as were written for sea-

8

men were books of pilotage. Examples will be found at the end of the Hakluyt Society's edition of *Hues Tractatus de globis*. The war-ships, Phœnician, Greek, Roman, Norse, Byzantine and Italian, throughout the middle ages, used sails only when not in action. They were rowed in battle, and the mast was lowered, or left on shore. Whenever they could they avoided passing the night at sea. Their galleys were beached or anchored close to the shore and the men landed. We know from Thucydides' narrative of the expedition to Syracuse that the crews were landed even for their meals; from the chronicle of Ramon de Muntaner we know that this was also the case with the best Mediterranean squadrons at the end of the 13th century. The Athenians, clinging to the coast, spent two months in going from Athens to Syracuse. Roger di Lauria, the admiral of Aragon, when coming from Sicily in circumstances of great urgency to Catalonia, went round by the coast of Africa and Spain. When under sails the ships of war and of commerce alike had, at the outside, very few sails, and generally only one great course, square and slung by the middle of the yard. It could be trained fore and aft by bowlines, so as to enable the vessel to sail on the wind. Under these restrictions seamanship was necessarily a limited art. From Marco Polo we learn that the seamen of the China Sea and of the Indian Ocean were coasters like their European contemporaries.

31. *Put a check before two of the following statements which make it almost certain that the Spanish sailors of the middle ages were afraid to venture far from land. Check only two.*

> Crews landed even for their meals.
> They did not stay on the sea at night.
> They were afraid of lack of wind.
> Lauria went from Sicily to Catalonia by the coast of Africa and Spain.
> Ships had few sails.

Marco Polo's statement.

Treatises on seamanship were chiefly about pilotage.

32. *Put a check before the two of the following which best show the fear of the open sea. Check only two.*

Books were on pilotage.

Chaucer's sailor.

*Hues Tractatus de globis.*

In sailing away from land they relied on regular trade winds.

Scant supply of food.

The sailors landed at night.

The use of primitive sails.

33. *How was the single sail trained so that the ship would go in the same direction as the wind?*

At right angles to the long axis of the ship.

By bowlines.

Parallel to the long axis of the ship.

34. *How was the single sail trained so that the ship would go at right angles to the wind?*

At right angles to the long axis of the ship.

By bowlines.

Parallel to the long axis of the ship.

35. *What fact stated in the paragraph gives a measure of how near the ships of the middle ages kept to the shore?*

They sailed by the hour.

Chaucer's sailor hardly lost sight of the coast.

Masts were left on shore during a battle.

They returned at night.

The Athenians' trip to Syracuse.

The crews landed for meals.

*Read this paragraph. Then read the question. Make a ( V ) check before the best answer to the question. Read the paragraph again as much as is necessary.*

The church cantata, solo or chorale is indistinguishable from a small oratorio or portion of an oratorio. In Bach's case many of the larger cantatas are actually called oratorios.

Many of Bach's greatest cantatas begin with an elaborate chorus followed by a couple of arias and recitatives, and end with a plain chorale. This has often been commented upon as an example of Bach's indifference to artistic climax in the work as a whole. But no one will maintain this who realizes the place which the church cantata occupied in the Lutheran church service. The text was carefully based upon the gospel or lessons for the day; unless the cantata was short the sermon probably took place after the first chorus or one of the arias, and the congregation joined in the final chorale. Thus the unity of the service was the unity of the music; and, in the cases where all the movements of the cantata were founded on one and the same chorale-tune, this unity has never been equalled, except by those 16th-century masses and motets which are founded upon the Gregorian tunes of the festival for which they are written.

36. *What feature is stated as giving some of Bach's cantatas extraordinary unity?*

> They begin with an elaborate chorus followed by a couple of arias, and end with a plain chorale.
>
> If the cantata was short, the sermon took place after the first chorus.
>
> His founding all the movements of the cantata on the same chorale tune.
>
> The text was based on the gospel of the day.
>
> The congregation joined in the final chorus.
>
> The unity of the service was the unity of the music.

## SUB-SERIES Q

### COMPLETIONS

1.  It must ............................ seem to the wisest............................
    men, when brought into contact with the great things
    of nature that ............................ they ............................ is

........................ nothing ....................... to the infinitude of ........................ they are ignorant.

2. It is a maxim that ........................ man ........................ ever written out of reputation ........................ by himself.

3. The American press ........................ ........................ ........................ above the moral level of the average good citizen,—in no country ........................ ........................ either expect or find it ........................ ........................ so,—but it is ........................ ........................ ........................ of the machine politicians in the cities.

4. David Hume ........................ ........................ founded the literary school of English historical writing, and ........................ ........................ of the more important doctrines of modern political economy, but also ........................ a paramount influence on the philosophic ........................ ........................ ........................ eighteenth ........................ .

5. Queen Anne was much ........................ to horseracing, and not only ........................ royal plates to be ........................ for, ........................ ran ........................ for them ........................ .

6. The mere practical man regards f a v o r a b l y ........................ the results of science, ........................ the ........................ through which these results are ........................ quite superfluous.

7. ........................ happens. ........................ ........................ relations of the Senate and the President are seldom cordial, ........................ ........................ confidential, ........................ ........................ he and the majority of the Senate belong to the same party, ........................ the Senate and the President are rival powers jealous ........................ ........................ ........................ .

8. Francis Bacon ........................ in his will, "For my n a m e a n d memory, I ........................ it to

......................................... charitable speeches, ................................
foreign nations, ........................... ................................. the
next ages.''

9. ................................... ..................................... wonderfully little genuine inventiveness in the ................................., and perhaps
................................. of all has been shown in.................................
................................. of political institutions.

10. The florid ................................. of the debating club or
................................. pomp of the funeral ................................. is
frequently used by orators when ................................. but
................................. of exposition is desirable.

### MATHEMATICS

There being only five single mathematical tasks in Sub-
series Q, each is counted as 2.

11. Let $pp^n$ mean any flat surface enclosed by straight
lines, the n denoting the number of sides it has. Let $E$
mean equiangular. What is the common name for
$Epp^4$?

12. Express in brief form, using $I, B$ and $D$: ''The illumi-
nation varies directly as the brightness of the light
and inversely as the square of the distance.'' Use
''$= K$ times'' for ''varies as.''

13. Let $n$ = any number
" $n_r$ = 1 divided by $n$
" $n_R$ = 10 " " $n$
" $n^S$ = the number raised to the same power as
itself.

What does $\left(\dfrac{a_R}{a_r}\right)^S$ equal?

14. Let $m, m_2, m_3$, etc., be any numbers.
Let $n$ be their number, that is, $n$ tells how many $m$'s
there are.

Let $S$ ( ) mean "the sum of".

What name will you give to $\dfrac{S(m\text{'s})}{n}$?

15. Let $A. D. =$ the average of the deviations of a set of numbers from their average, disregarding the signs of the deviations.

Find the $A. D.$ of $6, 9, 10, 11, 14$.

## VOCABULARY
### Directions and samples as in Sub-Series N.

| | |
|---|---|
| 21. radial | 1 light.....2 agitator.....3 straight line.....4 root.....5 ray |
| 22. sequestrate | 1 follow.....2 petition.....3 horseman.....4 confiscate.....5 redwood |
| 23. tactility | 1 tangibility.....2 grace.....3 subtlety.....4 extensibility.....5 manageableness |
| 24. apogee | 1 orbit.....2 nadir.....3 ellipse.....4 culmination.....5 zodiac |
| 25. nugatory | 1 candy.....2 belittling.....3 inoperative.....4 lump of gold.....5 hades |
| 26. sedulous | 1 muddied.....2 sluggish.....3 stupid.....4 assiduous.....5 corrupting |
| 27. umbel | 1 cluster.....2 canopy.....3 shadow.....4 pigment.....5 ribbing |
| 28. asseveration | 1 pluck.....2 oath.....3 continuance.....4 partition.....5 cleverness |
| 29. abjure | 1 swear.....2 recant.....3 refuse.....4 degraded.....5 illegal |
| 30. auricular | 1 golden.....2 heard.....3 jointed.....4 distinct.....5 clear |

## DIRECTIONS AND COMPREHENSION OF SENTENCES AND PARAGRAPHS.

The paragraph for questions 31, 32, 33 and 34 is "The American State" used in Sub-Series O. There being only six tasks instead of the usual ten, each is counted as $1\frac{2}{3}$.

31. Two words are used several times to indicate comparison. Which are they? ................................

...........................................................................

32. Name three states which are like plants which have grown from seeds spread by the wind. ........................

...........................................................................

33. What states may properly be thought of as being what they are as a result of ordinary political growth?

...........................................................................

34.  What part did nature play in deciding that Montana should comprise certain territory? ............................................

........................................................................................................................

*Read this and then write the answers.  Read it again if you need to.*

### DIRGE IN WOODS

A wind sways the pines,
   And below
Not a breath of wild air;
Still as the mosses that glow
On the flooring and over the lines
Of the roots here and there.
The pine tree drops its dead;
They are quiet, as under the sea.
Overhead, overhead
Rushes life in a race,
As the clouds the clouds chase;
   And we go,
And we drop like the fruits of the tree,
   Even we,
   Even so.

35.  What is as still as the mosses? ............................................

36.  Three words in the poem indicate comparison.  What are they? ............................................

Some of the sub-series intermediate between D and N may be found in Chapter VI.

We could have improved this series at the beginning if our resources for work had been more extensive.  We could improve it still more now with the knowledge which we have already gained from using it; and the reader should consider it more as an illustration of the method than as an ideal series of intellectual tasks.  It is, however, a reasonably satisfactory series for its purpose, as will be seen.  One possible criticism we may mention, as it concerns an important general question of method which we have not yet discussed.

We have defined intellect as that which produces intellectual products, succeeds with intellectual tasks. We thus include not only the native, inherent capacity which a person has for such successes, but also whatever education has added thereto, and whatever increment of success with intellectual tasks he has by virtue of working with better intellectual tools. For example, if A can succeed with the tasks of the first four sub-series shown whereas B can succeed with only the first three, we credit A with a higher altitude or level of intellect than B, even though we may be confident that if B had had the advantages of A, he would have surpassed him. We are measuring available power of intellectual achievement without any specification as to its genesis. A person who has acquired the intellectual tool, reading, probably has a considerable advantage over one of equal original capacity who has not acquired that tool, in the harder completions and directions. One who has studied arithmetic surely has a notable advantage in many of the arithmetical problems of our series over one of equal original capacity who has not studied it. This procedure would be open to criticism if we should assume that the score made in the series is a measure of original capacity to grow into or acquire intellect, without proving that it did so. We shall not; nothing about the causation of the ability measured by the series will be taken for granted.

The procedure will be criticized by others as a failure to separate original capacity from the circumstances of training and to select tasks which would measure the former alone. This is an attractive enterprise, but not, in our judgment, so important as the measurement of intellect as it actually exists and works. We also doubt whether it can be achieved until the latter has been. There is also danger that, if we include in a series of intellectual tasks only those in whose accomplishment differences of education can make little or no difference, we shall have a collection of freakish puzzles, irrelevant to the actual operations of intellect by persons twelve years or older in the United States to-day— or possibly have nothing at all.

Whatever be its defects, our series defines intellectual tasks and provides us with a rank order of sub-series, each of which represents all of Intellect CAVD and nothing but Intellect CAVD nearly enough so that its intellectual diffi- culty can be measured by the methods of the previous chap- ter. The number right out of $10C + 10A + 10V + 10D$ tasks at any one level correlates almost as closely with the number right out of twenty times as many tasks represent- ing twenty levels from very low to very high as its own self-correlation permits. Our proof of this statement is given in Appendices IV and V. It has to be somewhat ir- regular and roundabout, since we have been unable to ob- tain records from any individuals attempting the entire series. But it is conclusive.

We have now to consider what theoretical or practical significance this Intellect CAVD has.

### THE RELATION OF INTELLECT CAVD TO THE ABILITIES MEASURED BY ORDINARY INTELLIGENCE EXAMINATIONS

The ability which it measures is very much the same as that which is measured by the Stanford Binet, or by the Otis Self-Administering Group Test, or by the Terman Group Test for Grades 7 to 12, or by a combination of these three, or by the Thorndike Intelligence Examination for High School Graduates, or by the I. E. R. Tests of Selective and Relational Thinking, Generalization and Organization. This last is a selected team of tests representing a general consensus of psychological opinion concerning symptoms of intellect. That is, Intellect CAVD is very much the same as that which is measured by representative examinations for so-called general intelligence. The evidence for this is the correlations obtained. We report these briefly.

Using persons sixteen years old or older, with Stanford Mental Age of from 28 months to 59 months (all in asy-

lums for the mentally deficient), we find a correlation of
.73 (.68 Pearson, .78 Sheppard) between a summation score
for CAVD and Stanford Mental Age, the details being as
shown in Table 7. This is in fact probably as close as the
self-correlation of the Stanford Binet will permit. (In the
62 cases for which we have a second trial of the Stanford
Binet, the self-correlation is .53.) If the range were extended to include all persons sixteen years old or older,
this correlation of .73 would rise to about .98.[9]

At the other extreme we measured twenty adults, all
high-school graduates, chosen from professional and clerical workers, with the Thorndike Intelligence Examination
for High School Graduates (average of two forms), and
with an incomplete sampling of Intellect CAVD. The correlation is about .95, the facts being as shown in Table 8.
The self-correlation of the Thorndike Examination score
for this group would be only about .97$\frac{1}{2}$, the correlation
of one form with the other being .95. So Intellect CAVD
is nearly identical with the ability measured by the Thorndike Examination.

Clark ['25], using 180 pupils in Grades 7 to 12 of the
Lincoln School of New York City, finds the intercorrelations stated below among (1) a score based on a selection
of tasks from the arithmetical and sentence completion and
information sections of Intellect CAVDI, (2) the Otis Self-
Administering Group Test, (3) the Terman Group Test,
and (4) the Stanford Binet Mental Age.

|  | Raw Correlation |
|---|---|
| Part of Intellect CAVDI with Otis S. A. Test | .87 |
| "    "    "    "    " Terman Group Test | .94 |
| "    "    "    "    " Stanford M. A. | .78 |
| Otis S. A. Test with Terman Group Test | .88 |
| "    "    "    "    " Stanford M. A. | .77 |
| Terman Group Test with Stanford M. A. | .77 |

[9] The mean square variation of the random sample of the Army in Stanford Mental Age was over 34 months (Memoirs, p. 392); that of our group of
178 cases was under 8 months.

## TABLE 7.

THE CORRELATION BETWEEN CAVD SUMMATION SCORE AND STANFORD-BINET MENTAL AGE—IN THE CASE OF 178 IMBECILES SIXTEEN YEARS OLD OR OLDER, OF MENTAL AGE 28 MONTHS TO 59 MONTHS.

| Stanford-Binet M.A. | CAVD Score. | | | | | | | | | | | | | | | | | | | | | | | | |
|---|---|---|---|---|---|---|---|---|---|---|---|---|---|---|---|---|---|---|---|---|---|---|---|---|---|
| | 0 | 5 | 10 | 15 | 20 | 25 | 30 | 35 | 40 | 45 | 50 | 55 | 60 | 65 | 70 | 75 | 80 | 85 | 90 | 95 | 100 | 105 | 110 | 115 | 120 |
| 25–28 mos. | | | | 1 | | | | | | | | | | | | | | | | | | | | | |
| 29–32 " | | 2 | 1 | | | 1 | 1 | 1 | 1 | | | | | | | | | | | | | | | | |
| 33–36 " | | 1 | 2 | 2 | 2 | | 2 | 4 | 1 | 3 | 2 | 3 | 3 | | 1 | 1 | | | 1 | | | | | | |
| 37–40 " | | | 1 | | | 1 | 2 | | 4 | 1 | 2 | 3 | | 2 | 1 | 1 | 1 | | | | | | | | |
| 41–44 " | | | | | 1 | | | 4 | 2 | 1 | 6 | 4 | 2 | 1 | 2 | 3 | | 3 | | 1 | | | | | |
| 45–48 " | | | | | | 1 | 1 | 1 | 3 | 2 | 2 | 3 | 1 | 3 | 3 | 1 | 1 | 2 | 2 | | | 2 | · | | |
| 49–52 " | | | | | 1 | | | | 1 | 1 | 1 | 1 | 3 | 3 | 3 | 5 | 1 | 4 | 3 | 3 | 3 | 3 | | | 1 |
| 53–56 " | | | | | | | | | 1 | | 2 | 1 | | 1 | 1 | 1 | 3 | 6 | 3 | 2 | 2 | 2 | | 2 | |
| 57–60 " | | | | | | | | | | | 1 | | | | 2 | 1 | | | | | 1 | 2 | 2 | | |

The selection of tasks from the three fifths of Intellect CAVDI was meagre, so that even these three fifths were far from perfectly measured. Nor does one trial with an Otis or Terman or Stanford examination measure perfectly what would be found if a dozen alternative examinations of the same type were used. The correlations of Intellect CAVD or CAVDI with the ability as measured by a dozen alternative Otis Tests or Terman Tests would approximate to perfect correlation for the group in question. The obtained correlations are higher than the obtained intercorrelations of Otis, Terman and Stanford, and about as high as their self-correlations.[10]

One hundred and forty-six pupils at the very beginning of Grade 6 in one school were tested with a fairly extensive selection from CAVD, each being allowed time enough to do all that he could. A summation score was given with approximately equal weight to C, A, V, and D. These same pupils had been tested some months earlier with the National A and B. The correlation between the summation score in CAVD and the score in the National was about .76 (.81 by Pearson's, and .71 by Sheppard's formula). This is about as close as the correlation between the National and a repetition of itself. If we assume that the variability for a group of constant chronological age 12 is two times the variability of this selected grade population, the correlation for the former would be .92.

Dr. M. A. May measured a group of about 650 pupils in Grades 5 to 8 with a composite of our Vocabulary, Arithmetic, Completions, Information and Reading tasks. Pintner had measured the same pupils with the National Intelligence Examination. The correlation between a rough summation score for the former and the score in the latter was .84. This again is about as high as the self-correlations of the two would permit.

Sixty-one college sophomores were measured with Army Alpha and with 70 CAVD tasks. The correlation was .71

10 Just what these self-correlations would be for the group in question is not known; but they would certainly not be on the average much above .90.

TABLE 8.

THE CORRELATION BETWEEN SCORE IN THE THORNDIKE EXAMINATION FOR HIGH SCHOOL GRADUATES (AVERAGE OF TWO FORMS) AND AN INCOMPLETE SAMPLING OF INTELLECT CAVD.

| Score in Thorndike Exam. | Score in Sampling of Intellect CAVD | | | | | | | | | | | | | | | | | | | | | | | | |
|---|---|---|---|---|---|---|---|---|---|---|---|---|---|---|---|---|---|---|---|---|---|---|---|---|---|
| | 30 | 2 | 4 | 6 | 8 | 40 | 2 | 4 | 6 | 8 | 50 | 2 | 4 | 6 | 8 | 60 | 2 | 4 | 6 | 8 | 70 | 2 | 4 | 6 | 8 |
| 40 | 1 | | | | | | | | | | | | | | | | | | | | | | | | |
| 45 | | 1 | | | | | | | | | | | | | | | | | | | | | | | |
| 50 | | | 1 | | 1 | | | | | | | | | | | | | | | | | | | | |
| 55 | | | 1 | | | | | | | | | 1 | | | | | | | | | | | | | |
| 60 | | | | | | | | | | | | | | 1 | | | | | | | | | | | |
| 65 | | | | | | | | | | | | | | | | | | | | | | | | | |
| 70 | | | | | | | | | | | | | | | | | | | | | | | | | |
| 75 | | | | | | | | | | | | | | | | | | 1 | 1 | | | | | | |
| 80 | | | | | | | | | | | | | | | | | | 2 | | 1 | | | | | |
| 85 | | | | | | | | | | | | | | | | | | | 2 | 1 | 1 | | | | |
| 90 | | | | | | | | | | | | | | | | | | | | 1 | 1 | | | 1 | |
| 95 | | | | | | | | | | | | | | | | | | | | | | 2 | 1 | | |
| 100 | | | | | | | | | | | | | | | | | | | | | | | | 1 | |
| 105 | | | | | | | | | | | | | | | | | | | | | | | 1 | | |
| 110 | | | | | | | | | | | | | | | | | | | | | | | | | 1 |

by the Pearson and .81 by the Sheppard formula. The self-correlation of so short a selection from CAVD will not be above .80 within this group, and the self-correlation of Alpha will be little, if any, above .80. So the correlation of .71 or .76 is about as high as the self-correlations permit.

Three hundred and eighty-eight pupils in Grade 6 were tested with a composite of stock intelligence tests (the I. E. R. Tests of Selective and Relational Thinking, Generalization and Organization) and with a sampling of about 40 of the completions and about 40 of the arithmetical problems of CAVD, the score for these latter being a summation of credits. The correlation was .81. The self-correlation for the I. E. R. tests in such a group will be not over .85;[11] it will probably be about .80 for the sampling of C and A. So the composite of C and A correlates nearly as closely with the stock test as the reliabilities permit.

Intellect CAVD or CAVDI is then no more limited or unreal or remote from the practical management of intellect than the "intellects" which are measured by the scores in examinations representative of the best present practice. It is so nearly the same thing as they that what we learn about it will have an application nearly or quite as broad as present practice is.

### THE HOMOGENEITY OF DIFFICULTY CAVD

We have cured the main defect in the methods of measuring the intellectual difficulty of tasks which was brought forward in the previous chapter. We can make sure that a task (always now a composite of many single tasks) measures all of Intellect CAVD and nothing but Intellect CAVD by correlating it therewith, and then measure its difficulty.

We have now to consider or reconsider a number of other questions. The first is whether the tasks whose differences in difficulty we thus measure do really differ in the possession of varying amounts of some one thing which are

11 It is .82 for a group of 1,039 boys in Grades 9, 10, and 11, and .86 for a group of 16-year-old boys in Grades 9, 10, and 11.

properly represented by cardinal numbers. Do the sub-series or levels (A, B, C, . . . Q) form a progressive, homogeneous series enough like a series of lengths or weights or temperatures to be subject to the laws of mathematics?

We show elsewhere[12] that a sub-series of CAVD tasks at any level of difficulty measures closely the same ability as the total series (provided the sub-series contains enough single tasks fairly to sample the tasks at that level). In that sense Intellect CAVD is nearly or quite the same from its lowest to its highest levels. It is obviously the same in the sense that the tasks are throughout to supply words to complete sentences, to solve arithmetical problems, to understand single words, and to understand connected discourse.

It is also the same in the sense that any person who is accustomed to think scientifically about intellectual difficulty progresses up this series without any sense of shock or shift or qualitative change. The progress is, of course, not so obviously an increase in the amount of one characteristic which does not change its nature, as when one looks at straight lines of increasing length or cubes of increasing volume or lifts graded weights. But it seems logically fairly comparable to one's experience who looks at very irregular and differently shaped solids, such as cups, shoes, babies, wheels, steam radiators, chairs, and motor cycles, which form a series of increasing volumes.

Finally, there is a very close correlation between level or altitude of Intellect CAVD and range or width of intellect—between the degree of difficulty at which a person can succeed with CAVD tasks and the number of CAVD tasks that he can succeed with at any specified degree of difficulty.[13] Range at a given level is entirely measured by number, is a variable varying in nothing whatsoever save amount. Whatever correlates so closely with it may be expected also to exist as varying amounts of some one quality or characteristic.

12 Appendix IV and Appendix V.
13 The measurements of this are reported in Chapter XIII.

These facts probably warrant us in using the one term *Difficulty CAVD* to designate the variable, with cardinal numbers to designate the varying amounts of degrees or intensities of it.

Difficulty CAVD is not the same throughout its variations in the sense that any one unit of it can replace or be interchangeable with any other unit of it, in the way in which one inch or one cent can replace any other. We cannot put three tasks, each of difficulty 4, together and have a task of difficulty 12, nor can we subtract some part of any task of difficulty 10 from it so as to leave a task of difficulty 9 and add that fraction of the actual task to a task of difficulty 5 so as to make its difficulty 6. The meaning of arithmetical operations upon numbers representing degrees of difficulty of intellectual tasks must be considered with reference to the realities which these numbers represent.

This is the case, also, with numbers representing many variables such as volts, degrees of temperature, wavelengths or ages, to which arithmetic is none the less usefully applied. Dividing a temperature of 300 degrees (above the absolute zero) by 10 gives 30 degrees in a certain real and useful sense, but not in the same sense that dividing 300 dollars by 10 gives 30 dollars. We cannot take 5 years of age from 40 years old and use it to make a five-year-old into a ten-year-old. Multiplying short vibrations will not give long vibrations.

We shall return to a consideration of the applicability of arithmetic to the numbers representing different degrees of difficulty CAVD later, after we have gained more knowledge of them and shown more facts concerning the realities for which they stand. For the present it may serve to note that the numbers representing difficulty CAVD are roughly comparable to the numbers representing temperatures in respect of the meaning and use of arithmetical operations performed upon them.

THE INFERENCE FROM THE FORM OF DISTRIBUTION OF A GRADE
POPULATION IN STANDARD INTELLIGENCE EXAMINATION
SCORES TO THE FORM OF ITS DISTRIBUTION IN
LEVEL OR ALTITUDE OF INTELLECT CAVD

The next matter that needs consideration concerns our use of the scores in stock intelligence examinations in the investigations of the form of distribution of the variations of an individual; and of the variations among individuals in Grade 6, Grade 9, and Grade 12; and of the relation of the variability of an individual to his average degree of intellect. The scores in any one of these stock examinations represent the composite influence of level, or altitude, range or width, and facility or speed, in unknown proportions. In strict logic we should have used for our purpose a large number of examinations, each concerned with level or altitude alone, but made by different experts and without prejudice concerning the form of distribution of intellect, as was the case with the material which we did use. The form of distribution which we really needed for our argument is the form of distribution in respect of how hard things the varying intellect of an individual and the varying intellects of a group can succeed with. It would, however, have been utterly impracticable to have attempted to have experts make seventeen such examinations, and to have applied these to the large number of individuals needed to make the argument valid. The cost in time and labor would have been prohibitive. We therefore used the stock examinations which were available; and set up experiments to ascertain how closely the ability measured by these examinations is correlated with altitude or level of intellect as measured by the hardest intellectual tasks at which a person attains a given percentage of successes. Are we justified in inferring the form of distribution of level or altitude of Intellect CAVD from the form of distribution of the ability measured by these stock intelligence examinations?

It is impossible to answer this question by a straightforward experiment in which a group of several hundred pupils of, for example, Grade 9 should be given the graded tasks of Intellect CAVD and also be tested with a dozen or more stock tests of intelligence. The form of distribution found for the group in level or altitude measured by the graded tasks of Intellect CAVD depends upon the real differences in difficulty between the tasks which is precisely what we are trying to determine. We must argue indirectly, as by the correlation between level or altitude of Intellect CAVD and score in a stock test of intelligence.

We have already shown that, in general, summation scores in Intellect CAVD measure very closely the same ability as the stock intelligence examinations do. Consequently we may correlate a level or altitude score in Intellect CAVD with a summation score in Intellect CAVD. Such correlations will have closely the same meaning as correlations between a level score in Intellect CAVD and the official score in the stock intelligence examination. If the correlations are close, the abilities are similar and will have, in any given group, similar forms of distribution when measured in truly equal units.

The correlations between altitude or level score in CAVD and summation score in CAVD are reported in Chapter 13. They are well above .90 even in groups of rather narrow range. The correlations between altitude or level score in CAVD and official score in standard intelligence examinations are reported here. They show in general that if an individual is tested with any sufficiently extensive collection of intellectual tasks representing wide variations in difficulty, the level which he reaches is closely correlated with the score which he obtains by a summation of credits for work done within a certain time, after the fashion common in the stock examination.

In the case of 146 pupils of Grade 5½, the correlation between altitude or level score in CAVD and score in the National Examination (A + B) was .72 by one determination of altitude and .665 by an independent determination of altitude. The two independent measures of altitude or level correlated .755. The level score in CAVD thus correlates with the National Intelligence score nearly as closely as with itself (.69¼ compared with .75½).

Twenty individuals were measured in respect of a sampling from Intellect CAVD by the level at which they could succeed with fifty percent of the task elements, that is, could do correctly 20 of the 40 single tasks making up a composite task. Each was measured also by two alternative forms of the Thorndike Examination for High School Graduates. The correlations between the level score and the two stock examination scores are .92 and .90. One of the stock examination scores correlates with the other .95; and the level score would probably not correlate with that from another similar sampling from Intellect CAVD more than .97. So perfectly measured level or altitude CAVD and perfectly measured ability in this sort of stock examination would probably correlate about .95.

In this same group the correlation between the level score in CAVD and a summation score in a composite of C, A, V, and D, including the tasks used in determining the level score and many others, was .96. The correlations between this summation score and the scores in the two Thorndike Examinations were both .95. Thus level score in CAVD correlates with summation score in CAVD nearly or quite up to its probable self-correlation, and correlates with summation score in the Thorndike 91/95 as high as does the summation score from much more extensive testing.

Dr. John R. Clark secured measurements of one hundred eighty pupils in Grades 7 to 12 of the Lincoln School in the Stanford Binet, Terman Group Test and Otis Self-Administering Group Test, and in rough measures of level or altitude, range or width, and speed or facility in samplings from the arithmetic and completion tasks of Intellect CAVD. He found the correlations with level to be as shown in Table 9.

The three stock examinations correlate on the average .80 one with another, and correlate on the average .76 with arithmetic level score if the latter is perfectly measured, and .64 with completion level score if that is perfectly measured. They may fairly be expected to correlate almost perfectly with a level score for the sort of tasks which they themselves contain.

TABLE 9

THE CORRELATIONS BETWEEN SCORES IN STOCK INTELLIGENCE EXAMINATIONS AND LEVEL SCORES IN ARITHMETICAL PROBLEMS AND SENTENCE COMPLETIONS. 180 PUPILS IN GRADES 7 TO 12. DATA FROM CLARK ('24).

| | Otis | Terman | Arith. Level | Co. Level | Arith. Level if perfectly measured | Co. Level if perfectly measured |
|---|---|---|---|---|---|---|
| Stanford Binet | .74 | .77 | .57 | .57 | .65 | .65 |
| Otis Self Adm. | | .88 | .74 | .55 | .83 | .61 |
| Terman Group | | | .74 | .59 | .80 | .66 |
| Arith. Level | | | | .46 | | |
| Arith. Level perfectly measured | | | | | | .55 |

We may then assume with risk of only moderate error that achievement with the series of CAVD composite tasks represents an important ability closely allied to that which such stock intelligence examinations as the Stanford Binet, National, Otis, Terman, and Thorndike measure; that the level or altitude score attained in Intellect CAVD may properly be expressed as a cardinal number; that this level score, if measured in truly equal units, will show a rather close approach to Form A (the probability surface) in Grade 6, Grade 9, Grade 12, or any intervening grade; and that the correlation between a person's true level or altitude in Intellect CAVD and his score in any one of the subseries or composite tasks (A, B, C, . . . Q) will be very nearly as close as the self-correlation of the sub-series will permit.

We can then measure the differences in difficulty between any two of these composite tasks for any grade group between 6 and 12 which is so constituted that all of its individuals do not succeed, neither do all fail, with either of the two composite tasks in question.

# CHAPTER IV

## The Measurement of the Intellectual Difficulty of a Single Brief Task

In the previous chapter we have shown that if intellectual difficulty is defined as the difficulty of a perfectly representative sub-series of a total series of concretely specified tasks, it can be measured, at least over a range from tasks which the stupidest children in Grade 6 can do to tasks which only the brightest of college freshmen can do.

In the present chapter we have to consider the difficulties which confront us when the sub-series is only imperfectly representative of the total. As the title of the chapter indicates, we shall emphasize the extreme cases where the task is a very partial representative; but the discussion will provide also for the treatment of any degree of partiality and incompleteness.

We have seen that when we know that k percent of a group succeed with a task $t_1$ (k being $> 0$ and $< 100$) we may express the difficulty of the task as $M_{t_1} + A\sigma_{t_1}$ where $M_t$ is the central tendency of the group in the ability measured by t, $\sigma_{t_1}$ is the variability of the group in the ability measured by t, and A is a factor dependent for its sign and absolute value on k. We have seen that we cannot, without further knowledge to that effect, assume that $M_{t_1}$ is equal to the central tendency of the group in intellect or anything else save the ability measured by $t_1$; or that $\sigma_{t_1}$ is equal to the variability of the group in general intellect or anything else save the ability measured by $t_1$.

### THE PROBLEM IN THE CASE OF SINGLE TASKS, EACH OF WHICH MEASURES INTELLECT PLUS A MERE SAMPLING ERROR

We have now to consider the possibility of such further knowledge. Consider it first for cases where $t_1$ is a representative sample of intellectual tasks, and the measurement afforded by $t_1$ is a compound of perfectly measured intellect and error of sampling, and the error is of the same magnitude for any one $t_1$ as for any other, so that the average of a sufficient number of $t_1$'s would be a perfect measure of intellect, so that the correlation of any one $t_1$ with any other will be a constant. For such cases the knowledge needed is available and $M_i$ and $\sigma_i$, the central tendency and variability of the group in intellect, can be computed from $M_{t1}$ and $\sigma_{t1}$, when the amount of the error is known.

Since $M_i$ is the average of the N individuals of the group, each measured in $(t_1 + t_2 + t_3 + t_4 \cdots t_n)/n$, $M_i$ will, if N is large, approximate closely to $M_{t1}$, $M_{t2}$, $M_{t3}$, etc., and any one of these will approximate closely to any other of them. The effect of the error whereby the estimate of intellect by any t differs from that by the average of all the t's is as often plus as minus, and is negligible for our purposes so far as concerns the central tendency of a large group. $M_i$ may be taken as equal to $M_{t1}$.

Because of the sampling error, $\sigma_i$ will always be smaller than $\sigma_{t1}$. $\sigma_{t1}$ will equal $\sqrt{\sigma_p^2 + \sigma_e^2}$, where $\sigma_p$ is the variability of the N individuals each measured by $(t_1 + t_2 + t_3 + t_4 \cdots t_n)/n$, and $\sigma_e$ is the variability of the sampling error, dependent upon the variations of $t_1$, $t_2$, $t_3$, etc., in any individual from the average of $t_1$, $t_2$, $t_3$, etc., for that individual. $\sigma_e$ may be computed in various ways from various measures of the unlikeness of $t_1$, $t_2$, $t_3$, etc., in the same individual, such as the correlation of $t_1$ with $t_2$ in the group, or the correlation of $t_1$ or $t_2$ or $t_3$ with $(t_1 + t_2 + t_3 \cdots t_n)/n$, or the differences between $t_1$ and $t_2$ in individuals, or the variability of an individual in intellect as estimated first by $t_1$, then by $t_2$, then by $t_3$, and so on.

Thus $\sigma_i = \sigma_t \sqrt{r_{t_a t_b}}$ or $\sigma_t = \dfrac{\sigma_i}{\sqrt{r_{t_a t_b}}}$ [Kelley, '23, formula 166, p. 213] and since $r_{ti} = \sqrt{r_{t_a t_b}}$ [Kelley, '23, formula 160, p. 206], $\sigma_t = \dfrac{\sigma_i}{r_{ti}}$,[1] where

[1] This second formula is presented because it lends itself better to much of the material at our disposal. It is derived by Kelley directly from Spearman's formulas for the correlations of sums or averages. The reader of less mathe-

$\sigma_i$ = the variability of the group in intellect, which is here identical with $\sigma_p$, the variability of the group in $(t_1 + t_2 + t_3 \cdots t_n)/n$.

$r_{ti}$ = the correlation between the estimate of intellect by any one t in question and the estimate of intellect by $(t_1 + t_2 + t_3 \cdots t_n)/n$ in the group in question.

$\sigma_t$ = the variability of the group in the ability measured by the one t in question.

$r_{t_a t_b}$ = the correlation between the estimate of intellect by any one t and that by any other t.

For example, assume that the completion task 22 is one taken at random from a number of completions, each of which measures intellect plus a similar sampling error, the average of all of them measuring it exactly.

We found the difficulty of task 22 to be .098 times the $\sigma_{22}$ of the ninth grade group harder than the $M_{22}$ of that group. In accord with our assumptions, we may replace $M_{22}$ by $M_i$. The correlation between score in task 22 and intellect may be taken as approximately .40 for the group in question, since the obtained correlation with a fairly close representation of intellect is .37$\frac{1}{2}$. In place of .098 $\sigma_{22}$ we then put .098 $\dfrac{\sigma_i}{.40}$. The purely intellectual difficulty of task 22, freed from the effect of the sampling error, is now measured as .245 ($\sigma_i$ for 9th grade) and can be compared with that of any other task representing intellect plus the effect of sampling error for which we have the percent of correct responses in this group. Thus task 20, which

---

matical ability may easily derive it from the more familiar formula for the correction for attenuation, as follows:

Consider the ordinary Spearman attenuation formula for our case,

$$r_{t_\infty i} = \frac{r_{ti}}{\sqrt{r_{t_1 t_2} r_{i_1 i_2}}}$$

Let $i_1$ and $i_2$ be perfect measures of intellect.  Then $r_{i_1 i_2} = 1.00$.    $r_{t_\infty i}$ is 1.00 by hypothesis.

So $\sqrt{r_{t_1 t_2}} = r_{ti}$.

Substituting in $\sigma_t = \dfrac{\sigma_p}{\sqrt{r_{t_1 t_2}}}$ we have $\sigma_t = \dfrac{\sigma_p}{r_{ti}} = \dfrac{\sigma_i}{r_{ti}}$ in this case.

showed 60% of correct responses in this group, giving — $.2533\sigma_{20}$, has a correlation with the same fairly close representation of intellect just mentioned, of $.18\frac{1}{2}$. Its correlation with intellect may be taken as approximately .20. Assuming that it is a random sample from a set of tasks whose average measures intellect perfectly,[2] and each of which suffers an error of equal magnitude, we transmute ".2533 $\sigma_{20}$ easier than $M_{20}$ in Grade 9" into "$\dfrac{.2533\,\sigma_{19}}{.20}$ easier than $M_1$ in Grade 9," or — 1.27 $\sigma_{19}$. Task 20 is then 1.51 easier than task 22, the unit of measure being the mean square deviation of intellect in Grade 9.

If the error whereby the ability measured by a task differs from intellect is a random sampling error, so that perfectly measured intellect can be got by merely increasing the number of tasks strictly comparable to it drawn in the sample, we can then correct for it, the correction being a further application of the facts shown by Spearman ['04, '07, '10, and '13], Boas ['06], Thorndike ['13], and Kelley ['19, '21 and '23].

If the single tasks whose intellectual difficulty we wish to determine measured intellect perfectly, except for such a random sampling error, we could and should compute $r_{ti}$ (or $r_{ti(CAVD)}$) for each of them in each group used, and apply the corrections.

The effect of the correction may be illustrated by cases where we have reduced the sampling error empirically by using ten tasks in place of one.

Thus for 250 pupils in Grade $8\frac{1}{2}$, the median of the ten percents correct for the ten single word tasks and the percent scoring five or more correct responses out of the ten was as shown in Table 10 for each of the fourteen 10-word composites in the I. E. R. A–2 and B–2. Table 10

[2] This average will have to be computed from a larger number of $t$'s than would be needed in the case of the tasks from which task 22 was drawn as a random sample, since the error is here larger, making the correlation with i smaller.

also reports the $\sigma_1$ values and the $\sigma_{10}$ values which correspond to these percents. The percent is more remote from 50 when we shift from one right out of one to five or more right out of ten; and the value in terms of $\sigma_{10}$ is more remote from the median of the group.

TABLE 10.

THE EFFECT OF DECREASING THE ERROR OF ESTIMATING THE DIFFICULTY OF THE
MEDIAN TASK OF A COMPOSITE OF TEN BY THE USE OF THE PERCENT OF A
GROUP SCORING "5 OR MORE RIGHT OUT OF TEN" IN PLACE OF THE
MEDIAN OF THE TEN PERCENTS OF THE GROUP SCORING
"RIGHT" IN THE TASKS TAKEN ONE AT A TIME.
VOCABULARY TASKS IN THE CASE OF 250
PUPILS OF GRADE 8½.

| | | Median of the ten Percents | Percent Scoring 5 or more | Distance from the Median Ability of the Group | |
| --- | --- | --- | --- | --- | --- |
| | | | | In Terms of $\sigma_1$ | In Terms of $\sigma_{10}$ |
| Composite | 1 | 93.2 | 98.0 | $-1.49$ | $-2.05$ |
| " | 1a | 93.4 | 97.6 | $-1.51$ | $-1.98$ |
| " | 2 | 82.6 | 92.0 | $-0.94$ | $-1.41$ |
| " | 2a | 87.4 | 97.2 | $-1.15$ | $-1.91$ |
| " | 3 | 62.8 | 74.0 | $-0.32$ | $-0.64$ |
| " | 3a | 72.3 | 86.4 | $-0.60$ | $-1.10$ |
| " | 4 | 55.2 | 64.4 | $-0.13$ | $-0.37$ |
| " | 4a | 55.6 | 61.6 | $-0.14$ | $-0.30$ |
| " | 5 | 43.0 | 44.4 | $+0.18$ | $+0.15$ |
| " | 5a | 43.2 | 44.8 | $+0.17$ | $+0.13$ |
| " | 6 | 23.4 | 15.2 | $+0.73$ | $+1.03$ |
| " | 6a | 25.8 | 19.6 | $+0.65$ | $+0.86$ |
| " | 7 | 15.8 | 4.4 | $+1.00$ | $+1.71$ |
| " | 7a | 10.8 | .8 | $+1.24$ | $+2.41$ |

It may be realized more exactly by applying the formula to a few representative cases. Thus, tasks A, B and C, each being done correctly by the same percent (80) of a group (of normal form of distribution), but correlating with intellect to the extent of .20, .35 and .50, respectively, in that group, will be of *intellectual* difficulty $-4.208\,\sigma_1$, $-2.405\,\sigma_1$ and $-1.683\,\sigma_1$, respectively. Tasks C, D and E, although done correctly by very different percents of the group, are of equal intellectual difficulty, their differences in difficulty being counterbalanced by reverse differences in intellectualness.

| Task | % successful | Correlation with intellect | Difficulty | Intellectual Difficulty |
|------|------|------|------|------|
| A | 80 | .20 | $-.8416\sigma_A$ | $-4.208\sigma_i$ |
| B | 80 | .35 | $-.8416\sigma_B$ | $-2.405\sigma_i$ |
| C | 80 | .50 | $-.8416\sigma_C$ | $-1.683\sigma_i$ |
| D | 60.1 | .20 | $-.2559\sigma_D$ | $-1.280\sigma_i$ |
| E | 67.3 | .35 | $-.4482\sigma_E$ | $-1.280\sigma_i$ |
| F | 73.9 | .50 | $-.6403\sigma_F$ | $-1.280\sigma_i$ |

THE PROBLEM IN THE CASE OF SUCH SINGLE TASKS AS ARE USED IN CAVD OR IN STANDARD INTELLIGENCE EXAMINATIONS

Unfortunately we cannot be sure that a single task will measure intellect save for such a sampling error. This may be best realized by taking our Intellect CAVD as intellect for the moment, and considering a task made up of 20 completions, 20 arithmetical problems, 20 words and 20 directions, all of equal difficulty. The ability measured by such an 80-element task, if the elements are well selected, is approximately perfectly representative of ability CAVD.

Now if we take one of the eighty tasks at random, we do not have something which measures what the eighty together do plus an ordinary error of sampling. One word-knowledge test does not differ from one arithmetical problem test in the same way that one arithmetical problem test differs from another. The total is too varied a synthesis and the single task is too small a sample for the latter to represent the former plus an ordinary sampling error. In the eighty are four different sorts of tasks; in the twenty completions there may be four or five which require knowledge of specialized facts; amongst these four or five, there may be one which is very much easier for intellects which have lived in the country than for intellects, otherwise similar, which have lived in the city; and another of which the reverse is true.

The case is not so much like measuring a man's height a dozen times and taking one of the dozen to represent their average, as like measuring his head, his neck, his trunk, his legs to the knees, his shins, and his feet and adding the results to get his height. Our measures of intellect are *inventories;* we combine C, A, V and D as we might combine a man's real estate, ships, stocks, bonds, accounts receivable, merchandise, materials, and cash on hand. What he happened to own in the way of real estate in Boston would not in a useful sense represent his total wealth plus a sampling error.

Assume for the purpose of illustration that: (1) intellect is composed of C and A in equal parts, and is perfectly measured at the level in question by a task composed of 20 completions and 20 arithmetical problems, the two twenties having equal weight; (2) a task comprising the 20 completions will correlate perfectly with a task comprising 100 completions from which the 20 are a random sample; (3) a task comprising the 20 arithmetical problems will correlate perfectly with a task comprising 100 problems from which the 20 are a random sample; (4) the 20 completions or the 100 completions will correlate 0 with the 20 arithmetical problems or the 100 arithmetical problems.

If now N individuals composing a group distributed "normally" are measured in respect of their success with a task composed of 40 completions, and if a given percent succeed with the task (that is, have 20 or more of the 40 right), the difficulty of that 40-completion task is $M_{40C} +$ $x\sigma_{40C}$. The correlation between the score in 40C and the score in intellect, or $C + A$ measured by $20C + 20A$, is .707. The correlation between the score in 40C and the score in another 40C is 1.00.

By our assumptions

$$\sigma_{20C + 20A} = \sqrt{\sigma^2_{20C} + \sigma^2_{20A}} \qquad \text{since } r_{20C\ 20A} = 0.$$

$$\sigma_{20C + 20A} = \sqrt{2}\sigma_{20C} \qquad \text{since } \sigma_{20C} = \sigma_{20A}.$$

$$\sigma_{20C + 20A} = \frac{\sqrt{2}}{2}\sigma_{40C} \qquad \text{since } \sigma_{40C} = 2\sigma_{20C}, \text{ since } r_{20C\ 20C}$$

is 1.00.

$$\sigma_{20C + 20A} = .707\ \sigma_{40C}.$$

But by the formula $\left(\sigma_t = \dfrac{\sigma_i}{\sqrt{r_{t_1 t_2}}}\right)$ we should have

$$\sigma_{40C} = \frac{\sigma_{20C + 20A}}{\sqrt{r_{20C\ 20C}}},\ \text{giving}$$

$$\sigma_{40C} = \frac{\sigma_{20C + 20A}}{\sqrt{1}}$$

or $\sigma_{20C + 20A} = \sigma_{40C}$.

We see the reason for the discrepancy if we consider the attenuation formula

$$r_{C_\infty \text{ with } (C + A)_\infty} = \frac{r_{C40 \text{ with } C20 + A20}}{\sqrt{r_{C40\ C40}\ r_{(C20 + A20)(C20 + A20)}}}$$

With our present assumptions, $r_{C_\infty \text{ with } (C + A)_\infty}$ is *not* 1.00, because, no matter how many C's we take, we do not get all of intellect and nothing but intellect. It is in fact .707. So we do not have

$$\sqrt{r_{C40 \text{ with } C40}} = r_{C40 \text{ with } C20 + A20},\ \text{but}$$

$$\sqrt{r_{C40 \text{ with } C40}} = \frac{r_{C40 \text{ with } C20 + A20}}{.707}$$

If we substitute $r_{C40 \text{ with } C20 + A20}$ for $\sqrt{r_{C40\ C40}}$ in the formula $\sigma_t = \dfrac{\sigma_i}{\sqrt{r_{t_1 t_2}}}$, we have again the erroneous result

$\sigma_{20C + 20A} = \sigma_{40C}$.

Now the correlation between $C_\infty$ and $(C + A + V + D)_\infty$ or any other form of perfectly measured intellect is not perfect; and the correlation between $C_\infty$ and either $A_\infty$ or $V_\infty$ or $D_\infty$ or Picture Completions $_\infty$ or Geometrical Relations $_\infty$ is not in fact perfect. In general, if we sample by taking one small task, it has to be so limited that if we take a thousand tasks closely like it, the score therein need not correlate perfectly with the score in intellect, or with the score in a thousand tasks *closely like any other one| task* with which we might begin.  In particular, no single completion, or word to be defined, or problem in arithmetic, or sentence to be comprehended can safely be regarded as differing from intellect only by a sampling error such as may be adequately corrected for by

$$\sigma_t = \frac{\sigma_i}{\sqrt{r_{t_1 t_2}}} \text{or } \sigma_t = \frac{\sigma_i}{r_{ti}}.$$

A single task, $t_1$, measures not a large part of intellect plus a small error due to the action of a large number of factors of about equal magnitude, but a small part of intellect plus a large error.  The latter is due to the action of factors some of which, like residence in the city, access to books, formal training with arithmetical problems, special acquaintance with the particular word or sentence or problem, may be of very great magnitude in comparison with others.

More generally, $\sigma_i = \sigma_t \, r_{ti}$ or $\sigma_t = \dfrac{\sigma_i}{r_{ti}}$ is, as Kelley's discussion [p. 213] makes clear, true for a case where i is simply the average of many t's, each of which has closely the same $\sigma$ as any other and closely the same $r_{ti}$ as any other.  It is not true when we fail to get i by a collection of tasks however extensive.  And no matter how many completions we take, we shall never get an i made up of completions and arithmetical problems unless the correlation between sentence completion and solving arithmetical problems is perfect.

The quantitative importance of having a varied as well as a large sample may be illustrated by measurements of the correlation between i, as represented by the summation score in CAVD (40C + 40A + 40V + 40D), and Composites of 10 made up all of C or A or V or D on the one hand, and on the other, composites of 10 made up of 2C + 3A + 2V + 3D or of 3C + 2A + 3V + 2D.  In the case of 240 college graduates, the average of the former sort was .59 with a P.E. of ± .028; the average of the latter sort was .72 with a P.E. of ± .022.

It should also be noted that, even if the correlation between the score in an infinite number of completions and
the score in an infinite number of arithmetical problems
were perfect, so that we got all of intellect and nothing but
intellect as well by a sampling of one type of task as by a
mixed sampling (the reduction of $r_{t_1}$ below 1.00 being due
purely to sampling error), still the practical difficulties in
the way of applying the correction would make it far wiser
first to construct composite tasks. It is very laborious to
compute $r_{t_1}$ for each element. It will be low (roughly
from .20 to .60 for a group of individuals in the same school
grade), and the probable error of a low bi-serial r is such
that an enormous number of individuals must be tested to
obtain $r_{t_1}$ with a precision such that the probable error is
less than .01 (from 5,000 to more than 10,000 for $r = .40$,
according as the split of successes and failures is near .50,
.50, or remote therefrom).

The only safe and wise course is, then, to make sure that
the tasks whose difficulty we are to measure are alike in the
amount of intellect which each involves, and in the amount
of non-intellect by which each is contaminated, by using
composite tasks each containing many single tasks, representing with proper weight the various aspects or constituents of intellect. The nearer we come to having each of
them measure all of intellect and nothing but intellect, the
safer our course will be.

With composites which differ from i only by the sampling error the correction formulas are appropriate. In
proportion as the composite is made to include a large
sampling, the labor of computing $r_{t_1}$ or $r_{t_1 t_2}$ to a given degree of precision is reduced and the reliability of the correction is increased. With forty-element CAVD com-
posites, for example, it is safe to infer $\sigma_i$ from $\sigma_{t_1}$, either by
$\sigma_i = \sqrt{r_{t_1 t_2}} \sigma_{t_1}$ or by $\sigma_i = r_{t_1 i} \sigma_{t_1}$.

In constructing composite tasks whose difficulty will be
truly intellectual difficulty, freed from the sampling error

by having many tasks, and freed from the constant error by having a proper representation of all the elements of intellect, it may be desirable, other things being equal, to include in any one composite only tasks which would show approximately the same intellectual difficulty if, by a miracle, all of intellect, and nothing but intellect, could in each case be utilized for success. The measure of the difficulty of a composite of n tasks would be more reliable if this could be the case. The construction of composites of specified amounts of difficulty would be less a matter of trial and correction.

So, for this purpose, we may need to measure approximately something which, for lack of a better name, we may call the "intellectual difficulty" of single tasks, and to know how close the approximations are.

The facts which we shall present in this connection are also of importance in estimating the errors in scales[3] which have been constructed on the assumption that $\sigma_{t_1}$, $\sigma_{t_2}$, $\sigma_{t_3}$, $\sigma_{t_4}$, etc., are equal. They are also of importance in connection with the general technique of selecting single tasks to make a composite, even if we make no attempt to select them to be of the same intellectual difficulty, rather than of the same difficulty.

These facts are the percents of some group succeeding with the several tasks ($t_1$, $t_2$, $t_3$, etc.) whence we may compute M measures of their difficulty ($M_{t_1} + C_1 \sigma_{t_1}$, $M_{t_2} + C_2 \sigma_{t_2}$, $M_{t_3} + C_3 \sigma_{t_3}$, etc.); and the correlations ($r_{t_1i}$, $r_{t_2i}$, $r_{t_3i}$, etc., between each of many single tasks and intellect (CAVD or some other defined intellect), whence we may compute the extent to which $t_1$, $t_2$, $t_3$, etc. represent intellect, and so estimate their "intellectual difficulty." We have seen that with a large group, $M_{t_1}$, $M_{t_2}$, $M_{t_3}$, etc., will be closely equal. In proportion as $r_{t_1i}$, $r_{t_2i}$, $r_{t_3i}$, etc., are approximately equal, $\sigma_{t_1}$, $\sigma_{t_2}$, $\sigma_{t_3}$, etc., will be approximately equal, and $\sigma_i$ will be approximately the same fraction of each of them, equalling respectively $\sqrt{\sigma_i^2 + E_1^2}$, $\sqrt{\sigma_i^2 + E_2^2}$,

[3] Such as the Buckingham Spelling Scale, Trabue Completion Scales, Van Wagenen History Scales.

10

$\sqrt{\sigma_i{}^2 + E_3{}^2}$, where $E_1$ or $E_2$ or $E_3$ is the "error" by which the estimate of intellect by the single task diverges from the estimate of intellect from a properly weighted sum of all tasks. $E_1$, $E_2$, $E_3$, etc., will be approximately equal, if they produce approximately equal reductions from perfection in the correlations $r_{t_1 i}$, $r_{t_2 i}$, $r_{t_3 i}$, etc.

If, then, we select single tasks which are done by equal percents of a large group, *and also are approximately equally closely correlated* with intellect, we shall have equality in the sort of intellectual difficulty which we are discussing. For example, Table 11 shows, in the case of 30 reading tasks, the percents succeeding and the correlations (bi-serial r) with the combined score in two forms of a standard intelligence examination given a year apart (the I. E. R. Tests of Selective and Relational Thinking, Generalization and Organization[4]). The facts are given for 668 pupils in Grade 11. Using the facts of Table 11 as our guide, tasks 10, 15, and 24 may be expected to be of approximately equal "intellectual difficulty." They are approximately equally difficult because the percents succeeding are respectively 66, 65, and 67. They are approximately equally intellectual because the $r_{t_1 i}$'s are, respectively, .40, .41, and .38. We can also balance low degrees of %s (percent successful) against high degrees of $r_{t i}$ so as to get tasks that would be of equal intellectual difficulty in so far as the formula is applicable.

Even if it is not desirable to spend time in choosing tasks which are alike in the $+ -$ values of $\sigma_i$ as inferred from $\sigma_i = r_{t i}\sigma_t$, it will be very useful to know how much difference will be shown in the $r_{t i}$'s of single tasks in completing sentences, solving arithmetical problems, knowing word-meanings, following directions or answering questions about a paragraph, giving opposites, possessing and using information, completing pictures, supplying or selecting the proper related term as in the analogies test, and other stock forms of tasks used in instruments for measure-

---

[4] The self-correlation of this combined score is approximately $\frac{1.70}{1.85}$ or .92, in this group.

ment of intellect. For, other things being equal, the higher $r_{t1}$ is the more suitable the task is for inclusion in a composite to measure i.

TABLE 11

THE DIFFICULTY AND INTELLECTUALNESS OF 30 SINGLE TASKS IN UNDERSTANDING SENTENCES, MEASURED BY THE PERCENT OF 668 11TH GRADE PUPILS SUCCEEDING WITH EACH, AND BY THE CORRELATIONS OF SUCCESS IN EACH WITH THE AVERAGE SCORE IN TWO FORMS OF THE I.E.R. SEL. REL. GEN. ORG. EXAMINATION.

| Task | % Suc- ceeding | $r_{t1}$ | Unreliability of $r_{t1}$ $(\sigma_r)$ |
|---|---|---|---|
| D I A  1 | 93 | .43 | ± .07 |
| 2 | 94 | .30 | " .075 |
| 3 | 91 | .29 | " .065 |
| 4 | 84 | .55 | " .04 |
| 5 | 76 | .36 | " .045 |
| 6 | 83 | .45 | " .045 |
| 7 | 75 | .43 | " .04 |
| 8 | 82 | .53 | " .04 |
| 9 | 82 | .54 | " .04 |
| 10 | 66 | .40 | " .04 |
| 11 | 81 | .52 | " .04 |
| 12 | 69 | .48 | " .04 |
| 13 | 77 | .45 | " .04 |
| 14 | 57 | .28 | " .045 |
| 15 | 65 | .41 | " .04 |
| 16 | 75 | .48 | " .04 |
| 17 | 66 | .45 | " .04 |
| 18 | 65 | .46 | " .04 |
| 19 | 75 | .40 | " .045 |
| 20 | 70 | .49 | " .04 |
| 21 | 69 | .36 | " .045 |
| 22 | 56 | .33 | " .04 |
| 23 | 54 | .35 | " .04 |
| 24 | 67 | .38 | " .04 |
| 25 | 70 | .32 | " .045 |
| 26 | 66 | .52 | " .04 |
| 27 | 64 | .46 | " .04 |
| 28 | 64 | .49 | " .04 |
| 29 | 57 | .45 | " .04 |
| 30 | 64 | .53 | " .035 |

THE CORRELATIONS OF SINGLE TASKS WITH MEASURES OF INTELLECT

We have made the computations in the case of 24 other reading tasks and 55 vocabulary tasks, with the results shown in Table 12. We also give in Table 13 the facts for 10 completion tasks, 10 arithmetical tasks, and 10 vocabulary tasks, using a group of 240 college graduates. These data, together with those of Vincent (to be described shortly), make possible a general estimate of how much $r_{ti}$ may be expected to vary in the case of single tasks selected or devised by psychologists as suitable elements of an intelligence examination.

The obtained correlations vary very widely, but some of this variability is due to the unreliability of the determinations; and allowance must be made for this in order to estimate the true variation in $r_{ti}$ due to the differences among single tasks in the amount of i which each involves and the amount of non-i by which it is contaminated.

Consider first the facts from 99 tasks in reading and vocabulary, where the percent is between 5 and 95, in the case of 668 and 454 pupils, respectively, in Grade 11, shown in Table 14. We omit the very, very easy and very, very hard tasks, since we should measure their difficulty by a duller and by a brighter group, respectively.

It is obvious to inspection that the correlations vary more than can be accounted for by their unreliabilities. In the .40 to .60 group, we have a range from — .45 to .52, in the .60 to .80 group, a range from .11 to .56, and in the .80 to .95 group, a range from — .02 to .67.[5]

The variation which we should obtain with the unreliabilities cut to 0 by a sufficiently large group is to be found from $\sigma_{true} = \sqrt{\sigma^2_{obt.} - \sigma^2_{error}}$. Using medians as central tendencies, the facts are:

$$\sigma_{true\ .40-.60} = \sqrt{.0217-.0024} \text{ or } .139 \ (n = 20).$$

$$\sigma_{true\ .60-.80} = \sqrt{.0092-.0022} \text{ or } .084 \ (n = 35).$$

$$\sigma_{true\ .80-.95} = \sqrt{.0246-.0041} \text{ or } .143 \ (n = 38).$$

[5] The bi-serial r's in Tables 11, 12, and 13 were computed by an approximate method. They will diverge from r's computed accurately by not over .005, which is not of consequence in comparison with the variations which we are considering.

TABLE 12

PERCENTAGE SUCCEEDING AND CORRELATIONS WITH A CRITERION IN THE CASE OF
24 READING TASKS AND 52 VOCABULARY TASKS: GRADE 11: n = 668
FOR THE READING TASKS AND 454 FOR THE VOCABULARY TASKS.

| Task | | $\% s$ | $r_{t1}$ | $\sigma_r$ | Task | | $\% s$ | $r_{1t}$ | $\sigma_r$ |
|---|---|---|---|---|---|---|---|---|---|
| D I A | 66 | 72 | .39 ± .045 | | V B | 45 | 87 | .29 ± .07 | |
| | 67 | 81 | .28 " .045 | | | 46 | 85 | .39 " .06 | |
| | 68 | 83 | .31 " .05 | | | 47 | 85 | .45 " .06 | |
| | 69 | 88 | .39 " .055 | | | 48 | 97 | .40 " .11 | |
| | 70 | 80 | .24 " .045 | | | 49 | 20 | .15 " .06 | |
| | 71 | 94 | .30 " .075 | | | 50 | 66 | .33 " .055 | |
| | 72 | 42 | .13 " .05 | | | 51 | 77 | .24 " .055 | |
| | 73 | 80 | .23 " .045 | | | 52 | 73 | .52 " .05 | |
| | 74 | 81 | .41 " .045 | | | 53 | 26 | − .13 " .06 | |
| | 75 | 53 | .39 " .04 | | | 54 | 65 | .27 " .055 | |
| | 77 | 69 | .35 " .045 | | | 55 | 84 | − .02 " .07 | |
| | 78 | 90 | .31 " .065 | | | 56 | 96 | .58 " .085 | |
| | 79 | 73 | .32 " .045 | | | 57 | 44 | .48 " .05 | |
| | | | | | | 58 | 80 | .48 " .05 | |
| D II A | 1 | 47 | .17 " .045 | | | 59 | 90 | .36 " .07 | |
| | 2 | 41 | .35 " .045 | | | 60 | 82 | .50 " .05 | |
| | 3 | 34 | .13 " .05 | | | 61 | 87 | .54 " .06 | |
| | 4 | 54 | .22 " .045 | | | 62 | 66 | .29 " .055 | |
| | 5 | 51 | .25 " .045 | | | 63 | 43 | .35 " .05 | |
| | 17 | 22 | .31 " .045 | | | 64 | 85 | .04 " .07 | |
| | 18 | 2 | .44 " .005 | | | 65 | 95 | .31 " .095 | |
| | 19 | 49 | .45 " .04 | | | 66 | 91 | .34 " .07 | |
| | 20 | 14 | .37 " .055 | | | 67 | 91 | .67 " .07 | |
| | 21 | 4 | .12 " .08 | | | 68 | 74 | .11 " .06 | |
| | 22 | 9 | .61 " .05 | | | 69 | 43 | .05 " .055 | |
| | | | | | | 70 | 45 | .36 " .05 | |
| V B | 31 | 92 | − .01 " .085 | | | 76 | 69 | .45 " .05 | |
| | 32 | 92 | .27 " .075 | | | 77 | 53 | .00 " .055 | |
| | 33 | 88 | .34 " .055 | | | 78 | 85 | .47 " .06 | |
| | 34 | 98 | .07 " .135 | | | 79 | 63 | .36 " .05 | |
| | 35 | 83 | .14 " .06 | | | 80 | 78 | .40 " .055 | |
| | 36 | 60 | .18 " .055 | | | 81 | 43 | .18 " .055 | |
| | 37 | 95 | .20 " .095 | | | 82 | 56 | .40 " .05 | |
| | 38 | 92 | .24 " .08 | | | 83 | 65 | .56 " .045 | |
| | 39 | 97 | − .14 " .115 | | | 84 | 66 | .38 " .05 | |
| | 40 | 89 | .53 " .065 | | | 85 | 50 | .52 " .045 | |
| | 41 | 92 | .31 " .075 | | | 86 | 91 | .63 " .06 | |
| | 42 | 91 | .29 " .075 | | | 87 | 96 | .45 " .090 | |
| | 43 | 91 | .34 " .07 | | | 88 | 52 | .45 " .045 | |
| | | | | | | 89 | 70 | .41 " .05 | |
| | 44 | 97 | .50 " .105 | | | 90 | 73 | .37 " .055 | |

In the case of the 30 tasks done by the 240 college graduates, the correlations vary from .18 to .90.

$$\sigma_{true} = \sqrt{.0208 - .0059} \text{ or } .122 \quad (n = 30).$$

TABLE 13

PERMILLES SUCCEEDING AND CORRELATIONS WITH A CRITERION OF INTELLECT,
IN THE CASE OF 240 COLLEGE GRADUATES.

|  | Task | Permille's | $r_{ti}$ | $\sigma_{r_{ti}}$ |
|---|---|---|---|---|
| C O | 1 | 600 | .42 | ± .07 |
|  | 2 | 754 | .38 | " .08 |
|  | 3 | 775 | .55 | " .07 |
|  | 4 | 567 | .57 | " .06 |
|  | 5 | 654 | .43 | " .07 |
|  | 6 | 458 | .31 | " .07 |
|  | 7 | 521 | .18 | " .08 |
|  | 8 | 729 | .54 | " .07 |
|  | 9 | 733 | .24 | " .08 |
|  | 10 | 575 | .49 | " .06 |
| A Z | 1 | 792 | .39 | " .08 |
|  | 2 | 779 | .45 | " .08 |
|  | 3 | 642 | .23 | " .08 |
|  | 4 | 467 | .20 | " .08 |
|  | 5 | 421 | .33 | " .07 |
|  | 6 | 679 | .30 | " .08 |
|  | 7 | 671 | .29 | " .08 |
|  | 8 | 642 | .42 | " .07 |
|  | 9 | 700 | .43 | " .07 |
|  | 10 | 600 | .47 | " .07 |
| V A$_2$ | 61 | 671 | .59 | " .06 |
|  | 62 | 496 | .46 | " .07 |
|  | 63 | 775 | .51 | " .07 |
|  | 64 | 983 | .90 | " .09 |
|  | 65 | 308 | .48 | " .07 |
|  | 66 | 396 | .42 | " .07 |
|  | 67 | 650 | .41 | " .07 |
|  | 68 | 292 | .45 | " .07 |
|  | 69 | 650 | .31 | " .08 |
|  | 70 | 192 | .28 | " .09 |

TABLE 14

THE CORRELATIONS (BI-SERIAL r) OF EACH OF 99 READING AND VOCABULARY
TASKS WITH INTELLECT (I.E.R. SEL. REL., GEN. ORG.), GROUPED
ACCORDING TO THE PERCENT SUCCEEDING WITH
THE TASK.

| 5 to 20 | | 20 to 40 | | 40 to 60 | | 60 to 80 | | 80 to 95 | |
|---|---|---|---|---|---|---|---|---|---|
| $r_{ti}$ | $\sigma_{r_{ti}}$ | $r_{ti}$ | $\sigma_{r_{ti}}$ | $r_{ti}$ | $\sigma_{r_{ti}}$ | $r_{ti}$ | $\sigma_{r_{ti}}$ | $r_{ti}$ | $\sigma_{r_{ti}}$ |
| .37 ± .055 | | .13 ± .05 | | .28 ± .045 | | .36 ± .045 | | .43 ± .07 | |
| .61 " .05 | | .31 " .045 | | .33 " .04 | | .43 " .04 | | .30 " .075 | |
| | | .15 " .06 | | .35 " .04 | | .40 " .04 | | .29 " .065 | |
| | | —.13 " .06 | | .45 " .04 | | .48 " .04 | | .55 " .04 | |
| | | | | —.13 " .05 | | .45 " .04 | | .45 " .045 | |
| | | | | .39 " .04 | | .41 " .04 | | .53 " .04 | |
| | | | | .17 " .045 | | .48 " .04 | | .54 " .04 | |
| | | | | .35 " .045 | | .45 " .04 | | .52 " .04 | |
| | | | | .22 " .045 | | .46 " .04 | | .28 " .045 | |
| | | | | —.25 " .045 | | .40 " .045 | | .31 " .05 | |
| | | | | —.45 " .04 | | .49 " .04 | | .39 " .055 | |
| | | | | .48 " .05 | | .36 " .045 | | .24 " .045 | |
| | | | | .35 " .05 | | .38 " .04 | | .30 " .075 | |
| | | | | .05 " .055 | | .32 " .045 | | .23 " .045 | |
| | | | | —.36 " .05 | | .52 " .04 | | .41 " .045 | |
| | | | | .00 " .055 | | .46 " .04 | | .31 " .065 | |
| | | | | .18 " .055 | | .49 " .04 | | —.01 " .085 | |
| | | | | .40 " .05 | | .53 " .035 | | .27 " .075 | |
| | | | | .52 " .045 | | .39 " .045 | | .34 " .055 | |
| | | | | .45 " .045 | | .35 " .045 | | .14 " .06 | |
| | | | | | | .32 " .045 | | .24 " .08 | |
| | | | | | | .18 " .055 | | .53 " .065 | |
| | | | | | | .33 " .055 | | .31 " .075 | |
| | | | | | | .24 " .055 | | .29 " .075 | |
| | | | | | | .52 " .05 | | .34 " .07 | |
| | | | | | | .27 " .055 | | .29 " .07 | |
| | | | | | | .29 " .055 | | .39 " .06 | |
| | | | | | | .11 " .06 | | .45 " .06 | |
| | | | | | | .45 " .05 | | —.02 " .07 | |
| | | | | | | .36 " .05 | | .48 " .05 | |
| | | | | | | .40 " .055 | | .36 " .07 | |
| | | | | | | .56 " .045 | | .50 " .05 | |
| | | | | | | .38 " .05 | | .54 " .06 | |
| | | | | | | .41 " .05 | | .04 " .07 | |
| | | | | | | .37 " .055 | | .34 " .07 | |
| | | | | | | | | .67 " .07 | |
| | | | | | | | | .47 " .06 | |
| | | | | | | | | .63 " .06 | |

It is thus clear that only a small part (about one fifth) of the variation in the $r_{ti}$'s is due to the limitation to 668 or 454 or 240 cases.

Suppose now that we take the mere difficulty of a task as a measure of its "intellectual difficulty." How large an error do we make by such neglect of any correction for the magnitude of $r_{ti}$? Such a procedure is equivalent to treating as equal $\sigma_{t1}$, $\sigma_{t2}$, $\sigma_{t3}$, $\sigma_{t4}$, $\cdots$ $\sigma_{tn}$, which after the correction would be respectively

$$\frac{\sigma_i}{r_{t1i}}, \quad \frac{\sigma_i}{r_{t2i}}, \quad \frac{\sigma_i}{r_{t3i}}, \quad \text{and so on.}$$

Since $r_{ti}$ has a median of about .38 and a mean square variation of about .12 for Grade 11 when n is $\infty$, the sigmas which we treat as equal and which will in reality not all equal $\frac{\sigma_i}{.38}$, vary from about $\frac{\sigma_i}{.04}$ to about $\frac{\sigma_i}{.74}$; in about a sixth of the tasks $\sigma_t$ will be below $\frac{\sigma_i}{.26}$, and in about a sixth of them it will be above $\frac{\sigma_i}{.50}$. The sigmas will vary around $2.63\sigma_i$ with a mean square variation of .83$\sigma_i$. If the variability of an eleventh-grade population is one-fourth of the variability of all 17-year-olds, this equals .21$\sigma_{i \text{ of all 17-year-olds}}$ or nearly one-thirtieth of the entire range of adult human intellect.[6]

[6] It may be well to call attention to the effect of the variability of the group upon such correlations as we have presented. As is well known, a correlation of .99 between two measures of intellect for a group composed of a random selection of 20-year-olds will shrink greatly if, by selection for some characteristic closely related to intellect, we have a group varying only one-fifth as much as the random group.

This means of course that the error of a single small task, by its failure to utilize all of intellect and its adulteration by factors other than intellect, may be a small fraction of the total range of, say, adult human intellect, but a large fraction of the range of collegiate intellect.

The rise in the correlations between score in a single task and intellect with wider range of the group used does not impair the validity of anything hitherto stated in this chapter as an inference from the correlations found for any group. The correction for the error, assuming it to act as a chance

Obviously, we do not obtain a very close resemblance in "intellectual difficulty" within a composite of single tasks of equal difficulty. This, however, impairs the value of such a composite only slightly, since the variations of individuals' intellects in respect to how difficult any given single task is to each of them are so great. We use measures of intellectual difficulty to measure the level or height of individual intellects. If we did have a score of single tasks that were of absolutely equal intellectual difficulty for, say, eleventh-grade intellects all taken together, they would vary greatly in intellectual difficulty for those intellects taken one at a time, and they would also vary greatly in intellectual difficulty in the case of a thousand of these eleventh-grade intellects chosen to be all of identical intellectual level. If, for example, each of such a thousand intellects gave ten correct responses out of twenty, they would not all answer any one task correctly, nor all fail completely on any one. The single task does not measure all of intellect and nothing but intellect, and so may utilize a large fraction of A's intellect and a small fraction of B's; it may be solved by C largely by factors other than intellect, while in D there exist non-intellectual factors which prevent him from solving it.

Consequently, a score of single tasks, all with, say, 50% of successes, which after correction would be represented by twenty values ranging down even to Median $_{\text{grade 11}}$ — $2\sigma_{\text{i grade 11}}$, and even up to Median $_{\text{grade 11}}$ + $2\sigma_{\text{i grade 11}}$, will nevertheless be a very serviceable composite.

The two paragraphs preceding the last one are, however, really fallacious. Since a single word to be defined or sentence to be understood does not have any genuine intellectual difficulty in the sense of difficulty for all of intellect and nothing but intellect, we cannot properly attribute

---

sampling error, is in terms of the variability of the group for which the correlation is found. In absolute units the correction will be the same, the increase in the variability of the group exactly counterbalancing the effect of the increase in the correlation.

any amount of intellectual difficulty to it. We should not impute purely intellectual difficulty to any save purely intellectual tasks. A task cannot be purely intellectual when it correlates only .40 with intellect in a grade population or only .80 in an age population. We are back at the familiar point. We cannot measure the intellectual difficulty of a single brief task.

Moreover, in putting tasks together in a composite, we should pay attention to their equality in purely intellectual difficulty, if it could be measured, only after much more important desiderata had been provided.

In making up composites of tasks our chief aims are to make *composites* which will correlate highly with intellect and which will be of specified difficulty. This means that after the first element of the composite has been chosen, the merit of the next depends largely upon its *partial* correlation with intellect; and after two have been chosen, the merit of the next depends largely upon $r_{13.12}$, its partial correlation with intellect (after elimination of the influence of the first and second elements). And so on with the others. Getting high partials means getting different aspects of intellect represented and getting different non-intellectual factors counteracted. A moderate amount of wisdom in predicting what a given task will do in these respects will save much labor in computing $r_{t1}$'s.

So far as concerns the first aim, *equality* in the correlations ($r_{t1}$'s) is valueless. Among equally difficult tasks we would prefer those with the *highest* correlations and partial correlations.

So far as concerns obtaining a composite of precisely a certain specified difficulty, there is no practicable way of guaranteeing this beforehand. In practice, however, the matter is easy to arrange. We make up each composite from tasks of equal difficulty, and then measure the difficulty of the composites. If we have enough single tasks and over a wide enough range, we shall have a great number of composites differing progressively by small amounts of difficulty, and can usually find among them one close enough to the specified difficulty to serve. If such a one is not found, it can be created by combining two neighboring composites, taking half of the tasks from each, or four tenths from one and six tenths from the other, or whatever proportions are likely to give a composite of the desired degree of difficulty.

In the actual selection of elements for a composite, then, the main desiderata are to have the percents of successes equal and the $r_{ti}$'s either high or with high partials. The equality of the $r_{ti}$'s is an altogether minor matter.[7]

The facts about variation in the $r_{ti}$'s retain their importance because we do need to get high correlations with i, both for their intrinsic value and because one of the best practical ways to get high partial correlations with i is to find tasks which measure intellect with different data or different operations and still show high total correlations. It is a sound rule not to use any single task in a composite unless its $r_{ti}$ or the average $r_{ti}$ for it or for tasks like it is above .30 for a school-grade population of the level for which it is intended.[8]

Any information about the $r_{ti}$'s of representative tasks is therefore of general value; and we quote here the results obtained by Vincent ('24). Using data furnished by us, she measured the correlation between the score attained with a single sentence to be completed and the total score attained in an intelligence examination of two and a half hours, whose reliability coefficient is about .85 for such

[7] So far as concerns boredom from too easy or irritation and discouragement from too hard single tasks within the same composite, they are due chiefly to variations in *difficulty*, not in *intellectual difficulty*. They are prevented chiefly by including tasks which are equally difficult. The tasks should also be fairly free from environmental influences; and high "total" correlations with i are one symptom of this.

[8] More precisely, for any two minutes of work we should obtain $r_{ti}$ above .40 for Grades 3 to 5, .35 for Grades 6 to 8, .30 for Grades 9 to 11, and .20 for Grades 12 to 14. It is harder to get high correlations in the higher grades, where the range of intellect may be narrower and where the specialization of the environment is greater.

groups as she used. The first group consisted of candidates for entrance to college; the second consisted of sixth-grade pupils. The examination for the former was the Thorndike Intelligence Examination for High School Graduates; that

TABLE 15

OVERLAPPINGS AND BI-SERIAL R'S FOR 35 ELEMENTS

| Overlappings | Bi-serial r's with P.E.'s |
|---|---|
| 0.0 | .826 ± .046 |
| 5.2 | .752 " .049 |
| 6.4 | .726 " .046 |
| 8.9 | .588 " .057 |
| 9.1 | .639 " .054 |
| 10.0 | .406 " .082 |
| 11.7 | .431 " .083 |
| 12.3 | .558 " .061 |
| 12.4 | .559 " .068 |
| 12.5 | .463 " .068 |
| 12.6 | .559 " .060 |
| 15.2 | .551 " .048 |
| 15.8 | .597 " .061 |
| 16.5 | .542 " .041 |
| 18.7 | .665 " .031 |
| 20.7 | .520 " .037 |
| 21.2 | .475 " .043 |
| 21.5 | .480 " .051 |
| 21.6 | .444 " .044 |
| 22.9 | .427 " .045 |
| 23.3 | .398 " .045 |
| 27.9 | .416 " .053 |
| 28.1 | .352 " .045 |
| 28.6 | .163 " .047 |
| 30.4 | .160 " .083 |
| 31.7 | .377 " .055 |
| 31.8 | .372 " .081 |
| 31.9 | .343 " .073 |
| 35.1 | .359 " .076 |
| 35.6 | .276 " .068 |
| 36.2 | .168 " .064 |
| 36.7 | .145 " .066 |
| 36.9 | .261 " .073 |
| 37.7 | .323 " .062 |
| 40.9 | .307 " .083 |

for the latter was made up of Sentence Completions, Arithmetical Problems, Vocabulary, Sentence Comprehension, and a battery of stock intelligence tests. The correlation (using the bi-serial r) varies from .70 or higher to near 0.

TABLE 16

THE CORRESPONDENCE BETWEEN SUCCESS IN A SINGLE SMALL TASK AND INTELLECT, AS MEASURED BY THE OVERLAPPING OF THE SCORE IN INTELLECT OF THOSE FAILING WITH THE TASK PAST THE MEDIAN SCORE IN INTELLECT OF THOSE SUCCEEDING WITH THE TASK. COMPILED FROM THE ORIGINAL DATA OF VINCENT.

| % of Over-lapping | Candidates for College Entrance | | | | Sixth-Grade Pupils | | |
|---|---|---|---|---|---|---|---|
| | Frequencies | | | | | | |
| | C. | A. | D. | All | C. | A. | All |
| 0–4 | 2 | 3 | 2 | 7 | 1 | 2 | 3 |
| 5–9 | 4 | 4 | 3 | 11 | 5 | 8 | 13 |
| 10–14 | 5 | 11 | 14 | 30 | 6 | 12 | 18 |
| 15–19 | 15 | 25 | 19 | 59 | 5 | 7 | 12 |
| 20–24 | 40 | 22 | 19 | 81 | 5 | 5 | 10 |
| 25–29 | 21 | 21 | 18 | 60 | 2 | 4 | 6 |
| 30–34 | 19 | 17 | 17 | 53 | | 4 | 4 |
| 35–39 | 11 | 11 | 9 | 31 | 2 | | 2 |
| 40–44 | 2 | 5 | 10 | 17 | 1 | 1 | 2 |
| 45–49 | 1 | 1 | 3 | 5 | | | |
| 50–54 | | 3 | 2 | 5 | | | |
| 55–59 | 1 | 1 | | 2 | | | |
| 60–64 | 1 | 1 | | 2 | | | |
| 65–69 | | 1 | | 1 | | | |
| 70–74 | | | 1 | 1 | | | |
| n | 122 | 126 | 117 | 365 | 27 | 43 | 70 |
| Median | 24 | 24 | 25 | 24 | 16½ | 14 | 15 |
| Q | | | | 7 | | | 6¼ |

An overlapping of 25% corresponds to a correlation coefficient of from about .30 to about .42 according as the percent succeeding is remote from or near to 50.

An overlapping of 15% corresponds to a correlation coefficient of about .45 to about .60 according as the percent succeeding is remote from or near to 50.

The facts for 35 tasks are shown in Table 15. We may use, as a measure of the correspondence between score for one element and score in intellect measured perfectly or nearly perfectly, the smallness of the overlapping (in the total examination scores) of the failures past the median of the successes (success and failure referring to the single task in question). This ranges from 0 to nearly 50%, the latter figure corresponding to a correlation of zero.

From Vincent's original data we have compiled Table 16, which shows the percentages of overlapping for various tasks in completing sentences, understanding paragraphs, and solving arithmetic problems.

The overlappings of Table 16 would all be somewhat smaller if the measure of intellect were perfect. They would be less variable if the number of individuals used in the determinations were larger. This number ranged from 50 to 499 in the college group (two-thirds of the sentences being taken by fewer than 175 individuals) and was either about 175, or about 240, or about 375 in the sixth-grade group. They would become both smaller and less variable in proportion as any mistakes in scoring were eliminated. Those for the college group would become less variable if the tasks had been done with no limitations of time. The sixth-grade groups were allowed to use as much time as they wished; the college group were instructed to work as fast as they could without making mistakes, and were subject to a time limit which was rather generous in the case of the completion and the reading tasks, but rather limited in the case of the arithmetical tasks. The smaller overlappings (that is, higher correlations) for the sixth grade group are due probably partly to this fact and partly perhaps to a greater variability of the sixth-grade group in intellect.

The eleven cases of negative correlation in the college group are in some cases due to badly chosen tasks; in others they are due probably to some constant error in the scorers; in others they are due to the chance error attached to a determination from a limited number of cases.

## SUMMARY

The sum and substance of this chapter is an emphatic conclusion that for every theoretical and practical purpose in the measurement of intellectual difficulty, we should use collections of tasks rather than single small tasks. We ought to measure the *difficulty* of single tasks; but we can profitably measure *intellectual difficulty* only in the case of composites which contain enough kinds of tasks to represent a fair sampling of all of intellect as it operates at that level, and enough tasks to make the error closely the same for any one composite as for any other with which we wish to compare it in respect of difficulty.

When such composite tasks are attained we can infer the difficulty values in terms of $\sigma_i$ from the values in terms of $\sigma_{t1}$, $\sigma_{t2}$, $\sigma_{t3}$, etc., or, since $\sigma_{t1}$, $\sigma_{t2}$, $\sigma_{t3}$, etc., are closely equal, we can use $\sigma_t$ as the unit.

# CHAPTER V

THE MEASUREMENT OF THE INTELLECTUAL DIFFICULTY OF TASKS BY A CONSENSUS OF EXPERT OPINION

No one doubts that a certain validity attaches to human judgments of the difficulty of intellectual tasks,—that, for example, it is harder to find an opposite of "government" beginning with "a" than an opposite of "below" beginning with "a," or to answer correctly, "How many quarters of a quarter equal half of a half?" than to answer correctly, "How many cents are three cents and one cent?"

If a thousand psychologists or others who are acquainted with intellectual tasks are required to state which of two tasks is harder, the amount of agreement is a measure, or at least a symptom, of the magnitude of the real difference. If 910 of the thousand rank A as harder than K, whereas only 510 of the thousand rank B as harder than K, the difference A–K will be supposed by all sensible persons to be greater than the difference B–K, except for tasks in respect of which the thousand suffer from some illusion or constant error.

Given the truth of certain assumptions about the judges and the process of judging, the magnitude of the real difference may be determined from the percent of judges discerning it. These assumptions have been used as a provisional way to determine the magnitudes of differences in the general merit of handwriting and drawings by Thorndike ['10 and '13] and Kline and Carey ['23]; the general merit of compositions by Hillegas ['12]; and the beauty of designs by Thorndike ['16]. They have been used widely by Hollingworth, Strong and others in measuring various features of advertisements.

This method of deriving units of measure is more appropriate in the case of certain esthetic and ethical values, where to be more beautiful (amusing, sublime, refined, reverent, patriotic) is to be thought so, than in the case of intellectual difficulty, but it has obvious advantages in economy and ease of application, and, at the worst, it utilizes human judgments without exaggerating their intrinsic errors and without introducing any new errors.

What the intrinsic errors of human judgments of the difficulty of intellectual tasks are has not been known because hitherto there has been no extended or systematic study of such judgments, and no criterion against which to check their validity and precision.

## THE EXPERIMENTS

We have carried out two experiments with these impressionistic judgments of the difficulty of tasks. The first, which was reported in the *Journal of Educational Research,* February, 1924, [Thorndike, Bregman and Cobb, '24] used a hundred tasks as the material to be judged, and forty students of psychology and education as the judges. The raw correlation of the ranking for difficulty by the consensus with the ranking by the percentages of a group succeeding with the respective task elements was .88.

The second experiment used some twelve hundred tasks and twenty sets of judgments, these being made by Dr. E. M. Bailor, Dr. E. O. Bregman (2), M. V. Cobb (2), Dr. A. I. Gates, Z. F. Miner, Dr. R. Pintner, E. E. Robinson (2), G. J. Ruger, Dr. L. S. Hollingworth, Dr. Godfrey Thomson, Dr. L. M. Vincent (2), J. W. Tilton, Dr. B. D. Wood, Ella Woodyard (2), and E. L. Thorndike (2).

The number 2 in parenthesis means that the person in question made two sets of judgments. The instructions for the ratings and a few sample tasks including some near both extremes are quoted below.

### INSTRUCTIONS FOR GRADING

Each slip is a task in Arithmetic, Sentence Completion, Vocabulary, Directions, Reading, Information, or giving Opposites. The nature of each task will be apparent, if you remember that:

11

1. A single word preceded by a letter means that the task is to give an opposite to the word beginning with that letter, *e.g.*, "b......white" requires "black" as the response.

2. A word followed by 5 other words means that the task is to select that one of the five which means most nearly the same as the first word, *e.g.*, "powerful......holy......strong......during......sad......old" requires "strong" as the response.

3. A word followed by 4 or 5 pictures means that the task is to select that one of the pictures which best fits the word.

4. If the task is preceded by the word "oral," the task is not to be shown to the person in print, but put to him clearly orally, and repeated once, and a second time if he desires.

5. If the task is not preceded by the word "oral," the person doing the task is supposed to have the opportunity to read and re-read it. If he has difficulty in reading, he is supposed to have the task stated to him orally in whole or in part *as often as he wishes*.

The tasks are to be rated in 200 or more groups, in respect of their intellectual difficulty, for a group of persons twenty years old brought up in the United States, with an opportunity to go to school for at least 7 years, unless they were so dull as to be unable to learn at school. At one end will be the tasks which you think only the best intellects would do correctly; at the other end will be those which all save the lowest imbeciles would do correctly.

You should assume that the general nature of the task of giving an opposite, or of completing a sentence, or of selecting the word most nearly of the same meaning, has been stated in very simple language and illustrated by five easy samples, and that the tasks of any one sort are given at one time and in an order beginning with the easiest.

In all ratings pay no attention to the possibility of *chance* successes. Think of the difficulty of the task in every case as the difficulty of succeeding with it by real knowledge or ability.

In about one case out of 200 there was an omitted or ambiguous rating. To simplify later computations, an estimate was made of the probable intent of the judge in such cases, by consideration of his ratings of four tasks of approximately the same sort.

The basis for the judgments doubtless varies from one judge to another and from one task to another for the same judge, and for the same task for the same judge at different times. It would be interesting and perhaps valuable to discover what qualities in a task and what facts or fancies about it make any given judge regard it as hard. We shall, however, limit our inquiry to the ratings themselves regardless of how they were caused.

## TABLE 17.

THE CORRESPONDENCE BETWEEN THE SUM OF THE RATINGS OF TEN JUDGES AND THE SUM OF THE RATINGS OF THE OTHER TEN.

| Sum of 2nd ten | Sum of 1st ten | | | | | | | | | | | | | | | | | | | | | | | |
|---|---|---|---|---|---|---|---|---|---|---|---|---|---|---|---|---|---|---|---|---|---|---|---|---|
| | 10 | 80 | 160 | 240 | 320 | 400 | 480 | 560 | 640 | 720 | 800 | 880 | 960 | 1040 | 1120 | 1200 | 1280 | 1360 | 1440 | 1520 | 1600 | 1680 | 1760 | 1840 |
| 10 to 79 | 12 | 3 | | | | | | | | | | | | | | | | | | | | | | |
| 80 " 159 | 4 | 20 | 22 | 4 | | | | | | | | | | | | | | | | | | | | |
| 160 " 239 | | 1 | 15 | 10 | 1 | | | | | | | | | | | | | | | | | | | |
| 240 " 319 | | | 4 | 16 | 12 | 7 | | | | | | | | | | | | | | | | | | |
| 320 " 399 | | | | 5 | 21 | 19 | 5 | | | | | | | | | | | | | | | | | |
| 400 " 479 | | | | 1 | 15 | 20 | 4 | 2 | | | | | | | | | | | | | | | | |
| 480 " 559 | | | | 1 | 6 | 20 | 16 | 3 | 5 | | | | | | | | | | | | | | | |
| 560 " 639 | | | | | 1 | 8 | 13 | 13 | 13 | 2 | | 2 | | | | | | | | | | | | |
| 640 " 719 | | | | | | 3 | 14 | 5 | 16 | 15 | 5 | 5 | | | | | | | | | | | | |
| 720 " 799 | | | | | | | 4 | 10 | 9 | 29 | 18 | 6 | 1 | | | | | | | | | | | |
| 800 " 879 | | | | | | | | 3 | 6 | 7 | 30 | 17 | 7 | 2 | | | | | | | | | | |
| 880 " 959 | | | | | | | | 1 | 3 | 8 | 10 | 22 | 14 | 5 | 5 | | | | | | | | | |
| 960 " 1039 | | | | | | | | | | 5 | 4 | 6 | 12 | 13 | 11 | 1 | | | | | | | | |
| 1040 " 1119 | | | | | | | | | | | | 1 | 8 | 16 | 14 | 4 | | | | | | | | |
| 1120 " 1199 | | | | | | | | | | | | 1 | 4 | 16 | 15 | 16 | 7 | | | | | | | |
| 1200 " 1279 | | | | | | | | | | | | 2 | 3 | 6 | 14 | 21 | 7 | 3 | 2 | 2 | | | | |
| 1280 " 1359 | | | | | | | | | | | | | 3 | 3 | 6 | 8 | 13 | 18 | 11 | 4 | 1 | | | |
| 1360 " 1439 | | | | | | | | | | | | | | 4 | 2 | 7 | 9 | 17 | 15 | 11 | 4 | | | |
| 1440 " 1519 | | | | | | | | | | | | | | | 1 | 1 | 10 | 16 | 24 | 11 | 9 | 2 | | |
| 1520 " 1599 | | | | | | | | | | | | | | | | 2 | 4 | 10 | 6 | 18 | 16 | 6 | 1 | |
| 1600 " 1679 | | | | | | | | | | | | | | | | 1 | 2 | 3 | 6 | 11 | 19 | 5 | 2 | |
| 1680 " 1759 | | | | | | | | | | | | | | | | | | 2 | | 5 | 5 | 13 | 7 | |
| 1760 " 1839 | | | | | | | | | | | | | | | | | | | | | 1 | 3 | 10 | 1 |

## THE RATINGS

The ratings were combined by simple addition, the result being a series of arbitrary numbers from 32 to over 3,600 which represent accurately enough for all our purposes an order of difficulty by the consensus. Its statistical reliability is fairly high. The sum of the ratings by ten of the judges (Br., Mi., Ro. (2), Thom., Thor. (2), Vi. and Wo.(2)) corresponds closely with the sum of the ratings by the other ten. The facts appear in Table 17.

The reliability is about the same for any one sort of task, such as sentence completion, or arithmetical problem or word knowledge, as for the entire series. That is, the judges agreed about as closely when they compared two tasks of different sorts as when they compared two tasks of the same sort.

The correlations between the two sums of ten are as follows:

| | |
|---|---|
| Completion tasks | .973 |
| Arithmetic tasks | .988 |
| Vocabulary tasks | .954 |
| Directions tasks | .996 |
| Information tasks | .979 |
| Opposite tasks | .978 |

The average of the six is .978. The correlation when all are mixed together is .984.

This material is unsuitable for the computation of coefficients of correlation, the distributions being of very irregular form. The correlations given above are used only as rough indicators of the closeness of agreement between the two groups of ten judges.

The mean square error and the median or "probable" error of the sum of the twenty ratings for any task are as shown in Table 18.[1] The error varies, increasing in general

---

[1] These measures of unreliability are computed from the mean square deviations of the differences between the sum of the ratings of the first ten and the sum of the ratings of the second ten judges. The mean square error for a sum of ten equals $\dfrac{1}{\sqrt{2}} \sigma_{diff.}$. The mean square error for the average

with the difficulty of the tasks, but also decreasing at the two extremes of the set of tasks used. On the average, it is about one thirtieth of the difference between task I and task II, shown at the bottom of Table 18, for the mean square error, and about one forty-fifth thereof for the probable error.

TABLE 18

The Probable Divergence of a Difficulty Rating by 20 Experts from the Average of an Infinite Number of Difficulty Ratings of the Task, (Each Rating Being the Average of the Ratings of 20 Experts).

| | The unit being the same as that of the difficulty ratings by the 20 experts | | The unit being one hundredth of the difference[2] between Level A and Level O | | The unit being one hundredth of the difference between difficulty rating for Task I and Task II | |
|---|---|---|---|---|---|---|
| Tasks rated under | S.D. | P.E. | S.D. | P.E. | S.D. | P.E. |
| 400 (approx.) | 44 | 29 | 1.5 | 1.0 | 1.3 | .8 |
| 400 to 799 | 81 | 55 | 2.8 | 1.9 | 2.3 | 1.6 |
| 800 " 1199 | 97 | 66 | 3.3 | 2.2 | 2.8 | 1.9 |
| 1200 " 1599 | 99 | 67 | 3.4 | 2.3 | 2.9 | 1.9 |
| 1600 " 1999 | 110 | 74 | 3.7 | 2.5 | 3.2 | 2.1 |
| 2000 " 2399 | 129 | 87 | 4.4 | 3.0 | 3.7 | 2.5 |
| 2400 " 2799 | 117 | 79 | 4.0 | 2.7 | 3.4 | 2.3 |
| 2800 " 3199 | 108 | 73 | 3.7 | 2.5 | 3.1 | 2.1 |
| 3200 " 3599 | 86 | 58 | 2.9 | 2.0 | 2.4 | 1.7 |

I

1. Hold up your hand.
2. Show me your nose. Put your finger on your nose.
3. Show me your mouth. Put your finger on your mouth.

---

of two sums of ten equals $\frac{1}{\sqrt{2}} \times \frac{1}{\sqrt{2}} \times \sigma_{diff.}$. Since, however, we are using

the sum of twenty in place of the average of two sums of ten, our numbers are all twice as large as they would be for the average of two sums of ten. That is, the mean square error for a sum of twenty equals:

$$2 \times \frac{1}{\sqrt{2}} \times \frac{1}{\sqrt{2}} \times \sigma_{diff.} \text{ or simply } \sigma_{diff.}.$$

[2] Level A is the ability of adults of mental age a little under 36 months, and so with I.Q.'s of about 20.

Level O is approximately the ability of the average graduate of American colleges of high requirements.

II

1. Read this and then write the answers. Read it again if you need to.

COLERIDGE

I see thee pine like her in golden story
Who, in her prison, woke and saw, one day,
The gates thrown open—saw the sunbeams play
With only a web 'tween her and summer's glory;
Who, when the web—so frail, so transitory,
It broke before her breath—had fallen away,
Saw other webs and others rise for aye,
Which kept her prisoned till her hair was hoary.
Those songs half-sung that yet were all divine—
That woke Romance, the queen, to reign afresh—
Had been but preludes from that lyre of thine,
Could thy rare spirit's wings have pierced the mesh
Spun by the wizard who compels the flesh,
But lets the poet see how heav'n can shine.

Copy the first word of the line which implies there had not been a continuous stream of like songs.

2. Supply the missing words to make this a true and sensible sentence.

Speech, gesture and ............................... ............................... form of human

action are in ............................... ............................... run resolvable ...............................

............................... contraction.

3. Arrange these numbers and signs to form a true equation.
2/3   2   3   15   15   =   -   -   ×

So much of these unreliabilities as is due to the small number of judges can be reduced to any desired extent by increasing the number of judges. The crude summations of ranks can also be replaced by more precise and refined uses of the differences between the rankings for any two tasks. The general value of the method can, however, be studied well enough for our purposes with the sums of the twenty ranks as they stand.

The meaning of these sums of the twenty ranks in terms of the percentage of the judges who judge the direction of the difference correctly may be realized from the following facts:

Taking 618 pairs of tasks at random from those pairs which differ in the "sum of the twenty" by approximately 100 (95 to 105), we find that, in 263, eleven and a half or fewer of the twenty judges[3] judged correctly; in 114, twelve judged correctly; and in 241, twelve and a half or more judged correctly. A difference of 100 in the "sum of the twenty ranks" thus corresponds to a percentage of judges a little under 60.

Taking 853 pairs of tasks at random from those pairs which differ in the "sum of the twenty" by approximately 200 (195 to 205), we find that, in 404, thirteen or fewer of the judges judged correctly; in 49, thirteen and a half judged correctly; in 400, fourteen or more judged correctly. A difference of 200 in the sum of the twenty ranks thus corresponds almost exactly to a percentage of $67\frac{1}{2}$.

A percentage of $67\frac{1}{2}$ correct means a difference of .673 times the median deviation of the judges in ability to judge the intellectual difficulty of tasks, and 60% means a difference of .375 times it. So we may regard the median deviation (or difference observable by 75% of these judges) as a bit over 300 in the units of the "Sums of twenty."[4] The entire range is thus only about twelve times the amount of difference which 75% of these judges recognize, which means, of course, that our judgments of the intellectual difficulty of tasks are not acute.

### THE VALIDITY OF THE CONSENSUS

The important matter is, of course, the *validity* of the consensus,—its correspondence with intellectual difficulty when that is objectively determined. How far we have a right to use a consensus of expert opinion to measure the difficulty of a task depends upon the freedom of the consensus from systematic or "constant" errors, such as a

---

[3] When any judge assigned the same rank to the two tasks which the twenty put as 100 apart, he was scored as half right and half wrong.

[4] It will be a little less than that at the two extremes, and more than that in the middle, the agreement of the judges being closer for a difference of 100 or 200 at the extremes than for the same numerical difference in the middle ranges.

tendency to over-estimate the intellectual difficulty of completions in comparison with arithmetical problems, or to underestimate differences in intellectual difficulty at the hard end of the series, or to fail to see differences over a certain range of the scale.

We can determine intellectual difficulty objectively for certain composite tasks. Thus, for very dull adults the respective intellectual difficulties of the composites A, B, C, and D are determined by the facts that 159, 87, 23, and 1 out of 180 such dull adults succeed with these composites. That the composites measure Intellect CAVD is elsewhere proved. From the form of distribution of the group of 180, the differences between A, B, C, and D in intellectual difficulty may be found.

If now we examine the average consensus estimate of difficulty of the forty elements of composite A, and similarly for B, C, and D, we may easily compute the average differences between A, B, C, and D in intellectual difficulty as estimated by the consensus. The closeness of correspondence of the objectively and subjectively determined sets of differences in intellectual difficulty may be measured in various ways. A similar procedure can be carried out for composites used with a group of college graduates, or for any other set of composites, whose intellectual difficulty is objectively measured in suitable units. In proportion as the consensus agrees closely with the objective results in the case of composites where we have such objective results, we can trust the consensus[5] in the case of tasks where we lack objective results. It is therefore of great importance to inquire how close this correspondence is, how free the consensus is from errors other than the variable errors due to the small number of experts.

It will be useful to state in a summary manner the outcome of the inquiry before presenting its details.

Such a consensus, even from a thousand experts, will not be trustworthy throughout. It will make blunders, suffer

[5] Subject to due consideration of its variable errors, and within the range of difficulty and sort of task where it has been proved valid.

from "constant errors," some of them regrettably large. We shall see, for example, that it overestimates the difficulty of easy sentence-completions in comparison to that of directions or vocabulary or arithmetic tests, and that it fails to observe genuine differences in difficulty within a rather wide range of vocabulary tests. If composite tasks were made up on the basis of its estimates of the intellectual difficulty of tasks, the difficulty of these composites as composites would need to be carefully measured objectively.

The consensus would, on the other hand, often be near the truth and rarely be greatly in error. There will be a substantial correlation with objectively determined results. If such a consensus alone had been used to estimate the difficulty of single tasks, and CAVD composites of forty had been constructed on the basis of its estimates, they would have been serviceable composites, forming a gradation in intellectual difficulty, and containing in any one composite few single tasks which would appear puerile on the one hand or mystifying on the other to the individuals who could succeed with half of the tasks in that composite. After being evaluated as composites by objective methods, these composites would be not much inferior to those which we have constructed at enormous cost of time and labor spent in experimentation. Consequently, the use of estimates by a suitable consensus may well replace measurements of the percents succeeding in the case of single tasks, in the preliminary work of making composite tasks.

The evidence that the consensus is in certain respects definitely wrong is as follows:

We have four composites each made up of ten sentence-completions; four, each made up of ten arithmetical tasks; four, each made up of ten vocabulary tasks; four, each made up of ten directions, and four, each made up of ten information tasks. Each of 180 very dull adults was tested with each of these twenty 10-composite tasks, which we shall designate hereafter as

C   A,  B,  C, and  D
A   "   "   "   "   "
V   "   "   "   "   "
D   "   "   "   "   "
I   "   "   "   "   "

The results were as shown in Table 19, the 180 individuals being divided into two groups, of 100 at one institution, and 80 at another.

TABLE 19.

MEASURES OF THE DIFFICULTY OF 10-COMPOSITE TASKS.

| | | By Experiment | | | By the Consensus | |
| | | Percent Succeeding | | Distances from the Median. In terms of $\sigma_{10}$ | Median Sum of 20 Expert Ratings | No. of Tasks Rated |
|---|---|---|---|---|---|---|
| | | n = 100 | 80 | n = 100    80 | | |
| C | A | 84 | 82½ | − 1.19   − 1.13 | 800 | 8 |
| | B | 65 | 56 | − .51   − .20 | 830 | 2 |
| | C | 35 | 27½ | + .45   + .68 | 970 | 4 |
| | D | 3 | 0 | + 1.59   high | 1023 | 4 |
| A | A | 69 | 80 | − .65   − 1.03 | 309 | 3 |
| | B | 45 | 49 | + .15   + .03 | 536 | 2 |
| | C | 15 | 21 | + 1.05   + .87 | 458 | 2 |
| | D | 5 | 5 | + 1.47   + 1.47 | 858 | 3 |
| V | A | 80 | 81 | − 1.03   − 1.07 | 292 | 9 |
| | B | 49 | 57½ | + .03   − .25 | 562 | 9 |
| | C | 14 | 19 | + 1.09   + .93 | 925 | 7 |
| | D | 1 | 5 | + 1.78   + 1.47 | 848 | 6 |
| D | A | 90 | 86 | − 1.45   − 1.27 | not over 300 | |
| | B | 45 | 67½ | + .15   − .59 | ......... | |
| | C | 19 | 27½ | + .93   + .68 | 529 | 5 |
| | D | 12 | 14 | + 1.16   + 1.09 | 668 | 10 |
| I | A | 76 | 83½ | − .89   − 1.17 | 341 | 7 |
| | B | 51 | 59½ | − .03   − .32 | 618 | 4 |
| | C | 23 | 21½ | + .81   + .86 | 733 | 7 |
| | D | 3 | 4 | + 1.59   + 1.53 | 792 | 6 |

In the same table are shown the median summation scores for the single tasks in each of these composites so far as they were included in the 1200 rated, and the number so included.[6]

There is an obvious "constant error" in the direction of overestimating the difficulty of the sentence-completions, especially the easier ones. To be in line with the other tasks, the figures for them should be, respectively, about 500, 300, 350, and 200 lower than they are. There is a failure to distinguish the Arithmetic B's from the Arithmetic C's. There is a similar failure with the Vocabulary C's and D's.

TABLE 20.

DIFFERENCES IN DIFFICULTY OF VARIOUS COMPOSITE TASKS AND OF THE
MEDIAN SUMS OF 20 EXPERT RATINGS OF THE SINGLE TASKS OF THESE
COMPOSITES WHICH WERE RATED. EACH DIFFERENCE IS EX-
PRESSED AS A PERCENT OF THE DIFFERENCE BETWEEN THE
A AND THE D COMPOSITE OF ITS KIND.

| | Differences in Difficulty | | | Disagreements | | |
|---|---|---|---|---|---|---|
| | By Experiment $n = 100$ | 80 | By the Consensus | 100 with 80 | 100 with Consensus | 80 with Consensus |
| C B–C A | 24 | 30* | 10 | 6 | 34 | 20 |
| C C–C B | 35 | 28* | 65 | 7 | 30 | 37 |
| C D–C C | 41 | 42* | 25 | 1 | 16 | 17 |
| A B–A A | 38 | 42 | 41 | 4 | 3 | 1 |
| A C–A B | 42 | 34 | –14 | 8 | 56 | 48 |
| A D–A C | 20 | 24 | 73 | 4 | 53 | 49 |
| V B–V A | 38 | 32 | 49 | 6 | 11 | 17 |
| V C–V B | 38 | 46 | 65 | 8 | 27 | 19 |
| V D–V C | 25 | 21 | –14 | 4 | 39 | 35 |
| I B–I A | 35 | 31 | 61½ | 4 | 26½ | 30½ |
| I C–I B | 34 | 44 | 25½ | 10 | 8½ | 18½ |
| I D–I C | 31 | 25 | 13 | 6 | 18 | 12 |
| Sum of disagreements | | | | 68 | 322 | 304 |

* The difficulty of C D is estimated as + 2.00.

[6] The probable errors of these medians will be approximately 50 when $n = 2$, 40 when $n = 3$, 35 when $n = 4$, 31 when $n = 5$, 28½ when $n = 6$, 26½ when $n = 7$, 25 when $n = 8$, 23 when $n = 9$, and 22 when $n = 10$.

If we list the differences between the A and the B, the B and the C, and the C and the D tasks and express each as a percent of the difference between the A and the D tasks, we can observe more readily how closely the consensus parallels the objective results, when the kind of task is kept constant. The disagreement between the consensus and

TABLE 21.

FORM OF DISTRIBUTION USED IN THE CALCULATIONS OF TABLES 19 AND 20.
RELATIVE FREQUENCIES AT EQUAL SUCCESSIVE INTERVALS.

| Interval | Frequency |
|---|---|
| 0 to .99 | 5.5 |
| 1 " 1.99 | 5.5 |
| 2 " 2.99 | 11 |
| 3 " 3.99 | 11 |
| 4 " 4.99 | 17 |
| 5 " 5.99 | 17 |
| 6 " 6.99 | 22 |
| 7 " 7.99 | 28 |
| 8 " 8.99 | 33 |
| 9 " 9.99 | 33 |
| 10 " 10.99 | 34 |
| 11 " 11.99 | 39 |
| 12 " 12.99 | 38 |
| 13 " 13.99 | 39 |
| 14 " 14.99 | 39 |
| 15 " 15.99 | 39 |
| 16 " 16.99 | 39 |
| 17 " 17.99 | 39 |
| 18 " 18.99 | 44 |
| 19 " 19.99 | 45 |
| 20 " 20.99 | 44 |
| 21 " 21.99 | 45 |
| 22 " 22.99 | 44 |
| 23 " 23.99 | 44 |
| 24 " 24.99 | 45 |
| 25 " 25.99 | 44.5 |
| 26 " 26.99 | 38.5 |
| 27 " 27.99 | 33.7 |
| 28 " 28.99 | 27.8 |
| 29 " 29.99 | 22.3 |
| 30 " 30.99 | 16.6 |
| 31 " 31.99 | 11.2 |
| 32 " 32.99 | 5.5 |

the result of either experiment is about four times as great as the disagreement between the results of the two experiments. The facts are shown in Table 20.

In the calculations of Table 19 and Table 20, the form of distribution of these low imbeciles is taken to be that shown in Table 21. We ask the reader to take the validity of this form of distribution on faith for the present, or to turn to Appendix VI and examine the facts given in connection with its derivation there. To show that the present conclusion does not depend for its validity upon the particular form of distribution used, we have carried through the computations supposing it to be Form A (the "normal" form) and supposing it to be a rectangle. The results appear in Table 22 and Table 23.

The resemblances may also be measured crudely by correlation coefficients, after first expressing the estimates of difficulty as a rank order. The correlations[7] using

$$\rho = 1 - \frac{6\Sigma D^2}{n(n^2 - 1)} \text{ are}$$

.97 for the experiment with 100 with the experiment with 80;

.62 for the experiment with 100 with the consensus;

.70 for the experiment with 80 with the consensus.

We have records from 240 college graduates and from 189 candidates for college entrance with the composites of ten tasks listed in Table 24. We have also computed the medians of the 20-expert sums of ratings of such tasks in each composite as were rated by the experts. These and the measures of difficulty from the experiments with the 240 and the 189 are entered in Table 24. In this case the form of distribution of intellect in the 189 is known to be ap-

---

[7] We may here use $\rho$ for r without transmuting, since the form of distribution of these twenty composites in respect of difficulty is probably better represented by a rectangle than by a surface of Form A. If transmuted, all would be a trifle higher. In the ranks for the consensus, D A is put as 1 and D B as 5 on the basis of the ratings by the consensus of certain tasks closely resembling the tasks of D A and D B.

proximately of Form A; and that of the 240 may be treated as such with no damage to the present argument.[8]

A general inspection of Table 24 reveals notable irregularities in the measures by the consensus, as when A O is rated 178 points easier than A N, and D5 is rated 242 points easier than D4½. The consensus seems to fail to discriminate well in general among the D (reading) tasks.

TABLE 22.

MEASURES OF DIFFICULTY IF THE FORM OF DISTRIBUTION ASSUMED IS FORM A OR A RECTANGLE. DISTANCE FROM C.T. IN TERMS OF $\sigma$ AND OF Q/25.

| | | Percent Succeeding | | In terms of $\sigma$ assuming Form A | | In terms of Q/25 assuming a rectangle | |
|---|---|---|---|---|---|---|---|
| | | 100 | 80 | 100 | 80 | 100 | 80 |
| C | A | 84 | 82½ | − .995 | − .935 | − 34 | − 32½ |
| | B | 65 | 56 | − .385 | − .158 | − 15 | − 6 |
| | C | 35 | 27½ | + .385 | + .598 | + 15 | + 22½ |
| | D | 3 | 0 | + 1.881 | high | + 47 | high |
| A | A | 69 | 80 | − .496 | − .842 | − 19 | − 30 |
| | B | 45 | 49 | + .126 | + .031 | − 5 | + 1 |
| | C | 15 | 21 | + 1.036 | + .798 | + 35 | + 29 |
| | D | 5 | 5 | + 1.645 | + 1.645 | + 45 | + 45 |
| V | A | 80 | 81 | − .842 | − .883 | − 30 | − 31 |
| | B | 49 | 57½ | + .050 | − .189 | + 1 | − 7½ |
| | C | 14 | 19 | + 1.080 | + .887 | + 36 | + 31 |
| | D | 1 | 5 | + 2.326 | + 1.645 | + 49 | + 45 |
| D | A | 90 | 86 | − 1.282 | − 1.092 | − 40 | − 36 |
| | B | 45 | 67½ | + .126 | − .454 | + 5 | − 17½ |
| | C | 19 | 27½ | + .878 | + .598 | + 31 | + 22½ |
| | D | 12 | 14 | + 1.175 | + 1.092 | + 38 | + 36 |
| I | A | 76 | 83½ | − .706 | − .974 | − 26 | − 33½ |
| | B | 51 | 59½ | − .025 | − .240 | − 1 | − 9½ |
| | C | 23 | 21½ | + .739 | + .789 | + 27 | + 28½ |
| | D | 3 | 4 | + 1.881 | + 1.751 | + 47 | + 46 |

[8] By the best treatment which we are able to make of the available evidence, the form of distribution of level of intellect in the 240 college graduates diverges from Form A only in the manner and to the extent shown in Table 165 of Appendix VI.

TABLE 23

DIFFERENCES IN DIFFICULTY OF VARIOUS COMPOSITE TASKS AND OF THE MEDIAN SUMS OF 20 EXPERT RATINGS OF THE SINGLE TASKS OF THESE COMPOSITES WHICH WERE RATED. EACH DIFFERENCE IS EXPRESSED AS A PERCENT OF THE DIFFERENCE BETWEEN THE A AND THE D COMPOSITE OF ITS KIND.

| | Differences in difficulty between tasks | | | | | Disagreements | | | |
| | By experiment: Assuming the Form of Distribution to be Form A | | By experiment: Assuming the form of Distribution to be a Rectangle | | By the Consensus | 100 from 80: | | 100 from Consensus: | |
| | 100 | 80 | 100 | 80 | | Form A | Rectangle | Form A | Rectangle |
|---|---|---|---|---|---|---|---|---|---|
| C B–C A | 21 | 20* | 23½ | 32 | 10 | 1 | 8½ | 11 | 13½ |
| C C–C B | 27 | 19* | 37 | 34½ | 65 | 8 | 2½ | 38 | 28 |
| C D–C C | 52 | 61* | 39½ | 33½ | 25 | 9 | 6 | 27 | 14½ |
| A B–A A | 29 | 35 | 37½ | 41½ | 41 | 6 | 4 | 12 | 3½ |
| A C–A B | 42½ | 31 | 47 | 37½ | —14 | 11½ | 9½ | 56½ | 61 |
| A D–A C | 28½ | 34 | 15½ | 21 | 73 | 5½ | 5½ | 44½ | 57½ |
| V B–V A | 28 | 27½ | 40½ | 31 | 49 | ½ | 9½ | 21 | 8½ |
| V C–V B | 32½ | 42½ | 43 | 50½ | 65 | 10 | 7½ | 32½ | 22 |
| V D–V C | 39½ | 30 | 16½ | 18½ | —14 | 9½ | 2 | 53½ | 30½ |
| D B–D A | 57 | 29 | 57½ | 25½ | | | | | |
| D C–D B | 31 | 48 | 33½ | 55½ | | | | | |
| D D–D C | 12 | 23 | 9 | 19 | | | | | |
| I B–I A | 26 | 27 | 34 | 30 | 61½ | 1 | 4 | 35½ | 27½ |
| I C–I B' | 30 | 38 | 38½ | 48 | 25½ | 8 | 9½ | 4½ | 13 |
| I D–I C | 44 | 35 | 27½ | 22 | 13 | 9 | 5½ | 31 | 14½ |
| Sum of disagreements, omitting the Directions Tests | | | | | | 79 | 74 | 367 | 294 |

* The difficulty of C D is estimated as + 2.00.

The correlations, using $\rho = 1 - \dfrac{6\Sigma D^2}{n(n^2 - 1)}$ with the rank orders, are .94 for the 240 experiment with the 189 experiment, .79 and .72 for the correlations between experimental

TABLE 24.

DIFFICULTY OF TWELVE COMPOSITES BY THE RESULTS WITH 240 COLLEGE GRADU-
ATES AND 189 CANDIDATES FOR COLLEGE ENTRANCE, IN DISTANCES + AND −
FROM THE MEDIAN FOR THE 240, IN TERMS OF THE σ OF THE COM-
POSITE CONCERNED.   ALSO THE MEDIAN RATINGS BY THE CONSEN-
SUS OF SUCH TASKS IN EACH COMPOSITE AS WERE RATED.

|  | Difficulty | | By the consensus: Median | N | Estimated Probable Error of the Consensus Median |
|---|---|---|---|---|---|
|  | By the 240 | By the 189 | | | |
| C N | − 1.47 | − 1.29 | 3084 | 6 | 35 |
| O | − .87 | − .77 | 3279 | 2 | 60 |
| P | − .29 | − .00 | 3482 | 3 | 50 |
| Q | + .21 | + .86 | 3314 | 1 | 95 |
| A N | − 2.03 | − 2.07 | 2855 | 6 | 35 |
| O | − 1.23 | − 1.18 | 3047 | 3 | 50 |
| P | − .92 | − .67 | 2869 | 4 | 42 |
| Q | − .45 | − .36 | 3338 | 3 | 50 |
| D 4½ | − 1.79 | − 2.07 | 3191 | 4 | 42 |
| 5 | − 1.08 | − 1.54 | 2949 | 3 | 50 |
| 6 | − .64 | − 1.07 | 3258 | 3 | 50 |
| 7 | + .30 | + .16 | 3291 | 1 | 85 |

|  | Differences | | | Disagreements | | |
|---|---|---|---|---|---|---|
|  | By the 240 | By the 189 | By the Consensus | 240– 189 | 240– Cons. | 189– Cons. |
| C O–N | 36 | 24 | 85 | 12 | 49 | 61 |
| P–O | 34 | 36 | 88 | 2 | 54 | 52 |
| Q–P | 30 | 40 | − 73 | 10 | 103 | 113 |
| A O–N | 50½ | 52 | 39½ | 1½ | 11 | 12½ |
| P–O | 19½ | 30 | − 36½ | 10½ | 56 | 66½ |
| Q–P | 30 | 18 | 97 | 12 | 67 | 79 |
| D 5–4½ | 34 | 24 | − 242 | 10 | 276 | 266 |
| 6–5 | 21 | 21 | 309 | 0 | 288 | 288 |
| 7–6 | 45 | 55 | 33 | 10 | 12 | 22 |
| Sum of disagreements | | | | 68 | 916 | 960 |

results and the consensus. A treatment of the differences in terms of percents like that of Table 20 is presented in the lower half of Table 24. The disagreements between experiment and consensus are 13 or 14 times as large as the disagreements between the two experiments. The disagreements between experiment and consensus would, however, be reduced if we had ratings of five or six tasks instead of one in the C Q and D7 composites.

We have extensive experiments with the vocabulary composites 1a, 2a, 3a, 4a, 5a, 6a, and 7a with pupils in Grades 9, 10, and 11; and four of the tasks of each of these composites were rated by the consensus. The essential facts appear in Table 25. The consensus is badly in error in putting 1a much too low, or 2a much too high, or in doing both.[9] It also crowds 4a, 5a, and 6a close together, failing to distinguish fully the large differences which exist between these. It makes the sum of the differences between 1a and 2a and between 6a and 7a nearly four times as large as the entire difference between 2a and 6a, though the experimental results make the latter nearly twice the former. The disagreements between the consensus and any experiment are about seven times as large as the disagreements between any one experiment and any other. In spite of these notable errors, there remains a general correspondence between consensus estimates and experimental results. The rank-order correlation is indeed almost unity, Table 25 showing no reversals.

[9] It would not be fair to make this statement on the basis of the facts of Table 25 alone, since both V 1a and V 2a are so easy for pupils in Grade 9 and above that results from these grades are not suitable to measure the difficulty of either at all accurately. We have evidence from a group of 200 pupils in Grade 5½, however, to the effect that the difference between V 1a and V 2a is less than the difference between V 2a and V 3a. The percents correct are: 99.5, 89.5, and 58.0 Taken at their face value, these give differences of $.88\sigma$ for 1a to 2a and $1.50\sigma$ for 2a to 3a. The .88 may be too small because the one pupil in 200 who failed to get five of the 10 words in 1a is right may have been extremely careless. Very, very low percents are of course unreliable for n = 200, for many reasons. It is extremely unlikely, however, that the true $\sigma$ value for V 1a will be below $-3.20$, so as to make the difference between 1a and 2a actually greater than the difference between 2a and 3a.

12

We have also very extensive experiments with the D (reading) composites 1 to 7, the results from which are presented in Table 26. Unfortunately, the median consensus ratings for composites 1 and 7 are from only one task each. Even after liberal allowance for the large probable errors of these medians, there is a clear failure of the con-

TABLE 25.

MEASURES OF DIFFICULTY.

| | Grade 9 n = 1041 | Grade 10 n = 700 | Grade 11 n = 752 | Consensus Medians | n |
|---|---|---|---|---|---|
| V 1a n = 10 | − 2.457 | − 2.457 | − 3.090 | 2139 | 4 |
| " 2a " | − 2.576 | − 2.366 | − 3.090 | 2622 | " |
| " 3a " | − 1.366 | − 1.468 | − 1.995 | 2679 | " |
| " 4a " | − .719 | − .990 | − 1.483 | 2787 | " |
| " 5a " | + .068 | − .264 | − .845 | 2809 | " |
| " 6a " | + .904 | + .527 | + .050 | 2854 | " |
| " 7a " | + 2.120 | + 1.866 | + 1.259 | 3227 | " |

*Differences*

| | | | | |
|---|---|---|---|---|
| 2a–1a | .119 | .091 | .000 | 483 |
| 3a–2a | 1.210 | .898 | 1.095 | 57 |
| 4a–3a | .647 | .478 | .512 | 108 |
| 5a–4a | .787 | .726 | .638 | 22 |
| 6a–5a | .836 | .791 | .895 | 45 |
| 7a–6a | 1.216 | 1.339 | 1.209 | 373 |

*Differences Divided by the 7a–1a Difference*

| | | | | |
|---|---|---|---|---|
| 2a–1a | .026 | .021 | .000 | .444 |
| 3a–2a | .264 | .208 | .252 | .052 |
| 4a–3a | .141 | .111 | .118 | .099 |
| 5a–4a | .172 | .168 | .147 | .020 |
| 6a–5a | .183 | .183 | .206 | .041 |
| 7a–6a | .266 | .310 | .278 | .342 |

*Discrepancies*

| | 9–10 | 9–11 | 10–11 | 9–Con. | 10–Con. | 11–Con. |
|---|---|---|---|---|---|---|
| 2a–1a | .005 | .026 | .021 | .418 | .423 | .444 |
| 3a–2a | .056 | .012 | .044 | .212 | .156 | .200 |
| 4a–3a | .030 | .023 | .007 | .042 | .012 | .019 |
| 5a–4a | .004 | .025 | .021 | .125 | .148 | .127 |
| 6a–5a | .000 | .023 | .023 | .142 | .142 | .165 |
| 7a–6a | .044 | .012 | .032 | .076 | .032 | .064 |
| Sum | .139 | .121 | .148 | 1.042 | .913 | 1.019 |

sensus to distinguish differences in difficulty accurately amongst these reading tasks. The range from D1 to D7 represents the range from what two thirds of pupils in Grade 6 can do to what not one in twenty-five high-school seniors can do. By the experimental results, it is clear that

TABLE 26.

MEASURES OF DIFFICULTY.

|  | Grade 10 n = 1185 | Grade 11 n = 1053 | Grade 12 n = 742 | Consensus | n |
|---|---|---|---|---|---|
| D 1 | − 2.409 | − 2.878 | − 2.652 | 2713 | 1 |
| D 2 | − 1.398 | − 1.695 | − 1.812 | 2743 | 4 |
| D 3 | − .690 | − .999 | − 1.170 | 3118 | 2 |
| D 4 | − .055 | − .333 | − .516 | 3177 | 5 |
| D 5 | + .542 | + .306 | − .065 | 2949 | 3 |
| D 6 | + 1.243 | + .966 | + .824 | 3255 | 4 |
| D 7 | + 2.170 | + 1.896 | + 1.774 | 3291 | 1 |

*Differences*

|  | | | | | |
|---|---|---|---|---|---|
| D 2–1 | 1.011 | 1.183 | .840 | 30 | |
| D 3–2 | .708 | .696 | .642 | 375 | |
| D 4–3 | .635 | .664 | .654 | 59 | |
| D 5–4 | .597 | .641 | .451 | − 228 | |
| D 6–5 | .701 | .660 | .889 | 306 | |
| D 7–6 | .927 | .930 | .950 | 36 | |

*Differences Expressed as Fractions of the D7–D1 Difference*

|  | | | | | |
|---|---|---|---|---|---|
| D 2–1 | .221 | .248 | .190 | .052 | |
| D 3–2 | .155 | .146 | .145 | .649 | |
| D 4–3 | .139 | .139 | .148 | .102 | |
| D 5–4 | .130 | .134 | .102 | − .394 | |
| D 6–5 | .153 | .138 | .201 | .529 | |
| D 7–6 | .202 | .195 | .214 | .062 | |

*Disagreements*

|  | 10–11 | 10–12 | 11–12 | 10–Con. | 11–Con. | 12–Con. |
|---|---|---|---|---|---|---|
| D 2–1 | .027 | .031 | .058 | .169 | .196 | .138 |
| D 3–2 | .009 | .010 | .001 | .494 | .503 | .504 |
| D 4–3 | .000 | .009 | .009 | .037 | .037 | .046 |
| D 5–4 | .004 | .028 | .032 | .524 | .528 | .496 |
| D 6–5 | .015 | .048 | .063 | .376 | .391 | .328 |
| D 7–6 | .007 | .012 | .019 | .140 | .133 | .152 |
| Sum | .062 | .138 | .182 | 1.740 | 1.788 | 1.664 |

each step is a substantial increase in difficulty. But by the consensus we have great irregularities and reversals, and the differences 1 to 2 and 6 to 7, which should be the largest, are specially small (if we trust the single-task medians).

The comparisons of the last 10 pages are all subject to the criticism that the experimental results do not measure the truly intellectual difficulty of the composites in question, but rather their difficulty for whatever ability each involves, and that if by a miracle we could know how well people would succeed with these composites if each individual could use all of his intellect and nothing but intellect with each composite, the results thus obtained might correspond more closely with the consensus estimates than our actual experimental results do.

For this criticism to have force the $r_{t_1}$ correlations of the tasks which are put as unduly hard by the consensus would have to be lower than the others. For example, $r_{t_1}$ for the sentence-completions should be much lower than $r_{t_1}$ for the arithmetic, vocabulary, or directions. This is not the case. We have computed the correlations of each with a composite made up of completions, arithmetic, vocabulary, directions, information and opposites with approximately equal weights, using 176 of the 180 imbeciles. They are:[10]

| | |
|---|---|
| Completions with CAVDIO | .90 |
| Arithmetic with CAVDIO | .80 |
| Vocabulary with CAVDIO | .68 |
| Directions with CAVDIO | .92 |
| Information with CAVDIO | .85 |
| Opposites with CAVDIO | .92 |

The range is here very restricted, all the individuals being within a range of 28 to 58 months of mental age, with a σ of about 8 months. If the correlations were for all

[10] There is some spurious correlation in each of these, but this does not seriously damage the argument, since the amount is not large and is approximately equal for all.

twenty-year-olds or for adults, they would all be very much higher. If we take the variability of adults as $\sigma = 2.85$ years, as computed from the army data [Memoirs, p. 391], and apply the correction[11] for restricted range, we have:

| | |
|---|---|
| Completions with CAVDIO | .994 |
| Arithmetic with CAVDIO | .985 |
| Vocabulary with CAVDIO | .971 |
| Directions with CAVDIO | .995 |
| Information with CAVDIO | .990 |
| Opposites with CAVDIO | .995 |

In the case of 240 college graduates, the correlations of 10-composites made up of completions, arithmetical problems, vocabulary, and reading, respectively, with a CAVD summation score from 160 tasks averaged as follows:

| | |
|---|---|
| C | .69 |
| A | .49 |
| V | .51 |
| D | .56 or higher.[12] |

Nowhere in fact do we find any inferiority of C to A, V, and D in closeness of correlation with i or anything approximating to i.

Wherever and however we estimate it, the $r_{ti}$ for ten of our sentence-completions will not be below the average of the correlations for ten of our A's or V's or D's.

We can think of no good reason why the discrepancies in the case of the vocabulary and reading tasks should be any less on the whole if we should compare them with the difficulties found by experiment corrected for differences in $r_{ti}$, instead of with the mere difficulties. We may, it is true, hope that the experts' estimates of difficulty will disregard some of the sources of error to which the experi-

---

[11] $R_{12} \dfrac{\sigma_1}{\Sigma_1} = \dfrac{r_{12}}{\sqrt{1 - r^2_{12} + r^2_{12}(\Sigma_1/\sigma_1)^2}}$.   See [Kelley, '23, p. 225.]

[12] Some of the D composites had fewer than 10 elements, so that the average of .56 is somewhat too low.

mental determinations are subject, and so deviate from the experimental determinations toward the difficulty for intellect uncontaminated by non-intellectual factors. But the particular constant errors which we have described do not seem alleviated in this way.

SUMMARY

On the whole it is certain that we cannot trust any consensus of present opinion to provide an accurate measure of the difficulty or of the intellectual difficulty of a single brief task. Psychologists do not as yet know enough about intellect and intellectual difficulty to avoid occasional large constant errors, such as the over-estimation of the difficulty of easy completions, or to distinguish well amongst vocabulary or reading tasks. The psychologist cannot as yet know from inspecting a task what fraction of intellect it will call into action, how high degree of intellect will be needed to succeed with it, and what effect non-intellectual factors will have upon its solution, so as to answer the question of how hard it will be in an actual experiment or how hard it would be if each person in the group used all of his intellect and was entirely uninfluenced by non-intellectual factors. A consensus of experts cannot, in the present status of psychology, either relieve us from the need of experimental tests of difficulty or provide an escape from our previous conclusion that the measurement of intellectual difficulty may best limit itself to composites, varied enough to utilize all of intellect and to equalize non-intellectual factors.

On the other hand, the consensus estimates are in no sense fortuitous. The correlations of estimates with experimental results are always positive and fairly high, even within the very narrow range of low-grade imbeciles, or of college graduates. Over a wide range the correlations will of course be much higher. The correspondence of opinion with experiment is not close enough to justify us in accepting estimates of the difficulty or of the intellectual difficulty of single brief tasks as always even approximately true, or in leaving any result of any such estimates unchecked by experiment. But it is not so slight as to justify us in making no use of it. On the contrary, if we free it from its over- and under-estimation of the difficulty of certain types of tasks, it will give a serviceable first rough approximation to an order of intellectual difficulty. Even without any correction or amendment, composites formed by taking ten of C, ten of A, ten of V, and ten of D, all forty of which had

TABLE 27.

THE DIFFERENCES IN DIFFICULTY OF CAVD 40-COMPOSITE TASKS BY EXPERIMENT AND BY THE CONSENSUS OF 20 EXPERTS.

| | Percent which the Stated Difference is of the Difference P–A | | |
| | Difference | | |
| | By the Median of the Four Consensus Medians | By Experiment | Discrepancy |
|---|---|---|---|
| B–A | 16.8 | 8.0 | + 8.8 |
| C–B | 11.0 | 4.8 | + 6.2 |
| D–C | 7.4 | 4.1 | + 3.3 |
| E–D | 5.8 | 6.2 | – .4 |
| F–E | 2.6 | 6.1 | – 3.5 |
| G–F | 3.7 | 7.7 | – 4.0 |
| H–G | 4.2 | 9.4 | – 5.2 |
| I–H | 7.4 | 16.5 | – 9.1 |
| J–I | 10.0 | 14.6 | – 4.6 |
| K–J | 5.8 | 3.5 | + 2.3 |
| L–K | 5.3 | – .9 | + 6.2 |
| M–L | 5.3 | 6.0 | – .7 |
| N–M | 4.2 | 2.1 | + 2.1 |
| O–N | 6.3 | 5.7 | + .6 |
| P–O | 4.2 | 5.4 | – 1.2 |

identical consensus estimates, would be useful composite tasks. We have not had time actually to make and test such, but we have carried out the converse procedure of computing the median consensus estimates for the tasks of our experimentally determined composites. The results appear in Table 27.

The number of single tasks from the different composites which were rated by the consensus, ranged from 6 of P to 29 of F, being for A, B, C, D, E, F, G, H, I, J, K, etc., in order 20, 13, 18, 23, 18, 29, 20, 20, 13, 15, 17, 8, 12, 16, 13, and 6.

The derivation of the experimental results for composites A to P is given in Chapter IX.

# CHAPTER VI[1]

## LEVELS OF INTELLECT

We measure the level or altitude of an intellect by the difficulty of the intellectual tasks which it can perform successfully, or more exactly, by the difficulty of the tasks a certain defined percent of which it can perform successfully.

Such tasks, to be truly intellectual, have to be composites of a number of single tasks. In the case of Intellect CAVD, each should represent C, A, V, and D with approximately equal weight to each. Success with such a composite task may be taken to mean getting all of its single tasks right, or 99 percent or more of them, or any other defined fraction of them. For several reasons, the most useful

[1] This chapter should properly be preceded by a chapter presenting the facts concerning the difficulty of the single tasks used in constructing composites with which to measure altitude or level of intellect, and concerning their intellectualness as measured by $r_{ti}$, or some approximation thereto, where that information has been obtained.

In constructing the tests for intellectual level or altitude, we have made measurements of the difficulty of over three thousand tasks. The number of individuals concerned in one of these measurements varies from a hundred to over four thousand.

These measurements are of great value quite apart from the uses which we have made of them. They will assist future workers in the field to extend and refine the selection of tests for altitude of intellect. They provide a substantial beginning for the construction of tests of mental growth in its later and higher stages, including alternative forms. They provide material for many scientific studies, for example, of judgments of intellect, of the organization of intellect, of the nature of intellectual difficulty. They may be used in many ways in the practical work of examining for intellect. The publication of such an inventory of intellectual tasks with a rough measurement of the difficulty of each will encourage others to add to it, so that after some years we shall have a standard source of supply of intellectual tasks of any kind, at any desired level of difficulty.

The expense of ordinary publication is, however, prohibitive. Consequently, we have prepared a hundred sets in the form of volumes of mimeographed sheets. These will be sold at cost by the Bureau of Publications of Teachers College, Columbia University.

meaning to take is getting 50 percent or more of the single tasks right. We shall use this meaning, unless some other is specified.

### COMPOSITE TASKS

The sub-series presented in Chapter III are samples of the composite tasks which we have constructed; and additional ones are shown below.

### LEVEL I

*Write words on the dotted lines so as to make the whole sentence true and sensible. Write one word on each inch of dots.*

1. Hot weather comes in the ............................ and ............................ weather ............................ the winter.
2. The first ............................ after June is ............................ .
3. Children ............................ are rude ............................ not easily win friends.
4. The dog ............................ a useful ............................ because ............................ his intelligence and faithfulness.
5. The rose is a favorite ............................ because of ............................ fragrance and ............................ .
6. The poor little ............................has ............................ nothing to ............................; he is hungry.
7. He will come ............................ he is not ill.
8. Not ............................ persons are eager to work hard.
9. Divisor times quotient will ............................ dividend, if the ............................ is done correctly.
10. ............................ you look, ............................ will see flowers.

*Write the answers to these problems. Use the empty space to figure on.*

11. What will 4 eight-cent stamps and 1 three-cent stamp cost?
12. How many inches are there in 2 feet and 7 inches?
13. How many stamps are there in a sheet 8 stamps wide and 5 stamps long?

14. What does a pound of candy cost when you pay 10 cents for a quarter of a pound?
15. How much longer is 100 minutes than an hour?
16. 32 plus what number equals 36?
17. How much more is $7 \times 6$ than $2 \times 20$?
18. How long is it from seven o'clock in the morning to two o'clock in the afternoon?
19. The sum of two numbers is 40. One of the numbers is 14. What is the other number?
20. What number added to 16 gives a number 4 less than 27?

*Look at the first word in line 1. Find the other word in the line which means the same or most nearly the same. Write its number on the line at the right side of the page. Do the same in lines 2, 3, 4, etc. Lines A, B, C, and D show the way to do it. Do all the lines you can. Write only one number for each line.[2]*

| | | |
|---|---|---|
| beast | 1 afraid.....2 words.....3 large.....4 animal.....5 bird | 4 |
| baby | 1 cradle.....2 mother.....3 little child.....4 youth.....5 girl | 3 |
| raise | 1 lift up.....2 drag.....3 sun.....4 bread.....5 deluge | 1 |
| blind | 1 man.....2 cannot see.....3 game.....4 unhappy.....5 eyes | 2 |
| | | |
| confess | 1 agree.....2 mend.....3 deny.....4 admit.....5 mingle | .............. |
| backward | 1 downwards.....2 after.....3 toward the rear.....4 defense.....5 arrears | .............. |
| advertise | 1 detain.....2 explore.....3 give notice of.....4 adverse.....5 newspaper | .............. |
| combat | 1 fight.....2 dismay.....3 club.....4 expedition.....5 comb | .............. |
| blond | 1 polite.....2 dishonest.....3 dauntless.....4 coy.....5 fair | .............. |
| broaden | 1 efface.....2 make level.....3 elapse.....4 embroider.....5 widen | .............. |
| chubby | 1 indolent.....2 obstinate.....3 irritable.....4 plump.....5 muscular | .............. |
| concern | 1 see clearly.....2 engage.....3 furnish.....4 disturb.....5 have to do with | .............. |
| cargo | 1 load.....2 small boat.....3 hem.....4 draught.....5 vehicle | .............. |
| clutch | 1 exploit.....2 nest.....3 flit.....4 grasp.....5 cane | .............. |

*Read this and then write the answers. Read it again if you need to.*

> Then, upon one knee uprising,
> Hiawatha aimed an arrow;
> Scarce a twig moved with his motion,

---

[2] If it has not been given previously, practice or supervision should be given to insure that the individual tested understands these directions.

> Scarce a leaf was stirred or rustled;
> But the wary roebuck started,
> Stamped with all his hoofs together,
> Listened with one foot uplifted,
> Leaped as if to meet the arrow;
> Ah! the singing, fatal arrow;
> Like a wasp it buzzed and stung him!

31. What was Hiawatha trying to kill? ..................................
32. What word is used to describe the roebuck? ..........................
33. What is the arrow said to resemble? ..............................

*Read this and then write the answers. Read it again if you need to.*

There is an old saying, "As harmless as a fly"; and until recently the fly has been regarded only as an unpleasant but harmless nuisance. Had our forefathers known as much about flies as we now know, they might have made the proverb, "As dangerous as the fly." His origin and his habits are of the worst sort. He is, in short, a disgusting and dangerous pest.

The scientists have told us also how to keep clear of the flies. Houses and grounds should be kept free of decaying organic matter, and stables should be screened so as to cut them off from their breeding places. Our houses should be carefully screened and food kept free from their dangerous feet and mouths. Fly paper and fly traps can be bought everywhere. Your teacher, also, can probably tell you other means of protection. But don't forget that the "harmless fly" of the proverb is the dangerous fly of fact.

34. Did our great grandparents know as much about flies as men do now? ....................................................................

Should flies be prevented from reaching their breeding-places? ....................................................................

Is it desirable for a girl to be so gentle that she cannot bear to kill a fly? ....................................................................

[All three answers must be right in 34.]

*There are only four single D Tasks in level I, so each receives a credit of 2½.*

## LEVEL J.

*Write words on the dotted lines so as to make the whole sentence true and sensible. Write one word on each inch of dots.*

1. The ........................... way to ....................... is by airplane.
2. There is no ........................ on earth ........................ cannot bear ........................ misfortune.
3. Two pounds of silver are ........................ more than two pounds of iron.
4. He ........................ is cheerful will make friends.
5. A body of........................entirely surrounded by........................ is called an........................ .
6. The........................I think about it, the........................perplexed I am.
7. It........................strength to........................a heavy weight.
8. When........................lines are perpendicular to each other, they form a right........................ .
9. One........................times one half equals one fourth.
10. The........................of five and ten is fifteen.

*Write the answers to these problems. Use the blank sheets to figure on.*

11. What number minus 7 equals 23?
12. What number minus 16 equals 20?
13. 12 is $\frac{2}{5}$ of . . . .
14. If a present costing $9.45 is to be paid for by 27 men contributing equal amounts, what is one man's share?
15. Dick started from his house, walked two miles north, then two miles west, then two miles south. How far away from his house was he then?
16. A man bought land for $400. He sold it for $445, gaining $15 an acre. How many acres were there?
17. 12 is $\frac{3}{4} \times$ . . . .
18. Counting that 100 lb. will last 15 men for a week, how much will be required to last 30 men for 3 weeks?
19. A girl had 20 quarters, 16 dimes, 12 nickels and 8 pennies. She made four piles, Pile A, Pile B, Pile C and

Pile D. In Pile A she put half the quarters, one fourth of the dimes, one third of the nickels, and all of the pennies. How much money had she in Pile A?

20. At the rate of $2.25 per week how long will it take to save $90.00?

*Directions and samples as on page 161.*

| | | |
|---|---|---|
| 21. awe | 1 lamb....2 fear....3 tool....4 mound....5 opera | |
| 22. aged | 1 years....2 active....3 old....4 merciful....5 punctual | |
| 23. arrive | 1 answer....2 rival....3 enter....4 force....5 come | |
| 24. blunt | 1 dull....2 drowsy....3 deaf....4 doubtful....5 ugly | |
| 25. accustom | 1 disappoint....2 customary....3 encounter....4 get used....5 business | |
| 26. bade | 1 gaze....2 a tool....3 fetched....4 wait....5 ordered | |
| 27. bog | 1 ebb....2 disorder....3 swamp....4 field....5 difficulty | |
| 28. cascade | 1 hat....2 waterfall....3 firmament....4 disaster....5 box | |
| 29. bray | 1 cry of an ass....2 bowl....3 cry of an ox....4 frustrate....5 raven's cry | |
| 30. disembark | 1 unearth....2 ashore....3 dislodge....4 disparage....5 strip | |

*In each set of sentences, check the two which mean most nearly the same as the sentence printed in heavy type.*

**31. I weigh the man, not his title.**—(Wycherley.)

............'Tis not the king's stamp can make the metal better.

............Fine feathers make fine birds.

............Titles are the marks of honest men and wise.

............The rank is but the guinea stamp, the man's the gold, for a' that.

**32. Anyone can hold the helm when the sea is calm.**

............Sail when the wind blows.

............Untempted virtue is easily retained.

............The pilot cannot mitigate the billows or calm the winds.

............An unassaulted castle is easily held.

**33. In the presence of the greater malady, the lesser is forgot.**

............We see not the candle if the moon be shining.

............An ounce of prevention is worth a pound of cure.

............The greater glory dims the less.

............There are some remedies worse than the disease.

34. **What is failure? It is only a spur to the one who receives it in the right spirit.**

_____Every rebuff is a stepping stone to higher things.

_____To reach the port of heaven we must sail, and not drift, nor lie at anchor.

_____Failure makes the spirit within stir to go in once more and fight.

_____Not failure, but low aim is crime.

*The paragraph for task 35 is the Hiawatha paragraph on page 161.*

35. What two words are used to tell the noise the arrow made?

*The paragraph for tasks 36, 37, and 38 is the "Fly" on page 162.*

36. Where does the paragraph say the fly is born? _____

_____

37. Who or what informs us how to avoid the dangerous pest described in the paragraph printed above? _____

_____

38. Name three devices which protect us from the disgusting pest. _____

### EVERY HOME NEEDS A GARDEN

A MAGAZINE published to promote real gardening. Most people do not think much about their gardens at this time of the year, but if more people did, there would be more good gardens. If you live in the city where space is at a premium, we provide pleasure for you by suggesting how to grow flowers indoors. If you live in the country and have a garden and do not experience the satisfaction of seeing things grow as a result of your own efforts—then you need the X.Y.Z. magazine.

39. What is recommended for persons who fail to make things grow in their gardens? _____

_____

40. Which one of these words could best be used instead of *at a premium?* Draw a line under it.

    space    flowers    valuable    extension    extensive
    cheap    noble

## LEVEL K

*Write words on the dotted lines to make the whole sentence true and sensible. Write one word on each inch of dots.*

1. When a man is......................of sight,...................... ......................
   also very soon out......................mind.
2. No......................is powerful......................to......................
   two and two be five.
3. ......................you wish me to help you...................... ......................
   Latin, please......................me by telephone.
4. He is......................genteel who does......................deeds.
5. It may......................effort and a long......................but
   the result is sure.
6. This magazine is the......................of a new and progressive movement.
7. Four......................two is more......................seven.
8. No......................what happens wrong is......................right.
9. The......................source......................wealth in Denmark
   ......................agriculture.
10. In......................to maintain......................health, one
    should have nourishing.......................

*Write the answers to these problems. Use the blank sheets to figure on.*

11. A man spent two thirds of his money and had $8 left. How much had he at first?
12. I bought $4\frac{1}{2}$ yards of cloth, gave the clerk $2 and received 20 cents as correct change. What was the price of the cloth per yard?
13. A dealer bought some mules for $800. He sold them for $1,000, making $40 on each mule. How many mules were there?
14. How much more is the sum of $3\frac{1}{3}$ and $4\frac{1}{2}$ than the sum of $2\frac{3}{4}$ and $3\frac{1}{4}$?

15. $20 =$ how many times 12?

16. How many times must you add $1\frac{1}{2}$ to 6 to have 15 as a result?

17. How many times as long as 8 feet is 12 yds.?

18. $20 = \frac{2}{3} \times$ .................

19. 8 is $1\frac{1}{3} \times$ .................

20. 20 is $1\frac{1}{4} \times$ .................

*Directions and samples the same as on page 161.*

| | | |
|---|---|---|
| conspire | 1 plot.....2 breathe.....3 rely.....4 die.....5 outrun | ................. |
| check | 1 error.....2 stop.....3 flash.....4 rude.....5 haste | ................. |
| cherish | 1 dedicate.....2 happy.....3 covet.....4 hold dear.....5 marry | ................. |
| chirrup | 1 aspen.....2 joyful.....3 capsize.....4 chirp.....5 incite | ................. |
| accessible | 1 indefatigable.....2 successful.....3 limpid.....4 easy to reach.....5 liable | ................. |
| dingy | 1 afraid.....2 hostelry.....3 small bell.....4 midget.....5 dirty | ................. |
| edible | 1 auspicious.....2 eligible.....3 fit to eat.....4 sagacious.....5 able to speak | ................. |
| confound | 1 discovered.....2 fulfill.....3 establish.....4 mix up.....5 expire | ................. |
| concur | 1 agree.....2 race.....3 mongrel.....4 pounce.....5 ramble | ................. |
| contact | 1 tactful.....2 hate.....3 injunction.....4 touch.....5 oversight | ................. |

*In each set of sentences, check the two which mean most nearly the same as the sentence printed in heavy type.*

31. **Today is worth two tomorrows.**
.................Time is an herb that cures all diseases.
.................A bird in the hand is worth two in the bush.
.................To speed today is to be set back tomorrow.
.................There is no time like the present.

32. **Faint heart never won fair lady.**
.................Nothing venture; nothing gain.
.................Married in haste we repent at leisure.
.................Fools rush in where angels fear to tread.
.................Fortune favors the brave.

33. **Fight fire with fire.**
.................Set a thief to catch a thief.
.................Knavery is the best defence against a knave.
.................Sow the wind, reap the whirlwind.
.................Fire that's closest kept burns fiercest.

34. **One sorrow never comes but brings an heir.**
.................Two in distress makes sorrow less.
.................It never rains but it pours.

13

...............On horror's head horrors accumulate.

...............Sorrow's crown of sorrow is remembering happier things.

*The paragraph for task 35 is "Every Home Needs a Garden," on page 165.*

35. What does the advertisement say would be the result if people thought more about their gardens in the time of year referred to? ...............

*The paragraph for task 36 is the paragraph on Work on page 81.*

36. According to the paragraph what even would a prisoner welcome? ...............

*The paragraph for task 37 is "The American State," on page 84.*

37. In what respect are some of the original thirteen states and California unlike all the others? ...............

*The paragraph for tasks 38, 39, and 40 is "Dirge in Woods," on page 94.*

38. To whom does "we" refer? ...............
39. What veins the moss carpet? ...............
40. What event of man's career is like the falling of the fruits of the pine? ...............

### Level L

*Write words on the dotted lines so as to make the whole sentence true and sensible. Write one word on each inch of dots.*

1. Many new ............... are printed every year, but some wise ............... prefer to ............... the old ones.

2. Telephone and ............... were means of ............... unknown in the seventeenth ...............

3. Much of the débris ............... upon the ............... is valuable.

4. Most men _____ themselves _____ more
   kindly than their _____ judge them.
5. Power is generated _____ _____, gaso-
   line, and several _____ things.
6. A _____ of ease is _____ preparation for
   achievement.
7. Sailors fear most _____ and snowy _____
   because then there is most _____ of a collision
   between _____.
8. She was _____ to fashion fine _____
   from the cloth she had learned to _____.
9. The _____ of the river are being constantly
   _____ by the _____ of the water.
10. Any _____ will stick to a master _____ is
   _____ and kind to _____.

*In the lines below, each number is gotten in a certain
way from the numbers coming before it. Study out what
this way is in each line, and then write in the space left for
it the number that should come next. The first two lines
are already filled in as they should be.*

|  | SAMPLES | 2 | 4 | 6 | 8 | 10 | _12_ |
|---|---|---|---|---|---|---|---|
|  |  | 11 | 12 | 14 | 15 | 17 | _18_ |
| 11. |  |  | 85 | 79 | 73 | 67 | _____ |
| 12. |  |  | 90 | 81 | 72 | 63 | _____ |
| 13. |  |  | 76.3 | 85.3 | 94.3 | 103.3 | _____ |
| 14. |  |  | 64 | 32 | 16 | 8 | _____ |
| 15. |  |  | 240 | 120 | 60 | 30 | _____ |
| 16. |  | 12 | 16 | 22 | 26 | 32 | 36 | _____ |
| 17. | 7 | 11 | 15 | 16 | 20 | 24 | 25 | 29 | _____ |
| 18. |  |  | 13 | $12\frac{2}{3}$ | $12\frac{1}{3}$ | 12 | _____ |
| 19. |  |  | 46 | $45\frac{3}{4}$ | $45\frac{1}{2}$ | $45\frac{1}{4}$ | _____ |
| 20. | 2 | 5 | 7 | 8 | 11 | 13 | 14 | 17 | _____ |

*Directions and samples as on page 161.*

| downcast | 1 thrown down....2 neutral.....3 judicious.....4 sad.....5 broken | ............ |
| pact | 1 puissance.....2 remonstrance.....3 agreement.....4 skillet.....5 pressure | ............ |
| audible | 1 festive.....2 easy.....3 audit.....4 heard.....5 downy | ............ |
| solicitor | 1 lawyer.....2 chieftain.....3 watchman.....4 maggot.....5 constable | ............ |
| beguile | 1 entreat.....2 delight.....3 dispense.....4 deceive.....5 foster | ............ |
| dominate | 1 abide.....2 goad.....3 threaten.....4 control.....5 dissuade | ............ |
| average | 1 level....2 count.....3 evident.....4 ordinary.....5 distinct | ............ |

28. behave        1 act.....2 own.....3 keep still.....4 enable.....5 entitle

29. comely        1 ignoble.....2 handsome.....3 disagreeable.....4 enter.....5 in time

30. cycle         1 scythe.....2 cyclone.....3 circle.....4 ode.....5 junction

*In each set of sentences, check the two which mean most nearly the same as the sentence printed in heavy type.*

**31. Man's evil manners live in brass; their virtues we write in water.—(Shakespeare.)**

.............Some rise by sin and some by virtues fall.

.............The evil that men do lives after them; the good is oft interred with their bones.

.............He lives in fame that died in virtue's cause.

.............The memory of vices lives longer than the memory of virtues.

**32. In this world a man must either be anvil or hammer.**

.............To get along, a man must be a knocker.

.............Man must either do or be done.

.............Man cannot be neutral; he must accomplish something or lose out.

.............Might is right.

**33. No greater grief than to remember days of joy when misery is at hand.—(Dante.)**

.............Misery loves company.

.............Sorrows remembered sweeten present joy.

.............To recall past pleasures is but to aggravate our present miseries.

.............A sorrow's crown of sorrow is remembering happier things.

**34. It is a consolation to the wretched to have companions in misery.**

.............Society in shipwreck is a comfort to all.

.............Misery acquaints a man with strange bedfellows.

.............Company in misery makes it light.

.............When misery is highest, help is nighest.

**35. Nothing emboldens sin so much as mercy.**

.............Spare the rod and spoil the child.

.............Pardon one offense, and you encourage the commission of many.

............He that has no charity merits no mercy.

............Let the punishment fit the crime.

36. **He counsels best who lives best.**

............Practice what you preach.

............A poor cask may hold good wine.

............A good example is the best sermon.

............An ounce of prevention is worth a pound of cure.

37. **The fault is not in our stars but in ourselves, that we are underlings.**—(Shakespeare.)

............Every man is the architect of his own fortune.

............Man is the master of his destiny.

............We can't read our fates from the stars.

............If we are underlings, it is not our fault.

38. **Every white will have its black, and every sweet its sour.**

............It never rains but it pours.

............Birds of a feather flock together.

............Every cloud has a silver lining.

............You cannot pluck roses without thorns.

*The paragraph for task 39 is the "Fly" on page 162.*

39. What is meant by "his origin"? ..............................................

*The paragraph for task 40 is "Every Home Needs a Garden" on page 165.*

40. What feeling is usually said to be experienced by people who see things grow as a result of their efforts?

----

## Level M

*Write words on the dotted lines so as to make the whole sentence true and sensible. Write one word on each inch of dots.*

1. Modern ............ of communication should ............ ............ closer to each other.

2. Astronomers are uncertain ............ the planet Mars is ............ .

3. Cleanliness is a ............ item in securing and ............ good health.

4. More _____ were killed, more houses _____,
   more money _____ during the Great _____,
   than during any equal number of _____ in
   history.

5. In the _____ time squirrels store _____
   for food in the _____ when the _____
   is such that they cannot _____ for things to
   eat.

6. Columbus _____ America, but it was _____
   for another Italian, _____.

7. A boy on a farm _____ _____ things about
   animals and _____ which a city _____
   usually does not _____.

8. The wind _____ the streets _____ of
   every flake of _____.

9. The benefit to the _____ from the _____
   of science is incalculable.

10. The _____ old days are often _____ with
    the present.

Tasks 14 and 15 must both be right to secure credit.
There are thus only 8 tasks; and each counts as 1¼.

A 3 for 5c.          E 6 for 5c.          J 4 for 25c.
B 3 for 10c.         F 80c. per peck.     K 2½c. each.
C 3 for 25c.         G 40c. per lb.       L 1½c. per lb.
D 48c. per lb.       H 50c. per lb.       M 4½c. per lb.
                     I 8 for $1.00.

*A, B, C, D, etc., are articles costing as shown above. 1A
means 1 of A, 2A means 2 of A, 3A means 3 of A, etc. Supply the missing numbers in lines 11 to 15 as shown in lines
I, II, and III. Use the empty parts of the page to figure on.*

I. 3 A cost        ½     as much as 3 B.
II. 2½ lb. G cost  *just*  as much as 8 I.
III. 1 lb. H costs *2 times* as much as 4 J.

11.     ¼ lb.   H costs _____ as much as ¼ lb. G.
12.     1 lb.   D   "    _____    "    1 lb. G.
13.     1 peck  F   "    _____    "    1 lb. H.

14.       2 lbs. M "     ................       "       1 lb. L.
15.       1 lb. L "     ................       "       1 lb. M.

*Write the numbers and signs in each line below in the
proper order, so that they make a true equation as shown
in the three sample lines. Use the bottom of the page to
figure on if you need to.*

$$3\ 3\ 6 = +  \qquad\qquad 3 + 3 = 6$$

Sample lines $\begin{cases}4\ 7\ 8\ 20 = + \times \qquad\qquad 7 \times 4 = 20 + 8 \\ 2\ 3\ 3\ 7\ 18 = + - \times (\ ) \qquad 7 + 2 = 18 - (3 \times 3)\end{cases}$

16.       2   2   3   5   15   =   —   —   ×
17.       1   1   4   4   16   =   —   —   ×   ()
18.       2   5   6   7   10   =   +   +   —
19.       1   4   8   15   20   =   +   —   —

20. Counting that 25 dozen sheets of paper are worth ten
    cents, how many sheets of paper are worth a fifth
    of a cent?

*Directions and samples the same as on page 161.*

| | | |
|---|---|---|
| tion | 1 play.....2 deed.....3 mention.....4 opinion.....5 crime | ............ |
| varice | 1 ordinary.....2 various.....3 empress.....4 frailty.....5 greed | ............ |
| earing | 1 a large ring.....2 behavior.....3 cub.....4 commendation.....5 destination | ............ |
| lusion | 1 aria.....2 illusion.....3 eulogy.....4 dream.....5 reference | ............ |
| ynasty | 1 davenport.....2 very unpleasant.....3 framework.....4 ruling family.....5 engine | ............ |
| abitat | 1 dweller.....2 bodice.....3 prodigality.....4 habit.....5 home | ............ |
| lversity | 1 ill fortune.....2 dialogue.....3 advertisement.....4 dislike.....5 distemper | ............ |
| price | 1 value.....2 a star.....3 grimace.....4 whim.....5 inducement | ............ |
| nominious | 1 seductive.....2 not guilty.....3 incontestable.....4 ignorant.....5 shameful | ............ |
| astity | 1 dissension.....2 pursuit.....3 eminence.....4 purity.....5 punishment | ............ |

*In each set of sentences, check the two which mean most
nearly the same as the sentence printed in heavy type.*

**31. What a man has, so much is he sure of.**
    ................There's many a slip 'twixt the cup and the lip.
    ................He who hesitates is lost.
    ................Look before you leap.
    ................A bird in the hand is worth two in the bush.

**32. Tho the knowledge they (the ancients) have left
    us be worth our study, yet they exhausted not
    all its treasures; they left a great deal for the
    industry and sagacity of after ages.—(Locke.)**
    ................Worth is wholly dependent on long use.
    ................Build the present on a knowledge of the past.

...............Do not neglect the present in admiration of the past.

...............There is nothing new under the sun.

33. **Cowards die many times before their death.—** (Shakespeare.)

...............Fortune favors the brave.

...............Discretion is the better part of valor.

...............The valiant never taste of death but once.

...............They suffer more who fear than they who die.

34. **Some books are to be tasted, others to be swallowed, and some few to be chewed and digested.** —(Bacon.)

...............Reading is profitable to every one.

...............One should read only parts of some books, while others should be carefully studied.

...............Only a few books repay one for painstaking effort.

...............People's tastes differ in books.

35. **Write it on your heart that every day is the best day of the year.**—(Emerson.)

...............There is no time like the present.

...............Never do today what you can put off until tomorrow.

...............Anticipation is better than realization.

...............A common delusion is that the present hour is not the critical, decisive hour.

36. **Our virtues disappear when put in competition with our interests.**—(La Rochefoucauld.)

...............A dog with a bone knows no friend.

...............My teeth are nearer than my kindred.

...............Virtue is its own reward.

...............A good friend is my nearest relation.

37. **If men wish to be held in esteem, they must associate with those only who are estimable.**—(La Bruyere.)

...............What a man does shows what he is.

...............You cannot always judge a man by his surroundings.

...............He who comes from the kitchen smells of its smoke.

...............If you always live with those who are lame, you will yourself learn to limp.

38. **We too often forget that not only is there a soul of goodness in things evil, but very generally also a soul of truth in things erroneous.**—(Spencer.)

...............Falsity frequently has a nucleus of reality.

...............Beliefs that are shown to be untrue may, nevertheless, be based on some element of truth.

...............Benevolence sometimes has evil consequences.

...............Evil is commonly due to error.

39. **They build too low who build beneath the stars.**

...............Not failure, but low aim is crime.

...............Hitch your wagon to a star.

...............He that strives to touch a star often stumbles at a straw.

...............Wouldst thou reach stars because they shine on thee?

*The paragraph for task 40 is "Every Home Needs a Garden," on page 165.*

40. Copy the four words which most fully state the purpose of the X. Y. Z. magazine.

### THE CONSTRUCTION OF COMPOSITE TASKS

With the knowledge gained in the course of our investigations, we could now construct composite tasks for use in measuring altitude or intellect which would be much superior to these. But these will serve reasonably well.

If we had begun our work with the knowledge which we now have, we should also have proceeded somewhat differently in their construction. The procedures which we did use will consequently be reported here only very briefly. We shall preface them by a description of a more efficient and economical method of construction of such composite tasks, which we recommend for the future.

It is as follows: Select the special abilities which together constitute the sort of intellect (call it intellect abc . . . n) for which composite tasks are to be constructed. Select a sufficient number of single tasks to provide one hundred for each special ability that is included at each twentieth of the total range of intellect abc . . . n from the lowest thousandth of human adults to the highest thousandth (or the proper segment of such a collection, if the tasks are to cover only a part of this range). In this selection you trust your own knowledge and judgment. Have twenty or more competent judges rank these tasks for intellectual difficulty for the group whose intellect abc . . . n you plan to measure by the tasks. Let them use as fine a scale as is convenient up to two hundred compartments, and require the use of approximately the same number of compartments by each judge (say, 150 to 200, or 75 to 100, or 60 to 75, or 45 to 60, or 32 to 45, or 25 to 32, or 18 to 25). Express the results of this consensus by simple summing. Arrange the single tasks in order of difficulty as estimated by the consensus, and in series representing each the same special ability (unless some better way is found to insure that persons to be tested understand the general nature of the tasks, and do not fail because of misunderstanding directions).

Test with a cross-section of these tasks from fifteen hundred to twenty-five hundred individuals, taking about two hundred from each of ten groups selected to represent different altitudes of intellect abc . . . n, such as, college graduates, pupils in grade 12, pupils in grade 9, . . . adults of mental age 4. Let the tasks used always begin at a point where 95% of the group of two hundred can succeed with at least four out of five of the tasks. Be sure that each individual has sufficient time. It will be found most convenient to have each individual in the group attempt all of the tasks used with that group.

Enter the score as c, x, or — (correct, wrong or omitted) for each individual in each group for each task. Find the percent of successes for each task in each group. Make up composites containing 2 tasks of a, 2 tasks of b, 2 tasks of c . . . 2 tasks of n, putting in one such composite tasks most nearly alike in difficulty. Call such a composite a 2n-composite. Find the percent of successes for each 2n-composite in each group which was tested by all its tasks. Plot the successes and failures[3] in each 2n-composite in at least one group[4] against the total score (number of tasks correct), and compute the overlapping of the failures past the median of the successes in that group. Compute the biserial r.

Combine the 2n-composites into 4n or 6n or 8n or 10n or 12n composites, using 2n composites which are neighbors in difficulty, and making each composite large enough so that its $r_{ti}$ will be at least .90 for a grade population or other group of approximately the variability of a grade population. How large composites will be needed can be judged from the size of $r_{ti}$ for the 2n composites, the self-correlations of the 2n composites, and the self-correlation of the measure of i. This last[5] should be approximately 1.00.

The resulting composites should be nearly or quite as satisfactory for measuring intellect abc . . . n as the 40-composites described in this chapter are for measuring In-

---

[3] A success in a 2n-composite is a case which has n or more right. A failure is a case which has fewer than n right.

[4] Use the group which most nearly approximates 50% of successes with the 2n-composites.

[5] Let $r_{ti_1}$ = the average r from the 2n composites.

" $r_{t_1}$ = the average self-correlation for a 2n composite.

" $r_{i_1}$ = the self-correlation of the measure of i.

" $r_{tx}$ = the average self-correlation of a composite necessary to produce an $r_{ti}$ of .90.

Then $.90 = \dfrac{r_{ti_1}}{\sqrt{r_{tx} \cdot r_{i_1}}}$

and n, the number of 2n composites necessary to produce a self-correlation of $r_{tx}$ can be produced from

$$\frac{(r_{ti_1})^2}{.81 r_{i_1}} = \frac{n r_{t_1}}{1 + (n-1) r_{t_1}}$$

tellect CAVD. The $r_{ti}$ for any one of them should be very close to 1.00 for all adults, or for any group of the same chronological age. All the tasks in any one of them will be enough alike in difficulty to seem neither much too easy nor much too hard to those for whom the composite as a whole is suitable.

The same procedure may be followed in constructing levels for any ability which has what we have termed "altitude," that is, which has to master tasks varying in difficulty. The difficulty may be in words that are harder to spell, that is, require a higher altitude of spelling ability for success; or in temptations to dishonesty that are harder to resist, that is, require a higher altitude of honesty to pass; or in hundreds of other sorts of tasks. But wherever the concepts of difficulty and altitude are applicable, this method of constructing measuring instruments is applicable.

At the outset of our studies, we lacked the knowledge of how often and how far a consensus of expert judges could be trusted in its estimates of intellectual difficulty, and the knowledge of how many single elements are needed to give a reliable measure of intellectual difficulty, and the knowledge of the essential impossibility of measuring the intellectual difficulty of any single small task. So we did not proceed in the way outlined above, but began with single small tasks, estimated their difficulty by the percent of various groups which succeeded with each, combined these into composites by special abilities, that is, into sets of ten or twenty completions of approximately equal difficulty; sets of ten or twenty arithmetical problems of approximately equal difficulty, and so on. The 40 element composites were made by putting together a 10 completion composite, a 10 arithmetic composite, a 10 word knowledge composite, and a 10 sentence-comprehension composite, which were, as composite tasks, as nearly equal in difficulty as could be found in our material.

This method does have the advantage that we have means of conveniently measuring the difficulty of tasks in these four abilities separately, and have made many such measurements of value (these are reported in Chapter VIII). The disadvantages are that our composite tasks do not represent as narrow segments or slices of difficulty as they might have done; are not spaced apart as evenly as they might have been, and required much more labor in their construction than would have been the case by the other method.

We shall describe briefly the derivation of the word-knowledge composites of ten single tasks as a sample to show the nature and validity of the selection and the extent of the experimentation involved. In the case of the others we shall simply present the evidence that the elements of each composite of ten (occasionally fewer), do belong fairly in that rather than in an easier or harder composite. We shall then even more briefly relate samples of the evidence by which these composites of ten were put into composites of forty. Finally we shall state the facts concerning the value of the composites of forty as intellectual tasks the difficulty of which we shall later measure.

### 10-Composites in Word Knowledge or V

Consider the tasks shown below. Each 'Level' or 10-Composite is, by our definition of difficulty, harder than the preceding for such a group as persons twelve to twenty years old or older who have lived in the United States five years or more, since a smaller percentage of them will get five or more of the ten elements right. The difficulty is 'intellectual' to the extent that within any sub-group of equal age the greater intellects will show higher percents correct than the smaller intellects in the case of any word.

It may seem far-fetched and forced and an unhappy consequence of our definitions to argue thus that it requires more intellect to know such words as cloistered, madrigal and ignominious, than to know such words as confess, advertise and combat. A dull person, it may be said, could learn the former as well as the latter; and it is a matter of range rather than level that he does not. There is much force in this criticism, and we chose the case of Word Knowledge as one illustration of the measurement of difficulty, in order to state the answer to the criticism.

Word Knowledge is representative of many tasks of an informational character where many of the harder tasks might have been in the repertory of the dull so far as the essential difficulty of mastering them is concerned, but simply are not as a matter of observed fact. They are not there because the greater intellect can learn more per unit of time and has learned more at equal age; range is positively correlated with level. Also there is, for any locality and epoch, a certain rough order of acquisition, whereby people usually do not progress to learn certain things until they have learned certain other things. The former are then 'harder' by our definition although, if customs had been reversed, they might have been easier.

*Look at the first word in line 1. Find the other word in the line which means the same or most nearly the same. Write its number on the line at the right side of the page. Do the same in lines 2, 3, 4, etc. Lines A, B, C, and D show the way to do it. Do all the lines you can. Write only one number for each line.*

A. beast      1 afraid.....2 words.....3 large.....4 animal.....5 bird

B. baby       1 cradle.....2 mother.....3 little child.....4 youth.....5 girl

C. raise      1 lift up.....2 drag.....3 sun.....4 bread.....5 deluge

D. blind      1 man.....2 cannot see.....3 game.....4 unhappy.....5 eyes

## Level V1

*Begin:*

1. await       1 pace.....2 slow.....3 wait for.....4 tired.....5 quit

2. beautify    1 make beautiful.....2 intrude.....3 exaggerate.....4 insure.....5 blessed

3. bug         1 insect.....2 a vehicle.....3 fiber.....4 abuse.....5 din

4. arrange     1 put in order.....2 hasten.....3 distance.....4 frighten.....5 charge

5. different   1 not the same.....2 quarrelsome.....3 better.....4 complete.....5 not here

6. cotton      1 cloth.....2 small bed.....3 hut.....4 flour.....5 herd

7. blacken     1 a fern.....2 interpose.....3 impel.....4 make black.....5 slack

8. ablaze      1 ostensible.....2 on fire.....3 slightly.....4 loaf about.....5 urbane

9. avenue      1 justice.....2 arrival.....3 street.....4 jury.....5 library

10. bench      1 tool.....2 pull ashore.....3 opinion.....4 seat.....5 pond

## LEVEL V2

1. confess     1 agree.....2 mend.....3 deny.....4 admit.....5 mingle     .............
2. backward     1 downwards.....2 after.....3 toward the rear.....4 defense.....5 arrears     .............
3. advertise     1 detain.....2 explore.....3 give notice of.....4 adverse.....5 newspaper     .............
4. combat     1 fight.....2 dismay.....3 club.....4 expedition.....5 comb     .............
5. blond     1 polite.....2 dishonest.....3 dauntless.....4 coy.....5 fair     .............
6. broaden     1 efface.....2 make level.....3 elapse.....4 embroider.....5 widen     .............
7. chubby     1 indolent.....2 obstinate.....3 irritable.....4 plump.....5 muscular     .............
8. concern     1 see clearly.....2 engage.....3 furnish.....4 disturb.....5 have to do with     .............
9. cargo     1 load.....2 small boat.....3 hem.....4 draught.....5 vehicle     .............
0. clutch     1 exploit.....2 nest.....3 flit.....4 grasp.....5 cane     .............

## LEVEL V3

1. awe     1 lamb.....2 fear.....3 tool.....4 mound.....5 opera     .............
2. aged     1 years.....2 active.....3 old.....4 merciful.....5 punctual     .............
3. arrive     1 answer.....2 rival.....3 enter.....4 force.....5 come     .............
4. blunt     1 dull.....2 drowsy.....3 deaf.....4 doubtful.....5 ugly     .............
5. accustom     1 disappoint.....2 customary.....3 encounter.....4 get used.....5 business     .............
6. bade     1 gaze.....2 a tool.....3 fetched.....4 wait.....5 ordered     .............
7. bog     1 ebb.....2 disorder.....3 swamp.....4 field.....5 difficulty     .............
8. cascade     1 hat.....2 waterfall.....3 firmament.....4 disaster.....5 box     .............
9. bray     1 cry of an ass.....2 bowl.....3 cry of an ox.....4 frustrate.....5 raven's cry     .............
0. disembark     1 unearth.....2 go ashore.....3 dislodge.....4 disparage.....5 strip     .............

## LEVEL V4

1. conspire     1 plot.....2 breathe.....3 rely.....4 die.....5 outrun     .............
2. check     1 error.....2 stop.....3 flash.....4 rude.....5 haste     .............
3. cherish     1 dedicate.....2 happy.....3 covet.....4 hold dear.....5 marry     .............
4. chirrup     1 aspen.....2 joyful.....3 capsize.....4 chirp.....5 incite     .............
5. accessible     1 indefatigable.....2 successful.....3 limpid.....4 easy to reach.....5 liable     .............
6. dingy     1 afraid.....2 hostelry.....3 small bell.....4 midget.....5 dirty     .............
7. edible     1 auspicious.....2 eligible.....3 fit to eat.....4 sagacious.....5 able to speak     .............
8. confound     1 discovered.....2 fulfill.....3 establish.....4 mix up.....5 expire     .............
9. concur     1 agree.....2 race.....3 mongrel.....4 pounce.....5 ramble     .............
0. contact     1 tactful.....2 hate.....3 injunction.....4 touch.....5 oversight     .............

## LEVEL V5

1. downcast     1 thrown down.....2 neutral.....3 judicious.....4 sad.....5 broken     .............
2. pact     1 puissance.....2 remonstrance.....3 agreement.....4 skillet.....5 pressure     .............
3. audible     1 festive.....2 easy.....3 audit.....4 heard.....5 downy     .............
4. solicitor     1 lawyer.....2 chieftain.....3 watchman.....4 maggot.....5 constable     .............
5. beguile     1 entreat.....2 delight.....3 dispense.....4 deceive.....5 foster     .............
6. dominate     1 abide.....2 goad.....3 threaten.....4 control.....5 dissuade     .............
7. average     1 level.....2 count.....3 evident.....4 ordinary.....5 distinct     .............
8. behave     1 act.....2 own.....3 keep still.....4 enable.....5 entitle     .............
9. comely     1 ignoble.....2 handsome.....3 disagreeable.....4 enter.....5 in time     .............
0. cycle     1 scythe.....2 cyclone.....3 circle.....4 ode.....5 junction     .............

## LEVEL V6

51. action    1 play.....2 deed.....3 mention.....4 opinion.....5 crime
52. avarice   1 ordinary.....2 various.....3 empress.....4 frailty.....5 greed
53. bearing   1 a large ring.....2 behavior.....3 cub.....4 commendation.....5 destination
54. allusion  1 aria.....2 illusion.....3 eulogy.....4 dream.....5 reference
55. dynasty   1 davenport.....2 very unpleasant.....3 framework.....4 ruling family.....
              5 engine
56. habitat   1 dweller.....2 bodice.....3 prodigality.....4 habit.....5 home
57. adversity 1 ill fortune.....2 dialogue.....3 advertisement.....4 dislike.....5 distemper
58. caprice   1 value.....2 a star.....3 grimace.....4 whim.....5 inducement
59. ignominious 1 seductive.....2 not guilty.....3 incontestable.....4 ignorant.....5 shameful
60. chastity  1 dissension.....2 pursuit.....3 eminence.....4 purity.....5 punishment

## LEVEL V7

61. gainsay    1 persuade.....2 beshrew.....3 deny.....4 profit.....5 imprint
62. eclogue    1 obituary.....2 a poem.....3 carousal.....4 epigram.....5 portrait
63. cloistered 1 miniature.....2 bunched.....3 arched.....4 malady.....5 secluded
64. reciprocal 1 saturnine.....2 mutual.....3 receptive.....4 morose.....5 careless
65. accolade   1 salutation.....2 anchovy.....3 procession.....4 bivouac.....5 acolyte
66. benighted  1 fraudulent.....2 weary.....3 insuperable.....4 ignorant.....5 venal
67. madrigal   1 song.....2 mountebank.....3 lunatic.....4 ribald.....5 sycophant
68. pinnace    1 a boat.....2 doublet.....3 pinnacle.....4 hold fast.....5 forfeiture
69. broach     1 dodge.....2 clasp.....3 open.....4 top.....5 edify
70. nectarine  1 bouillon.....2 a fruit.....3 a jewel.....4 a drink.....5 diurnal

Intellectual tasks range in this respect between two extremes. At one extreme the tasks are, in and of themselves, almost or quite impossible for the dull person regardless of which things the world tries to teach him. At the other the tasks are such as he can master nearly or quite as easily as he can master any intellectual tasks, the question being rather how many a dull person can master at a given age or with a given set of opportunities. For example, two of our very hard word tasks are:

reciprocal    saturnine.............mutual.............receptive.............
        morose.............careless
nectarine     bouillon.............a fruit.............a jewel.............a
        drink.............diurnal

A person twenty years old with a mental age of four not only would not know the meaning of *reciprocal*, but also probably never could be taught it. The idea involves thinking of things by aspects and in relationships in a way that is probably beyond his degree of intellect. He would not, save in rare instances, know *nectarine*; but with proper training he could know *nectarine* instead of some word, say *apple,* which he does know.

Theoretically it is best to measure level or "altitude" of intellect by tasks that lie toward the former extreme; and for practical purposes also, we may, in general, expect better results per hour of time spent from using such. They are likely to involve more of intellect, and to be less adulterated by other influences than intellect, and to be more representative of level and less of width or range.[6] However, the standard tests used for measuring intelligence contain tasks that range far toward the other extreme, and it is obviously desirable to measure the difficulty of these tasks and ascertain how much of it is due to intellect pure and simple, and how much of it is due to other factors.

Word Knowledge is a specially suitable case for study, because it has been approved by Terman as one of the very best single measures of intellect, and is involved to some degree in many of our better tests, such as oral and printed directions, paragraph reading or comprehension, sentence completion, opposites, and other tests of relations presented in words.

We began with four hundred words chosen originally to make an instrument for measuring word knowledge without regard to the merits or demerits of any one of them as a measure of intellect.

The selection amongst these was made solely on grounds of the percentages right in certain groups, the end sought being to have for any one level word-tasks which were approximately equally hard in the sense of being done correctly by approximately equal percents of the group; and

---

[6] These matters will be treated in connection with new experimental data, to be presented in Chapter XV. We shall there see that the theoretical and practical advantages are much less than has been supposed.

to have, at the next higher level, words which were done by fewer of the group.

The procedure was as follows: 400 words, ranging from very common words to words outside the first twenty thousand as listed in the Thorndike Teachers Word Book, were used in the case of 278 pupils in grade nine. On the basis of the percents correct, 110 of the tasks were chosen,

| | | | | | |
|---|---|---|---|---|---|
| 10 done correctly by | 276 or 277 | or | 99.3 to 99.6% | of the pupils |
| 10 " " | " 271 to 273 | or | 97.1 to 97.8% | " " " |
| 15 " " | " 257 to 261 | or | 92.4 to 93.9% | " " " |
| 15 " " | " 228 to 236 | or | 82.1 to 84.9% | " " " |
| 15 " " | " 185 to 194 | or | 66.6 to 69.8% | " " " |
| 15 " " | " 134 to 143 | or | 48.2 to 51.5% | " " " |
| 15 " " | " 79 to 90 | or | 28.4 to 32.4% | " " " |
| 15 " " | " 37 to 51 | or | 13.3 to 18.3% | " " " |

These 110 tasks were experimented with in the case of 430 pupils in grades 11 or 12, 500 pupils in grades 9 or 10, 250 pupils in grade $8\frac{1}{2}$, and 514 pupils in grade 6, and smaller groups of college students.

From them were chosen the seven 'Levels' of ten tasks each shown above. Levels 1 and 2 were constructed chiefly on the basis of the results with the 514 pupils of grade 6. Levels 3, 4, and 5 were constructed chiefly on the basis of the results with pupils of grades 9 to 12. Levels 6 and 7 were constructed chiefly on the basis of the results with pupils in grades 11, 12, 13, and 17. The tasks within any one level vary in difficulty somewhat widely and it is possible that results from as many thousands as we have hundreds might show some tasks in adjacent levels which actually should be transposed.

Greater equality within and distinctness between levels could have been attained by reducing the number from ten to eight or fewer, but this did not, on the whole, seem desirable. The order of difficulty of these tasks varies so much from group to group, and so enormously from one individual to another that, at levels where a person gets from 20% to 80% right, the percent which an individual has correct from one of our sets of ten is probably a more re-

liable measure of the percent which he would have correct
from a hundred tasks each of exactly the same difficulty as
the median task of the ten than is the percent which he
would have correct of the middle eight of the ten. Difficulty is taken in the above to be difficulty for the sort of
persons who get about half right at the level in question.

The essential facts concerning the percentages correct
for each of the 110 tasks are shown in Table 28.

TABLE 28

PERCENTS CORRECT FOR EACH SINGLE WORD OF SEVEN 10-WORD COMPOSITE
TASKS IN EACH OF VARIOUS GROUPS OF INDIVIDUALS

| | Grade<br>City<br>Number of<br>Individuals | 6a<br>N.Y.<br><br>514 | 8½<br>N.Y.<br><br>250 | 9<br>Mix.<br><br>278 | 9 + 10<br>K<br><br>500 | 11 + 12<br>K<br><br>430 | 12<br>K₁<br><br>200 | 12<br>K₂<br><br>200 |
|---|---|---|---|---|---|---|---|---|
| 1 | await | 94.9 | 90.0 | 99.6 | 92.8 | 97.9 | 95.5 | 96.5 |
| 3 | beautify | 94.3 | 93.2 | 99.3 | 94.6 | 94.2 | 97.5 | 94.0 |
| 6 | bug | 94.6 | 94.4 | 99.6 | 97.8 | 99.5 | 99.5 | 99.0 |
| 7 | arrange | 96.0 | 95.6 | 99.3 | 97.2 | 99.3 | 98.5 | 98.5 |
| 9 | different | 94.5 | 93.0 | 99.3 | 97.4 | 100.0 | 99.5 | 96.5 |
| 10 | cotton | 93.4 | 93.2 | 99.6 | 96.4 | 98.8 | 98.0 | 96.5 |
| 12 | blacken | 95.2 | 94.4 | 97.5 | 98.0 | 99.3 | 98.5 | 98.0 |
| 13 | ablaze | 89.9 | 95.6 | 97.8 | 94.6 | 99.3 | 99.0 | 97.0 |
| 18 | avenue | 94.6 | 93.2 | 97.8 | 98.0 | 99.5 | 98.5 | 98.5 |
| 21 | bench | 92.0 | 90.8 | 93.5 | 92.2 | 96.3 | 92.0 | 95.5 |
| 22 | confess | 62.4 | 86.0 | 93.9 | 92.2 | 96.7 | 99.0 | 98.0 |
| 25 | backward | 70.9 | 88.4 | 92.4 | 87.6 | 90.5 | 95.0 | 94.5 |
| 26 | advertise | 69.0 | 82.0 | 93.1 | 79.6 | 88.8 | 89.0 | 89.0 |
| 28 | combat | 59.6 | 88.4 | 92.4 | 89.2 | 97.4 | 99.0 | 99.0 |
| 30 | blond | 62.4 | 63.2 | 92.8 | 87.2 | 96.0 | 97.5 | 98.0 |
| 31 | broaden | 62.9 | 83.2 | 93.1 | 94.6 | 99.1 | 97.5 | 98.0 |
| 32 | chubby | 64.6 | 78.8 | 93.5 | 92.4 | 95.8 | 97.5 | 98.5 |
| 33 | concern | 65.1 | 74.0 | 93.5 | 87.6 | 94.7 | 97.0 | 95.5 |
| 34 | cargo | 67.1 | 89.2 | 93.9 | 84.0 | 89.1 | 92.5 | 95.5 |
| 35 | clutch | 60.2 | 80.4 | 92.4 | 89.8 | 94.0 | 97.5 | 97.5 |
| 36 | awe | 29.4 | 62.8 | 82.4 | 69.0 | 83.5 | 89.0 | 86.0 |
| 37 | aged | 53.8 | 69.6 | 83.5 | 73.8 | 85.8 | 88.5 | 90.0 |
| 39 | arrive | 43.0 | 68.8 | 83.8 | 63.8 | 68.8 | 73.5 | 74.5 |
| 40 | blunt | 41.0 | 66.8 | 84.5 | 85.8 | 92.3 | 96.5 | 94.0 |
| 41 | accustom | 45.6 | 62.4 | 82.4 | 52.0 | 68.6 | 70.0 | 68.0 |
| 42 | bade | 45.1 | * | 84.9 | 72.6 | 82.8 | 84.5 | 83.5 |
| 43 | bog | 40.2 | 56.8 | 84.2 | 66.6 | 79.3 | 87.5 | 88.0 |
| 44 | cascade | 39.9 | 56.8 | 82.1 | 65.6 | 75.3 | 87.5 | 92.5 |

* Omitted because of a misprint in test.

| | Grade | 6a | 8½ | 9 | 9 + 10 | 11 + 12 | 12 | 12 |
|---|---|---|---|---|---|---|---|---|
| | City | N. Y. | N. Y. | Mix. | K | K | K₁ | K₂ |
| | Number of Individuals | 514 | 250 | 278 | 500 | 430 | 200 | 200 |
| 46 | bray | 54.7 | 62.0 | 84.2 | 79.4 | 85.8 | 93.0 | 95.5 |
| 50 | disembark | 50.4 | 66.0 | 82.4 | 65.4 | 81.4 | 89.5 | 95.0 |
| 51 | conspire | 29.6 | 70.8 | 69.1 | 61.0 | 85.8 | 94.5 | 93.0 |
| 54 | check | 28.0 | 67.6 | 69.8 | 50.6 | 71.4 | 80.5 | 77.0 |
| 56 | cherish | 22.9 | 40.4 | 68.4 | 48.4 | 70.5 | 72.0 | 79.0 |
| 57 | chirrup | 39.4 | 56.8 | 68.0 | 66.0 | 70.2 | 73.0 | 71.0 |
| 58 | accessible | 29.8 | 58.8 | 68.4 | 54.8 | 82.3 | 94.0 | 94.0 |
| 59 | dingy | 27.9 | 53.6 | 66.6 | 71.0 | 87.2 | 93.5 | 92.0 |
| 61 | edible | 30.2 | 42.4 | 69.1 | 57.2 | 73.0 | 91.5 | 87.0 |
| 62 | confound | 27.1 | 47.2 | 68.4 | 43.2 | 56.0 | 52.5 | 52.5 |
| 63 | concur | 40.8 | 56.4 | 68.0 | 61.6 | 79.3 | 83.5 | 80.0 |
| 64 | contact | 21.1 | 54.0 | 66.6 | 57.2 | 81.9 | 85.0 | 88.5 |
| 66 | downcast | 21.3 | 44.0 | 51.5 | 42.4 | 61.4 | 64.0 | 61.0 |
| 67 | pact | 19.2 | 38.8 | 49.3 | 29.2 | 63.7 | 77.5 | 77.0 |
| 69 | audible | 5.0 | 52.8 | 49.3 | 38.8 | 60.7 | 83.0 | 80.5 |
| 70 | solicitor | 45.0 | 57.2 | 49.3 | 39.8 | 47.0 | 71.0 | 68.5 |
| 71 | beguile | | 45.6 | 48.6 | 44.4 | 59.1 | 47.5 | 51.0 |
| 73 | dominate | | 42.0 | 49.3 | 42.2 | 70.7 | 79.0 | 82.5 |
| 75 | average | | 26.8 | 48.2 | 52.1 | 61.6 | 72.5 | 67.5 |
| 78 | behave | | 35.6 | 48.2 | 39.8 | 43.0 | 70.0 | 64.5 |
| 79 | comely | | 45.2 | 48.6 | 39.0 | 42.8 | 62.5 | 64.5 |
| 94 | cycle | | 40.4 | 31.7 | 37.6 | 50.7 | 64.5 | 67.0 |
| 81 | action | | 24.0 | 29.5 | 23.4 | 33.3 | 46.5 | 42.0 |
| 84 | avarice | | 31.6 | 29.2 | 31.0 | 42.3 | 60.5 | 58.5 |
| 86 | bearing | | 34.8 | 32.4 | 29.0 | 34.9 | 54.0 | 43.5 |
| 87 | allusion | | 17.2 | 31.7 | 22.8 | 32.1 | 43.0 | 43.0 |
| 90 | dynasty | | 22.8 | 32.1 | 23.8 | 56.5 | 70.5 | 77.5 |
| 91 | habitat | | 15.6 | 32.4 | 26.0 | 44.9 | 54.0 | 49.5 |
| 92 | adversity | | 25.2 | 28.8 | 22.6 | 41.6 | 67.5 | 67.5 |
| 93 | caprice | | 22.0 | 29.2 | 21.2 | 40.5 | 55.0 | 61.5 |
| 105 | ignominious | | 17.2 | 17.6 | 17.6 | 30.7 | 41.5 | 42.0 |
| 107 | chastity | | 26.0 | 16.9 | 25.2 | 38.4 | 64.0 | 64.0 |
| 88 | gainsay | | 22.0 | 32.1 | 18.8 | 24.9 | 30.0 | 37.5 |
| 89 | eclogue | | 40.4 | 30.9 | 23.8 | 23.3 | 33.0 | 35.0 |
| 97 | cloistered | | 12.0 | * | 10.8 | 14.2 | 31.0 | 24.0 |
| 98 | reciprocal | | 10.0 | 13.3 | 11.0 | 20.0 | 26.0 | 25.5 |
| 99 | accolade | | 16.0 | 13.3 | 11.8 | 12.3 | 15.0 | 17.0 |
| 100 | benighted | | 11.2 | 14.7 | 7.5 | 13.3 | 16.0 | 17.0 |
| 102 | madrigal | | 22.4 | 17.6 | 8.2 | 11.4 | 21.0 | 28.0 |
| 104 | pinnace | | 15.6 | 13.3 | 8.4 | 10.7 | 14.5 | 13.5 |
| 106 | broach | | 16.4 | 18.3 | 14.6 | 27.4 | 39.0 | 34.5 |
| 110 | nectarine | | 5.6 | 18.3 | 6.8 | 14.9 | 13.5 | 12.0 |

* Omitted because of a misprint in test.

Ninety tasks were chosen to represent harder words than level 7, and were used with one hundred college graduates. From these ninety, four composites of ten each were chosen to be most alike in difficulty within a ten and most widely apart between tens. These four sets of ten were used with 240 college graduates who were also tested with levels 6 and 7. The results are shown in Table 29. We thus obtain level 8 of about the same difficulty as 7, and levels 9, 10, and 11 progressively harder. These levels from 1 to 11 are competent to measure word knowledge from below the level of the average ten-year-old to far above the level of the average college graduate.

Composites 1a, 2a, 3a, 4a, 5a, 6a, and 7a, of approximately the same difficulty as 1, 2, 3, 4, 5, 6, and 7, were constructed by testing many pupils in grades 6, $8\frac{1}{2}$, 9, 10, 11, 12, and 100 college graduates with composites 1 to 7 and also with 240 new tasks, obtaining the percents succeeding with each of the 310 and selecting sets of ten from the 240 to match sets 1, 2, 3, 4, 5, 6, and 7, respectively. The facts are shown in Tables 30 and 31.

At the low end of the ability, the four sets A, B, C, and D shown below were constructed by selection from about twice as many on the basis of trials with 180 individuals 16 years old or older of mental age from 2 to 4. The facts are shown in Table 32.

Composites of ten intermediate between D and I were constructed on the basis of the ratings of about 160 single tasks by the consensus of twenty experts, and trials of these with a hundred adults of mental age 6.0 to 7.0, with 50 feeble-minded individuals in the same educational "class" in an institution for the feeble-minded, with 101 pupils fifteen years old or over in special classes in a large city, and with 162 pupils in grade 4B (second half). The facts concerning these word-knowledge tasks appear in Table 33.

These composites intermediate in difficulty between V D and V I are imperfect in three respects. The difficulty of each single task element is not determined from enough cases. The oral picture selection tests are not equated accurately enough with the oral word-selection tests. The difficulty of written word-selection tests has not been equated accurately against the difficulty of the same sort of test given orally.

In general, we have devoted most of our work in the preparation of composite tasks to making effective instruments to measure altitude of Intellect CAVD from an altitude corresponding roughly to a mental age of ten up to very high levels. Our work with composites at lower levels has been aimed first at demonstrating that Intellect CAVD can be measured at the altitude of low imbecility, and that we can, subject to certain limitations, locate an absolute zero point for intellect and so, by later studies which will bridge the interval between imbecility and our level I, attach approximate absolute values to all the levels. We have not been able to give adequate attention to the construction of CAVD composites to bridge this interval and our composites between D and I are not so well made as the easier and harder ones.

## LEVEL 1A

*Begin:*

1. boyhood    1 childhood.....2 mischief.....3 hardihood.....4 cap.....5 cherub
2. churchman    1 janitor.....2 member of a church.....3 elector.....4 disciple.....5 steeplejack
3. boyish    1 naughty.....2 male.....3 impudent.....4 like a boy.....5 informal
4. cocoa    1 chocolate.....2 a drug.....3 chrysalis.....4 biscuit.....5 trivial
5. bottomless    1 artless.....2 deeper.....3 unreasonable.....4 ultimate.....5 without bottom
6. assistant    1 orator.....2 perseverant.....3 progressive.....4 at hand.....5 helper
7. chauffeur    1 carter.....2 stove.....3 hot water.....4 coachman.....5 automobile driver
8. dine    1 sprawl.....2 visit.....3 make a noise.....4 have dinner.....5 bespeak
9. blouse    1 whisk.....2 storm.....3 below.....4 pouch.....5 waist
10. cafe    1 chaperon.....2 theater.....3 restaurant.....4 flask.....5 festivity

## LEVEL 2A

11. dandruff    1 ruffle.....2 scamp.....3 bald.....4 dastard.....5 disease of the scalp
12. abashed    1 ashamed.....2 overpowered.....3 overlooked.....4 bruised.....5 lowered
13. bethink    1 dream.....2 molest.....3 forget.....4 ascertain.....5 call to mind
14. comical    1 funny.....2 coming.....3 placid.....4 typical.....5 alert
15. apology    1 excuse.....2 verdict.....3 tribulation.....4 conclusion.....5 disease
16. clung    1 held fast.....2 part of a wheel.....3 stung.....4 part.....5 nestled
17. amidst    1 among.....2 drenched.....3 middle.....4 lost.....5 partly

baste            1 sew.....2 list.....3 calico.....4 wallow.....5 dump                                    .....18
causeless        1 eventual.....2 without reason.....3 ineffective.....4 highway.....5 faultless           .....19
aster            1 flower.....2 bitter.....3 matin.....4 star.....5 guilder                                .....20

## LEVEL 3A

ballot           1 song.....2 vote.....3 ammunition.....4 dance.....5 award                               .....21
rinse            1 scald.....2 wash.....3 smear.....4 wrench.....5 grin                                   .....22
barge            1 seaport.....2 knock.....3 tonnage.....4 expansive.....5 boat                           .....23
acquit           1 do.....2 free of blame.....3 leave.....4 aquatic.....5 pipe                            .....24
cambric          1 brittle.....2 linen.....3 moccasin.....4 leather.....5 crochet                         .....25
brawn            1 strength.....2 brood.....3 brine.....4 burnt.....5 bolster                             .....26
appreciation     1 forbearance.....2 accomplishment.....3 speech.....4 sympathetic
                   recognition..... 5 sermon                                                              .....27
alliance         1 league.....2 enchantment.....3 slander.....4 hypocrisy.....5 assembly                  .....28
deceiver         1 detective.....2 illusion.....3 spy.....4 cavalier.....5 cheat                          .....29
calculate        1 marvel.....2 administer.....3 plaster.....4 reckon.....5 convene                       .....30

## LEVEL 4A

childlike        1 innocent.....2 saucy.....3 foolish.....4 piteous.....5 affectionate                    .....31
betwixt          1 confused.....2 braided.....3 between.....4 bewitched.....5 pinched                      .....32
crafty           1 meager.....2 difficult.....3 adjacent.....4 sly.....5 artistic                         .....33
outstrip         1 subside.....2 outer edge.....3 outskirt.....4 satiate.....5 out-run                    .....34
available        1 hidden.....2 at hand.....3 economical.....4 lamentable.....5 useful                     .....35
certify          1 exhort.....2 ascertain.....3 boast.....4 fuse.....5 assure                             .....36
annihilate       1 dead.....2 crucify.....3 enamor.....4 nihilist.....5 destroy                           .....37
contentedly      1 fully.....2 heretofore.....3 without a stop.....4 cheerfully.....5 massy                .....38
carcass          1 mold.....2 body.....3 cargo.....4 rind.....5 hold of a ship                            .....39
console          1 alone.....2 qualify.....3 visit.....4 thin sole.....5 soothe                           .....40

## LEVEL 5A

amen             1 so be it.....2 hymn.....3 proverb.....4 farewell.....5 communion                       .....41
brawl            1 pouch.....2 roast.....3 hoot.....4 quarrel.....5 lie at length                         .....42
debase           1 degrade.....2 base.....3 chastise.....4 blaspheme.....5 unfounded                      .....43
adventurous      1 clamorous.....2 casual.....3 bold.....4 travel.....5 advancing                         .....44
adequate         1 capricious.....2 conscientious.....3 enough.....4 added.....5 water supply              .....45
amiable          1 tractable.....2 trusty.....3 passionate.....4 pleasing.....5 odious                    .....46
ally             1 league.....2 associate.....3 council.....4 factor.....5 navigator                      .....47
benefactor       1 patron.....2 churchman.....3 tourist.....4 sexton.....5 advantage                      .....48
bethought        1 perhaps.....2 credulous.....3 forget.....4 bewildered.....5 considered                 .....49
aperture         1 through.....2 precipice.....3 opening.....4 raiment.....5 opportunity                  .....50

## LEVEL 6A

ascribe          1 attribute.....2 pertain.....3 clerk.....4 write.....5 upbraid                          .....51
default          1 defeat.....2 blame.....3 failure.....4 libel.....5 displace                            .....52
apparition       1 ghost.....2 insurrection.....3 apparent.....4 farce.....5 apparel                      .....53
appliance        1 request.....2 adjustment.....3 conformity.....4 device.....5 pliant                    .....54
churlish         1 craven.....2 rude.....3 reckless.....4 contemptible.....5 envious                      .....55
sexton           1 cube.....2 janitor.....3 compass.....4 archbishop.....5 six singers                    .....56
buckler          1 keel.....2 servant.....3 stag.....4 shield.....5 scraper                               .....57
animosity        1 hatred.....2 animation.....3 disobedience.....4 diversity.....5 friendship              .....58
conflagration ? 1 carnival.....2 celebration.....3 decoration with flags.....4 contagion.....5 fire       .....59
confidential     1 respectable.....2 secure.....3 sensitive.....4 secret.....5 confident                 .....60

## Level 7a

| | | |
|---|---|---|
| 61 scrivener | 1 searcher.....2 forger.....3 chaplain.....4 clerk.....5 sceptic | .....61 |
| 62. beaker | 1 cup.....2 binnacle.....3 beak.....4 slanderer.....5 bottle | .....62 |
| 63. emanate | 1 populate.....2 free.....3 prominent.....4 rival.....5 come | .....63 |
| 64. landau | 1 pier.....2 coach.....3 postern.....4 gable.....5 headdress | .....64 |
| 65. amaranthine | 1 jubilant.....2 bitter.....3 maritime.....4 ungracious.....5 purple | .....65 |
| 66. athwart | 1 alongside.....2 above.....3 alert.....4 across.....5 thwarted | .....66 |
| 67. conscientious | 1 guilty.....2 cautious.....3 efficient.....4 good.....5 knowing | .....67 |
| 68. ingenuous | 1 ungenerous.....2 unselfish.....3 dull.....4 frank.....5 unthinking | .....68 |
| 69. betimes | 1 hereby.....2 sometimes.....3 meantime.....4 early.....5 now and then | .....69 |
| 70. lambrequin | 1 knapsack.....2 drapery.....3 raw wool.....4 matting.....5 chandelier | .....7 |

### TABLE 29

#### Permilles Correct in the Single Tasks of Word Knowledge

10—Composite Tasks 8, 9, 10 and 11

| | T.C. Grad. n = 100 | L. Grad. n = 240 | | T.C. Grad. n = 100 | L. Grad. n = 240 |
|---|---|---|---|---|---|
| **8** | | | **10** | | |
| 1. monomania | 550 | 392 | 1. shrievalty | 250 | 283 |
| 2. saturnalian | 520 | 375 | 2. sessile | 210 | 179 |
| 3. pristine | 510 | 421 | 3. teleological | 210 | 221 |
| 4. quaternion | 540 | 346 | 4. peccancy | 210 | 358 |
| 5. predatory | 520 | 571 | 5. cacophony | 240 | 413 |
| 6. persiflage | 500 | 521 | 6. pediment | 250 | 254 |
| 7. encomium | 480 | 600 | 7. licentiate | 190 | 154 |
| 8. abattoir | 480 | 613 | 8. ambulatory | 220 | 317 |
| 9. meticulous | 510 | 658 | 9. murrain | 230 | 133 |
| 10. largess | 500 | 429 | 10. cantilena | 230 | 288 |
| **9** | | | **11** | | |
| 1. radial | 400 | 408 | 1. saltatory | 190 | 121 |
| 2. sequestrate | 350 | 529 | 2. amerce | 110 | 154 |
| 3. tactility | 360 | 204 | 3. distrain | 130 | 458 |
| 4. apogee | 320 | 363 | 4. besom | 090 | 154 |
| 5. nugatory | 320 | 525 | 5. rhodolite | 090 | 138 |
| 6. sedulous | 350 | 363 | 6. rune | 130 | 112 |
| 7. umbel | 350 | 129 | 7. hermeneutic | 100 | 021 |
| 8. asseveration | 340 | 254 | 8. devolution | 070 | 046 |
| 9. abjure | 340 | 342 | 9. palindromic | 100 | 112 |
| 10. auricular | 320 | 321 | 10. carmagnole | 120 | 120 |

## TABLE 30.

PERMILLES CORRECT FOR EACH SINGLE WORD OF THE SEVEN 10-WORD COMPOSITE
TASKS 1A, 2A, 3A, 4A, 5A, 6A, 7A IN EACH OF VARIOUS
GROUPS OF INDIVIDUALS.

| | | 6b<br>n = 139 | 6c<br>n = 105 | 8½<br>250 | 9k<br>306 | 10k<br>311 | 11k<br>224 | 12k<br>195 |
|---|---|---|---|---|---|---|---|---|
| 1 | boyhood | 777 | 990 | 904 | 917 | 927 | 933 | 933 |
| 2 | churchman | 820 | 971 | 928 | 933 | 960 | 964 | 970 |
| 3 | boyish | 777 | 942 | 932 | 891 | 940 | 946 | 964 |
| 4 | cocoa | 805 | 990 | 848 | 911 | 921 | 937 | 949 |
| 5 | bottomless | 683 | 933 | 935 | 968 | 982 | 982 | 979 |
| 7 | assistant | 640 | 895 | 952 | 952 | 960 | 982 | 985 |
| 9 | chauffeur | 604 | 942 | 976 | 968 | 976 | 991 | 979 |
| 10 | dine | 626 | 933 | 952 | 952 | 972 | 996 | 990 |
| 13 | blouse | 604 | 914 | 956 | 968 | 966 | 996 | 990 |
| 15 | cafe | 546 | 933 | 932 | 981 | 976 | 991 | 990 |
| 11 | dandruff | 590 | 790 | 896 | 965 | 969 | 991 | 990 |
| 16 | abashed | 661 | 628 | 752 | 757 | 828 | 812 | 872 |
| 17 | bethink | 460 | 752 | 892 | 863 | 886 | 875 | 923 |
| 22 | comical | 554 | 809 | 952 | 964 | 985 | 996 | 995 |
| 23 | apology | 446 | 834 | 964 | 912 | 921 | 937 | 954 |
| 24 | clung | 496 | 866 | 928 | 967 | 966 | 991 | 970 |
| 31 | amidst | 446 | 781 | 856 | 843 | 892 | 914 | 923 |
| 32 | baste | 446 | 743 | 640 | 824 | 857 | 914 | 913 |
| 34 | causeless | 410 | 790 | 820 | 819 | 914 | 954 | 970 |
| 39 | aster | 417 | 657 | 532 | 889 | 950 | 946 | 659 |
| 33 | ballot | 424 | 514 | 756 | 771 | 824 | 825 | 816 |
| 35 | rinse | 388 | 581 | 676 | 637 | 683 | 749 | 852 |
| 42 | barge | 395 | 638 | 836 | 752 | 737 | 888 | 831 |
| 45 | acquit | 453 | 457 | 724 | 523 | 647 | 852 | 841 |
| 47 | cambric | 460 | 343 | 504 | 706 | 747 | 861 | 887 |
| 58 | brawn | 316 | 486 | 736 | 569 | 700 | 834 | 846 |
| 59 | appreciation | 374 | 571 | 708 | 676 | 786 | 847 | 821 |
| 61 | alliance | 244 | 447 | 728 | 667 | 728 | 830 | 826 |
| 64 | deceiver | 252 | 609 | 732 | 775 | 721 | 812 | 826 |
| 86 | calculate | 093 | 371 | 720 | 598 | 728 | 843 | 836 |
| 36 | childlike | 496 | 324 | 356 | 500 | 528 | 602 | 718 |
| 46 | betwixt | 230 | 343 | 464 | 572 | 631 | 772 | 785 |
| 52 | crafty | 273 | 457 | 752 | 542 | 583 | 669 | 657 |
| 60 | outstrip | 244 | 324 | 660 | 539 | 670 | 727 | 713 |
| 67 | available | 173 | 257 | 504 | 494 | 715 | 852 | 852 |

TABLE 30—*Continued.*

| | | 6b<br>n = 139 | 6c<br>n = 105 | 8½<br>520 | 9k<br>306 | 10k<br>311 | 11k<br>224 | 12k<br>195 |
|---|---|---|---|---|---|---|---|---|
| 68 | certify | 108 | 447 | 532 | 543 | 570 | 683 | 677 |
| 78 | annihilate | 201 | 171 | * | 507 | 667 | 825 | 841 |
| 80 | contentedly | 302 | 486 | 588 | 549 | 686 | 754 | 785 |
| 94 | carcass | 144 | 352 | 580 | 549 | 615 | 731 | 881 |
| 113 | console | 065 | 228 | 556 | 509 | 663 | 785 | 821 |
| 50 | amen | 237 | 466 | 564 | 425 | 480 | 629 | 559 |
| 54 | brawl | 266 | 305 | 568 | 350 | 441 | 598 | 636 |
| 79 | debase | 273 | 267 | 432 | 294 | 438 | 665 | 682 |
| 84 | adventurous | 122 | 257 | 432 | 399 | 486 | 500 | 584 |
| 89 | adequate | 187 | 114 | 336 | 363 | 425 | 598 | 657 |
| 93 | amiable | 209 | 238 | 448 | 363 | 460 | 624 | 667 |
| 100 | ally | 201 | 219 | 416 | 366 | 441 | 611 | 672 |
| 103 | benefactor | 173 | 314 | 384 | 355 | 409 | 558 | 652 |
| 108 | bethought | 137 | 152 | 520 | 359 | 502 | 549 | 616 |
| 109 | aperture | 093 | 133 | 416 | 342 | 460 | 566 | 616 |
| 63 | ascribe | 345 | 324 | 256 | 275 | 316 | 317 | 416 |
| 69 | default | 108 | 219 | 256 | 271 | 316 | 352 | 390 |
| 85 | apparition | 151 | 124 | 360 | 164 | 219 | 415 | 605 |
| 88 | appliance | 165 | 162 | 224 | 157 | 267 | 406 | 498 |
| 101 | churlish | 230 | 162 | 292 | 229 | 283 | 312 | 359 |
| 107 | sexton | 216 | 162 | 300 | 228 | 332 | 379 | 462 |
| 112 | buckler | 165 | 228 | 220 | 211 | 267 | 526 | 374 |
| 125 | animosity | 065 | 124 | 364 | 176 | 264 | 388 | 482 |
| 137 | conflagration | 022 | 048 | 260 | 160 | 293 | 459 | 451 |
| 138 | confidential | 124 | 057 | 216 | 121 | 216 | 357 | 457 |
| C 53 | scrivener | | | | 058 | 146 | 158 | 185 |
| C 73 | beaker | | | | 106 | 158 | 231 | 431 |
| C 76 | emanate | | | | 067 | 091 | 098 | 154 |
| C 79 | landau | | | | 080 | 101 | 133 | 190 |
| C 83 | amaranthine | | | | 102 | 126 | 150 | 159 |
| C 88 | athwart | | | | 067 | 101 | 197 | 113 |
| C 89 | conscientious | | | | 061 | 126 | 115 | 195 |
| C 90 | ingenuous | | | | 128 | 154 | 171 | 195 |
| C 93 | betimes | | | | 054 | 032 | 051 | 082 |
| C 95 | lambrequin | | | | 096 | 066 | 098 | 149 |

* Omitted because of misprint in test.

THE CONSTRUCTION OF 10-COMPOSITE TASKS IN SENTENCE COM-
PLETION, ARITHMETICAL PROBLEMS, AND THE UNDER-
STANDING OF SENTENCES AND PARAGRAPHS

The 10-composites for C, A, and D were constructed by
the process of trying many single tasks with various groups
and selecting tasks of similar difficulty, which has been described and illustrated in the case of V.  Only the main results will be presented here.  They are in the form of tables

TABLE 31.

PERMILLES OBTAINING FIVE OR MORE RIGHT OUT OF TEN IN THE VOCABULARY
COMPOSITES 1, 1A, 2, 2A, 3, 3A, ETC.

| | Grade | 5½ N. Y. | 8½ N. Y. | 9 K | 10 K | 11 K | 12 K |
|---|---|---|---|---|---|---|---|
| | n = | 148 | 250 | 1089 | 723 | 769 | 643 |
| V 1 | | 993 | 980 | 993 | 996 | 997 | 994 |
| V 1a | | 993 | 976 | 993 | 993 | 999 | 997 |
| V 2 | | 905 | 920 | 989 | 989 | 996 | 994 |
| V 2a | | 959 | 972 | 995 | 991 | 999 | 1000 |
| V 3 | | 615 | 740 | 913 | 924 | 967 | 975 |
| V 3a | | 601 | 864 | 914 | 929 | 977 | 987 |
| V 4 | | | 645 | 749 | 801 | 936 | 946 |
| V 4a | | | 618 | 764 | 839 | 931 | 962 |
| V 5 | | | 440 | 428 | 560 | 748 | 824 |
| V 5a | | | 448 | 473 | 604 | 801 | 846 |
| V 6 | | | 152 | 129 | 290 | 473 | 560 |
| V 6a | | | 236 | 183 | 299 | 480 | 593 |
| V 7 | | | 044 | 017 | 030 | 061 | 107 |
| V 7a | | | 060 | 017 | 031 | 104 | 137 |

giving the percent of successes for each single task in each
group.  The constitution of the group sometimes varies
within a table, because sometimes in a certain group some
tasks would be assigned to only a part of the group.  Where
this is the case, the fact is noted by printing the new $n$ in
the body of the table.  The $n$ at the top of a column applies
to all entries in that column unless a second $n$ appears in

the column. If a second $n$ appears in the column, it applies to all entries below it unless a third $n$ appears; and so on. Percents are strictly comparable only where they are for the same $n$.

The sentence-completion 10-composites are A, B, C, D, E, F, G, I, J, K, L, M, N, O, P, and Q. The main facts concerning these are shown in Tables 34, 35, and 36. We also

TABLE 32.

PERCENTS CORRECT IN THE SINGLE TASKS OF WORD KNOWLEDGE: COMPOSITE TASKS A, B, C AND D.  180 ADULT IMBECILES.

| | | $n = 100$ | $n = 80$ | | | $n = 100$ | $n = 80$ |
|---|---|---|---|---|---|---|---|
| A | 1 | 76 | 81 | C | 1 | 26 | 36 |
| | 2 | 71 | 79 | | 2 | 25 | 15 |
| | 3 | 74 | 75 | | 3 | 24 | 31 |
| | 4 | 76 | 80 | | 4 | 24 | 49 |
| | 5 | 76 | 89 | | 5 | 23 | 19 |
| | 6 | 73 | 85 | | 6 | 22 | 22½ |
| | 7 | 72 | 73 | | 7 | 21 | 30 |
| | 8 | 72 | 79 | | 8 | 20 | 24 |
| | 9 | 67 | 77½ | | 9 | 21 | 25 |
| | 10 | 67 | 76 | | 10 | 21 | 30 |
| B | 1 | 48 | 55 | D | 1 | 12 | 21 |
| | 2 | 49 | 52½ | | 2 | 15 | 9 |
| | 3 | 51 | 61 | | 3 | 11 | 9 |
| | 4 | 46 | 62½ | | 4 | 14 | 16 |
| | 5 | 44 | 42½ | | 5 | 15 | 12½ |
| | 6 | 47 | 54 | | 6 | 9 | 12½ |
| | 7 | 40 | 36 | | 7 | 14 | 17½ |
| | 8 | 43 | 50 | | 8 | 9 | 7½ |
| | 9 | 41 | 57½ | | 9 | 6 | 6 |
| | 10 | 39 | 56 | | 10 | 4 | 12½ |

have certain provisional completion 10-composites I–J and R which will be useful until better ones are constructed.

Some of these composites and also some of the arithmetic and directions composites to be presently described could probably be improved by transfers of some elements. We have not made these transfers, because the gain would not be great and the labor of recomputing the composite-

## TABLE 33.

PERCENTS CORRECT IN THE SINGLE TASKS OF WORD KNOWLEDGE E, F, G, AND H.

| | | | | n = 100 | n = 50 | n = 101 Spec. | n = 162 4B |
|---|---|---|---|---|---|---|---|
| V E | 1 | gasoline (picture selection) | | 59 | 100 | —.— | —.— |
| | 2 | crayon | " " | 51 | 64 | | |
| | 3 | tresses | " " | 55 | 20 | | |
| | 4 | refrigerator | " " | 48 | 70 | | |
| | 5 | plume | " " | 48 | 96 | | |
| | 6 | entrance | " " | 46 | 32 | | |
| | 7 | porridge | " " | 44 | 74 | | |
| | 8 | hide | " " | 42 | 76 | | |
| | 9 | drummer | " " | 35 | 68 | | |
| | 10 | ram | " " | 38 | 60 | | |
| V F | 1 | rock | (verbal selection) | 26 | 94 | 94.1 | 98.1 |
| | 2 | people | " " | 25 | 92 | 85.1 | 97.5 |
| | 3 | large | " " | 23 | 90 | 90.1 | 96.9 |
| | 4 | heaven | " " | 23 | 88 | 88.1 | 92.6 |
| | 5 | speak | " " | 22 | 88 | 84.2 | 95.7 |
| | 6 | mountain | " " | 22 | 92 | 96.0 | 95.1 |
| | 7 | dark | " " | 23 | 94 | 80.2 | 93.8 |
| | 8 | kind | " " | 21 | 94 | 77.2 | 96.9 |
| | 9 | quiet | " " | 20 | 80 | 77.2 | 90.1 |
| | 10 | short | " " | 20 | 90 | 79.2 | 93.2 |
| V G | 1 | good | " " | 20 | 70 | 69.3 | 87.7 |
| | 2 | still | " " | 16 | 70 | 68.3 | 95.1 |
| | 3 | warm | " " | 21 | 72 | 81.2 | 95.1 |
| | 4 | walk | " " | 17 | 72 | 69.3 | 95.1 |
| | 5 | behind | " " | 17 | 76 | 73.3 | 94.4 |
| | 6 | near | " " | 16 | 58 | 72.3 | 92.0 |
| | 7 | fast | " " | 21 | 74 | 71.3 | 95.7 |
| | 8 | once | " " | 12 | 62 | 80.2 | 98.1 |
| | 9 | sweet | " " | 12 | 58 | 71.3 | 90.1 |
| | 10 | bring | " " | 7 | 70 | 71.3 | 87.7 |
| V H | 1 | love | " " | 18 | 62 | 61.4 | 84.6 |
| | 2 | lift | " " | 6 | 58 | 61.4 | 83.3 |
| | 3 | great | " " | 8 | 70 | 63.4 | 91.4 |
| | 4 | nation | " " | 6 | 58 | 53.5 | 71.6 |
| | 5 | space | " " | 5 | 38 | 44.6 | 73.5 |
| | 6 | none | " " | 4 | 60 | 72.3 | 90.7 |
| | 7 | every | " " | 4 | 38 | 36.6 | 70.4 |
| | 8 | before | " " | 11 | 56 | 66.3 | 84.6 |
| | 9 | pair | " " | 0 | 48 | 47.5 | 74.1 |
| | 10 | today | " " | 7 | 38 | 49.5 | 75.3 |

task scores and correlations which have been obtained from these 10-composites would greatly outweigh the gain.

The arithmetical 10-composites were constructed in the same way by trial, selection, and retrial. It is difficult to secure large groups to take long experimental tests, and

TABLE 34.

PERCENTS SUCCEEDING WITH EACH SINGLE TASK OF VARIOUS 10-COMPOSITES IN TWO GROUPS OF ADULT IMBECILES.

| | | n = 100 | n = 80 | | | | n = 100 | n = 80 | | | | n = 100 | n = 80 |
|---|---|---|---|---|---|---|---|---|---|---|---|---|---|
| C A | 1 | 78 | 84 | A A | 1 | 67 | 64 | D A | 1 | 83 | 87½ |
| | 2 | 77 | 79 | | 2 | 53 | 57½ | | 2 | 85 | 84 |
| | 3 | 78 | 81 | | 3 | 75 | 73 | | 3 | 65 | 69 |
| | 4 | 82 | 81 | | 4 | 56 | 67½ | | 4 | 80 | 80 |
| | 5 | 68 | 72½ | | 5 | 67 | 65 | | 5 | 81 | 86 |
| | 6 | 59 | 71 | | 6 | 64 | 73 | | 6 | 85 | 84 |
| | 7 | 69 | 74 | | 7 | 67 | 72½ | | 7 | 72 | 70 |
| | 8 | 67 | 62½ | | 8 | 61 | 67½ | | 8 | 80 | 86 |
| | 9 | 63 | 66 | | 9 | 72 | 64 | | 9 | 73 | 75 |
| | 10 | 81 | 73 | | 10 | 60 | 71 | | 10 | 63 | 73 |
| C B | 1 | 46 | 56 | A B | 1 | 28 | 50 | D B | 1 | 59 | 65 |
| | 2 | 65 | 56 | | 2 | 55 | 46 | | 2 | 43 | 57½ |
| | 3 | 57 | 38 | | 3 | 49 | 42 | | 3 | 58 | 66 |
| | 4 | 56 | 55 | | 4 | 40 | 44 | | 4 | 47 | 50 |
| | 5 | 53 | 50 | | 5 | 40 | 54 | | 5 | 40 | 44 |
| | 6 | 50 | 45 | | 6 | 55 | 51 | | 6 | 43 | 75 |
| | 7 | 56 | 45 | | 7 | 42 | 42½ | | 7 | 49 | 44 |
| | 8 | 51 | 49 | | 8 | 27 | 49 | | 8 | 42 | 59 |
| | 9 | 48 | 56 | | 9 | 44 | 49 | | 9 | 40 | 74 |
| | 10 | 40 | 39 | | 10 | 57 | 40 | | 10 | | 47½ |
| C C | 1 | 26 | 26 | A C | 1 | 26 | 24 | D C | 1 | 35 | 34 |
| | 2 | 37 | 30 | | 2 | 20 | 24 | | 2 | 24 | 29 |
| | 3 | 34 | 35 | | 3 | 34 | 24 | | 3 | 27 | 36 |
| | 4 | 44 | 34 | | 4 | 23 | 29 | | 4 | 17 | 32½ |
| | 5 | 36 | 32½ | | 5 | 38 | 17 | | 5 | 23 | 19 |
| | 6 | 37 | 31 | | 6 | 9 | 20 | | 6 | 19 | 27½ |
| | 7 | 27 | 26 | | 7 | 16 | 30 | | 7 | 20 | 22½ |
| | 8 | 31 | 22½ | | 8 | 21 | 32 | | 8 | 30 | 35 |
| | 9 | 30 | 27½ | | 9 | 15 | 22 | | 9 | 20 | 24 |
| | 10 | 22 | 17½ | | 10 | 21 | 19 | | 10 | 22 | 25 |
| C D | 1 | 35 | | A D | 1 | 24 | 5 | D D | 1 | 16 | 26 |
| | 2 | 17 | 19 | | 2 | 18 | 16 | | 2 | 8 | 10 |
| | 3 | 12 | | | 3 | 11 | 10 | | 3 | 16 | 25 |
| | 4 | 19 | 15 | | 4 | 11 | 11 | | 4 | 10 | 16 |
| | 5 | 2 | | | 5 | 13 | 14 | | 5 | 16 | 24 |
| | 6 | 2 | 6 | | 6 | 23 | 11 | | 6 | 8 | 22½ |
| | 7 | 9 | 4 | | 7 | 22 | 14 | | 7 | 13 | 30 |
| | 8 | 1 | 2½ | | 8 | 12 | 12 | | 8 | 14 | 17½ |
| | 9 | 13 | 14 | | 9 | 21 | 10 | | 9 | 16 | 17½ |
| | 10 | 11 | 1 | | 10 | 17 | 5 | | 10 | 22 | 9 |

TABLE 35.

PERCENTS SUCCEEDING WITH EACH SINGLE TASK OF VARIOUS 10-COMPOSITES IN FOUR GROUPS: 100 ADULTS OF MENTAL AGE 6, 50 FEEBLE-MINDED OF CLASS 3 IN AN INSTITUTION, PUPILS IN SPECIAL CLASSES IN A LARGE CITY, AND PUPILS IN GRADE 4 (SECOND HALF)

**C E**

| | M.A.6 n=100 | F.M. 50 | Spec. 101 | 4B 162 |
|---|---|---|---|---|
| 1 | 50 | 78 | 91 | 96.3 |
| 2 | 49 | 90 | 92 | 94.4 |
| 3 | 58 | 92 | 93 | 98.8 |
| 4 | 46 | 78 | 92 | 98.8 |
| 5 | 60 | 82 | 85 | 96.9 |
| 6 | 49 | 98 | 86 | 95.7 |
| 7 | 41 | 82 | 83 | 96.9 |
| 8 | 43 | 90 | 97 | 93.2 |
| 9 | 45 | 82 | 86 | 72.8 |
| 10 | 47 | 100 | …. | 99.4 |

**C F**

| | M.A.6 n=100 | F.M. 50 | Spec. 101 | 4B 162 |
|---|---|---|---|---|
| 1 | 31 | 80 | 83 | 96.3 |
| 2 | 31 | 82 | 79 | 98.1 |
| 3 | 24 | 90 | 81 | 87.7 |
| 4 | 20 | 84 | 89 | 97.5 |
| 5 | 24 | 74 | 73 | 77.2 |
| 6 | 36 | 56 | 82 | 84.0 |
| 7 | 37 | 64 | 65 | 80.2 |
| 8 | 27 | 82 | …. | 87.7 |
| 9 | 34 | 80 | …. | 92.6 |
| 10 | 25 | 76 | …. | 82.1 |

**A E**

| | M.A.6 100 | F.M. 50 | Spec. 101 | 4B 162 |
|---|---|---|---|---|
| 1 | 46 | 86 | | |
| 2 | 45 | 84 | | |
| 3 | 49 | 92 | 91 | 99.4 |
| 4 | 48 | 92 | 100 | 99.4 |
| 5 | 57 | | | |
| 6 | 51 | | | |
| 7 | 48 | | | |
| 8 | 49 | | | |
| 9 | 59 | | | |
| 10 | 47 | | | |

**A F**

| | M.A.6 100 | F.M. 50 | Spec. 101 | 4B 162 |
|---|---|---|---|---|
| 1 | 33 | 78 | 89 | 96.9 |
| 2 | 23 | 76 | 87 | 97.5 |
| 3 | 26 | 88 | 93 | 100.0 |
| 4 | 22 | 76 | 99 | 97.5 |
| 5 | 24 | 82 | 97 | 96.9 |
| 6 | 20 | 90 | 96 | 97.5 |
| 7 | 35 | 86 | 98 | 97.5 |
| 8 | 22 | 78 | 91 | 98.8 |
| 9 | 22 | 82 | 92 | 98.1 |
| 10 | 23 | 84 | 96 | 100.0 |

**D E**

| | M.A.6 100 | F.M. 50 | Spec. 101 | 4B 162 |
|---|---|---|---|---|
| 1 | 37 | 86 | 85 | |
| 2 | 31 | 86 | 88 | |
| 3 | 48 | 84 | 80 | |
| 4 | 53 | 88 | 88 | |
| 5 | 59 | 88 | 82 | |
| 6 | 38 | 84 | 79 | |
| 7 | 56 | 90 | 96 | |
| 8 | 38 | 96 | 97 | |
| 9 | 38 | 90 | 97 | 85.2 |
| 10 | 50 | 80 | 94 | 93.2 |

**D F**

| | M.A.6 100 | F.M. 50 | Spec. 101 | 4B 162 |
|---|---|---|---|---|
| 1 | 35 | 60 | 71 | |
| 2 | 34 | 80 | 74 | |
| 3 | 27 | 68 | 90 | |
| 4 | 27 | 80 | 95 | 95.1 |
| 5 | 25 | 76 | 87 | 85.8 |
| 6 | 23 | 50 | 67 | 82.7 |
| 7 | 19 | 68 | 86 | 80.2 |
| 8 | 29 | 94 | 92 | 90.7 |
| 9 | 12 | 70 | 85 | 82.7 |
| 10 | 17 | 82 | 85 | 75.3 |

## TABLE 35 (continued).

| C G | M. A. 6 n=100 | F.M. 50 | Spec. 101 | 4B 162 |
|---|---|---|---|---|
| 1 | 10 | 38 | 47 | 87.7 |
| 2 | 6 | 36 | 62 | 76.5 |
| 3 | 13 | 44 | | 57.4 |
| 4 | 11 | 60 | | 60.5 |
| 5 | 21 | 44 | | 66.0 |
| 6 | | 38 | | 66.7 |
| 7 | | 40 | | 67.9 |
| 8 | | 56 | | 50.0 |
| 9 | | 36 | | 63.0 |
| 10 | | 36 | | 67.9 |

| A G | M. A. 6 100 | F.M. 50 | Spec. 101 | 4B 162 |
|---|---|---|---|---|
| 1 | 17 | 64 | 85 | 92.0 |
| 2 | 11 | 48 | 84 | 93.2 |
| 3 | 5 | 64 | 90 | 95.7 |
| 4 | 7 | 76 | 90 | 94.4 |
| 5 | 4 | 64 | 87 | 95.7 |
| 6 | 8 | 68 | 93 | 95.1 |
| 7 | 6 | 56 | 85 | 94.4 |
| 8 | 8 | 54 | 93 | 90.7 |
| 9 | 7 | 68 | 88 | 95.1 |
| 10 | 7 | 72 | 85 | 95.7 |

| A H | M. A. 6 100 | F.M. 50 | Spec. 101 | 4B 162 |
|---|---|---|---|---|
| 1 | 11 | 56 | 62 | 79.6 |
| 2 | 6 | 62 | 81 | 90.1 |
| 3 | 1 | 28 | 64 | 80.2 |
| 4 | 3 | 60 | 65 | 92.0 |
| 5 | 4 | 34 | 54 | 86.4 |
| 6 | 6 | 46 | 58 | 74.1 |
| 7 | 0 | 34 | 54 | 90.1 |
| 8 | 1 | 48 | 54 | 93.2 |
| 9 | 3 | 40 | 69 | 81.5 |
| 10 | 0 | 28 | 59 | 75.3 |

| D G | M. A. 6 100 | F.M. 50 | Spec. 101 | 4B 162 |
|---|---|---|---|---|
| 1 | | 48 | 69 | 64.2 |
| 2 | | 56 | 51 | 63.0 |
| 3 | | 34 | 71 | 67.9 |
| 4 | | 42 | 70 | 76.5 |
| 5 | | 60 | 68 | 67.9 |
| 6 | | 50 | 63 | 65.4 |
| 7 | | 56 | 58 | 71.6 |
| 8 | | 56 | 64 | 41.4 |
| 9 | | 54 | 75 | 59.3 |
| 10 | | 50 | 52 | 69.1 |

| D H | M. A. 6 100 | F.M. 50 | Spec. 101 | 4B 162 |
|---|---|---|---|---|
| 1 | | 42 | 45 | 60.5 |
| 2 | | 34 | 54 | 63.6 |
| 3 | | 50 | 55 | 66.0 |
| 4 | | 34 | 45 | 56.8 |
| 5 | | 38 | 49 | 58.0 |
| 6 | | 54 | 60 | 43.8 |
| 7 | | 38 | 48 | 40.1 |
| 8 | | 42 | 47 | 64.2 |
| 9 | | 56 | 51 | 48.1 |
| 10 | | 30 | 45 | 59.9 |

TABLE 36.

THE PERMILLES SUCCEEDING WITH EACH SINGLE TASK OF VARIOUS
10-COMPOSITES OF SENTENCE COMPLETIONS.

| Grade<br>n = | 5½<br>205 | 8½<br>250 | 6 (1)<br>61 | 6 (2)<br>100 | 6 (3)<br>107 | 6 (4)<br>140 | 17 or +<br>60 |
|---|---|---|---|---|---|---|---|
| | | | C I | | | | |
| 1 | 654 | | 787 | 490 | 738 | 650 | 933 |
| 2 | 654 | | 672 | 610 | 682 | 593 | 950 |
| 3 | 693 | | 443 | 530 | 748 | 564 | 900 |
| 4 | 746 | 812 | 607 | 460 | 757 | 578 | 1000 |
| 5 | 634 | 804 | 639 | 380 | 682 | 564 | 950 |
| 6 | 634 | 824 | 623 | 460 | 626 | 585 | 800 |
| | | | n = 162 | n = 80 | n = 75 | n = 104 | |
| 7 | 649 | 840 | 667 | 362 | 787 | 510 | 933 |
| 8 | 639 | 796 | 543 | 500 | 773 | 779 | 983 |
| 9 | 580 | 800 | 617 | 413 | 667 | 519 | 891 |
| 10 | 751 | 832 | 630 | 587 | 667 | 693 | 983 |
| | | | C J | | | | |
| 1 | 541 | 580 | 630 | 437 | 720 | 712 | 941 |
| | | | | n = 49 | n = 52 | n = 140 | n = 59 |
| 2 | 605 | 696 | | 531 | 692 | 690 | 893 |
| | | | n = 375 | n = 177 | n = 186 | n = 248 | |
| 3 | 498 | 780 | 501 | 429 | 613 | 564 | 783 |
| 4 | 532 | 776 | 481 | 350 | 600 | 539 | 983 |
| 5 | 493 | 704 | | | | | 925 |
| 6 | 341 | 736 | 443 | 260 | 495 | 436 | 958 |
| 7 | 463 | 664 | 377 | 290 | 542 | 364 | 717 |
| 8 | 358 | 708 | 278 | 150 | 547 | 443 | 891 |
| 9 | 294 | 681 | 279 | 280 | 402 | 450 | 900 |
| 10 | 206 | 673 | 352 | 79 | 414 | 314 | 925 |
| | | | C K | | | | |
| | | | | | n = 116 | | n = 59 |
| 1 | 376 | 364 | | | 379 | | 890 |
| | | | n = 184 | n = 49 | n = 53 | n = 126 | |
| 2 | 225 | 432 | 386 | 122 | 547 | 238 | 825 |
| 3 | 270 | 644 | 288 | 41 | 679 | 262 | 867 |
| 4 | 196 | 336 | 255 | 184 | 453 | 333 | 917 |
| | | | | n = 49 | n = 52 | n = 140 | |
| 5 | 377 | 564 | | 61 | 442 | 155 | 861 |
| 6 | 279 | 568 | | | | | |
| 7 | 353 | 580 | 123 | 250 | 293 | 202 | 808 |
| 8 | 225 | 336 | 185 | 137 | 280 | 192 | 683 |
| 9 | 152 | 476 | 246 | 110 | 299 | 150 | 983 |
| 10 | 191 | 476 | 180 | 90 | 280 | 186 | 908 |

TABLE 36—*Continued*.

## C L

This is the least satisfactory 10-composite. It was used because, as a composite, it filled a certain place. The 10 single tasks in order showed percents correct of 60, 59, 60, 54, 42½, 41, 15½, 11, 5½ and ½ in a group of 200 pupils in grade 9.

## C M

The 10 single tasks in order showed percents correct in a group of 200 pupils in grade 9 of 22, 20, 36, 38, 30, 25, 28, 20, 26½, and 25.

| Grade n = | 5½ 205 | 8½ 250 | NS(1) 100 | NS(2) 100 | NS 135 | NS 87 | 17or+ 60 | 17or+ 28 | 17or+ 17 | S.Sch. 35 | 10,11,12 82 |
|---|---|---|---|---|---|---|---|---|---|---|---|
| | | | | | | C N | | | | | |
| 1 | 020 | 200 | 470 | 530 | 482 | 678 | 830 | 821 | 882 | 857 | 350 |
| 2 | 083 | 160 | 690 | 530 | 467 | 609 | 817 | 821 | 824 | 771 | 386 |
| 3 | 005 | 080 | 530 | 420 | 297 | 483 | 830 | 964 | 882 | 886 | 446 |
| 4 | 167 | 240 | 600 | 570 | 526 | 713 | 733 | 786 | 647 | 914 | 349 |
| 5 | 010 | 108 | 410 | 470 | 341 | 540 | 667 | 964 | 647 | 829 | 277 |
| 6 | 020 | 164 | 450 | 500 | 356 | 506 | 770 | 893 | 706 | 714 | 578 |
| 7 | 010 | 92 | 540 | 550 | 400 | 575 | 746 | 893 | 647 | 857 | 602 |
| 8 | 025 | 100 | 420 | 400 | 259 | 506 | 627 | 964 | 824 | 600 | 747 |
| 9 | 034 | 192 | 380 | 580 | 326 | 609 | 686 | 893 | 824 | 771 | 482 |
| 10 | 108 | 148 | 680 | 710 | 511 | 759 | 885 | 893 | 882 | 943 | 482 |
| | | | | | | C O | | | | | |
| 1 | | | 090 | 160 | 126 | 253 | 600 | | | | |
| 2 | | | 290 | 220 | 200 | 264 | 577 | | | | |
| 3 | | | 430 | 380 | 363 | 391 | 551 | | | | |
| 4 | | | 110 | 150 | 097 | 172 | 433 | | | | |
| 5 | | | 280 | 210 | 297 | 368 | 442 | | | | |
| 6 | | | 260 | 330 | 259 | 448 | 596 | | | | |
| 7 | | | 250 | 230 | 297 | 253 | 619 | | | | |
| 8 | | | 410 | 490 | 445 | 586 | 636 | | | | |
| 9 | | | 350 | 430 | 304 | 425 | 593 | | | | |
| 10 | | | 210 | 190 | 208 | 345 | 610 | | | | |
| | | | | | | C P | | | | | |
| 1 | | | 040 | 020 | 067 | 000 | | | | | |
| 2 | | | 150 | 170 | 193 | 207 | | | | | |
| 3 | | | 050 | 040 | 030 | 034 | | | | | |
| 4 | | | 100 | 060 | 059 | 161 | | | | | |
| 5 | | | 100 | 050 | 082 | 149 | | | | | |

TABLE 36—*Continued.*

| Grade | 5½ | 8½ | NS(1) | NS(2) | NS | NS | 17or+ | 17or+ | 17or+ | S.Sch. | 10,11,12 |
| n = | 505 | 520 | 100 | 100 | 135 | 87 | 60 | 28 | 17 | 35 | 82 |
| 6 | | | 120 | 090 | 119 | 138 | | | | | |
| 7 | | | 260 | 240 | 297 | 310 | | | | | |
| 8 | | | 100 | 100 | 082 | 149 | | | | | |
| 9 | | | 030 | 090 | 052 | 080 | | | | | |
| 10 | | | 110 | 100 | 111 | 057 | | | | | |
| | | | | | C Q | | | | | | |
| 1 | | | 080 | 080 | 082 | 115 | | 750 | 353 | 171 | |
| 2 | | | 000 | 050 | 015 | 000 | | 429 | 235 | 114 | |
| 3 | | | 000 | 020 | 008 | 023 | | 571 | 765 | 229 | |
| 4 | | | 030 | 030 | 015 | 023 | | 500 | 765 | 257 | |
| 5 | | | 020 | 040 | 030 | 023 | | 500 | 824 | 257 | |
| 6 | | | 000 | 040 | 000 | 000 | | 429 | 588 | 171 | |
| 7 | | | 020 | 020 | 015 | 011 | | 536 | 529 | 229 | |
| 8 | | | 020 | 030 | 000 | 000 | | 607 | 471 | 229 | |
| 9 | | | 000 | 010 | 000 | 000 | | 571 | 706 | 171 | |
| 10 | | | 000 | 010 | 000 | 000 | | 393 | 706 | 086 | |
| | | | | | C R | | | | | | |
| 1 | | | 000 | 000 | 000 | 000 | 321 | | | | |
| 2 | | | 000 | 000 | 000 | 000 | 464 | | | | |
| 3 | | | 000 | 010 | 000 | 000 | 429 | | | | |
| 4 | | | 000 | 000 | 000 | 000 | 250 | | | | |
| 5 | | | 000 | 000 | 000 | 000 | 500 | | | | |
| 6 | | | 000 | 000 | 000 | 000 | 250 | | | | |
| 7 | | | 000 | 000 | 000 | 000 | 393 | | | | |
| 8 | | | 000 | 000 | 000 | 000 | 250 | | | | |
| 9 | | | 000 | 000 | 000 | 000 | 286 | | | | |
| 10 | | | 000 | 000 | 000 | 000 | 536 | | | | |

when they have been secured, it is especially hard to obtain time enough to exhaust abilities in arithmetical problems. A patient adult may work for half an hour at a single problem. We fear that the tasks which happen to come late in the series as first printed showed fewer successes in our returns than they would have shown if they had been attempted first. In general, we feel less security that the percents of successes correspond closely with degrees of difficulty in the case of the arithmetical problems than in the

TABLE 37.

THE PERMILLES SUCCEEDING WITH EACH SINGLE TASK OF VARIOUS 10-COMPOSITES
OF ARITHMETICAL PROBLEMS.

| Grade | Sp | Sp | 5½ | A I 8½ | 9 I | 9 II |
|---|---|---|---|---|---|---|
| n = | 50 | 52 | 189 | 126 | 246 | 264 |
| 1 | 260 | 346 | 751 | | | |
| 2 | 340 | 192 | 682 | | | |
| 3 | 340 | 288 | 661 | | | |
| 4 | 340 | 404 | 762 | | | |
| 5 | 380 | 308 | 857 | | | |
| 6 | 620 | 673 | 831 | | | |
| 7 | 300 | 365 | 857 | | | |
| 8 | 440 | 423 | 788 | | | |
| 9 | 280 | 250 | 815 | | | |
| 10 | 140 | 135 | 656 | | | |
| | | | | A J | | |
| 1 | | | 302 | ........ | 646 | 792 |
| 2 | | | 233 | ........ | 626 | 739 |
| 3 | | | 296 | 818 | 672 | 708 |
| 4 | | | 545 | 778 | 846 | 799 |
| 5 | | | 217 | 627 | 512 | 538 |
| 6 | | | 370 | 690 | 667 | 633 |
| 7 | | | 217 | 643 | 715 | 610 |
| 8 | | | 344 | 603 | 768 | 527 |
| 9 | | | 217 | 540 | 732 | 564 |
| 10 | | | 328 | 611 | 821 | 652 |
| | | | | A K | | |
| 1 | | | 317 | 532 | | |
| 2 | | | 143 | 643 | | |
| 3 | | | 175 | 571 | | |
| 4 | | | 307 | 603 | | |
| 5 | | | 206 | 524 | | |
| 6 | | | 058 | 429 | | |
| 7 | | | 228 | 540 | | |
| 8 | | | 196 | 587 | | |
| 9 | | | 139 | 579 | | |
| 10 | | | 105 | 341 | | |

TABLE 37—(*Continued*).

| Grade | 5½ | 8½ | 9I | 9II | NS(1) | NS(2) | NS | NS | 17 |
|-------|-----|-----|-----|-----|-------|-------|-----|-----|-----|
| n = | 189 | 250 | 246 | 264 | 100 | 100 | 135 | 87 | 240 |

| | | | A L | | | | | | |
|---|---|---|---|---|---|---|---|---|---|
| 1 | 296 | 544 | | | | | | | |
| 2 | 296 | 484 | | | | | | | |
| 3 | 190 | 448 | | | | | | | |
| 4 | 206 | 424 | | | | | | | |
| 5 | 185 | 396 | | | | | | | |
| 6 | 153 | 416 | | | | | | | |
| 7 | 238 | 516 | | | | | | | |
| 8 | 148 | 436 | | | | | | | |
| 9 | 127 | 376 | | | | | | | |
| 10 | 201 | 484 | | | | | | | |

| | | | A M | | | | | | |
|---|---|---|---|---|---|---|---|---|---|
| 1 | | | 059 | 174 | 680 | 570 | 437 | 563 | |
| 2 | | | 093 | 246 | 730 | 650 | 481 | 598 | |
| 3 | | | 102 | 220 | 700 | 650 | 452 | 644 | |
| 4 | | | 089 | 133 | 720 | 650 | 496 | 621 | |
| 5 | | | 065 | 140 | 680 | 630 | 504 | 736 | |
| 6 | | | 053 | 171 | 580 | 430 | 341 | 609 | |
| 7 | | | 057 | 129 | 650 | 600 | 407 | 701 | |
| 8 | | | 057 | 095 | 600 | 510 | 348 | 667 | |

| | | | A N | | | | | | |
|---|---|---|---|---|---|---|---|---|---|
| 1 | | | | | 630 | 480 | 252 | 391 | 762 |
| 2 | | | | | 400 | 390 | 185 | 322 | 725 |
| 3 | | | | | 420 | 290 | 185 | 379 | 762 |
| 4 | | | | | 310 | 260 | 222 | 230 | 662 |
| 5 | | | | | 470 | 370 | 185 | 333 | 742 |
| 6 | | | | | 530 | 420 | 378 | 517 | 829 |
| 7 | | | | | 470 | 450 | 326 | 437 | 683 |
| 8 | | | | | 410 | 430 | 326 | 471 | 817 |
| 9 | | | | | 340 | 300 | 178 | 310 | 742 |
| 10 | | | | | 340 | 260 | 200 | 379 | 712 |

TABLE 37—(Continued).

| Grade | | NS(1) | NS(2) | NS | NS | 17 |
|---|---|---|---|---|---|---|
| n = | | 100 | 100 | 135 | 87 | 240 |

A O

| 1 | | 120 | 140 | 104 | 161 | 792 |
| 2 | | 120 | 130 | 081 | 230 | 779 |
| 3 | | 130 | 090 | 104 | 149 | 642 |
| 4 | | 030 | 040 | 022 | 034 | 467 |
| 5 | | 000 | 040 | 022 | 057 | 421 |
| 6 | | 030 | 040 | 022 | 115 | 679 |
| 7 | | 020 | 030 | 067 | 092 | 671 |
| 8 | | 010 | 040 | 044 | 057 | 642 |
| 9 | | 020 | 040 | 052 | 057 | 700 |
| 10 | | 020 | 050 | 059 | 092 | 600 |

A P

| 1 | | | | | | 546 |
| 2 | | | | | | 617 |
| 3 | | | | | | 400 |
| 4 | | | | | | 504 |
| 5 | | | | | | 650 |
| 6 | | | | | | 579 |
| 7 | | | | | | 629 |
| 8 | | | | | | 562 |
| 9 | | | | | | 612 |
| 10 | | | | | | 675 |

A Q

| 1 | | | | | | 519 |
| 2 | | | | | | 343 |
| 3 | | | | | | 423 |
| 4 | | | | | | 502 |
| 5 | | | | | | 218 |

case of C or V or D. However, the errors in this respect
are probably very small in comparison with the difference
in difficulty from Arithmetic A to Arithmetic P.

The main facts for the arithmetical 10-composites A, B,
C, D, E, F, G, H, I, J, K, L, M, N, O, P, and Q are given in
Tables 34, 35, and 37. We have also certain provisional

TABLE 38.
THE PERCENTS SUCCEEDING WITH EACH SINGLE TASK OF VARIOUS 10-COMPOSITES OF DIRECTIONS AND READINGS.

| de 4 | 5 | Ad | 9I | 9II | 10 | 11(1) | 11(2) | 11(3) | 11(4) | 12(1) | 12(2) | 12(3) | A |
|---|---|---|---|---|---|---|---|---|---|---|---|---|---|
| 162 | 311 | 44 | 246 | 236 | 100 | 100 | 100 | 100 | 63 | 100 | 100 | 84 | 4 |
| | | | | | D ½ | | | | | | | | |
| 51.9 | 71.1 | 75.0 | 95.1 | | 96 | 100 | 96 | 97 | 98.4 | | | | |
| 26.5 | 46.0 | 63.6 | 91.9 | | 95 | 99 | 92 | 97 | 96.8 | | | | |
| 5.6 | 20.3 | 56.8 | 81.3 | | 96 | 98 | 96 | 99 | 100.0 | | | | |
| 34.6 | 50.2 | 77.3 | 91.5 | | 92 | 99 | 98 | 94 | 98.4 | | | | |
| | | | | | D 1 | | | | | | | | |
| 37.7 | 51.4 | 65.9 | 88.2 | | 85 | 84 | 94 | 84 | 88.9 | | | | |
| 56.2 | 62.4 | 65.9 | 80.9 | | 91 | 94 | 89 | 94 | 90.5 | | | | |
| 6.2 | 11.3 | 38.6 | 82.9 | | 89 | 95 | 90 | 88 | 87.3 | | | | |
| 35.2 | 37.9 | 59.1 | 72.0 | | 92 | 92 | 92 | 89 | 96.8 | | | | |
| 40.1 | 47.6 | 63.6 | 82.9 | | 91 | 95 | 94 | 91 | 98.4 | | | | |
| 26.5 | 32.5 | 52.3 | 65.0 | | 82 | 85 | 93 | 86 | 98.4 | | | | |
| 24.1 | 35.7 | 34.1 | 76.4 | | 92 | 90 | 90 | 80 | 96.8 | | | | |
| 41.4 | 60.1 | 65.9 | 91.9 | | 95 | 96 | 93 | 86 | 95.2 | | | | |
| 6.2 | 17.7 | 50.0 | 79.4 | | 83 | 98 | 93 | 90 | 94.0 | | | | |
| 46.9 | 55.3 | 47.7 | 58.9 | | 81 | 94 | 91 | 87 | 90.5 | | | | |
| | | | | | D 2 | | | | | | | | |
| 17.3 | 20.3 | 50.0 | 62.2 | 52.6 | 75 | 82 | 81 | 79 | 79.4 | | | | |
| 5.6 | 8.7 | 38.6 | 47.6 | 45.8 | 69 | 85 | 83 | 82 | 81.0 | | | | |
| 25.9 | 27.7 | 52.3 | 57.7 | 53.8 | 68 | 88 | 77 | 73 | 79.4 | | | | |
| 13.6 | 9.6 | 47.7 | 41.9 | 39.0 | 70 | 79 | 79 | 82 | 79.4 | | | | |
| 5.6 | 15.4 | 45.5 | 42.7 | | 79 | 78 | 85 | 73 | 88.9 | | | | |
| 16.0 | 23.1 | 47.7 | 42.7 | | 77 | 83 | 77 | 75 | 74.6 | | | | |
| 4.3 | 16.1 | 52.3 | 78.5 | | 74 | 84 | 76 | 75 | 84.1 | | | | |
| 19.8 | 30.2 | 43.2 | 65.4 | | 78 | 78 | 83 | 76 | 81.0 | | | | |
| 9.3 | 22.2 | 40.9 | 69.5 | | 78 | 83 | 72 | 78 | 76.2 | | | | |
| 16.7 | 16.4 | 40.9 | 44.3 | | 66 | 77 | 77 | 76 | 76.2 | | | | |
| | | | | | D 2½ | | | | | | | | |
| 8.6 | 13.8 | | 52.4 | 48.3 | 74 | 72 | 78 | 73 | 79.4 | 72 | 71 | 77.4 | |
| 11.7 | 15.4 | | 32.5 | 38.6 | 64 | 77 | 72 | 70 | 77.8 | 66 | 69 | 79.8 | |
| 15.4 | 19.6 | | 58.1 | 58.1 | 63 | 76 | 76 | 68 | 73.0 | 85 | 69 | 76.2 | |
| 3.7 | 3.9 | | 39.4 | 24.2 | 66 | 71 | 74 | 72 | 69.8 | 79 | 76 | 85.7 | |
| 9.3 | 15.8 | | 59.3 | | 71 | 72 | 68 | 78 | 82.5 | 76 | 68 | 75.0 | |

TABLE 38 (*continued*).

| Grade 4 n= 162 | 5 311 | Ad 44 | 9I 246 | 9II 236 | 10 100 | 11(1) 100 | 11(2) 100 | 11(3) 100 | 11(4) 63 | 12(1) 100 | 12(2) 100 | 12(3) 84 |
|---|---|---|---|---|---|---|---|---|---|---|---|---|
| 6 | | | | 53.8 | 67 | 77 | 74 | 64 | 67.7 | 81 | 79 | 83.3 |
| 7 | | | | 20.8 | 56 | 71 | 71 | 72 | 69.2 | 68 | 69 | 60.7 |
| 8 | | | | 42.0 | 54 | 62 | 73 | 64 | 69.2 | 68 | 67 | 70.2 |
| 9 | | | | 33.3 | 61 | 66 | 64 | 68 | 69.2 | 68 | 68 | 70.2 |
| 10 | | | | 34.1 | 48 | 63 | 66 | 61 | 60.0 | 71 | 67 | 61.9 |
| | | | | | | D 3 | | | | | | |
| 1 | | | 43.1 | 37.7 | 67 | 66 | 65 | 57 | 55.6 | 70 | 73 | 61.9 |
| 2 | | | 31.7 | 23.7 | 64 | 73 | 71 | 65 | 77.8 | 69 | 66 | 66.7 |
| 3 | | | 40.7 | 22.5 | 64 | 67 | 66 | 54 | 58.7 | 60 | 61 | 63.1 |
| 4 | | | 46.7 | 42.0 | 62 | 64 | 68 | 63 | 63.5 | 76 | 78 | 65.5 |
| 5 | | | 48.8 | 38.6 | 65 | 62 | 65 | 62 | 69.8 | 74 | 74 | 72.7 |
| 6 | | | 43.5 | 42.8 | 60 | 64 | 69 | 66 | 65.1 | 72 | 80 | 71.4 |
| 7 | | | 49.6 | 39.4 | 65 | 64 | 69 | 66 | 61.9 | 67 | 74 | 73.8 |
| 8 | | | 22.4 | 14.0 | 69 | 64 | 64 | 67 | 74.6 | 63 | 71 | 63.1 |
| 9 | | | 39.8 | | 56 | 69 | 70 | 65 | 77.8 | 79 | 72 | 78.6 |
| 10 | | | 41.1 | 17.0 | 59 | 71 | 72 | 67 | 76.2 | 74 | 64 | 72.7 |
| | | | | | | D 4 | | | | | | |
| 1 | | | 38.6 | 30.5 | 44 | 41 | 54 | 55 | 57.1 | 52 | 53 | 47.6 |
| 2 | | | 41.5 | 28.8 | 58 | 50 | 52 | 51 | 55.6 | 48 | 68 | 47.6 |
| 3 | | | 42.3 | 28.4 | 45 | 46 | 49 | 52 | 57.1 | 58 | 73 | 58.3 |
| 4 | | | 25.2 | 19.9 | 47 | 49 | 60 | 56 | 58.7 | 65 | 59 | 65.5 |
| 5 | | | 42.3 | 25.0 | 47 | 49 | 44 | 54 | 52.4 | 49 | 48 | 47.6 |
| 6 | | | 36.2 | 25.4 | 43 | 55 | 51 | 53 | 52.4 | 56 | 56 | 54.8 |
| 7 | | | 45.1 | 27.1 | 46 | 54 | 51 | 54 | 44.4 | 66 | 64 | 65.5 |
| 8 | | | 40.2 | 25.9 | 43 | 55 | 48 | 54 | 44.4 | 61 | 52 | 60.7 |
| 9 | | | 19.5 | 15.3 | 40 | 45 | 52 | 52 | 50.8 | 60 | 45 | 61.9 |
| 10 | | | 32.9 | 12.6 | 41 | 49 | 43 | 42 | 42.9 | 41 | 47 | 38.1 |
| | | | | | | D 4½ | | | | | | |
| 1 | | | | | 41 | 42 | 42 | 46 | 60.3 | 56 | 41 | 59.5 |
| 2 | | | | | 51 | 58 | 45 | 48 | 47.7 | 54 | 45 | 51.2 |
| 3 | | | | | 63 | 50 | 52 | 42 | 47.7 | 67 | 59 | 58.3 |
| 4 | | | | | 47 | 68 | 57 | 51 | 58.5 | 65 | 60 | 67.9 |
| 5 | | | | | 42 | 59 | 62 | 61 | 56.9 | 63 | 62 | 54.8 |

TABLE 38 (*continued*).

| 9<br>236 | 10<br>100 | 11(1)<br>100 | 11(2)<br>100 | 11(3)<br>100 | 11(4)<br>63 | 12(1)<br>100 | 12(2)<br>100 | 12(3)<br>84 |
|---|---|---|---|---|---|---|---|---|
| | 42 | 67 | 57 | 64 | 52.3 | 60 | 71 | 66.7 |
| | 30 | 52 | 39 | 37 | 46.2 | 55 | 49 | 46.4 |
| | 33 | 62 | 48 | 37 | 43.1 | 59 | 51 | 55.9 |
| | 47 | 49 | 52 | 61 | 63.1 | 52 | 44 | 48.8 |
| | 47 | 50 | 59 | 53 | 61.5 | 49 | 58 | 59.5 |
| | | D 5 | | | | | | |
| | 44 | 46 | 33 | 40 | 49.2 | 54 | 46 | 55.9 |
| | 32 | 39 | 39 | 37 | 25.4 | 34 | 32 | 32.1 |
| | 43 | 47 | 35 | 47 | 46.0 | 55 | 52 | 64.3 |
| | 31 | 43 | 39 | 38 | 36.5 | 43 | 41 | 46.4 |
| | 27 | 30 | 35 | 32 | 33.3 | 53 | 35 | 42.9 |
| | 27 | 37 | 31 | 34 | 34.9 | 38 | 22 | 44.0 |
| | 28 | 40 | 37 | 25 | 49.2 | 45 | 41 | 40.5 |
| | 25 | 43 | 30 | 46 | 46.0 | 38 | 41 | 38.1 |
| | 26 | 42 | 41 | 37 | 36.9 | 47 | 37 | 44.0 |
| | 41 | 30 | 38 | 41 | 33.8 | 33 | 33 | 40.5 |
| | | D 6 | | | | | | |
| | 16 | 17 | 24 | 16 | 14.3 | 25 | 22 | 28.6 |
| | 17 | 21 | 17 | 18 | 23.8 | 21 | 16 | 21.4 |
| | 30 | 26 | 21 | 21 | 32.3 | 27 | 24 | 23.9 |
| | 08 | 16 | 17 | 09 | 15.4 | 17 | 08 | 13.1 |
| | 19 | 21 | 20 | 22 | 16.9 | 17 | 24 | 21.4 |
| | 20 | 24 | 17 | 05 | 26.2 | 27 | 18 | 28.6 |
| | | D 7 | | | | | | |
| | 02 | 00 | 03 | 02 | 0.15 | 00 | 03 | 02.4 |
| | 02 | 12 | 06 | 10 | 40.0 | 15 | 21 | 11.9 |
| | 02 | 03 | 03 | 05 | 06.1 | 11 | 01 | 04.8 |
| | 00 | 03 | 03 | 01 | 01.5 | 16 | 07 | 04.8 |
| | 09 | 08 | 05 | 04 | 16.9 | 13 | 10 | 09.5 |
| | 05 | 05 | 08 | 08 | 12.3 | 16 | 09 | 09.5 |

TABLE 38 (*continued*).

| | N.S.(1) 100 | N.S.(2) 100 | N.S. 135 | N.S. 87 |
|---|---|---|---|---|
| | | D 5½ | | |
| 1 | 31 | 37 | 27.4 | 46.0 |
| 2 | 27 | 34 | 26.7 | 29.9 |
| 3 | 52 | 44 | 40.7 | 39.1 |
| 4 | 54 | 49 | 34.8 | 43.7 |
| 5 | 20 | 40 | 27.4 | 23.0 |
| 6 | 37 | 46 | 38.5 | 28.7 |
| 7 | 42 | 42 | 34.8 | 31.0 |
| 8 | 41 | 45 | 34.1 | 36.8 |
| 9 | 47 | 40 | 39.3 | 26.4 |
| 10 | 31 | 26 | 25.9 | 19.5 |
| | | D 6½ | | |
| 1 | 29 | 31 | 23.7 | 23.0 |
| 2 | 10 | 9 | 5.9 | 5.1 |
| 3 | 24 | 21 | 18.5 | 17.2 |
| 4 | 8 | 8 | 3.0 | 5.7 |
| 5 | 7 | 10 | 10.4 | 6.9 |
| 6 | 32 | 27 | 23.7 | 11.5 |

arithmetical 10-composites, I J, J I, K I, and L I, which will be useful.

In the case of comprehension of directions and paragraphs, we have composites of from six to ten elements A, B, C, D, E, F, G, 1, 1½, 2, 2½, 3, 3½, 4, 4½, 5, 5½, 6, 6½, and 7, and have provisional composites H and ½. The facts concerning the difficulty of the constituent elements of these composites are given in Tables 34, 35, and 38.

## THE DIFFICULTY OF THE 10-COMPOSITES

After the composites of ten have been obtained for sentence completions, arithmetical tasks, and understanding sentences, by such experimentation and selection as has been described for the word-knowledge tasks, the difficulty of each composite in comparison with one or more others was measured in several groups of individuals. As many different composites were used in each group of individuals as was feasible. It is hard to secure the cooperation of large groups in taking such long examinations as are necessary to put a large number of these composites in comparison for the same group; but in one way or another, we have accumulated a very large body of facts (shown in Tables 39 to 50).

We use these 10-composites to make 40-composites each containing 10C, 10A, 10V, and 10D.[7] They will also be available for special scales for sentence completion, arithmetical reasoning, vocabulary knowledge, and comprehension of sentences and paragraphs. The arithmetical series, for example, is unquestionably a better instrument for measuring arithmetical ability of the problem-solving sort than has hitherto been available.

In Tables 39 to 50 there are sometimes two forms of entry: "%s" (percent successes) means the percent of the group in question having 50% or more of the single tasks right; "σ distance" means the difference in difficulty between the 10-composite in question and a 10-composite of the same kind which exactly half of the group would succeed with in the sense of having 50% or more of the single tasks correct. σ distance is in terms of the mean square deviation of the group in the ability measured by the 10-composite in question. The σ distances even for the same group are not then strictly comparable, since the mean square deviation of the group in the ability measured by, say, C I, may not be identical with its mean square deviation in the ability measured by C J, or by A I, etc. Two 10-composites of identical σ distances will not, however, be far apart in difficulty.

Minus (—) means easier than the median difficulty defined by the 10-composite which exactly half of the group succeed with; plus (+) means harder than it. The form of distribution is arbitrarily assumed to be "normal" in the case of all the abilities in all the groups. This is often

---

[7] In some cases the number is less than 10. Each single task is then given a weight so that a perfect score would count 10.

erroneous and always doubtful, but will do no harm if its arbitrariness is kept in mind. The σ distances are rough approximate measures convenient for comparison. The actual fact is always the %s.

TABLE 39.

THE DIFFICULTY OF 10-COMPOSITE C—A, B, C, AND D; A—A, B, C, AND D; V—A, B, C, AND D; AND D—A, B, C, AND D, IN THE CASE OF 180 ADULT IMBECILES.

| | | n | %s 100 | %s 80 | σ distance 100 | σ distance 80 | | | n | %s 100 | %s 80 | σ distance 100 | σ distance 80 |
|---|---|---|---|---|---|---|---|---|---|---|---|---|---|
| C | A | 84 | 82½ | | − 1.19 | − 1.13 | V | A | 80 | 81 | | − 1.03 | − 1.07 |
| | B | 65 | 56 | | − .51 | − .20 | | B | 49 | 57½ | | + .03 | − .25 |
| | C | 35 | 27½ | | + .45 | + .68 | | C | 14 | 19 | | + 1.09 | + .93 |
| | D | 3 | 0 | | + 1.59 | high | | D | 1 | 5 | | + 1.78 | + 1.47 |
| A | A | 69 | 80 | | − .65 | − 1.03 | D | A | 90 | 86 | | − 1.45 | − 1.27 |
| | B | 45 | 49 | | + .15 | + .03 | | B | 45 | 67½ | | + .15 | − .59 |
| | C | 15 | 21 | | + 1.05 | + .87 | | C | 19 | 27½ | | + .93 | + .68 |
| | D | 5 | 5 | | + 1.47 | + 1.47 | | D | 12 | 14 | | + 1.16 | + 1.09 |

TABLE 40.

THE DIFFICULTY OF 10-COMPOSITES C—E, F, G AND I, A—E, F, G AND H, V—E, F, G AND H, AND D—E, F, G AND H, IN VARIOUS GROUPS. (σ DISTANCES ARE OMITTED FROM THIS TABLE.)

| | | 100 M.A. 6 | %s 50 Class 3 | 101 Special Class | | | 100 M.A. 6 | %s 50 Class 3 | 101 Special Class |
|---|---|---|---|---|---|---|---|---|---|
| C | E | 56 | 94 | 93 | V | E | ...... | 94 | ...... |
| | F | 25 | 94 | 88 | | F | 23 | 96 | 96 |
| | G | 7 | 42 | 74 | | G | 15 | 84 | 85 |
| | I | ...... | 20 | 18 | | H | 4 | 64 | 62 |
| A | E | 55 | 92 | 100 | D | E | 45 | 96 | 98 |
| | F | 20 | 90 | 96 | | F | 23 | 92 | 97 |
| | G | 5 | 74 | 93 | | G | 6 | 58 | 75 |
| | H | ...... | 88 | 73 | | H | ...... | 44 | 57 |

The Sentence Completion and Arithmetical tasks were done in June, 1924; the Vocabulary and Directions-Reading tasks were done in September, 1924. We treat them together, since the differences due to an interval of less than three months are small.

The following composites had fewer than 10 single tasks: Directions-Reading $\frac{1}{2}$, which had 4, $2\frac{1}{2}$, which had 5, and 3, which had 6. 2 right, 3 right, and 3 right are used respectively, in these cases, instead of 5 right.

TABLE 41.

THE DIFFICULTY OF 10-COMPOSITES C—F, G, I, J, AND K, A—F, G, H, I, J, AND K, V—F, G, H, 2, 3, AND 4, AND D—F, G, H, ½, 1, 2, AND 2½, IN VARIOUS GROUPS IN %S.

| n = | 4B 162 | 5A 125 | 5B 186 | | 4B 162 | 5A 125 | 5B 186 |
|---|---|---|---|---|---|---|---|
| C F | 100.0 | | | V F | 98.8 | | |
| G | 83.3 | | | G | 98.1 | | |
| I | 35.2 | 47.2 | 67.6 | H | 87.0 | 93.6 | 100.0 |
| J | 22.2 | 25.6 | 44.6 | 2 | 50.6 | 57.6 | 75.3 |
| K | 1.2 | 9.6 | 6.4 | 3 | 25.9 | 35.2 | 53.8 |
| | | | | 4 | 5.6 | 5.6 | 9.7 |
| A F | 100.0 | | | D F | 93.8 | | |
| G | 98.8 | | | G | 82.1 | | |
| H | 96.3 | 95.2 | 98.4 | H | 75.9 | 80.8 | 91.9 |
| I | 72.8 | 77.6 | 86.6 | ½ | 36.4 | 52.8 | 68.3 |
| J | 6.8 | 8.0 | 25.3 | 2 | 3.1 | 5.6 | 10.2 |
| K | 0 | 3.2 | 15.6 | 2½ | 1.9 | 0.8 | 5.4 |

Of the 53 adult students, only 45 were measured with the completion tasks, and only 28 of these attempted the Q and R composites. We have estimated as well as we can how the individuals in question would have succeeded if they had attempted all.

THE COMBINATION OF 10-COMPOSITES INTO 40-COMPOSITES

These 10-composites were combined into 40-composites by putting together a C, an A, a V, and a D which, from the data at hand, seemed of nearly equal difficulty as composites. Some of the 10-composites were constructed especially to fit others in this way. Into the history of the procedure by which the final arrangement of the 40-composites

## TABLE 42.

DIFFICULTY OF 10-COMPOSITES MEASURED BY THE PERCENTS OF 147 PUPILS IN GRADE 5½ SUCCEEDING WITH FIVE OR MORE OF THE TEN SINGLE TASKS, AND BY DISTANCES + OR − FROM THE MEDIAN DIFFICULTY FOR GRADE 5½, IN UNITS OF THE MEAN SQUARE VARIATION OF GRADE 5½ IN LEVEL OF WHATEVER ABILITY THE 10-COMPOSITE MEASURES IN EACH CASE. THE 147 PUPILS FOR 205 PUPILS AND 200 PUPILS IN GRADE 5½. THE 147 PUPILS ARE THOSE WHO WERE INCLUDED IN BOTH THE 205 AND THE 200.

| 10-Composite | % s 147 | % s 205 | σ distance 147 | σ distance 205 |
|---|---|---|---|---|
| C  I | 83.1 | 80.6 | − .96 | − .86 |
| J | 43.2 | 44.4 | + .17 | + 0.14 |
| K | 20.9 | 20.0 | + .81 | + 0.84 |
| N | 1.4 | 1.0 | + 2.20 | + 2.33 |
| O | 0.0 | 0.0 | | |
| A  IK | 91.9 | 93.2 | − 1.40 | − 1.49 |
| IJ | 74.3 | 68.3 | − .65 | − .48 |
| KI | 34.5 | 35.1 | + .40 | + .38 |
| J | | 26.8 | | + .62 |
| K | 19.6 | 18.5 | + .86 | + .90 |
| L | | 15.6 | | + 1.01 |

| 10-Composite | % s 147 | % s 200 | σ distance 147 | σ distance 200 |
|---|---|---|---|---|
| 1 | 100 | 99.5 | | − 2.58 |
| 1a | 100 | 99.5 | | − 2.58 |
| 2 | 93.2* | 89.5 | − 1.49* | − 1.25 |
| 2a | | 95.5 | | − 1.69½ |
| 3 | 55.4** | 60.5 | − .14** | − .40 |
| 3a | | 58.0 | | − .20 |
| D G(−4) | 100.0 | | | |
| H(−3) | 100.0 | | | |
| I(−2) | 100.0 | | | |
| K(O) | 92.5 | | − 1.44 | |
| J(−1) | 95.9 | | − 1.74 | |
| ½ | 88.5 | | − 1.20 | |
| 1 | 74.3 | | − .65 | |
| 2 | 30.4 | | + .51 | |
| 2½ | 14.9 | | + 1.04 | |
| 3 | 6.1 | | + 1.55 | |

* Average of the results for 2 and 2a.
** Average of the results for 3 and 3a.

TABLE 43.

THE DIFFICULTY OF VARIOUS 10-COMPOSITES IN THE CASE OF 44 ADULTS:
RECRUITS IN THE UNITED STATES ARMY.

| %s | | | %s | | | %s | | | %s | |
|---|---|---|---|---|---|---|---|---|---|---|
| C F | 100.0 | A F | 100.0 | V F | 100.0 | D F | 100.0 |
| G | 86.4 | G | 100.0 | G | 100.0 | G | 95.5 |
| | | H | 100.0 | H | 100.0 | H | 88.6 |
| I | 77.3 | I | 95.5 | 1 | 100.0 | ½ | 79.6 |
| J | 70.5 | I-J | 70.5 | 2 | 90.9 | 1 | 61.4 |
| K | 50.0 | | | 3 | 81.8 | 2 | 47.7 |
| | | | | 4 | 61.4 | 2½ | 38.6 |
| | | | | 5 | 45.5 | 3 | 38.6 |
| | | | | 6 | 11.4 | 4 | 18.2 |
| | | | | 7 | 2.3 | 5 | 09.1 |

TABLE 44.

DIFFICULTY OF 10-COMPOSITES MEASURED BY THE PERMILLES OF SUCCESSES
AND BY DISTANCES + OR − FROM THE MEDIAN DIFFICULTY FOR GRADE
8½, IN UNITS OF THE MEAN SQUARE DEVIATION OF GRADE 8½
IN THE ABILITY MEASURED BY THE COMPOSITE.

| 10-Composites | Permille s | σ distance |
|---|---|---|
| C I | 972 | − 1.91 |
| J | 876 | − 1.15½ |
| K | 472 | + .07 |
| N | 72 | + 1.46 |
| A KI | 564 | − .16 |
| L | 440 | + .15 |
| V 1 | 980 | − 2.05 |
| 1a | 976 | − 1.98 |
| 2 | 920 | − 1.41 |
| 2a | 972 | − 1.91 |
| 3 | 740 | − .64 |
| 3a | 864 | − 1.10 |
| 4 | 644 | − .37 |
| 4a | 618 | − .30 |
| 5 | 440 | + .15 |
| 5a | 448 | + .13 |
| 6 | 152 | + 1.03 |
| 6a | 236 | + .72 |
| 7 | 44 | + 1.71 |
| 7a | 60 | + 1.55 |
| Inf. 3 (1) | 984 | − 2.14 |
| 4 (2) | 716 | − .57 |
| 5 (3) | 500 | .00 |
| 6 (4) | 356 | + .37 |
| 7 (5) | 324 | + .46 |
| 8 (6) | 200 | + .84 |

TABLE 45.

DIFFICULTY OF 10-COMPOSITES MEASURED BY THE PERCENTS OF TWO GROUPS
(246 PUPILS IN GRADE 9 AND 264 PUPILS IN GRADE 9) SUCCEEDING WITH
FIVE OF MORE OF THE TEN SINGLE TASKS, AND BY DISTANCES + OR −
FROM THE MEDIAN DIFFICULTY FOR THE GROUP IN UNITS OF THE
MEAN SQUARE DEVIATION OF THE GROUP IN THE ALTITUDE OF
WHATEVER ABILITY THE 10-COMPOSITE MEASURES.

| 10-Composite | 9 I Permille s | σ distance | 9II Permille s | σ distance |
|---|---|---|---|---|
| C I | 967 | − 1.84 | | |
| I J | 951 | − 1.65 | | |
| J | 967 | − 1.84 | 936 | − 1.52 |
| K | 805 | − .86 | 689 | − .49 |
| L1 | 350 | + .39 | 295 | + .54 |
| M1 | 191 | + .88 | 178 | + .92 |
| N | | | 30 | + 1.88 |
| O | | | 0 | |
| A I | 1000 | .............. | | |
| I-J | 980 | − 2.05 | | |
| J | 886 | − 1.21 | 773 | − .75 |
| J1 | 943 | − 1.58 | 784 | − .79 |
| K1 | 545 | − .11 | 333 | + .43 |
| K | 671 | − .44 | 500 | .00 |
| L | 439 | + .15 | 258 | + .65 |
| L1 | | | 629 | − .33 |
| M | | | 167 | + .97 |
| N | | | 72 | + 1.46 |
| V 1 | 996 | − 2.65 | 996 | − 2.65 |
| 1a | | | | |
| 2 | 967 | − 1.84 | 977 | − 2.00 |
| 2a | | | | |
| 3 | 866 | − 1.11 | 826 | − .94 |
| 3a | | | | |
| 4 | 703 | − − .53 | 678 | − .45 |
| 4a | | | | |
| 5 | 492 | + .02 | 405 | + .24 |
| 5a | | | | |
| 6 | 150 | + 1.04 | 144 | + 1.06 |
| 6½a | | | 49 | + 1.65 |
| 7 | 20 | + 2.05 | 23 | + 2.00 |
| 7a | | | 11 | + 2.29 |

[1] In the case of the L and M completions with those pupils of Group 9 I
who did not have time to do everything to their satisfaction, an estimated
score was derived on the basis of what they did as far as they went and of
what they did with the completions of K.

TABLE 45—*Continued.*

| 10-Composite | 9I | | 9II | |
| --- | --- | --- | --- | --- |
| | Permille s | σ distance | Permille s | σ distance |
| D ½ | 992 | − 2.41 | | |
| 1 | 951 | − 1.65 | | |
| 2 | 683 | − .48 | | |
| 2½ | 600 | − .25* | | |
| 3 | 362 | + .35 | 205 | + .82 |
| 3½ | 293 | + .54 | | |
| 4 | 289 | + .56 | 133 | + 1.11 |
| 4½ | | | | |
| 5 | 126 | + 1.15 | 27 | + 1.93 |
| 6 | | | 23 | + 2.00 |
| 7 | | | 0 | |

TABLE 46.

DIFFICULTY OF 10-COMPOSITES MEASURED BY THE σ DISTANCES + OR − FROM
THE MEDIAN DIFFICULTY OF A GIVEN GRADE IN UNITS OF THE MEAN
SQUARE DEVIATION OF THE POPULATION OF THAT GRADE IN
THE ABILITY MEASURED BY THE 10-COMPOSITES.

| | Grade 9 | Grade 10 | Grade 11 | Grade 12 |
| --- | --- | --- | --- | --- |
| | n = 1089 | n = 723 | n = 769 | n = 643 |
| V 1 | − 2.457 | − 2.652 | − 2.748 | − 2.512 |
| 2 | − 2.290 | − 2.290 | − 2.652 | − 2.512 |
| 3 | − 1.360 | − 1.433 | − 1.838 | − 1.960 |
| 4 | − .671 | − .845 | − 1.522 | − 1.607 |
| 5 | + .182 | − .151 | − .668 | − .931 |
| 6 | + 1.131 | + .553 | + .068 | + .151 |
| 7 | + 2.120 | + 1.881 | + 1.546 | + 1.243 |
| | n = 1041 | n = 700 | n = 752 | n = 637 |
| V 1a | − 2.457 | − 2.457 | − 3.090 | − 2.748 |
| 2a | − 2.576 | − 2.366 | − 3.090 | |
| 3a | − 1.366 | − 1.468 | − 1.995 | − 2.226 |
| 4a | − .719 | − .990 | − 1.483 | − 1.774 |
| 5a | + .068 | − .264 | − .845 | − 1.019 |
| 6a | + .904 | + .527 | + .050 | − .235 |
| 7a | + 2.120 | + 1.866 | + 1.259 | + 1.094 |
| | | n = 1185 | n = 1053 | n = 742 |
| D 1 | | − 2.409 | − 2.878 | − 2.652 |
| 2 | | − 1.398 | − 1.695 | − 1.812 |
| 3 | | − .690 | − .999 | − 1.170 |
| 4 | | − .055 | − .335 | − .516 |
| 5 | | + .542 | + .306 | − .065 |
| 6 | | + 1.243 | + .966 | + .824 |
| 7 | | + 2.170 | + 1.896 | + 1.774 |

* 71.5% had 2 right out of 5.   48.4% had 3 right out of 5.
16

TABLE 47.

THE DIFFICULTY OF VARIOUS 10-COMPOSITES MEASURED BY THE PERCENT SUC-
CEEDING AND BY THE DISTANCE FROM THE MEDIAN IN TERMS OF THE MEAN
SQUARE DEVIATION OF THE GROUP. 422 NORMAL SCHOOL SENIORS. THE
FORM OF DISTRIBUTION IS ASSUMED TO BE "NORMAL." THE DIVISION
INTO TWO GROUPS OF 150 AND 185 IS APPROXIMATELY AT RANDOM.
THE GROUP OF 87 REPRESENTED A SOMEWHAT SUPERIOR SELECTION
AND TOOK CERTAIN ADDITIONAL TESTS.

| n = | %s 150 | 185 | 87 | 422 | σ distances 150 | 185 | 87 | 422 |
|---|---|---|---|---|---|---|---|---|
| C M$^2$ | 98.7 | 96.2 | 98.9 | 97.6 | − 2.23 | − 1.77 | − 2.29 | − 1.98 |
| MNs | 92.0 | 80.5 | 94.3 | 87.4 | − 1.41 | − .86 | − 1.58 | − 1.15 |
| N | 65.3 | 45.9 | 75.9 | 59.0 | − .39 | + .10 | − .70 | − .23 |
| Na | 54.0 | 53.0 | 69.0 | 56.6 | − .10 | − .08 | − .50 | − .17 |
| No | 17.3 | 19.5 | 20.7 | 19.0 | + .94 | + .86 | + .82 | + .88 |
| O | 18.7 | 20.5 | 35.6 | 23.0 | + .89 | + .82 | + .37 | + .74 |
| OP | 04.7 | 08.1 | 04.6 | 06.2 | + 1.67 | + 1.40 | + 1.68 | + 1.54 |
| P | 00.7 | 04.3 | 03.4 | 02.8 | + 2.46 | + 1.72 | + 1.83 | + 1.91 |
| Pa | 13.0 | 04.9 | 03.4 | 03.3 | + 2.23 | + 1.65 | + 1.83 | + 1.84 |
| Q | 00.0 | 00.5 | 00.0 | 00.2 | ∞ | + 2.58 | ∞ | + 2.88 |
| Qa | 00.0 | 00.0 | 00.0 | 00.0 | ∞ | ∞ | ∞ | ∞ |
| A X$_{1-8}$ | 90.7 | 73.5 | 83.9 | 81.8 | − 1.30 | − .63 | − .99 | − .91 |
| X$_{9-16}$ | 77.3 | 51.9 | 75.9 | 65.9 | − .75 | − .05 | − .70 | − .41 |
| X$_a$ | 94.7 | 85.4 | 96.6 | 91.0 | − 1.62 | − 1.05 | − 1.83 | − 1.34 |
| X$_b$ | 84.0 | 62.7 | 79.3 | 73.7 | − .99 | − .32 | − .78 | − .63 |
| X$_y$ | 72.7 | 44.9 | 69.0 | 59.7 | − .60 | + .13 | − .50 | − .25 |
| Y | 46.7 | 22.2 | 36.8 | 33.9 | + .08 | + .77 | + .34 | + .42 |
| Ya | 45.3 | 26.5 | 42.5 | 36.5 | + .12 | + .63 | + .19 | + .35 |
| Yz | 11.3 | 06.5 | 24.1 | 11.8 | + 1.21 | + 1.51 | + .70 | + 1.19 |
| Z$_1$ | 00.7 | 03.2 | 06.9 | 03.1 | + 2.46 | + 1.85 | + 1.48 | + 1.87 |
| Z$_2$ | 05.3 | 02.2 | 14.9 | 05.9 | + 1.62 | + 2.01 | + 1.04 | + 1.56 |
| Z$_a$ | Not taken off—so few got it. | | | | | | | |
| V 4a | 99.3 | 95.7 | 98.9 | 97.6 | − 2.46 | − 1.72 | − 2.29 | − 1.98 |
| 5a | 91.3 | 80.5 | 93.1 | 87.0 | − 1.36 | − .86 | − 1.48 | − 1.13 |
| 6a | 72.7 | 52.4 | 73.6 | 64.0 | − .60 | − .06 | − .63 | − .36 |
| 6½ | 44.7 | 35.7 | 50.6 | 41.9 | + .13 | + .37 | − .02 | + .20 |
| 7 | 18.0 | 16.2 | 20.7 | 17.8 | + .92 | + .99 | + .82 | + .92 |
| D 4½$^3$ | 96.7 | 81.6 | 90.8 | 88.9 | − 1.84 | − .90 | − .87 | − 1.22 |
| 5 | | | 66.7 | | | | − .43 | |
| 5½ | 38.7 | 22.7 | 24.1 | 28.7 | + .29 | + .75 | + .70 | + .56 |
| 6$^2$ | 54.7 | 42.2 | 34.5 | 45.0 | − .12 | + .20 | + .40 | + .13 |
| 6½$^4$ | 07.3 | 04.3 | 04.9 | 05.7 | + 1.45 | + 1.72 | + 1.65 | + 1.58 |
| 7$^4$ | 10.7 | 04.3 | 08.0 | 07.3 | + 1.24 | + 1.72 | + 1.41 | + 1.45 |

[2] Only six of the ten single tasks were used.

[3] Only nine of the ten single tasks were used. A person thus had to
succeed with 55½% to score a success; hence the % is too low.

[4] This composite has only six single tasks.

## TABLE 48.

THE DIFFICULTY OF 10-COMPOSITES MEASURED BY THE PERCENTS OF 240 COLLEGE GRADUATES AND 100 STUDENTS OF EDUCATION (COLLEGE OR NORMAL SCHOOL GRADUATES) SUCCEEDING, AND BY DISTANCES + OR − FROM THE MEDIAN DIFFICULTY FOR THE COLLEGE GRADUATES IN QUESTION, IN UNITS OF THE MEAN SQUARE DEVIATION OF THE COLLEGE GRADUATES IN QUESTION IN ALTITUDE OF WHATEVER ABILITY THE 10-COMPOSITE MEASURES IN EACH CASE.

| | | % | | σ distance | | | | % | | σ distance | |
|---|---|---|---|---|---|---|---|---|---|---|---|
| n = | | 240 | 100 | 240 | 100 | | | 240 | 100 | 240 | 100 |
| C | N | 92.9 | 95 | − 1.47 | − 1.64½ | Vocab. | 5 | 99.6 | 100 | − 2.65 | |
| | O | 80.8 | 82 | − .87 | − .91½ | " | 5a | 100.0 | 100 | | |
| | P | 61.3 | 56 | − .29 | − .15 | " | 6 | 99.6 | 100 | − 2.65 | |
| | Q | 41.7 | 44 | + .21 | + .15 | " | 6a | 94.6 | 99 | − 1.61 | − 2.33 |
| | R | 18.3 | | + .90 | | " | 7 | 68.4 | 75 | − .48 | − .67½ |
| | | | | | | " | 7a | 69.6 | 77 | − .51 | − .74 |
| | | | | | | " | 8 | 53.3 | 56 | − .08 | − .15 |
| | | | | | | " | 9 | 29.6 | 31 | + .54 | + .50 |
| A | N | 87.5 | 91 | − 1.15 | − 1.34 | " | 10 | 14.2 | 10 | + 1.07 | + 1.28 |
| | O | 82.1 | 79 | − .92 | − .81 | " | 11 | 1.7 | 4 | + 2.02 | + 1.75 |
| | P | 67.5 | 80 | − .45 | − .84 | | | | | | |
| | Q | 39.2 | | + .27 | | | | | | | |
| | | | | | | Inf. | 3 (1) | | 100 | | |
| | | | | | | " | 4 (2) | | 100 | | |
| D | 4½ | 96.3 | | − 1.79 | | " | 5 (3) | | 100 | | |
| | 5 | 85.9 | | − 1.08 | | " | 6 (4) | | 97 | | − 1.88 |
| | 5½ | | 74 | | − .64 | " | 7 (5) | | 81 | | − .88 |
| | 6 | 73.8 | | − .64 | | " | 8 (6) | | 60 | | − .25 |
| | 6½ | | 33 | | + .44 | | | | | | |
| | 7 | 38.3 | | + .30 | | | | | | | |

As given to these groups A Q contained only 5 tasks, D 5 contained only 8, D 6 contained only 6, D 6½ contained only 6, and D 7 contained only 6.

TABLE 49.

DIFFICULTY OF 10-COMPOSITES MEASURED BY THE PERCENTS OF 53 ADULT STU-
DENTS SUCCEEDING, AND BY DISTANCES + OR − FROM THE MEDIAN DIFFICULTY
FOR THE GROUP, IN UNITS OF THE MEAN SQUARE DEVIATION OF THE
GROUP IN THE ABILITY MEASURED BY THE COMPOSITE.

|   |   | Permilles | $\sigma$ distance |
|---|---|-----------|-------------------|
| C | M | 1000 | |
|   | N | 962 | − 1.77 |
|   | O | 887 | − 1.19 |
|   | P | 774 | − .75 |
|   | Q | 453 | + .12 |
|   | R | 245 | + .69 |
| | | | |
| A | J | 1000 | |
|   | K | 1000 | |
|   | L | 962 | − 1.77 |
|   | M | 943 | − 1.58 |
|   | N | 887 | − 1.21 |
|   | O | 717 | − .57½ |
|   | P | 736 | − .63 |

TABLE 50.

DIFFICULTY OF 10-COMPOSITES MEASURED BY THE PERCENTS OF 63 UNIVERSITY
STUDENTS SUCCEEDING.

|   |   |   |   |   |   |
|---|---|------|---|------|------|
| C | N | 98.4 | V | 6½a | 98.4 |
|   | O | 95.2 |   | 7 | 82.6 |
|   | P | 74.6 |   | 8 | 57.1 |
|   | Q | 33.3 |   | 9 | 20.6 |
|   | R | | | | |
| | | | | | |
| A | M | | D | 5 | 93.7 |
|   | N | 81.0 |   | 6 | 77.8 |
|   | O | 69.9 |   | 6½ | 27.0 |
|   | P | 60.3 |   | 7 | 39.7 |
|   | Q | 14.3 | | | |

was arrived at, we need not enter. The combinations made
are as shown below:

| 40-Composite | 10-Composite | | | |
| --- | --- | --- | --- | --- |
| | C | A | V | D |
| A | A | A | A | A |
| B | B | B | B | B |
| C | C | C | C | C |
| D | D | D | D | D |
| E | E | E | E | E |
| F | F | F | F | F |
| G | G | G | G | G |
| H | ...... | H | H | H |
| I | I | I | 2 | ½ |
| J | J | J | 3 | 2 |
| K | K | K | 4 | 2½ |
| L | L | L | 5 | 3 |
| M | M | M | 6 | 4 |
| N | N | N | 6½a | 5 |
| O | O | O | 7 | 6 |
| P | P | P | 8 | 6½ |
| Q | Q | Q | 9 | 7 |
| R | R | | 10 | |

The chief facts concerning the likeness in difficulty of
the four 10-composites making each 40-composite are summarized in Table 51, which gives the percents succeeding
for each of the four for each group which was tested with
all four, and some other data.

Not all of the facts of Tables 39–50 were available when
the process of putting the 10-composites together to make
40-composites was begun. If they had been, better combinations could have been made. In some cases a 10-com-
posite which is itself inferior is used because its difficulty
as a composite fits a certain place. Such happened with
Co L. In some cases 10-composites which seemed nearly
enough equal in difficulty to belong well together, were
found from wider experience not to be very closely alike,
but the discovery was made too late to allow amendments
to be made.

TABLE 51.

SUMMARY OF THE FACTS CONCERNING THE DIFFICULTY OF THE FOUR
10-COMPOSITES CONSTITUTING EACH 40-COMPOSITE.

|   | C | A | V | D | Group | n |
|---|---|---|---|---|---|---|
| A | 84 | 69 | 80 | 90 | im. 3 | 100 |
|   | 82½ | 80 | 81 | 86 | " | 80 |
| B | 65 | 45 | 49 | 45 | " | 100 |
|   | 56 | 49 | 57½ | 67½ | " | 80 |
| C | 35 | 15 | 14 | 19 | " | 100 |
|   | 27½ | 21 | 19 | 27½ | " | 80 |
| D | 3 | 5 | 1 | 12 | " | 100 |
|   | 0 | 5 | 5 | 14 | " | 80 |
| E | 56 | 55 | ...... | 45 | im. 6 | |
|   | 94 | 92 | 94 | 96 | f. | |
|   | 93 | 100 | ...... | 98 | sp. | |
| F | 25 | 20 | 23 | 23 | im. 6 | |
|   | 94 | 90 | 96 | 92 | f. | |
|   | 88 | 96 | 96 | 97 | sp. | |
|   | 100 | 100 | 99 | 94 | 4 | |
|   | 100 | 100 | 100 | 100 | ad. | |
| G | 7 | 5 | 15 | 6 | im. 6 | |
|   | 42 | 74 | 84 | 58 | f. | |
|   | 74 | 93 | 85 | 75 | sp. | |
|   | 83 | 99 | 98 | 82 | 4 | |
| H | | ...... | 4 | ...... | im. 6 | |
|   | | 88 | 64 | 44 | f. | |
|   | | 73 | 62 | 57 | sp. | |
|   | | 96 | 87 | 76 | 4b | |
|   | | 95 | 94 | 81 | 5a | |
| I | | 98 | 100 | 92 | 5b | |
|   | 20 | 14 | 24 | 12 | f. | |
|   | 18 | 20 | 37 | ...... | sp. | |
|   | 35 | 73 | 51 | 36 | 4b | |
|   | 47 | 78 | 58 | 53 | 5a | |
|   | 68 | 87 | 75 | 68 | 5b | |
|   | 83 | 92 | 93 | 89 | 5½ | |
|   | 97 | 100 | 97 | 99 | 9 I | |

TABLE 51 (continued).

|   | C | A | V | D | Group | n |
|---|---|---|---|---|---|---|
| J | 22 | 7 | 26 | 3 | 4b | |
| | 26 | 8 | 35 | 6 | 5a | |
| | 45 | 25 | 54 | 10 | 5b | |
| | 43 | 27 | 55 | 30 | 5½ | |
| | 97 | 89 | 87 | 68 | 9 I | |
| | 94 | 77 | 83 | ...... | 9 II | |
| K | 1 | 0 | 6 | 2 | 4b | |
| | 10 | 3 | 6 | 1 | 5a | |
| | 6 | 16 | 10 | 5 | 5b | |
| | 21 | 16 | ...... | 15 | 5½ | |
| | 81 | 67 | 70 | 60 | 9 I | |
| | 69 | 50 | 68 | ...... | 9 II | |
| L | 35 | 44 | 49 | 36 | 9 I | |
| | 30 | 26 | 41 | 21 | 9 II | |
| M | 18 | 17 | 14 | 13 | 9 II | |
| | ...... | 66 | 64 | ...... | N.S. | 422 |
| N | 3 | 7 | 5 | 3 | 9 II | |
| | 59 | 34 | 42 | ...... | N.S. | 422 |
| | 93 | 88 | ...... | 86 | 17 Law | |
| | 95 | 91 | ...... | ...... | 17–18 Ed. | |
| | 98 | 81 | 98 | 94 | Univ. | 63 |
| O | 23 | 3 | 18 | 45 | N.S. | 422 |
| | 81 | 82 | 68 | 74 | 17 Law | |
| | 82 | 79 | 75 | ...... | 17–18 Ed. | |
| | 95 | 70 | 83 | 78 | Univ. | 63 |
| P | 3 | 6 | ...... | 7 | N.S. | 422 |
| | 61 | 68 | 53 | ...... | 17 Law | |
| | 56 | 80 | 56 | 33 | 17–18 Ed. | |
| | 75 | 60 | 57 | 27 | Univ. | 63 |
| Q | 42 | 39 | 30 | 38 | 17 Law | |
| | 44 | ...... | 31 | ...... | 17–18 Ed. | |
| | 33 | 14 | 21 | 40 | Univ. | 63 |
| R | 18 | ...... | 14 | ...... | 17 Law | |
| | ...... | ...... | 10 | ...... | 17–18 Ed. | |

In general, however, these 40-composites are satisfactory. All the single tasks within any one of them are nearly enough alike in difficulty to prevent an individual for whom the composite as a whole is a suitable test, from being either bored or bewildered by any item of it. They rise in difficulty by steps which are small enough so that (as will be demonstrated later) a very finely graduated and reasonably precise measurement of altitude of Intellect CAVD is possible. In particular, composites J to Q furnish a very convenient series of defined and graded tasks. Each of them measures very nearly the same ability as the one below it or above it, and correlates with the score in the entire series of CAVD tasks nearly or quite as closely as its own self-correlation permits.

The methods used for obtaining CAVD 40-composite tasks, each of which measures all of Intellect CAVD and nothing but it, save for a small chance error which can safely be corrected for by $\sigma_1 = \sigma_t\ r_{t1}$ or by $\sigma_1 = \sigma_t\sqrt{r_{t1t2}}$, are applicable to any other form of intellect. We could have taken, in place of CAVD, Intellect OGAnS (O standing for the ability to give or select opposites, G standing for the ability to perceive the common element in $n$ facts and select other facts containing it, An standing for the ability to perceive and apply relations as in an Analogies test, and S standing for the ability to put together to make a sensible total, a series of elements as in a dissected sentences test.

Or we could have taken in place of CAVD, a non-verbal Intellect CRPF made up of Picture Completions, Geometrical Relations, Picture Sequences, and Forms to be cut up so as to produce specified parts. Or we could have taken an Intellect NIL made up of novel problems of the sort used in Burt's Reasoning Test,[8] informational tasks, and tasks in learning.[9] Or we could have taken any combination of all these.

[8] Shown in Chapter XVI.

[9] Such as the substitution test of the Army Beta, The National Intelligence Test, The Pintner-Non Verbal, and other examinations.

In place of attaching approximately equal weight to each sort of tasks, we may use any specified weights. We may also weight the single tasks of the same sort (C or A or V or D) differently one from another, provided the statistical consequences are allowed for consistently.

We may use the same situation and task as an element in composites at different levels according to the quality of the performance. Thus to give "mean" as the opposite of "grand" may count as a right in levels a, $a + k$, and $a + 2k$, whereas to give "little" may count as a right for a and $a + k$, but as a wrong for level $a + 2k$.

The essentials are that whatever intellect we claim to measure be defined by an actual series of tasks, and that each composite task measure the ability.

The difficulty of these CAVD 40-composites A, B, C, $\cdots$ Q is intellectual and it can be measured for each of them by means of the facts stated in Chapters II and IV, together with certain others. We shall carry through these measurements. But in order to do so, certain facts will be needed; and it will be most instructive to present these facts as parts of a general discussion of the meaning of the scores assigned in standard intelligence examinations. So the next two chapters will be in some respects a digression.

# CHAPTER VII

## The Transformation of the Scores of Standard Examinations into Terms of Scales with Equal Units

### THE METHOD OF TRANSFORMATION : ILLUSTRATED BY THE THORNDIKE EXAMINATION AND ARMY ALPHA

We have shown that the form of distribution of altitude of intellect measured in truly equal units is approximately Form A for any grade population from Grade 6 to college freshmen. We can then transmute the scores in any examination which is closely symptomatic of intellect, into terms of truly equal units, if we have the distributions of scores in grade populations. Consider, for example, the facts of Table 52, which shows the essential steps in such a transformation and two further steps by which the measures in truly equal units are adapted to the general scale of the original scoring.

The first column is a series of points on the scale of the original scores 54, 57, 60, 63, and so on. The second column gives the permille of individuals in the grade in question whose scores are below the point at which they are entered. Thus up to 54, there were 23; up to 57, there were 30; up to 60, there were 43, and so on. The third column gives the distance below or above the central tendency for the grade in terms of the mean square deviation of the grade. The sign is — until the entry in column 2 passes 500, when it changes to +. The fourth column gives the successive differences, the entry on a line with 57 giving the true difference between the score of 54 and the score of 57; the entry on a line with 60 giving the true difference between the score of 57 and the score of 60; and so on. These are the essentials.

If we desire to put these differences in such shape as to compare each readily with the difference which it replaces,

TABLE 52.

THORNDIKE EX. H.S. GRADS. PART I, FORMS D AND N. GRADE 12. n = 1527.

| 1 | 2 | 3*<br>x | 4 | 5 | 6 | 7 |
|---|---|---|---|---|---|---|
| Points on Original Scale | Permille up to Stated Point | − or +<br>Deviation from the Median in Equal Units | △<br>Value of Intervals in Equal Units | △/.05400** | Corrected Points on Scale | Column 6 − Column 1 |
| 54 | 23 | − 1.995393 | | | 54.77 | .77 |
| 57 | 30 | − 1.880794 | .114599 | 2.12 | 56.89 | − .11 |
| 60 | 43 | − 1.716886 | .163908 | 3.04 | 59.93 | − .07 |
| 63 | 59 | − 1.563224 | .153662 | 2.84 | 62.77 | − .23 |
| 66 | 75 | − 1.439531 | .123693 | 2.29 | 65.06 | − .84 |
| 69 | 95 | − 1.310579 | .128952 | 2.39 | 67.45 | − 1.55 |
| 72 | 136 | − 1.098468 | .212111 | 3.93 | 71.38 | − .62 |
| 75 | 166 | − .970093 | .128365 | 2.38 | 73.76 | − 1.24 |
| 78 | 214 | − .792619 | .177474 | 3.29 | 77.05 | − .95 |
| 81 | 263 | − .634124 | .158495 | 2.93 | 79.98 | − 1.02 |
| 84 | 330 | − .439913 | .194211 | 3.60 | 83.58 | − .42 |
| 87 | 391 | − .276714 | .163199 | 3.02 | 86.60 | − .40 |
| 90 | 463 | − .092878 | .183836 | 3.40 | 90. | .00 |
| 93 | 536 | + .090361 | .183239 | 3.39 | 93.39 | .39 |
| 96 | 600 | + .253347 | .162986 | 3.02 | 96.41 | .41 |
| 99 | 656 | + .401571 | .148224 | 2.75 | 99.16 | .16 |
| 102 | 720 | + .582841 | .181270 | 3.36 | 102.52 | .52 |
| 105 | 770 | + .738847 | .156006 | 2.89 | 105.41 | .41 |
| 108 | 807 | + .866894 | .128047 | 2.37 | 107.78 | − .22 |
| 111 | 852 | + 1.045050 | .178156 | 3.30 | 111.08 | .08 |
| 114 | 885 | + 1.200359 | .155309 | 2.88 | 113.96 | − .04 |
| 117 | 916 | + 1.378659 | .188300 | 3.49 | 117.45 | .45 |
| 120 | 934 | + 1.506262 | .127603 | 2.36 | 119.81 | − .19 |
| 123 | 954 | + 1.684941 | .178679 | 3.31 | 123.12 | .12 |
| 126 | 966 | + 1.825007 | .140066 | 2.60 | 125.72 | − .28 |
| 129 | 980 | + 2.053749 | .228742 | 4.24 | 129.96 | .96 |

always 3 in this case, we may divide the entries of column 4 by whatever σ value is on the average equal to 1 in the original scores. The result of such a division appears as column 5. If we desire to use the true differences to form a

* Computed from the Kelley-Wood table [Kelley, '23, p. 373 ff.].

** .054 is the average σ value corresponding to a difference of 1.00 in the original scale.

true scale of the same general location and extent as the original scores, we can do so by taking any point of the original scale arbitrarily and replacing all the other points by the values derived from the true differences. Column 6 shows the result of this operation, 90 being taken as the point of coincidence of the original and true values.

Column 7 is simply a convenient way of showing how and how far the measures in truly equal units diverge from

TABLE 53.

THORNDIKE INT. EX. H.S. GRADS. PART I, FORMS D AND N; SCORES FROM 54 TO 129 CORRECTED TO BE IN TRULY EQUAL UNITS.

| Original | Corrected | Original | Corrected | Original | Corrected |
|---|---|---|---|---|---|
| 54 | 54.8 | 80 | 79.0 | 106 | 106.2 |
| 55 | 55.5 | 81 | 80.0 | 107 | 107.0 |
| 56 | 56.2 | 82 | 81.2 | 108 | 107.8 |
| 57 | 56.9 | 83 | 82.4 | 109 | 108.9 |
| 58 | 57.9 | 84 | 83.6 | 110 | 110.0 |
| 59 | 58.9 | 85 | 84.6 | 111 | 111.1 |
| | | | | | |
| 60 | 59.9 | 86 | 85.6 | | |
| 61 | 60.9 | 87 | 86.6 | 112 | 112.1 |
| 62 | 61.8 | 88 | 87.8 | 113 | 113.1 |
| 63 | 62.8 | 89 | 88.9 | 114 | 114.0 |
| 64 | 63.6 | 90 | 90.0 | 115 | 115.2 |
| | | | | | |
| 65 | 64.4 | 91 | 91.2 | 116 | 116.4 |
| 66 | 65.1 | 92 | 92.3 | 117 | 117.5 |
| 67 | 65.9 | 93 | 93.4 | 118 | 118.3 |
| 68 | 66.7 | 94 | 94.4 | 119 | 119.1 |
| 69 | 67.5 | 95 | 95.4 | 120 | 119.8 |
| | | | | | |
| 70 | 68.8 | 96 | 96.4 | 121 | 120.9 |
| 71 | 70.1 | 97 | 97.4 | 122 | 122.0 |
| 72 | 71.4 | 98 | 98.3 | 123 | 123.1 |
| 73 | 72.2 | 99 | 99.2 | 124 | 124.0 |
| 74 | 73.0 | 100 | 100.3 | 125 | 124.9 |
| | | | | | |
| 75 | 73.8 | 101 | 101.4 | 126 | 125.7 |
| 76 | 74.9 | 102 | 102.5 | 127 | 127.1 |
| 77 | 76.0 | 103 | 103.5 | 128 | 128.5 |
| 78 | 77.0 | 104 | 104.5 | 129 | 130.0 |
| 79 | 78.0 | 105 | 105.4 | | |

those by the original scores. In the illustration the divergences are small and irregular, so that for many purposes the original scores can be taken as approximately the scores in truly equal units. Finally, we may by interpolation arrange a table giving the true-unit equivalents to any desired detail. When interpolating, one may also smooth the results if he has good reason to believe that the irregularities

TABLE 54.

ARMY ALPHA:  GRADE 9:  n = 1721.

| Points on Original Scale | Permille up to Stated Point | x - or + Deviations from tne Median in Equal Units | Δ Value of Interval in Equal Units | Δ/.0399 |
|---|---|---|---|---|
| 55 | 30 | − 1.880794 | | |
| 60 | 47 | − 1.674665 | .206129 | 5.17 |
| 65 | 76 | − 1.432503 | .242162 | 6.07 |
| 70 | 117 | − 1.190118 | .242385 | 6.07 |
| 75 | 174 | − .938476 | .251642 | 6.31 |
| 80 | 238 | − .712751 | .225725 | 5.66 |
| 85 | 307 | − .504372 | .208379 | 5.23 |
| 90 | 398 | − .258527 | .245845 | 6.16 |
| 95 | 473 | − .067731 | .190796 | 4.78 |
| 100 | 564 | + .161119 | .228850 | 5.73 |
| 105 | 630 | + .331853 | .170734 | 4.28 |
| 110 | 700 | + .524401 | .192558 | 4.83 |
| 115 | 755 | + .690309 | .165908 | 4.16 |
| 120 | 809 | + .874217 | .183908 | 4.61 |
| 125 | 856 | + 1.062519 | .188302 | 4.72 |
| 130 | 902 | + 1.293032 | .230513 | 5.78 |
| 135 | 936 | + 1.522036 | .229004 | 5.74 |
| 140 | 959 | + 1.739198 | .217162 | 5.44 |
| 145 | 971 | + 1.895698 | .156500 | 3.92 |
| 150 | 980 | + 2.053749 | .158051 | 3.96 |

are due to the small size of the population rather than to inequalities in alleged units. In the case of the illustration, we present (in Table 53) the results of interpolation without smoothing.

We have made the calculations necessary to obtain values in truly equal units for scores in Army Alpha, National A,

Otis Advanced Examination, Haggerty Intelligence Examination Delta 2, Terman Group Test of Mental Ability, Myers Mental Measure, Pintner Non-Language Mental Test, I. E. R. Tests of Selective and Relational Thinking, Generalization and Organization, Army Examination a, the Trabue Mentimeter, and the Brown University Psychological Examination. The results appear in Tables 54 to 94.

TABLE 55.

ARMY ALPHA:　GRADE 12:　n = 1387.

| Points on Original Scale | Permille up to Stated Point | x − or + Deviations from the Median | △ Value of Interval in Equal Units | △/.0411 |
|---|---|---|---|---|
| 75 | 18 | − 2.096927 | | |
| 80 | 40 | − 1.750686 | .346241 | 8.42 |
| 85 | 52 | − 1.625763 | .124923 | 3.04 |
| 90 | 74 | − 1.446632 | .179131 | 4.36 |
| 95 | 102 | − 1.270237 | .175395 | 4.27 |
| 100 | 142 | − 1.071377 | .198860 | 4.84 |
| 105 | 195 | − .859617 | .211760 | 5.15 |
| 110 | 267 | − .621912 | .237705 | 5.78 |
| 115 | 343 | − .404289 | .217623 | 5.29 |
| 120 | 422 | − .196780 | .207509 | 5.05 |
| 125 | 497 | − .007520 | .189260 | 4.60 |
| 130 | 581 | + .204452 | .211972 | 5.16 |
| 135 | 647 | + .377234 | .172782 | 4.20 |
| 140 | 711 | + .556308 | .179074 | 4.36 |
| 145 | 779 | + .768820 | .212512 | 5.17 |
| 150 | 838 | + .986271 | .217451 | 5.29 |
| 155 | 883 | + 1.190118 | .203847 | 4.96 |
| 160 | 924 | + 1.432503 | .242485 | 5.90 |
| 165 | 951 | + 1.654628 | .222125 | 5.41 |
| 170 | 968 | + 1.852180 | .197552 | 4.81 |
| 175 | 986 | + 2.197286 | .345106 | 8.40 |

In each of these cases we have material from several grade populations, which it is necessary to combine. The methods of combination may be illustrated by Army Alpha. For the upper range of scores 75 to 175 or higher, we have three large grade populations: 1,721 in Grade 9, 1,387 in Grade 12, and 2,545 college freshmen (Ohio). Each of these groups is submitted to the same treatment as was illustrated in the first four columns of Table 52. The results appear in Tables 54, 55, and 56 (columns 1 to 4). The differences in truly equal units are then divided in each of the three tables by the $\sigma$ difference corresponding to the average raw Alpha score point for the interval 75 to 150

TABLE 56.

ARMY ALPHA:   COLLEGE FRESHMEN (OHIO):   n = 2545.

| Points on Original Scale | Permille up to Stated Point | x – or + Deviations from the Median | $\Delta$ Value of Interval in Equal Units | $\Delta$/.0337 |
|---|---|---|---|---|
| 65 | 20 | – 2.053749 | | |
| 70 | 28 | – 1.911036 | .142713 | 4.23 |
| 75 | 36 | – 1.799118 | .111918 | 3.32 |
| 80 | 51 | – 1.635234 | .163884 | 4.86 |
| 85 | 70 | – 1.475791 | .159443 | 4.73 |
| 90 | 94 | – 1.316519 | .159272 | 4.73 |
| 95 | 125 | – 1.150349 | .166170 | 4.93 |
| 100 | 162 | – .986271 | .164078 | 4.87 |
| 105 | 206 | – .820379 | .165892 | 4.92 |
| 110 | 257 | – .652622 | .167757 | 4.98 |
| 115 | 309 | – .498687 | .153935 | 4.57 |
| 120 | 379 | – .308108 | .190579 | 5.81 |
| 125 | 442 | – .145900 | .162208 | 4.81 |
| 130 | 495 | – .012533 | .132367 | 3.93 |
| 135 | 565 | + .163658 | .176191 | 5.23 |
| 140 | 624 | + .316003 | .152345 | 4.52 |
| 145 | 701 | + .527279 | .211276 | 6.27 |
| 150 | 763 | + .715986 | .188707 | 5.60 |
| 155 | 818 | + .907770 | .191784 | 5.69 |
| 160 | 871 | + 1.131131 | .223361 | 6.63 |
| 165 | 906 | + 1.316519 | .185388 | 5.50 |
| 170 | 939 | + 1.546433 | .229914 | 6.82 |
| 175 | 961 | + 1.762410 | .215977 | 6.41 |
| 180 | 981 | + 2.074855 | .312445 | 9.27 |

(that is, by $(X_{150} - X_{75})/75$). This interval is taken because it is common to all three of the grade populations, so that its use gives strictly comparable results from all three. These results appear as the last columns in Tables 54, 55, and 56, and again in Table 57, where they are averaged for each 5-point interval of the original scores. The last column of Table 57 gives the unreliability in terms of $\sigma_{t-o}$ (mean square error) of each average. We have rather reliable measures in truly equal units from 75 to 155, and less reliable measures down to 55 and up to 175.

TABLE 57.

ARMY ALPHA: GRADES 9, 12 AND 13 (COLLEGE FRESHMEN): VALUES OF SUCCESSIVE 5-POINT INTERVALS OF THE ORIGINAL SCORES, IN EQUAL UNITS.

| Interval: Original Score | Values in Equal Units | | | | $\sigma_{t-o}$ |
|---|---|---|---|---|---|
| | Grade 9 $n = 1721$ | Grade 12 $n = 1387$ | Grade 13 $n = 2545$ | Average | |
| 55 to 59 | 5.17 | | | 5.17 | |
| 60 to 64 | 6.07 | | | 6.07 | |
| 65 to 69 | 6.07 | | 4.23 | 5.15 | .66 |
| 70 to 74 | 6.31 | | 3.32 | 4.82 | 1.06 |
| 75 to 79 | 5.66 | 8.42 | 4.86 | 6.31 | .87 |
| 80 to 84 | 5.23 | 3.04 | 4.73 | 4.33 | .54 |
| 85 to 89 | 6.16 | 4.36 | 4.73 | 5.08 | .45 |
| 90 to 94 | 4.78 | 4.27 | 4.93 | 4.66 | .16 |
| 95 to 99 | 5.73 | 4.84 | 4.87 | 5.15 | .24 |
| 100 to 104 | 4.28 | 5.15 | 4.92 | 4.78 | .21 |
| 105 to 109 | 4.83 | 5.78 | 4.98 | 5.20 | .24 |
| 110 to 114 | 4.16 | 5.29 | 4.57 | 4.67 | .27 |
| 115 to 119 | 4.61 | 5.05 | 5.81 | 5.16 | .29 |
| 120 to 124 | 4.72 | 4.60 | 4.81 | 4.71 | .05 |
| 125 to 129 | 5.78 | 5.16 | 3.93 | 4.96 | .44 |
| 130 to 134 | 5.74 | 4.20 | 5.23 | 5.06 | .37 |
| 135 to 139 | 5.44 | 4.36 | 4.52 | 4.77 | .28 |
| 140 to 144 | 3.92 | 5.17 | 6.27 | 5.12 | .56 |
| 145 to 149 | 3.96 | 5.29 | 5.60 | 4.95 | .41 |
| 150 to 154 | 4.32 | 4.96 | 5.69 | 4.99 | .32 |
| 155 to 159 | | 5.90 | 6.63 | 6.27 | .27 |
| 160 to 164 | | 5.41 | 5.50 | 5.46 | .03 |
| 165 to 169 | | 4.81 | 6.82 | 5.82 | .74 |
| 170 to 174 | | 8.40 | 6.41 | 7.41 | .70 |

For the lower range of scores (from 95 down) we have three grade populations (263, 281, and 321), though not so large ones as is desirable. They also are treated in the same manner as has been illustrated, up to the point of the differences in equal units, the results appearing in Tables

58, 59, and 60. These differences are then divided by $(X_{85} - X_{25})/60$. The results of the divisions appear as the three last columns of Tables 58, 59, and 60, and again in Table 61, where they are averaged for each 5-point interval of the original scores. We thus have measures in truly equal units for all the range from 20 to 85, though not so reliable ones as we should like to have. As an addition to these determinations, we have used in a similar manner the records from 242 12th-grade boys, 393 12th-grade girls, and 400 college freshmen. The results appear in Table 62.

We have combined all these results from these three determinations, giving weights of 3 to the determination from 5,653 individuals (1,721 + 1,387 + 2,545), 1 to the determination from 865 individuals (263 + 281 + 321), and 1 to the determination from 1,035 individuals (242 + 393 + 400).[1] The results appear in Table 63.

In Table 64 we give the results of interpolation with rather liberal smoothing. In the smoothing, we have been guided by three facts. First, the ups and downs from about 55 to about 145 are quite irregular and, in view of the probable errors, may well be chances of the sampling. Second, the data of Table 61 for the interval 15 to 20 and the general drift of the Army results support the hypothesis that original scores from 10 to 20 will have a true-unit value even higher than our 13.67 for 20 to 30; so that the increase from 10.81 for 40 to 50, to 11.67 for 30 to 40, and 13.67 for 20 to 30 may be considered real. Third, the facts of Table 62 and the facts of Table 65 for Alpha scores of a college-graduate group show that the true-unit values per interval of 5 score-points continue, above 175, the rise shown in our table from 150 to 170. We take 100 as the point of coinci-

[1] Before combining them we have multiplied all the results from the 865 determination (Grades 5, 6, and 7) by 1.08, which puts their total value from 65 to 95 on a parity with the total value from 65 to 95 of the 5623 series; we have also multiplied all the results from the 1035 determination by 1.03, which puts their total value from 110 to 155 on a parity with the total value from 110 to 155 of the 5623 series. These multiplications serve to keep our systems of values consistent.

TABLE 58.

ARMY ALPHA: GRADE 5: n = 263.

| Points on Original Scale | Permille up to Stated Point | x − or + Deviation from the Median | Δ Value of Interval in Equal Units | Δ/.0588 |
|---|---|---|---|---|
| 15 | 34 | − 1.825007 | | |
| 20 | 106 | − 1.248085 | .576922 | 9.81 |
| 25 | 190 | − .877896 | .370189 | 6.29 |
| 30 | 293 | − .544642 | .333254 | 5.67 |
| 35 | 395 | − .266311 | .278331 | 4.73 |
| 40 | 494 | − .015040 | .251271 | 4.27 |
| 45 | 589 | + .224973 | .240013 | 4.08 |
| 50 | 692 | + .501527 | .276554 | 4.70 |
| 55 | 768 | + .732276 | .230749 | 3.92 |
| 60 | 848 | + 1.027893 | .295617 | 5.03 |
| 65 | 905 | + 1.310579 | .282686 | 4.81 |
| 70 | 939 | + 1.546433 | .235854 | 4.01 |
| 75 | 970 | + 1.880794 | .334361 | 5.69 |
| 80 | 989 | + 2.290370 | .409576 | 6.96 |
| 85 | 996 | + 2.652070 | .361700 | 6.15 |

TABLE 59.

ARMY ALPHA: GRADE 6: n = 281.

| Points on Original Scale | Permille up to Stated Point | × − or + Deviation from the Median | Δ Value of Interval in Equal Units | Δ/.0551 |
|---|---|---|---|---|
| 20 | 14 | − 2.197286 | | |
| 25 | 39 | − 1.762410 | .435876 | 7.91 |
| 30 | 89 | − 1.346939 | .415471 | 7.54 |
| 35 | 132 | − 1.116987 | .229952 | 4.17 |
| 40 | 214 | − .792619 | .324368 | 5.89 |
| 45 | 299 | − .527279 | .265340 | 4.81 |
| 50 | 427 | − .184017 | .343252 | 6.23 |
| 55 | 566 | − .166199 | .350216 | 6.36 |
| 60 | 630 | + .331853 | .165654 | 3.01 |
| 65 | 737 | + .634124 | .302271 | 5.49 |
| 70 | 797 | + .830953 | .196829 | 3.57 |
| 75 | 836 | + .978150 | .147197 | 2.67 |
| 80 | 886 | + 1.205527 | .227377 | 4.13 |
| 85 | 939 | + 1.546433 | .340906 | 6.19 |
| 90 | 964 | + 1.799118 | .252685 | 4.58 |
| 95 | 985 | + 2.170090 | .370972 | 6.73 |

dence of the scale of the original scores and the scale of their equivalents in truly equal units. If we use the values of Table 63, we reach 65.92 as the equivalent of 65, and 149.90 as the equivalent of 150. The .10 deficiency we simply disregard and go from 100 to 150 by steps of 1.0. The .92 excess we distribute over the interval from 80 to 90,

TABLE 60.
ARMY ALPHA: GRADE 7: n = 321.

| Points on Original Scale | Permille up to Stated Point | x − or + Deviation from the Median | Δ Value of Interval in Equal Units | Δ/.04915 |
|---|---|---|---|---|
| 25 | 15 | − 2.170090 | | |
| 30 | 22 | − 2.014091 | .155999 | 3.17 |
| 35 | 56 | − 1.589268 | .424823 | 8.64 |
| 40 | 87 | − 1.359463 | .229805 | 4.68 |
| 45 | 140 | − 1.080319 | .279144 | 5.68 |
| 50 | 196 | − .855996 | .224323 | 4.56 |
| 55 | 290 | − .553385 | .302611 | 6.16 |
| 60 | 371 | − .329206 | .224179 | 4.56 |
| 65 | 449 | − .128188 | .201018 | 4.09 |
| 70 | 539 | + .097914 | .226102 | 4.60 |
| 75 | 626 | + .321278 | .223364 | 4.54 |
| 80 | 732 | + .618873 | .297595 | 6.05 |
| 85 | 782 | + .778966 | .160093 | 3.26 |
| 90 | 826 | + .938476 | .159490 | 3.24 |
| 95 | 863 | + 1.093897 | .155421 | 3.16 |
| 100 | 910 | + 1.340755 | .246858 | 5.02 |
| 105 | 931 | + 1.483280 | .142525 | 2.90 |
| 110 | 963 | + 1.786614 | .303334 | 6.17 |
| 115 | 969 | + 1.866296 | .079682 | 1.62 |
| 120 | 984 | + 2.144411 | .278115 | 5.66 |

which seems the most likely place for it to belong. From 65 down and from 150 up, we increase the values following the general course of the results of our determinations.

Two hundred and sixteen first-year law students,[2] all college graduates, were tested with Army Alpha. The distribution was as shown in Table 65. We do not know pre-

[2] Omitting two foreign students.

cisely the form of distribution of intellect measured in truly equal units for such a group as this, but the facts given in Appendix VI make it safe to assume that the upper half of the distribution has a form not much unlike Form A. By Form A the values of the intervals from the median up are:

| | |
|---|---|
| 180 to 184 | $.4565\sigma$ |
| 185 to 189 | $.3089\sigma$ |
| 190 to 194 | $.3609\sigma$ |
| 195 to 199 | $.5586\sigma$ |
| 200 to 204 | $.6807\sigma$ |

TABLE 61.

ARMY ALPHA, GRADES 5, 6 AND 7. VALUES OF SUCCESSIVE 5-POINT INTERVALS OF THE ORIGINAL SCORES, IN EQUAL UNITS.

| Interval Original Score | Values in Equal Units | | | | $\sigma_{t-o}$ |
|---|---|---|---|---|---|
| | Grade 5 n = 263 | Grade 6 n = 281 | Grade 7 n = 321 | Average | |
| 15 to 19 | 9.81 | | | 9.81 | |
| 20 to 24 | 6.29 | 7.91 | | 7.10 | .50 |
| 25 to 29 | 5.67 | 7.54 | 3.17 | 5.28 | 1.04 |
| 30 to 34 | 4.73 | 4.17 | 8.64 | 5.85 | 1.15 |
| 35 to 39 | 4.27 | 5.89 | 4.68 | 4.95 | .40 |
| 40 to 44 | 4.08 | 4.81 | 5.68 | 4.86 | .38 |
| 45 to 49 | 4.70 | 6.23 | 4.56 | 5.16 | .44 |
| 50 to 54 | 3.92 | 6.36 | 6.16 | 5.48 | .64 |
| 55 to 59 | 5.03 | 3.01 | 4.56 | 4.20 | .50 |
| 60 to 64 | 4.81 | 5.49 | 4.09 | 4.80 | .33 |
| 65 to 69 | 4.01 | 3.57 | 4.60 | 4.06 | .34 |
| 70 to 74 | 5.69 | 2.67 | 4.54 | 4.30 | .72 |
| 75 to 79 | 6.96 | 4.13 | 6.05 | 5.71 | 1.18 |
| 80 to 84 | 6.15 | 6.19 | 3.26 | 5.20 | .79 |
| 85 to 89 | | 4.58 | 3.24 | 3.91 | .47 |
| 90 to 94 | | 6.73 | 3.16 | 4.95 | 1.26 |
| 95 to 99 | | | 5.02 | 5.02 | |
| 100 to 104 | | | 2.90 | 2.90 | |
| 105 to 109 | | | 6.17 | 6.17 | |
| 110 to 114 | | | 1.62 | 1.62 | |
| 115 to 119 | | | 5.66 | 5.66 | |

TABLE 62.

ARMY ALPHA: GRADES 12 AND 13; SUPPLEMENTAL VALUES OF SUCCESSIVE
5-POINT INTERVALS OF THE ORIGINAL SCORES, IN EQUAL UNITS.

| Interval Original Score | Grade 12 Boys $n = 242$ | Values in Equal Units Grade 12 Girls $n = 393$ | Yale Freshman $n = 400$ | Average | $\sigma_{t-o}$ |
|---|---|---|---|---|---|
| 75 to 79 | 8.05 | | | 8.05 | |
| 80 to 84 | 2.20 | 3.00 | | 2.60 | .28 |
| 85 to 89 | 2.13 | 1.08 | | 1.61 | .37 |
| 90 to 94 | 5.36 | 3.80 | | 4.58 | .55 |
| 95 to 99 | 1.80 | 5.16 | | 3.48 | 1.19 |
| 100 to 104 | 5.56 | 5.84 | | 5.70 | .10 |
| 105 to 109 | 4.89 | 6.05 | | 5.47 | .41 |
| 110 to 114 | 4.76 | 5.83 | 7.13 | 5.91 | .56 |
| 115 to 119 | 5.01 | 5.70 | 3.52 | 4.74 | .53 |
| 120 to 124 | 3.29 | 4.56 | 4.06 | 3.97 | .30 |
| 125 to 129 | 6.14 | 5.06 | 5.47 | 5.56 | .26 |
| 130 to 134 | 2.24 | 5.57 | 4.76 | 4.19 | .82 |
| 135 to 139 | 4.26 | 4.11 | 2.94 | 3.77 | .34 |
| 140 to 144 | 7.19 | 4.71 | 5.45 | 5.78 | .60 |
| 145 to 149 | 5.35 | 4.25 | 4.66 | 4.75 | .26 |
| 150 to 154 | 5.23 | 3.09 | 4.99 | 4.44 | .55 |
| 155 to 159 | 6.64 | 5.63 | 6.13 | 5.68 | .35 |
| 160 to 164 | 3.37 | 6.52 | 5.00 | 4.96 | .74 |
| 165 to 169 | 6.58 | 4.95 | 5.86 | 5.80 | .39 |
| 170 to 174 | 10.29 | | 7.96 | 9.13 | .89 |
| 175 to 179 | | | 7.64 | 7.64 | |
| 180 to 184 | | | 7.95 | 7.95 | |
| 185 to 189 | | | 6.67 | 6.67 | |
| 190 to 194 | | | 6.01 | 6.01 | |

The values for the two intervals next below the median are:

| 170 to 174 | $.3136\sigma$ |
| 175 to 179 | $.2585\sigma$ |

These last and the values for 180 to 189 will not be very
different if any reasonable assumption is made about the
form of distribution.

Expressing the values for 190 and above in terms of the
170 to 190 difference, which is $1.327626\sigma$, we have the following results:

$$190 \text{ to } 194 = .272$$
$$195 \text{ to } 199 = .421$$
$$200 \text{ to } 204 = .513$$

TABLE 63.

FINAL ESTIMATE OF RELATIVE VALUES OF ARMY ALPHA SCORES IN EQUAL UNITS.

| Interval | Weighted Average: Intervals of 5 | Weighted Average: Intervals of 10 |
|---|---|---|
| 20 to 24 | 7.67 | |
| 25 to 29 | 5.70 | 13.67 |
| 30 to 34 | 6.32 | |
| 35 to 39 | 5.35 | 11.67 |
| 40 to 44 | 5.24 | |
| 45 to 49 | 5.57 | 10.81 |
| 50 to 54 | 5.92 | |
| 55 to 59 | 4.54 | 10.46 |
| 60 to 64 | 5.18 | |
| 65 to 69 | 4.96 | 10.14 |
| 70 to 74 | 4.78 | |
| 75 to 79 | 6.28 | 11.06 |
| 80 to 84 | 4.26 | |
| 85 to 89 | 4.23 | 8.49 |
| 90 to 94 | 4.81 | |
| 95 to 99 | 4.76 | 9.57 |
| 100 to 104 | 5.06 | |
| 105 to 109 | 5.31 | 10.37 |
| 110 to 114 | 5.03 | |
| 115 to 119 | 5.09 | 10.12 |
| 120 to 124 | 4.56 | |
| 125 to 129 | 5.15 | 9.71 |
| 130 to 134 | 4.88 | |
| 135 to 139 | 4.55 | 9.43 |
| 140 to 144 | 5.33 | |
| 145 to 149 | 4.94 | 10.27 |
| 150 to 154 | 4.89 | |
| 155 to 159 | 6.17 | 11.06 |
| 160 to 164 | 5.37 | |
| 165 to 169 | 5.86 | 11.23 |
| 170 to 174 | 7.91 | |
| 175 to 179 | 7.87 | 15.78 |
| 180 to 184 | 8.19 | |
| 185 to 189 | 6.87 | 15.06 |
| 190 to 194 | 6.19 | |

TABLE 64.

EQUIVALENTS FOR ARMY ALPHA SCORES FROM 20 TO 170 IN A SCALE WITH EQUAL
UNITS, 1 OF THIS SCALE EQUALLING .89/90 OF THE DIFFERENCE BETWEEN
60 AND 150 OF THE ORIGINAL ALPHA SCORES, OR APPROXIMATELY 1/100
OF THE DIFFERENCE BETWEEN 50 AND 150 OF THE ORIGINAL
ALPHA SCORES.

| Orig. | Cor. | Orig. | Cor. | Orig. | Cor. | Orig. | Cor. | Orig. | Cor. |
|---|---|---|---|---|---|---|---|---|---|
| 20 | 14.1 | 50 | 50.4 | 80 | 81.0 | 110 | 110 | 140 | 140 |
| 21 | 15.5 | 51 | 51.5 | 81 | 81.9 | 111 | 111 | 141 | 141 |
| 22 | 16.9 | 52 | 52.6 | 82 | 82.8 | 112 | 112 | 142 | 142 |
| 23 | 18.3 | 53 | 53.6 | 83 | 83.7 | 113 | 113 | 143 | 143 |
| 24 | 19.7 | 54 | 54.7 | 84 | 84.6 | 114 | 114 | 144 | 144 |
| 25 | 21.1 | 55 | 55.8 | 85 | 85.5 | 115 | 115 | 145 | 145 |
| 26 | 22.5 | 56 | 56.8 | 86 | 86.4 | 116 | 116 | 146 | 146 |
| 27 | 23.9 | 57 | 57.9 | 87 | 87.3 | 117 | 117 | 147 | 147 |
| 28 | 25.2 | 58 | 58.9 | 88 | 88.2 | 118 | 118 | 148 | 148 |
| 29 | 26.5 | 59 | 60.0 | 89 | 89.1 | 119 | 119 | 149 | 149 |
| 30 | 27.8 | 60 | 61 | 90 | 90 | 120 | 120 | 150 | 150 |
| 31 | 29.0 | 61 | 62 | 91 | 91 | 121 | 121 | 151 | 151.1 |
| 32 | 30.2 | 62 | 63 | 92 | 92 | 122 | 122 | 152 | 152.2 |
| 33 | 31.4 | 63 | 64 | 93 | 93 | 123 | 123 | 153 | 153.3 |
| 34 | 32.6 | 64 | 65 | 94 | 94 | 124 | 124 | 154 | 154.4 |
| 35 | 33.8 | 65 | 66 | 95 | 95 | 125 | 125 | 155 | 155.5 |
| 36 | 35.0 | 66 | 67 | 96 | 96 | 126 | 126 | 156 | 156.6 |
| 37 | 36.1 | 67 | 68 | 97 | 97 | 127 | 127 | 157 | 157.7 |
| 38 | 37.2 | 68 | 69 | 98 | 98 | 128 | 128 | 158 | 158.8 |
| 39 | 38.3 | 69 | 70 | 99 | 99 | 129 | 129 | 159 | 159.9 |
| 40 | 39.4 | 70 | 71 | 100 | 100 | 130 | 130 | 160 | 161.0 |
| 41 | 40.5 | 71 | 72 | 101 | 101 | 131 | 131 | 161 | 162.1 |
| 42 | 41.6 | 72 | 73 | 102 | 102 | 132 | 132 | 162 | 163.2 |
| 43 | 42.7 | 73 | 74 | 103 | 103 | 133 | 133 | 163 | 164.3 |
| 44 | 43.8 | 74 | 75 | 104 | 104 | 134 | 134 | 164 | 165.4 |
| 45 | 44.9 | 75 | 76 | 105 | 105 | 135 | 135 | 165 | 166.6 |
| 46 | 46.0 | 76 | 77 | 106 | 106 | 136 | 136 | 166 | 167.7 |
| 47 | 47.0 | 77 | 78 | 107 | 107 | 137 | 137 | 167 | 168.8 |
| 48 | 48.2 | 78 | 79 | 108 | 108 | 138 | 138 | 168 | 170.0 |
| 49 | 49.3 | 79 | 80 | 109 | 109 | 139 | 139 | 169 | 171.1 |
|  |  |  |  |  |  |  |  | 170 | 172.2 |

In our series as constructed from the extensive data in
Grades 5, 6, 7, 9, 12, and 13 the 170 to 190 difference is .3084.
So in the terms of that series 190 to 194 = 8.39, 195 to 199
= 12.98, and 200 to 204 = 15.82.

TABLE 64a.

PROVISIONAL EQUIVALENTS FOR ARMY ALPHA SCORES FROM 170 TO 209; SCALE AS IN TABLE 64.

| Orig. | Cor. | Orig. | Cor. | Orig. | Cor. | Orig. | Cor. |
|-------|------|-------|------|-------|------|-------|------|
| 170 | 172.2 | 180 | 187.2 | 190 | 203 | 200 | 223 |
| 171 | 173.7 | 181 | 188.8 | 191 | 205 | 201 | 225 |
| 172 | 175.2 | 182 | 190.4 | 192 | 207 | 202 | 228 |
| 173 | 176.7 | 183 | 192. | 193 | 209 | 203 | 231 |
| 174 | 178.2 | 184 | 193.6 | 194 | 211 | 204 | 234 |
| 175 | 179.7 | 185 | 195.2 | 195 | 213 | 205 | 237 |
| 176 | 181.2 | 186 | 196.7 | 196 | 215 | 206 | 240 |
| 177 | 182.7 | 187 | 198.3 | 197 | 217 | 207 | 243 |
| 178 | 184.2 | 188 | 199.8 | 198 | 219 | 208 | 246 |
| 179 | 185.7 | 189 | 201.4 | 199 | 221 | 209 | 249 |

Averaging the two determinations for 190 to 194 (6.19 and 8.39), we have 7.28 as the best estimate for that. We have 12.98 as the best estimate for 195 to 199, and 15.82 as the best estimate for 200 to 204. This would give us 20.26 for the interval 190 to 199, with a probability that the interval from 200 to 209 would be still larger.

We have not incorporated these determinations with the others, because they are less secure. There can be no doubt, however, that anyone will be much nearer the truth by using them than by using the original score values for Army Alpha. There can be little doubt also that the units of Alpha represent in general progressively greater increments of ability from 130 to 210. Subject to further investigations we offer Table 64a as a scale of provisional equivalents in truly equal units for Army Alpha scores of 170 to 209.

The values of the letter-grade intervals used in the Army reports are as follows, in equal units:

| Original | | Corrected |
|----------|-------------------------------------------------|-----------|
| 209 to 135 | High End of A   to High End of B − | 249 to 135 |
| 134 to 105 | High End of B − to High End of C + | 134 to 105 |
| 104 to  75 | High End of C + to High End of C | 104 to  76 |
|  74 to  45 | High End of C   to High End of C − |  75 to  45 |
|  44 to  25 | High End of C − to High End of D |  44 to  21 |
|  24 to  15 | High End of D   to High End of D − |  20 to  ? |
|  14 to   0 | High End of D − to Low End of D − |  ? to  ? |

THE NATIONAL INTELLIGENCE EXAMINATION A

Consider next the case of the National Intelligence Examination A. We use first the scores from 1,668 pupils in Grade 6 and 494 pupils in Grade 9. The results of the derivation of values in equal units are shown in Table 66. The procedure by which these are obtained is just the same as that shown in detail in the case of Army Alpha. The two sets of values are combined with weights of 3 and 1.

TABLE 65.

ARMY ALPHA DISTRIBUTION OF SCORES OF 216 COLLEGE GRADUATES.

| | |
|---|---|
| 100 to 104 | 1 |
| 105 to 109 | |
| 110 to 114 | 2 |
| 115 to 119 | 2 |
| 120 to 124 | |
| 125 to 129 | 3 |
| 130 to 134 | 5 |
| 135 to 139 | 1 |
| 140 to 144 | 4 |
| 145 to 149 | 6 |
| 150 to 154 | 8 |
| 155 to 159 | 9 |
| 160 to 164 | 6 |
| 165 to 169 | 15 |
| 170 to 174 | 24 |
| 175 to 179 | 22 |
| 180 to 184 | 38 |
| 185 to 189 | 22 |
| 190 to 194 | 20 |
| 195 to 199 | 18 |
| 200 to 204 | 8 |
| 205 to 209 | 2 |

We next use scores from 1,679 pupils in Grade 7 and 482 pupils in Grade 8, the results, weighted by 3 and 1, being as shown in Table 67. The values here are, in the last column, divided by a factor such that the total difference 70 to 170 is the same as for the determinations from Grades 6 and 9.

TABLE 66.

NATIONAL A: GRADES 6 (n = 1668) AND 9 (n = 494).

| A | 6 | | | 9 | | | H | I |
|---|---|---|---|---|---|---|---|---|
| | B | C | D | E | F | G | | |
| Point on Original Scale | Permille up to Stated Point | Δ6 Value of Interval in Equal Units | Δ6/.045 | Permille up to Stated Point | Δ9 Value of Interval in Equal Units | Δ9/.0546 | Weighted Average 3D+G/4 | Interval |
| 50 | 8 | .151887 | 3.38 | | | | 3.38 | 50 to 54 |
| 55 | 12 | .137057 | 3.04 | | | | 3.04 | 55 " 59 |
| 60 | 17 | .105981 | 2.35 | | | | 2.35 | 60 " 64 |
| 65 | 22 | .202180 | 4.50 | | | | 4.50 | 65 " 69 |
| 70 | 35 | .175677 | 3.91 | | | | 3.91 | 70 " 74 |
| 75 | 51 | .243490 | 5.42 | | | | 5.42 | 75 " 79 |
| 80 | 82 | .216757 | 4.82 | | | | 4.82 | 80 " 84 |
| 85 | 120 | .168123 | 3.74 | | | | 3.74 | 85 " 89 |
| 90 | 157 | .234671 | 5.22 | | | | 5.22 | 90 " 94 |
| 95 | 220 | .248152 | 5.52 | | | | 5.52 | 95 " 99 |
| 100 | 300 | .218560 | 4.76 | | | | 4.76 | 100 " 104 |
| 105 | 380 | .202528 | 4.50 | 38 | .168752 | 3.10 | 4.15 | 105 " 109 |
| 110 | 459 | .210948 | 4.69 | 70 | .298691 | 5.47 | 4.89 | 110 " 114 |
| 115 | 543 | .255815 | 5.69 | 96 | .171106 | 3.15 | 5.06 | 115 " 119 |
| 120 | 642 | .201298 | 4.48 | 157 | .297821 | 5.48 | 4.73 | 120 " 124 |
| 125 | 714 | .203712 | 4.53 | 222 | .241408 | 4.44 | 4.51 | 125 " 129 |
| 130 | 779 | .217451 | 4.84 | 309 | .266769 | 4.91 | 4.86 | 130 " 134 |
| 135 | 838 | .229689 | 5.11 | 433 | .329946 | 6.07 | 5.35 | 135 " 139 |
| 140 | 888 | .230672 | 5.13 | 545 | .281780 | 5.18 | 5.15 | 140 " 144 |
| 145 | 926 | .238309 | 5.30 | 671 | .329637 | 6.06 | 5.49 | 145 " 149 |
| 150 | 954 | .258193 | 5.74 | 782 | .336290 | 6.18 | 5.85 | 150 " 154 |
| 155 | 974 | | | 881 | .401035 | 7.37 | 7.37 | 155 " 159 |
| 160 | | | | 948 | .445676 | 8.20 | 8.20 | 160 " 164 |
| 165 | | | | 972 | .285273 | 5.25 | 5.25 | 165 " 169 |
| 170 | | | | 986 | .286250 | 5.26 | 5.26 | 170 " 174 |
| 175 | | | | | | | | |

TABLE 67.

NATIONAL A: GRADES 7 (n = 1679) AND 8 (n = 482)

| A | 7 | | | 8 | | | H | I |
|---|---|---|---|---|---|---|---|---|
| Point on Original Scale | Permille up to Stated Point | Value of Interval in Equal Units Δ | Δ/.047 | Permille up to Stated Point | Value of Interval in Equal Units Δ | Δ/.491 | Weighted Average $\frac{3D+G}{4}$ | H/.971 |
| 45 | 1.8 | .121 | 2.55 | | | | 2.55 | 2.63 |
| 50 | 2.4 | .106 | 2.23 | | | | 2.23 | 2.30 |
| 55 | 4.2 | .228 | 4.80 | | | | 4.80 | 4.94 |
| 60 | 7.7 | .082 | 1.73 | | | | 1.73 | 1.78 |
| 65 | 9.5 | .176 | 3.71 | 8.3 | | | 3.71 | 3.82 |
| 70 | 14.9 | .132 | 2.78 | 10.4 | .108 | 2.20 | 2.64 | 2.72 |
| 75 | 20.8 | .263 | 5.54 | 16.6 | .184 | 3.75 | 5.09 | 5.24 |
| 80 | 38.1 | .164 | 3.45 | 31.1 | .258 | 5.25 | 3.90 | 4.02 |
| 85 | 53.6 | .165 | 3.47 | 53.9 | .263 | 5.36 | 3.94 | 4.06 |
| 90 | 73.8 | .217 | 4.57 | 83.0 | .222 | 4.52 | 4.56 | 4.70 |
| 95 | 109.6 | .193 | 4.06 | 120.3 | .211 | 4.30 | 4.12 | 4.25 |
| 100 | 150.0 | .226 | 4.76 | 159.8 | .179 | 3.65 | 4.51 | 4.65 |
| 105 | 209.0 | .1895 | 3.99 | 222.0 | .2295 | 4.67 | 5.16 | 5.32 |
| 110 | 267.4 | .2368 | 4.98 | 307.0 | .261 | 5.32 | 5.07 | 5.22 |
| 115 | 346.6 | .228 | 4.80 | 390.0 | .225 | 4.58 | 4.75 | 4.89 |
| 120 | 413.2 | .213 | 4.48 | 477.2 | .222 | 4.52 | 4.49 | 4.63 |
| 125 | 518.8 | .201 | 4.23 | 543.6 | .144 | 2.93 | 3.91 | 4.03 |
| 130 | 597.4 | .216 | 4.55 | 630.7 | .2475 | 5.04 | 4.67 | 4.81 |
| 135 | 677.8 | .218 | 4.59 | 717.8 | .242 | 4.93 | 4.68 | 4.82 |
| 140 | 751.6 | .268 | 5.64 | 784.2 | .212 | 4.32 | 5.31 | 5.47 |
| 145 | 828.5 | .274 | 5.77 | 867.2 | .325 | 6.62 | 5.98 | 6.16 |
| 150 | 889.2 | .298 | 6.27 | 900.0 | .1685 | 3.43 | 5.56 | 5.73 |
| 155 | 935.7 | .332 | 6.99 | 958.5 | .4525 | 9.22 | 7.55 | 7.78 |
| 160 | 968.4 | .438 | 9.22 | 983.4 | .396 | 8.07 | 8.93 | 9.20 |
| 165 | 989.3 | .285 | 6.01 | 993.8 | .360 | 7.33 | 6.34 | 6.53 |
| 170 | 995.2 | .466 | 9.68 | | | | 9.68 | 9.97 |
| 175 | 998.8 | | | | | | | |

TABLE 68.

NATIONAL A. SUMMARY OF DETERMINATIONS OF VALUES IN EQUAL UNITS.

| Interval | By Grades 6 and 9 | By Grades 7 and 8 | Average |
|---|---|---|---|
| 45 to 49 | | 2.63 | 2.63 |
| 50 " 54 | 3.38 | 2.30 | 2.84 |
| 55 " 59 | 3.04 | 4.94 | 3.99 |
| 60 " 64 | 2.35 | 1.78 | 2.07 |
| 65 " 69 | 4.50 | 3.82 | 4.16 |
| 70 " 74 | 3.91 | 2.72 | 3.32 |
| 75 " 79 | 5.42 | 5.24 | 5.33 |
| 80 " 84 | 4.82 | 4.02 | 4.42 |
| 85 " 89 | 3.74 | 4.06 | 3.90 |
| 90 " 94 | 5.22 | 4.70 | 4.96 |
| 95 " 99 | 5.52 | 4.25 | 4.89 |
| 100 " 104 | 4.76 | 4.65 | 4.71 |
| 105 " 109 | 4.15 | 5.32 | 4.74 |
| 110 " 114 | 4.89 | 5.22 | 5.06 |
| 115 " 119 | 5.06 | 4.89 | 4.98 |
| 120 " 124 | 4.73 | 4.63 | 4.68 |
| 125 " 129 | 4.51 | 4.03 | 4.27 |
| 130 " 134 | 4.86 | 4.81 | 4.84 |
| 135 " 139 | 5.35 | 4.82 | 5.09 |
| 140 " 144 | 5.15 | 5.47 | 5.31 |
| 145 " 149 | 5.49 | 6.16 | 5.83 |
| 150 " 154 | 5.85 | 5.73 | 5.79 |
| 155 " 159 | 7.37 | 7.78 | 7.58 |
| 160 " 164 | 8.20 | 9.20 | 8.70 |
| 165 " 169 | 5.25 | 6.53 | 5.89 |
| 170 " 174 | 5.26 | 9.97 | 7.62 |

| Interval | By Grades 6 and 9 | By Grades 7 and 8 | Average | $\sigma_{t-o}$ |
|---|---|---|---|---|
| 50 to 59 | 6.42 | 7.24 | 6.83 | .41 |
| 60 " 69 | 6.85 | 5.60 | 6.23 | .625 |
| 70 " 79 | 9.33 | 7.76 | 8.55 | .78 |
| 80 " 89 | 8.56 | 8.08 | 8.32 | .24 |
| 90 " 99 | 10.74 | 8.95 | 9.85 | .895 |
| 100 " 109 | 8.91 | 9.97 | 9.44 | .53 |
| 110 " 119 | 9.95 | 10.11 | 10.03 | .08 |
| 120 " 129 | 9.24 | 8.66 | 8.95 | .29 |
| 130 " 139 | 10.21 | 9.63 | 9.92 | .29 |
| 140 " 149 | 10.64 | 11.63 | 11.14 | .505 |
| 150 " 159 | 13.22 | 13.51 | 13.37 | .15 |
| 160 " 169 | 13.45 | 15.73 | 14.59 | 1.14 |

In Table 68 the results of the 6, 9 and of the 7, 8 determinations are put side by side and averaged, and measures of the unreliability of the averages are attached.

We have made a provisional extension of the transmutations for National A down to original scores of 20 by using the assumption that Grades 5 and 4 will show approximately normal distribution of perfectly measured in-

TABLE 69.
NATIONAL A: GRADE 4 (n = 1677) AND GRADE 5 (n = 2487)

| Interval | Original Distributions | | Values in Equal Units | | Average | Average × |
|---|---|---|---|---|---|---|
| | 4 | 5 | 4 | 5 | age | .924 |
| 10– 19 | 10 | 3 | | | | |
| 20– 29 | 33 | 7 | 11.51 | 9.30 | 10.40 | 9.61 |
| 30– 39 | 69 | 23 | 9.92 | 10.19 | 10.06 | 9.30 |
| 40– 49 | 113 | 63 | 8.24 | 10.44 | 9.34 | 8.63 |
| 50– 59 | 214 | 118 | 10.07 | 9.42 | 9.75 | 9.01 |
| 60– 69 | 285 | 275 | 9.87 | 12.00 | 10.94 | 10.02 |
| 70– 79 | 311 | 347 | 9.99 | 10.02 | 10.01 | 9.25 |
| 80– 89 | 257 | 417 | 9.36 | 10.13 | 9.75 | 9.01 |
| 90– 99 | 200 | 412 | 10.26 | 10.01 | 10.14 | 9.37 |
| 100–109 | 106 | 350 | 9.49 | 10.27 | 9.88 | 9.13 |
| 110–119 | 55 | 226 | 10.85 | 9.55 | 10.20 | 9.42 |
| 120–129 | 7 | 147 | 7.69 | 10.83 | 9.26 | 8.56 |
| | 2 | 66 | 10.59 | 10.44 | 10.52 | 9.71 |
| | | 22 | | | | |
| | | 11 | | | | |
| | | 1 | | | | |
| | | 1 | | | | |

tellect. Table 69 shows the original distributions, the values of the intervals in equal units by the assumption, the quotients when these are divided by 1/50 of the difference between 70 and 120 of the original scale, the averages for the two grades, and these averages after multiplication by a factor which equates the 70 to 120 difference with the 70 to 120 difference of the scale derived by the use of Grades 6 and 9.

TABLE 70.

EQUIVALENTS FOR NATIONAL A SCORES FROM 20 TO 170, IN A SCALE WITH
EQUAL UNITS 1 = APPROXIMATELY 1/50 OF THE DIFFERENCE BE-
TWEEN 100 AND 150 OF THE ORIGINAL SCALE.

| Orig. | Cor. | Orig. | Cor. | Orig. | Cor. | Orig. | Cor. | Orig. | Cor. |
|---|---|---|---|---|---|---|---|---|---|
| 20 | 30.2 | 50 | 57.8 | 80 | 82.4 | 110 | 110 | 140 | 139 |
| 1 | 31.2 | 1 | 58.6 | 1 | 83.2 | 1 | 111 | 1 | 140.1 |
| 2 | 32.2 | 2 | 59.4 | 2 | 84.1 | 2 | 112 | 1 | 141.2 |
| 3 | 33.2 | 3 | 60.2 | 3 | 85.0 | 3 | 113 | 3 | 142.3 |
| 4 | 34.1 | 4 | 61.0 | 4 | 85.8 | 4 | 114 | 4 | 143.4 |
| 5 | 35.1 | 5 | 61.8 | 5 | 86.6 | 5 | 115 | 5 | 144.5 |
| 6 | 36.1 | 6 | 62.6 | 6 | 87.4 | 6 | 116 | 6 | 145.6 |
| 7 | 37.0 | 7 | 63.4 | 7 | 88.2 | 7 | 117 | 7 | 146.7 |
| 8 | 38.0 | 8 | 64.2 | 8 | 89.0 | 8 | 118 | 8 | 147.8 |
| 9 | 38.9 | 9 | 65.0 | 9 | 89.8 | 9 | 119 | 9 | 148.9 |
| 30 | 39.8 | 60 | 65.7 | 90 | 90.7 | 120 | 120 | 150 | 150.0 |
| 1 | 40.8 | 1 | 66.5 | 1 | 91.6 | 1 | 120.9 | 1 | 151.3 |
| 2 | 41.8 | 2 | 67.3 | 2 | 92.6 | 2 | 121.8 | 2 | 152.6 |
| 3 | 42.7 | 3 | 68.1 | 3 | 93.6 | 3 | 122.7 | 3 | 154.0 |
| 4 | 43.6 | 4 | 68.9 | 4 | 94.6 | 4 | 123.6 | 4 | 155.3 |
| 5 | 44.6 | 5 | 69.7 | 5 | 95.6 | 5 | 124.5 | 5 | 156.6 |
| 6 | 45.5 | 6 | 70.5 | 6 | 96.5 | 6 | 125.4 | 6 | 158.0 |
| 7 | 46.4 | 7 | 71.3 | 7 | 97.5 | 7 | 126.7 | 7 | 159.3 |
| 8 | 47.3 | 8 | 72.1 | 8 | 98.5 | 8 | 127.2 | 8 | 161.6 |
| 9 | 48.2 | 9 | 73.0 | 9 | 99.5 | 9 | 128.1 | 9 | 162.0 |
| 40 | 49.1 | 70 | 73.8 | 100 | 100.5 | 130 | 129.0 | 160 | 163.4 |
| 1 | 50.0 | 1 | 74.6 | 1 | 101.4 | 1 | 130 | 1 | 164.8 |
| 2 | 50.9 | 2 | 75.5 | 2 | 102.4 | 2 | 131 | 3 | 166.2 |
| 3 | 51.8 | 3 | 76.3 | 3 | 103.3 | 3 | 132 | 3 | 167.6 |
| 4 | 52.7 | 4 | 77.2 | 4 | 104.3 | 4 | 133 | 4 | 169.0 |
| 5 | 53.6 | 5 | 78.0 | 5 | 105.2 | 5 | 134 | 5 | 170.5 |
| 6 | 54.5 | 6 | 78.9 | 6 | 106.2 | 6 | 135 | 6 | 172.0 |
| 7 | 55.3 | 7 | 79.8 | 7 | 107.1 | 7 | 136 | 7 | 173.5 |
| 8 | 56.2 | 8 | 80.6 | 8 | 108.1 | 8 | 137 | 8 | 175.0 |
| 9 | 57.0 | 9 | 81.5 | 9 | 109.0 | 9 | 138 | 9 | 176.5 |
| | | | | | | | | 170 | 178.0 |

We combine these results with that from Grades 6, 7, 8, and 9, allowing equal weight to each of the two, and so have, as provisional values for these low intervals, the following:

| | |
|---|---|
| 20–29 | 9.61 |
| 30–39 | 9.30 |
| 40–49 | 8.63 |
| 50–59 | 7.92 |
| 60–69 | 8.12 |

Using these values up to 70 and that of Table 68 from 70 on, and making the original scale and the scale in equal units coincide at 120, we have Table 70 as our transmuting table.

## THE OTIS ADVANCED EXAMINATION

In the case of the Otis Advanced Examination we have the distributions shown in Table 71. We obtain the $\sigma$ values in equal units for each interval for each group, as shown in the case of Army Alpha. In Groups I, II, and III we then divide each of these by the difference between 70 and 140 (in equal units); average I and II with respective weights of 2 and 1; combine this average with III, giving equal weight to Grade 6 and to Grade 9. In Group IV we divide each of the $\sigma$ values by the difference between 100 and 170 (in equal units) and then multiply each by a factor which makes the 100 to 170 difference for Group IV equal to that for the I, II, III weighted average. The I, II, III weighted average and the IV result are then averaged with weights of 3 and 1, respectively. The essential steps in these computations are shown in Table 72, the last column of which shows the combined estimate of the relative values of the 10-point intervals from 30 to 200 in terms of equal units. For convenience in interpretation these values are divided by 1.06, which makes the unit of the equal-unit scale 1/100 of the difference between 70 and 170 of the original scale. By interpolation and smoothing, letting the two scales coincide at 100, we obtain the equivalents of Table 73. It may be noted that what scant data we have above 200 indicate that the rise from 12.52 to 17.77 (or 11.81 and 16.76, after division by 1.06) is not a matter of the sampling error. The data give 21.60 (or 20.38) as the value for 200 to 209.

The interval from 20 to 29 has a value of 18.30 (17.26 after division by 1.06) by the sixth-grade groups, but this is too unreliable for use without confirmation. We have considered the facts for a fifth-grade population of 3,058 individuals and a fourth-grade population of 1,500 pupils. We do not, of course, know that in these grades the distri-

TABLE 71.

OTIS ADVANCED: DISTRIBUTIONS.

| Interval | I Grade 6 n = 4298 | II Grade 6 n = 1654 | III Grade 9 n = 3627 | IV Grade 12 n = 1226 |
|---|---|---|---|---|
| 10 to 19 | 3 | 1 | | |
| 20 " 29 | 19 | 12 | | |
| 30 " 39 | 74 | 23 | | |
| 40 " 49 | 168 | 56 | | |
| 50 " 59 | 334 | 107 | 9 | |
| 60 " 69 | 504 | 183 | 40 | |
| 70 " 79 | 659 | 243 | 79 | |
| 80 " 89 | 738 | 268 | 174 | 6 |
| 90 " 99 | 587 | 244 | 262 | 23 |
| 100 " 109 | 499 | 209 | 443 | 38 |
| 110 " 119 | 346 | 135 | 520 | 58 |
| 120 " 129 | 193 | 93 | 541 | 95 |
| 130 " 139 | 97 | 45 | 547 | 153 |
| 140 " 149 | 51 | 25 | 409 | 187 |
| 150 " 159 | 20 | 8 | 317 | 191 |
| 160 " 169 | 5 | 1 | 190 | 187 |
| 170 " 179 | | | 62 | 139 |
| 180 " 189 | 1 | 1 | 24 | 85 |
| 190 " 199 | | | 10 | 50 |
| 200 " 209 | | | | 13 |
| 210 " 219 | | | | 1 |

butions of truly measured intellect are of Form A; but their low end will not diverge enough from the corresponding sections of Form A to invalidate the comparisons which we shall make.

Assuming the low end to be of the geometrical form of the corresponding section of Form A, and expressing the true values of the interval 10 to 19, and of the interval 20 to 29 in terms of the interval 30 to 39, we find the following:

The relevant facts are that in Grade 4 we have 33 cases (out of a total of 1,500) from 0 to 9, 121 cases from 10 to 19, 246 cases from 20 to 29, and 248 cases from 30 to 39; in Grade 5 we have 6, 41, 112 and 257 (out of the total of 3,058) in these same intervals.

| Interval | Grade 4 | Grade 5 | Average |
|---|---|---|---|
| 10–19 | 1.65 | 1.37 | 1.51 |
| 20–29 | 1.43 | 1.00 | 1.22 |

We allow equal weights in averaging, because the larger population of Grade 5 is offset by the larger proportion of Grade 4 in the intervals studied.

TABLE 72.

OTIS ADVANCED: EQUIVALENTS FOR EACH 10-POINT INTERVAL OF THE ORIGINAL SCALE IN EQUAL UNITS.

| Interval | A<br>6<br>n = 4298 | B<br>6<br>n = 1654 | C<br>2A + B<br>3 | D<br>9<br>n = 3627 | E<br>C + D<br>2 | F<br>12<br>n = 1226 | G<br>3E+ F<br>4 | H<br><br>G/1.06 |
|---|---|---|---|---|---|---|---|---|
| 30 to 39 | 14.29 | 10.04 | 12.86 | | 12.86 | | 12.86 | 12.1 |
| 40 to 49 | 11.89 | 10.80 | 11.53 | | 11.53 | | 11.53 | 10.9 |
| 50 to 59 | 11.74 | 10.54 | 11.34 | | 11.34 | | 11.34 | 10.7 |
| 60 to 69 | 10.91 | 11.18 | 11.00 | | 11.00 | | 11.00 | 10.4 |
| 70 to 79 | 10.89 | 10.80 | 10.86 | 10.13 | 10.50 | | 10.50 | 9.9 |
| 80 to 89 | 10.99 | 10.46 | 10.81 | 10.69 | 10.75 | | 10.75 | 10.1 |
| 90 to 99 | 9.47 | 9.84 | 9.60 | 9.35 | 9.48 | | 9.48 | 8.9 |
| 100 to 109 | 10.00 | 10.31 | 10.10 | 10.74 | 10.42 | 10.52 | 10.45 | 9.9 |
| 110 to 119 | 10.23 | 9.18 | 9.88 | 9.90 | 9.89 | 9.10 | 10.09 | 9.5 |
| 120 to 129 | 9.63 | 10.45 | 9.87 | 9.56 | 9.72 | 9.74 | 9.72 | 9.2 |
| 130 to 139 | 11.54 | 9.38 | 10.82 | 10.41 | 10.62 | 11.27 | 10.78 | 10.2 |
| 140 to 149 | | | | 9.77 | 9.77 | 11.24 | 10.14 | 9.6 |
| 150 to 159 | | | | 11.23 | 11.23 | 10.96 | 11.15 | 10.5 |
| 160 to 169 | | | | 13.10 | 13.10 | 12.08 | 12.84 | 12.1 |
| 170 to 179 | | | | 10.16 | 10.16 | 12.27 | 10.69 | 10.1 |
| 180 to 189 | | | | | | 12.52 | 12.52 | 11.8 |
| 190 to 199 | | | | | | 17.77 | 17.77 | 16.8 |

Multiplying the 12.86 of Column G and the 12.1 (more exactly 12.13) of Column H of Table 72 by 1.51 and 1.22, we have these values for the intervals:

10–19    19.42 (or 18.32 when divided by 1.06).
20–29    15.69 (or 14.80 when divided by 1.06).

We may use these as provisional values subject to further investigation. They are used in the extension of Table 73 by Table 73a.

#### THE HAGGERTY EXAMINATION, DELTA 2

In the case of the Haggerty Delta 2 we have the distributions shown in Table 74. After estimating the frequencies

18

TABLE 73.

Equivalents for Otis Advanced Scores from 30 to 200 in a Scale with Equal Units. $1 = \dfrac{1}{120}$ of the Difference between 50 and 170 of the Original Scores.

| O | C | O | C | O | C | O | C | O | C |
|---|---|---|---|---|---|---|---|---|---|
| 30 | 26.4 | 70 | 70.6 | 110 | 109.5 | 150 | 147.8 | 190 | 192.3 |
| 31 | 27.7 | 71 | 71.6 | 111 | 110.5 | 151 | 148.9 | 191 | 193.6 |
| 32 | 28.9 | 72 | 72.6 | 112 | 111.4 | 152 | 149.9 | 192 | 195.1 |
| 33 | 30.2 | 73 | 73.6 | 113 | 112.4 | 153 | 151.0 | 193 | 196.6 |
| 34 | 31.4 | 74 | 74.6 | 114 | 113.3 | 154 | 152.0 | 194 | 198.1 |
| 35 | 32.6 | 75 | 75.6 | 115 | 114.3 | 155 | 152.9 | 195 | 199.7 |
| 36 | 33.8 | 76 | 76.6 | 116 | 115.2 | 156 | 154.0 | 196 | 201.3 |
| 37 | 35.0 | 77 | 77.6 | 117 | 116.2 | 157 | 155.0 | 197 | 203.0 |
| 38 | 36.2 | 78 | 78.6 | 118 | 117.1 | 158 | 156.1 | 198 | 204.7 |
| 39 | 37.4 | 79 | 79.6 | 119 | 118.1 | 159 | 157.2 | 199 | 206.5 |
| 40 | 38.6 | 80 | 80.6 | 120 | 119.0 | 160 | 158.3 | 200 | 208.3 |
| 41 | 39.7 | 81 | 81.6 | 121 | 120.0 | 161 | 159.4 | | |
| 42 | 40.8 | 82 | 82.5 | 122 | 120.9 | 162 | 160.5 | | |
| 43 | 41.9 | 83 | 83.5 | 123 | 121.9 | 163 | 161.6 | | |
| 44 | 43.0 | 84 | 84.5 | 124 | 122.8 | 164 | 162.7 | | |
| 45 | 44.1 | 85 | 85.4 | 125 | 123.8 | 165 | 163.8 | | |
| 46 | 45.2 | 86 | 86.4 | 126 | 124.7 | 166 | 164.9 | | |
| 47 | 46.3 | 87 | 87.4 | 127 | 125.7 | 167 | 166.0 | | |
| 48 | 47.4 | 88 | 88.3 | 128 | 126.6 | 168 | 167.1 | | |
| 49 | 48.4 | 89 | 89.3 | 129 | 127.6 | 169 | 168.2 | | |
| 50 | 49.5 | 90 | 90.3 | 130 | 128.6 | 170 | 169.3 | | |
| 51 | 50.6 | 91 | 91.3 | 131 | 129.5 | 171 | 170.4 | | |
| 52 | 51.6 | 92 | 92.2 | 132 | 130.5 | 172 | 171.5 | | |
| 53 | 52.7 | 93 | 93.2 | 133 | 131.4 | 173 | 172.6 | | |
| 54 | 53.8 | 94 | 94.2 | 134 | 132.4 | 174 | 173.7 | | |
| 55 | 54.9 | 95 | 95.1 | 135 | 133.4 | 175 | 174.8 | | |
| 56 | 56.0 | 96 | 96.1 | 136 | 134.3 | 176 | 175.9 | | |
| 57 | 57.0 | 97 | 97.1 | 137 | 135.3 | 177 | 177.0 | | |
| 58 | 58.1 | 98 | 98.0 | 138 | 136.2 | 178 | 178.1 | | |
| 59 | 59.2 | 99 | 99.0 | 139 | 137.2 | 179 | 179.3 | | |
| 60 | 60.2 | 100 | 100.0 | 140 | 138.2 | 180 | 180.5 | | |
| 61 | 61.3 | 101 | 101.0 | 141 | 139.1 | 181 | 181.6 | | |
| 62 | 62.3 | 102 | 101.9 | 142 | 140.1 | 182 | 182.8 | | |
| 63 | 63.4 | 103 | 102.9 | 143 | 141.0 | 183 | 183.9 | | |
| 64 | 64.4 | 104 | 103.9 | 144 | 142.0 | 184 | 185.1 | | |
| 65 | 65.5 | 105 | 104.8 | 145 | 143.0 | 185 | 186.3 | | |
| 66 | 66.5 | 106 | 105.7 | 146 | 143.9 | 186 | 187.5 | | |
| 67 | 67.5 | 107 | 106.7 | 147 | 144.9 | 187 | 188.7 | | |
| 68 | 68.6 | 108 | 107.6 | 148 | 145.8 | 188 | 189.9 | | |
| 69 | 69.6 | 109 | 108.6 | 149 | 146.8 | 189 | 191.1 | | |

TABLE 73a.

PROVISIONAL VALUES FOR OTIS ADVANCED SCORES FROM 10 TO 29.

| O | C | O | C | O | C | O | C |
|---|---|---|---|---|---|---|---|
| 10 | – 6.7 | 15 | 2.6 | 20 | 11.6 | 25 | 19.1 |
| 11 | – 4.8 | 16 | 4.4 | 21 | 13.1 | 26 | 20.6 |
| 12 | – 3.0 | 17 | 6.2 | 22 | 14.6 | 27 | 22.1 |
| 13 | – 1.1 | 18 | 8.0 | 23 | 16.1 | 28 | 23.6 |
| 14 | .8 | 19 | 9.8 | 24 | 17.6 | 29 | 25 |

in intervals of 10 from the irregular arrangement of III and IV, the values of each interval of each group in equal units are computed. These values for I, II, and III are put in terms of the difference between original 70 and original 130, to make them comparable. The two Grade 9 determinations are then combined with weights of 1 and 3, respectively. With these averages are combined the determinations from Grade 6, with weights of 2 for the former and 1 for the latter. The determinations from Grade 12 are

TABLE 74.

HAGGERTY DELTA 2 DISTRIBUTIONS

| Interval | I Grade 6 n = 916 | II Grade 9 n = 473 | III Grade 9 n = 1995 | | IV Grade 12 n = 668 |
|---|---|---|---|---|---|
| 10 to 19 | 1 | | | | |
| 20 | | | 25 to 42 | 1 | |
| 30 | 4 | | | | |
| 40 | 12 | | 43 to 54 | 3 | |
| 50 | 39 | 1 | 55 to 65 | 10 | |
| 60 | 87 | 5 | 66 to 76 | 29 | |
| 70 | 127 | 6 | | | |
| 80 | 161 | 36 | 77 to 86 | 73 | 1 |
| 90 | 164 | 54 | 87 to 99 | 225 | 13 |
| 100 | 154 | 89 | 100 to 114 | 555 | 45 |
| 110 | 86 | 109 | 115 to 119 | 212 | 36 |
| 120 | 61 | 79 | 120 to 129 | 415 | 121 |
| 130 | 17 | 73 | 130 to 139 | 283 | 162 |
| 140 | 2 | 42 | 140 to 149 | 155 | 170 |
| 150 to 159 | 1 | 12 | 150 to 159 | 31 | 102 |
| 160 to 169 | | 1 | 160 to 169 | 3 | 16 |
| | | | 170 to 179 | | 2 |

made comparable with this composite determination by multiplying them by a factor such as makes the 100 to 150 difference the same for the Grade 12 group as for the composite. They are then combined with the composite determination, the weights being 1 for the Grade 12 items and 3 for the composite. The essentials of these computations appear in Table 75, the last column of which gives the final estimate. The units of the Haggerty Delta 2 score become progressively "harder" (that is, larger) when put in equal units, from some point in the 70's up to 160.

TABLE 75.

HAGGERTY DELTA 2: VALUES IN EQUAL UNITS.

| Interval | A n = 916 | B n = 473 | C n = 1995 | D $\dfrac{B+3C}{4}$ | E $\dfrac{A+2D}{3}$ | F n = 668 | G $\dfrac{3E+F}{4}$ |
|---|---|---|---|---|---|---|---|
| 50 to 59 | 10.85 | | | | 10.85 | | 10.85 |
| 60 to 69 | 10.55 | | | | 10.55 | | 10.55 |
| 70 | 9.31 | 5.20 | 9.29 | 8.27 | 8.62 | | 8.62 |
| 80 | 9.19 | 13.25 | 8.38 | 9.62 | 9.48 | | 9.48 |
| 90 | 9.03 | 9.62 | 9.08 | 9.21 | 9.15 | | 9.15 |
| 100 | 10.30 | 10.42 | 11.06 | 10.90 | 10.70 | 10.05 | 10.54 |
| 110 | 8.78 | 11.48 | 10.67 | 10.87 | 10.17 | 9.50 | 10.01 |
| 120 | 13.41 | 9.82 | 11.53 | 11.10 | 11.87 | 12.61 | 12.06 |
| 130 | | 16.61 | 11.87 | 13.06 | 13.06 | 12.86 | 13.01 |
| 140 | | 10.37 | 16.16 | 14.71 | 14.71 | 15.46 | 19.86 |
| 150 | | | | | | 20.88 | 20.88 |

Interpolating, smoothing, expressing the values in terms of 1/60 of the difference between original 60 and original 120, and letting the two series coincide at 90, we have the equivalents of Table 76.

### THE TERMAN GROUP TEST

In the case of the Terman Group Test of Mental Ability, we have the scores of 5,582 pupils in Grade 7, 9,087 in Grade 8, 10,881 in Grade 9, 6,730 in Grade 10, 4,206 in Grade 11, and 4,886 in Grade 12. [Terman, '23, p. 9.] These are reported in the form of the point on the scale

TABLE 76.

EQUIVALENTS FOR HAGGERTY DELTA 2 SCORES FROM 50 TO 160, IN A SCALE
WITH EQUAL UNITS.

| O | C | O | C | O | C |
|---|---|---|---|---|---|
| 50 | 50.6 | 87 | 87.1 | 124 | 124.8 |
| 51 | 51.7 | 88 | 88.1 | 125 | 126.0 |
| 52 | 52.8 | 89 | 89.0 | 126 | 127.2 |
| 53 | 53.9 | 90 | 90.0 | 127 | 128.4 |
| 54 | 55.0 | 91 | 90.9 | 128 | 129.6 |
| 55 | 56.1 | 92 | 91.8 | 129 | 130.8 |
| 56 | 57.2 | 93 | 92.7 | 130 | 132.0 |
| 57 | 58.3 | 94 | 93.7 | 131 | 133.3 |
| 58 | 59.4 | 95 | 94.6 | 132 | 134.6 |
| 59 | 60.5 | 96 | 95.6 | 133 | 135.9 |
| 60 | 61.5 | 97 | 96.5 | 134 | 137.2 |
| 61 | 62.6 | 98 | 97.4 | 135 | 138.5 |
| 62 | 63.7 | 99 | 98.3 | 136 | 139.8 |
| 63 | 64.7 | 100 | 99.3 | 137 | 141.1 |
| 64 | 65.8 | 101 | 100.3 | 138 | 142.4 |
| 65 | 66.9 | 102 | 101.4 | 139 | 143.7 |
| 66 | 67.9 | 103 | 102.4 | 140 | 145.0 |
| 67 | 69.0 | 104 | 103.4 | 141 | 146.9 |
| 68 | 70.0 | 105 | 104.5 | 142 | 148.8 |
| 69 | 71.0 | 106 | 105.5 | 143 | 150.7 |
| 70 | 72.0 | 107 | 106.5 | 144 | 152.6 |
| 71 | 72.9 | 108 | 107.6 | 145 | 154.5 |
| 72 | 73.8 | 109 | 108.6 | 146 | 156.4 |
| 73 | 74.7 | 110 | 109.7 | 147 | 158.3 |
| 74 | 75.5 | 111 | 110.7 | 148 | 160.2 |
| 75 | 76.4 | 112 | 111.7 | 149 | 162.1 |
| 76 | 77.2 | 113 | 112.8 | 150 | 164.0 |
| 77 | 78.1 | 114 | 113.8 | 151 | 166.1 |
| 78 | 79.0 | 115 | 114.8 | 152 | 168.2 |
| 79 | 79.8 | 116 | 115.9 | 153 | 170.3 |
| 80 | 80.7 | 117 | 116.9 | 154 | 172.4 |
| 81 | 81.6 | 118 | 117.9 | 155 | 174.5 |
| 82 | 82.5 | 119 | 119.0 | 156 | 176.6 |
| 83 | 83.4 | 120 | 120.0 | 157 | 178.7 |
| 84 | 84.3 | 121 | 121.2 | 158 | 180.8 |
| 85 | 85.2 | 122 | 122.4 | 159 | 183.0 |
| 86 | 86.2 | 123 | 123.6 | 160 | 185.0 |

TABLE 77.

TERMAN GROUP TEST.

| A | B | C | D | E | F | G | H | I | J | K | L | M |
|---|---|---|---|---|---|---|---|---|---|---|---|---|
| | Scale Points Corresponding to Permille Entries. | | | | | | Differences in Equal Units Corresponding to the Intervals between Successive Scale Points of Columns B to G. | | | | | |
| Per-mille | Grade 7 | Grade 8 | Grade 9 | Grade 10 | Grade 11 | Grade 12 | Grade 7 | Grade 8 | Grade 9 | Grade 10 | Grade 11 | Grade 12 |
| 10 | 20 | 30 | 35 | 48 | 55 | 63 | 12.21 | 12.38 | 12.59 | 12.63 | 13.42 | 13.23 |
| 25 | 25 | 36 | 44 | 58 | 66 – | 74 | 10.50 | 10.64 | 10.83 | 10.86 | 11.54 | 11.38 |
| 50 | 31 | 43 | 53 – | 67 – | 77 | 86 | 12.11 | 12.27 | 12.49 | 12.52 | 13.31 | 13.12 |
| 100 | 38 | 52 | 63 – | 79 | 90 | 100 | 8.17 | 8.28 | 8.42 | 8.45 | 8.98 | 8.85 |
| 150 | 43 | 58 | 71 | 86 | 99 | 109 | 6.49 | 6.58 | 6.69 | 6.72 | 7.14 | 7.03 |
| 200 | 47 | 64 – | 76 | 92 | 105 | 112 | 5.57 | 5.65 | 5.74 | 5.76 | 6.12 | 6.03 |
| 250 | 51 | 69 | 81 | 98 | 112 | 122 | 5.00 | 5.07 | 5.15 | 5.17 | 5.50 | 5.42 |
| 300 | 54 | 73 | 86 | 103 | 118 | 128 | 9.03 | 9.16 | 9.31 | 9.34 | 9.93 | 9.78 |
| 400 | 61 | 81 | 95 | 113 | 128 | 138 | 8.44 | 8.56 | 8.70 | 8.73 | 9.28 | 9.14 |
| 500 | 68 | 89 | 104 | 122 | 138 | 147 | 8.44 | 8.56 | 8.70 | 8.73 | 9.28 | 9.14 |
| 600 | 75 | 97 | 113 | 131 | 147 | 156 | 9.03 | 9.16 | 9.31 | 9.34 | 9.93 | 9.78 |
| 700 | 83 | 107 | 123 | 141 | 158 | 165 | 5.00 | 5.07 | 5.15 | 5.17 | 5.50 | 5.42 |
| 750 | 88 | 112 | 128 | 147 – | 163 | 169 | 5.57 | 5.65 | 5.74 | 5.76 | 6.12 | 6.03 |
| 800 | 93 | 118 | 135 | 152 | 168 | 174 | 6.49 | 6.58 | 6.69 | 6.72 | 7.14 | 7.03 |
| 850 | 100 | 126 | 142 | 159 | 174 | 179 | 8.17 | 8.28 | 8.42 | 8.45 | 8.98 | 8.85 |
| 900 | 109 | 135 | 151 – | 166 | 180 | 185 | 12.11 | 12.27 | 12.49 | 12.52 | 13.31 | 13.12 |
| 950 | 122 | 148 – | 164 | 177 | 189 | 194 | 10.50 | 10.64 | 10.83 | 10.86 | 11.54 | 11.38 |
| 975 | 134 | 159 | 172 | 185 | 196 | 200 | 12.21 | 12.38 | 12.59 | 12.63 | 13.42 | 13.23 |
| 990 | 147 – | 170 | 181 | 194 | 203 | 207 | | | | | | |

below which a certain permille of the group lies. Thus Table 77 states that 10 permille or 1 percent of the population of Grade 7 had scores up to 20, 25 permille had scores up to 25, 50 permille had scores up to 31, and so on.

TABLE 78.

TERMAN GROUP TEST.

Sample of the Six Sets of Values in Equal Units Whence the General Transmutation Table Is Derived.

|  | Gr. 7 | Gr. 8 | Gr. 9 | Gr. 10 | Gr. 11 | Gr. 12 | Average |
|---|---|---|---|---|---|---|---|
| 100 | 100.00 | 100.00 | 100.00 | 100.00 | 100.00 | 100.00 | 100. |
| 101 | 100.91 | 100.92 | 100.99 | 101.04 | 101.19 | 100.98 | 101. |
| 102 | 101.82 | 101.84 | 101.98 | 102.08 | 102.38 | 101.97 | 102. |
| 103 | 102.72 | 102.76 | 102.97 | 103.11 | 103.57 | 102.95 | 103. |
| 104 | 103.63 | 103.67 | 103.97 | 104.04 | 104.76 | 103.93 | 104. |
| 105 | 104.54 | 104.58 | 104.94 | 104.98 | 105.95 | 104.92 | 105. |
| 106 | 105.45 | 105.50 | 105.90 | 105.91 | 106.82 | 105.90 | 106. |
| 107 | 106.36 | 106.41 | 106.87 | 106.85 | 107.70 | 106.88 | 107. |
| 108 | 107.26 | 107.42 | 107.83 | 107.78 | 108.57 | 107.87 | 108. |
| 109 | 108.17 | 108.44 | 108.79 | 108.71 | 109.45 | 108.85 | 109. |
| 110 | 109.10 | 109.45 | 109.76 | 109.65 | 110.32 | 111.19 | 110. |
| 111 | 110.03 | 110.46 | 110.73 | 110.58 | 111.19 | 113.54 | 111. |
| 112 | 110.96 | 111.48 | 111.70 | 111.52 | 112.07 | 115.88 | 112. |
| 113 | 111.90 | 112.42 | 112.67 | 112.45 | 112.99 | 116.48 | 113. |
| 114 | 112.83 | 113.36 | 103.60 | 113.42 | 113.90 | 117.09 | 114. |
| 115 | 113.76 | 114.30 | 104.53 | 114.39 | 114.82 | 117.69 | 115. |
| : | : |  |  | : | : | : | : |
| : | : |  |  | : | : | : | : |
| : | : |  |  | : | : | : | : |
| 190 |  |  |  | 195.75 | 198.69 | 199.79 | 198. |
| 191 |  |  |  | 197.15 | 200.34 | 201.25 | 200. |
| 192 |  |  |  | 198.56 | 201.99 | 202.70 | 201. |
| 193 |  |  |  | 199.96 | 203.64 | 204.16 | 203. |
| 194 |  |  |  | 201.36 | 205.29 | 205.62 | 204. |
| 195 |  |  |  |  | 206.94 | 207.52 | 207. |
| 196 |  |  |  |  | 208.58 | 209.41 | 209. |
| 197 |  |  |  |  | 210.50 | 211.31 | 211. |
| 198 |  |  |  |  | 212.42 | 213.21 | 213. |
| 199 |  |  |  |  | 214.34 | 215.10 | 215. |
| 200 |  |  |  |  | 216.26 | 217.00 | 217. |

We therefore find the value in equal units for the given intervals, rather than for successive intervals of 5 or 10. These values are then divided by:

1/86 of the difference between 61 and 147 in the case of Grade 7.

1/84 of the difference between 64 and 148 in the case of Grade 8.

1/88 of the difference between 63 and 151 in the case of Grade 9.

1/80 of the difference between 67 and 147 in the case of Grade 10.

1/81 of the difference between 66 and 147 in the case of Grade 11.

1/84 of the difference between 63 and 147 in the case of Grade 12.

The results appear as the last six columns of Table 77. We then construct a transmutation table of values for each grade, in each case coinciding with the original scale at 100. A sample piece of this table is shown as Table 78.

A final transmutation table (Table 79) is obtained by averaging all six values for each point of the original scale, or all five values, if there are only five, or all four or three, if there are only four or three. The table does not extend down or up beyond the points where three grade distributions were available.

### THE MYERS MENTAL MEASURE

Using the scores of 724 pupils in Grade 6 and 311 pupils in Grade 9 in the Myers Mental Measure, we find the facts of Table 80 and construct Table 81 as the transmuting table. The two scales coincide at 46.

### THE PINTNER NON-LANGUAGE TEST

For the Pintner Non-Language Mental Test we have the scores of 1,237 pupils in Grade 6 and 258 in Grade 9 shown in Table 82 (columns I and II). From these we derive the values in true units for each twenty-point interval and express them in terms of one two-hundredth of the difference between 260 and 460. They appear as columns III and IV of Table 82. When they are averaged, with weights

TABLE 79.

TERMAN GROUP TEST OF MENTAL ABILITY: VALUES IN EQUAL UNITS OF EACH POINT ON THE ORIGINAL SCALE FROM 35 TO 193.

| O | C | O | C | O | C | O | C | O | C |
|---|---|---|---|---|---|---|---|---|---|
| 35 | 21 | 70 | 68 | 100 | 100 | 130 | 129 | 160 | 158 |
| 6 | 22 | 1 | 69 | 1 | 101 | 1 | 129 | 1 | 159 |
| 7 | 24 | 2 | 71 | 2 | 102 | 2 | 130 | 2 | 160 |
| 8 | 25 | 3 | 72 | 3 | 103 | 3 | 131 | 3 | 161 |
| 9 | 27 | 4 | 73 | 4 | 104 | 4 | 132 | 4 | 162 |
| 40 | 28 | 75 | 74 | 105 | 105 | 135 | 133 | 165 | 163 |
| 1 | 30 | 6 | 75 | 6 | 106 | 6 | 134 | 6 | 165 |
| 2 | 31 | 7 | 76 | 7 | 107 | 7 | 135 | 7 | 166 |
| 3 | 33 | 8 | 77 | 8 | 108 | 8 | 136 | 8 | 167 |
| 4 | 34 | 9 | 78 | 9 | 109 | 9 | 137 | 9 | 168 |
| 45 | 36 | 80 | 80 | 110 | 110 | 140 | 138 | 170 | 170 |
| 6 | 37 | 1 | 81 | 1 | 111 | 1 | 139 | 1 | 171 |
| 7 | 39 | 2 | 82 | 2 | 112 | 2 | 140 | 2 | 172 |
| 8 | 40 | 3 | 83 | 3 | 113 | 3 | 141 | 3 | 174 |
| 9 | 41 | 4 | 84 | 4 | 114 | 4 | 142 | 4 | 175 |
| 50 | 43 | 85 | 85 | 115 | 115 | 145 | 143 | 175 | 176 |
| 1 | 44 | 6 | 86 | 6 | 116 | 6 | 144 | 6 | 178 |
| 2 | 46 | 7 | 87 | 7 | 117 | 7 | 145 | 7 | 179 |
| 3 | 47 | 8 | 88 | 8 | 118 | 8 | 146 | 8 | 181 |
| 4 | 49 | 9 | 89 | 9 | 118 | 9 | 147 | 9 | 182 |
| 55 | 50 | 90 | 90 | 120 | 119 | 150 | 148 | 180 | 183 |
| 6 | 51 | 1 | 91 | 1 | 120 | 1 | 149 | 1 | 185 |
| 7 | 52 | 2 | 92 | 2 | 121 | 2 | 150 | 2 | 186 |
| 8 | 54 | 3 | 93 | 3 | 122 | 3 | 151 | 3 | 188 |
| 9 | 55 | 4 | 94 | 4 | 123 | 4 | 152 | 4 | 189 |
| 60 | 56 | 95 | 95 | 125 | 124 | 155 | 153 | 185 | 191 |
| 1 | 58 | 6 | 96 | 6 | 125 | 6 | 154 | 6 | 192 |
| 2 | 59 | 7 | 97 | 7 | 126 | 7 | 155 | 7 | 194 |
| 3 | 60 | 8 | 98 | 8 | 127 | 8 | 156 | 8 | 195 |
| 4 | 61 | 9 | 99 | 9 | 128 | 9 | 157 | 9 | 197 |
| 65 | 63 | | | | | | | 190 | 198 |
| 6 | 64 | | | | | | | 1 | 200 |
| 7 | 65 | | | | | | | 2 | 201 |
| 8 | 66 | | | | | | | 3 | 203 |
| 9 | 67 | | | | | | | 4 | 204 |

TABLE 80.

Myers Mental Measure; Grade 6 (n = 724) and Grade 9 (n = 311): Values of Intervals in Terms of Equal Units, Expressed as Multiples of $\frac{1}{45} \times$ (Difference Between 36 and 81).

| Interval | Grade 6 | Grade 9 | Average |
|---|---|---|---|
| 21 to 25 | 9.69 | | 9.69 |
| 26 " 30 | 6.78 | | 6.78 |
| 31 " 35 | 7.89 | 11.83 | 9.86 |
| 36 " 40 | 6.98 | 6.10 | 6.54 |
| 41 " 45 | 5.44 | 7.36 | 6.40 |
| 46 " 50 | 5.89 | 4.95 | 5.42 |
| 51 " 55 | 5.01 | 5.23 | 5.12 |
| 56 " 60 | 6.43 | 5.38 | 5.91 |
| 61 " 65 | 3.19 | 3.46 | 3.33 |
| 66 " 70 | 4.57 | 4.39 | 4.48 |
| 71 " 75 | 3.86 | 5.62 | 4.74 |
| 76 " 80 | 3.61 | 1.62 | 2.62 |
| 81 " 85 | | 5.35 | 5.35 |

TABLE 81.

Equivalents of Scores from 21 to 86 for Myers Mental Measure: In Equal Units.

| O | C | O | C | O | C | O | C |
|---|---|---|---|---|---|---|---|
| 21 | 5.7 | 41 | 39.6 | 61 | 61.0 | 81 | 78.0 |
| 22 | 7.7 | 42 | 40.9 | 62 | 62.0 | 82 | 79.0 |
| 23 | 9.7 | 43 | 42.2 | 63 | 62.9 | 83 | 80.0 |
| 24 | 11.6 | 44 | 43.4 | 64 | 63.9 | 84 | 81.0 |
| 25 | 13.5 | 45 | 44.7 | 65 | 64.8 | 85 | 82.0 |
| 26 | 15.4 | 46 | 46.0 | 66 | 65.7 | 86 | 82.9 |
| 27 | 16.7 | 47 | 47.0 | 67 | 66.7 | | |
| 28 | 18.1 | 48 | 48.1 | 68 | 67.6 | | |
| 29 | 19.4 | 49 | 49.2 | 69 | 68.5 | | |
| 30 | 20.8 | 50 | 50.3 | 70 | 69.4 | | |
| 31 | 22.2 | 51 | 51.4 | 71 | 70.3 | | |
| 32 | 24.2 | 52 | 52.4 | 72 | 71.3 | | |
| 33 | 26.2 | 53 | 53.4 | 73 | 72.2 | | |
| 34 | 28.2 | 54 | 54.4 | 74 | 73.1 | | |
| 35 | 30.2 | 55 | 55.5 | 75 | 74.0 | | |
| 36 | 32.1 | 56 | 56.5 | 76 | 74.9 | | |
| 37 | 34.4 | 57 | 57.4 | 77 | 75.5 | | |
| 38 | 35.7 | 58 | 58.3 | 78 | 76.1 | | |
| 39 | 37.0 | 59 | 59.2 | 79 | 76.7 | | |
| 40 | 38.3 | 60 | 60.1 | 80 | 77.3 | | |

of 4 and 1, we have column V.   The transmutation table, which coincides with the original scale at 300, appears as Table 83.

#### THE I. E. R. TEST OF SELECTIVE AND RELATIONAL THINKING, GENERALIZATION AND ORGANIZATION

For the I. E. R. Test of Selective and Relational Thinking, Generalization and Organization, we have scores from

TABLE 82.

PINTNER NON-LANGUAGE MENTAL TEST.   ORIGINAL SCORES AND VALUES OF INTERVALS IN EQUAL UNITS.

| Interval | I Original Scores Grade 6 n = 1237 | II Original Scores Grade 9 n = 258 | III Values of Intervals in Equal Units Grade 6 | IV Values of Intervals in Equal Units Grade 9 | V Weighted Average Value |
|---|---|---|---|---|---|
| 0 to 19 | 1 | | | | |
| 20 " 39 | ` | | | | |
| 40 " 59 | 2 | | | | |
| 60 " 79 | 2 | | | | |
| 80 " 99 | 6 | | | | |
| 100 " 119 | 11 | | 19.6 | | 19.6 |
| 120 " 139 | 17 | | 22.0 | | 22.0 |
| 140 " 159 | 32 | | 13.5 | | 13.5 |
| 160 " 179 | 28 | 1 | 13.7 | | 13.7 |
| 180 " 199 | 37 | 1 | 12.3 | | 12.3 |
| 200 " 219 | 41 | | 12.2 | | 12.2 |
| 220 " 239 | 48 | 1 | 12.2 | | 12.2 |
| 240 " 259 | 56 | 5 | 19.3 | 29.7 | 21.4 |
| 260 " 279 | 101 | 6 | 15.5 | 19.7 | 16.3 |
| 280 " 299 | 92 | 13 | 19.8 | 26.4 | 21.1 |
| 300 " 319 | 125 | 13 | 18.6 | 18.2 | 18.5 |
| 320 " 329 | 119 | 11 | 17.7 | 12.7 | 16.7 |
| 340 " 359 | 108 | 27 | 23.4 | 25.3 | 23.8 |
| 360 " 379 | 126 | 21 | 19.3 | 16.8 | 18.8 |
| 380 " 399 | 85 | 28 | 23.2 | 21.1 | 22.8 |
| 400 " 419 | 78 | 26 | 17.4 | 19.4 | 17.8 |
| 420 " 439 | 42 | 25 | 23.9 | 19.8 | 23.1 |
| 440 " 459 | 38 | 23 | 20.9 | 20.7 | 20.9 |
| 460 " 479 | 20 | 17 | | 18.7 | 18.7 |
| 480 " 499 | 10 | 14 | | 19.8 | 19.8 |
| 500 " 519 | 7 | 14 | | 30.3 | 30.3 |
| 520 " 539 | 3 | 6 | | 23.0 | 23.0 |
| 540 " 559 | 1 | 2 | | | |
| 560 " 579 | | 3 | | | |
| 580 | 1 | 1 | | | |

TABLE 83.

EQUIVALENTS FOR PINTNER NON-LANGUAGE SCORES FROM 100 TO 380, IN A SCALE WITH EQUAL UNITS. O AND C REFER TO THE ORIGINAL SCORES AND THE SCORES TRANSMUTED INTO A SCALE WITH EQUAL UNITS.

| O | C | O | C | O | C | O | C | O | C | O | C | O | C |
|---|---|---|---|---|---|---|---|---|---|---|---|---|---|
| 100 | 136 | 140 | 177 | 180 | 205 | 220 | 229 | 260 | 263 | 300 | 300 | 340 | 341 |
| 1 | 137 | 1 | 178 | 1 | 205 | 1 | 230 | 1 | 263 | 1 | 301 | 1 | 341 |
| 2 | 138 | 2 | 179 | 2 | 206 | 2 | 230 | 2 | 264 | 2 | 302 | 2 | 342 |
| 3 | 139 | 3 | 179 | 3 | 206 | 3 | 231 | 3 | 265 | 3 | 303 | 3 | 343 |
| 4 | 140 | 4 | 180 | 4 | 207 | 4 | 231 | 4 | 266 | 4 | 303 | 4 | 344 |
| 5 | 141 | 5 | 181 | 5 | 208 | 5 | 232 | 5 | 267 | 5 | 304 | 5 | 345 |
| 6 | 142 | 6 | 182 | 6 | 208 | 6 | 233 | 6 | 268 | 6 | 305 | 6 | 346 |
| 7 | 143 | 7 | 183 | 7 | 209 | 7 | 233 | 7 | 268 | 7 | 306 | 7 | 347 |
| 8 | 144 | 8 | 183 | 8 | 209 | 8 | 234 | 8 | 269 | 8 | 307 | 8 | 348 |
| 9 | 145 | 9 | 184 | 9 | 210 | 9 | 235 | 9 | 270 | 9 | 308 | 9 | 349 |
| 110 | 146 | 150 | 185 | 190 | 211 | 230 | 235 | 270 | 271 | 310 | 308 | 350 | 350 |
| 1 | 147 | 1 | 185 | 1 | 211 | 1 | 236 | 1 | 272 | 1 | 309 | 1 | 351 |
| 2 | 148 | 2 | 186 | 2 | 212 | 2 | 236 | 2 | 273 | 2 | 310 | 2 | 352 |
| 3 | 148 | 3 | 187 | 3 | 213 | 3 | 237 | 3 | 273 | 3 | 311 | 3 | 353 |
| 4 | 149 | 4 | 187 | 4 | 213 | 4 | 238 | 4 | 274 | 4 | 312 | 4 | 354 |
| 5 | 150 | 5 | 188 | 5 | 214 | 5 | 238 | 5 | 275 | 5 | 313 | 5 | 355 |
| 6 | 151 | 6 | 189 | 6 | 214 | 6 | 239 | 6 | 276 | 6 | 313 | 6 | 356 |
| 7 | 152 | 7 | 189 | 7 | 215 | 7 | 239 | 7 | 277 | 7 | 314 | 7 | 357 |
| 8 | 153 | 8 | 190 | 8 | 216 | 8 | 240 | 8 | 277 | 8 | 315 | 8 | 357 |
| 9 | 154 | 9 | 191 | 9 | 216 | 9 | 241 | 9 | 278 | 9 | 316 | 9 | 358 |
| 120 | 155 | 160 | 192 | 200 | 217 | 240 | 241 | 280 | 279 | 320 | 317 | 360 | 359 |
| 1 | 156 | 1 | 192 | 1 | 217 | 1 | 242 | 1 | 280 | 1 | 318 | 1 | 360 |
| 2 | 158 | 2 | 193 | 2 | 218 | 2 | 243 | 2 | 281 | 2 | 319 | 2 | 362 |
| 3 | 159 | 3 | 194 | 3 | 219 | 3 | 244 | 3 | 282 | 3 | 320 | 3 | 363 |
| 4 | 160 | 4 | 194 | 4 | 219 | 4 | 246 | 4 | 283 | 4 | 322 | 4 | 364 |
| 5 | 161 | 5 | 195 | 5 | 220 | 5 | 247 | 5 | 284 | 5 | 323 | 5 | 365 |
| 6 | 162 | 6 | 196 | 6 | 221 | 6 | 248 | 6 | 285 | 6 | 324 | 6 | 366 |
| 7 | 163 | 7 | 196 | 7 | 221 | 7 | 249 | 7 | 286 | 7 | 325 | 7 | 367 |
| 8 | 164 | 8 | 197 | 8 | 222 | 8 | 250 | 8 | 287 | 8 | 326 | 8 | 368 |
| 9 | 165 | 9 | 198 | 9 | 222 | 9 | 251 | 9 | 288 | 9 | 327 | 9 | 370 |
| 130 | 166 | 170 | 198 | 210 | 223 | 250 | 252 | 290 | 289 | 330 | 329 | 370 | 371 |
| 1 | 167 | 1 | 199 | 1 | 224 | 1 | 253 | 1 | 291 | 1 | 330 | 1 | 372 |
| 2 | 169 | 2 | 200 | 2 | 224 | 2 | 254 | 2 | 292 | 2 | 331 | 2 | 373 |
| 3 | 170 | 3 | 200 | 3 | 225 | 3 | 255 | 3 | 293 | 3 | 332 | 3 | 374 |
| 4 | 171 | 4 | 201 | 4 | 225 | 4 | 256 | 4 | 294 | 4 | 333 | 4 | 375 |
| 5 | 172 | 5 | 202 | 5 | 226 | 5 | 257 | 5 | 295 | 5 | 335 | 5 | 376 |
| 6 | 173 | 6 | 202 | 6 | 227 | 6 | 258 | 6 | 296 | 6 | 336 | 6 | 378 |
| 7 | 174 | 7 | 203 | 7 | 227 | 7 | 259 | 7 | 297 | 7 | 337 | 7 | 379 |

3,231 pupils in Grade 9 and from two groups (of 1,666 and 972) in Grade 12, as shown in Table 84. The values of ten-point intervals in true units derived from facts of Table 84 appear in Table 85. Table 86 is the transmutation table

TABLE 84.

I.E.R. TESTS OF SELECTIVE AND RELATIONAL THINKING, GENERALIZATION AND ORGANIZATION: DISTRIBUTIONS IN GRADE 9 AND GRADE 12.

| | Grade 9 n = 3231 | Grade 12 n = 1666 | n = 972 |
|---|---|---|---|
| 40 to 49 | 2 | | |
| 50 " 59 | 6 | | |
| 60 " 69 | 15 | 1 | |
| 70 " 79 | 15 | | |
| 80 " 89 | 32 | 1 | 1 |
| 90 " 99 | 66 | 1 | 3 |
| 100 " 109 | 82 | 6 | |
| 110 " 119 | 127 | 7 | 4 |
| 120 " 129 | 168 | 11 | 13 |
| 130 " 139 | 200 | 20 | 20 |
| 140 " 149 | 271 | 32 | 20 |
| 150 " 159 | 258 | 39 | 37 |
| 160 " 169 | 295 | 56 | 31 |
| 170 " 179 | 272 | 79 | 51 |
| 180 " 189 | 303 | 94 | 65 |
| 190 " 199 | 246 | 119 | 76 |
| 200 " 209 | 228 | 119 | 76 |
| 210 " 219 | 195 | 129 | 95 |
| 220 " 229 | 143 | 142 | 71 |
| 230 " 239 | 115 | 145 | 86 |
| 240 " 249 | 74 | 134 | 66 |
| 250 " 259 | 49 | 145 | 72 |
| 260 " 269 | 26 | 103 | 59 |
| 270 " 279 | 20 | 77 | 32 |
| 280 " 289 | 8 | 54 | 36 |
| 290 " 299 | 5 | 47 | 30 |
| 300 " 309 | 4 | 41 | 9 |
| 310 " 319 | 4 | 30 | 6 |
| 320 " 329 | 1 | 12 | 5 |
| 330 " 339 | | 8 | 5 |
| 340 " 349 | 1 | 10 | 1 |
| 350 " 359 | | 4 | |
| 360 " 369 | | | |
| 370 " 379 | | 1 | 1 |

without smoothing. For rough work, it is sufficient to take the original scores at their face value. They are very, very close to the true values from 130 to 250, and are nowhere more than 3.7 points off.

TABLE 85.

I.E.R. Test of Selective and Relational Thinking, Generalization and Organization. Values of Intervals of Original Scale in Equal Units.

| Interval | Grade 9 n = 3231 | Grade 12 n = 1666 | Grade 12 n = 972 | Grade 12 Average | Grades 9 and 12 Average |
|---|---|---|---|---|---|
| 90 to 99 | 11.9 | | | | 11.9 |
| 100 " 109 | 9.7 | | | | 9.7 |
| 110 " 119 | 10.6 | | | | 10.6 |
| 120 " 129 | 10.4 | | | | 10.4 |
| 130 " 139 | 9.8 | 10.4 | 13.5 | 11.9 | 10.9 |
| 140 " 149 | 11.1 | 10.7 | 8.8 | 9.75 | 10.4 |
| 150 " 159 | 9.3 | 9.1 | 11.4 | 10.25 | 9.8 |
| 160 " 169 | 10.0 | 9.9 | 7.4 | 8.65 | 9.3 |
| 170 " 179 | 9.0 | 10.4 | 9.7 | 10.05 | 9.6 |
| 180 " 189 | 10.5 | 9.9 | 10.3 | 10.1 | 10.3 |
| 190 " 199 | 9.3 | 10.5 | 10.3 | 10.4 | 9.9 |
| 200 " 209 | 10.0 | 9.4 | 9.4 | 9.4 | 9.7 |
| 210 " 219 | 10.3 | 9.3 | 11.2 | 10.25 | 10.3 |
| 220 " 229 | 9.7 | 9.9 | 8.3 | 9.1 | 9.4 |
| 230 " 239 | 10.9 | 10.2 | 10.7 | 10.45 | 10.7 |
| 240 " 249 | 10.3 | 10.1 | 8.9 | 9.5 | 9.9 |
| 250 " 259 | | 12.1 | 11.2 | 11.65 | 11.7 |
| 260 " 269 | | 10.3 | 11.5 | 10.9 | 10.9 |
| 270 " 279 | | 9.3 | 7.9 | 8.6 | 8.6 |
| 280 " 289 | | 8.0 | 11.8 | 9.9 | 9.9 |
| 290 " 299 | | 9.0 | 16.1 | 12.55 | 12.6 |
| 300 " 309 | | 11.1 | 7.7 | 9.4 | 9.4 |
| 310 " 319 | | 12.6 | 7.2 | 9.9 | 9.9 |

## THE BROWN UNIVERSITY PSYCHOLOGICAL EXAMINATION

The results of similar computations for the Brown University Psychological Examination appear in Tables 87 and 88.

| O | C | O | C | O | C | O | C | O | C | O | C | O | C | O | C |
|---|---|---|---|---|---|---|---|---|---|---|---|---|---|---|---|
| 90 | 87.2 | 120 | 119.4 | 150 | 151.1 | 180 | 179.8 | 210 | 209.7 | 240 | 240.1 | 270 | 272.6 | 300 | 303.7 |
| 1 | 88.4 | 1 | 120.5 | 1 | 152 | 1 | 180.8 | 1 | 210.8 | 1 | 241 | 1 | 273.5 | 1 | 304.6 |
| 2 | 89.6 | 2 | 121.6 | 2 | 153 | 2 | 181.8 | 2 | 211.9 | 2 | 242 | 2 | 274.3 | 2 | 305.5 |
| 3 | 90.8 | 3 | 122.6 | 3 | 154 | 3 | 182.9 | 3 | 213 | 3 | 243 | 3 | 275.2 | 3 | 306.4 |
| 4 | 92 | 4 | 123.6 | 4 | 155 | 4 | 183.9 | 4 | 214 | 4 | 244 | 4 | 276.1 | 4 | 307.4 |
| 5 | 93.1 | 5 | 124.7 | 5 | 156 | 5 | 184.9 | 5 | 215 | 5 | 245 | 5 | 277 | 5 | 308.3 |
| 6 | 94.3 | 6 | 125.7 | 6 | 157 | 6 | 186 | 6 | 216 | 6 | 246 | 6 | 277.8 | 6 | 309.3 |
| 7 | 95.5 | 7 | 126.7 | 7 | 158 | 7 | 187 | 7 | 217 | 7 | 247 | 7 | 278.6 | 7 | 310.3 |
| 8 | 96.7 | 8 | 127.8 | 8 | 159 | 8 | 188 | 8 | 218 | 8 | 248 | 8 | 279.4 | 8 | 311.3 |
| 9 | 97.9 | 9 | 128.8 | 9 | 160 | 9 | 189 | 9 | 219 | 9 | 249 | 9 | 280.3 | 9 | 312.3 |
| 100 | 99.1 | 130 | 129.8 | 160 | 160.9 | 190 | 190.1 | 220 | 220 | 250 | 250 | 280 | 281.2 | 310 | 313.3 |
| 1 | 100 | 1 | 130.9 | 1 | 161.8 | 1 | 191 | 1 | 221 | 1 | 251.1 | 1 | 282.1 | 1 | 314.3 |
| 2 | 101 | 2 | 132 | 2 | 162.7 | 2 | 192 | 2 | 222 | 2 | 252.3 | 2 | 283.1 | 2 | 315.3 |
| 3 | 102 | 3 | 133.1 | 3 | 163.7 | 3 | 193 | 3 | 223 | 3 | 253.4 | 3 | 284.1 | 3 | 316.2 |
| 4 | 103 | 4 | 134.2 | 4 | 164.6 | 4 | 194 | 4 | 224 | 4 | 254.6 | 4 | 285.1 | 4 | 317.2 |
| 5 | 104 | 5 | 135.3 | 5 | 165.5 | 5 | 195 | 5 | 224.9 | 5 | 255.7 | 5 | 286.1 | 5 | 318.2 |
| 6 | 105 | 6 | 136.4 | 6 | 166.4 | 6 | 196 | 6 | 225.8 | 6 | 256.9 | 6 | 287.1 | 6 | 319.2 |
| 7 | 106 | 7 | 137.4 | 7 | 167.3 | 7 | 197 | 7 | 226.7 | 7 | 258.1 | 7 | 288.1 | 7 | 320.2 |
| 8 | 106.9 | 8 | 138.5 | 8 | 168.3 | 8 | 198 | 8 | 227.6 | 8 | 259.3 | 8 | 289.1 | 8 | 321.2 |
| 9 | 107.9 | 9 | 139.6 | 9 | 169.2 | 9 | 199 | 9 | 228.5 | 9 | 260.5 | 9 | 290.1 | 9 | 322.2 |
| 110 | 108.8 | 140 | 140.7 | 170 | 170.2 | 200 | 200 | 230 | 229.4 | 260 | 261.7 | 290 | 291.1 | 320 | 323.2 |
| 1 | 109.9 | 1 | 141.8 | 1 | 171.1 | 1 | 201 | 1 | 230.5 | 1 | 262.8 | 1 | 292.3 | | |
| 2 | 111 | 2 | 142.9 | 2 | 172.1 | 2 | 202 | 2 | 231.6 | 2 | 263.9 | 2 | 293.6 | | |
| 3 | 112 | 3 | 144 | 3 | 173 | 3 | 203 | 3 | 232.6 | 3 | 265 | 3 | 294.8 | | |
| 4 | 113 | 4 | 145 | 4 | 174 | 4 | 204 | 4 | 233.7 | 4 | 266 | 4 | 296.1 | | |
| 5 | 114 | 5 | 146 | 5 | 175 | 5 | 205 | 5 | 234.7 | 5 | 267.1 | 5 | 297.4 | | |
| 6 | 115 | 6 | 147 | 6 | 176 | 6 | 206 | 6 | 235.8 | 6 | 268.2 | 6 | 298.7 | | |
| 7 | 116.1 | 7 | 148 | 7 | 177 | 7 | 207 | 7 | 236.9 | 7 | 269.3 | 7 | 300 | | |
| 8 | 117.2 | 8 | 149 | 8 | 178 | 8 | 207.9 | 8 | 238 | 8 | 270.4 | 8 | 301.2 | | |
| 9 | 118.3 | 9 | 150 | 9 | 178.9 | 9 | 208.8 | 9 | 239 | 9 | 271.5 | 9 | 302.4 | | |

TABLE 87.

Brown University Psychological Examination. Grades 12, N = 3333 and 13, N = 2118.

| Interval | Δ Value of interval in equal units | | Values in terms of 1/35 of the difference between 35 and 70 | | Average |
|---|---|---|---|---|---|
| | Grade 12 n = 3333 | Grade 13 n = 2118 | Grade 12 | Grade 13 | |
| 20 to 24 | .5304 | | 6.25 | | 6.25 |
| 25 " 29 | .5800 | | 6.84 | | 6.84 |
| 30 " 34 | .4764 | | 5.62 | | 5.62 |
| 35 " 39 | .4500 | .4260 | 5.30 | 5.13 | 5.22 |
| 40 " 44 | .3780 | .3741 | 4.46 | 4.50 | 4.48 |
| 45 " 49 | .4172 | .3442 | 4.92 | 4.14 | 4.53 |
| 50 " 54 | .3976 | .3851 | 4.69 | 4.63 | 4.66 |
| 55 " 59 | .4179 | .4500 | 4.93 | 5.42 | 5.18 |
| 60 " 64 | .4263 | .4495 | 5.02 | 5.41 | 5.22 |
| 65 " 69 | .4805 | .4798 | 5.67 | 5.77 | 5.72 |
| 70 " 74 | | .4908 | | 5.91 | 5.91 |
| 75 " 79 | | .6048 | | 7.28 | 7.28 |

TABLE 88.

Equivalents of Scores from 20 to 80 for the Brown University Psychological Examination, in Equal Units.

| O | C | O | C | O | C |
|---|---|---|---|---|---|
| 20 | 17.0 | 40 | 41.0 | 60 | 59.8 |
| 1 | 18.2 | 1 | 41.9 | 1 | 60.8 |
| 2 | 19.5 | 2 | 42.8 | 2 | 61.9 |
| 3 | 20.7 | 3 | 43.7 | 3 | 63.0 |
| 4 | 22.0 | 4 | 44.6 | 4 | 64.0 |
| 25 | 23.4 | 45 | 45.5 | 65 | 65.1 |
| 6 | 24.6 | 6 | 46.4 | 6 | 66.2 |
| 7 | 26.0 | 7 | 47.3 | 7 | 67.4 |
| 8 | 27.4 | 8 | 48.2 | 8 | 68.5 |
| 9 | 28.8 | 9 | 49.1 | 9 | 69.6 |
| 30 | 30.2 | 50 | 50 | 70 | 70.8 |
| 1 | 31.3 | 1 | 51 | 1 | 72.0 |
| 2 | 32.4 | 2 | 52 | 2 | 73.1 |
| 3 | 33.6 | 3 | 52.9 | 3 | 74.3 |
| 4 | 34.7 | 4 | 53.8 | 4 | 75.5 |
| 35 | 35.8 | 55 | 54.7 | 75 | 76.7 |
| 6 | 36.9 | 6 | 55.7 | 6 | 78.1 |
| 7 | 38.0 | 7 | 56.7 | 7 | 79.6 |
| 8 | 39.0 | 8 | 57.8 | 8 | 81.0 |
| 9 | 40.0 | 9 | 58.8 | 9 | 82.5 |
| | | | | 80 | 84.0 |

TABLE 89.

ARMY EXAMINATION A: DISTRIBUTION OF PUPILS IN GRADES 4, 5, 6, 7, 8, 9 AND 13.

| Interval | 4<br>n = 463 | 5<br>n = 570 | 6<br>n = 672 | 7<br>n = 685 | 8<br>n = 630 | 13<br>n = 701 |
|---|---|---|---|---|---|---|
| 0– 9 | 4 | | | | | |
| 10–19 | 9 | | | | | |
| 20–29 | 16 | 4 | 1 | 2 | | |
| 30–39 | 21 | 5 | | | | |
| 40 | 36 | 10 | 2 | | 1 | |
| 50 | 41 | 21 | 6 | 1 | | |
| 60 | 46 | 26 | 3 | 7 | 2 | |
| 70 | 57 | 48 | 15 | 6 | | |
| 80 | 53 | 45 | 32 | 11 | 4 | |
| 90 | 47 | 64 | 41 | 20 | 2 | |
| 100 | 40 | 53 | 53 | 27 | 6 | |
| 110 | 31 | 61 | 54 | 36 | 21 | 1 |
| 120 | 22 | 61 | 64 | 56 | 30 | 1 |
| 130 | 20 | 55 | 78 | 55 | 28 | |
| 140 | 11 | 43 | 84 | 63 | 37 | |
| 150 | 7 | 28 | 80 | 65 | 46 | 3 |
| 160 | 1 | 20 | 53 | 53 | 52 | 3 |
| 170 | 1 | 11 | 24 | 79 | 56 | 5 |
| 180 | | 6 | 26 | 56 | 61 | 5 |
| 190 | | 8 | 23 | 47 | 55 | 20 |
| 200 | | 1 | 8 | 44 | 42 | 25 |
| 210 | | | 9 | 16 | 45 | 25 |
| 220 | | | 7 | 16 | 36 | 31 |
| 230 | | | 5 | 18 | 33 | 53 |
| 240 | | | | 3 | 28 | 58 |
| 250 | | | 2 | 1 | 15 | 61 |
| 260 | | | 1 | 2 | 13 | 68 |
| 270 | | | | | 9 | 75 |
| 280 | | | | 1 | 6 | 66 |
| 290 | | | | | 1 | 48 |
| 300 | | | 1 | | | 51 |
| 310 | | | | | 1 | 39 |
| 320 | | | | | | 20 |
| 330 | | | | | | 16 |
| 340 | | | | | | 12 |
| 350 | | | | | | 13 |
| 360 | | | | | | 2 |

19

## THE ARMY EXAMINATION A

For special reasons, we have investigated the values of scores in the Army Examination *a,* although it is not in present use. We have distributions from Grades 6, 7, 8, and from college freshman, nearly seven hundred in each [Memoirs, p. 537], shown in Table 89. We shall also use to

TABLE 90.

ARMY EXAMINATION A: EQUIVALENTS FOR EACH 10-POINT INTERVAL OF THE ORIGINAL SCALE IN EQUAL UNITS. RESULTS FROM GRADES 6, 7 AND 8.

| Original Interval | Value in Equal Units | | | Average |
| | Gr. 6 | Gr. 7 | Gr. 8 | |
| --- | --- | --- | --- | --- |
| 60 to 69 | 18.7 | 18.95 | | 18.8 |
| 70 to 79 | 15.65 | 6.9 | | 11.3 |
| 80 to 89 | 12.3 | 9.15 | 15.6 | 12.4 |
| 90 to 99 | 11.6 | 11.0 | 4.0 | 8.9 |
| 100 to 109 | 9.6 | 9.7 | 9.5 | 9.6 |
| 110 to 119 | 10.1 | 9.7 | 17.1 | 12.3 |
| 120 to 129 | 11.55 | 11.4 | 14.1 | 12.4 |
| 130 to 139 | 12.65 | 9.45 | 9.2 | 10.4 |
| 140 to 149 | 13.65 | 9.6 | 9.8 | 11.0 |
| 150 to 159 | 11.3 | 9.4 | 10.05 | 10.3 |
| 160 to 169 | 6.4 | 7.65 | 9.9 | 8.0 |
| 170 to 179 | 8.65 | 12.2 | 9.9 | 10.3 |
| 180 to 189 | 10.6 | 10.05 | 10.5 | 10.4 |
| 190 to 199 | 5.2 | 10.35 | 9.8 | 8.4 |
| 200 to 209 | 7.5 | 13.2 | 7.9 | 9.5 |
| 210 to 219 | 9.4 | 6.7 | 9.6 | 8.6 |
| 220 to 229 | 11.25 | 9.6 | 8.9 | 9.9 |
| 230 to 239 | 0.00 | 20.7 | 10.05 | 10.3 |
| 240 to 249 | 9.28 | 7.3 | 11.8 | 9.5 |
| 250 to 259 | 13.48 | 5.5 | 8.45 | 9.1 |
| 260 to 269 | | | 11.3 | 11.3 |
| 270 to 279 | | | 12.9 | 12.9 |

some extent the distributions of 570 pupils in Grade 5 and 463 pupils in Grade 4, which are also shown in Table 89.

The values of each 10-point interval from 60 to 270 in equal units are computed for Grades 6, 7, and 8, by the methods previously used, and made strictly comparable by being divided by the difference between 90 and 230 of the original scale. They are then averaged. The true values of the intervals from 10 to 100 are computed for Grades 4 and 5, assuming that the low ends of these distributions are distributed like the low end of Form A. They are made strictly comparable and averaged. The averages are then multiplied by a factor such that the difference 60 to 100 is represented by the same amount in the series of true values

TABLE 91.

ARMY EXAMINATION A: EQUIVALENTS FOR CERTAIN 10-POINT INTERVALS OF THE ORIGINAL SCALE IN EQUAL UNITS. RESULTS FROM GRADES 4 AND 5.

| Interval | Values in Equal Units Gr. 4 | Gr. 5 | Av. | Av. × 1.28 |
|---|---|---|---|---|
| 10 to 19 | 16.4 | | 16.4 | 21.0 |
| 20 " 29 | 13.15 | | 13.15 | 16.8 |
| 30 | 10.1 | 10.3 | 10.2 | 13.1 |
| 40 | 11.9 | 10.5 | 11.2 | 14.3 |
| 50 | 10.1 | 12.2 | 11.65 | 14.3 |
| 60 | 9.7 | 9.5 | 9.6 | 12.3 |
| 70 | 10.8 | 11.9 | 11.35 | 14.5 |
| 80 | 10.0 | 8.6 | 9.3 | 11.9 |
| 90 " 99 | 9.7 | 10.4 | 10.05 | 12.9 |

obtained from Grades 6, 7, and 8, and in the series obtained from Grades 4 and 5. The 6, 7, 8 series is then extended by the values from 10 to 100 obtained from Grades 4 and 5, allowing equal weight to the two sets of values from 60 to 99.

The values of the intervals from 200 to 360 are computed from the facts for college freshmen (Grade 13). They are then multiplied by a factor such that the difference 200 to 260 is represented by the same amount in the two series of true values (from Grades 6, 7, 8, and from Grade 13) The 6, 7, 8 series is then extended by the values for 260 to 360 obtained from Grade 13.

The essentials of these procedures and their results appear in Tables 90, 91, and 92.

A transmutation table in steps of 10 is then made, letting the two scales coincide at 170. This appears as Table 93.

TABLE 92.

ARMY EXAMINATION A: EQUIVALENTS IN EQUAL UNITS. RESULTS FROM GRADES 6, 7, AND 8; 4 AND 5; 13; AND COMPOSITE FROM ALL.

| Original Interval | Value in Equal Units | | | |
| | By Grades 6, 7 and 8 | By Grades 4 and 5 | By Grade 13 | Composite |
|---|---|---|---|---|
| 1– 9 | | | | |
| 10– 19 | | 21.0 | | 21.0 |
| 20– 29 | | 16.8 | | 16.8 |
| 30– 39 | | 13.1 | | 13.1 |
| 40– 49 | | 14.3 | | 14.3 |
| 50– 59 | | 14.3 | | 14.3 |
| 60– 69 | 18.8 | 12.3 | | 15.6 |
| 70– 79 | 11.3 | 14.5 | | 12.9 |
| 80– 89 | 12.4 | 11.9 | | 12.2 |
| 90– 99 | 8.9 | 12.9 | | 10.9 |
| 100–109 | 9.6 | | | 9.6 |
| 110–119 | 12.3 | | | 12.3 |
| 120–129 | 12.4 | | | 12.4 |
| 130–139 | 10.4 | | | 10.4 |
| 140–149 | 11.0 | | | 11.0 |
| 150–159 | 10.3 | | | 10.3 |
| 160–169 | 8.0 | | | 8.0 |
| 170–179 | 10.3 | | | 10.3 |
| 180–189 | 10.4 | | | 10.4 |
| 190–199 | 8.4 | | | 8.4 |
| 200–209 | 9.5 | | | 9.5 |
| 210–219 | 8.6 | | | 8.6 |
| 220–229 | 9.9 | | | 9.9 |
| 230–239 | 10.3 | | | 10.3 |
| 240–249 | 9.5 | | | 9.5 |
| 250–259 | 9.1 | | | 9.1 |
| 260–269 | 11.3 | | 8.7 | 10.0 |
| 270–279 | 12.9 | | 9.2 | 11.1 |
| 280–289 | | | 10.3 | 10.3 |
| 290–299 | | | 9.7 | 9.7 |
| 300–309 | | | 8.1 | 8.1 |
| 310–319 | | | 10.3 | 10.3 |
| 320–329 | | | 10.8 | 10.8 |
| 330–339 | | | 7.7 | 7.7 |
| 340–349 | | | 8.6 | 8.6 |
| 350–359 | | | 9.7 | 9.7 |

TABLE 93.

TRANSMUTATION TABLE FOR ARMY EXAM. A.

| Original Scale | Scale in Equal Units |
|---|---|
| 10 | − 34.1 |
| 20 | − 13.1 |
| 30 | 3.7 |
| 40 | 16.8 |
| 50 | 31.1 |
| 60 | 44.4 |
| 70 | 60.0 |
| 80 | 72.9 |
| 90 | 85.1 |
| 100 | 96.0 |
| 110 | 105.6 |
| 120 | 117.9 |
| 130 | 130.3 |
| 140 | 140.7 |
| 150 | 151.7 |
| 160 | 162.0 |
| 170 | 170.0 |
| 180 | 180.3 |
| 190 | 190.7 |
| 200 | 199.1 |
| 210 | 208.6 |
| 220 | 217.2 |
| 230 | 228.1 |
| 240 | 238.4 |
| 250 | 247.9 |
| 260 | 257.0 |
| 270 | 267.0 |
| 280 | 278.1 |
| 290 | 288.4 |
| 300 | 298.1 |
| 310 | 306.2 |
| 320 | 316.5 |
| 330 | 327.3 |
| 340 | 335.0 |
| 350 | 343.6 |
| 360 | 353.3 |

## TABLE 94.

EQUIVALENTS FOR ARMY EXAMINATION a SCORES FROM 10 TO 360 IN A SCALE WITH EQUAL UNITS. 1 = 1/80 OF THE DIFFERENCE BETWEEN 130 AND 210 OF THE ORIGINAL SCALE.

From 130 to 210 the values of the two scales are identical.

| O | C | O | C | O | C | O | C | O | C | O | C | O | C |
|---|---|---|---|---|---|---|---|---|---|---|---|---|---|
| 10 | −34 | 50 | 31 | 90 | 85 | 210 | 210 | 250 | 248 | 290 | 288 | 330 | 327 |
| 11 | −32 | 51 | 32 | 91 | 86 | 211 | 211 | 251 | 249 | 291 | 289 | 331 | 328 |
| 12 | −30 | 52 | 34 | 92 | 87 | 212 | 212 | 252 | 250 | 292 | 290 | 332 | 329 |
| 13 | −28 | 53 | 35 | 93 | 88 | 213 | 213 | 253 | 251 | 293 | 291 | 333 | 330 |
| 14 | −26 | 54 | 36 | 94 | 89 | 214 | 214 | 254 | 252 | 294 | 292 | 334 | 330 |
| 15 | −24 | 55 | 38 | 95 | 90 | 215 | 215 | 255 | 253 | 295 | 293 | 335 | 331 |
| 16 | −22 | 56 | 40 | 96 | 91 | 216 | 216 | 256 | 254 | 296 | 294 | 336 | 332 |
| 17 | −20 | 57 | 41 | 97 | 92 | 217 | 217 | 257 | 255 | 297 | 295 | 337 | 333 |
| 18 | −17 | 58 | 42 | 98 | 93 | 218 | 218 | 258 | 256 | 298 | 296 | 338 | 334 |
| 19 | −15 | 59 | 44 | 99 | 94 | 219 | 219 | 259 | 257 | 299 | 297 | 339 | 335 |
| 20 | −13 | 60 | 45 | 100 | 95 | 220 | 219 | 260 | 258 | 300 | 298 | 340 | 336 |
| 21 | −11 | 61 | 46 | 101 | 96 | 221 | 220 | 261 | 259 | 301 | 299 | 341 | 337 |
| 22 | −9 | 62 | 48 | 102 | 97 | 222 | 221 | 262 | 260 | 302 | 300 | 342 | 338 |
| 23 | −7 | 63 | 49 | 103 | 98 | 223 | 222 | 263 | 261 | 303 | 300 | 343 | 339 |
| 24 | −5 | 64 | 50 | 104 | 100 | 224 | 223 | 264 | 262 | 304 | 301 | 344 | 340 |
| 25 | −3 | 65 | 52 | 105 | 101 | 225 | 224 | 265 | 263 | 305 | 302 | 345 | 340 |
| 26 | −1 | 66 | 53 | 106 | 102 | 226 | 225 | 266 | 264 | 306 | 303 | 346 | 341 |
| 27 | 0 | 67 | 55 | 107 | 103 | 227 | 226 | 267 | 265 | 307 | 304 | 347 | 342 |
| 28 | 2 | 68 | 56 | 108 | 104 | 228 | 227 | 268 | 266 | 308 | 305 | 348 | 343 |
| 29 | 3 | 69 | 58 | 109 | 105 | 229 | 228 | 269 | 267 | 309 | 306 | 349 | 344 |
| 30 | 4 | 70 | 60 | 110 | 106 | 230 | 229 | 270 | 268 | 310 | 307 | 350 | 345 |
| 31 | 6 | 71 | 61 | 111 | 107 | 231 | 230 | 271 | 269 | 311 | 308 | 351 | 346 |
| 32 | 7 | 72 | 62 | 112 | 108 | 232 | 231 | 272 | 270 | 312 | 309 | 352 | 347 |
| 33 | 8 | 73 | 64 | 113 | 110 | 233 | 232 | 273 | 271 | 313 | 310 | 353 | 348 |
| 34 | 10 | 74 | 65 | 114 | 111 | 234 | 233 | 274 | 272 | 314 | 311 | 354 | 349 |
| 35 | 11 | 75 | 67 | 115 | 112 | 235 | 234 | 275 | 273 | 315 | 312 | 355 | 350 |
| 36 | 12 | 76 | 68 | 116 | 113 | 236 | 235 | 276 | 274 | 316 | 313 | 356 | 350 |
| 37 | 13 | 77 | 70 | 117 | 115 | 237 | 236 | 277 | 275 | 317 | 314 | 357 | 351 |
| 38 | 15 | 78 | 71 | 118 | 116 | 238 | 237 | 278 | 276 | 318 | 315 | 358 | 352 |
| 39 | 16 | 79 | 72 | 119 | 117 | 239 | 238 | 279 | 277 | 319 | 316 | 359 | 353 |
| 40 | 17 | 80 | 73 | 120 | 118 | 240 | 239 | 280 | 278 | 320 | 317 | 360 | 354 |
| 41 | 18 | 81 | 74 | 121 | 119 | 241 | 240 | 281 | 279 | 321 | 318 |  |  |
| 42 | 20 | 82 | 75 | 122 | 120 | 242 | 241 | 282 | 280 | 322 | 319 |  |  |
| 43 | 21 | 83 | 76 | 123 | 122 | 243 | 242 | 283 | 281 | 323 | 320 |  |  |
| 44 | 22 | 84 | 78 | 124 | 123 | 244 | 243 | 284 | 282 |  |  |  |  |
|  |  | 85 | 79 | 125 | 124 |  |  | 285 | 283 |  |  |  |  |

From 130 to 360, the original scale value may be used
with little error, but from 130 down the true values of the
original scale units increase so that these 120 points of the
original scale are equal to about 164 elsewhere.   Table 94
presents a detailed transmutation table made with some
smoothing.

# CHAPTER VIII

## The Form of Distribution of Intellect in Man

The orthodox doctrine is that the form of distribution of intellect in human beings of the same sex and age is Form A, shown in Fig. 15, representing a fact whose variations up and down from its average condition are caused by a large number of uncorrelated factors each of which exer-

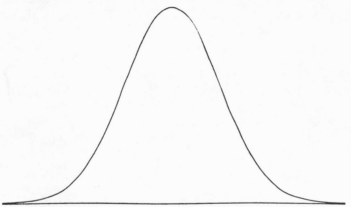

Fig. 15.    Form A, The Normal Probability Surface.

cises about the same amount of influence on intellect as any other, and being a surface enclosed by a curve approximating the normal probability curve $y = \dfrac{1}{\sigma\sqrt{2\pi}} e^{\frac{-x^2}{2\sigma^2}}$ where $\sigma$ is the mean square variation.

This doctrine was urged by Francis Galton, on the basis partly of analogy with the facts in the case of certain bodily dimensions, and partly of his own shrewd observations of human abilities. Since his day it has gained very wide acceptance. This is partly because the measurements of intellect and of other mental abilities in children of the same age (their units being taken at their face value) have uniformly shown continuity clustering around one mode, with diminishing frequencies in proportion to remoteness from that mode, and with no notable departure from symmetry toward any one special form of asymmetry. It is partly because some assumption had to be made in one investigation after another for purposes of quantitative treatment, and this assumption was about as safe as any other one assumption, and much easier to operate with. Hence we gradually slid into the habit of using the doctrine. This fashion became so strong that in recent years psychologists have assumed symmetry, even though the units taken at their face value produced a markedly skewed distribution.

## GENERAL CONSIDERATIONS

Many of those who have made extensive use of this assumption have been aware of its highly hypothetical nature. The argument from analogy is weak because so many bodily variables are clearly skewed in distribution. Such are weight, longevity, girth of chest, strength of arm pull. The argument from mental measurements is weak, not only because of the general ambiguity of the units, but still more because the "error" has been a large proportion of the variation in many of the investigations. The "error" being symmetrical and "normal" tends to add a spurious symmetry and normality to the variability. Moreover, sometimes the selection is such that normality in the group measured may well be an argument in favor of skewness for man in general. So, for example, with sixteen-year olds in high school, or twenty-five-year olds in universities.

In general the form of distribution of any variable trait is due to the number of causes that influence variations in its amount, their magnitudes and their interrelations.[1] Since we do not know what the causes of the variations in

[1] There is a certain regrettable vagueness, not to say ignorance, concerning the causation of variations, as when psychologists consider the amount of intellect to be a consequence of the presence or absence of a single Mendelian determiner, and yet to be distributed unimodally in Form A. Either of these beliefs really denies the other.

intellect in human beings of the same age are, we cannot as yet count them or measure their magnitudes or determine their correlations. We should then be very skeptical of *a priori* assumptions of Form A as the form of distribution of intellect in human beings of the same age. They are very much stronger in the case of children in the same school grade.

In the case of children in the same school grade the causes are our own acts; and we do know that school authorities have a rough standard of the educational ability which belongs in a certain grade, say Grade 7, that intellect correlates closely with educational ability, that departures from this standard (that is, mistakes in grading) are rare in some proportion to their magnitude, that they are due to many causes (the different teachers' judgments with all the experiences upon which they are based, and the ideals and prejudices which they exemplify, and the other causes of error to which they are subject), and that many of these causes are only loosely inter-correlated. These are all features of a status productive of symmetry and normality.

In the case of children of the same age (or age and sex and race) the causes are acts of nature, many of them happening millenniums ago; and we do not even know whether the hereditary factors of variability in intellect are six big ones or sixty small ones. We do not know whether the words heard and acts seen in the first three years of life are of almost zero consequence, as used to be thought when favored children were turned over to healthy peasants during this period; or are of enormous consequence, as is asserted by Freud and (but for different reasons) by Watson.[2] So we may best consider the facts of the distribution of intellect in man with little or no pre-disposition.

[2] There is one special set of major causes of variation about whose action we do know something. Certain diseases and certain accidents, either before or during or after birth, act to prevent or reduce the development of intellect. In some cases one of these causes may act to prevent intellect from reaching more than a certain very lowly status regardless of what might have happened had its action been withheld. The result may be that whatever the distribution apart from these causes, there is combined with it a very small distribution with a mode at a very low degree of intellect, as shown in Fig. 16.

TABLE 36.

NATIONAL INTELLIGENCE EXAMINATION: DISTRIBUTION OF SCORES FOR WHITE PUPILS, AGE 11.

| Interval | Frequencies in Grades 3 to 8 |  |  |  |  |  |  |  |  |  |  |  | Total | Permille: intervals of |  |
|---|---|---|---|---|---|---|---|---|---|---|---|---|---|---|---|
|  | 3A | 3B | 4A | 4B | 5A | 5B | 6A | 6B | 7A | 7B | 8A | 8B |  | 5 | 10 |
| 10– 14 | 2 |  | 2 |  |  |  |  |  |  |  |  |  | 4 | 2 |  |
| 15– 19 | 2 | 1 | 1 |  |  |  |  |  |  |  |  |  | 5 | 3 | 5 |
| 20 | 4 | 1 | 3 | 2 | 1 |  |  |  |  |  |  |  | 10 | 6 |  |
| 25 | 3 |  | 6 | 2 |  |  |  |  |  |  |  |  | 10 | 6 | 12 |
| 30 | 1 | 2 | 6 | 1 | 1 |  |  |  |  |  |  |  | 14 | 8 |  |
| 35 | 3 | 1 | 2 | 1 | 3 | 1 |  | 1 |  |  |  |  | 7 | 4 | 13 |
| 40 | 2 | 1 | 6 | 1 | 7 | 1 |  |  |  |  |  |  | 18 | 11 |  |
| 45 | 3 | 3 | 10 | 3 | 7 | 6 | 2 |  |  |  |  |  | 26 | 16 | 27 |
| 50 |  | 1 | 20 | 4 | 4 | 5 |  |  |  |  |  |  | 30 | 18 |  |
| 55 | 2 | 1 | 18 | 6 | 12 | 14 | 3 | 1 |  |  |  |  | 47 | 29 | 47 |
| 60 |  | 3 | 15 | 13 | 33 | 10 | 8 | 2 |  |  |  |  | 70 | 43 |  |
| 65 |  | 3 | 13 | 3 | 27 | 20 | 8 | 3 | 1 |  |  |  | 63 | 38 | 81 |
| 70 |  | 1 | 10 | 14 | 26 | 25 | 6 | 5 | 2 |  |  |  | 72 | 44 |  |
| 75 |  |  | 12 | 9 | 40 | 16 | 12 | 9 | 1 |  |  |  | 92 | 56 | 100 |
| 80 |  |  |  | 7 | 40 | 16 | 15 | 5 | 2 |  |  |  | 88 | 54 |  |
| 85 |  |  | 3 | 8 | 43 | 24 | 18 | 10 | 1 |  |  |  | 99 | 60 | 114 |
| 90 | 1 |  | 10 | 7 | 46 | 21 | 24 | 11 | 1 |  |  |  | 99 | 60 |  |
| 95 |  | 1 | 8 | 5 | 56 | 18 | 20 | 13 | 2 | 1 |  |  | 122 | 74 | 135 |
| 100 |  |  | 7 | 3 | 44 | 13 | 28 | 12 | 4 |  |  |  | 110 | 67 |  |
| 105 |  |  | 2 | 4 | 35 | 17 | 37 | 13 | 6 |  |  |  | 93 | 57 | 124 |
| 110 |  |  |  | 3 | 25 | 8 | 33 | 9 | 6 |  |  |  | 87 | 53 |  |
| 115 |  |  | 2 | 1 | 21 | 4 | 33 | 12 | 8 |  |  |  | 97 | 59 | 112 |
| 120 |  |  | 2 | 1 | 24 | 2 | 30 | 14 | 6 | 2 |  |  | 86 | 52 |  |
| 125 |  |  | 1 |  | 15 | 3 | 25 | 7 | 2 | 1 |  |  | 71 | 43 | 96 |
| 130 |  |  |  |  | 8 |  | 10 | 6 | 7 | 1 |  |  | 62 | 38 |  |
| 135 |  |  | 2 |  | 6 |  | 9 | 4 | 5 | 3 |  |  | 56 | 34 | 72 |
| 140 |  |  |  |  | 2 | 1 | 11 | 2 | 2 |  |  |  | 39 | 24 |  |
| 145 |  |  |  | 1 | 1 | 1 |  |  | 1 | 1 |  |  | 19 | 12 | 36 |
| 150 |  |  |  |  | 1 |  | 2 | 1 | 5 |  |  |  | 14 | 8 |  |
| 155 |  |  |  |  |  |  | 2 | 1 | 2 |  |  |  | 17 | 10 | 19 |
| 160 |  |  |  |  |  |  |  |  | 2 | 1 |  |  | 5 | 3 |  |
| 165–169 |  |  |  |  |  |  |  |  | 2 |  |  |  | 6 | 4 | 7 |
| Total | 23 | 19 | 161 | 97 | 528 | 226 | 369 | 142 | 63 | 10 | 0 | 0 | 1638 | 996 | 1000 |

The results stated in Chapter VII permit us to free the evidence of the past from the ambiguity and misleading of units whose real value was unknown.  If we had the time and facilities, we could free them also from the constant tendency toward symmetry and normality due to the error of measurement, but that work must be delayed.  What we can do now is to show the form of distribution of children of the same year-age in respect of intellect in so far as it is measured by the Haggerty or by the Otis or by the National A, and in so far as the children examined are a random sampling of the children at that age.  We do not separate

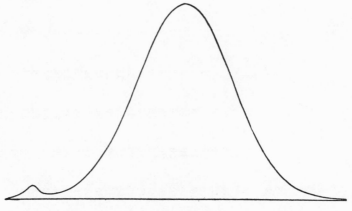

FIG. 16

the sexes, because the sex differences are small and the separation would leave us with too small populations.  We do not separate races, because that cannot be done in the records available.  Negro schools are very rarely, if ever, included in the records; but negro children and children of mixed parentage doubtless are sometimes reported without distinction, and so included in the distributions.

The ages used are 11, 12, 13, and 14, at which years certain very dull children have been excluded from school at home or in institutions.  Some 14-year olds have left school.  The measurements were taken in schools, so that there is

| Interval | 3A | 3B | 4A | 4B | 5A | 5B | 6A | 6B | 7A | 7B | 8A | 8B | Total | Permille: intervals of 5 | Permille: intervals of 10 |
|---|---|---|---|---|---|---|---|---|---|---|---|---|---|---|---|
| 10–14 | 1 | | | | | | | | | | | | 1 | 0.6 | 2 |
| 15–19 | 1 | | | | | | | 1 | | | | | 2 | 1 | |
| 20 | 1 | | 3 | | | | | | | | | | 4 | 3 | 6 |
| 25 | 2 | 1 | 4 | 1 | | | | | | | | | 5 | 3 | |
| 30 | 1 | 3 | 2 | 2 | 1 | | | | | | | | 10 | 7 | 10 |
| 35 | 2 | | 7 | 2 | 3 | 1 | | | | | | | 6 | 4 | |
| 40 | 1 | 1 | 1 | 1 | 3 | 2 | | 1 | | | | | 21 | 14 | 22 |
| 45 | | 1 | 3 | 4 | 6 | 4 | | 1 | | | | | 12 | 8 | |
| 50 | 2 | 1 | 8 | 3 | 2 | 2 | 3 | 1 | | | | | 13 | 9 | 34 |
| 55 | 1 | | 3 | 6 | 5 | 6 | 3 | 3 | | | | | 38 | 25 | |
| 60 | 1 | | 3 | 4 | 14 | 5 | 3 | 3 | | | | | 30 | 20 | 52 |
| 65 | 1 | | 3 | 1 | 16 | 8 | 10 | 7 | | | | | 49 | 32 | |
| 70 | | | 7 | 2 | 26 | 9 | 13 | 6 | | | | | 51 | 34 | 80 |
| 75 | | | 7 | 3 | 25 | 11 | 7 | 8 | 1 | | | | 71 | 47 | |
| 80 | | | 1 | 4 | 34 | 18 | 30 | 11 | 1 | | | | 62 | 41 | 78 |
| 85 | | | 3 | 1 | 19 | 15 | 28 | 21 | 3 | 1 | | | 56 | 37 | |
| 90 | | | 1 | 1 | 20 | 9 | 19 | 16 | 1 | | | | 78 | 51 | 110 |
| 95 | | | 2 | 3 | 20 | 13 | 34 | 16 | 10 | 2 | 1 | | 89 | 59 | |
| 100 | | | | | 14 | 10 | 35 | 14 | 20 | 6 | | | 79 | 52 | 118 |
| 105 | | | | | 11 | 17 | 37 | 12 | 13 | 3 | | | 101 | 66 | |
| 110 | | | | | 12 | 9 | 22 | 17 | 15 | 7 | 1 | | 92 | 61 | 131 |
| 115 | | | | | 11 | 11 | 20 | 9 | 27 | 5 | 2 | 1 | 106 | 70 | |
| 120 | | | | | 5 | 4 | 21 | 5 | 31 | 8 | 6 | | 85 | 56 | 103 |
| 125 | | | | | 4 | 3 | 16 | 1 | 23 | 5 | 2 | | 71 | 47 | |
| 130 | | | | | 5 | 1 | 20 | 5 | 36 | 10 | 3 | | 70 | 46 | 85 |
| 135 | | | | | 5 | 2 | 13 | 2 | 24 | 6 | 2 | 1 | 59 | 39 | |
| 140 | | | | | 2 | 1 | 13 | 1 | 29 | 12 | 1 | | 61 | 40 | 79 |
| 145 | | | | | 2 | | 9 | | 22 | 5 | 3 | | 59 | 39 | |
| 150 | | | | | 1 | | 1 | | 26 | 6 | 4 | | 49 | 32 | 59 |
| 155 | | | | | | | 2 | | 24 | 3 | 3 | | 41 | 27 | |
| 160 | | | | | | | | | 15 | 3 | 1 | | 20 | 13 | 23 |
| 165 | | | | | | | | | 9 | 1 | 1 | | 15 | 10 | |
| 170 | | | | | | | | | 3 | 1 | 1 | | 6 | 4 | 8 |
| 175–179 | | | | | | | | | 3 | | 1 | 1 | 6 | 4 | |
| Total | 14 | 7 | 55 | 38 | 266 | 161 | 359 | 161 | 337 | 84 | 33 | 3 | 1518 | 1002 | |

Frequencies in Grades 3 to 8

too small a representation of truants and of sickly children. City children are more fully represented than country children. The schools are predominantly public schools; so that Catholic children are insufficiently represented. The age is doubtless sometimes in error, and is a year wide. The latter fact should spread and flatten all the distributions a little.

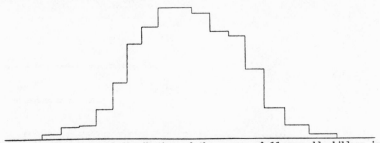

FIG. 17.  The form of distribution of the scores of 11-year-old children in National A, transmuted into a scale with equal units.

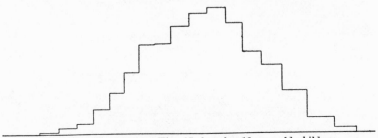

FIG. 18.  The same as Fig. 17, but for 12-year-old children.

It seems unwise to tamper with the records in an effort to allow for these various factors and make the distributions more exactly representative of "all white children of the United States of age x." The process of allowance would probably make improvements, but they would be small and uncertain and very tedious to make and to understand. So we shall take the facts just as Haggerty, Otis, and the National Committee give them; and do nothing to them save transmute each scale interval into units which are truly equal, construct the resulting distributions, and measure certain of their properties. In our inferences from the results we shall, of course, try to bear all the conditioning factors in mind.

Consider first Tables 95 to 98, which give the facts in the case of the National A. Tables 95, 96, and 97 give the original data. Table 98 gives the data for constructing the surfaces of frequency in the shape of the true values for each interval, which are taken as lengths along the abscissa line, and the quotients of the permille numbers each divided by its corresponding abscissa length. These quotients give

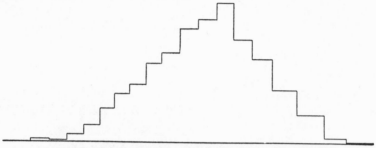

FIG. 19.  The same as Fig. 17, but for 13-year-old children.

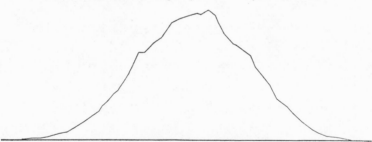

FIG. 20.  An approximate composite of Figs. 17, 18, and 19.

the relative magnitudes of the ordinates or heights of the rectangles erected over the corresponding abscissa lengths. Figs. 17, 18, and 19 show the resulting surfaces of frequency with equal units. Fig. 20 shows a rough composite picture of the form of distribution of National A ability in children of the same year-age. It contains the three separate distributions centered on their medians.

Tables 99 and 100 show the original data in the case of the Otis Advanced Examination. Table 101 shows the ab-

TABLE 97.

NATIONAL INTELLIGENCE EXAMINATION A: DISTRIBUTION OF SCORES FOR WHITE PUPILS, AGE 13.

| Interval | Frequencies in Grades 3 to 8 | | | | | | | | | | | | Total | Permille intervals of 5 | Permille intervals of 10 |
|---|---|---|---|---|---|---|---|---|---|---|---|---|---|---|---|
| | 3A | 3B | 4A | 4B | 5A | 5B | 6A | 6B | 7A | 7B | 8A | 8B | | | |
| 10–14 | | | | | 1 | | | | | | | | 1 | 0.8 | |
| 15–19 | | 1 | 1 | | | | | | | | | | 2 | 2 | 2.8 |
| 20–24 | | | | | 1 | | | | | | | | 1 | 0.8 | |
| 25 | | | | 1 | 1 | | | | | | | | 1 | 0.8 | 1.6 |
| 30 | | | 1 | 1 | 3 | 1 | 1 | | | | | | 4 | 3 | |
| 35 | | 1 | 1 | 1 | 1 | 1 | 1 | 1 | | | | | 5 | 4 | 7 |
| 40 | | | 1 | 1 | 1 | 2 | 2 | | | | | | 4 | 3 | |
| 45 | | 1 | | | 9 | 4 | 1 | 2 | | | | | 15 | 12 | 15 |
| 50 | | | 4 | 3 | 9 | 5 | 1 | | | | | | 17 | 14 | |
| 55 | | | 2 | 2 | 6 | 6 | 5 | | | | | | 17 | 14 | 28 |
| 60 | | | 1 | 2 | 12 | 8 | 1 | 2 | | | | | 24 | 19 | |
| 65 | | | 6 | | 14 | 3 | 5 | 1 | 1 | | 1 | | 28 | 22 | 41 |
| 70 | | | 1 | 3 | 16 | 8 | 8 | 2 | 2 | | | | 39 | 31 | |
| 75 | | | | 4 | 9 | 3 | 6 | 1 | 2 | | | | 25 | 20 | 51 |
| 80 | | | 3 | 3 | 7 | 8 | 6 | 9 | 9 | | | | 47 | 37 | |
| 85 | | | 1 | 1 | 10 | 6 | 19 | 6 | 8 | 2 | 4 | | 40 | 31 | 68 |
| 90 | | | | 2 | 6 | 13 | 16 | 7 | 13 | 3 | 3 | 2 | 67 | 53 | |
| 95 | | | | | 5 | 4 | 18 | 10 | 8 | 3 | 6 | 3 | 49 | 39 | 92 |
| 100 | | | | | 7 | 6 | 10 | 16 | 13 | 3 | 5 | 1 | 69 | 54 | |
| 105 | | | | 2 | 4 | 6 | 19 | 15 | 25 | 8 | 9 | 2 | 73 | 57 | 111 |
| 110 | | | | | 1 | 2 | 20 | 8 | 19 | 13 | 9 | 7 | 73 | 57 | |
| 115 | | | | | 3 | 4 | 17 | 16 | 33 | 6 | 9 | 5 | 90 | 71 | 128 |
| 120 | | | | | 1 | 3 | 12 | 9 | 28 | 15 | 5 | 3 | 83 | 65 | |
| 125 | | | | | | 5 | 8 | 6 | 24 | 23 | 10 | 7 | 82 | 65 | 130 |
| 130 | | | | | | 1 | 11 | 4 | 29 | 14 | 6 | 6 | 64 | 50 | |
| 135 | | | | | | 1 | 6 | 6 | 22 | 13 | 11 | 5 | 71 | 56 | 106 |
| 140 | | | | | | | 4 | 2 | 19 | 18 | 8 | 3 | 58 | 46 | |
| 145 | | | | | | | 5 | 3 | 23 | 22 | 9 | 7 | 64 | 50 | 96 |
| 150 | | | | | | | 2 | 1 | 19 | 16 | 9 | 6 | 57 | 45 | |
| 155 | | | | | | | 2 | 1 | 13 | 10 | 4 | 2 | 36 | 28 | 73 |
| 160 | | | | | | | 1 | | 9 | 11 | 8 | 4 | 33 | 26 | |
| 165 | | | | | | | | | 5 | 6 | 4 | | 20 | 16 | 42 |
| 170 | | | | | | | | | 4 | | 2 | | 6 | 5 | |
| 175 | | | | | | | | | 1 | | 1 | | 2 | 2 | 7 |
| 180 | | | | | | | | 1 | | | | | 1 | 0.8 | |
| | | | | | | | 109 | 261 | 266 | 186 | 114 | 42 | 1268 | 1000.2 | |

TABLE 98.

NATIONAL A.  DATA FOR SURFACE OF FREQUENCY IN EQUAL UNITS.

| Original Interval | Abscissa Length in Equal Units | Ordinate Heights to Make the Areas Equal to the Corresponding Permille Entries of Tables—95, 96 and 97 | | |
|---|---|---|---|---|
| | | Age 11 | Age 12 | Age 13 |
| 10–19 | 10.00 (Est.) | 5 | 2 | 2.5 |
| 20–29 | 9.61 | 12.5 | 6.2 | 1.6 |
| 30 | 9.30 | 14.0 | 10.8 | 7.5 |
| 40 | 8.63 | 31.3 | 25.5 | 17.4 |
| 50 | 7.92 | 59.3 | 42.9 | 35.4 |
| 60 | 8.12 | 99.8 | 64.0 | 50.5 |
| 70 | 8.55 | 117.0 | 93.6 | 59.6 |
| 80 | 8.32 | 137.0 | 93.8 | 81.7 |
| 90 | 9.85 | 137.0 | 112.0 | 93.4 |
| 100 | 9.44 | 131.0 | 125.0 | 118.0 |
| 110 | 10.03 | 112.0 | 131.0 | 128.0 |
| 120 | 8.95 | 107.0 | 115.0 | 145.0 |
| 130 | 9.92 | 72.6 | 85.7 | 106.8 |
| 140 | 11.14 | 32.3 | 71.0 | 86.3 |
| 150 | 13.37 | 14.2 | 44.1 | 54.5 |
| 160 | 14.59 | 4.8 | 15.8 | 28.8 |
| 170 | 15.00 (Est.) | | 5.3 | 4.7 |
| 180 | 16.00 (Est.) | | | 0.7 |

scissa lengths in equal units and the ordinate heights obtained by dividing each original permille number by the corresponding abscissa length in equal units.  Figs. 21, 22, 23, and 24 show the surfaces drawn according to Table VII.

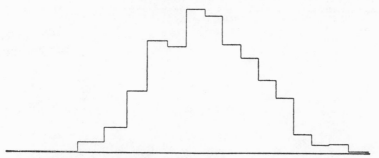

FIG. 21.  The form of distribution of the scores of 11-year-old children in Otis Advanced, transmuted into a scale with equal units.

20

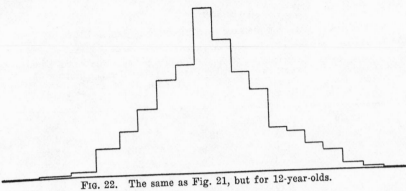

FIG. 22.   The same as Fig. 21, but for 12-year-olds.

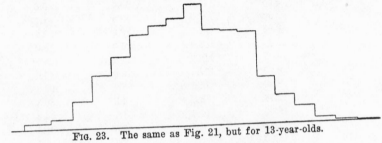

FIG. 23.   The same as Fig. 21, but for 13-year-olds.

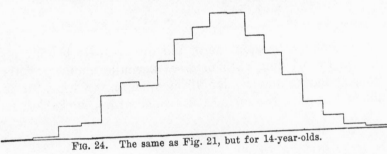

FIG. 24.   The same as Fig. 21, but for 14-year-olds.

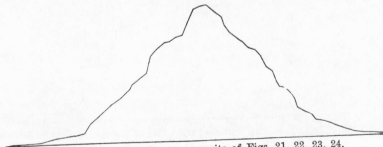

FIG. 25.   An approximate composite of Figs. 21, 22, 23, 24.

Fig. 25 is a composite repeating Figs. 21 to 24, with the four medians coinciding.

Table 102 shows the original data for the Haggerty Delta 2; Table 103 shows the lengths and heights when

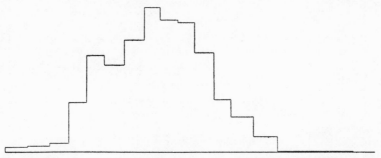

FIG. 26.   The form of distribution of the scores of 11-year-old children in the Haggerty Delta Two, transmuted into a scale with equal units.

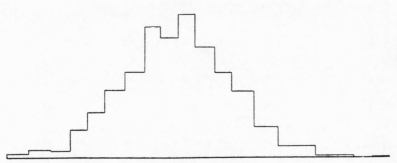

FIG. 27.   The same as Fig. 26, but for 12-year-olds.

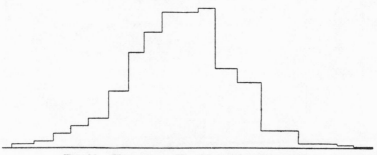

FIG. 28.   The same as Fig. 26, but for 13-year-olds.

TABLE 99.

OTIS ADVANCED EXAMINATION: DISTRIBUTION OF SCORES: AGES 11 AND 12.

Columns grouped as: **Age 11** — Frequencies in Grades 4 to 9, then Total and Per-mille; **Age 12** — Frequencies in Grades 4 to 10, then Total and Per-mille.

| Interval | A11 · 4 | A11 · 5 | A11 · 6 | A11 · 7 | A11 · 8 | A11 · 9 | A11 · Total | A11 · Per-mille | A12 · 4 | A12 · 5 | A12 · 6 | A12 · 7 | A12 · 8 | A12 · 9 | A12 · 10 | A12 · Total | A12 · Per-mille |
|---|---|---|---|---|---|---|---|---|---|---|---|---|---|---|---|---|---|
| 0– 9 | 1 |  |  |  |  |  | 1 | 2 | 1 |  |  |  |  |  |  | 1 | 1 |
| 10–19 |  | 1 |  |  |  |  | 1 | 2 | 1 | 2 |  |  |  |  |  | 3 | 4 |
| 20–29 | 6 | 4 |  |  |  |  | 10 | 16 | 3 | 3 |  |  |  |  |  | 6 | 7 |
| 30 | 4 | 16 |  |  |  |  | 20 | 32 | 2 | 22 | 5 |  |  |  |  | 29 | 34 |
| 40 | 8 | 27 | 7 | 1 |  |  | 43 | 70 |  | 29 | 12 | 1 |  |  |  | 42 | 49 |
| 50 | 6 | 60 | 9 | 1 |  |  | 77 | 125 | 2 | 31 | 25 | 3 | 1 |  |  | 62 | 72 |
| 60 | 3 | 50 | 15 | 3 |  |  | 71 | 115 | 1 | 29 | 41 | 11 | 4 |  |  | 86 | 100 |
| 70 | 2 | 55 | 30 | 3 | 1 |  | 92 | 150 | 1 | 29 | 52 | 12 | 2 |  |  | 96 | 112 |
| 80 | 1 | 44 | 32 | 8 | 2 |  | 85 | 138 |  | 33 | 74 | 31 | 3 |  |  | 141 | 165 |
| 90 |  | 23 | 37 | 6 | 3 |  | 67 | 109 |  | 9 | 63 | 27 | 14 | 1 |  | 114 | 133 |
| 100 |  | 16 | 35 | 6 | 1 |  | 58 | 94 |  | 5 | 41 | 21 | 14 | 2 | 1 | 84 | 98 |
| 110 |  | 9 | 30 | 4 | 1 | 1 | 44 | 72 |  | 3 | 33 | 11 | 19 | 1 | 2 | 69 | 81 |
| 120 |  | 2 | 16 | 4 | 1 |  | 22 | 36 |  | 2 | 13 | 9 | 10 | 3 |  | 37 | 43 |
| 130 |  | 2 | 6 | 3 | 2 |  | 12 | 19 |  |  | 7 | 4 | 13 | 6 | 2 | 33 | 39 |
| 140 |  |  | 1 | 2 | 2 |  | 5 | 8 |  |  | 4 | 2 | 11 | 5 | 1 | 23 | 27 |
| 150 |  |  | 1 | 2 |  | 1 | 6 | 10 |  |  | 1 | 3 | 9 | 4 | 1 | 19 | 22 |
| 160 |  |  | 1 |  |  |  | 1 | 2 |  |  | 1 |  | 4 | 2 | 2 | 7 | 8 |
| 170 |  |  |  |  |  |  |  |  |  |  |  |  | 1 | 1 | 1 | 3 | 4 |
| 180 |  |  |  |  |  |  |  |  |  |  |  |  | 1 |  |  | 1 | 1 |
| 190 |  |  |  |  |  |  |  |  |  |  |  |  |  |  |  |  |  |
| 200 |  |  |  |  |  |  |  |  |  |  |  |  |  |  |  |  |  |
| 210 |  |  |  |  |  |  |  |  |  |  |  |  |  |  |  |  |  |
| Total | 31 | 309 | 220 | 43 | 13 | 2 |  |  | 11 | 197 | 372 | 135 | 106 | 25 | 10 |  |  |

equal units are used.   Figs. 26, 27, 28, and 29 are the resulting surfaces of frequency; Fig. 30 is their composite.

Fig. 31 is a composite of the three composites, Figs. 20,
25 and 30.

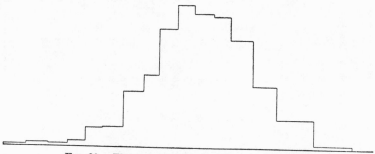

FIG. 29.   The same as Fig. 26, but for 14-year-olds.

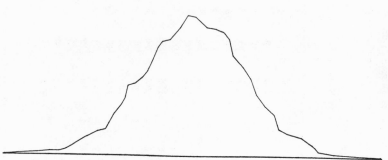

FIG. 30.   An approximate composite of Figs. 26, 27, 28, and 29.

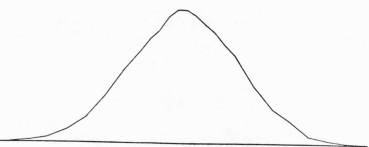

FIG. 31.   A composite of three composites.

## TABLE 100.

### Otis Advanced Examination: Distribution of Scores: Ages 13 and 14.

| Interval | Age 13 Frequencies in Grades 4 to 11 | | | | | | | | | | Age 14 Frequencies in Grades 5 to 11 | | | | | | | | |
|---|---|---|---|---|---|---|---|---|---|---|---|---|---|---|---|---|---|---|---|
| | 4 | 5 | 6 | 7 | 8 | 9 | 10 | 11 | Total | Per-mille | 5 | 6 | 7 | 8 | 9 | 10 | 11 | Total | Per-mille |
| 0–9 | | | | | | | | | | | | | | | | | | | |
| 10–19 | 1 | 5 | 2 | 1 | | | | | 9 | 9 | 1 | | | | | | | 1 | 1 |
| 20 | | 5 | 5 | 1 | 1 | | | | 12 | 12 | 1 | 2 | | | | | | 4 | 4 |
| 30 | 1 | 12 | 11 | 3 | 3 | | | | 30 | 31 | 7 | 6 | 2 | 1 | | | | 15 | 16 |
| 40 | 1 | 26 | 23 | 8 | | | | | 58 | 59 | 6 | 5 | 4 | 1 | | | | 16 | 17 |
| 50 | | 31 | 21 | 10 | 12 | 2 | | | 76 | 77 | 15 | 14 | 7 | 3 | 1 | | | 41 | 45 |
| 60 | | 21 | 45 | 16 | 12 | | | | 94 | 96 | 9 | 19 | 7 | 17 | 2 | | | 54 | 59 |
| 70 | | 8 | 39 | 21 | 28 | 3 | | | 99 | 102 | 4 | 21 | 6 | 14 | 2 | 1 | | 48 | 52 |
| 80 | | 5 | 29 | 17 | 41 | 11 | 4 | | 107 | 109 | 3 | 13 | 10 | 25 | 11 | 1 | | 69 | 75 |
| 90 | | 3 | 25 | 22 | 44 | 18 | 6 | | 118 | 120 | 1 | 14 | 11 | 40 | 19 | 8 | | 88 | 96 |
| 100 | | 1 | 11 | 10 | 48 | 16 | 6 | | 92 | 94 | 1 | 10 | 6 | 40 | 30 | 3 | 1 | 97 | 105 |
| 110 | | | 7 | 8 | 47 | 17 | 12 | 1 | 92 | 94 | | 2 | 10 | 37 | 41 | 10 | 1 | 109 | 118 |
| 120 | | | 1 | 5 | 39 | 31 | 13 | 1 | 90 | 92 | | | 7 | 31 | 53 | 17 | 1 | 109 | 119 |
| 130 | | | | 3 | 20 | 16 | 7 | | 46 | 47 | | | 1 | 26 | 48 | 17 | | 88 | 96 |
| 140 | | | | | 10 | 13 | 7 | | 30 | 31 | | | 1 | 7 | 39 | 11 | 3 | 72 | 78 |
| 150 | | | | | 4 | 12 | 2 | 1 | 19 | 19 | | | | 7 | 34 | 25 | 1 | 56 | 61 |
| 160 | | | | | 2 | 2 | 1 | | 5 | 5 | | | | 2 | 14 | 12 | 1 | 30 | 33 |
| 170 | | | | | | 2 | | | 2 | 2 | | | | | 8 | 14 | | 15 | 16 |
| 180 | | | | | | 1 | | | 1 | 1 | | | | | 1 | 5 | | 5 | 5 |
| 190 | | | | | | | | | | | | | | | 1 | 3 | | 3 | 3 |
| 200 | | | | | | | | | | | | | | | | 2 | | | |
| 210 | | | | | | | | | | | | | | | | | | | |
| Total | 3 | 117 | 219 | 125 | 311 | 144 | 58 | 3 | | | 48 | 106 | 72 | 252 | 304 | 129 | 9 | | |

The ability which is measured by the score of any one of the commonly used intelligence examinations is thus shown to be distributed in children of the same age (from 11 to 14 in rather close approximation to Form A. There are no demonstrable departures from unimodality or from

TABLE 101.

OTIS ADVANCED EXAMINATION: DATA BY WHICH THE SURFACES OF FREQUENCY ARE CONSTRUCTED.

| Intervals by Original Scores | Values of Intervals in Equal Units | Heights of the Surface of Frequency with Equal Units to Make the Areas Equal to the Corresponding Permille Entries | | | |
|---|---|---|---|---|---|
| | | 11 | 12 | 13 | 14 |
| 0– 9 | 20.0 (Est.) | 1.0 | 0.5 | | |
| 10–19 | 18.3 | 1.1 | 2.2 | | .5 |
| 20–29 | 14.8 | 10.8 | 4.7 | 6.6 | 2.5 |
| 30 | 12.2 | 26.2 | 27.9 | 9.8 | 13.4 |
| 40 | 10.9 | 64.2 | 45.0 | 28.4 | 16.0 |
| 50 | 10.7 | 116.9 | 67.3 | 55.2 | 41.7 |
| 60 | 10.4 | 110.5 | 96.2 | 74.1 | 56.5 |
| 70 | 10.0 | 150.0 | 112.0 | 96.0 | 52.2 |
| 80 | 9.7 | 142.3 | 170.0 | 105.0 | 77.2 |
| 90 | 9.7 | 112.4 | 137.0 | 112.0 | 98.9 |
| 100 | 9.5 | 98.9 | 103.0 | 126.0 | 110.9 |
| 110 | 9.5 | 75.8 | 85.3 | 99.0 | 125.0 |
| 120 | 9.6 | 37.5 | 44.8 | 98.0 | 123.9 |
| 130 | 9.6 | 19.8 | 40.7 | 95.9 | 99.7 |
| 140 | 9.6 | 8.3 | 28.2 | 49.0 | 81.5 |
| 150 | 10.5 | 9.5 | 21.0 | 29.6 | 58.0 |
| 160 | 11.0 | 1.8 | 7.3 | 17.3 | 29.7 |
| 170 | 11.2 | | 3.6 | 4.5 | 14.6 |
| 180 | 11.8 | | .9 | 1.7 | 4.7 |
| 190 | 16.0 | | | .6 | 2.1 |

symmetry; the decrease in frequency as we pass from the mode is slow, then more rapid, and then slow again.

### THE FORM OF DISTRIBUTION AT AGES UP TO FIFTEEN

It is reasonable to infer that the form of distribution which is found for these examination scores, when transformed into a scale with equal units, will be found with very

little change for any valid measures of the altitude of Intellect CAVD, or of Intellect GOPI (letting G refer to geometrical tasks, O to opposites, P to picture completions, I
to information), or of any representative sampling of intellectual tasks. It is reasonable to carry the inference on to
any valid measures of the histological and physiological
basis of altitude of intellect. It is probably safe also to ex-

TABLE 102.

HAGGERTY DELTA 2; DISTRIBUTION OF SCORES.   DATA FROM MADSEN [ '22].

|  | Age 11 Grades 3 to 8 | | Age 12 Grades 3 to 10 | | Age 13 Grades 3 to 10 | | Age 14 Grades 3 to 11 | |
|---|---|---|---|---|---|---|---|---|
|  | n | Per-mille | n | Per-mille | n | Per-mille | n | Per-mille |
| 0– 9 | 5 | 6 | 4 | 5 |  |  | 1 | 2 |
| 10– 19 | 6 | 7 | 8 | 10 | 4 | 5 | 3 | 5 |
| 20– 29 | 8 | 10 | 6 | 7 | 6 | 8 | 2 | 3.5 |
| 30– 39 | 39 | 48 | 22 | 28 | 11 | 14 | 9 | 6 |
| 40– 49 | 78 | 96 | 35 | 44 | 16 | 21 | 11 | 19 |
| 50– 59 | 80 | 98 | 62 | 79 | 26 | 34 | 13 | 23 |
| 60– 69 | 99 | 122 | 74 | 94 | 48 | 62 | 32 | 57 |
| 70– 79 | 106 | 130 | 92 | 117 | 65 | 85 | 37 | 66 |
| 80– 89 | 106 | 130 | 93 | 118 | 88 | 114 | 66 | 117 |
| 90– 99 | 100 | 123 | 107 | 136 | 99 | 129 | 76 | 135 |
| 100–109 | 89 | 109 | 95 | 121 | 115 | 149 | 83 | 147 |
| 110–119 | 44 | 54 | 69 | 88 | 112 | 145 | 77 | 136 |
| 120–129 | 36 | 44 | 65 | 83 | 76 | 99 | 76 | 135 |
| 130–139 | 17 | 21 | 33 | 42 | 68 | 88 | 47 | 83 |
| 140–149 | 1 | 1 | 18 | 23 | 26 | 34 | 28 | 50 |
| 150–159 | 1 | 1 | 3 | 4 | 7 | 9 | 4 | 7 |
| 160–169 |  |  |  |  | 2 | 3 |  |  |
| 170–179 |  |  | 1 | 1 | 1 | 1 |  |  |
| Total | 815 |  | 787 |  | 770 |  | 565 |  |

tend the inference back to ages eleven to one, since there is
no evidence that mortality from one to twelve is selective
in respect of altitude of intellect to any considerable extent, or that the environment acts during those years to
reduce and counteract tendencies to multimodality, skewness, and other departures from Form A. With a little less
assurance, we may extend it back to the germ cells and

assert that, to a close approximation, the original capacities of white children in the United States to manifest given altitudes of intellect are distributed in a surface that is approximately unimodal, symmetrical, and of Form A.

## THE FORM OF DISTRIBUTION IN ADULTS

Extending the inference to later ages is a very different matter. If the distribution is "normal" at 14, it may still become skewed at 24. This would happen if the gains made by those of different degrees of intellect at 14 differed in certain ways and by certain amounts. For example, suppose that the altitude of intellect of fourteen-year-olds is distributed as shown in column I of Table 104, and that from fourteen to twenty-four those individuals of abilities 1, 2, 3, 4, and 5 gain 0, while those of abilities 6 to 19 gain as shown below:

| Ability | Gain | | |
|---|---|---|---|
| 6 | 0 | to | .15 |
| 7 | .15 | to | .35 |
| 8 | .35 | to | .55 |
| 9 | .55 | to | 1.3 |
| 10 | 1.3 | to | 2.0 |
| 11 | 2 | to | 5 |
| 12 | 5 | to | 10 |
| 13 | 10 | to | 16 |
| 14 | 16 | to | 40 |
| 15 | 40 | to | 80 |
| 16 | 80 | to | 150 |
| 17 | 150 | to | 300 |
| 18 | 300 | to | 600 |
| 19 | 600 | to | 1000 |

The distribution at age twenty-four would then have its low extreme at 1 as before, its mode and median at about 11, and an enormous skew running up to about 1,000. To take a much less extreme state of affairs which might be real, suppose the condition at fourteen to be as in columns II and III of Table 104, and the gains to be as shown in column IV. Then the condition at twenty-four will be as shown in column V with a clear skew.

We also have evidence that a positive relation of gain to ability exists in the case of the ages above fourteen, though we do not know its exact nature or amount. Imbeciles notoriously gain very little. Thorndike has shown ['23] that the sort of pupil who attends high school gains up to eighteen at least, in the ability measured by stock intelligence tests, and that the white pupils gain much more than the colored pupils.

TABLE 103.

HAGGERTY DELTA 2.    DATA FOR SURFACE OF FREQUENCY IN EQUAL UNITS.

| Original Interval | Abscissa Length in Equal Units | Ordinate Heights to Make the Areas Equal to the Corresponding Per-mille Entries of Tables | | | |
|---|---|---|---|---|---|
| | | Age 11 | Age 12 | Age 13 | Age 14 |
| 0– 9 | 12.00 (Est.) | 5 | 4 | | 2 |
| 10–19 | 12.00 (Est.) | 6 | 8 | 4 | 4 |
| 20–29 | 10.70 | 9 | 7 | 7 | 3 |
| 30 | 9.50 | 51 | 29 | 15 | 6 |
| 40 | 9.33 | 103 | 47 | 23 | 20 |
| 50 | 10.85 | 90 | 73 | 31 | 21 |
| 60 | 10.55 | 116 | 89 | 59 | 54 |
| 70 | 8.62 | 151 | 136 | 99 | 77 |
| 80 | 9.48 | 137 | 124 | 120 | 123 |
| 90 | 9.15 | 134 | 149 | 141 | 148 |
| 100 | 10.54 | 103 | 115 | 141 | 139 |
| 110 | 10.01 | 54 | 88 | 145 | 136 |
| 120 | 12.06 | 36 | 69 | 82 | 112 |
| 130 | 13.01 | 16 | 32 | 68 | 64 |
| 140 | 19.86 | 0.5 | 12 | 17 | 25 |
| 150 | 20.88 | 0.5 | 2 | 4 | 3 |

The differential gain could be caused by several different factors. Inner mental growth is less in amount in the dull at all ages; it may, and probably does, slow up and approach zero earlier in the dull. Insofar as ability with intellectual tasks is due to environment and training, the expectation will be that each added acquisition will be a stimulus to others and an aid in acquiring them. So learning to read commonly leads to the acquisition of a wider vocabulary and a better score in opposite tests and completion tests than would have been attained by oral intercourse alone. The more intellectual the individual is, also, the more will he give his free time to intellectual pursuits. Finally, vocational selection is such that the more intellec-

TABLE 104.

THE EFFECT OF CORRELATION BETWEEN STATUS AND GAIN WHEN GAIN IN-
CREASES IN A GEOMETRIC RATIO.

| I Status | II Frequency at 14 Grouped by 1's | III Grouped by 3's | IV Gain 14 to 24 | V Frequency at 24 |
|---|---|---|---|---|
| 0 | | | | |
| 1 | .02 | .2 | .1 + | 0.2 |
| 2 | .19 | | .125 | |
| 3 | 1.14 | | .156 | |
| 4 | 4.85 | 21.5 | .195 | 21.5 |
| 5 | 15.50 | | .244 | |
| 6 | 38.76 | | .305 | |
| 7 | 77.52 | 242 | .381 | 242 |
| 8 | 125.97 | | .477 | |
| 9 | 167.96 | | .596 | |
| 10 | 184.76 | 521 | .745 | 510 |
| 11 | 167.96 | | .931 | |
| 12 | 125.97 | | 1.16 | |
| 13 | 77.52 | 242 | 1.45 | 214 |
| 14 | 38.76 | | 1.82 | |
| 15 | 15.50 | | 2.27 | |
| 16 | 4.85 | 21.5 | 2.84 | 53 |
| 17 | 1.14 | | 3.55 | |
| 18 | .19 | | 4.44 | |
| 19 | .02 | .2 | 5.55 | 6 |
| 20 | | | | |
| 21 | | | | |
| 22 | | | | |
| 23 | | | | 0.2 |
| 24 | | | | |
| 25 | | | | 0.02 |

tual individuals continue in school and engage in clerical and professional work that involves intellectual activities, while the dull leave school for labor which requires little thought, and sometimes does not even permit it.

There may of course be a marked increase of gain for those of higher abilities without producing skewness. If $g = as + b$, no skewness will be produced, no matter how steep the relation line may be. The variability will increase, but the form will still be Form A, as shown in Table

TABLE 105.

THE EFFECT OF CORRELATION BETWEEN STATUS AND GAIN WHEN $G = AS + B$.

| Status | Frequency at 14 | Gain 14 to 24 | Frequency at 24 |
|--------|-----------------|---------------|-----------------|
| 1 | 1 | 2 | |
| 2 | 10 | 4 | |
| 3 | 45 | 6 | 1 |
| 4 | 120 | 8 | |
| 5 | 210 | 10 | |
| 6 | 252 | 12 | 10 |
| 7 | 210 | 14 | |
| 8 | 120 | 16 | |
| 9 | 45 | 18 | 45 |
| 10 | 10 | 20 | |
| 11 | 1 | 22 | |
| 12 | | | 120 |
| 13 | | | |
| 14 | | | |
| 15 | | | 210 |
| 16 | | | |
| 17 | | | |
| 18 | | | 252 |
| 19 | | | |
| 20 | | | |
| 21 | | | 210 |
| 22 | | | |
| 23 | | | |
| 24 | | | 120 |
| 25 | | | |
| 26 | | | |
| 27 | | | 45 |
| 28 | | | |
| 29 | | | |
| 30 | | | 10 |
| 31 | | | |
| 32 | | | |
| 33 | | | 1 |

105, where the abilities 1, 2, 3, 4, 5, 6, etc., have gains of 2, 4, 6, 8, 10, 12, etc.

The causes which influence differences in gains in intellect up to about fourteen do seem to produce them in a rough proportion to the differences in ability, so that the form does remain that of Form A.

The only data that we have found for measuring the form of distribution of anything approximating a random sampling for any age above fifteen are the well-known Army records with Alpha, Beta, and Examination *a*. We have no satisfactory means of determining the value of Beta scores in a scale of equal units. So we limit our inquiry to Alpha and Examination *a*.

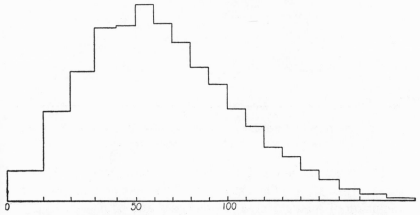

FIG. 32.   The form of distribution of the scores of recruits in Army Alpha transmuted into a scale with equal units.

Using the equal-unit values for Alpha and *a* derived in Chapter VII, and proceeding as in the case of the National, Otis, and Haggerty scores for children, we obtain the results shown in Fig. 32 for 51,620 native-born whites of the draft [Data from the National Academy of Sciences Memoirs, '21, p. 764].

The equal-unit values of the interval from 0 to 20 in Army Alpha and from 0 to 30 in Examination *a* are estimates from exceedingly scant data.

The lower end of Fig. 32 would be extended if the illiterates who were exempt from Alpha had been included. It would have been extended still further if the men rejected for dullness by the examining boards had been included. The upper end would be extended if the officers had been included.

Using the equal-unit values for Examination $a$ in the same manner, we obtain the results shown in Fig. 33 for

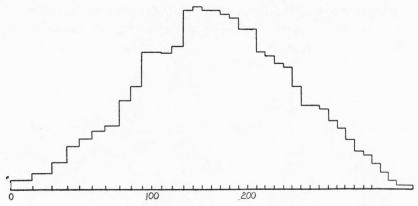

FIG. 33.   The form of distribution of the scores of recruits in Army Examination $a$, transmuted into a scale with equal units.

63,647 enlisted men in four camps. [Data from the Memoirs, '21, p. 492.] The same considerations concerning the inclusion of men rejected for dullness and of officers apply as applied in the case of Alpha. In these four camps, 13.9% had been excluded from examination as illiterate.

It is difficult to reach any secure conclusion from the facts of Fig. 32 and Fig. 33, except that there is no evidence of negative skewness. From Alpha alone in the general draft it would appear that even after generous allowance for the dullness of the illiterates and others who were excluded from examination, the distribution was skewed positively, i.e., toward the high end. With Examination $a$ in the four camps, however, the skewness of the original scores disappears when the values in equal units are used.

We cannot even estimate with surety what the distribution of 51,620 of the native-born whites would have been if they had been measured with Examination $a$, or what the distribution of the 63,647 enlisted men in the four camps would have been if they had been measured with Alpha. That is, we cannot decide how far the difference between Fig. 32 and Fig. 33 is caused by the tests used and how far it is caused by the groups tested.

On the whole,[3] we may provisionally regard the sort of intellect measured by Alpha and $a$ as distributed in the adult native-born white population of the United States with some positive skewness. We may provisionally assign, as the cause of the change from the symmetry and normality found in children, a differential gain from the age of fourteen to twenty and beyond, whereby some individuals increase these abilities very greatly, whereas others increase them little or not at all. This should be only provisional. The whole matter of adult intellect should sometime be studied with the care which it deserves.

For the ages from 14 up to 17 or 18, we may assume symmetry and normality without much probability of more than a small error. Or, we may have a slightly greater prospect of correctness if we allow for a very little positive skewness, increasing year by year.

[3] Certain facts of the distribution of men in occupations, of the distribution of wages, of the distribution of schooling, and the like rather favor the supposition that adult intellect is distributed with positive skewness.

# CHAPTER IX

## A Scale for Measuring Altitude of Intellect

It was not a part of our original plan to make an actual scale for measuring intellectual difficulty, but only to find methods whereby this could be done. We have proved that the form of distribution of altitude of intellect in grade populations from Grade 6 to the first year of college can be known, so that the degree of intellectual difficulty of a composite task which is truly intellectual can be measured by the percentage of successes in such a grade population. We have also shown that the form of distribution of intellect of an age population 10 to 14 is approximately of Form A, that of the normal probability surface, so that the same procedure can be followed in one of these age groups. It is highly probable that it can be followed in lower age groups.

Although we did not plan for scaling the difficulty of actual tasks and are not able to do it precisely with the time and facilities at our disposal, it seems best to make a beginning, if only to illustrate the workings of the principles and techniques involved in an actual case.

The work on this scale may best be considered in two parts, that which evaluates the differences in difficulty of Composites I to Q, and that which evaluates the differences in difficulty of Composites A to I. The latter was done primarily to put the values for I, J, K $\cdots$ Q in relation to the absolute zero, for which purpose chance errors in the determinations of B–A, C–B, D–C $\cdots$ I–H are of minor importance, since they tend to equalize one another. These lower intervals are less precisely determined than those from I to Q; and we report them and their derivations separately in the latter part of the chapter.

THE DIFFICULTY OF COMPOSITES I, J, K, L, M, N, O, P, AND Q

We present first the measurement of differences in difficulty between tasks I and J, between J and K, between K and L, and so on with M, N, O, P, and Q. The facts at our disposal for the measurement of differences in difficulty amongst these composite tasks are the percentages correct in various groups as shown in Table 106. Group 5½ refers to the 147 pupils measured at the end of Grade 5 and at the beginning of Grade 6 with composites I, J, and K. Group 9I refers to the 246 pupils of Grade 9 who are measured with composites I, J, K, L, and M. Group 9II refers to the 192 pupils of Grade 9 who are measured with composites

TABLE 106.

PERCENTS OF VARIOUS GROUPS SUCCEEDING WITH 20 OR MORE SINGLE TASKS OF CAVD 40-COMPOSITES I TO Q.

| Composite | Percents Succeeding | | | | |
|---|---|---|---|---|---|
| | 5½ | 9I | 9II | 13 | 17 |
| I | 91.2 | 99.6 | | | |
| J | 29.1 | 89.4 | | | |
| K | 11.5 | 61.4 | 47.0 | | |
| L | | 32.9 | 16.3 | | |
| M | | 5.3 | 7.2 | | |
| N | | | 1.1 | 81.5 | 95.4 |
| O | | | | 48.1 | 77.1 |
| P | | | | 27.5 | 56.7 |
| Q | | | | 3.7 | 22.9 |

K, L, M, and N. Group 13 refers to the 189 candidates for entrance to college who were measured with composites N, O, P, and Q. Group 17 refers to the 240 college graduates who were measured with N, O, P, and Q.

If we know the form of distribution of a group and the percent of the group succeeding with a task, it requires only straight-forward mensuration to find the point on the base line corresponding to that percent, and the distance of that point plus or minus from the median (or mode, or other point of reference defined by the distribution of the

21

group) in terms of the mean square variation (or other defined measure of variability) of the group in whatever ability is measured by that task.

The form of distribution is taken as normal for each of the grade groups, $5\frac{1}{2}$, 9I, 9II, and 13, in consequence of the facts outlined in Chapter II and presented in detail in Appendix III. The form of distribution of Group 17, which was composed of first-year law-school students, all college graduates, was determined by a special investigation which is reported in Appendix VI. The same has been done for

TABLE 107.

THE DIFFICULTY OF COMPOSITES I TO Q IN VARIOUS GROUPS EXPRESSED IN EACH CASE AS A DEVIATION FROM THE DIFFICULTY FOR THE MEDIAN OF THAT GROUP, IN TERMS OF THE $\sigma$ OF THAT GROUP IN THE ABILITY MEASURED BY SUCCESS WITH THE COMPOSITE IN QUESTION. – IS EASIER, + IS HARDER.

| Composite | | | Difficulty | | |
|---|---|---|---|---|---|
| | $5\frac{1}{2}$ | 9I | 9II | 13 | 17 |
| I | – 1.35 | – 2.65 | | | |
| J | + .55 | – 1.25 | | | |
| K | + 1.20 | – .29 | + .08 | | |
| L | | + .44 | + .98 | | |
| M | | + 1.62 | + 1.46 | | |
| N | | | + 2.29 | – .897 | – 1.862 |
| O | | | | + .048 | – .714 |
| P | | | | + .598 | – .153 |
| Q | | | | + 1.787 | + .738 |

the form of distribution of certain groups used, later in this chapter, namely, for the 180 adult imbeciles of mental age from $2\frac{1}{2}$ to 5 years, for the 100 adult feeble-minded of mental age near $6\frac{1}{2}$, for the group of 50 feeble-minded at or near mental age 8, for the group of 101 dull pupils 13 years old or over, in special classes in New York City, for the population of Grade 4 (second half year) and for the population of Grade 5. The evidence and argument in all these cases appear in Appendix VI.

Table 107 gives the difficulty of various 40-composites in various groups, expressed in each case as a distance from the difficulty which 50% of that group can succeed with and in terms of $\sigma_{t_1}$ (the mean square deviation of whatever ability is measured by that composite in that group). The next procedure in constructing a scale of difficulty is to make all these different measurements of difficulty commensurate and put them all into relation to the same point of reference. This is a complicated procedure involving the following steps:

Each measurement in $\sigma_{t_1}$ for a given group is to be turned into a measurement in $\sigma_i$ for that group, $\sigma_i$ being the mean square variation of the group in altitude of intellect perfectly measured in truly equal units.

Each measurement in the $\sigma_i$ of a certain group must be made commensurable with measurements in the $\sigma_i$ of any other group, by finding the comparative magnitudes of $\sigma_i$ of the 240 graduates, $\sigma_i$ of the 189 college entrants, $\sigma_i$ of the 246 pupils in Grade 9I, $\sigma_i$ of the 192 pupils in Grade 9II, and so on. All of the different $\sigma_i$ values may then be multiplied or divided by numbers so that all will be expressed in the same units. We shall use the mean square deviation of pupils in Grade 9 as our unit for this purpose.

The measurements, now in units of $\sigma_{19}$, must be expressed, not as distances plus or minus from the CAVD difficulty for the median now of one group now of another, but all from some common point of reference such as the median for Grade 9.

ESTIMATING $\sigma_i$ FROM $\sigma_{t_1}$

We turn the measurements in $\sigma_{t_1}$ into terms of $\sigma_i$ by using $\sigma_i = \sigma_{t_1} \sqrt{r_{t_1 t_2}}$ or by using $\sigma_i = \sigma_{t_1} r_{t_1 i}$.

The self-correlation $r_{t_1 t_2}$ is, of course, for a 40-composite with another 40-composite of equal difficulty, not for an infinitely extensive set of tasks of a certain difficulty with another equally extensive set. Also $r_{t_1 t_2}$ is the correlation for the specific group of restricted range which is being used, not the correlation for a group of wide range, such as all persons of age 20.

For precise determinations of $\sqrt{r_{t_1 t_2}}$ or of $r_{t_1 i}$ we need measurements with more extensive groups and alternate forms of our 40-composite tasks. With the material at our disposal we can hope only for approximate results.

We measure or infer $r_{t_1 t_2}$ separately for each composite with each group. We may, however, wisely modify the estimate for each composite with each group in view of the facts concerning $r_{t_1 t_2}$ for the same composite in other groups, or for other neighboring composites in the same group.

Consider, for example, the 40-composites K, L, and M. The correlations of each of these with a 40-composite of different content but similar difficulty estimated by $\dfrac{2r_{20,\ 20}}{1 + r_{20,\ 20}}$ are as shown below according to the group and kind of coefficient computed.

|  | K | | L | | M | |
|---|---|---|---|---|---|---|
| Group 246 (Sheppard) | .74 + | .70 | .86 | .86 | .69 | .68½ |
| Group 246 (Pearson) | .65 + | | .86 | | .68 | |
| Group 192 (Sheppard) | .80 + | .77 | .86 | .87½ | .73 | .75½ |
| Group 192 (Pearson) | .73 + | | .89 | | .78 | |

The correlations of each of them with a 40-composite of different content but similar difficulty may also be estimated by adding .03[1] to their average correlations with their nearest neighbor composites (or, with some justification, by adding .02 or .01 or even 0). Using .03, we have the results shown below.

|  | K | | L | | M | |
|---|---|---|---|---|---|---|
| Group 246 (Sheppard) | .70 | .69½ | .68 | .68½ | .66 | .68 |
| Group 246 (Pearson) | .69 | | .69 | | .70 | |
| Group 192 (Sheppard) | .50 | .57 | .65 | .67½ | .75½ | .75 |
| Group 192 (Pearson) | .64 | | .70 | | .75 | |

Combining the two sorts of estimates, we have

|  | K | L | M |
|---|---|---|---|
| Group 246 | .70 | .77 | .68 |
| Group 192 | .67 | .77½ | .75 |

[1] See Appendix IV for the derivation and justification of this allowance for remoteness.

Moreover, we may consider that chance played some part in making the self-correlation of L higher than the other two; and so lower its $r_{t_1t_2}$ and raise theirs somewhat to balance. Similarly we may consider that chance played some part in making these $r_{t_1t_2}$'s higher in the 192 group than in the 246 group, and allow somewhat for that. Thus we may replace the last set of figures by

|  | K | L | M |
|---|---|---|---|
| Group 246 | .72 | .76 | .70 |
| Group 192 | .67 | .74½ | .75 |

in which slight smoothing by these allowances is made.

In Table 108 is collected all the information concerning the $r_{t_1t_2}$'s for each 40-composite in each group. I and II refer to the two methods of determining $r_{t_1t_2}$. In I we use the correlation between the two halves of a 40-composite obtained by taking $5C + 5A + 5V + 5D$ at random, the second half being composed of the remaining $5C + 5A + 5V + 5D$; and estimate $r_{40, 40}$ by $\dfrac{2r_{20, 20}}{1 + r_{20, 20}}$. That is, $r_{t_1t_2} = \dfrac{2r_{20, 20}}{1 + r_{20, 20}}$. In II we use the obtained correlation between the 40-composite in question and its nearest neighbor composites,[2] adding .03.

The correlations for composites N, O, P, and Q in group 17 under "By other data" were obtained as follows: A composite almost identical with N was correlated with another of very closely equal difficulty, giving r = .72. A composite almost identical with O was correlated with a composite of very closely equal difficulty, giving r = .75. The composite almost identical with N was also correlated with a composite almost identical with O, giving r = .73. The composite almost identical with O was correlated with Q, giving r = .73. From these correlations, allowing + .03 for

---

[2] The results by method I are in general higher. The differences (Method I – Method II) are: .09 .12 0 .17½ .00½ .20 .20 .00½ .05½ – .07 .05 .05 – .06, averaging .063.

TABLE 108.

$r_{t_1t_2}$ as Estimated from Correlations Between Number of Single Tasks Correct in One-half of a 40-Composite and Number of Single Tasks Correct in the Other Half; and also as Estimated from Correlations Between Number Correct in a 40-Composite and Number Correct in a Neighboring 40-Composite.

| Group 5½ | 40 Composite $r_{t_1t_2}=\dfrac{2r_{20,20}}{1+r_{20,20}}$ | | | | Method II $r_{t_1t_2}=.03+r_{40}$ with nearest 40 | | | | | By other data | Average | | | | |
|---|---|---|---|---|---|---|---|---|---|---|---|---|---|---|---|
| | 9I | 9II | 13 | 17 | 5½ | 9I | 9II | 13 | 17 | 17 | 5½ | 9I | 9II | 13 | 17 |
| I | .71 | | | | .78 | .62 | | | | | .78 | .66½ | | | |
| J | .78½ | | | | .78 | .62½ | | | | | .78 | .72½ | | | |
| K | .70 | | | | | .70 | .57 | | | | | .70 | .67 | | |
| L | .86 | .87½ | | | | .68½ | .67½ | | | | | .77½ | .77½ | | |
| M | .68½ | .75½ | | | | .68 | .75 | | | | | .68 | .75 | | |
| N | | .75 | .66 | | | | .69½ | .73 | .86 | .74 | | | .72 | .69½ | .80 |
| O | | | .81 | | | | | .76 | .86½ | .75½ | | | | .78½ | .81 |
| P | | | .81 | | | | | .76 | .79½ | | | | | .78½ | .79½ |
| Q | | | .66 | | | | | .72 | .72 | .76 | | | | .69 | .74 |

one step of remoteness, we have the self-correlation of N as .72 or .76, averaging .74; that of O as .75 or .76, averaging .75½; and that of Q as .76.

9I and 9II differ almost nil in the general magnitude of $r_{t_1 t_2}$ for the three 40-composites used with both of these groups, the average difference (I–II) being — .013 with a

TABLE 109.

VALUES OF $r_{t_1 t_2}$ DERIVED FROM TABLE 108, AND THE VALUES OF $\sqrt{r_{t_1 t_2}}$ USED TO OBTAIN TABLE 110 FROM TABLE 107.

|  | | $r_{t_1 t_2}$ | | | | | $\sqrt{r_{t_1 t_2}}$ | | |
|  | 5½ | 9I | 9II | 13 | 17 | 5½ | 9I | 9II | 13 | 17 |
|---|---|---|---|---|---|---|---|---|---|---|
| I | .78 | .66½ | | | | .883 | .815 | | | |
| J | .78 | .72½ | | | | .883 | .851 | | | |
| K | | .68½ | .68½ | | | | .828 | .828 | | |
| L | | .77½ | .77½ | | | | .880 | .880 | | |
| M | | .70 | .73 | | | | .837 | .854 | | |
| N | | | .72 | .72½ | .77 | | | .848½ | .851½ | .877½ |
| O | | | | .77 | .82½ | | | | .877½ | .908 |
| P | | | | .77 | .81 | | | | .877½ | .900 |
| Q | | | | .69 | .74 | | | | .831 | .860 |

mean square error of ± .033, three times as great as the difference. So we shall probably be nearer the truth by using .68½ and .68½ in place of the .70 and .67, and .70 and .73 in place of the .68 and .75.

In general $r_{t_1 t_2}$ is .04½ higher in 17 than in 13, and the use of this fact to smooth out the irregularities in the values for N, O, P, and Q will probably be an improvement. Thus, columns 3 and 4 below are probably truer than column 1 and 2. The totals for each group and for each composite are unaltered by the amendments.

|  | From the table | | Amended | |
|  | 1 | 2 | 3 | 4 |
|---|---|---|---|---|
| N | 69½ | 80 | 72½ | 77 |
| O | 78½ | 81 | 77 | 82½ |
| P | 78½ | 79½ | 77 | 81 |
| Q | 69 | 74 | 69 | 74 |

We make the amendments noted in the last two paragraphs and so use the $r_{t_1 t_2}$'s listed in Table 109 in estimating the difficulty in terms of $\sigma_i$ for each composite in each group. The results are shown in Table 110.

TABLE 110.

THE INTELLECTUAL DIFFICULTY OF COMPOSITES I TO Q IN GROUPS 5½, 9I, 9II, 13 AND 17. EXPRESSED IN TERMS OF $\sigma_{i\,5\frac{1}{2}}$, $\sigma_{i\,9I}$, $\sigma_{i\,9II}$, $\sigma_{i\,13}$ OR $\sigma_{i\,17}$; AS DEVISED BY THE USE OF TABLE 109.

| Composite | Difficulty | | | | |
|---|---|---|---|---|---|
| | In $\sigma_{i\,5\frac{1}{2}}$ | In $\sigma_{i\,9I}$ | In $\sigma_{i\,9II}$ | In $\sigma_{i\,13}$ | In $\sigma_{i\,17}$ |
| I | − 1.53 | − 3.25 | | | |
| J | + .62 | − 1.47 | | | |
| K | + 1.36 | − .35 | + .10 | | |
| L | | + .50 | + 1.11 | | |
| M | | + 1.94 | + 1.71 | | |
| N | | | + 2.70 | − 1.054 | − 2.120 |
| O | | | | + .055 | − .786 |
| P | | | | + .681 | − .170 |
| Q | | | | + 2.150 | + .858 |

Estimating the $\sigma_i$'s by $\sigma_i = \sigma_{t_1} r_{t_1 i}$, we obtain $r_{t_1 i}$ by $r_{t_1 i} = \dfrac{r_{t_1 i_1}}{\sqrt{r_{i_1 i_2}}}$, in which $r_{t_1 i_1}$ is the obtained correlation between the 40-composite in question and the summation score in a long CAVD series, and $r_{i_1 i_2}$ is the self-correlation of this summation score. In certain cases we have to estimate $r_{i_1 i_2}$, but the error of the estimate is small,[3] and its effect is reduced since only the square root of $r_{i_1 i_2}$ is used. The values of $r_{t_1 i_1}$ and $r_{i_1 i_2}$ used are those used for another purpose in Appendix V. The results of the computations are shown in Table 111.

Using the estimates of $r_{t_1 i}$ of Table 111, we obtain the estimates of the difficulty of each composite for each group in terms of the $\sigma_i$ of that group which are presented in

[3] For a grade population the empirical values of $r_{i_1 i_2}$ vary from .91 to .95. In group 5½ and group 17 where we estimate, the summation score is from a very long series, so we use .95.

Table 112. These differ on the average from those of Table 110, as shown below, the median difference regardless of signs being .03 and the average difference .05.

$$\sigma_i \ (\text{by} \ \sqrt{r_{t_1 t_2}}) - \sigma_i \ (\text{by} \ r_{t_1 i})$$

| | |
|---|---|
| $-.15$ to $-.06$ | 4 |
| $-.05$ to $+.04$ | 12 |
| $+.05$ to $+.14$ | 3 |
| $+.15$ to $+.24$ | 1 |

TABLE 111.

VALUES OF $r_{t_1 i}$ ESTIMATED FROM CORRELATIONS BETWEEN NUMBER OF SINGLE TASKS CORRECT IN A 40-COMPOSITE AND NUMBER CORRECT IN A LONG CAVD SERIES.

| Composite | 5½ | 9I | $r_{t_1 i}$ 9II | 13 | 17 |
|---|---|---|---|---|---|
| I | .933 | .759 | | | |
| J | .882 | .907 | | | |
| K | | .854 | .819 | | |
| L | | .944 | .896 | | |
| M | | .849 | .922 | | |
| N | | | .819 | | |
| O | | | | .824 | .872 |
| P | | | | .917 | .944 |
| Q | | | | .948 | .913 |
| | | | | .790 | .882 |

Except in the case of composite I in group 9I, it does not matter much whether we use the estimates of Table 110 or those of Table 112 or averages of the two. We have averaged each pair of determinations with the results shown in Table 113 which are used as the $\sigma_i$ values in all that follows.

EXPRESSING THE $\sigma_i$ OF EACH GROUP IN TERMS OF A COMMON UNIT

We make the $\sigma_i$'s of two groups, A and B, commensurate by finding the difference in difficulty between two tasks in terms of $\sigma_{iA}$ and in terms of $\sigma_{iB}$, provided the two groups overlap sufficiently. Thus, we find, in the case of the group

(17) of 240 college graduates and the group (13) of high school graduates, that:

Composite O — Composite N $= 1.12\sigma_{i\ 13}$ and $1.36\sigma_{i\ 17}$.
Composite P — Composite O $= .61\sigma_{i\ 13}$ and $.60\sigma_{i\ 17}$.
Composite Q — Composite P $= 1.55\sigma_{i\ 13}$ and $1.02\sigma_{i\ 17}$.

$\sigma_{i\ 13} = 1.21\sigma_{i\ 17}$ or $.99\sigma_{i\ 17}$ or $.66\sigma_{i\ 17}$, according to the successive pair of composites used. If we take the most remote composites which include all the data, Q and N, we have $3.28\sigma_{i\ 13} = 2.98\sigma_{i\ 17}$, whereby $\sigma_{i\ 13} = .91\sigma_{i\ 17}$.

TABLE 112.

THE INTELLECTUAL DIFFICULTY OF COMPOSITES I TO Q IN TERMS OF $\sigma_{i\ 5\frac{1}{2}}$, $\sigma_{i\ 9I}$, ETC.; AS DEVISED BY THE USE OF TABLE 111.

| Composite | In $\sigma_{i\ 5\frac{1}{2}}$ | In $\sigma_{i\ 9I}$ | Difficulty<br>In $\sigma_{i\ 9II}$ | In $\sigma_{i\ 13}$ | In $\sigma_{i\ 17}$ |
|---|---|---|---|---|---|
| I | − 1.45 | − 3.49 | | | |
| J | + .59 | − 1.38 | | | |
| K | + 1.29 | − .34 | + .10 | | |
| L | | + .47 | + 1.09½ | | |
| M | | + 1.91 | + 1.58 | | |
| N | | | + 2.80 | − 1.09 | − 2.13½ |
| O | | | | + .05 | − .76 |
| P | | | | + .63 | − .17 |
| Q | | | | + 2.26 | + .84 |

In the same way, we find, in the case of the Group 9I of 246 pupils in Grade 9 and the Group 9II of 192 pupils in Grade 9, that:

Composite L — Composite K $= .84\sigma_{i\ 9I}$ and $1.00\sigma_{i\ 9II}$.
Composite M — Composite L $= 1.44\sigma_{i\ 9I}$ and $.55\sigma_{i\ 9II}$.

$\sigma_{i\ 9I} = 1.19\sigma_{i\ 9II}$ or $.38\sigma_{i\ 9II}$, according to the pair of composites used. If we take the most remote pair which include all the data, M and K, we have $2.28\sigma_{i\ 9I} = 1.55\sigma_{i\ 9II}$, whereby $\sigma_{i\ 9I} = .68\sigma_{i\ 9II}$.

In the same way, we find, with Group 5½ and Group 9I, that:

Composite J — Composite I $= 2.10\sigma_{i\ 5\frac{1}{2}}$ and $1.94\sigma_{i\ 9I}$.
Composite K — Composite J $= .72\sigma_{i\ 5\frac{1}{2}}$ and $1.09\sigma_{i\ 9I}$.

$\sigma_{i\ 5\frac{1}{2}} = .92\sigma_{i\ 9I}$ or $1.51\sigma_{i\ 9I}$ according to the pair of composites used. If we use K and I, which include all the data, we have $2.82\sigma_{i\ 5\frac{1}{2}} = 3.02\sigma_{i\ 9I}$, whereby $\sigma_{i\ 5\frac{1}{2}} = 1.07\sigma_{i\ 9I}$.

For precise work in scale construction, the groups should be large and close enough together to have a considerable overlapping. The measurement of the $\sigma_i$ of any one group in terms of the $\sigma_i$ of any other group may then be determined with as small an error as is desired.

Our groups are obviously not large enough, since there are so great differences between the estimates of the com-

TABLE 113.

THE INTELLECTUAL DIFFICULTY OF COMPOSITES I TO Q. AVERAGES OF THE
DETERMINATIONS OF TABLE 110 AND TABLE 112.

| Composite | Difficulty | | | | |
| --- | --- | --- | --- | --- | --- |
| | In $\sigma_{i\ 5\frac{1}{2}}$ | In $\sigma_{i\ 9I}$ | In $\sigma_{i\ 9II}$ | In $\sigma_{i\ 13}$ | In $\sigma_{i\ 17}$ |
| I | − 1.49 | − 3.37 | | | |
| J | + .61 | − 1.43 | | | |
| K | + 1.33 | − .35 | + .10 | | |
| L | | + .49 | + 1.10 | | |
| M | | + 1.93 | + 1.65 | | |
| N | | | + 2.75 | − 1.07 | − 2.13 |
| O | | | | + .05 | − .77 |
| P | | | | + .66 | − .17 |
| Q | | | | + 2.21 | + .85 |

parative variabilities according to the composites which we use. There is particular risk in using the estimates of comparative variabilities in different groups which depend upon a composite that is very easy or one that is very hard for the group. In the case of the very easy composites carelessness may play a part that affects the results. In the case of the composites which are very difficult for a group, lack of effort and persistence and interest may be a disturbing factor; and it is possible that, in spite of care taken to give what seemed to be abundant time, certain individuals may not have exhausted their abilities for lack of sufficient time. The eccentricity of the results with Composite M in Group 9I may be due to this fact. In general, Group 9I was superior to Group 9II and the reversal to notable inferiority with Composite M may be explainable by the fact that this was the hardest composite taken. It was not truly the last in point of time, since all the C's were done in one division of the examination, all the A's in another division of it, all the V's in another division of it, and all the D's in another division of it.

In cases where the material is not notably richer than this of ours and in cases where the groups are spaced so far apart that there is little or no overlapping, valuable aid may be derived from a general consideration of the comparative variability of groups similar in school grade or other indication of intellect to the particular groups which are used in scaling the difficulty of the composite tasks. Moreover, facts concerning the comparative variability of grade populations are valuable as a check on even the best determinations made by using two or more composites with two or more groups. Consequently we have made a rather exhaustive study of the variability of grade populations from 6 through 13, using all the data that we could discover which had sufficiently large populations to make the determinations of variability reasonably precise.

In order to discover the relative variability of different grade populations from 6 through 13, if each individual were measured in truly equal units, we may proceed in either one of two ways:

We may argue after the fashion of the argument in Appendix III that inequalities in the face-value units will neutralize each other so that the general average result from many tests, each with its own sort of inequality, will be near the truth. In this case, we simply take the sigmas by the original scoring for these different grades and get their general drift. Dr. Bregman has done this for all the material available with populations large enough to give reliable sampling of the grades. The results are shown in Table 115 and in more detail in Table 114.

The second method is to transmute the face-value measures for such tests as Army Alpha, National A, Otis Advanced, etc., into terms of equal units before computing the sigmas. The results of the investigations reported in Chapter VII enable us to do this, since in that chapter we determined the value in equal units of each interval of the

TABLE 114.

DATA FOR COMPUTING RELATIVE VARIABILITIES OF DIFFERENT GRADES IN INTELLECT; AND FOR COMPUTING DISTANCES BETWEEN MEDIANS OF DIFFERENT GRADES IN INTELLECT.

Original median refers to the median by the standard method of scoring; corrected median refers to the median by a scale in equal units; original σ refers to the mean square deviation by the standard method of scoring; corrected σ refers to the mean square deviation by a scale in equal units.

| | | Median | | σ | |
|---|---|---|---|---|---|
| Grade | Number | Original | Corrected | Original | Corrected |
| *Army Alpha** | | | | | |
| 6 | 281 | 54.9 | 55.6 | 18.4 | 19.1 |
| 9 | 1721 | 97.94 | 97.94 | 24.0 | 24.2 |
| 10 | 1223 | | | | 24.0 |
| 11 | 977 | | | | 23.8 |
| 12 | 1387 | 125.39 | 125.39 | 24.24 | 24.8 |
| 12 | 766 | 128.04 | 128.04 | 24.13 | 24.9 |
| Coll.  1 | 2545 | 128.50 | 128.50 | 28.20 | 29.2 |
| "  1 | 400 | 157.8 | 158.5 | 19.99 | 23.3 |
| *Army Examination A** | | | | | |
| 6 | 742 | 139.8 | 139.8 | 36.9 | 38.94 |
| 7 | 685 | 158.6 | 158.6 | 39.2 | 40.90 |
| 8 | 630 | 186.1 | 186.1 | 43.04 | 43.39 |
| 9 | 311 | 204.36 | 204.36 | 45.89 | 45.53 |
| 12 | 53 | 276 | 274 | 36 | 36 |
| Coll.  1 | 701 | 267.33 | 265.33 | 40.63 | 39.25 |
| *National A*** | | | | | |
| 6 | 1668 | 111.9 | 111.9 | 22.8 | 21.8 |
| 9 | 494 | 141.75 | 140.85 | 16.8 | 16.5 |

* All computations exact.

** Sigmas in equal units are computed by ½ the distance required to exclude 15.87% at each extreme.

TABLE 114 (Continued).

| Grade | Number | Median Original | Median Corrected | σ Original | σ Corrected |
|---|---|---|---|---|---|
| *Otis** | | | | | |
| 6 | 5952 | 86.8 | 87.2 | 24.3 | |
| 7 | 3896 | 96.98 | 97.1 | 24.4 | |
| 8 | 4598 | 111.93 | 111.4 | 25.08 | |
| 9 | 3627 | 125.04 | 123.8 | 24.62 | |
| 12 | 1226 | 151.83 | 149.7 | 24.06 | |
| *Haggerty** | | | | | |
| 6 | 916 | 91.4 | 91.3 | 20.4 | 20.7 |
| 7 | 737 | 105.07 | 105.2 | 20.2 | |
| 8 | 689 | 113.9 | 113.7 | 19.46 | |
| 9 | 473 | 113.7 | 113.5 | 17.5 | 19.54 |
| 9 | 1995 | 116.5 | 116.4 | 18.2 | 23.25 |
| 12 | 668 | 135.83 | 139.3 | 15.31 | 22.4 |
| *I. E. R. Form A*** | | | | | |
| 6 | 379 | 83.9 | 81.0 | 32.41 | |
| 9 | 3231 | 173.4 | 173.4 | 42.9 | |
| 10 | 1935 | 191.1 | 191.1 | 40.3 | |
| 11 | 1533 | 202.6 | 202.6 | 42.4 | |
| 12 | 972 | 219.81 | 219.8 | 44.99 | |
| 12 | 1666 | 227.79 | 227.5 | 45.85 | |
| *I. E. R. Form B*** | | | | | |
| 10 | 1656 | 209.0 | | 43.55 | |
| 11 | 1453 | 219.7 | | 44.0 | |
| 12 | 1207 | 229.9 | | 44.7 | |
| *Terman Group Test**** | | | | | |
| 9 | 1438 | 102.16 | 102.16 | 32.0 | |
| 12 | 4886 | 144.55 | 142.55 | 32.61 | |

* All computations exact.

** The sigmas in equal units will vary inappreciably from the sigmas by the original scale and are not computed.

*** The effect of inequalities in the units will be almost identical for Grade 9 and for Grade 12; hence the relative values of the sigmas will not be influenced thereby. Consequently the sigmas for values in equal units have not been computed.

original scale for Army Alpha, National, Otis, Haggerty, Army *a*, Terman Group Test, and several others. We have made these computations with results as shown in Table 114.

TABLE 114 (Continued).

| Grade | Number | Median | | σ | |
|---|---|---|---|---|---|
| | | Original | Corrected | Original | Corrected |
| *Brown University** | | | | | |
| 12 | 3333 | 45.69 | 46.2 | 11.59 | |
| Coll. 1 | 2118 | 56.62 | 56.3 | 11.11 | |
| *Myers Mental Measure*** | | | | | |
| 6 | 724 | 46.3 | 46.3 | 13.1 | 12.6 |
| 7 | 696 | 49.61 | 49.8 | 14.65 | |
| 8 | 950 | 54.15 | 54.55 | 13.72 | |
| 9 | 311 | 57.1 | 57.5 | 13.05 | 13.75 |
| *Pintner Non-Language*** | | | | | |
| 6 | 1237 | 316.7 | 313.7 | 86.7 | 86.5 |
| 7 | 755 | 339.0 | 339.0 | 73.18 | |
| 8 | 530 | 379.6 | 381.6 | 73.24 | |
| 9 | 258 | 400.6 | 403.0 | 75.0 | 78.5 |
| *Pressey Cross-Out**** | | | | | |
| 6 | 1057 | 51.18 | | 10.30 | |
| 7 | 998 | 56.10 | | 10.30 | |
| 8 | 725 | 63.12 | | 10.0 | |
| 9 | 303 | 72.5 | | 10.0 | |
| *Trabue Completion**** | | | | | |
| 6 | 1454 | 21.8 | | 5.5 | |
| 7 | 1456 | 25.39 | | 5.67 | |
| 8 | 1740 | 27.61 | | 6.29 | |
| 9 | 273 | 30.05 | | 5.9 | |

* The inequalities of units in the scale are such as balance one another and leave the relative values of the sigmas by the original units undisturbed. Consequently new values are not computed.

** The sigmas according to a scale with equal units are computed by finding ½ the distance required to exclude 15.87% at each extreme.

*** Scores in equal units have not been determined.

The data which we have used to measure comparative variabilities are the same as those which will be used later to measure the differences between the medians of various grade groups in intellect. We present them in Table 114 classified according to the examination used. In connection with each examination we record the results for Grades 6, 9, 12, and 13 (or first year of college) and occasionally for other grades or groups. We report the number of individuals; the median score, taking the

TABLE 114 (Concluded).

| Grade | Number | Median Original | Median Corrected | σ Original | σ Corrected |
|-------|--------|--------|-----------|----------|-----------|
| *Illinois Examination** | | | | | |
| 6 | 588 | 75.52 | | 17.01 | |
| 9 | 380 | 101.4 | | 18.5 | |
| *Thorndike Intelligence Examination, Part I** | | | | | |
| 12 | 1527 | 91.4 | | 18.1 | |
| Coll. 1 | 166 | 101.7 | | 17.6 | |
| " 1 | 466 | 108.4 | | 17.0 | |
| " 1 | 319 | 107.1 | | 18.5 | |
| " 1 | Weighted average (weights 1, 2 and 2) | 106.5 | | 17.7 | |

\* Scores in equal units have not been determined.

units at their face value; the median score in a scale with equal units; the mean square deviation, taking the units at their face value; the mean square deviation, using a scale with equal units. In the latter case the sigmas have been computed exactly, where it was possible, but in many cases we have had to resort to approximations. In cases where the scale with equal units was so closely similar to the original scale that little, if any, difference would be made in the mean square deviation, we have used the original figures. Notes are appended to Table 114 descriptive of what was done in this regard in each case.

From the facts of Table 114 are computed the ratios of Table 115.

From the facts of Table 115 we may conclude that the forces of selection and gradation which determine the variability of grade populations result in a slight increase from Grade 6 to 9, which we may estimate as 4 percent (giving twice as much weight to the results from equal-unit scaling

TABLE 115.

THE RELATIVE VARIABILITY OF DIFFERENT GRADE POPULATIONS.

| Examination | Using the Original Scale Units | | | | Using Scales with Equal Units | | | |
|---|---|---|---|---|---|---|---|---|
| | $\dfrac{\sigma_{16}}{\sigma_{19}}$ | $\dfrac{\sigma_{112}}{\sigma_{19}}$ | $\dfrac{\sigma_{113}}{\sigma_{19}}$ | $\dfrac{\sigma_{113}}{\sigma_{112}}$ | $\dfrac{\sigma_{16}}{\sigma_{19}}$ | $\dfrac{\sigma_{112}}{\sigma_{19}}$ | $\dfrac{\sigma_{113}}{\sigma_{19}}$ | $\dfrac{\sigma_{113}}{\sigma_{112}}$ |
| Army Alpha | .77 | 1.01 | 1.00 | 1.00 | .79 | 1.03 | 1.09 | 1.06 |
| Army a | .80 | .78½ | .88½ | 1.13 | .85½ | .79 | .86 | 1.09 |
| National A | 1.36 | | | | 1.32 | | | |
| Otis Adv. | .99 | .98 | | | .99 | .98 | | |
| Haggerty | 1.13 | .85 | | | .93 | 1.00 | | |
| I.E.R. Sel. Gen. | .76 | 1.06 | | | .76 | 1.06 | | |
| Terman Group | | 1.0? | | | | 1.02 | | |
| Brown Univ. | | | | .96 | | | | .96 |
| Myers Mental | 1.00 | | | | .92 | | | |
| Pintner | 1.16 | | | | 1.10 | | | |
| Th. Part I N | | | | .97 | | | | |
| Trabue Comp. | .93 | | | | | | | |
| Illinois | .92 | | | | | | | |
| Pressey | 1.03 | | | | | | | |
| Median | .99 | .99½ | .94 | .98½ | .92½ | 1.01 | .97½ | 1.06 |
| Average | .99 | .95 | .94 | 1.01½ | .96 | .98 | .97½ | 1.04 |

as to those from the original scores). From 9 to 12 there is little or no change. The medians for the $\dfrac{\sigma_{112}}{\sigma_{19}}$ ratios average 1.00½. The .78½ and .79 of Army $a$ which make the averages lower (.95 and .98) are from a very small group of 53, which should be given very little weight. This group was used because it enriched somewhat our very scanty material on the $\dfrac{\sigma_{113}}{\sigma_{112}}$ comparison. We may then estimate the

22

variabilities of Grades 6, 9, and 12 as 96, 100, and 100. Comparing Grade 13 with both Grade 9 and Grade 12, we find for the original-scale units a median $\dfrac{\sigma_{113}}{\sigma_{112} \text{ or } \sigma_{19}}$ of .98 and an average of .99; for the scales in equal units, there is a median of 1.06 and an average of 1.01. The best estimate, in view of the fact that the .88½ and .86 by Army $a$ deserve less weight than the other determinations, seems to be about 102. We then have 96, 100, 100, and 102 as the relative variabilities of Grades 6, 9, 12, and 13.

These general facts may be used to correct the eccentric and unreliable determinations from the composites themselves (see page 304 f.). The use of the entire stretch of overlapping gave $\sigma_{15\frac{1}{2}}$ as $1.07\sigma_{19I}$, for our particular group, but in general $\sigma_{15\frac{1}{2}}$ may be expected to be about $.96\sigma_{19}$. We know of no facts which make it probable that our groups 5½ and 9I differ from Grades 5½ and 9 in general in such a way as to make a variation of $\dfrac{\sigma_{15\frac{1}{2}}}{\sigma_{19}}$ up from .96, any more probable than a variation down. The scientific procedure would be to apply the same examinations to these two particular groups, and compute the variabilities in units of known value, but this was not practicable. The best thing to be done in the circumstances is to attach some reasonable weights to the two lines of evidence, and so obtain a working estimate. Giving the general facts about Grades 6 and 9 a weight of 4, and the particular facts from the composites used in both groups a weight of 1, the ratio $\dfrac{\sigma_{15\frac{1}{2}}}{\sigma_{19I}}$ is .98.

The next matter to be cleared up is the comparative variability of 9I and 9II. $\dfrac{\sigma_{19I}}{\sigma_{19II}}$ was 1.19 by L–K and .38 by M–L. We shall disregard these determinations entirely and treat the variability of 9I as equal to that of 9II, for the following reason. These two groups were constituted by a division of all the pupils in Grade 9 in a certain school at random, so far as is known. There is nothing in their summation scores to show that one is more variable than the other. The L–K and M–L determinations are enormously at variance, and so deserve very little weight.

Between 9 and 13 there is no overlapping, so that the general facts of grade variability are the only means of estimate. As has been stated, our group 13 is a group of candidates for college entrance, not of actual freshmen. They were, however, candidates already selected by certain tests and were of intellect comparable to the freshman groups reported in Table 114, differing probably toward less variability rather than toward more, if they differed at all in this respect. 1.02 or 1.00 is then suitable as the $\frac{\sigma_{113}}{\sigma_{19}}$ ratio, so far as is known.

The last comparison to be considered is of group 13 and group 17. The determinations from the composites taken in common were: $\frac{\sigma_{113}}{\sigma_{117}} = 1.21$ or .99 or .66, with a median of .99 and an average of .95. The use of the widest stretch between composites gave .91. The .66 and .91 and .95 are probably too low, inasmuch as all depend on the $+2.21$ for composite Q in the 13 group. This is the most unreliable of the eight determinations, and is probably too high. The difference between the general level of ability of group 17 and that of group 13 is 1.06 by composite N, .82 by O, .83 by P, and 1.56 by Q. The median .99 is the most probable estimate from the composites used in both groups. The general drift of the facts for Grades 6, 9, 12, and 13 gives the expectation that the variability in Grade 17 will be somewhat but not much higher than that in Grades 12 or 13, perhaps 1.04 or 1.05 times the variability of Grade 9, giving a ratio for $\frac{\sigma_{113}}{\sigma_{117}}$ of about .95.

The records for Examination a with 136 college students of Grades 14, 15, and 16, and with 27 graduate students show, however, decreases in variability much below that of

Grade 9, making $\frac{\sigma_{i13}}{\sigma_{i17}}$ well above 1.05. So the general considerations can hardly be used to favor change from 1.00 in either direction. On the whole .99 for $\frac{13}{17}$ or 1.01 for $\frac{17}{13}$ is fairly well justified by both methods.

The values recommended for turning the various $\sigma_i$'s into $\sigma_{i9}$'s are then:

$$\frac{\sigma_{15\frac{1}{2}}}{\sigma_{i9I} \text{ or } \sigma_{i9II}} = .98$$

$$\sigma_{i9I} = \sigma_{i9II}$$

$$\frac{\sigma_{I13}}{\sigma_{i9I} \text{ or } \sigma_{i9II}} = 1.02$$

$$\frac{\sigma_{I17}}{\sigma_{i9I} \text{ or } \sigma_{i9II}} = 1.03$$

Nothing in the particular comparisons from the composites themselves is inconsistent with these estimates. What has been done is to use general considerations to locate ratios within the limits of those which were reasonable in view of the particular comparisons. Using them the measures of Table 113 become those of Table 116.

### EXPRESSING THE MEASURES OF DIFFICULTY AS DISTANCES FROM A COMMON POINT OF REFERENCE

The differences in difficulty of composites I, J, and K plus and minus from the median of group $5\frac{1}{2}$ may be expressed as differences from the median of group 9I, by finding the differences between the difficulty for the median of group $5\frac{1}{2}$ and the difficulty for the median of group 9I. This may be found by using the composite tasks which were used with both groups. Thus composite I is, by Table 116, $1.52\sigma_{i9}$ easier than the task which just 50% of group $5\frac{1}{2}$ can master and $3.37\sigma_{i9}$ easier than the task which just 50% of group 9I can master. By this determination, the difficulty of the median task for $5\frac{1}{2}$ is 1.85 less than the difficulty of the median task for 9I. Using the facts of Table 116 for composites J and K in the same manner, gives $2.05\sigma_{19}$ and $1.71\sigma_{19}$. The average is $1.87\sigma_{19}$; the median is $1.85\sigma_{19}$.

In the same manner, K is $.35\sigma_{19}$ easier than the task which just 50% of group 9I can master and $.10\sigma_{19}$ harder than the task which just 50% of group 9II can master. By this determination, the difficulty of the median task for 9I is $.45\sigma_{19}$ greater than the difficulty of the median task for 9II. Using the facts for composites L and M gives $.61\sigma_{19}$ greater and $.28\sigma_{19}$ less. The average of the three determinations is $.26\sigma_{19}$; the median is $.45\sigma_{19}$.

Composite N is $2.75\sigma_{19}$ harder than the task at which 50% of 9II succeed, and $1.05\sigma_{19}$ easier than the task at which 50% of group 13 succeed. So the difficulty of the median task for group 13 is $3.8\sigma_{19}$ greater than that of the median task for 9II.

Using N, O, P, and Q in similar manner, the difficulty of the median task for Group 17 is found to be $1.02\sigma_{19}$ or $.80\sigma_{19}$, or $.81\sigma_{19}$, or $1.34\tfrac{1}{2}\sigma_{19}$ greater than the difficulty of the median task for Group 13. The average is $.99\tfrac{1}{2}\sigma_{19}$; the median is $.92\sigma_{19}$.

Relating the difficulty of the median task for each group to the difficulty of the median task for a group half-way between 9I and 9II, we have:

|  | Computed by average | Computed by medians |
|---|---|---|
| The median for $5\frac{1}{2}$ — Median 9I + 9II | $-1.74$ | $-1.62\frac{1}{2}$ |
| The median for 9I — Median 9I + 9II | $+ .13$ | $+ .22\frac{1}{2}$ |
| The median for 9II — Median 9I + 9II | $- .13$ | $- .22\frac{1}{2}$ |
| The median for 13 — Median 9I + 9II | $+3.80$ | $+3.80$ |
| The median for 17 — Median 9I + 9II | $+4.80$ | $+4.72$ |

The reasonableness of these estimates may be checked by the facts for the difference between the median scores in Grade $5\frac{1}{2}$ and Grade 9 and Grade 13 in intelligence examinations in general, expressed in terms of the variability of Grade 9, or in some other unit of measure.

We have collected the available facts concerning the median scores of Grade 6, Grade 9, Grade 12, and the first-year of college, in Army Alpha, Army Examination *a,* National A, Otis Advanced, Haggerty, I. E. R. Sel. Rel. Gen. Org., Terman Group, the Brown University Examination, the Myers Mental Measure, the Pintner Non-Language Test, the Trabue Completion, the Illinois Examination, and the Pressey Cross-Out Test. They are reported in Table 114 (on pages 307 to 310, inclusive). For all save the last three, we have computed what the differences between the medians in question are by a scale of equal units. The results, both by the original scale and by the scale with equal units, are shown in Table 117.

TABLE 116.

THE INTELLECTUAL DIFFICULTY OF COMPOSITE TASKS I TO Q IN TERMS OF $\sigma_{19}$.

| Composite | By 5½ | By 9I | Difficulty By 9II | By 13 | By 17 |
|---|---|---|---|---|---|
| I | − 1.52 | − 3.37 | | | |
| J | + .62 | − 1.43 | | | |
| K | + 1.36 | − .35 | + .10 | | |
| L | | + .49 | + 1.10 | | |
| M | | + 1.93 | + 1.65 | | |
| N | | | + 2.75 | − 1.05 | − 2.07 |
| O | | | | + .05 | − .75 |
| P | | | | + .65 | − .16½ |
| Q | | | | + 2.17 | + .82½ |

The variabilities used in computing Table 117 are, of course, the variabilities of the respective groups *in the ability measured by the particular instrument used,* such as Army Alpha or National A. ($\sigma$ is $\sigma_{alpha}$ or $\sigma_{National}$;

$$\frac{m_9 - m_6}{\sigma_9} \text{ is } \frac{m_{Alpha9} - m_{Alpha6}}{\sigma_{Alpha9}} \text{ or}$$

$$\frac{m_{Nat.9} - m_{Nat.6}}{\sigma_{Nat.9}} \text{ or the like; and will be smaller than}$$

$$\frac{m_{CAVD9} - m_{CAVD6}}{\sigma_{CAVD}} \text{ or } \frac{m_{19} - m_{16}}{\sigma_i}, \text{ since } \sigma_{alpha} \text{ or } \sigma_{Nat.9} \text{ will be}$$

larger than $\sigma_{19}$.)

$\sigma_{Alpha}$ should be treated just as we treated $\sigma_{ti}$'s. We have to estimate $\sigma_{i9}$ from $\sigma_{Alpha9}$ or $\sigma_{Nat.9}$ or $\sigma_{Otis9}$. This has to be done rather crudely since neither the self-correlations of most of these tests, nor their correlations with any such criterion as the score of one of our long CAVD series, have been worked out. The self-correlation of the I. E. R. for

TABLE 117.

DIFFERENCE BETWEEN GRADES IN SCORES ATTAINED IN VARIOUS INTELLIGENCE EXAMINATIONS.

| | Using the original scores | | Using scores in Equal Units | | | |
|---|---|---|---|---|---|---|
| | $\dfrac{m_9 - m_6}{\sigma_9}$ | $\dfrac{m_{13} - m_{12}}{\sigma_9}$ | $\dfrac{m_9 - m_6}{\sigma_9}$ | $\dfrac{m_{12} - m_9}{\sigma_9}$ | $\dfrac{m_{13} - m_9}{\sigma_9}$ | $\dfrac{m_{13} - m_{12}}{\sigma_9}$ |
| Army Alpha | | | 1.75 | 1.28 | 2.50 | |
| Army $a$ | | | 1.42 | | 1.38½ | |
| National | | | 1.76 | | | |
| Otis Adv. | | | 1.49 | 1.05 | | |
| Haggerty | | | 1.09 | 1.21 | | |
| I. E. R. | | | 2.15 | 1.20 | | |
| Terman | | | | 1.26 | | |
| Brown | | | | | | .87 |
| Myers | | | .81 | | | |
| Pintner | | | 1.14 | | | |
| Thorndike | | .83½ | | | | |
| Trabue | 1.40 | | | | | |
| Illinois | 1.40 | | | | | |
| Pressey | 2.13 | | | | | |
| Median | 1.40 | | 1.45½ | 1.21 | 1.94 | |
| Average | 1.64 | | 1.45 | 1.20 | | |
| $\dfrac{\text{Median} + \text{Average}}{2}$ | 1.52 | .83½ | 1.45 | 1.21 | 1.94 | .87 |

two different forms of the examination taken a year apart is .82 for 1,000 boys of Grades 9, 10, and 11, and is .86 for 489 sixteen-year-old boys in these grades [Bailor, '24, p. 8]. We have computed the self-correlation of the Terman Group Test for 209 cases of high school pupils in Grades 9, 10, and 11, finding it to be .92. The correlation of the Haggerty test against a combined score in Army Alpha, Thurstone, Otis, Pressey, and other tests is .89 for a group of 60 college seniors. This would make the self-correlation about .80. The self-correlation in "an entire school," the two trials being on the same day, is .90 [Haggerty, '23, p. 54]. From the data given in the Memoirs ['21, pp. 315–17], we estimate the self-correlation of Army $a$ as about .80 for a grade population. The Otis Self-Administering correlates .88 with the Terman Group Test in a group covering Grades 7 to 12 [Clark, '25, p. 15].

Allowing for the restriction of the range in our groups as compared with those reported above, we may expect the self-correlations of these various examinations within one grade to vary around a central tendency of about .80 for $r_{t_1 t_2}$. Dividing by $\sqrt{.80}$, we have, for the data from equal-unit scores:

$$m_9 - m_6 = 1.62\sigma_{i9}.$$
$$m_{12} - m_9 = 1.35\sigma_{i9}.$$
$$m_{13} - m_9 = 2.17\sigma_{i9}.$$
$$m_{13} - m_{12} = .973\sigma_{i9}.$$

The same divisor with the data from original scores gives:

$$m_9 - m_6 = 1.70\sigma_{i9}.$$
$$m_{13} - m_{12} = .934\sigma_{i9}.$$

Allowing a weight of 4 to the determinations from scores in equal units and a weight of 1 to the determinations from the original scores, we have:

$$m_9 - m_6 = 1.64\sigma_{i9}.$$
$$m_{12} - m_9 = 1.35\sigma_{i9}.$$
$$m_{13} - m_9 = 2.17\sigma_{i9}.$$
$$m_{13} - m_{12} = .96\tfrac{1}{2}\sigma_{i9}.$$

We have two independent estimates of $m_{13} - m_9$, $2.17\sigma_{i9}$ by the direct comparison and $2.31\tfrac{1}{2}\sigma_{i9}$ by the comparison *via* Grade 12. Allowing equal weight to each gives $2.24\sigma_{i9}$ as the combined estimate.

The $1.64\sigma_{19}$ for $m_9 - m_6$ agrees very well with the observed results of the Av., $-1.74\sigma_{19}$, and the Median, $-1.62\sigma_{19}$, for $m_9 - m_{5\frac{1}{2}}$; and we may reasonably accept $-1.74\sigma_{19}$ or $-1.62\sigma_{19}$ or the average $-1.68\sigma_{19}$. We shall take the last, and use $-1.7\sigma_{19}$ as the $m_9 - m_{5\frac{1}{2}}$ difference. The observed comparison of 9I and 9II may be taken as it stands, there being no relevance of the general facts to it. So 9I is $.13\sigma_{19}$ or $.22\frac{1}{2}\sigma_{19}$ above $m_9$ and 9II is $.13\sigma_{19}$ or $.22\frac{1}{2}\sigma_{19}$ below it. We use $+ .2\sigma_{19}$ and $- .2\sigma_{19}$.

The $2.24\sigma_{19}$ is much below the observed result of $3.60\sigma_{19}$ for our Group 13 — Group 9; and, since this $3.60\sigma_{19}$ depends upon the single determination by Composite N, it is wise to consider possible amendments of it in view of the general facts.

The following additional facts will help in the decision. The individuals of Groups 13 and 17 were tested with half of the Composite M and with $D4\frac{1}{2}$, which is only a little harder than D4. We can infer approximately what the percent of successes with Composite M would have been, if it had all been given, by allowance for the missing C (Completion M) and for the replacement of D4 by $D4\frac{1}{2}$.

In the case of the 189 individuals of Group 13 there were four who might perhaps have failed to have 20 or more right out of 40 in Composite M if they had been tested with it. By our estimates two probably would have so failed. This gives 1.06% or $2.34\sigma_{t13}$ below the median difficulty for Group 13. This, in terms of $\sigma_{t13}$ would be 2.75; in terms of $\sigma_{19}$ it would be 2.70. This would make the 9 median $4.5\sigma_{19}$ below the 13 median.

Among the 240 of Group 17 there was no individual who would not have had 20 or more right if he had been tested with all the 40 tasks. There were some who probably would have had only 22, 23, 24, or 25 right. By our estimates

2 would have scored 22.
1    "        "       "    23.
3    "        "       "    24.
2    "        "       "    25.

The level of Composite M is then probably more than $-3\sigma_{t17}$ below the median of Group 17, but not much more than that. A reasonable placement would be $-3.2\sigma_{t17}$. This in terms of $\sigma_{117}$ would be 3.64; in terms of $\sigma_{19}$ it would be 3.53. This would make the 9 median $5.32\sigma_{19}$ below the 17 median or about $4.3\sigma_{19}$ below the 13 median.

In view of these additional facts it seems best to consider that our Group 13 differs more from our Group 9 than the college freshmen classes of our general survey differed from the ninth grades of that survey, and that the $3.60\sigma_{19}$ is approximately correct. This means that we are treating Groups 13 and 9 as if only about one in ten of the latter were equal or superior to the lowest tenth of the former in altitude of Intellect CAVD; and this would not, in our opinion, seem too small an overlapping to anyone who knew the two groups.

The difference ($1.00\sigma_{19}$ av. or $.92\sigma_{19}$ median) between Group 13 and Group 17 is determined from four different composites and with a mean square error of only .11. There is no reason to alter this in one direction rather than in another.

So we put all the measures of difficulty of Table 116 into differences from the difficulty of the task at which 50 percent of our Group 9 would succeed by the following:

$$-1.7\sigma_{19} \text{ for Group } 5\tfrac{1}{2}$$
$$+ .2\sigma_{19} \text{ `` `` } 9\mathrm{I}$$
$$- .2\sigma_{19} \text{ `` `` } 9\mathrm{II}$$
$$+3.6\sigma_{19} \text{ `` `` } 13$$
$$+4.6\sigma_{19} \text{ `` `` } 17$$

The results are shown in Table 118.

The average values, allowing equal weight to each determination, are:

$$\mathrm{I} = -3.2\sigma_{19} \qquad \mathrm{M} = +1.8\sigma_{19}$$
$$\mathrm{J} = -1.2\sigma_{19} \qquad \mathrm{N} = +2.6\sigma_{19}$$
$$\mathrm{K} = - .2\sigma_{19} \qquad \mathrm{O} = +3.8\sigma_{19}$$
$$\mathrm{L} = + .8\sigma_{19} \qquad \mathrm{P} = +4.4\sigma_{19}$$
$$\mathrm{Q} = +5.6\sigma_{19}$$

The differences, all in terms of $\sigma_{19}$, are:

$$J\text{–}I = 2.0^4 \qquad\qquad N\text{–}M = .8$$
$$K\text{–}J = 1.0^4 \qquad\qquad O\text{–}N = 1.2$$
$$L\text{–}K = 1.0 \qquad\qquad P\text{–}O = .6$$
$$M\text{–}L = 1.0 \qquad\qquad Q\text{–}P = 1.2$$

The measurement of the unreliabilities of these determinations is beyond our facilities both of time and skill. They are doubtless large, perhaps as large as .15. They are, however, not as large by far (relative to the differences to be measured) as are those of the best forms of the Binet.

TABLE 118.

THE INTELLECTUAL DIFFICULTY OF TASKS I TO Q EXPRESSED IN EACH CASE AS A
DIFFERENCE FROM THE MEDIAN DIFFICULTY FOR GROUP 9, IN UNITS OF $\sigma_{19}$.

| Task | By 5½ | By 9I | Difficulty By 9II | By 13 | By 17 |
|------|-------|-------|-------------------|-------|-------|
| I | − 3.22 | − 3.17 | | | |
| J | − 1.08 | − 1.23 | | | |
| K | − .34 | − .15 | − .10 | | |
| L | | + .69 | + .90 | | |
| M | | + 2.13 | + 1.45 | | |
| N | | | + 2.55 | + 2.55 | + 2.53 |
| O | | | | + 3.65 | + 3.85 |
| P | | | | + 4.25 | + 4.43½ |
| Q | | | | + 5.77 | + 5.42½ |

THE DIFFICULTY OF COMPOSITES A, B, C, D, E, F, G, AND H[5]

As was stated at the beginning of the chapter, the measurements of these lower levels of difficulty are less secure than those of tasks I to Q, since investigations of the form of distribution of the various groups used and of their differences in central tendency and variability comparable to the investigations in the case of Grades 6 to 13 have not

[4] These estimates will be amended by the results from other large groups to become 1.9 for J–I and 1.1 for K–J.

[5] Composite H contained only 30 single tasks, having no sentence completions.

been made. The results of such investigations as we have made are reported in Appendix VI.

The basal facts for measuring the differences in difficulty between A and B, B and C, C and D, and so on, are the results of experiments with 180 adult imbeciles of Stanford Mental Age from about $2\frac{1}{2}$ years to 5 years, 100 adults of mental age 6 (a few over 84 months), 50 feeble-minded comprising all the children graded as Class III in one institution for the feeble-minded,[6] 101 pupils in ungraded classes in a large city,[7] 163 pupils in Grade 4 (second half), 311 pupils in Grade 5, and 44 adults, recruits in the United States Army. These groups will be referred to in order as: im. 3, im. 6, f., sp., 4, 5, and ad. (The use of im. and f. involves no theory of classification, but is solely for convenience.)

In groups im. 3, im. 6, f., and sp., the tasks were given orally. In groups f. and sp. (and in some cases in group im. 6), the individual tested was allowed to look at the booklet as the questions were asked, and read it if he could. In groups 4 and 5, the tasks were all presented in print. The comparative difficulty for any given group of oral and printed presentation has not been determined. In the computations of differences between groups in variability and central tendency which follow, the assumption is made that the pupils in Grades 4B and 5 would do better, but vary about as much, if they were tested in the manner used with the lower-level groups, as they did when tested with the printed booklets. The amount of allowance made will be described when the differences of groups below group 4 from groups 4 and above are computed.

The percent succeeding for each of the 40-composite tasks is reported for such of the groups as were measured by that task, in Table 119. Table 119 thus corresponds to Table 106.

[6] This Class III corresponds roughly to grade 3 of an ordinary school. The chronological ages ranged from 9 to 21, only 6 being below 12 and only 2 over 18.

[7] The distribution of ages reported was: 15 from 13–0 to 13–11, 37 from 14–0 to 14–11, 39 from 15–0 to 15–11, and 10 from 16–0 to 16–11.

Using for the respective groups the forms of distribution derived and described in Appendix VI, the difficulty of each 40-composite is found in terms of its difference from the difficulty of that 40-composite which exactly half of the group in question would have succeeded with, in terms of the mean square deviation of the group in question in the ability measured by that 40-composite. These measures appear in Table 120, which corresponds to Table 107.

TABLE 119.

PERCENTS SUCCEEDING WITH VARIOUS COMPOSITES IN GROUPS IM3, IM6, F, SP, 4, 5, AND AD.

| | Groups in Institutions for the Feeble-Minded | | | Special Classes | Regular School Classes | | Adult Recruits |
| | im3 | im6 | f | sp | 4 B | 5 | ad |
| | MA 2½ to 5 $n = 180$ | MA 6 to 7 $n = 100$ | MA 7– to 10 + $n = 50$ | $n = 101$ | $n = 163$ | $n = 311$ | $n = 44$ |
|---|---|---|---|---|---|---|---|
| A | 88.3 | | | | | | |
| B | 48.3 | | | | | | |
| C | 12.8 | 98.0 | | | | | |
| D | 00.6 | 73.0 | | | | | |
| E | | 45.0 | 96.0 | 98.0 | | | |
| F | | 14.0 | 94.0 | 96.0 | 100.0 | | 100.0 |
| G | | 03.0 | 66.0 | 88.1 | 98.8 | | 100.0 |
| H | | | 68.0 | 67.3 | 91.4 | 97.7 | 97.7 |
| I | | | 06.0 | 34.7 | 35.6 | 63.3 | 70.5 |
| J | | | | | 03.1 | 13.2 | 56.8 |
| K | | | | | 00.0 | 00.3 | 47.7 |

ESTIMATING $\sigma_i$ FROM $\sigma_{t_1}$

By means of determinations of $r_{t_1 t_2}$ for the various 40-composites in the various groups, the measures in units of $\sigma_{A\ im3}$, $\sigma_{C\ im6}$, and the like, are transmuted into units of $\sigma_{i\ im3}$, $\sigma_{i\ im6}$, and the like. The essential facts of these determinations are shown below. The results appear in Table 122, which corresponds to Table 113.

In general, we have measured $r_{t_1 t_2}$ both by the Spearman formula using two twenties, and by the correlations of neighboring forties. To economize time, only one method is used in the case of group im. 3 and group im. 6 and group ad.; and only 98 of the 180 individuals are used in group im. 3.

The self-correlation of one random half of a 40-composite with the other half for 98 of the imbeciles of mental age $2\frac{1}{2}$ to 5 years was found to be .86$\frac{1}{2}$ for A, .77$\frac{1}{2}$ for B, .86 for C, and .76 for D. The self-correlation of one 40-composite with another at the same level may then be estimated $\left(\text{by } r_{40} = \dfrac{2r_{20}}{1 + r_{20}}\right)$ as .927 for A, .874 for B, .924 for C, and .864 for D.

TABLE 120.

THE DIFFICULTY OF COMPOSITES A TO K, IN VARIOUS GROUPS EXPRESSED AS A DEVIATION FROM THE DIFFICULTY FOR THE MEDIAN OF THAT GROUP, IN TERMS OF THE σ OF THAT GROUP IN THE ABILITY MEASURED BY SUCCESS WITH THE COMPOSITE IN QUESTION.

| Group n | im 3 180 | im 6 100 | f 50 | sp 101 | 4 163 | 5 311 | ad 44 |
|---|---|---|---|---|---|---|---|
| A | - 1.68 | | | | | | |
| B | + .05 | | | | | | |
| C | + 1.13 | - 1.90 | | | | | |
| D | + 1.83 | - .45 | | | | | |
| E | | + .29 | - 1.33 | - 2.61 | | | |
| F | | + 1.25 | - 1.25 | - 2.31 | <- 3.10 | | |
| G | | + 2.08 | - .33 | - 1.54 | - 2.26 | | <- 3.10 |
| H | | | - .41 | - .44 | - 1.37 | - 2.00 | - 2.00 |
| I | | | + 1.17 | + .36 | + .37 | - .34 | - 1.00 |
| J | | | | | + 1.87 | + 1.12 | - .35 |
| K | | | | | > + 3.10 | + 2.75 | + .06 |

Dividing the entries under im 3 in Tables 120 by $\sqrt{.927}$, $\sqrt{.874}$, $\sqrt{.924}$, and $\sqrt{.864}$, respectively, we obtain values in terms of $\sigma_{i \text{ im3}}$ from the values for $\sigma_{A \text{ im3}}$, $\sigma_{B \text{ im3}}$, etc. They are: — 1.74, + .05, + 1.18, and + 1.97, as shown in Table 122.

The inter-correlations of the 40-composites C, D, E, F, and G in the case of the 100 adults of mental age 6 were as shown in Table 121. The correlations with neighboring composites were .685 for A, .703 for B, .725 for C, .769 for D, and .809 for E. We add .03 to obtain estimated $r_{t_1t_2}$'s.

Dividing the entries in the im 6 column of Table 120 by $\sqrt{.715}$, $\sqrt{.733}$, $\sqrt{.755}$, $\sqrt{.799}$, and $\sqrt{.839}$, respectively, we obtain values in terms of $\sigma_{i\ im6}$ from the values for $\sigma_{C\ im6}$, $\sigma_{D\ im6}$, $\sigma_{E\ im6}$, etc. They are: $-2.25, -.53, +.33, +1.40$, and $+2.27$ as shown in Table 122.

The self-correlation of one random half of a 40-composite with the other half for group f (the 50 feeble-minded in class 3) was found to be .638 for E, .809 for F, .638 for G, .876 for H, and .588 for I. The self-correlation of one 40-

TABLE 121.

RAW INTERCORRELATIONS OF COMPOSITES C, D, E, F AND G IN THE CASE OF 100 INDIVIDUALS CHRONOLOGICALLY SIXTEEN OR OVER, AND MENTALLY SIX.

|   | D | E | F | G |
|---|---|---|---|---|
| C | .685 | .685 | .588 | .426 |
| D |  | .721 | .638 | .426 |
| E |  |  | .729 | .509 |
| F |  |  |  | .809 |

composite with another at the same level of difficulty is thus $\left(\text{by } r_{40} = \dfrac{2r_{20}}{1 + r_{20}}\right)$ .779 for E, .894 for F, .779 for G, .934 for H, and .741 for I.

The inter-correlations of the 40-composites E, F, G, H, and I for group f, were: E with $F = .59$, F with $G = .81$, G with $H = .88$, and H with $I = .81$. The correlations with neighboring composites are thus .59 for E, .70 for F, $.84\frac{1}{2}$ for G, $.84\frac{1}{2}$ for H, and .81 for I. Adding .03 as an allowance for remoteness gives .62, .73, $.87\frac{1}{2}$, $.87\frac{1}{2}$, and .84.

Allowing equal weight to these two determinations, the values of $r_{t_1t_2}$ are, respectively, .70, .81, .83, .90, and .79. Dividing the entries in column f in Table 120 by $\sqrt{.70}$, $\sqrt{.81}$, $\sqrt{.83}$, $\sqrt{.90}$, and $\sqrt{.79}$, respectively, we obtain values in terms of $\sigma_{if}$ from the values of $\sigma_{Ef}$, $\sigma_{Ff}$, $\sigma_{Gf}$, $\sigma_{Hf}$, and $\sigma_{If}$.

They are $-1.59$, $-1.39$, $-.36$, $-.43$, and $+1.32$, as shown in Table 122.

In group sp (the 101 pupils in special classes) the intercorrelations of neighboring composites were: F with G $=$ .62, G with H $= .77\frac{1}{2}$, H with I $= .86$. Adding .03 allowance for remoteness, $r_{t_1t_2}$ is .65 for F, .73 for G, .82 for H, and .89 for I.

The self-correlation of one random half of a 40-composite with the other half in group sp is .73 for F, .54 for G, .64 for H, and .82 for I. The correlation of a 40-composite with another of equal difficulty, that is, $r_{t_1t_2}$, may by these facts be estimated $\left( \text{by } r_{40} = \dfrac{2r_{20}}{1 + r_{20}} \right)$ as .844 for F, .701 for G, .780 for H, and .901 for I.

Giving equal weight to these two determinations, we have, as values of $r_{t_1t_2}$, .75, $.71\frac{1}{2}$, .80, and $.89\frac{1}{2}$ for F, G, H, and I in group sp. Dividing the entries in the sp column of Table 120 by $\sqrt{.75}$, $\sqrt{.715}$, $\sqrt{.80}$, and $\sqrt{.895}$, respectively, we have values in terms of $\sigma_{1\ sp}$ from the values of $\sigma_{E\ sp}$, $\sigma_{F\ sp}$, etc. They are $-2.67$, $-1.82$, $-.49$, and $+.38$, as entered in Table 122.

In group 4 (the 163 cases of Grade 4B) the intercorrelations were: G with H $= .83\frac{1}{2}$; H with I $= .86$; I with J $= .63$; J with K $= .47$. Adding .03 as allowance for remoteness, $r_{t_1t_2}$ is $.86\frac{1}{2}$ for G, .88 for H, $.77\frac{1}{2}$ for I, and .58 for J.

In group 4 the self-correlations of one half with the other half of each 40-composite were .69 for G, .79 for H, .83 for I, and .65 for J. The correlation of a 40-composite with another of equal difficulty is thus .817 for G, .883 for H, .907 for I, and .788 for J.

Giving equal weight to the two determinations of $r_{t_1t_2}$, we have .84, .88, .84, and $.68\frac{1}{2}$ for G, H, I, and J, respectively. Dividing the entries in the 4 column of Table 120 by $\sqrt{.84}$, $\sqrt{.88}$, $\sqrt{.84}$, and $\sqrt{.68\frac{1}{2}}$, respectively, we have values in terms of $\sigma_{14}$ from the values of $\sigma_{F\ 4}$, $\sigma_{G\ 4}$, $\sigma_{H\ 4}$, etc. They are $-2.47$, $-1.47$, $+.40$, and $+2.26$, as entered in Table 122.

The intercorrelations in the case of the 311 pupils of Grade 5 were: H with I = .77, I with J = .85, J with K = .61. The correlations with neighboring composites, elevated .03 to allow for remoteness, are thus: .80 for H, .84 for I, .76 for J, and .63 for K.

The self-correlations in this group, using 20 elements with 20, are: .68, .77, .70, and .51 for H, I, J, and K in order. The correlation of one 40-composite with another of equal difficulty would then be .81 for F, .87 for I, $.82\frac{1}{2}$ for J, and $.67\frac{1}{2}$ for K.

Allowing equal weight to the two determinations of $r_{t_1t_2}$,

TABLE 122.

THE DIFFICULTY OF COMPOSITES A TO K IN TERMS OF $\sigma_{im3}$, $\sigma_{im6}$, $\sigma_t$, ETC.

|   | im3 | im6 | f | sp | 4 | 5 | ad |
|---|---|---|---|---|---|---|---|
| A | − 1.74 | | | | | | |
| B | + .05 | | | | | | |
| C | + 1.18 | − 2.25 | | | | | |
| D | + 1.97 | − .53 | | | | | |
| E | + .33 | − 1.59 | | | | | |
| F | + 1.40 | − 1.39 | − 2.67 | | | | |
| G | + 2.27 | − .36 | − 1.82 | − 2.47 | | | |
| H | | − .43 | − .49 | − 1.46 | − 2.23 | − 2.34 | |
| I | | + 1.32 | + .38 | + .40 | − .37 | − 1.09 | |
| J | | | | + 2.26 | + 1.26 | − .35 | |
| K | | | | | + 3.41 | + .06 | |

we have $.80\frac{1}{2}$ for H, $.85\frac{1}{2}$ for I, .79 for J, and .65 for K. Dividing the entries in Column 5 of Table 120 by $\sqrt{.805}$, $\sqrt{.855}$, $\sqrt{.79}$, and $\sqrt{.65}$, respectively, we have values in terms of $\sigma_{i5}$ from the values for $\sigma_{H\,5}$, $\sigma_{I\,5}$, $\sigma_{J\,5}$, $\sigma_{K\,5}$. They are — 2.23, — .37, + 1.26, and + 3.41, as shown in Table 122.

In the case of the 44 adults, the intercorrelations of the 40-composites were: G with H = .75, H with I = .65, I with J = .96, and J with K = .91. Allowing + .03 for remoteness, we have .78, .73, $.83\frac{1}{2}$, $.95\frac{1}{2}$, and .94 as the probable correlation of G, H, I, J, K, each with another 40-composite of equal difficulty. Dividing the entries in Column ad of

23

Table 120 by $\sqrt{.73}$, $\sqrt{.835}$, $\sqrt{.955}$, and $\sqrt{.94}$, respectively, we have values in terms of $\sigma_{\text{1 ad}}$ from the values of $\sigma_{\text{G ad}}$, $\sigma_{\text{H ad}}$, $\sigma_{\text{I ad}}$, $\sigma_{\text{J ad}}$, and $\sigma_{\text{K ad}}$. They are — .2.34, — 1.09, — .35, and + .06, as shown in Table 122.

### EXPRESSING THE $\sigma_1$ OF EACH GROUP IN TERMS OF $\sigma_{19}$

In accordance with the earlier findings, $\sigma_{19\text{I}}$ and $\sigma_{19\text{II}}$ are treated as equal.

The $\sigma_1$ of group 5 (311 pupils in Grade 5) is made comparable with $\sigma_{19}$ by finding the difference in difficulty between two tasks in terms of $\sigma_{15}$ and in terms of $\sigma_{19\text{I}}$, which is equal to $\sigma_{19}$. Thus

K–J $= 2.15\sigma_{15}$ and $1.09\sigma_{19\text{I}}$, whereby $\sigma_{15} = .51\sigma_{19\text{I}}$.

J–I $= 1.63\sigma_{15}$ and $1.94\sigma_{19\text{I}}$, whereby $\sigma_{15} = 1.19\sigma_{19\text{I}}$.

It is also possible to proceed indirectly by way of $\sigma_{15\frac{1}{2}}$, which was found to equal $.98\sigma_{19}$. Thus

K–J $= 2.15\sigma_{15}$ and $.72\sigma_{15\frac{1}{2}}$ or $.705\sigma_{19}$, whereby $\sigma_{15} = .33\sigma_{19}$.

J–I $= 1.63\sigma_{15}$ and $2.10\sigma_{15\frac{1}{2}}$ or $2.06\sigma_{19}$, whereby $\sigma_{15} = 1.26\sigma_{19}$.

It is also true in general that the variability of Grade 5 in intellect will not be much different from that of Grade $5\frac{1}{2}$.

If an estimate had to be made from general considerations, $\sigma_{15}$ would be expected to be at least $.95\sigma_{19}$. We assign equal weight to .85 (the median of the .51, 1.19, .33, and 1.26) and to .95; and use $.90\sigma_{19}$ as the value of $\sigma_{15}$. The — 2.23, — .37, + 1.26, and + 3.41 of Table 122 in terms of $\sigma_{15}$ thus become the — 2.01, — .33, + 1.13, and + 3.07 of Table 123 in terms of $\sigma_{19}$.

Next, the $\sigma_{14}$ is put in terms of $\sigma_{19}$ both directly and *via* $\sigma_{15}$.

J–I $= 1.86\sigma_{14}$ and $1.94\sigma_{19}$, whereby $\sigma_{14} = 1.04\sigma_{19}$.

J–I $= 1.86\sigma_{14}$ and $1.63\sigma_{15}$, whereby $\sigma_{14} = .88\sigma_{15}$ or $.79\sigma_{19}$.

I–H $= 1.86\sigma_{14}$ and $1.86\sigma_{15}$, whereby $\sigma_{14} = 1.00\sigma_{15}$ or $.90\sigma_{19}$.

From these facts, $\sigma_{14}$ is taken to be approximately equal to $.94\sigma_{15}$ or $.85\sigma_{19}$. The — 2.47, — 1.46, + .40, and + 2.26 of

Table 122 in terms of $\sigma_{i4}$ thus become $-2.10, -1.24, +.34$, and $+1.92$ of Table 123 in terms of $\sigma_{i9}$.

Next the $\sigma_{isp}$ (the 101 special class pupils) is put in terms of $\sigma_{i9}$ *via* $\sigma_{i5}$ and *via* $\sigma_{i4}$.

H–G $= 1.33\sigma_{i9}$ and $1.01\sigma_{i4}$, whereby $\sigma_{isp} = .76\sigma_{i4}$ or $.65\sigma_{i9}$.

I–H $= .87\sigma_{isp}$ and $1.86\sigma_{i4}$, whereby $\sigma_{isp} = 2.14\sigma_{i4}$ or $1.93\sigma_{i9}$.

Nothing is known precisely of the general tendency of pupils over 13 in such special-class populations to vary, though the expectation would be that the variation would be fairly wide, from pupils who really belonged in an institution for the feeble-minded to pupils who really belonged in a regular Grade 4. Giving equal weight to the three determinations, $\sigma_{isp} = 1.47\sigma_{i9}$. Giving equal weight to the I–H and the H–G pairs, $\sigma_{isp} = 1.26\sigma_{i9}$. We use the latter.

In a similar manner $\sigma_{if}$, $\sigma_{i\ im3}$, and $\sigma_{i\ im6}$ are put in terms of $\sigma_{i9}$. The essential facts are:

I–H $= 1.75\sigma_{if}$ or $1.86\sigma_{i5}$ or $1.86\sigma_{i4}$ or $.87\sigma_{isp}$, whereby
$$\sigma_{if} = 1.06\sigma_{i5} \text{ or } .95\sigma_{i9},$$
$$\text{or } \sigma_{if} = 1.06\sigma_{i4} \text{ or } .90\sigma_{i9},$$
$$\text{or } \sigma_{if} = .50\sigma_{isp} \text{ or } .63\sigma_{i9}.$$

H–F $= .96\sigma_{if}$ or $2.18\sigma_{isp}$, whereby $\sigma_{if} = 2.27\sigma_{isp}$ or $2.86\sigma_{i9}$. We take the median of these four observations, $.92\frac{1}{2}\sigma_{i9}$.

G–F $= .87\sigma_{i\ im6}$ and $1.03\sigma_{if}$ and $.85\sigma_{isp}$, whereby
$$\sigma_{i\ im6} = 1.18\sigma_{if} \text{ or } 1.09\sigma_{i9} \text{ or}$$
$$\sigma_{i\ im6} = .97\sigma_{isp} \text{ or } 1.22\sigma_{i9}.$$

F–E $= 1.07\sigma_{i\ im6}$ and $.20\sigma_{if}$, whereby $\sigma_{i\ im6} = .187\sigma_{if}$ or $.17\sigma_{i9}$.

Since group im6 contains only individuals of Stanford Mental Age 6,[8] it may be assumed to be much less variable than group f or group im3, or any other group used here. The average of the three determinations ($1.09\sigma_{i9}$, $1.22\sigma_{i9}$, and $.17\sigma_{i9}$) which is $.83\sigma_{i9}$, is used, giving in terms of $\sigma_{i9}$ $-1.87, -.44, +.27, +1.16$, and $+1.88$ as the entries in Table 123.

[8] Plus two individuals of mental age 7.

$D\text{--}C = .79\sigma_{i\ im3}$ or $1.72\sigma_{i\ im6}$, whereby
$$\sigma_{i\ im3} = 2.18\sigma_{i\ im6} \text{ or } 1.81\sigma_{i9}.$$

Using $\sigma_{i\ im3} = 1.81\sigma_{i9}$, the entries for Table 123 are $-3.15$, $+.09$, $+2.14$, and $+3.57$.

The facts for the adult group are:

$K\text{--}J = .41\sigma_{iad}$ or $1.09\sigma_{i9}$ whereby $\sigma_{iad} = 2.67\sigma_{i9}$.

$J\text{--}I = .74\sigma_{iad}$ or $1.94\sigma_{i9}$ whereby $\sigma_{iad} = 2.62\sigma_{i9}$.

$I\text{--}H = 1.25\sigma_{iad}$ or $1.86\sigma_{i5}$ or $1.86\sigma_{i4}$ or $.87\sigma_{isp}$ or $1.75\sigma_{if}$.

By these four indirect computations, $\sigma_{iad} = 1.49\sigma_{i5}$ or $1.34\sigma_{i9}$.
$$\sigma_{iad} = 1.49\sigma_{i4} \text{ or } 1.27\sigma_{i9}.$$
$$\sigma_{iad} = .70\sigma_{isp} \text{ or } .88\sigma_{i9}.$$
$$\sigma_{iad} = 1.40\sigma_{if} \text{ or } 1.30\sigma_{i9}.$$

TABLE 123.

THE DIFFICULTY OF COMPOSITES A TO K, IN TERMS OF $\sigma_{i9}$.

|   | im3 | im6 | f | sp. | 4 | 5 | ad. | 5½ | 9I |
|---|------|------|------|------|------|------|------|------|------|
| A | $-3.15$ | | | | | | | | |
| B | $+.09$ | | | | | | | | |
| C | $+2.14$ | $-1.87$ | | | | | | | |
| D | $+3.57$ | $-.44$ | | | | | | | |
| E | | $+.27$ | $-1.47$ | | | | | | |
| F | | $+1.16$ | $-1.29$ | $-3.36$ | | | | | |
| G | | $+1.88$ | $-.33$ | $-2.29$ | $-2.10$ | | | | |
| H | | | $-.40$ | $-.62$ | $-1.24$ | $-2.01$ | $-5.12$ | | |
| I | | | $+1.22$ | $+.48$ | $+.34$ | $-.33$ | $-2.39$ | $-1.52$ | $-3.37$ |
| J | | | | | $+1.92$ | $+1.13$ | $-.77$ | $+.62$ | $-1.43$ |
| K | | | | | | $+3.07$ | $+.13$ | $+1.36$ | $-.35$ |

We weight each of the direct comparisons as equal to the median of the four indirect comparisons and thus by averaging, have, as the estimate used, $\sigma_{i\ ad} = 2.19\sigma_{i9}$. This value is not unreasonable, since the group of adults included men of schooling all the way from Grade 3 to Grade 12. The entries for Table 123, derived from Column ad in Table 122, are then: $-5.12$, $-2.39$, $-.77$, and $+.13$.

## EXPRESSING THE MEASURES OF DIFFICULTY AS DISTANCES FROM A COMMON POINT OF REFERENCE

The measures of Table 123 are in every case distances from the median difficulty for the group in question. We shall express each (in Table 124) as a distance from the median difficulty for Grade $9I + II$, in terms of $\sigma_{19}$ as a unit, by estimating the distance of the median difficulty for group $5\frac{1}{2}$ from the median difficulty for group $9I + II$, and similarly for the median difficulty for each of groups ad, 5, 4, sp, f, im6, and im3. The essential facts and procedures are stated below. We use $M_{9I + II}$ to denote the difficulty of the task which exactly 50% of the Grade 9 group will succeed with, $M_5$ to denote the difficulty of the task which exactly 50% of the group 5 will succeed with, and similarly for $M_{im3}$, $M_{im6}$, $M_f$, $M_{sp}$, $M_4$, $M_{ad}$, $M_{5\frac{1}{2}}$, $M_{9I}$, and $M_{9II}$.

$K = M_{5\frac{1}{2}} + 1.36\sigma_{19}$.

$\quad = M_5 \ + 3.07\sigma_{19}$, whence $M_{5\frac{1}{2}} - M_5 = 1.71\sigma_{19}$.

$J = M_{5\frac{1}{2}} + \ .62\sigma_{19}$

$\quad = M_5 \ + 1.13\sigma_{19}$, whence $M_{5\frac{1}{2}} - M_5 = \ .51\sigma_{19}$.

$I = M_{5\frac{1}{2}} - 1.52\sigma_{19}$.

$\quad = M_5 \ - \ .33\sigma_{19}$, whence $M_{5\frac{1}{2}} - M_5 = 1.19\sigma_{19}$.

$J = M_{5\frac{1}{2}} + \ .62\sigma_{19}$.

$\quad = M_4 \ + 1.92\sigma_{19}$, whence $M_{5\frac{1}{2}} - M_4 = 1.30\sigma_{19}$.

$I = M_{5\frac{1}{2}} - 1.52\sigma_{19}$.

$\quad = M_4 \ + \ .34\sigma_{19}$, whence $M_{5\frac{1}{2}} - M_4 = 1.86\sigma_{19}$.

$J = M_5 \ + 1.13\sigma_{19}$.

$\quad = M_4 \ + 1.92\sigma_{19}$, whence $M_{5\frac{1}{2}} - M_4 = \ .79\sigma_{19}$.

$I = M_5 \ + \ .33\sigma_{19}$.

$\quad = M_4 \ + \ .34\sigma_{19}$, whence $M_5 \ - M_4 = \ .67\sigma_{19}$.

$H = M_5 \ - 2.01\sigma_{19}$.

$\quad = M_4 \ - 1.24\sigma_{19}$, whence $M_5 \ - M_4 = \ .77\sigma_{19}$.

In view of the above, we take:

$.70\sigma_{19}$ as the difference between $M_4$ and $M_5$,

$.90\sigma_{19}$ as the difference between $M_5$ and $M_{5\frac{1}{2}}$, and

$1.60\sigma_{19}$ as the difference between $M_4$ and $M_{5\frac{1}{2}}$.

These figures fit everything well, except the determination of $M_{5\frac{1}{2}} - M_5$ by K; and this we believe deserves less weight than the others.

$I = M_{5\frac{1}{2}} - 1.52\sigma_{19}$
  $= M_{sp} + .48\sigma_{19}$, whence $M_{5\frac{1}{2}} - M_{sp} = 2.00\sigma_{19}$ and
                $M_4 - M_{sp} = 2.00\sigma_{19} - 1.60\sigma_{19}$, or $.40\sigma_{19}$.

$I = M_5 - .33\sigma_{19}$
  $= M_{sp} + .48\sigma_{19}$, whence $M_5 - M_{sp} = .81\sigma_{19}$ and
                $M_4 - M_{sp} = .81_{19} - .70\sigma_{19}$, or $.11\sigma_{19}$.

$H = M_5 - 2.01\sigma_{19}$
  $= M_{sp} - .62\sigma_{19}$, whence $M_5 - M_{sp} = 1.39\sigma_{19}$ and
                $M_4 - M_{sp} = 1.39\sigma_{19} - .70\sigma_{19}$, or $.69_{19}$.

$I = M_4 + .34\sigma_{19}$
  $= M_{sp} + .48\sigma_{19}$, whence $M_4 - M_{sp} = -.14\sigma_{19}$.

$H = M_4 - 1.24\sigma_{19}$
  $= M_{sp} - .62\sigma_{19}$, whence $M_4 - M_{sp} = -.62\sigma_{19}$.

$G = M_4 - 2.10\sigma_{19}$
  $= M_{sp} - 2.29\sigma_{19}$, whence $M_4 - M_{sp} = .19\sigma_{19}$.

Taking these six differences at their face value, there is a median difference of $.15\sigma_{19}$ and an average difference of $.11\sigma_{19}$. We have to allow for the fact that presentation was oral to group sp. Lacking experimental evidence, this allowance is arbitrary. We allow $.27\sigma_{19}$, making the special class $.40\sigma_{19}$ below group 4.

$I = M_{5\frac{1}{2}} - 1.52\sigma_{19}$
  $= M_t + 1.22\sigma_{19}$, whence $M_{5\frac{1}{2}} - M_t = 2.74\sigma_{19}$ and
                $M_{sp} - M_t = .74\sigma_{19}$.

$I = M_5 - .33\sigma_{19}$
  $= M_t + 1.22\sigma_{19}$, whence $M_5 - M_t = 1.55\sigma_{19}$ and
                $M_{sp} - M_t = .45\sigma_{19}$.

$H = M_5 - 2.01\sigma_{19}$
  $= M_t - .40\sigma_{19}$, whence $M_5 - M_t = 1.61\sigma_{19}$ and
                $M_{sp} - M_t = .51\sigma_{19}$.

$I = M_4 + .34\sigma_{19}$
  $= M_t + 1.22\sigma_{19}$, whence $M_4 - M_t = .88\sigma_{19}$ and
                $M_{sp} - M_t = .48\sigma_{19}$.

$H = M_4 \quad -1.24\sigma_{19}$
$\quad = M_f \quad - \quad .40\sigma_{19}$, whence $M_4 \quad -M_f = .84\sigma_{19}$ and
$$M_{sp} - M_f = .44\sigma_{19}.$$

$G = M_4 \quad -2.10\sigma_{19}$
$\quad = M_f \quad - \quad .33\sigma_{19}$, whence $M_4 \quad -M_f = 1.77\sigma_{19}$ and
$$M_{sp} - M_f = 1.27\sigma_{19}.$$

$I = M_{sp} + .48\sigma_{19}$
$\quad = M_f \quad + 1.22\sigma_{19}$, whence $M_{sp} - M_f = .74\sigma_{19}.$

$I = M_{sp} - .62\sigma_{19}$
$\quad = M_f \quad - .40\sigma_{19}$, whence $M_{sp} - M_f = .22\sigma_{19}.$
$\quad = M_{sp} - 2.29\sigma_{19}$
$\quad = M_f \quad - .33\sigma_{19}$, whence $M_{sp} - M_f = 1.86\sigma_{19}.$
$\quad = M_{sp} - 3.36\sigma_{19}$
$\quad = M_f \quad -1.29\sigma_{19}$, whence $M_{sp} - M_f = 2.07\sigma_{19}.$

The four direct comparisons with the sp group which had oral presentation are the most important. Their average is $1.22\sigma_{19}$; their median, $1.30\sigma_{19}$. The average of the other six is $.65\sigma_{19}$; their median, $50\sigma_{19}$. We use $1.10\sigma_{19}$, which is very close to the result obtained by weighting the result from direct comparison 3 and the result from indirect comparison 1. This puts the f group as $1.50\sigma_{19}$ below group 4, which is not unreasonable, since these feeble-minded individuals were doing approximately the work of a regular school grade 3.

$G = M_{sp} \quad -2.29\sigma_{19}$
$\quad = M_{im\ 6} + 1.88\sigma_{19}$, whence $M_{sp} - M_{im\ 6} = 4.17\sigma_{19}$ and
$$M_f - M_{im\ 6} = 3.07\sigma_{19}.$$

$F = M_{sp} \quad -3.36\sigma_{19}$
$\quad = M_{im\ 6} + 1.16\sigma_{19}$, whence $M_{sp} - M_{im\ 6} = 4.52\sigma_{19}$ and
$$M_f - M_{im\ 6} = 3.42\sigma_{19}.$$

$G = M_f \quad - .33\sigma_{19}$
$\quad = M_{im\ 6} + 1.88\sigma_{19}$, whence $M_f - M_{im\ 6} = 2.21\sigma_{19}.$

$F = M_f \quad -1.29\sigma_{19}$
$\quad = M_{im\ 6} + 1.16\sigma_{19}$, whence $M_f - M_{im\ 6} = 2.45\sigma_{19}.$

$E = M_f \quad -1.47\sigma_{19}$
$\quad = M_{im\ 6} + .27\sigma_{19}$, whence $M_f - M_{im\ 6} = 1.74\sigma_{19}.$

The average of the five determinations is $2.58\sigma_{19}$; the median is $2.45\sigma_{19}$. We use $2.50\sigma_{19}$.

$D = M_{im\ 6} - .44\sigma_{19}$
$= M_{im\ 3} + 3.57\sigma_{19}$, whence $M_{im\ 6} - M_{im\ 3} = 4.01\sigma_{19}$.
$C = M_{im\ 6} - 1.87\sigma_{19}$
$= M_{im\ 3} + 2.14\sigma_{19}$, whence $M_{im\ 6} - M_{im\ 3} = 4.01\sigma_{19}$.
We use $4.00\sigma_{19}$.

These determinations of differences are obviously far less reliable than is desirable, and should some time be made precisely. They are, however, presumably free from constant errors, and the variable errors do not prevent them from satisfying one main purpose of relating the measures of I, J, K, L, M, N, O, and P to an approximate absolute zero. We find the differences between $M_9$ and $M_5$ and $M_4$, etc., as follows:

$M_9 \quad - M_{5\frac{1}{2}} = 1.70\sigma_{19}$, by the data presented earlier in the chapter.

$M_{5\frac{1}{2}} - M_5 = .90\sigma_{19}$ and $M_9 - M_5 = 2.60\sigma_{19}$.

$M_5 \quad - M_4 = .70\sigma_{19}$, so $M_{5\frac{1}{2}} - M_4 = 1.60\sigma_{19}$,
and $M_9 - M_4 = 3.30\sigma_{19}$.

$M_4 \quad - M_{sp} = .40\sigma_{19}$, so $M_{5\frac{1}{2}} - M_{sp} = 2.00\sigma_{19}$,
and $M_9 - M_{sp} = 3.70\sigma_{19}$.

$M_{sp} \quad - M_f = 1.10\sigma_{19}$, so $M_{5\frac{1}{2}} - M_f = 3.10\sigma_{19}$,
and $M_9 - M_f = 4.80\sigma_{19}$.

$M_f \quad - M_{im\ 6} = 2.50\sigma_{19}$, so $M_{5\frac{1}{2}} - M_{im\ 6} = 5.60\sigma_{19}$,
and $M_9 - M_{im\ 6} = 7.30\sigma_{19}$.

$M_{im\ 6} - M_{im\ 3} = 4.00\sigma_{19}$, so $M_{5\frac{1}{2}} - M_{im\ 3} = 9.60\sigma_{19}$,
and $M_9 - M_{im\ 3} = 11.30\sigma_{19}$.

These facts are used to put all the entries of Table 123 into differences from the median difficulty of group 9. The result is Table 124, which is thus a continuation of Table 118.

The adult group is given its location by the following:

$K = M_{ad} + .13\sigma_{19}$
$= M_{9I} - .35\sigma_{19}$, whence $M_{9I} - M_{ad} = .48\sigma_{19}$.

$J = M_{ad} - .77\sigma_{19}$
$= M_{9I} - 1.43\sigma_{19}$, whence $M_{9I} - M_{ad} = .66\sigma_{19}$.

$I = M_{ad} - 2.39\sigma_{19}$
$= M_{9I} - 3.37\sigma_{19}$, whence $M_{9I} - M_{ad} = .98\sigma_{19}$.

$K = M_{ad} + .13\sigma_{19}$
$= M_{5\frac{1}{2}} + 1.36\sigma_{19}$, whence $M_{ad} - M_{5\frac{1}{2}} = 1.23\sigma_{19}$.

$J = M_{ad} - .77\sigma_{19}$
$= M_{5\frac{1}{2}} + .62\sigma_{19}$, whence $M_{ad} - M_{5\frac{1}{2}} = 1.39\sigma_{19}$.

$I = M_{ad} - 2.39\sigma_{19}$
$= M_{5\frac{1}{2}} - 1.52\sigma_{19}$, whence $M_{ad} - M_{5\frac{1}{2}} = .87\sigma_{19}$.

TABLE 124.

THE INTELLECTUAL DIFFICULTY OF TASKS A TO K EXPRESSED AS A DIFFERENCE
FROM THE MEDIAN DIFFICULTY FOR GROUP 9, IN UNITS OF $\sigma_{19}$.

|   | im3 | im6 | f | sp. | 4 | 5 | ad. | 5½ | 9I |
|---|---|---|---|---|---|---|---|---|---|
| A | -14.45 | | | | | | | | |
| B | -11.21 | | | | | | | | |
| C | - 9.16 | -9.17 | | | | | | | |
| D | - 7.73 | -7.74 | | | | | | | |
| E | | -7.03 | -6.27 | | | | | | |
| F | | -6.14 | -6.09 | -7.06 | | | | | |
| G | | -5.42 | -5.13 | -5.99 | -5.40 | | | | |
| H | | | -5.20 | -4.32 | -4.54 | -4.61 | -5.65 | | |
| I | | | -3.58 | -3.22 | -2.96 | -2.93 | -2.92 | -3.32 | -3.17 |
| J | | | | | -1.38 | -1.47 | -1.30 | -1.08 | -1.23 |
| K | | | | | + .47 | - .41 | - .34 | - .15 | |

Thus $M_{ad}$ is on the average $.71\sigma_{19}$ below $M_{9I}$, or $.51\sigma_{19}$ below $M_9$ and $1.16\sigma_{19}$ above $M_{5\frac{1}{2}}$. Since $M_9$ is $1.70\sigma_{19}$ above $M_{5\frac{1}{2}}$, this second determination is equivalent to $.56\sigma_{19}$ below $M_9$. We use the average, $.53\sigma_{19}$, and so transmute the $-5.12$, $-2.39$, $-.77$, and $+.13$ of Table 123, into $-5.65$, $-2.92$, $-1.30$, and $-.41$ in Table 124.

The data from groups $5\frac{1}{2}$ and 9I are also repeated in Table 124. Table 124 then has four determinations of the difficulty of K, five determinations of the difficulty of J, seven determinations of the difficulty of I, and so on.

We first consider whether there is any need to modify our earlier estimate of the difficulty of K, J, and I in view of the extensive new facts.

K was — $.2\sigma_{19}$ from the median of Group 9, by the average of three determinations (— .34, — .15, and — .10) from Groups $5\frac{1}{2}$, 9I, and 9II. It is — $.51\sigma_{19}$ by the adults and $+ .47\sigma_{19}$ by Group 5. In view of the great discrepancy, and the fact that K is perhaps too hard a task to enlist full effort from pupils in Grade 5, we leave the — .2 as the estimate for K. J was — $1.16\sigma_{19}$ from the median of Group 9. It is — $1.38\sigma_{19}$ by the averages of the determinations from 4, 5, and ad. Then $1.3\sigma_{19}$ is more probable than $1.2\sigma_{19}$ as its value. I was — $3.2\sigma_{19}$ by Groups $5\frac{1}{2}$ and 9I. It is — $3.12\sigma_{19}$ by the average of the five new determinations. We leave it as — $3.2\sigma_{19}$. So we may use — $3.2\sigma_{19}$ for I, — $1.3\sigma_{19}$ for J, and — $.2\sigma_{19}$ for K. The difference J–I is then $1.9\sigma_{19}$ instead of $2.0\sigma_{19}$, and the difference K–J is $1.1\sigma_{19}$ instead of $1.0\sigma_{19}$.

The difficulty of H is — $4.7\sigma_{19}$ or — $4.6\sigma_{19}$ (average and median); that of G is — $5.4\sigma_{19}$; that of F is — $6.4\sigma_{19}$ or — $6.1\sigma_{19}$; the difficulties of E, D, C, B, and A are, in order, — $6.6\frac{1}{2}\sigma_{19}$, — $7.7\sigma_{19}$, — $9.2\sigma_{19}$, — $11.2\sigma_{19}$, and — $14.4\frac{1}{2}\sigma_{19}$.

The difficulties for L, M, N, O, P, and Q were found (in Table 118) to be respectively $+ .8\sigma_{19}$, $+ 1.8\sigma_{19}$, $+ 2.5\sigma_{19}$, $+ 3.7\frac{1}{2}\sigma_{19}$, $+ 4.4\sigma_{19}$, and $+ 5.6\sigma_{19}$.

These measures are all deviations from the difficulty for the median of Group 9I + II. Expressed as deviations from the difficulty of Task A, they are, in the A, B, C order,

A = 0, B = $3.2\frac{1}{2}$, C = $5.2\frac{1}{2}$, D = $6.7\frac{1}{2}$, E = 7.8, F = 8.2, G = 9.0, H = 9.8, I = 11.3, J = $13.1\frac{1}{2}$, K = $14.2\frac{1}{2}$, L = $15.2\frac{1}{2}$, M = $16.2\frac{1}{2}$, N = $16.9\frac{1}{2}$, O = 18.2, P = $18.8\frac{1}{2}$, and Q = $20.0\frac{1}{2}$.

## THE SCALE

In Chapter X it will be shown that the distance from an approximate absolute zero of intellectual difficulty to the difficulty of Composite A is about 4.35 times the difference in difficulty between Composite A and Composite C, which is 5.28½. So the difficulties of A, B, C, etc., measured from an approximate absolute zero are,[9] in units of $\sigma_{19}$:

| | | | |
|---|---|---|---|
| A | 23 | J | 36¼ or 36.1 |
| B | 26¼ | K | 37¼ or 37.2 |
| C | 28¼ | L | 38¼ or 38.2 |
| D | 29¾ | M | 39¼ or 39.2 |
| E | 30¾ | N | 40 or 40.0 |
| F | 31¼ | O | 41¼ or 41.2 |
| G | 32 | P | 41¾ or 41.8 |
| H | 32¾ | Q | 43 or 43.0 |
| I | 34¼ or 34.2 | | |

The unit $\sigma_{19}$ may now be given a more realistic definition. It is one-twentieth of the difference in difficulty between such composites as an adult of approximately mental age three can succeed with (in the sense of obtaining 20 or more right of the single tasks) and such as only the ablest fifth of college graduates can succeed with. It is one-twentieth of the difference between tasks at which over 999 per thousand adults can succeed, and tasks at which only about ten per thousand can succeed. It is one-tenth of the difference between tasks at which nineteen out of twenty pupils in Grade 5 can succeed, and those at which only a fifth of college graduates can succeed. It corresponds to about 1½ average years of mental age from 6 to 12.

The relative magnitudes from 23 for A to 43 for Q will seem preposterous to many critics who will deem it incredible that the intellects of the top one percent of men should be less than twice as "high" as the intellects of the lower ranges of asylum inmates; or that a child of three has attained two-thirds of the intellectual altitude which he ever will attain.

The relative magnitudes are far from secure, depending so much as they do on the experimental determinations

[9] The first column gives the measures to the nearest quarter-unit, which is even closer than the data justify for tasks A to H. The second column gives measures to the nearest tenth of a unit for tasks I to Q.

from the im3 group and the expert ratings to be described in the next chapter. The 23 for A may conceivably be in truth only 13 or 10 or even lower, though we have no evidence that it is likely to be lower rather than higher. Even if it were as low as 10 or 12, the critics would still find the relative magnitudes nearly as preposterous. The difficulty is probably due to a confusion of altitude of intellect with intellect *in toto,* a confusion which the Binet and other tests seem to have stimulated. Intellect *in toto* is proportional to altitude only if the number of tasks is approximately equal at each level of difficulty. The number selected to make an examination, such as the Binet, or our CAVD series, may be so, but we shall show that the number of tasks that are or can be made increases with their difficulty, so that what we may call the "area" of an intellect of altitude 40 may be, not two times that of an intellect of altitude 20, but twenty or two hundred or perhaps two thousand times it. Any further discussion of these matters may best be deferred until after the treatment of the location of zero difficulty in Chapter X, and the treatment of the measurement of width and "area" of intellect in Chapter XII.

# CHAPTER X

## The Absolute Zero of Intellectual Difficulty

We may expect the same sort and amount of advantage to the scientific study of intellect from a determination of its absolute zero as accrues to the study of temperature or electrical resistance from the determination of their absolute zeros. Just as we cannot properly add or subtract or average numbers representing degrees of intellectual difficulty until we know that the units called equal are really equal, so we cannot properly make the "times as much" judgment, or divide one amount of intellectual difficulty by another to form a ratio, until we can state these amounts as differences from a true absolute zero meaning just barely not any intellectual difficulty.

Knowledge of the location of zero intellectual difficulty not only will put all our measures of difficulty, or altitude of intellect, into numbers capable of treatment in ratios, but also will put all our measures of what may be called the total "surface" or "area" of intellect,[1] into numbers capable of similar treatment.

Relations within the field of intellect, and relations between it and other facts measurable in known units from a known absolute zero will then be susceptible of simple, straightforward study and presentation as lines in the $+ +$ quadrant of a system of coördinates. In place of our present laborious and somewhat ambiguous determinations by correlations and regressions, that such and such an excess over or deficiency below the central tendency for a certain group in trait Y is related to such and such an excess over or deficiency below the central tendency of the same group in trait X, we shall have simple and definite statements that $y = ax + b$, found by plotting the straight line of best fit,

[1] These terms will be defined in Chapter XI.

just as the physicist or engineer does. Where the relation is curvilinear and intricate, the gain will be even greater, since in such cases the correlation and regression technique is especially laborious and subject to ambiguity and misleading.

We shall also be stimulated to study psychological relations over a large part of the range of intellect from near zero to near its maximum. The intellects of dogs, cats, primates, and men will more easily be made commensurate and put in relation to the same fact in the same plot.

### LOCATING ZERO DIFFICULTY BY EXPERIMENT

By the methods previously described, we can measure differences in difficulty in Intellect CAVD from tasks such as only one adult in a thousand can do down to tasks of level A (shown in Chapter III) which over nine hundred and ninety-nine adults in a thousand can do. Tasks in giving the opposites of words or in answering informational questions can be measured in respect of their intellectual difficulty from an equally high down to an equally low level.

Consider now such a series of tasks as AA to AAAAA below. Adult imbeciles and idiots who cannot do twenty out of forty tasks as hard as those of Level A, may succeed with twenty out of forty as hard as AA. A hundred dogs or cats of specified age and training could be measured as to their ability in composites of tasks like AA to AAAA. Amphibians and fishes of specified selection and training could be measured as to their ability in composites of tasks like AAA to AAAAA.[2]

AA    Responds to the direction "Come here."
AAA   Can find his way to some very familiar place, such as his own sleeping-place.
AAAA  Will not try to eat a familiar nasty-tasting object.
AAAAA Will not try to bite off his own toes.

2 We are, of course, here concerned with the difficulty of tasks learned by intellect, not with that of tasks provided for by original nature.

A Program of Tasks to Use in Measuring Tasks of Very
Little Intellectual Difficulty.

Composite Task.    Groups in Which the Percent of Successes Is between 100 and 0.

| | | |
|---|---|---|
| I | Earthworms | |
| II | " | |
| III | " | Crabs |
| IV | " | " |
| V | Fishes | " |
| VI | " | " |
| VII | " | Frogs |
| VIII | " | " |
| IX | Turtles | " |
| X | " | " |
| XI | " | Rats |
| XII | " | " |
| XIII | Cats | " |
| XIV | " | " |
| XV | " | Dogs |
| XVI | " | " |
| XVII | Monkeys | " |
| XVIII | " | " |
| XIX | " | Chimpanzees |
| XX | " | " |
| XXI | Human adults, A[3] | " |
| XXII | " | " |
| XXIII | " | Human adults, B[3] |
| XXIV | " | " |
| XXV | Human adults, C[3] | " |
| XXVI | " | " |
| A[4] | " | Human adults, D[3] |
| B[4] | " | " |
| C[4] | Human adults, E | " |
| D[4] | | " |

[3] The A, B, C, D, and E groups of human adults are to have means and mean square variations in mental months of about $12 \pm 4$, $20 \pm 4$, $30 \pm 4$, $39 \pm 4$, and $48 \pm 4$.

[4] These tasks A, B, C and D are the CAVD composites A, B, C and D or tasks equal to these in intellectual difficulty.

With sufficient care and ingenuity, we could doubtless devise composite tasks I, II, III, IV, V, and so on, such that there would be percents between 100 and 0 succeeding within each of the groups shown above and overlapping of groups as shown in the program above. It is probable that the number of test composites and of animal groups necessary will be much less than the program shows. We could then measure the differences in difficulty from A down to that intellectual task which earthworms can master, by the same general methods as we have used from high levels down to A.

The difficulty of the intellectual task which the earthworm's intellect can master is so near zero difficulty that a level slightly below it may safely be accepted as an approximate absolute zero of intellectual difficulty, sufficiently close for all purposes, theoretical or practical.

It is to be hoped that such a determination of zero intellectual difficulty by actual experimentation will sometime be made. The time and facilities required made it impracticable to include it among our investigations. We have had to content ourselves with cruder methods.

### LOCATING ZERO DIFFICULTY BY A CONSENSUS

What we have done is to utilize a consensus of psychologists, especially such as are expert in animal and infant psychology, or the psychology of the very dull. Each of them in entire independence of all the others ranked 56 tasks shown below (but presented in a random order) in accordance with the following instructions:

Please rank the tasks or achievements described on the enclosed slips according to their intellectual difficulty, that is, according to the degree of intellect required for a man to perform each, supposing the man to have lived 20 years with the average opportunities of a person born and bred in an average English-speaking home (or institution, if his intellect is so slight that he has to be brought up in an institution for the feeble-minded). Mark the task or achievement that requires least intellect, 1; the one that requires next to least, 2; the one that requires second to least, 3; and so on. Use your own conception of intellect in doing so. If any of the tasks or achievements seem equally difficult, assign them the same rank.

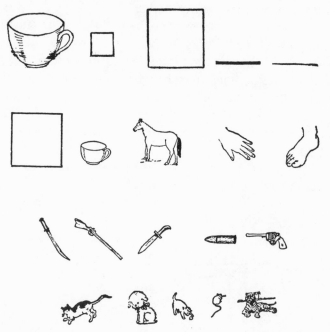

FIG. 34.  Drawings used with tasks 57, 58, 81, and 82.  Reduced to about 2/3 original size.

57. Responds correctly to the direction "Draw a line around the cup," Fig. 34a being shown.

58. Responds correctly to the direction "Make a cross in the square," Fig. 34b being shown.

69. Can answer correctly "What is the person that you send for when you are sick?"

70. Can answer correctly "Tell me something that walks on four legs."

75. Can recognize four fingers when four are held up and he is asked "How many?" in three trials out of five, the trials being interspersed with other tasks.

24

76. The experimenter shows a box is empty and shows five pennies clearly and puts them in the box. He then takes out four pennies from the box and shows these clearly and asks "How many cents are in the box?" Two correct responses out of three are required, the trials being interspersed with other tasks.

81. Can respond correctly when told "Put your finger on the pistol," or "Point to the pistol," or "Find the pistol," or "Which is the pistol?" or other familiar expression of similar meaning, Fig. 34c being shown.

82. Can respond correctly when told "Put your finger on the tiger," or "Point to the tiger," or "Find the tiger," or "Which is the tiger?" or other familiar expression of similar meaning, Fig. 34d being shown.

55. Responds correctly to the direction "Make the other arm on this man." (Pointing.)

FIG. 35.   Drawing used with task 55.   Reduced to about 2/3 original size.

63. Responds correctly to the direction "Stand back of your chair."

65. Can answer correctly "Is this morning or afternoon or evening?  Which is it?"

66. Can answer correctly "Tell me something that you are afraid of."

74. The experimenter shows that a box is empty.  He holds up one penny and puts it in the box.  He then holds up

two pennies, both clearly in view, and puts them in the box. He then asks "How many cents are in the box?" (Two correct responses out of three are required, the three trials beng interspersed with other tasks.)

79. Can respond correctly when told "Put your finger on the window," or "Point to the window," or "Find the window," or "Which is the window?" or other familiar expression of similar meaning, Fig. 36a being shown.

FIG. 36.   Drawings used with tasks 79 and 80.   Reduced to about 2/3 original size.

80. Can respond correctly when told "Put your finger on the envelope," or "Point to the envelope," or "Find the envelope," or "Which is the envelope?" or other familiar expression of similar meaning, Fig. 36b being shown.

51. Responds correctly to the direction "Make a line like this," the experimenter showing him by drawing a line on a sheet of paper. (Anything approximating a straight line is to be scored correct.)

52. Responds correctly to the direction "Make a cross like this." (Two lines that cross anywhere are to be scored correct.)

59. Can answer "What do you wear on your head when you go out?"

60. Can answer "Tell me something that is good to eat. Something else.  Something else." (3 required.)

71. Can respond correctly to "Show me the littlest square; show me the littlest one of all," showing three as here.

(Three squares with sides respectively ½″, 1″ and 1½″ are shown.)

72. Can respond correctly to "Show me the biggest square; show me the biggest one of all," showing three as here. (Three squares shown as in 71.)

77. Can respond correctly when told "Put your finger on the apple," or "Point to the apple," or "Find the apple," or "Which is the apple?" or other familiar expression of similar meaning, Fig. 37a being shown.

FIG. 37.    Drawings used with tasks 77 and 78.    Reduced to about 2/3 original size.

78. Can respond correctly when told "Put your finger on the dog," or "Point to the dog," or "Find the dog," or "Which is the dog?" or other familiar expression of similar meaning, Fig. 37b being shown.

45. Can give a correct response to "Tell me the name of something you eat."

49. Can give a correct response when someone shows him a watch and says "Tell me what this is."

46. Can give a correct response when someone shows him a penny and says "Tell me what this is."

4. Responds to the direction "Give me the pencil," assuming that a pencil is in clear view before him and that you are near enough for him to hand it to you.

5. Responds to the direction "Take the pencil," supposing one to be in clear view within his reach.

42. Can give a correct answer to "What do you call this?" (the questioner touching the nose of the one questioned).

29. Will not try to put a large object through a hole less than one-fourth its size, for example, will not try to put a baseball into an inkwell or put a football into his pocket.

50. Can get into bed and cover himself with the bedclothes.

31. Will be disturbed if, after turning away from two cherished objects (such as two pieces of cake) he turns back to find only one left.

18. Can open a door by turning an ordinary knob.

11. Responds to the direction "Shake hands" by holding out his hand.

3. Responds to the direction "Hold up your hand."

17. Can put on his hat.

40. Familiar and attractive food being on his plate, he will be able to put it in his mouth with a spoon.

1. Responds to the direction, "Stand up."

7. Responds to the direction, "Come here."

33. Can find his way to some very familiar place, such as the dining-room, his own bedroom or the bathroom.

26. Will not walk off a roof or wharf or the like where the distance to the ground or water is 20 feet or more.

10. Responds to the direction, "Come here, John" (supposing "John" to be his own name and assuming also that the person giving the direction is a familiar friend speaking in a pleasant voice, with a smile and with open arms, representing a very habitual situation to which approach has been the response).

23. Will go toward an object six feet off in case it is a familiar, attractive, desired object.

24. Will go around a familiar object, or push it out of his way, if it is movable, that is an obstacle in the way of his passage to some attractive, desired, familiar object which he is approaching.

16. Understands the meaning of "bad boy," spoken in a harsh voice with disapproving looks. (Use "girl" for "boy" in the case of a female.)

39. Familiar and attractive food being on his plate, he will be able to get it into his mouth somehow or other.

35. Being in the presence of some familiar source of great heat (wood fire, coal fire, gas flame, or the like, according to his environment), will not put his hand in it.

28. Will not try to eat a familiar nasty-tasting object, such as soap or ashes or a shoe.

14. Understands his own name so as at least to feel or think differently when it is spoken than when some other word is.

34. Being in the presence of some familiar, attractive, desired object, such as food when he is hungry, will go toward it rather than away from it.

41. Will bend his head or body to avoid a blow directed from in front straight at his nose.

32. Responds to his best and kindest friend, for example, mother or nurse, differently from his response to strangers.

27. Will not try to pull off his own fingers or toes.

38. Familiar and attractive food being offered him in a familiar way, will take it.

37. Having an object of bitter, nasty taste in his mouth, will spit it out more often than hold it there.

36. Having an object of sweet, pleasant taste in his mouth, will keep it there more often than spit it out.

A point somewhere between the last two tasks listed (36 and 37) and tasks 27 and 32 may fairly be taken to represent approximately zero intellectual difficulty, since tasks 36 and 37 are comparable to acts done by animals that cannot learn or can learn only in an infinitesimal way, and are done by human beings probably without any learning. Tasks 27 and 32 ("Will not try to pull off his own fingers or toes" and "Responds to his best and kindest friend

. . .'') are such as very dull animals can learn. Tasks 51, 52, 59, 60, 71, 72, 77, and 78 are a sampling from our level A. Tasks 55, 63, 65, 66, 74, 79, and 80 are a sampling from our level B. Tasks 57, 58, 69, 70, 75, 76, 81, and 82 are a sampling from our level C. We know from experiment the difference in difficulty between A and B, and between B and C. If we can measure the differences C–B and B–A, we have extended our scale to an approximate absolute zero. We make this measurement by measuring the following distances:

36, 37 to 27, 32, which are of nearly equal difficulty *inter se.*

27, 32 to 14, 28, 35, 39, which are of nearly equal difficulty *inter se.*

14, 28, 35, 39 to 10, 26, 33, which are of nearly equal difficulty *inter se.*

10, 26, 33 to 3, 11, 18, 31, 50, which are of nearly equal difficulty *inter se.*

 3, 11, 18, 31, 50 to 46, 49, which are of nearly equal difficulty *inter se.*

46, 49 to the level A tasks, which are of nearly equal difficulty *inter se.*

The level A to the level B tasks, which are of nearly equal difficulty *inter se.*

The level B to the level C tasks, which are of nearly equal difficulty *inter se.*

The measurements, in terms of the size of the minority (that is, the number of judges placing the one task as harder than the other, though it is in truth easier), are shown in Table 125. The corresponding distances in terms of the variability of expert opinion, assuming it to be of Form A, and taking 1.00 as its Q or Median Variation, are also given in Table 125.[5]

The difference between 36, 37, and A is 4.7 times the difference between A and C. The difference between 27, 32,

---

[5] These values will be in approximately the same proportions by any reasonable assumption about the form of the distribution, since we are using only minorities between 6 and 15 out of 40.

and A is 4 times the difference between A and C. We may then set the absolute zero of intellectual difficulty provisionally at A — 4.35 (C — A). C — A equals $5.28\sigma_{19}$ by the facts reported in Chapter IX, whereby zero is $23\sigma_{19}$ below A or A has a difficulty of $23\sigma_{19}$ measured from zero or just not any intellectual difficulty. We estimate the unreliability of this 23 due to the small number of judges as a probable error of about 2.

TABLE 125.

THE ESTIMATED DIFFERENCES IN DIFFICULTY OF INTELLECTUAL TASKS FROM ZERO DIFFICULTY TO THE DIFFICULTY OF COMPOSITE C.

|  |  | Average Minority | % | Difference in Difficulty |
|---|---|---|---|---|
| 36, 37, | to 27, 32, | 10.25 | 25.6 | .97 |
| 27, 32, | " 14, 28, 35, 39, | 9.75 | 24.4 | 1.03 |
| 14, 28, 35, 39, | " 10, 26, 33, | 10.33 | 25.7 | .97 |
| 10, 26, 33, | " 3, 11, 18, 31, 50 | 9.97 | 24.9 | 1.00 |
| 3, 11, 18, 31, 50 | " 46, 49, | 8.40 | 21.0 | 1.19 |
| 46, 49, | " A | 6.72 | 16.8 | 1.42 |
| A | " B[6] | 10.95 | 27.4 | .89 |
| B | " C[6] | 14.66 | 36.6 | .51 |
| 36, 37, | " A |  |  | 6.58 |
| 27, 32, | " A |  |  | 5.61 |
| A | " C |  |  | 1.40 |

We present all the facts concerning all the ratings in Table 126. The distance from zero to A can be determined *via* different tasks from those which we have used, but the result will be substantially the same provided that enough tasks are used to reduce the effect of chance.

[6] In the case of the A to B, and B to C comparisons, it would perhaps be better to use the median minority rather than the average minority, because of the irregularities in the separate comparisons. The two medians which would then replace 10.95 and 14.66 are 9.0 and 15.5. The differences in difficulty would then be 1.02 and .42, giving a total of 1.44 for the C–A difference in place of the 1.40. The end result is thus almost the same. If the median minority is used for the 46, 49 to A comparison, we have 6.75 in place of 6.72.

# TABLE 126.

The Number of Psychologists (out of 40) Judging a Certain Task to Be More Difficult Intellectually than a Certain Other, and the Number Judging the Two Tasks to Be Equally Difficult. The table reads: "Task 36 was judged harder than Task 37 by 13 and equal to it in difficulty by 7, Task 36 was judged harder than Task 38 by 2 and equal to it in difficulty by 3, Task 36 was judged harder than Task 27 by 10 and equal to it in difficulty by 2," and so on.

| | 37 | | 38 | | 27 | | 32 | | 41 | | 34 | | 14 | | 28 | | 35 | | 39 | | 16 | | 24 | | 23 | | 10 | | 26 | | 33 | | 7 | | 1 | |
|---|---|---|---|---|---|---|---|---|---|---|---|---|---|---|---|---|---|---|---|---|---|---|---|---|---|---|---|---|---|---|---|---|---|---|---|---|
| | > | = | > | = | > | = | > | = | > | = | > | = | > | = | > | = | > | = | > | = | > | = | > | = | > | = | > | = | > | = | > | = | > | = | > | = |
| 36 | 13 | 7 | 2 | 3 | 10 | 2 | 6 | 1 | 6 | 1 | 3 | | 2 | | 4 | 1 | 6 | | 1 | 1 | 1 | 1 | 2 | | 3 | | | | | | | | | | | |
| 37 | | | 6 | 2 | 12 | 2 | 10 | 1 | 6 | 1 | 5 | | 2 | | 6 | 1 | 6 | | 3 | | 2 | 1 | 3 | | 4 | | | | | | | | | | | |
| 38 | | | | | 20 | 1 | 22 | 2 | 15 | 1 | 11 | 2 | 7 | 2 | 11 | 3 | 12 | 1 | 1 | 2 | 7 | 1 | 4 | | 5 | | | | | | | | | | | |
| 27 | | | | | | | 22 | 1 | 18 | | 15 | | 12 | | 11 | | 11 | | 15 | | 12 | 1 | 9 | 1 | 11 | | | | | | | | | | | |
| 32 | | | | | | | | | 19 | | 12 | | 2 | 1 | 10 | | 9 | | 7 | | 1 | 2 | 2 | | 3 | | | | | | | | | | | |
| 41 | | | | | | | | | | | 23 | 1 | 18 | | 16 | | 16 | 1 | 17 | | 15 | 1 | 15 | | 15 | | 3 | 2 | 8 | 1 | 4 | 2 | 3 | | 1 | 1 |
| 34 | | | | | | | | | | | | | 12 | 2 | 14 | 3 | 14 | 4 | 7 | 3 | 13 | | 4 | 4 | 5 | 4 | 6 | 1 | 11 | 1 | 13 | | 2 | | 3 | 1 |
| 14 | | | | | | | | | | | | | | | 21 | 2 | 17 | 2 | 20 | 2 | 16 | 1 | 13 | 1 | 17 | 1 | 11 | 1 | 8 | 1 | 7 | 1 | 7 | | 4 | 1 |
| 28 | | | | | | | | | | | | | | | | | 20 | 5 | 15 | 4 | 14 | | 13 | 2 | 16 | 2 | 8 | 2 | 11 | 2 | 9 | 1 | 7 | | 4 | 1 |
| 35 | | | | | | | | | | | | | | | | | | | 17 | 3 | 16 | | 12 | 3 | 14 | 3 | | | | | | | | | | |
| 39 | | | | | | | | | | | | | | | | | | | | | 17 | | 15 | 2 | 15 | 2 | 10 | 1 | 15 | 1 | 9 | 1 | 7 | | 5 | 2 |
| 16 | | | | | | | | | | | | | | | | | | | | | | | 18 | | 20 | 1 | 11 | 1 | 18 | 1 | 17 | | 7 | | 5 | |
| 24 | | | | | | | | | | | | | | | | | | | | | | | | | 29 | 4 | 12 | 2 | 16 | 2 | 11 | 2 | 8 | | 7 | 1 |
| 23 | | | | | | | | | | | | | | | | | | | | | | | | | | | 10 | 2 | 14 | 2 | 4 | 1 | 4 | | 2 | 1 |
| 10 | | | | | | | | | | | | | | | | | | | | | | | | | | | | | 18 | 1 | 17 | | 3 | 3 | 8 | 3 |
| 26 | | | | | | | | | | | | | | | | | | | | | | | | | | | | | | | 19 | | 17 | | 13 | 1 |
| 33 | | | | | | | | | | | | | | | | | | | | | | | | | | | | | | | | | 18 | | 14 | |
| 7 | | | | | | | | | | | | | | | | | | | | | | | | | | | | | | | | | | | 13 | |

## TABLE 126—(Continued).

| | 40 ≧= | 17 ≧= | 3 ≧= | 11 ≧= | 18 ≧= | 31 ≧= | 50 ≧= | 29 ≧= | 42 ≧= | 4 ≧= | 5 ≧= | 46 ≧= | 49 ≧= | 45 ≧= | 51 ≧= | 52 ≧= | 59 ≧= | 60 ≧= |
|---|---|---|---|---|---|---|---|---|---|---|---|---|---|---|---|---|---|---|
| 10 | 13 1 | 12 2 | 5 1 | 4 1 | 10 | 9 | 6 | 5 2 | 2 2 | 2 | 3 | 5 | 4 | 4 | | | | |
| 26 | 17 | 14 1 | 10 | 10 | 12 | 12 | 11 | 13 | 9 | 10 | 9 | 3 | 4 | 1 | | | | |
| 33 | 13 | 14 | 14 | 12 1 | 11 | 10 1 | 10 2 | 8 | 7 | 5 1 | 7 | 1 | 1 | 1 | | | | |
| 7 | 19 1 | 16 | 9 2 | 9 1 | 14 | 11 1 | 12 | 10 2 | 4 1 | 2 | 3 1 | | | | | | | |
| 1 | 21 1 | 20 2 | 10 3 | 10 2 | 15 1 | 13 | 2 | 12 1 | 4 | 3 1 | 3 1 | 3 | 3 | 1 | | | | |
| 40 | | 15 2 | 16 1 | 12 2 | 14 1 | 10 1 | 4 | 13 1 | 7 | 9 | 9 1 | 3 | 2 | 3 | | | | |
| 17 | | | 15 2 | 14 2 | 11 3 | 15 | 9 1 | 16 1 | 7 | 10 | 11 | 4 | 4 | 3 | | | | |
| 3 | | | | 18 2 | 17 2 | 13 | 14 1 | 16 | 11 1 | 6 1 | 6 1 | 6 | 5 | 3 | | | | |
| 11 | | | | | 20 1 | 15 | 19 2 | 18 | 11 1 | 10 1 | 10 1 | 9 | 8 | 3 1 | | | | |
| 18 | | | | | | 17 | 14 2 | 18 2 | 10 1 | 14 | 14 | 4 1 | 3 1 | 3 1 | | | | |
| 31 | | | | | | | 19 | 18 2 | 20 | 21 | 21 1 | 12 | 13 | 7 1 | | | | |
| 50 | | | | | | | | 22 1 | 18 | 16 1 | 17 | 12 | 11 | 6 | | | | |
| 29 | | | | | | | | | 15 | 18 | 18 1 | 7 | 7 | 5 | | | | |
| 42 | | | | | | | | | | 23 | 22 1 | 4 4 | 5 4 | 2 1 | | | | |
| 4 | | | | | | | | | | | 21 6 | 8 | 10 1 | 8 | 1 | | 6 | 4 |
| 5 | | | | | | | | | | | | 7 | 9 1 | 7 | 1 | 1 | 5 | 4 |
| 46 | | | | | | | | | | | | | 20 8 | 10 | 12 1 | 6 1 | 7 | 8 |
| 49 | | | | | | | | | | | | | | 8 | 8 | 5 | 6 | 6 |
| 45 | | | | | | | | | | | | | | | 20 | 16 1 | 12 3 | 2 2 |

TABLE 126—(Concluded).

| | 71 | | 72 | | 77 | | 78 | | 55 | | 63 | | 65 | | 66 | | 74 | | 79 | | 80 | | 57 | | 58 | | 69 | | 70 | | 75 | | 76 | | 81 | | 82 | |
|---|---|---|---|---|---|---|---|---|---|---|---|---|---|---|---|---|---|---|---|---|---|---|---|---|---|---|---|---|---|---|---|---|---|---|---|---|---|---|
| | > | = | > | = | > | = | > | = | > | = | > | = | > | = | > | = | > | = | > | = | > | = | > | = | > | = | > | = | > | = | > | = | > | = | > | = | > | = |
| 4 | | | 1 | | 5 | | 5 | | | | | | | | | | | | | | | | | | | | | | | | | | | | | | | |
| 5 | | | 1 | | 5 | | 5 | | | | | | | | | | | | | | | | | | | | | | | | | | | | | | | |
| 46 | 3 | | 4 | | 7 | | 9 | | | | | | | | | | | | | | | | | | | | | | | | | | | | | | | |
| 49 | 4 | | 4 | | 8 | | 9 | | | | | | | | | | | | | | | | | | | | | | | | | | | | | | | |
| 45 | 12 | | 13 | | 18 | 1 | 17 | 1 | | | | | | | | | | | | | | | | | | | | | | | | | | | | | | |
| 51 | | | | | | | | | 1 | 1 | 24 | | 5 | 1 | 9 | | 2 | | 15 | 1 | 10 | | | | | | | | | | | | | | | | | |
| 52 | | | | | | | | | 2 | | 27 | | 7 | | 11 | | 1 | | 19 | | 15 | | | | | | | | | | | | | | | | | |
| 59 | | | | | | | | | 7 | | 22 | 2 | 3 | | 6 | 1 | 1 | | 14 | | 9 | | | | | | | | | | | | | | | | | |
| 60 | | | | | | | | | 14 | | 26 | 1 | 4 | | 7 | | 2 | 1 | 18 | | 12 | 1 | | | | | | | | | | | | | | | | |
| 71 | | | | | | | | | 11 | | 33 | | 9 | | 15 | | 1 | 1 | 19 | | 14 | 2 | | | | | | | | | | | | | | | | |
| 72 | | | | | | | | | 9 | 1 | 33 | | 8 | | 15 | | 1 | 1 | 18 | | 15 | 1 | | | | | | | | | | | | | | | | |
| 77 | | | | | | | | | 5 | 2 | 25 | | 7 | | 10 | | 5 | | 3 | 4 | 1 | 1 | | | | | | | | | | | | | | | | |
| 78 | | | | | | | | | 4 | 2 | 26 | | 7 | | 9 | | 4 | | 3 | | 1 | 2 | | | | | | | | | | | | | | | | |
| 55 | | | | | | | | | | | | | | | | | | | | | | | 15 | 1 | 17 | | 18 | | 16 | | 16 | | 2 | 1 | 17 | | 21 | |
| 63 | | | | | | | | | | | | | | | | | | | | | | | 2 | | 4 | | 7 | | 8 | | 8 | 1 | | | 8 | | 10 | |
| 65 | | | | | | | | | | | | | | | | | | | | | | | 24 | | 23 | 1 | 27 | | 23 | | 25 | | 5 | | 19 | 2 | 25 | |
| 66 | | | | | | | | | | | | | | | | | | | | | | | 19 | | 16 | | 20 | 1 | 14 | 2 | 17 | | 6 | | 16 | 1 | 17 | 1 |
| 74 | | | | | | | | | | | | | | | | | | | | | | | 26 | 1 | 27 | | 27 | | 23 | | 30 | 1 | 2 | 1 | 22 | | 24 | |
| 79 | | | | | | | | | | | | | | | | | | | | | | | 11 | | 9 | | 15 | | 13 | | 11 | | 2 | | 5 | | 5 | |
| 80 | | | | | | | | | | | | | | | | | | | | | | | 15 | 1 | 13 | | 16 | | 15 | | 14 | | 2 | | 8 | 2 | 14 | 1 |

# CHAPTER XI

## THE MEASUREMENT OF THE ALTITUDE OF AN INDIVIDUAL INTELLECT

It will, of course, very rarely happen that an individual will have exactly twenty single tasks right out of the forty in any composite. We have to estimate the level at which he would have exactly fifty percent right from such a record as that shown below.

| Composite Difficulty | I | J | K | L | M | N | O | P | Q |
|---|---|---|---|---|---|---|---|---|---|
| Numbers Correct | | | 24 | 18 | 11 | 8 | 1 | | |

We may use all or part of his record, bearing in mind that percents near zero and 100 (that is, numbers right out of forty near zero and forty) are of less value than those nearer 50 percent. To use his record most effectively we need to know the general form of the curve (especially near the 50 percent point) and to perform the equivalent of plotting the particular curve of this general form which best fits the observations. We have determined the general form of the curve from 10 percent of successes to 90 percent of successes by the method described below.

### THE FORM OF THE CURVE OF PERCENT CORRECT IN RELATION TO DIFFICULTY

All the cases of group 17 and 13 are grouped into five groups according to their general altitude as shown by the sum of their scores (number right) in N, O, P, and Q.

The median score at each of the four levels for each of the five groups is computed; and the five curves are drawn. They appear in Fig. 38.

These curves are subject to a very slight error due to the fact that they were computed using a value 41.9 for the difficulty of composite P, which was later found to be 0.1 off from the correct value (41.8). The difference to the general argument is so trifling that we have not recomputed the measures or redrawn the curves.

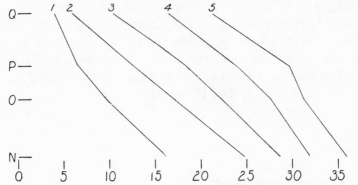

FIG. 38. Curves of percent correct in relation to difficulty; Groups 13 and 17.

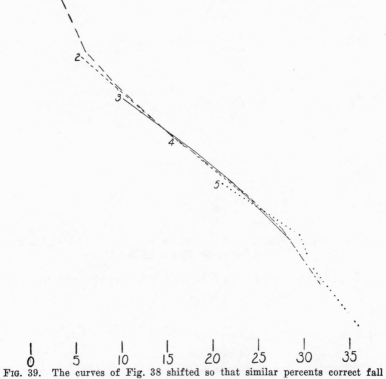

FIG. 39. The curves of Fig. 38 shifted so that similar percents correct fall approximately on the same points.

The four curves other than that for the middle group are then shifted up or down until each fits the curve for the middle group as closely as may be for such part of the range from zero to forty correct as they have in common. The result is shown in Fig. 39. A curve (Fig. 40) representing the central tendency of all the five in Fig. 39 is drawn. Fig. 40 represents the most probable general form of the curve of decrease in percentage correct with increase in difficulty so far as groups 17 and 13 reveal it.

FIG. 40. The probable form of the decrease in percent correct with increase in difficulty, for Groups 13 and 17.

Fig. 40 has heights as follows (in terms of tenths of $\sigma_{19}$):

   5 correct, $+ 30\frac{1}{2}$.
  10 correct, $+ 16$
  15 correct, $+ 7\frac{1}{2}$
  20 correct,    $0.$
  25 correct, $- 9.$
  30 correct, $- 18.$
  35 correct, $- 31\frac{1}{2}.$

All the cases of group 9I are grouped into five groups according to the sum of their scores in I, J, K, L, and M. The median score at each of the five levels is computed for each of the five groups; and the five curves are drawn. They appear in Fig. 41, being curves 6, 7, 8, 9, and 10.

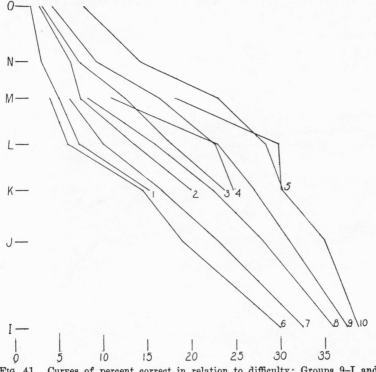

FIG. 41.   Curves of percent correct in relation to difficulty; Groups 9–I and 9–II.

The four curves for 9I other than that for the middle group are then shifted up or down until each fits the curve for the middle group as closely as may be for such part of the range from zero to forty correct as they have in common. The result is shown in Fig. 42. A curve (Fig. 44a) representing the central tendency of all the five in Fig. 42 is drawn.

All the cases of group 9II are grouped into five groups according to the sum of their scores in K, L, M, N, and O. The median score at each of the five levels is computed for each of the five groups; and the five curves are drawn. They appear in Fig. 41, being curves 1, 2, 3, 4, and 5.

The four curves for 9II other than that for the middle group are then shifted up or down until each fits the curve

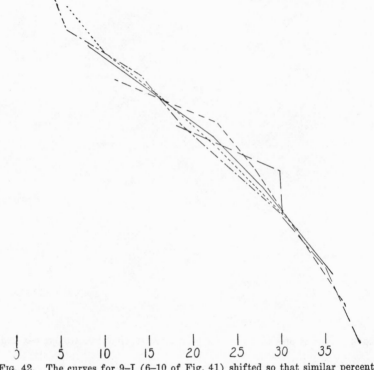

FIG. 42.  The curves for 9–I (6–10 of Fig. 41) shifted so that similar percents correct fall approximately on the same points.

for the middle group as closely as may be for such part of the range from zero to forty correct as they have in common. The result is shown in Fig. 43. A curve (Fig. 44b) representing the central tendency of all the five in Fig. 43 is drawn. The curve of Fig. 44b is then shifted down so as to fit Fig. 44a over that part of the range which they have in common and an average of the two is drawn.   This is Fig. 45, which represents the most probable general form of the curve of decrease in number correct with increase in difficulty so far as groups 9I and 9II reveal it.

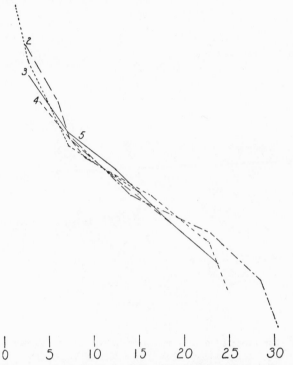

FIG. 43.   The curves for 9–II (1–5 of Fig. 41) shifted so that similar percents correct fall approximately on the same points.

This curve has heights as follows (in terms of tenths of $\sigma_{19}$):

5 correct, $+ 28.$
10 correct, $+ 15.$
15 correct, $+ \ 8.$
20 correct, $\quad 0.$
25 correct, $- \ 8.$
30 correct, $-18.$
35 correct, $-32.$

25

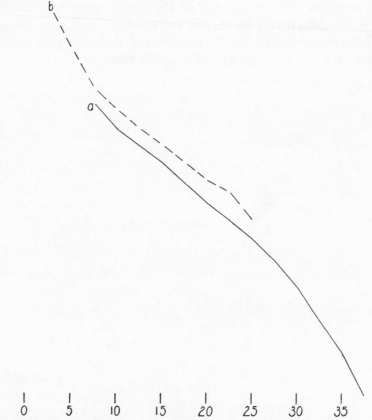

FIG. 44. The central tendency of the five curves of Fig. 42 (a), and the central tendency of the five curves of Fig. 43 (b).

Fig. 40 and Fig. 45 are very closely alike in form, and each is well represented by a curve with heights (in terms of tenths of $\sigma_{19}$) as follows:

$$5 \text{ correct}, \ + 30.$$
$$10 \text{ correct}, \ + 18.$$
$$15 \text{ correct}, \ + \ 8.$$
$$20 \text{ correct}, \ \ \ 0.$$
$$25 \text{ correct}, \ - \ 8.$$
$$30 \text{ correct}, \ - 18.$$
$$35 \text{ correct}, \ - 30.$$

All the cases of Groups 4 and 5 are grouped into six groups according to the sum of their scores in H, I, J, and

K. The six curves are drawn (Fig. 46), and shifted up or down so that similar numbers correct fall on approximately

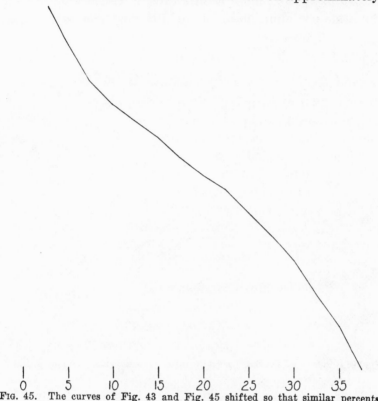

FIG. 45. The curves of Fig. 43 and Fig. 45 shifted so that similar percents correct fall approximately on the same points.

the same points (Fig. 47), and combined to form a curve (Fig. 48) representing the central tendency for number correct in relation to increase in difficulty in the same way that Fig. 40 was formed from the facts of Fig. 38. This curve has heights as follows (in terms of tenths of $\sigma_{19}$) :

5 correct, $+ 28\frac{1}{2}$.

10 correct, $+ 15\frac{1}{2}$.

15 correct, $+ 6\frac{1}{2}$.

20 correct, 0.

25 correct, $- 7$.

30 correct, $- 14$.

35 correct, $- 24\frac{1}{2}$.

The cases of Group im3 are grouped into five groups according to the sum of their scores in A, B, C, and D; and the same procedure followed as hitherto. The facts appear

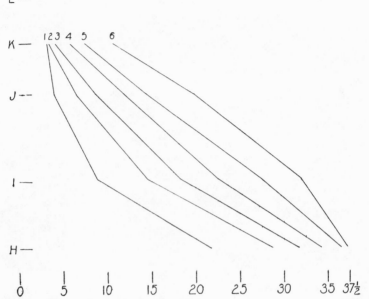

FIG. 46.   Curves of percent correct in relation to difficulty; Groups 4 and 5.

in Figs. 49, 50, and 51. Fig. 51 has heights as follows (in terms of tenths of $\sigma_{19}$):

$$5 \text{ correct, } + 34\tfrac{1}{2}.$$
$$10 \text{ correct, } + 21.$$
$$15 \text{ correct, } + 9\tfrac{1}{2}.$$
$$20 \text{ correct, } \quad 0.$$
$$25 \text{ correct, } - 9\tfrac{1}{2}.$$
$$30 \text{ correct, } - 22.$$
$$35 \text{ correct, } - 36.$$

The cases of Group im6 are grouped into three groups according to the sum of their scores in C, D, E, F, and G; and the same procedure followed. The facts appear in

Figs. 52, 53, and 54.   Fig. 54 has heights as follows (in terms of tenths of $\sigma_{19}$):

5 correct,  + 16.
10 correct,  + 11.
15 correct,  +  6.
20 correct,    0.
25 correct,  —  $6\frac{1}{2}$.
30 correct,  — $15\frac{1}{2}$.
35 correct,  — $31\frac{1}{2}$ (approx.)

The facts whence Figs. 38 to 54 are derived are presented in Table 127.

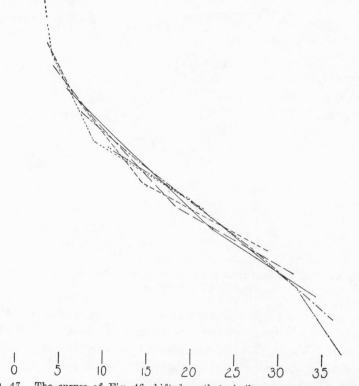

IG. 47.   The curves of Fig. 46 shifted so that similar percents correct fall on approximately the same points.

From Composite Q down to Composite I, or from the College-Graduate group down through Grade 5, there is a notable similarity not only in the shape but also in the amount of slope of the curves. From 5 correct to 35 correct equals $6.2\sigma_{19}$ at or near Composites O and P, $6.0\sigma_{19}$ at or near Composites L and M, and $5.3\sigma_{19}$ at or near Composites J and K. At lower levels there is considerable

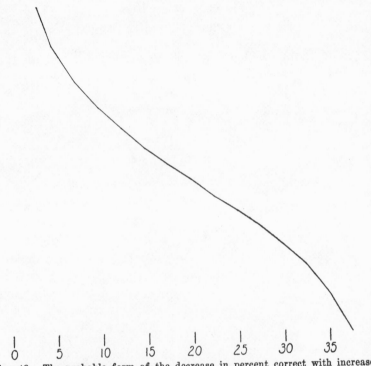

FIG. 48. The probable form of the decrease in percent correct with increase in difficulty, for Groups 4 and 5.

disparity, the spread around Composites B and C being $7.0\sigma_{19}$, while that around Composites E, F, and G is only about $4.8\sigma_{19}$. The determinations around levels A to G are much less reliable than those from I to Q. A combination of Figs. 51 and 54 with equal weight gives (in terms of tenths of $\sigma_{19}$) $+25, +16, +8, 0, -8, -19,$ and $-34$, with a spread of $5.9\sigma_{19}$.

ESTIMATING THE CAVD ALTITUDE OF AN INDIVIDUAL

From I to Q the altitude at which an individual will have exactly twenty right out of forty can be estimated from Table 128, which approximately represents a curve of the general form of Figs. 40, 45, and 48, running from $+ 3.0\sigma_{19}$ at 5 correct to $- 3.0\sigma_{19}$ at 35 correct.

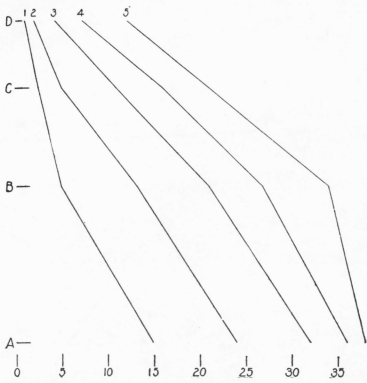

FIG. 49.  Curves of percent correct in relation to difficulty; Group im 3.

Table 129 is a similar table for Composites A to H, which may be used provisionally until the difficulties of these tasks and the nature of the relation between difficulty and number correct at these levels are more accurately determined.

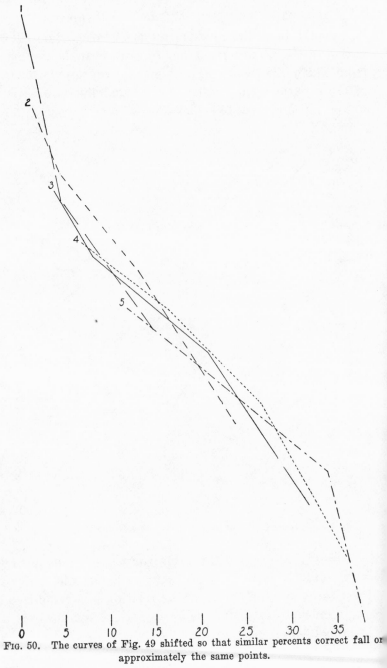

FIG. 50.   The curves of Fig. 49 shifted so that similar percents correct fall or approximately the same points.

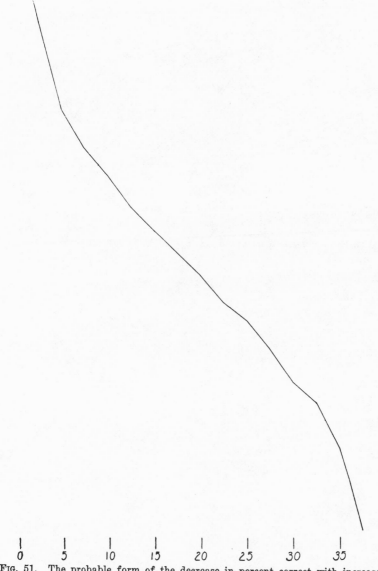

|   |   |   |   |   |   |   |   |
|---|---|---|---|---|---|---|---|
| 0 | 5 | 10 | 15 | 20 | 25 | 30 | 35 |

FIG. 51.  The probable form of the decrease in percent correct with increase in difficulty, for Group im 3.

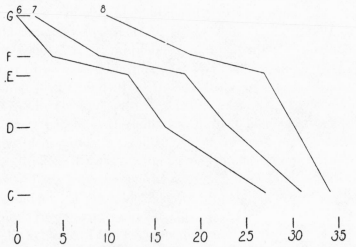

FIG. 52. Curves of percent correct in relation to difficulty: Group im 6.

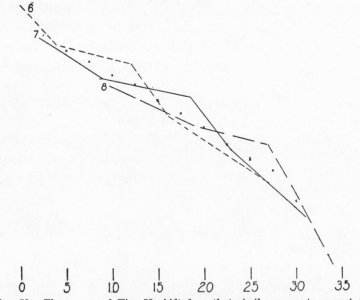

FIG. 53. The curves of Fig. 52 shifted so that similar percents correct fall on approximately the same points.

Any 40-composite task at which an individual has more than zero and less than forty of the single tasks correct can be used to estimate the level or altitude at which he would probably have exactly 20 right.  Scores near zero or forty deserve, however, relatively little weight, because the former are so much affected by chance successes in the case of the vocabulary tasks, and the latter are so much affected by careless slips.

A simple and impartial procedure which works very well in general is to utilize for any individual the three succes-

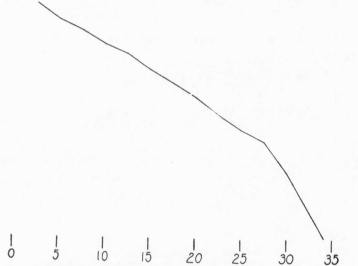

FIG. 54.   The probable form of the decrease in percent correct with increase in difficulty, for Group im 6.

sive levels whose sum of rights is nearest to 60, and to attach equal weight to each of them.  This is the procedure used in all the measurements of altitude which are reported in later chapters.

A possibly better procedure is to take the two successive levels whose sum of rights is nearest 40, and the neighboring level above or below which is nearest 20.  This seems to be somewhat quicker in operation, and is less likely to include levels with extremely low or high percents correct.

TABLE 127.

MEDIAN OF THE SCORES (NUMBER RIGHT OUT OF 40) FOR EACH OF TWENTY-NINE GROUPS WITH EACH OF FOUR OR MORE NEIGHBORING COMPOSITES.

| Group | A | B | C | D | E | F | G | H | I | J | K | L | M | N | O | P | Q |
|---|---|---|---|---|---|---|---|---|---|---|---|---|---|---|---|---|---|
| im3a | 15 | 5 | 2.5 | 1 | | | | | | | | | | | | | |
| b | 24 | 13.1 | 5 | 2 | | | | | | | | | | | | | |
| c | 32 | 21 | 11 | 4.3 | | | | | | | | | | | | | |
| d | 36 | 26.8 | 16 | 7.3 | | | | | | | | | | | | | |
| e | 38 | 34 | 21 | 12.2 | | | | | | | | | | | | | |
| im6a | | | 27 | 16.2 | 12.2 | 4 | 0 | | | | | | | | | | |
| b | | | 31 | 22.9 | 18.3 | 9 | 2 | | | | | | | | | | |
| c | | | 34 | 30.3 | 27 | 19 | 9.8 | | | | | | | | | | |
| 4 + 5a | | | | | | | | 21.7 | 8.9 | 4.1 | 3.3 | | | | | | |
| b | | | | | | | | 28.8 | 14.6 | 6.5 | 3.4 | | | | | | |
| c | | | | | | | | 32.7 | 18.3 | 8.8 | 4.2 | | | | | | |
| d | | | | | | | | 34.3 | 22.6 | 11.9 | 5.8 | | | | | | |
| e | | | | | | | | 36.6 | 27.4 | 14.4 | 7.5 | | | | | | |
| f | | | | | | | | 37.4 | 32.0 | 19.9 | 10.7 | | | | | | |
| 9Ia | | | | | | | | | 30.0 | 19 | 14.5 | 6 | 4.0 | | | | |
| b | | | | | | | | | 32.5 | 23 | 16.7 | 10 | 6.2 | | | | |
| c | | | | | | | | | 36.0 | 28 | 22.4 | 16 | 8.3 | | | | |
| d | | | | | | | | | 37.5 | 31 | 27.3 | 23 | 11.0 | | | | |
| e | | | | | | | | | 39.0 | 35 | 30.3 | 30 | 18.3 | | | | |
| 9IIa | | | | | | | | | | | 15.3 | 7.3 | 5.0 | 3.0 | 1.7 | | |
| b | | | | | | | | | | | 20.0 | 13.5 | 7.3 | 6.3 | 2.7 | | |
| c | | | | | | | | | | | 23.8 | 17.8 | 12.6 | 7.3 | 3.0 | | |
| d | | | | | | | | | | | 24.8 | 22.8 | 16.5 | 9.3 | 4.3 | | |
| e | | | | | | | | | | | 30.4 | 28.5 | 23.2 | 14.4 | 7.9 | | |
| 13 + 17a | | | | | | | | | | | | | | 16.3 | 9.7 | 6.5 | 4.0 |
| b | | | | | | | | | | | | | | 24.8 | 17.2 | 12.5 | 6.0 |
| | | | | | | | | | | | | | | 28.7 | 22.6 | 18.4 | 10.5 |
| | | | | | | | | | | | | | | | 27.7 | 24.0 | 16.5 |

TABLE 128.

ALTITUDES CORRESPONDING TO ANY NUMBER CORRECT FROM 5 TO 35 OUT OF 40 FOR TASKS I TO Q.

|    | I | J | K | L | M | N | O | P | Q |
|----|------|------|------|------|------|------|------|------|------|
| 5  | 31.2 | 33.1 | 34.2 | 35.2 | 36.2 | 37.0 | 38.2 | 38.8 | 40.0 |
| 6  | 31.4 | 33.3 | 34.4 | 35.4 | 36.4 | 37.2 | 38.4 | 39.0 | 40.2 |
| 7  | 31.7 | 33.6 | 34.7 | 35.7 | 36.7 | 37.5 | 38.7 | 39.3 | 40.5 |
| 8  | 31.9 | 33.8 | 34.9 | 35.9 | 36.9 | 37.7 | 38.9 | 39.5 | 40.7 |
| 9  | 32.2 | 34.1 | 35.2 | 36.2 | 37.2 | 38.0 | 39.2 | 39.8 | 41.0 |
| 10 | 32.4 | 34.3 | 35.4 | 36.4 | 37.4 | 38.2 | 39.4 | 40.0 | 41.2 |
| 11 | 32.6 | 34.5 | 35.6 | 36.6 | 37.6 | 38.4 | 39.6 | 40.2 | 41.4 |
| 12 | 32.8 | 34.7 | 35.8 | 36.8 | 37.8 | 38.6 | 39.8 | 40.4 | 41.6 |
| 13 | 33.0 | 34.9 | 36.0 | 37.0 | 38.0 | 38.8 | 40.0 | 40.6 | 41.8 |
| 14 | 33.2 | 35.1 | 36.2 | 37.2 | 38.2 | 39.0 | 40.2 | 40.8 | 42.0 |
| 15 | 33.4 | 35.3 | 36.4 | 37.4 | 38.4 | 39.2 | 40.4 | 41.0 | 42.2 |
| 16 | 33.6 | 35.5 | 36.6 | 37.6 | 38.6 | 39.4 | 40.6 | 41.2 | 42.4 |
| 17 | 33.7 | 35.6 | 36.7 | 37.7 | 38.7 | 39.5 | 40.7 | 41.3 | 42.5 |
| 18 | 33.9 | 35.8 | 36.9 | 37.9 | 38.9 | 39.7 | 40.9 | 41.5 | 42.7 |
| 19 | 34.0 | 35.9 | 37.0 | 38.0 | 39.0 | 39.8 | 41.0 | 41.6 | 42.8 |
| 20 | 34.2 | 36.1 | 37.2 | 38.2 | 39.2 | 40.0 | 41.2 | 41.8 | 43.0 |
| 21 | 34.4 | 36.3 | 37.4 | 38.4 | 39.4 | 40.2 | 41.4 | 42.0 | 43.2 |
| 22 | 34.5 | 36.4 | 37.5 | 38.5 | 39.5 | 40.3 | 41.5 | 42.1 | 43.3 |
| 23 | 34.7 | 36.6 | 37.7 | 38.7 | 39.7 | 40.5 | 41.7 | 42.3 | 43.5 |
| 24 | 34.8 | 36.7 | 37.8 | 38.8 | 39.8 | 40.6 | 41.8 | 42.4 | 43.6 |
| 25 | 35.0 | 36.9 | 38.0 | 39.0 | 40.0 | 40.8 | 42.0 | 42.6 | 43.8 |
| 26 | 35.2 | 37.1 | 38.2 | 39.2 | 40.2 | 41.0 | 42.2 | 42.8 | 44.0 |
| 27 | 35.4 | 37.3 | 38.4 | 39.4 | 40.4 | 41.2 | 42.4 | 43.0 | 44.2 |
| 28 | 35.6 | 37.5 | 38.6 | 39.6 | 40.6 | 41.4 | 42.6 | 43.2 | 44.4 |
| 29 | 35.8 | 37.7 | 38.8 | 39.8 | 40.8 | 41.6 | 42.8 | 43.4 | 44.6 |
| 30 | 36.0 | 37.9 | 39.0 | 40.0 | 41.0 | 41.8 | 43.0 | 43.6 | 44.8 |
| 31 | 36.2 | 38.1 | 39.2 | 40.2 | 41.2 | 42.0 | 43.2 | 43.8 | 45.0 |
| 32 | 36.5 | 38.4 | 39.5 | 40.5 | 41.5 | 42.3 | 43.5 | 44.1 | 45.3 |
| 33 | 36.7 | 38.6 | 39.7 | 40.7 | 41.7 | 42.5 | 43.7 | 44.3 | 45.5 |
| 34 | 37.0 | 38.9 | 40.0 | 41.0 | 42.0 | 42.8 | 44.0 | 44.6 | 45.8 |
| 35 | 37.2 | 39.1 | 40.2 | 41.2 | 42.2 | 43.0 | 44.2 | 44.8 | 46.0 |

In the rare cases where it is desirable to estimate altitude from a score below 5 or above 35, the following may be used: For 1, 2, 3 and 4, subtract 4.3, 3.9, 3.6 and 3.3 respectively from the score for 20. For 36, 37, 38 and 39, add 3.3, 3.6, 3.9 and 4.3 respectively to the score for 20.

TABLE 129.

APPROXIMATE PROVISIONAL ALTITUDES CORRESPONDING TO ANY NUMBER CORRECT FROM 5 TO 35 OUT OF 40 FOR TASKS A TO H.

|    | A | B | C | D | E | F | G | H |
|----|------|------|------|------|------|------|------|------|
| 5  | 20.0 | 23.2 | 25.3 | 26.7 | 27.8 | 28.3 | 29.0 | 29.8 |
| 6  | 20.2 | 23.4 | 25.5 | 26.9 | 28.0 | 28.5 | 29.2 | 30.0 |
| 7  | 20.5 | 23.7 | 25.8 | 27.2 | 28.3 | 28.8 | 29.5 | 30.3 |
| 8  | 20.7 | 23.9 | 26.0 | 27.4 | 28.5 | 29.0 | 29.7 | 30.5 |
| 9  | 21.0 | 24.2 | 26.3 | 27.7 | 28.8 | 29.3 | 30.0 | 30.8 |
| 10 | 21.2 | 24.4 | 26.5 | 27.9 | 29.0 | 29.5 | 30.2 | 31.0 |
| 11 | 21.4 | 24.6 | 26.7 | 28.1 | 29.2 | 29.7 | 30.4 | 31.2 |
| 12 | 21.6 | 24.8 | 26.9 | 28.3 | 29.4 | 29.9 | 30.6 | 31.4 |
| 13 | 21.8 | 25.0 | 27.1 | 28.5 | 29.6 | 30.1 | 30.8 | 31.6 |
| 14 | 22.0 | 25.2 | 27.3 | 28.7 | 29.8 | 30.3 | 31.0 | 31.8 |
| 15 | 22.2 | 25.4 | 27.5 | 28.9 | 30.0 | 30.5 | 31.2 | 32.0 |
| 16 | 22.4 | 25.6 | 27.7 | 29.1 | 30.2 | 30.7 | 31.4 | 32.2 |
| 17 | 22.5 | 25.7 | 27.8 | 29.2 | 30.3 | 30.8 | 31.5 | 32.3 |
| 18 | 22.7 | 25.9 | 28.0 | 29.4 | 30.5 | 31.0 | 31.7 | 32.5 |
| 19 | 22.8 | 26.0 | 28.1 | 29.5 | 30.6 | 31.1 | 31.8 | 32.6 |
| 20 | 23.0 | 26.2 | 28.3 | 29.7 | 30.8 | 31.3 | 32.0 | 32.8 |
| 21 | 23.2 | 26.4 | 28.5 | 29.9 | 31.0 | 31.5 | 32.2 | 33.0 |
| 22 | 23.3 | 26.5 | 28.6 | 30.0 | 31.1 | 31.6 | 32.3 | 33.1 |
| 23 | 23.5 | 26.7 | 28.8 | 30.2 | 31.3 | 31.8 | 32.5 | 33.3 |
| 24 | 23.6 | 26.8 | 28.9 | 30.3 | 31.4 | 31.9 | 32.6 | 33.4 |
| 25 | 23.8 | 27.0 | 29.1 | 30.5 | 31.6 | 32.1 | 32.8 | 33.6 |
| 26 | 24.0 | 27.2 | 29.3 | 30.7 | 31.8 | 32.3 | 33.0 | 33.8 |
| 27 | 24.2 | 27.4 | 29.5 | 30.9 | 32.0 | 32.5 | 33.2 | 34.0 |
| 28 | 24.4 | 27.6 | 29.7 | 31.1 | 32.2 | 32.7 | 33.4 | 34.2 |
| 29 | 24.6 | 27.8 | 29.9 | 31.3 | 32.4 | 32.9 | 33.6 | 34.4 |
| 30 | 24.8 | 28.0 | 30.1 | 31.5 | 32.6 | 33.1 | 33.8 | 34.6 |
| 31 | 25.0 | 28.2 | 30.3 | 31.7 | 32.8 | 33.3 | 34.0 | 34.8 |
| 32 | 25.3 | 28.5 | 30.6 | 32.0 | 33.1 | 33.6 | 34.3 | 35.1 |
| 33 | 25.5 | 28.7 | 30.8 | 32.2 | 33.3 | 33.8 | 34.5 | 35.3 |
| 34 | 25.8 | 29.0 | 31.1 | 32.5 | 33.6 | 34.1 | 34.8 | 35.6 |
| 35 | 26.0 | 29.2 | 31.3 | 32.7 | 33.8 | 34.3 | 35.0 | 35.8 |

# CHAPTER XII

THE MEASUREMENT OF WIDTH AND AREA OF INTELLECT

The width or range of intellect at any altitude or level of difficulty is measured by the number of tasks mastered at that altitude. Thus, suppose that Intellect X is measured with ten 40-composite tasks ($N_1$, $N_2$, $N_3$, etc.), each equal to Composite N in difficulty; and has the following score:

Number of single tasks right in $N_1 = 20$.
"      "      "      "      "      " $N_2 = 19$.
"      "      "      "      "      " $N_3 = 21$.
"      "      "      "      "      " $N_4 = 20$.
"      "      "      "      "      " $N_5 = 20$.
"      "      "      "      "      " $N_6 = 18$.
"      "      "      "      "      " $N_7 = 19$.
"      "      "      "      "      " $N_8 = 21$.
"      "      "      "      "      " $N_9 = 22$.
"      "      "      "      "      " $N_{10} = 20$.

Success at one of these 40-composite tasks means attaining 20 or more single tasks correct. The width of Intellect X at Altitude N is 7 out of 10 for Tasks $N_1$ to $N_{10}$. It may also under certain conditions be considered as 200 out of 400 for the single tasks composing $N_1$ to $N_{10}$, or as a certain number out of 40 for the same single tasks grouped in 10-composites, or as a certain number out of 100 for the same tasks grouped in 4-composites.

## WIDTH OF INTELLECT IN THE CASE OF TRULY INTELLECTUAL TASKS

Consider first the first and most correct meaning, that is, the number of composite-tasks correct, here 7 out of 10 for Tasks $N_1$ to $N_{10}$. If the ten are a representative sampling of tasks of intellectual difficulty N, Intellect X may be expected to have approximately 70 successes out of 100, or 700 out of 1,000, or in general approximately 70 percent of successes with tasks at the intellectual altitude of N. If there are 200 such tasks, his probable width is 140; if there are 60,000 such, his probable width is 42,000. If, when measured in respect of ten 40-composite tasks representative of intellectual difficulty M, his scores are 25, 25, 22, 24, 26, 25, 23, 24, 26, and 21, he may be expected to have 100 percent of successes with tasks of intellectual difficulty M. If there are 150 such tasks, his probable width is 150. If there are 40,000, his probable width is 40,000.

This illustration directs our attention to two meanings of width, namely, width of intellect in the sample examined and width of intellect in the entire series which the sample represents; and also to the fact that the sample examined may have a larger representation of tasks at one altitude than of tasks at another.

Suppose, for example, that the sample contains

40 single tasks between difficulty 30.0 and 30.99,
40    "    "    "    "    35.0 and 35.99, and
40    "    "    "    "    40.0 and 40.99, and

that there really are one million CAVD tasks between 30.0 and 30.99, two million between 35.0 and 35.99, and three million between 40.0 and 40.99. Then the sample has twice as large a representation of level 35.0 to 35.99 as it has of level 40.0 to 40.99, and three times as large a representation of level 30.0 to 30.99 as it has of level 40.0 to 40.99. If an individual can do 9 out of 10 of the sample at level 30.0 to 30.99, he can probably do 500,000 tasks at that level. But if he can do half of the tasks of the sample at level 40.0 to 40.99, he can probably do 1,500,000 tasks at that level.

If each of the tasks, the number of which measures width, is perfectly intellectual, depending for success upon all of intellect and nothing but intellect, the change from one hundred percent of successes to zero percent of successes, as the intellect in question is tested at higher and

higher altitudes, will be instantaneous.   When a small
amount of inadequacy and error is present, as in our 40-
composites for Intellect CAVD, the change will still be very
sudden.   The conditions in representative intellects, each
measured by a score or more of tasks like our 40-composites

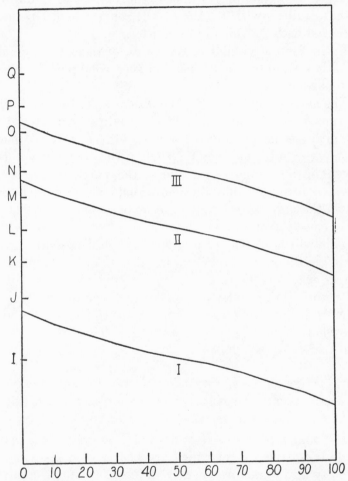

FIG. 55.  The probable percentages of successes of three intellects, I, II
and III, in a series of 360 tasks, 20 of difficulty A, 20 of difficulty B, and
so on, each task having $r_{1t}$ = approximately .9.  The drawings are not from
precise computations, being for illustration only, not for mensuration of the
effect.

26

at each altitude in Intellect CAVD, will be roughly as shown in Fig. 55.

The evidence for this is the correlations between one 40-composite and another at or near the same level, and the infrequency of reversals from failure to success in our series of tasks. For example, in the 240 individuals of Group 17, of those failing with P (103 in all), only 4 or 3.9 percent succeeded with Q, which is 1.1 harder.

In the 246 individuals of Group 9I, of those failing with K (93 in all), only 9 or 9.7 percent succeeded with L, which is 1.0 harder.

The measurement of CAVD width at any altitude, in the rigorous sense of number of intellectual tasks mastered at that altitude, is thus given for most altitudes by the measurement of altitude itself. Nearly up to that altitude the percent is one hundred; above it the percent very soon drops to zero. Within the short distance of uncertainty the widths may be determined by experiment or estimated fairly closely from the altitude.

This will hold true of any sort of intellect defined and treated in the same manner as Intellect CAVD. In proportion as each task depends for success upon all of intellect and nothing but intellect, a smaller and smaller increase in difficulty will cause a shift from success to failure, the altitude where it does so varying with the intellect that is being measured.

### WIDTH OF INTELLECT IN THE SENSE OF THE NUMBER OF SINGLE SHORT TASKS MASTERED, ANY ONE OF THESE TASKS BEING ONLY A VERY PARTIAL REPRESENTATION OF INTELLECT

For many purposes it is desirable to know how many single tasks from a set which are nearly or quite alike in difficulty and which are nearly or quite as intellectual as any short single tasks can be, a given intellect can succeed with. If, for example, two intellects A and B have identical CAVD altitudes exactly at Level N, and if A has average scores at Levels K, L, M, N, O, P, and Q of 39, 36, 29, 20, 17,

11, and 6, whereas B has scores of 30, 28, 27, 20, 18, 6, and 0, there is a difference between A and B which may need expression. Between 40 and 20 right, and between 19 and zero right in the case of such 40-composites as the CAVD series, there are ranges of difference which may be of great importance for theory or for practice or for both.

The measurement is, of course, a simple count of successes in the sample used in the examination, and an estimated count for the entire series which is represented by the sample. If the single tasks in K represent a selection of 40 out of 10,000, while those in L represent a selection of 40 out of 15,000, and those in M represent a selection of 40 out of 25,000, A's scores of 39, 36, and 29 in the examination mean probabilities of success with $\frac{39}{40} \times 10,000$, $\frac{36}{40} \times$ 15,000, and $\frac{29}{40} \times 25,000$, or with 9,750, 13,500, and 18,125 single tasks of the sort chosen as components of Composites K, L, and M, respectively.

A series of names is needed to designate different sorts of width, from the width of an intellect in perfectly intellectual tasks, down through its width in various composite tasks less and less representative of all of intellect and nothing but intellect, to its width in such tasks as giving the opposite of one word, or understanding one sentence, or tracing a way through one maze, or repeating one series of five digits backward. We suggest the use of a series of W's, each followed by a notation describing the tasks, and being in each case the percent of successes.

Thus, W(10C + 10A + 10V + 10D) would refer to the percent of successes with 40-composite tasks made up equally of C, A, V, and D; W(1C or 1A or 1V or 1D)N would refer to the percent of successes with a series of tasks made up of single C's, A's, V's, and D's. W(10M) would refer to the percent of successes with a series of composite tasks each made up of ten mazes. The altitude at which W is measured will require very careful description in every case.

AREA OF INTELLECT

*Area* or *volume* seems the best term to use to mean the total number of tasks of some specified sort at which an intellect succeeds; and *area* seems preferable. Area, like width, will have two distinct meanings, namely, the number of successes in the sample set of tasks examined, and the number of estimated successes in the entire inventory of tasks which have been or can be made, and of which the examination-tasks are a representative sample.

Area of intellect, like width, is, in the strictest usage, the number of truly intellectual tasks, each of which measures all of intellect and nothing but intellect. In this sense the area found will be a function of the altitude; Intellect X, of Altitude N, will succeed with all tasks up to that altitude, and with none beyond it.

As in the case of width, it will be desirable to use area of intellect in a loose sense to mean the total number of tasks mastered which are proper components of composites which, as totals, are intellectual, all the way down from composites which are nearly perfectly intellectual to short single tasks like the single C's, A's, V's, and D's. A notation like A(10C + 10A + 10V + 10D), A(1C or 1A or 1V or 1D)N, A(10M), and the like may usefully be adopted to describe the kind of "area" that is being measured.

We shall consder as a typical case the measurement of A(1C or 1A or IV or 1D). Everything is simple so far as concerns finding this area for the sample examined. But the effort to estimate the area as a fraction of all the different sentence-completions that might be desired, all the different arithmetical problems which could be collected or invented, all the word-knowledge tasks (Shall other than English words be used?) possible, and all the sentences or paragraphs or books that might be heard or read, and so to estimate effective A(1C or 1A or 1V or 1D) brings us up squarely against great difficulties due to lack of knowledge of the relative frequency of different C's, A's, V's, and D's at different levels of difficulty.

If we know the width of an intellect at each level in an adequate sample of tasks, we can measure its total "area," provided we know the number of tasks at each level. Thus, if the C, A, V, and D single tasks of Intellect CAVD at levels zero to forty[1] number, in order, 100, 100, 100, 100, 100, 200, 200, 200, 200, 200, 300, 300, 300, 300, 300, 400, 400, 400, 400, 400, 500, 500, 500, 500, 500, 700, 700, 700, 700, 700, 1000, 1000, 1000, 1000, 1000, 2000, 2000, 2000, 2,000, and 2000, and if Intellect JS, when measured with a representative sampling of 40 at each level, scores 40 at each level up through level 30, and 38, 32, 24, 20, 10, 4, 0, 0, 0, 0 in order thereafter, we find his A(1C or 1A or 1V or 1D) as 14,200 out of a possible 26,000. If there had been 650 tasks at each level, the same record in the examination would have meant 21,580 out of a possible 26,000.

Such a computation of the area of an intellect would not be a mere theoretical curiosity or statistical *tour de force,* but would be a systematic and accurate way of measuring something of very great importance. Common-sense thought and action about intellect often deal with something which this concept of area makes definite and objective. Just as terms like acuity, originality, and intellectual genius refer to intellect with especial emphasis on its altitude, so terms like breadth, scope, and intellectual power refer to intellect with especial emphasis on its "area." We should not expect common sense to make clean-cut distinctions or to avoid confusions, for the very good reason that altitude and area are closely correlated, so that for most practical purposes, we can describe a man's intelligence adequately by simply rating him for intelligence as a unit. But the concept of a man's general average probability of correct response to intellectual or semi-intellectual tasks has been real and useful; and it will be more so now that it can be made definite and measurable.

[1] Level 0 includes all C, A, V or D tasks from 0 difficulty up to a difficulty of 1.00, 1 includes all from 1.00 up to 2.00, 2 includes all from 2.00 up to 3.00, and so on.

It is possible to discover approximately the number of single tasks at each level of Intellect CAVD or any other defined intellect, though such estimates are beset by many difficulties. The enumeration of the C or A or V or D tasks harder than the average of those in Composite N and easier than the average of those in Composite O is, indeed, probably comparable in complexity to the enumeration of all the species of animals.

The chief and most obvious difficulty is that of deciding how much one task must differ from another in order that they shall be counted as two rather than one. Consider, for example, these fourteen tasks to be given orally:

1. John is 5 years old now.   How old will he be in 3 years?
2. Tom is 5 years old now.   How old will he be in 3 years?
3. John is 5 years old now.   Tom is 3 years older than John.  How old is Tom?
4. John is 5 years old.   Will is 3 years older than John.  How old is Will?
5. John has 5 cents now.   How much will he have if his father gives him 3 cents?
6. John has 5 cents now.   How much will he have if his mother gives him 3 cents?
7. How many dollars are five dollars and 3 dollars?
1a. John is 6 years old now.   How old will he be in 3 years?
2a. Tom is 6 years old now.   How old will he be in 3 years?
3a. John is 6 years old now.   Tom is 3 years older than John.  How old is Tom?
4a. John is 6 years old.   Will is 3 years older than John.  How old is Will?
5a. John has 6 cents now.   How much will he have if his father gives him 3 cents?
6a. John has 6 cents now.   How much will he have if his mother gives him 3 cents?
7a. How many dollars are 6 dollars and 3 dollars?

How many different tasks are there? All competent students of intellect will deny that there are fourteen. By any reasonable view, we should not count 2 as a different arithmetical task from 1. Whether the problem is put about John or Tom or Will or Mary, does not, we think, make any difference to it as an arithmetical or intellectual task. Our thinking is probably sound, and we shall later state the facts and principle which justify it. But note that if we think in a stiff pseudo-logical way that the name of the boy makes no difference, we shall err. Let Tom, well known to be of age ten, be sitting in full sight and the task is now not quite the same, requiring for success that the intellect shall not be misled by the temptation to think of the present Tom. Or let the problem be stated as "Sneezer Snoop Squibb is 5 years old now. How old will Sneezer Snoop Squibb be in 3 years?" and the task is not quite the same, requiring that the intellect be not distracted by the seductive name into inattention to the numbers.

If a psychologist should list all the arithmetical tasks that ever have been set, and add to them all that a decade of ingenious thought could devise, and then try to cull out the duplicates, he would find some that would be indubitably so, and some that would be as unlike as arithmetical tasks can be; but with many he could only say that the two tasks were somewhat different. So he would have to set up some standard of the amount of difference which would qualify two tasks to be counted as two, or some scheme for fractional counts.

The facts which he should use for these purposes are the facts of the differences of the tasks as tasks for intellects. By this is meant not merely that the facts are facts in the minds or neurones of individuals, but also that they are facts in the action of intellects to which the tasks are presented for solution. Two sentences differing in print only by an apostrophe or comma may differ enormously in the intellectual actions which they evoke in an intellect set upon solving them, and two questions which have not a word in common may arouse very similar behavior, as is the case with "Solve $2x^2 + x = 21$" and "What does y equal if $2y^2 + y = 21$?" for competent students of algebra. And either may arouse very different behavior according as the person reacts to it as a task to be solved or as, say, a mere question to contemplate.

So the investigator seeking to measure the differences amongst tasks (apart from differences in difficulty) must be expert in the psychology of thinking, and must be skilful in examining and cross-examining individuals who do the tasks in question and report what they did. He will often have to make subtle distinctions in cases where two tasks arouse different action in two intellects, and when it is doubtful how much of the difference lies in the tasks and how much in the intellects.

The objective method of correlation will be helpful. Obviously, if an intellect can do task 1 and cannot do task 2, then the two tasks are different for that intellect; two tasks are not perfectly alike as tasks for intellect, unless every intellect that can do one can do the other. Other things being equal, the more individuals there are within any given group who can do the one task and not the other, the greater the difference between the two (for that group) will be. More generally, the differences with which we are concerned here are measured, other things being equal, by the lack of perfect correlation between the ability to succeed with one and the ability to succeed with the other, in some defined group of intellects, difficulty being kept constant. If two tasks are identical as tasks for intellects, $r_{t_1t_2}$ will be 1.00. If they are of equal difficulty, the more unlike they are the lower $r_{t_1t_2}$ will be until it reaches a minimum which represents the amount of likeness which two tasks must have to be included in the series of arithmetical tasks which is to be enumerated.

This argument from correlation will not hold good if a task is a composite where success is defined as obtaining a certain percent of successes with the elementary tasks, or attaining a certain score by some system of credits. Two such composites may show very high correlations in respect of success as just defined, and yet have hardly a single detail of one like any detail of the other. The correlations are between scores, each of which measures chiefly ability in what is summed up in or common to all the single tasks of the composite, not what is characteristic of any one of them as a totality. The composites *are* closely alike in the sense that what is summed up in or common to all the single tasks of A, is closely like what is summed up in or common to all the single tasks of B.

## PROPORTIONAL COUNTS

For some purposes, the relative numbers of tasks at the different levels of difficulty will serve in place of the absolute numbers. Thus, if we wish to know what percent of A's area B's area is, we will do as well by knowing that the numbers of tasks are in the proportions K, 3K, 9K, 27K, 81K, as by knowing their absolute amounts.

It may well be that such proportional counts may be made with greater accuracy, as well as with greater ease and speed, than absolute counts. Certain factors of error may act alike at all levels and so do no harm to the proportional counts. Certain arbitrary schemes of fractional allowance for overlapping tasks may also act alike at all levels and so do no harm to proportional counts. Even such proportional counts, however, will require much sagacity and industry to achieve even approximate truth for even a small fraction of intellect. A reasonably satisfactory proportional count of the number of tasks at each level of even so small a representation of intellect as CAVD is, will indeed require an enormous amount of observation and experiment. New tasks, like new species of animals, are coming into existence while we count them; tasks a and c seem enough different to count as two, and tasks b and d seem enough different to count as two, but when a, b, c, and d are considered together, they do not seem to deserve a credit of four; it seems as if some sorts of tasks at some levels of difficulty were innumerable; when task X is simply a task where both a and b must be performed successfully to bring success in X, shall we count a and b and X as 3 or as 2? These difficulties, together with those which have been mentioned and others which might be, may make perfect or even approximately correct counts impossible.

The best way to find out what is possible is to begin work at actual counts. We have begun, but have not progressed far enough to report results, save one. This one, which the reader's sagacity may have anticipated, is that the number of different tasks per unit of altitude of intellect is not equal, but increases as we go up from zero altitude.

That this is true for sentence completions can be easily realized if one will try to make as many different C tasks as he can between the average difficulty of those in A and the average difficulty of those in B (23 to 26¼), and to do the same for the stretch of difficulty from N to Q (40 to 43). It will be found very hard and perhaps impossible to devise five hundred of the former, whereas there seems almost no limit to the possible number of the latter. Apparently the harder the task, the greater the number possible, though it is not easy to devise extremely hard completions which are linguistic rather than informational in their difficulty.

In the case of the arithmetical tasks the number of different tasks surely increases from the very easy levels up to a certain point, after which there is some doubt. The doubt seems, however, to be due mainly to our averseness to fabricating problems whch are so elaborate and intricate as to be extremely unreal, rather than to the paucity of such. In the case of the disarranged-equation task, it is obvious that the number of different ones possible increases rapidly with increased difficulty and has no limit.

In the case of vocabulary, the fact is unquestioned if other languages than English are included, and probably holds true for English alone.

In the case of the understanding of sentences and paragraphs, the increase is obscured by the facts that people usually try to make their statements as easily intelligible as may be, and that the number of persons who are concerned with very subtle and intricate ideas is few. Also, the number of different statements and questions of even a moderate degree of difficulty which can be fabricated is so enormous that comparisons are very difficult. Also, only persons of very high directions ability can frame statements which are sensible and correct but very hard to understand, and still free from any great informational difficulty. Sentence comprehension cannot, however, well be kept distinct from informational abilities; and if informational difficulties are allowed to enter freely, the number of sentences very hard to understand is practically infinite. Even if one abstains from these rather rigorously, the number of very hard D's that can be made is enormously greater than one would expect from the number found in reading. Merely by combining and permuting causal, conditional, and concessive clauses and pronoun references, one can produce an enormous number of different tasks like, "A change in ab would cause a similar change in og if ek did not produce its usual effect upon il, although ek did act upon um, and ba would cause an increase in ab, provided bi did not occur in unison with bo. What will happen to og if ba and bi and ek happen shortly subsequent to bo, provided the ek–il action is neutralized by bo, and um does not occur?"

We have not even begun a count for the entire series of tasks which might reasonably be made constituents in composites designed to measure intellect in general. Consequently, we are not able to make more than a very rough estimate of how much number increases with altitude, or of the way in which the increase comes. We think the increase for Intellect CAVD is so great as to make the number of different tasks at level 40 to 40.99 at least a hundred times the number at level 20 to 20.99. We also think that it comes smoothly and with acceleration, at least up to a certain level, after the pattern of Fig. 56 or Fig. 57 or Fig. 58. Intellect CAVD can hardly be said to have an appreciable

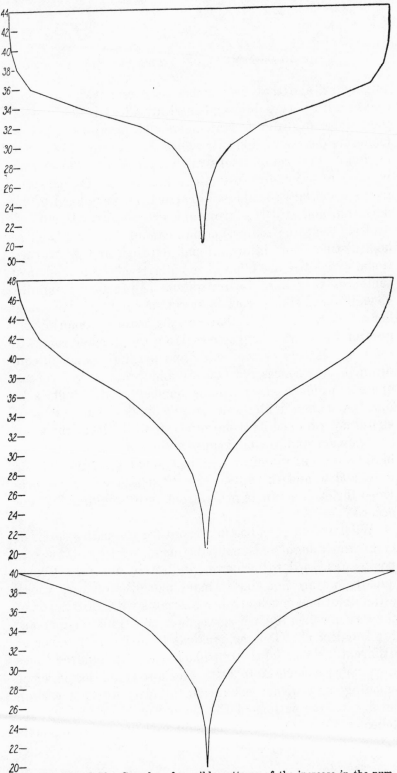

FIGS. 56, 57 and 58. Samples of possible patterns of the increase in the number of different intellectual tasks with increase in intellectual difficulty.

area below level 20, since it probably requires an altitude of 20 to complete ten out of any twenty sentences, no matter how easy, or to solve ten out of any twenty arithmetical tasks. The increase for intellect in general will be found, we think, to increase to a similar degree and in a similar manner, with at least fifty times as many tasks at 40 as at 20, and at least several hundred times as many at 40 as at 10.

An intellect of altitude 40 may then have an area, not twice that of an intellect of altitude 20, but ten or twenty or perhaps two hundred times it. The common-sense view that the greatest intellect of a thousand men is many times as great as the worst intellect of the thousand may be entirely correct, if we mean by "great" something corresponding to area.

Moreover, if we think of intellect as a hierarchy of unit connections or bonds between ideas or between the neural correspondents of ideas, the number of different connections required to enable a person to respond correctly to 20 out of 40 of the elements of task N at level 40 may be not twice the number required to enable one to respond correctly to 20 out of 40 of a task 3 below A, but ten or twenty or two hundred times it.

Intellectual altitude, by our definition, shows a small relative rise from the imbecile to the average and then to the gifted adult, by the argument followed in Chapter IX, so small as to arouse astonishment and incredulity concerning the usefulness of the definition and the validity of the argument, at first thought. If, however, the altitudes of the imbecile, average and gifted were in the proportions of 5, 15, and 20, or 1, 11, and 16, instead of about 25, 35, and 40, we might find the relative areas of intellect in the three groups much more preposterous in the reverse way. The scale of altitude must not be criticized for the lack of attributes which are appropriate only for a scale of area, unless it can be shown that width is approximately the same at all altitudes. It is not.

# CHAPTER XIII

## The Relations of Altitude to Width, Area, and Speed

The number of CAVD tasks at any given level of difficulty is unknown. Consequently all the relations with width which are considered in this chapter are relations with percents. No comparison or conclusion will appear which involves the absolute number of tasks in two levels.

### THE RELATION BETWEEN ALTITUDE AND W $(10c + 10a + 10v + 10d)$, I.E., NUMBER OF 40-COMPOSITE CAVD TASKS SUCCEEDED WITH AT A GIVEN LEVEL OF DIFFICULTY

N individuals are measured, each with, say, a score of CAVD composite tasks, each composite being of the same difficulty as any other, and each, consisting of so many single tasks that the correlation between the number right in any one composite and the number right in any other is perfect. Then any one of the N individuals who succeeds with any one of these composites (in the sense of having 50 percent or more of the single tasks correct) will succeed with any other of them; and the W of any individual will be one hundred percent or zero percent. Suppose that the same N individuals are measured perfectly in respect of altitude of Intellect CAVD. The correlation between altitude CAVD and W $(10C + 10A + 10V + 10D)$ will be perfect, every one of the individuals who succeeds with these composites having a higher altitude than any one of those who fail with them. If each task at a certain level of difficulty is extensive enough to represent and measure all of CAVD difficulty and no other difficulty—all of CAVD intellect as it operates with tasks at that level of difficulty and nothing but it—then everyone who succeeds with these will have a CAVD altitude as high as, or higher than, the altitude which they represent and no one who fails with them

388

will have a CAVD altitude as high as the altitude which
they represent. That is, if each task measures all the
CAVD intellect which can operate at that level and nothing
but it, the percent of tasks mastered at that level will be
zero or one hundred and will correlate perfectly with altitude CAVD.

Stated in another way, any individual who succeeds with
any task of difficulty d which measures CAVD perfectly as
it operates at that level of difficulty, will succeed with all
tasks of less difficulty than d, if these also measure CAVD
perfectly as it operates at their respective levels of difficulty; and any individual who fails with any task of difficulty d will fail with all tasks of greater difficulty than d,
if these also measure CAVD perfectly as it operates at
their respective levels.

These are not axioms necessitated logically by the definition of Intellect CAVD and of difficulty CAVD; but conclusions reached by observations of facts. The facts could
be otherwise. Some men might conceivably succeed with
tasks like O, P, and Q and fail with tasks like M, N, and O.

We do not give an absolute empirical proof of these conclusions, because we have not any tasks which measured all
of the CAVD intellect which operates at any given level of
difficulty. All the evidence, however, goes to prove their
truth.

Evidence may be found in the correlation between the
altitude measure and the score of success or failure in
20-composites $(5C + 5A + 5V + 5D)$ corrected for attenuation, so as to give the correlation between a precise measure of altitude and the number of s's in an examination
with a very large number of such 20-composites. For example, the average correlation (bi-serial r) of the measure of altitude with success in a CAVD 20-composite in the
case of 98 adult imbeciles was .984 for A, .916 for B, .875
for C, and .757 for D, averaging .883. The self-correlation
of the altitude measure is .94, the inter-correlations of the
three determinations whose average it is being .92, .77, and

.83. The self-correlation (tetrachoric r) of a CAVD 20-composite in this group is .96 for A, .76 for B, .79 for C, and .99 for D, averaging .87½. The correlation between a precise measure of altitude and success in 50 percent or more of a number of CAVD 20-composites of equal difficulty may then be expected to be $\dfrac{.984}{\sqrt{.96 \times .94}}$ for A, $\dfrac{.916}{\sqrt{.76 \times .94}}$ for B, $\dfrac{.875}{\sqrt{.77 \times .94}}$ for C, and $\dfrac{.757}{\sqrt{.99 \times .94}}$ for D, or, on the average, $\dfrac{.883}{\sqrt{.875 \times .94}}$, or .97.

Also the correlations between altitude and W(1C or 1A or 1V or 1D) are very near unity, as will be demonstrated in the next section. The correlations between altitude and W(10C + 10A + 10V + 10D) *a fortiori* will be near unity.

In view of such evidence the conclusions stated in the first two pages of this chapter may be accepted as true. There is no reason to expect that the case will be different with any fairly catholic form of intellect (such as Picture-Completions + Opposites + Geometrical Relations + Reasoning Problems of the type devised by Burt + Information; or Analogies + Number-Completions + Arithmetical Computation + a Common Element test of the type devised by Otis) from what it is with CAVD.

THE RELATION BETWEEN ALTITUDE AND W(1C OR 1A OR 1V OR 1D), I.E., THE NUMBER OF SINGLE TASKS SUCCEEDED WITH AT A GIVEN LEVEL

This correlation is very close. There are a certain number of individuals who are, relatively to others, much better (or worse) in arithmetical tasks than they are in the linguistic tasks, and whose records prevent perfect correlation. Also, there are probably other minor specializations within Intellect CAVD. But on the whole, individuals would be found to follow rather closely the general pattern of CAVD intellect shown in Fig. 59 if each of them had been tested with several hundred tasks (one-fourth being C; one-fourth, A; one-fourth, V; and one-fourth, D) at each level of difficulty from 0 to 44. In general, that is, if intellect A has a higher altitude than intellect B, intellect A will also show a greater W(1C or 1A or 1V or 1D) than B at all levels between those where both A and B have one hundred percent right and those where both A and B have zero percent right; and the amount of superiority of A to B in W will be closely similar to the amount of superiority in altitude.

To prove this, we have to estimate the relation as it will be found with a very large number of single tasks at the level of difficulty in question, from data where this number is only 40 or less. The evidence is as follows:

In the case of 237 individuals of group 17, the correlations between altitude CAVD and percent succeeding in tasks N, O, P, and Q were as follows (P means the Pearson r; Sh means the Sheppard r):

| | P | Sh |
|---|---|---|
| N | .86 | .76 |
| O | .93 | .94 |
| P | .91 | .91 |
| Q | .81 | .86 |
| Average | .88 | .87 |

The self-correlations for % s in N, O, P, and Q in this group may be taken as approximately .76, using the data given in Appendix V, which show that the correlations of neighboring 40-composites average .73 in this group. .03 is added for the effect of the slight remoteness. The self-correlation of the measure of altitude in this group is computed as .90 from the intercorrelations of the three independent measures of altitude of which it is the average. They are .80, .76, and .71, averaging .757. By the well-known formula of Spearman, $r_{3 \text{ with } 3}$ will equal $\dfrac{3(.757)}{1 + 2(.757)}$.

By this determination, a precise measure of altitude will

27

correlate with a precise measure of W(C or A or V or D) to the extent of $\dfrac{.875}{\sqrt{.76 \times .90}}$ or 1.06.

As a check on this determination, we have computed the obtained correlation between the measure of altitude and the sum of the numbers of rights in N, O, P, and Q. It is .99. The correlation between a precise measure of altitude and a precise measure of W(C or A or V or D) should be higher than this obtained correlation.

In the case of 189 individuals of group 13, the correlations between altitude CAVD and % s in tasks N, O, P, and Q were as follows:

|  | P | Sh |
|---|---|---|
| N | .875 | .84 |
| O | .925 | .90½ |
| P | .916 | .89 |
| Q | .782 | .83 |
| Average | .874 | .866 |

The average self-correlation for % s in N, O, P, and Q in this group may be taken as .74, from the data given in Appendix IV. The self-correlation of the measure of altitude in this group is found by the Spearman formula to be .89. The intercorrelations of the three independent measures of altitude of which it is the average are .71, .64, and .81. The correlation between altitude and W(C or A or V or D), both being measured accurately, will thus be $\dfrac{87}{\sqrt{.74 \times .89}}$ or 1.07. As a check, we have a correlation of .95 between the obtained measure of altitude and the sum of the numbers correct in N, O, P, and Q, and a part of M.

In the case of 246 individuals of group 9I, altitude CAVD correlates with % s in composites I, J, K, L, and M as follows: .58 for I, .82 for J, .92 for K, .82½ for L, and .64½ for M (all by the Sh formula). The self-correlations of % s in I, J, K, L, and M in this group are respectively .73, .80, .74, .86, and .69. The self-correlation of the measure of

altitude in this group is .79, the intercorrelation of the
three measures of which it is the average being .56, .58,
and .52. It is perhaps unwise to average correlations such
as these which show wide and regular differences. So we
correct each for attenuation separately and have, as the
five resulting determinations of the correlation between
altitude and W(C or A or V or D), .76, 1.03, 1.20, 1.00, and
.87. The average of these is .97; the median is 1.00. As a
check we have the correlation between the altitude measure
and the sum of the numbers correct in I, J, K, L, and M. It
is .91.

In the case of 192 individuals of group 9II, altitude
CAVD correlates with % s in composites K, L, M, and N as
follows: .73 for K, .90 for L, .91 for M, and .66 for N. The
average is .80. The self-correlations of K, L, M, and N are
respectively .76½, .87½, .75½, and .75, averaging .80. The
self-correlation of the measure of altitude in this group may
be taken as .83, the intercorrelations of the three measures
of which it is the altitude being .50, .635, and .73. So a precise measure of altitude will correlate with a precise measure of W(C or A or V or D) to the extent of .99 (.91 by K,
1.07 by L, 1.15 by M, and .84 by N). As a check we have
a correlation of .96 between the measure of altitude and the
sum of the numbers right in K, L, M, and N.

In the case of 63 university students the correlations
between altitude CAVD and % s in tasks N, O, P, and Q
were as follows:

|   | Sh |
|---|---|
| N | .77 |
| O | .92 |
| P | .90 |
| Q | .70 |

The intercorrelations of N, O, P, and Q are: N with O,
.58; O with P, .70; and P with Q, .73. The self-correlations
of N, O, P, and Q may be estimated as .61, .67, .74½, and .76
by adding .03 to the correlation between neighboring com-

posites. The self-correlation of the measure of altitude in this group may be taken as .83, the three measures of which it is the average having intercorrelations of .80, .54, and .50. The correlation between a precise measure of altitude and a precise measure of width is then computed as 1.08 for N, 1.23 for O, 1.14½ for P, and .88 for Q, averaging 1.08.

As a check on this result, we have the correlation of .98 between the measure of altitude and the sum of the numbers right in N, O, P, and Q.

We have thus five determinations of what the correlation between altitude CAVD and W would be if both were measured precisely, namely,

| | | |
|---|---|---|
| for group | 17 | 1.06 |
| " | 13 | 1.07 |
| " | 9I | .97 |
| " | 9II | .99 |
| " | Univ. students | 1.06 |

with an average of 1.03 ± a mean square error of .019.

There is an element of insecurity in these corrections for attenuation, especially in so far as the self-correlations for W(C or A or V or D) are estimated by adding .03 to the obtained correlations for neighboring composites. However, the empirical correlations between the obtained altitude measure and the obtained sum of the W's (.99, .95, .96 .91, and .98) show that the corrected correlations should be near unity.

The same close correlations obtain in groups at low altitudes. In the case of the 100 individuals of group im6, the correlations of the measure of altitude with % s in C, D, E, F, and G, respectively, were .79, .86, .89, .86, and .54, averaging .79. The self-correlations of the measures of % s were, respectively, .80, .86, .84, .83, and .81, averaging .83. The self-correlation of the measure of altitude in this group is .67 by the Spearman correction, the average intercorrelation of the three determinations of which it is the average being only .407. The correlation between a precise measure of altitude and a precise measure of W(C or A or V or D) is then 1.06 by this determination.

The correlation of the obtained measure of altitude with the sum of the numbers right in C, D, E, F, and G was .93.

In the case of the 50 f, the correlation between the obtained altitude measure and the sum of the number right in E, F, G, H, and I was .98.

In the case of 162 individuals of group 4, the correlations between altitude CAVD and % s in tasks F, G, H, I, J, and K were .48, .83, .93, .95, .75, and .53, respectively. The intercorrelations of % s in F, % s in G, and so on, are: F with G = .67; G with H = .81; H with I = .85$\frac{1}{2}$; I with J = .63; J with K = .51. The self-correlations may therefore be taken as .70 for F, .77 for G, .86 for H, .77 for I, .60 for J, and .54 for K. The self-correlation of the measure of altitude is .81, the average intercorrelation of the three measures of which it is the average being .59. The most probable correlation between a precise measure of altitude and a precise measure of width is then .64 for F, 1.05 for G, 1.11$\frac{1}{2}$ for H, 1.20 for I, 1.08 for J, and .80 for K, with an average of .98.

As a check on this determination, we have computed the correlation between the measure of altitude and the sum of the numbers of rights in F, G, H, I, J, and K. It is .96.

A rough calculation of the correlations for the 180 cases of group im3 shows that with them the raw correlations of the altitude measure with W(1C or 1A or 1V or 1D) in composites A, B, C, and D will be around .90 and that the corrected coefficients will be near unity.

The closeness of these correlations indicates that each individual would, if adequately measured by a large number of single tasks at each level of difficulty, show a pattern closely of the type of Fig. 59. Individuals might be of widely different patterns, such as those shown in Fig. 60, Fig. 61, and Fig. 62, so that individuals of the same altitude would differ widely in width at any level. But, in fact, such large divergences in pattern are very scarce in Intellect CAVD.

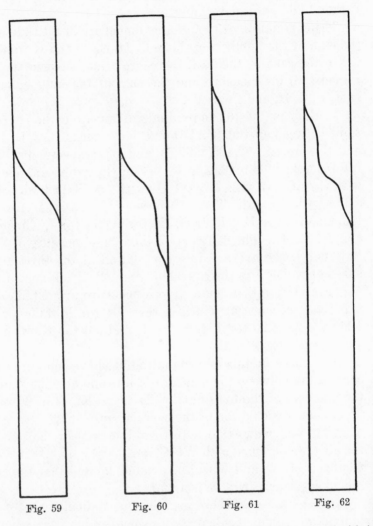

Fig. 59    Fig. 60    Fig. 61    Fig. 62

FIG. 59.   The pattern of decrease in percent of single tasks correct with increase in difficulty, which corresponds to close correlations between altitude and W(1C or 1A or 1V or 1D).

FIGS. 60, 61 and 62.   Patterns of decrease in percent of single tasks correct with increase in difficulty such as individuals would show if the correlations between altitude and W(1C or 1A or 1V or 1D) were much below 1.00.

How small and scarce they will be in other forms of intellect, that is, how close a resemblance between altitude and width will be found for any other form of intellect, will depend upon the constitution of the form in question.  In $CAPI_{ma}$, with picture completions and information about music and art replacing vocabulary and directions tasks, the correlations will probably be lower.  However, so long as the constituents of our composite tasks all concern the ability to deal with ideas and symbols for ideas, the amount of specialization will be small in comparison with the total variation in ability, so that the correlations will be high.

### THE RELATION BETWEEN ALTITUDE AND AREA OF INTELLECT

The facts brought forward in the first and second sections of this chapter prove that the $A(10C + 10A + 10V + 10D)$ of any intellect and the altitude of that intellect are determined almost or quite entirely by the same cause or causes.

The facts of the third and fourth sections prove that to a very considerable extent this is true for the $A(1C$ or $1A$ or $1V$ or $1D)$ of any intellect and its altitude.  A verification of this by the direct measurement of $A(1C$ or $1A$ or $1V$ or $1D)$ is not yet possible because the number of tasks at each level of difficulty is unknown.  Indirectly, it may be partially verified as follows: If n single tasks are taken from each level from zero to forty-five, one-fourth being C, one-fourth A, one-fourth V, and one-fourth D, and individuals are measured in respect of these, n being sufficiently large, the A's so obtained will have the same rank as A's obtained by an examination where the intellects are tested with all tasks at all levels.  The area for the selection of n at 0, + n at 1, + n at 2, + n at 3, and so on, may be taken to be approximately the area found by assuming that each intellect will succeed with all or nearly all of the single elements at levels below the highest level where it obtains 100 percent right and will fail with all or nearly all of the single elements at levels above the lowest level where it obtains zero percent right (or only that percent which mere chance guessing could give).

By permitting some estimating of scores, this procedure may be carried out. The results appear in Fig. 63. The cases entered in Fig. 63 are all taken at random so far as

FIG. 63.   The relation between CAVD altitude and area in a sampling of tasks comprising N tasks for each unit of altitude.

the relation in question is concerned. Those used were all that had 37 or more right in the easiest altitude with which they were tested, or a random selection from all such. The groups used were im3, f, 4, 9I, 17 and the group of 63 university students. The area number was computed as follows: I. Assume that, at each unit of altitude up to the easiest altitude at which the person was measured, he had 40 (i.e., all) right. II. Count the number he had right over the range at which he was measured; and estimate from this how many he would have had right had he been tested with 40 single tasks at each unit of altitude over this range. III. Estimate the number which he would have had right at all altitudes above the highest at which he was tested, using arbitrarily the number which he had right at the highest altitude at which he was tested. The area number is the sum of the three numbers obtained by I, II, and III.

The area number thus ranges possibly from 957 for an im3 who had 37 right in Composite A and none right in any higher composite, to 1,800 for a person who had 40 right in N and also in O, P, and Q. The lowest actual area number among the cases used was 1,063; the highest was 1,760. The very close interdependence of area and altitude shown by Fig. 63 would be little if at all reduced if more extensive and precise measures were available.[1]

There is thus a high degree of genuine unity to Intellect CAVD, not assumed but discovered. We began with a measurement in the form of an inventory, differing from a bare enumeration of success or failure with actual tasks only in that the tasks were graded in difficulty. We end with measurements of altitude, width and area which intercorrelate so closely that they may reasonably be treated as results of a closely knit set of causes. Whatever makes one intellect able to do much harder CAVD tasks than another intellect

[1] It would be reduced inasmuch as some of the errors now involved act in the same direction on the altitude measurement and on the area measurement. It would be increased inasmuch as the purely chance fraction of the error acts to reduce the correlation.

also makes it able to do many more tasks than that other can do. After the necessary data have been collected, width at any altitude, and so total area, will be predictable in the case of Intellect CAVD (and presumably in the case of other forms of intellect) rather precisely from altitude alone.

### THE RELATION OF ALTITUDE OR LEVEL OF INTELLECT TO SPEED

It is important to know the relation between level and speed for two reasons. If the relation is very close, the speed of performing tasks which all can perform would be an admirable practical measure of intellect. The record would be in time, an unimpeachable and most convenient unit. If, on the other hand, the correlation is very low, the practice of giving credit for speed in group examinations should probably be amended.

Dr. Hunsicker ['25] has made extensive individual measurements upon 82 adults and 81 school children, taking the time for easy problems in arithmetic and for easy completions, such as appear in our composites E, F, and G; and then testing the person with harder and harder tasks until the level was reached where he could not obtain fifty percent right.

The correlations which she obtained between altitude and rate (the reciprocal of the time required for tasks done with no, or very, very few errors) are shown in Table 130. They are much too low to make it advisable to use the speed at easy tasks as a measure of the altitude or width or area of intellect, except possibly in the case where the time available for the examination is very short. They are indeed so low that it seems unwise to attach much weight to speed in intelligence examinations in general.[2] A graded or ladder test of thirty minutes containing 5 levels each consisting of ten words and five arithmetical problems[3] using small num-

[2] Except, of course, in the case of tests (such as the substitution test) where speed measures the speed of learning.

[3] Or containing ten opposites and ten questions of arithmetical information, or containing five directions and five arithmetical problems.

bers, will in all probability show a closer correlation with any reasonable criterion of intellect than will a thirty minutes' speed test.

TABLE 130.

CORRELATIONS, RAW AND CORRECTED FOR ATTENUATION, BETWEEN RATE AND
LEVEL. (AFTER HUNSICKER, '25, TABLE V.)

| Individual Testing | No. in group | Arithmetic | | Completion | | |
|---|---|---|---|---|---|---|
| | | Raw r | Corrected r | Raw r | Corrected r | Average |
| W. C. ............... | 28 | .29 | .35 | .50 | .56 | .46 |
| S. C. ............... | 54 | .46 | .55 | .19 | .23 | .39 |
| P. S. 189 .......... | 32 | .49 | .58 | .49 | .64 | .61 |
| P. S. 6 ............. | 49 | .29 | .35 | .41 | .50 | .43 |
| Average ........ | | | .46 | | .48 | .47 |

We have extended Dr. Hunsicker's work by a measurement of the speed of doing a collection of CAVD tasks chosen from levels I and below in the case of 63 university students for whom a measure of CAVD altitude was obtained by the use of composites N, O, P, Q, and a still harder composite.

There were some errors in the easy tasks, so we have computed $r_{sa.e}$, the partial correlation between speed and altitude, for those making equal numbers of errors in the rate test.

$$r_{sa} = +.403 \qquad r_{se} = -.084 \qquad r_{ae} = -.484,$$
hence $r_{sa.e} = .416$.

The self-correlation of the measure of altitude is .83 for this group; the self-correlation of the measure of speed is not known but is almost certainly between .7 and .9. If the .403 were corrected for attenuation, the result for CAVD would thus be fairly close to Dr. Hunsicker's results for A and C.

# CHAPTER XIV

## The Meaning of Scores Obtained in Standard Intelligence Examinations

### THE MEANING OF THE BINET MENTAL AGE

A Binet Mental age is a rough measure of relative altitude A D Inf Ot, using Ot to mean "other tasks found or alleged to deserve inclusion in a battery to measure intelligence"; or, more exactly, of the relative A(1a or 1d or 1inf or 1ot) of a sampling of a certain number of tasks at each of certain levels. This A will correlate closely with altitude. Up to about M. A. 14, Binet scores are defined by the probable median or average chronological age of those who would obtain such a score, in the group by which the examination was standardized. Above M. A. 14, the scores are arbitrary.

Until the numbers of tasks at each level of difficulty are known, and perhaps even after they are known, a Binet Mental Age may best be treated as a measure of altitude— of how hard tasks the person can succeed with. If this is done, nothing will be lost from sound present uses and certain misapprehensions will be avoided. For example, everyone will understand that a very small increment of mental age at the high ages may mean a very large increment in area of intellect or percentage of success with the total mass of intellectual tasks which life may offer, and that a very large increment of mental age at the low ages may mean a relatively small increase in the total number of tasks achievable or in the total number of connections formed.

The great merit of the Binet Test is that it is a graded scale for intellectual difficulty, and it is only weakened by being interpreted loosely as a measure of some mysterious essence called intelligence which grows in man. The weakening is not disastrous simply because, as was shown in the previous chapter, altitude and width (and consequently area) of intellect are so closely correlated.

Miss Rowell is measuring the values of Stanford Binet M. A. 10, M. A. 11, M. A. 12, etc., in terms of the absolute units of the CAVD scale in so far as one can be said to measure the equivalence of two series of magnitudes which may not be measures of exactly the same fact in nature, and of which one (the Binet) may not measure varying amounts of the same fact. We have found that adults of Stanford Binet Mental Age 48 months, or 4 years, will show an altitude of about 26 in Intellect CAVD; and that adults of Stanford Binet Mental Age 78 months, or 6½ years, will show an altitude of about 30 in Intellect CAVD. When, by these measurements or by others, the differences in the M. A. scores are put in equal units and referred to the absolute zero of intellectual difficulty as located by us, or as more accurately located by future workers, the Binet scale and measurements will have a much greater value than they now have.

What has been said of the Binet applies equally to the Herring Examination, which is an alternative Binet.

### THE MEANING OF SCORES OBTAINED IN STANDARD GROUP EXAMINATIONS

The significance of scores in group tests such as the Army Alpha, National, Otis, may best first be considered with disregard of the factor of speed; that is, on the assumption that the scores of individuals represent what they can do with time enough allowed to exhaust their abilities.

The score does not measure either altitude or width or area of intellect. It does not measure altitude, because the number of tasks between levels equally far apart is not necessarily the same. It does not measure width, because the score is not divided up into a number of sub-scores, each representing the number of successes at a certain level. It does not measure area, because it measures neither altitude nor width, and because the percent which the tasks are of those that might be had at any level of difficulty is not known.

Although one of these group tests does not in a rigorous sense measure any one of the three, the score in it is about as closely symptomatic of altitude as the score in any test requiring so short a time could be. It is also closely symptomatic of the average width of intellect at and near the levels of difficulty represented by its tasks. One of these group examinations is in fact very much like what we have when we put together five or six of our CAVD 40-composites that are in a sequence for difficulty. The difference between a set of these CAVD composites from about G to N and Army Alpha or the National or the Otis (no time limit being set) is that in the case of the CAVD composites, we know how many single tasks there are at each level of difficulty, and we know how far apart the levels of difficulty are, and we can not only make a summation of credits, but also can make an altitude score, and a width score at each level. In Army Alpha or the National or the Otis, the total summation score is not susceptible of such an analysis.

Except for the speed element, then, one of these stock intelligence examinations may be regarded as a series of composites unequal in the number of their elements, and undefined as to the distances between levels. The addition of the speed element complicates matters and theoretically makes the significance of the score incapable of interpretation except in terms of what people of a certain sort do in that kind of a test when it is scored in that way.

Practically, however, the speed element does not make the scores in these examinations, as they are administered in the case of most of the individuals who are measured by them, very much different in significance from the scores which would be obtained with no time limits set. A few persons are nervously upset by the instructions to work as fast as they can; a few cautious, critical workers do not have time enough to do as many of the hard tasks as they are really able to do; a few persons are scored unduly high because they utilize the time especially shrewdly, while a few others are scored unduly low because they dally too long over tasks at which they fail, or leave tasks undone which the use of a little more time would have enabled them to finish. But, in general, the scores in these speed tests correlate very closely with the scores obtained when a longer time allowance is given, partly because the correlation between speed and altitude is positive, but more because the standard time allowance is long enough to enable most of the candidates to do most of the tasks which they could under any circumstances do.

The experiments of the Army psychologists on the result of doubling the time allowance for the Alpha and Beta examinations are well known [*Memoirs*, '21, pages 415–420]. The general result was that there was a slight improvement in the correlation with officers' ratings for intelligence, and a close correlation between the score in single time and the score in double time ($r = .967$), which is probably as high as the self-correlation of the determinations would permit.

Dr. J. R. Clark has investigated the influence of altitude and of speed upon the abilities measured by the Stanford Binet, the Otis Self-Administering Test, and the Terman Group Test, in the case of school pupils from Grades 7 to 12.

His results are not entirely clear, because his measures of speed are afflicted by rather large variable errors, and are perhaps also disturbed by the presence of an altitude factor; but on the whole they indicate that scores in these stock examinations are determined much more by altitude than by speed, and perhaps are determined almost entirely by altitude and width. The average of the six speed correlations (speed in arithmetic and speed in completions with Binet, Otis, and Terman) each being corrected for attentuation, is .54. The average of the corresponding altitude correlations is .70. The average of the four correlations between speed and altitude is not given, nor all the data whence to obtain it. Ar speed with Ar altitude (corrected r) is .76; Co speed with Co altitude is .40; the average is thus .58. The other two r's are not given. They would presumably be lower. If their average is estimated, we can compute the partial correlations of speed with Binet, Otis, and Terman for persons of equal altitude in Ar or Co and of altitude with Binet, Otis, and Terman for persons of equal speed in Ar or Co. Estimating this average as .48, the partial correlations are .28 for speed and .58 for altitude. A more instructive set of measurements is of the relations between speed in general and altitude in general to scores in Binet in general, Otis in general, and Terman in general.[1] These Dr. Clark has made. He finds that differences amongst individuals in the score in one of these examinations are almost perfectly correlated with differences in what is common to their two altitudes, and much less closely correlated with differences in what is common to their two speeds. We quote his results.

$$``r_{\text{general level and Binet}} = \sqrt{\frac{(r_{\text{ar. level and Binet}})(r_{\text{co. level and Binet}})}{(r_{\text{ar. level and co. level}})(r_{\text{Binet and Binet}})}}$$

$$= \sqrt{\frac{.65 \times .65}{(.55)(.90^*)}} = .93.$$

Similarly

$$r_{\text{general level and Otis}} = \sqrt{\frac{(r_{\text{ar. level and Otis}})(r_{\text{co. level and Otis}})}{(r_{\text{ar. level and co. level}})(r_{\text{Otis and Otis}})}}$$

$$= \sqrt{\frac{.83 \times .61}{(.55)(.90^*)}} = .98,$$

and

$$r_{\text{general level and Terman}} =$$

[1] "Binet in general" means the average score in an infinite number of tests patterned after the Stanford Binet.

* Estimated.

$$\sqrt{\frac{\left(r_{\text{ar. level and Terman}}\right)\left(r_{\text{co. level and Terman}}\right)}{(.55) \quad (.90^*)}}$$

$$= \sqrt{\frac{.80 \times .66}{(.55)(.90^*)}} = \text{Approx. 1.}$$

In the same way, the relationship between 'general speed' scores and intelligence test scores is found to be:

$$r_{\text{general speed and Binet}} = \sqrt{\frac{.55 \times .49}{(.50)(.90^*)}} = .59.$$

$$r_{\text{general speed and Otis}} = \sqrt{\frac{.71 \times .49}{(.50)(.90^*)}} = .77.$$

$$r_{\text{general speed and Terman}} = \sqrt{\frac{.67 \times .32}{(.50)(.90^*)}} = .49.$$

The mean of these correlations is .62.''—[Clark, '25, p. 33f.]

If partial correlations are computed using .97, .62, and any reasonable estimate for the intercorrelation of speed in general with altitude in general, they are very high for altitude and very low for speed. For example, let r for speed in general with altitude in general in this group be .65. We then have .95 and .00. Letting it be .60, we have .95 and .20. Letting it be .70, we have .96 and — .34.

Even with time limits, then, the scores in standard group examinations may properly be treated approximately as summation-of-credit scores of the same fundamental nature as a Stanford-Binet summation score or as a CAVD summation score. The chief difference for practical purposes is that the Stanford-Binet summation is of rights in a series of tasks specified as to difficulty, six for the interval from Chr. Age 3.0 to Chr. Age 4.0; six for the interval from Chr. Age 4.0 to Chr. Age 5.0; and so on; and the CAVD summation score is of tasks specified as Diff. 23, Diff. $26\frac{1}{4}$, Diff. $28\frac{1}{4}$, and so on; whereas the Army Alpha or National or Terman Group summations are from an undefined collection of tasks.

* Estimated.

We may expect that, in the future, all these group examinations which have proved themselves so convenient in getting quickly and cheaply an approximate measure of something which is reasonably called "intelligence," will retain these advantages and gain those of clearer interpretation by certain changes in the method of construction which are recommended by the principles which we have formulated. Instead of being a collection of small tasks of undefined location as to difficulty, they will be made in levels with a definite number in each level, and the levels will be placed, at least approximately, equally far apart. A more liberal time allowance will be given, and each individual who is examined will be instructed to take as much time as he needs and to go as far as he can. The group test can then be scored by a summation of credits just as now, but that summation will have resulted from a combination of scores of the number right at each of various levels of known difficulty. An altitude score can be inferred from it, since its correlation with altitude will be nearly as high as its own self-correlation permits. Or an altitude score can be computed more directly by some such procedure as was described in the case of CAVD in Chapter II.

### THE MEANING OF SCORES OBTAINED IN TESTS OF THE ABILITY TO LEARN AND TO IMPROVE

The only test of ability to learn which has been widely used as a measure of intellect is the substitution test.[2] There has been far too little experimentation with ability to learn as a test of intellect. The early work seemed discouraging, the correlations with a criterion being apparently much lower per unit of time in testing and labor in scoring for tests of improvement than for tests of status. We have elsewhere shown [Thorndike, '24] that this may be due in large measure to the peculiar action of the error

2 The form used in the National is typical. The amount done correctly in a given time depends largely on how quickly and accurately the individual learns the key.

of measurement upon the relation between initial ability and gain. Thomson ['24] has provided the requisite correction formula. While the recognition of this error and the correction for its influence on the correlation does not improve the actual diagnostic or predictive value of a short learning test, it does demonstrate that a test which is long enough to measure improvability accurately may have a much greater diagnostic and predictive value than had seemed possible. Another difficulty which has discouraged experimentation with tests of improvability is the lack of any sound general theory for comparing gains from different starting points; and this may greatly limit the scope of such tests. On the other hand, measures of improvability have exceptional advantages in respect of universality of application and freedom from improper training. They may also be much less susceptible to environmental differences than are the ordinary measures of status.

An investigation of the altitude of *learning,* that is, of how hard things a person can learn to do; and of the speed of learning certain things which all or nearly all can learn if they have time enough, is very much needed. Until such an investigation is made, the sound procedure with scores in substitution tests and the like is to treat the varying scores as representing success with tasks varying in difficulty. A score of $K + 2$ thus means success with a harder task than does a score of $K + 1$, and so on. The differences in difficulty corresponding to the differences in the scores can then be measured by the principles and techniques presented in this volume.

There are two final matters which concern all existing tests and scales for intellect. The first is the matter of the selection of the tasks. The second is the matter of the reliability of the measure.

In all of them the selection of the single tasks has been narrow and more or less arbitrary. Binet chose tasks which older children did and younger children could not do. In the National the choice was made in view of a criterion consisting of grade reached in school, intelligence as estimated by teachers, and the like. A general fund of knowledge that such and such tasks are allied to various symptoms and assumed criteria of intelligence is more or less wisely used. In none of them has the selection been made so as to represent or sample in any defined way any total series of tasks which the authors of the examination regarded as being the totality of intellectual tasks.

This is not a serious defect for the ordinary purposes of ranking individuals according to that ill-defined trait known as intelligence, for two reasons. First, most of the examinations in common use are made up of verbal and numerical and factual tasks in somewhat the same proportions; and, second, the intercorrelations of different sorts of tasks, so long as all concern the ability to manage ideas, are all fairly close.

However, there is no loss and a considerable gain, especially for rigorous treatment, if a definite plan for the selection of tasks is used, as in the CAVD series, so that the nature of the fact measured is clearly defined. If the Army Alpha, for example, were called D, A, Cs, So, Di, Ac, An, Inf, and constructed so that there were three of each of these sorts of tasks at each of eight levels, it would be a more useful instrument.

In respect of the reliability of the determination, our examinations have been far too lax, especially at the high levels, to serve well for scientific purposes or for such practical purposes as require any considerable exactitude. The meaning of any score is obscured by the fact that so large a portion of it is chance error. At the high levels a small error in altitude may mean a very large error in area. The neglect of this matter has indeed been almost scandalous, since in the case of many widely used intelligence examinations, the amount of the chance error is not even known.

In connection with our inquiry, Miss Woodyard is conducting a careful investigation of the nature and amount and causation of the chance error in mental measurements, which will be treated in a separate report. We present here only the facts concerning the reliability of a determination of CAVD altitude such as results from a measurement of an individual with four 40-composite tasks near his level of difficulty. To obtain such a measurement in an individual examination will require about thirty minutes of exploratory testing and about two hours with the four composites. To obtain it in a group examination will require usually that the group be tested with five 40-composites requiring from three hours at levels H to L, up to five hours at levels N to R.

The mean square error of an altitude determined from the three successive 40-composite scores whose sum is nearest to 60 is as shown below for various groups.

MEAN SQUARE ERROR OF A CAVD ALTITUDE IN UNITS OF THE CAVD SCALE ($1.00$ EQUALLING $\sigma_{i9}$)

The median error is reported for each group.

| | |
|---|---|
| 100 adults of mental age $2\frac{1}{2}$ to $4\frac{1}{2}$ | .41 |
| 100 adults of mental age 6 | .32 |
| 115 pupils in Grade 4 | .40 |
| 100 pupils in Grade 9 | .29 |
| 63 university students | $.37\frac{1}{2}$ |

The mean square error is thus about .35, or about one fiftieth of the difference between a low grade imbecile of mental age 3 years and a very gifted adult, one person in a thousand.

By improving the CAVD composites, the error doubtless can be reduced somewhat. Also, further investigation may disclose a procedure more serviceable than the "60" rule (described in Chapter XI, p. 369), and not more complicated or time-consuming. But the decreases will probably be small. In the main, decrease in the error must be attained by increase in the time of the examination.

The existing stock intelligence examinations may be superior to CAVD in this respect, but the probability is that they are inferior to it. It has the advantage of building upon the results gained by them, and of choosing from the best task-material known to date.

# CHAPTER XV

## The Nature of Intellect

We have learned to think of intellect as the ability to succeed with intellectual tasks, and to measure it by making an inventory of a fair sampling from these tasks, arranging these in levels of intellectual difficulty, and observing how many the intellect in question succeeds with at each level (and, if we wish, how long a time each success takes). From this graded inventory, we may compute measures of altitude or level, of width or range or extent at each level, and of total area. For Intellect CAVD, the pattern for a sample with $n$ tasks at each level, if $n$ is large enough, is very similar for all individuals of roughly similar training. Consequently, the altitude, the total area, and the width at any level are closely interdependent.

Any defined intellect can be treated as we have treated Intellect CAVD.

Such a definition in terms of tasks accomplishable, and such a measurement in terms of the contents of a graded inventory is sound and useful, but is not entirely satisfying. One cherishes the hope that some simpler, more unitary fact exists as the cause of intellect and that variations in the magnitude of this fact may provide a single fundamental scale which will account for levels and range and surface. Moreover, one realizes the desirability of search for the physiological cause of intellect, regardless of whether that cause be single and simple or manifold and complex.

Our consideration of these matters has led us to a hypothesis concerning the nature and causation of intellect for which we have found fairly substantial evidence. It is the purpose of this chapter to present and discuss this hypothesis.

## A WORKING DEFINITION OF INTELLECT

Since this hypothesis concerns intellect in general as well as any defined segment of it such as Intellect CAVD, we may revert to vaguer and more catholic conceptions. The fact of human life of whose nature we seek a more exact description is the ability to deal with things or persons or ideas by the use of ideas. We contrast intellectual power over things, as by ideas about length or weight or heat, with non-intellectual power over things, as by strength or skill or acuity of vision. We contrast intellectual power over people, as by consideration of facts about them, with non-intellectual power over them, as by good temper or courage or physical charm. We contrast intellectual power over ideas, as by using other ideas to gain success with them, with non-intellectual power over them, as by industry or patience.

The facts and arguments which we shall present do not, however, depend for relevance or value upon the acceptance of this particular identification and demarcation of intellect. They will apply nearly or quite as well to any preliminary description which any competent psychologist would devise for those features of life wherein the Aristotles differ most widely from the inmates of asylums for idiots, and wherein the life of a man thinking effectively about mathematics or medicine or manufacturing differs from the life the same man eating, drinking, swimming or playing tennis without, as we say, an idea in his head.

If a score of competent psychologists should list on the one hand all the products whose production depends primarily upon intellect—all the tasks for success with which intellect is the *sine qua non*; and on the other all the products or tasks which they regarded as non-intellectual—success thereat being independent of intellect—they would show very substantial agreement. Where they appeared to differ, the differences would be unimportant for our purpose. Very seldom would the same task appear on opposite sides of the ledger. When it did, the difference would resolve itself into a difference in favor of a narrower restriction of intellect (for example, to ability to deal with abstract ideas or to ability to deal with relations), or in favor of a wider extension of it (for example, to certain tasks where ideas are not at work, at least not obviously). The facts and arguments which we shall present will apply regardless of such shrinkage or swelling in the area regarded as intellectual.

Intellect may be CAVD, or CAVD plus ability in giving the opposites of words, making it CAVDO; or that, plus insight into spatial relations, making it CAVDOS; or that plus ability in inductive and deductive reasonings, making it CAVDOSR, and so on.

Beginning, then, with this loosely determined group of products which intellect produces, tasks at which intellect brings success, we may inquire concerning its observable or surface nature as a fact in human behavior or its deeper nature as a fact of fundamental processes in the mind or brain. We may investigate the thinking and action of men who have much intellect to discover more precisely and fully the features in which they differ from men who have little; or we may try to discover more ultimate causes of these differences. We may compare a man's obvious life, when he is using his intellect little or not at all, with his life when he makes large use of it, other factors remaining the same, to see just what the differences are; or we may try to discover hidden forces which produce these differences. We may study the nature of intellectual tasks, the production of intellectual products, or the nature of the ultimate power or powers whereby a man can succeed with such tasks. There may be, of course, much to be revealed concerning facts intermediate between the description of intellectual tasks and the discovery of their ultimate cause.

The standard orthodox view of the surface nature of intellect has been that it is divided rather sharply into a lower half, mere connection-forming or the association of ideas, which acquires information and specialized habits of thinking; and a higher half characterized by abstraction, generalization, the perception and use of relations and the selection and control of habits in inference or reasoning, and ability to manage novel or original tasks. The orthodox view of its deeper nature, so far as this has received attention, has been that the mere connection or association of ideas depends upon the physiological mechanism whereby a nerve stimulus is conducted to and excites action in neurones A, B, C, rather than any others, but that the higher processes depend upon something quite different. There would be little agreement as to what this something was, indeed little effort to think or imagine what it could be, but there would be much confidence that it was *not* the mechanism of habit formation.

## THE HYPOTHESIS THAT QUALITY OF INTELLECT DEPENDS UPON QUANTITY OF CONNECTIONS

The hypothesis which we present and shall defend admits the distinction in respect of surface behavior, but asserts that in their deeper nature the higher forms of intellectual operation are identical with mere association or connection forming, depending upon the same sort of physiological connections but requiring *many more of them*. By the same argument the person whose intellect is greater or higher or better than that of another person differs from him in the last analysis in having, not a new sort of physiological process, but simply a larger number of connections of the ordinary sort.

More exactly our hypothesis is as follows: Let $c$ represent whatever anatomical and physiological fact corresponds to the possibility of forming one connection or association or bond between an idea or any part or aspect or feature thereof and a sequent idea or movement or any part or aspect or feature thereof. Then if individuals $I_1$, $I_2$, $I_3$, $I_4$, etc., differing in the number of $c$'s which they possess but alike in other respects, are subjected to identical environments, the amount or degree of intellect which any one of them manifests, and the extent to which he manifests "higher" intellectual processes than the other individuals, will be closely proportional to the number of $c$'s which he possesses. If we rank them by intelligence-examination scores, the order will be that of the number of $c$'s. If we rank intellectual processes in a scale from lower, such as mere information, to higher, such as reasoning, the individuals who manifest the highest processes will have the largest number of $c$'s.

The view of common sense, of educational science, and of those who have constructed tests for measuring intellect, has been that intellect is a power to respond *correctly*, that the *quality* of the responses is a primary criterion of the degree of intellect. The teacher and the test-maker would insist that correct judgments and valid inferences required more intellect than the wrong judgments and faulty inferences.

The hypothesis which we present accepts this view, but makes a sharp distinction in this regard between the original intellectual capacity which a man has and the actual intellectual products which he produces. It credits the quality of the ideas that a man acquires, and the truth or falsity of the judgments which he makes, and, to some extent, even the validity of the inferences which he draws from any given data, largely to his training. The average man today has better ideas about lightning than Aristotle had, can make more correct judgments about eclipses than Moses could, and, if trained in science, may well draw more valid inferences from observing the action of acids on metals than either Aristotle or Moses did. With approximate equality of training, the quality of intellectual responses is an essential index of intellectual capacity, but it may be deceptive if the inequalities are great.

Our hypothesis limits itself to the original capacity. If by original nature, apart from all training, a man possesses tendencies to be right rather than wrong in his judgments, to hold true rather than false ideas, to make justifiable rather than unjustifiable inferences, more or less than other men, in so far forth those tendencies are due to his having more or fewer $c$'s than other men.

The essential element of our hypothesis is that it offers a purely quantitative fact, the number of $c$'s, as the cause of qualitative differences either in the kind of operation (*e.g.*, association *versus* reasoning) or in the quality of the result obtained (*e.g.*, truth *versus* error, wisdom *versus* folly), so far as these qualitative differences are caused by original nature.

We need to make clearer what is meant by "one connection or association or bond between an idea or any part or aspect or feature thereof, or a group of ideas and a sequent idea or movement or any part or feature or aspect thereof." By "connection or association or bond between $a$ and $b$," is meant the probability or certainty that if $a$ occurs in a person, $b$ will occur in him shortly thereafter (say within a second) unless some counteracting force prevents. For the sake of simplicity, we may think of all cases as cases of certainty. The existence of the connection $a \rightarrow b$ then means that whenever $a$ occurs, $b$ will follow within a very short time interval, unless restrained by some contrary force. Thus in a child who has learned the multiplication table, the idea 2 times 5 will always be followed by the idea 10, unless some contrary force prevents.

The $b$ which follows $a$ may be the suppression or prevention of an idea or movement as truly as its appearance. Connections where $a$ inhibits some event may indeed well be as numerous as connections where $a$ releases or produces some event. The $b$ may also be one step toward an event or one partial condition of it so that, for example, $a_1$ may be followed by $b_1$ with no obvious difference in the person, and $a_2$ may be followed by $b_2$, again with no observable difference in the person, but if $a_1$ and $a_2$ act closely together in time, an obvious difference $c$ in the person may always follow. Similarly the $b$ may be one step toward or one partial condition of the inhibition of some occurrence, so that, for example, $a_1$ alone may not prevent $c$, and $a_2$ alone may not prevent $c$, but $a_1 + a_2$ in close enough temporal proximity may entirely prevent $c$ from occurring.

By an "idea" is meant any small portion of the stream of thought, such as a precept, or an image, or a meaning, or a word of inner speech.[1] It is intended to omit unorganized sensory stuff such as the person does not ever isolate or identify or name, and emotional stuff such as excitement, irritability, or fear. But no sharp lines need be drawn, for the hypothesis will remain valid even if "ideas" are interpreted loosely to include more than we have in mind; and the hypothesis will be fruitful even if "ideas" are interpreted very, very narrowly, say to include only words. It is not intended to beg the question of consciousness or bodily action by the use of the word image. Whether "ideas" be envisaged as facts of conscious awareness or as facts of bodily behavior is a matter of indifference to the hypothesis.

There remains to be clarified the apparently innocent and unambiguous word "one," which really conceals a nest of difficulties. We think readily about "one idea," "part of an idea," "many ideas," "two images that are nearly alike," "ten thousand percepts," and the like; and the treatment of percepts, images, and relations as separable and capable of enumeration is doubtless useful and in a certain correspondence with reality. Yet it is hard to decide when and why the reader's percept of, say, the word "Adam" shall be counted as one percept of a word, or four percepts each of one letter, or ten percepts each of one line; or when and why his visual image of a square shall be counted as one image of a square, or as eight images of lines and angles, or as a fraction of a total visual image of a square on a certain background. Naïve common-sense calls "Two and three are five" one idea, and with a certain

---

[1] Sensori-motor connections, such as are formed in learning to swim, dive, box, or wrestle, and moral or temperamental connections, such as are formed in keeping one's temper, or being courageous, are thus considered as, at least partially, outside of intellect.

suitability, but that sort of a *"one"* is obviously different from the "one" used when a person has the idea of two, or the idea of three, or the idea of "and-ness."

In strictness the entire status of the mind (or of the central nervous system) at any instant connects with or leads to its entire status at the next instant, and any segregation of a part of this total status as one idea, and any attribution of a part of the sequent status to this idea's associative potency, is an incomplete statement of what happens.

These difficulties and others of like nature may best be met, not by trying to set up rigorous criteria for what shall be one idea, what a part of an idea, and what a group of ideas, nor, on the other hand, by a refusal to use the analyses which common sense and science have found profitable, but rather by realizing that ideas are not like eggs in a basket nor like eggs in an omelet, but are what they are. If we must liken them to something, let it be tones in a symphony or factions in a party or neurones in the brain, or some other case of a very complex organization where science can and should separate the total into parts, but where these parts are splitting and combining from time to time and are being influenced in their action by more or less of the total organization.

We must, of course, be consistent, in any comparative enumerations, not calling the same fact now one idea, now two, and now ten, to the prejudice of the truth.

The next matter to note is that there may be associations or bonds from different ideas, from $a$ to $b$, from $a$ to $c$, from $a$ to $d$, and so on, according to slightly different conditions in the general status of which $a$ is a part. Thus the idea of "12" may call up "$11 + 1$," or "$10 + 2$," or "$4 \times 3$," or "$6 \times 2$," or "dozen," or "not prime," or "a number," or "XII," according to relatively minor conditions attached to "12." There may likewise be connections from many different ideas to the same idea, or to the same movement, as when we think "yes" or nod the head to a hundred different questions. This does not mean that the same cause can have different results or different causes have the same result, any more in the mind than in physical nature. Different total statuses of the person never do lead to one absolutely identical status. It means simply that when certain accessories are neglected, one same consequence follows a hundred different stimuli.

We can then analyze the stream or web or panorama of intellectual life, finding in it ideas. These occur not haphazard, but always by some cause. Chief among the causes are the bonds or links whereby one idea tends to be followed by a certain other idea. One man may have per day or per lifetime many more different ideas than another man. Of two men having the same number of ideas, one may have many more different connections than the other man has. For example, individuals A and B may each be capable of the ideas $a, b, c, d$, and the movement $e$. A may have only the connections $a \rightarrow e$, $b \rightarrow e$, $c \rightarrow e$, and $d \rightarrow e$. B may have the connections $a \rightarrow bc$, $b \rightarrow ac$, $c \rightarrow db$, $d \rightarrow ae$, $ab \rightarrow abcc$, $ac \rightarrow bbcd$, $ad \rightarrow abce$, $bc \rightarrow abcd$, $bd \rightarrow aace$, and others.

This greater fund of ideas and connections is partly due to larger life and more varied and stimulating life, but it may be and certainly is partly due to original nature. It has some anatomical or physiological cause or parallel. Our hypothesis regards this anatomical cause or correspondent of the original possibility of having more such connections (call it C) as the cause of the original differences in intellect among men. It also supposes that the correspondence is such that C can be analyzed into a number of $c$'s so that a C which allows the formation of many connections with ideas has many $c$'s, whereas a C which allows the formation of only a few has few $c$'s. As we stated it, C consisted of $c$'s, one $c$ meaning the possibility of the formation of one connection, two $c$'s meaning the possibility of forming two connections, and so on. This form of statement was chosen primarily for clearness and brevity. It needs amendment, or at least explanation.

Whether there is any such one to one corespondence between facts of anatomy and physiology, and facts of mental association, bonds or links in behavior is, however, not of much consequence to the hypothesis. What is essential to the hypothesis is that by original nature, men differ in respect of the number of connections or associations with ideas which they can form, so that despite identical outside environments, some of them would have many more than others. "The number of $c$'s a man has" means simply the original constitutional basis of the number of ideational connections which he has. It is highly probable that the original basis of quantity of connections is itself a matter of quantity, that a more potent C is one that has more of something than a less potent C has. But it is not necessary for the hypothesis that this should be so. So our hypothesis may better be amended to read:

Let $C_a$, $C_{a+b}$, $C_{a+b+c}$, $C_{a+b+c+d}$, and so on, represent original natures such that with identical outside environments, the man having $C_a$ will form $a$ connections, the man having $C_{a+b}$ will form $a + b$ connections, and so on. Then, with identical outside environments, the amount of intellect which a man manifests, and the extent to which he manifests "higher" powers than other men, will depend largely upon his C.[2]

Negatively, the hypothesis asserts that no special qualitative differences are required to account for differences in degree of intellect; the higher processes or powers have no other basis in original nature than that which accounts for differences in the number of bonds of the associative type.

The reader who is impatient with these subtleties may forget them all with no great loss. The gist of our doctrine is that, by original nature, the intellect capable of the highest reasoning and adaptability differs from the intellect of

[2] Certain other inner conditions, such as the strength of curiosity, the satisfyingness of thought for thought's sake, and the appeal of non-intellectual activities, in so far as they are distinct from the man's C, would have to be allowed for to make a perfect prediction.

an imbecile only in the capacity for having more connections of the sort described.

The bearing of the hypothesis upon the problem of measurement lies in the fact that we may be able for many purposes *to replace our measurement via a sample inventory of tasks, by a more or less direct measurement of C.* If we can get access to C so as to measure it (and if the hypothesis is valid) we can measure intellectual capacity, and can measure it perhaps at a very early age. If also one C does vary from another simply by consisting of a larger number of *c*'s we have a single variable in the most convenient of all units.

Any person familiar with the finer anatomy of the brain will at once think of the number of possible contacts (or possibly coalescences) of the fibrils of axones with dendritic processes in the associative neurones which act in perception, thought, and speech as a highly probable C. We have had it in mind as the possible C which we should investigate first if opportunity offered. We do not, however, make the hypothesis depend upon this particular C.

EXPERIMENTAL VERIFICATION OF THE QUANTITY HYPOTHESIS

The hypothesis may be submitted to an almost crucial test by determining the correlations within the upper half of intellect, those within the lower half, and those between the upper and the lower halves. Do the "higher" abilities of selective and relational thinking, abstraction, generalization and organization display close interdependence among themselves and marked independence of the "lower" or purely associative abilities?

At our suggestion, Mr. J. W. Tilton has made this test in the case of 250 boys at the time of graduation from Grade 8. As measures of the "higher" or "control" abilities, he used sentence completions, arithmetical problems, and analogies tests. As measures of the more purely "associative" abilities, he used vocabulary tests, routine and informational arithmetic, and information tests.

The following is a sample of the arithmetic:

## I. E. R. ARITHMETIC, ASSOC., II

*Add:*

| *a.* | *b.* | *c.* | *d.* | *e.* | *f.* | *g.* |
|---|---|---|---|---|---|---|
| $\frac{3}{8}$ | | $9\frac{1}{2}$ | $9\frac{3}{4}$ | 3 wk. 4 da. | 7 lb. 12 oz. | $1\frac{1}{3}$ |
| $\frac{7}{8}$ | 1 | 2 | $5\frac{7}{8}$ | 4 wk. 2 da. | 8 lb. 5 oz. | $2\frac{7}{8}$ |
| $\frac{5}{8}$ | 1 | $5\frac{3}{4}$ | $6\frac{1}{2}$ | 2 wk. 6 da. | 6 lb. 14 oz. | $1\frac{1}{2}$ |

*Multiply:*

| *h.* | *i.* | *j.* | *k.* | *l.* |
|---|---|---|---|---|
| 254 | 9.6 | 3 ft. 5 in. | 16 | $12\frac{5}{8}$ |
| 6 | 4 | 5 | $2\frac{1}{4}$ | 16 |

*Divide:*

| *m.* | *n.* | *o.* | *p.* |
|---|---|---|---|
| $50 \div 7 =$ | $6 \overline{)\ .138}$ | $3\frac{1}{2} \div 9 =$ | $\frac{5}{4} \div \frac{3}{5} =$ |

*Write the answers to these questions:*

*q.* 1 cent is how many mills? ..........

*r.* 1 pint is how many gills? ..........

*s.* 1 square mile is how many acres? ..........

*t.* How much is 20% of $60? ..........

*u.* How much is $5\frac{1}{4}$% of $200? ..........

*v.* Which months have only 30 days? ..........

*w.* 1 rod is how many feet? ..........

*x.* 1 acre is how many square rods? ..........

*y.* 1 meter is how many inches? ..........

*z.* What is the square root of 64? ..........

*aa.* What is the cube root of 64? ..........

*bb.* $6^3$ equals how many? ..........

## The following is a sample of the information tests:

### I. E. R. INFORMATION, E 2 AND F 1

Write or print your name and age and grade in school here very plainly.

Name .......................... Age .......................... Grade ..........................

*In each of the sentences below, you have a choice among four words. Draw a line under the one of these four words which makes the truest sentence.*

E 2

1. The Gnome engine is chiefly used in airplanes automobiles tractors motorcycles.
2. Vinegar is made from picric acid apples bark lemons.
3. Adobe is the name of a building material Indian tribe Chinese official flower.
4. One of the books of the Bible is Jacob Jesse Joshua Judah.
5. Oxo is the name of a meat extract automobile cigar toothpowder.
6. Lille is in Belgium England France Switzerland.
7. Queen Elizabeth of England was born about 1425 1525 1625 1725.

8. From Leningrad to Moscow is about    500 mi.  1,000 mi.  1,500 mi. 2,000 mi.
9. Corot is the name of a    musician  painter  pigment  general.
10. The angle of incidence is equal to the angle of    coincidence  reflection  refraction  subsidence.

F 1

1. The namber of rows of kernels on an average ear of corn is about 5  15  25  35
2. The ten commandments are called the    decagon  decalog  decament decemvirate.
3. The ratio of the size of Africa to that of Europe is about    2 to 1  3 to 1  6 to 1  9 to 1.
4. Brahmaputra is the name of a    flower  goddess  language  river.
5. A pint can full of lead would weigh about    6 lb.  12 lb.  18 lb. 24 lb.
6. Hydrogen becomes liquid at about    $-300°$ C.  $-150°$ C.  $-10°$ C. $+60°$ C.
7. The number of a crab's legs is    four  six  eight  ten.
8. One inch equals about    2 cm.  $2\frac{1}{4}$ cm.  $2\frac{1}{2}$ cm.  $2\frac{3}{4}$ cm.
9. An irregular four-sided figure is called a    scolium  trapezium  parallelogram  pentagon.
10. One of the books of the Bible is    David  Eleazar  Leviticus  Uzziah.

The correlations (corrected for attenuation), which are presented in Table 131, give a clear answer. In this group the "higher" abilities correlate as closely with the associative abilities as the higher do *inter se,* or as the associative abilities do *inter se.* The average of these six cases is .558 ± .029 (P. E.). The average of the three cases of "higher" with "higher" is .544. The average of the three cases of "associative" with "associative" is .571. The average of the six cases of "higher" with "associative" where the content differs just as much as it does in the "higher with higher" and in the "associative with associative," is .577 ± .021 (P. E.). The three cases Co. with Voc., Ar. Cont. with Arith. Ass., and Anal. with Inf. where the content is similar (words, numbers, and facts), have an average correlation of .71.

If we apply the attenuation formula so as to measure the relation between (a) what is common to any two of the associative tests with words, numbers, and facts, and (b) what is common to any two of the "higher" tests with words, numbers, and facts, we obtain nine correlations[5] whose average is 1.07 $\pm$ .05($\sigma$). If we eliminate the influence of the correlations between higher and lower with similar content (not using $r_{Cov}$, $r_{AnInt}$, or $r_{AcAa}$) the correlation between what is common to the associative abilities and what is common to the higher abilities, has an average[6] of 1.00 $\pm$ .03($\sigma$).

There thus seems reason to refer the higher, originating, directing abilities to much the same fundamental causes as the associative. The higher powers are in their causation as much like the lower as like one another. This is not because the correlations are insensitive indices. On the contrary, similarity in the content or data thought about, raises the correlation from .58 to .71. Nor is it because the subjects of the experiments did not have and use the higher abilities.

We have extended, and, in general, confirmed, Mr. Tilton's findings by experiments of the same general nature.

458 pupils in Grade 11 in city K were tested with 350 vocabulary tasks and also with two forms of the I. E. R. Selective and Relational Thinking, Generalization and Organization examination.[7]

676 pupils in Grade 11 in city K, closely similar in ability to the 458 just mentioned, were tested with over a hundred reading tasks and also with the two forms of the I. E. R. Sel. Rel. Gen. Org. examination.

The raw correlations of the general intelligence score with the total vocabulary score (sum of rights) and with the total reading score (sum of rights) were .72 and .73, respectively. The correlation of the general intelligence score with that from another similar pair of examinations is .92 by the Spearman-Brown formula, the correlation of one

---

[5] 1.01, 1.06, .82, 1.31, 1.26$\frac{1}{2}$, 1.07$\frac{1}{2}$, 1.11, 1.05, and .97$\frac{1}{2}$, with a median of 1.06.

[6] 1.00, 99$\frac{1}{2}$, .77, 1.09, 1.09, 1.04, 1.01, 1.06$\frac{1}{2}$, and .90, with a median of 1.01.

[7] This is a composite of stock tests of so-called general intelligence.

form with the other being .85.  The correlation of the vocabulary score with that of another similar examination is .98 by the Spearman-Brown formula, the correlation between two random halves thereof being .97.  The correlation of the reading score with that of another similar examination is not known, but will not be far from .9.  Using .92, .98, and .90 for these self-correlations, we have .76 and .80 as the

TABLE 131.

INTERCORRELATIONS (CORRECTED FOR ATTENUATION) OF SENTENCE COMPLETION (CO), VOCABULARY (V), ARITHMETIC CONTROL (AC), ARITHMETICAL ASSOCIATION (AA), ANALOGIES (AN), AND INFORMATION (INF), IN 250 PUPILS OF GRADE 8½.  (COMPILED FROM TABLES OF TILTON [ '25], p. ——).

| Control with Control | | Control with Asso. (content different) | | Control with Asso. (content similar) | |
|---|---|---|---|---|---|
| Co An | .522 | Co Inf | .722 | Co V | .865 |
| Co Ac | .523 | Co Aa | .550 | An Inf | .604 |
| An Ac | .587 | An V | .563 | Ac Aa | .643 |
|  |  | An Aa | .486 |  |  |
|  |  | Ac V | .491 |  |  |
|  |  | Ac Inf | .575 |  |  |
| Asso. with Asso. | | | | | |
| V Inf. | .787 | | | | |
| V Aa | .433 | | | | |
| Inf. Aa | .592 | | | | |
| Self-Correlations | | | | | |
| V–I V–II | .815 ± .0143 | | | | |
| Inf I Inf II | .600 ± .0273 | | | | |
| Aa I Aa II | .829 ± .0133 | | | | |
| Co I Co II | .744 ± .0190 | | | | |
| An I An II | .920 ± .0103 | | | | |
| Ac I Ac II | .950 ± .0041 | | | | |

coefficients corrected for attenuation between a stock intelligence score and vocabulary and reading, respectively. The mere knowledge of single words seems almost as "intellectual" as the comprehension of paragraphs.

If we use for each individual a level score representing the degree of difficulty at which he can succeed with 50% of the tasks, a similar result is obtained.  The coefficients of correlation for the group in question are:

$$Corrected\ for$$
Raw    attenuation[8]

General intelligence score with vocab-
ulary ............................................................................ .72         .77
General intelligence score with compre-
hension of paragraphs ........................... .66         .76

We have measured 100 university students in (1) a composite of sentence completions, and comprehension of paragraphs, (2) a composite of picture completions, pictorial analogies, and geometrical analogies, (3) arithmetical problems,[9] (4) a vocabulary test, and (5) an extensive information test.[10] The intercorrelations are shown in Table 132.

The "higher" abilities show an average corrected correlation among themselves of .48 by P and .35 by S; the "lower" show a correlation of .67 by P and .59 by S. The average for a "higher" with a "lower" is .47 by P and .38 by S. In general, the correlation is nearly as close between a "higher' and a "lower" as within the higher or within the lower.

The estimated correlation between what is common to C and A and what is common to V and Inf is .90. The estimated correlation between what is common to C and Pic and what is common to V and Inf is .78. The estimated correlation between what is common to A and Pic and what is common to V and Inf is .56. The average is .75 ± .08($\sigma$).

Additional evidence is found in the correlation in the case of 126 pupils in Grade 5½ for each of whom summation

[8] The self-correlation of the vocabulary level-score is .94. The self-correlation of the reading level-score is approximately .80 (.77 with a level-score from a less extensive test).

[9] The arithmetical tasks were not hard enough to measure the ability of the group well, and the correlations would probably be considerably higher with an adequate set of mathematical tasks. But they would hardly surpass the information correlations.

[10] This was not as purely a test of associative thinking as would have been most desirable, a certain amount of organization and inference being of assistance in some of the tasks; but it was so to an enormously greater extent than the other composite.

## TABLE 132.

THE INTERCORRELATION OF FOUR TESTS OF THE HIGHER (CO. READ, ARITH., AND PIC.) AND TWO TESTS OF ASSOCIATIVE THINKING (VOC. AND INF.). 100 UNIVERSITY STUDENTS. P = BY PEARSON FORMULA; SH = BY SHEPPARD FORMULA.

| | Raw Correlations | | | | | | | | Correlations Corrected for Attenuation | | | | | | | |
| | Arith. | | Pic. | | Voc. | | Inf. | | Arith. | | Pic. | | Voc. | | Inf. | |
| | P | SH | P | SH | P | SH | P | SH | P | SH | P | SH | P | SH | P | SH |
|---|---|---|---|---|---|---|---|---|---|---|---|---|---|---|---|---|
| (1) Co. Read. | .28 | .34 | .44 | .31 | .58 | .54 | .51 | .37 | .33 | .39 | .52 | .40 | .63 | .58 | .58 | .43 |
| (3) Arith. | | | .48 | .40 | .23 | .22 | .42 | .40 | | | .59 | .53 | .25 | .24½ | .49 | .48 |
| (2) Pic. | | | | | .29 | .16 | .43½ | .25 | | | | | .33 | .20 | .53 | .33 |
| (4) Voc. | | | | | | | .61 | .59 | | | | | | | .67 | .65½ |

scores in C, A, V, D, and Inf were available. The reliabilities of these scores have not been determined at all exactly, but they are high and approximately equal, each representing about 40 minutes of work. Table 133 presents these correlations. The average of the intercorrelations of C, A, and D is .66. The correlation between V and Inf is .81. The average of the intercorrelations of C or A or D with V or Inf is .62. The change from "higher" to "lower" abilities does not reduce the correlations as much as the change from words to numbers within the higher abilities. C and D correlate .81, whereas C and A correlate only .64; and D and A only .52.

TABLE 133.

THE INTERCORRELATIONS OF THREE TESTS OF THE HIGHER AND TWO TESTS OF THE LOWER OR ASSOCIATIVE THINKING. 126 PUPILS IN GRADE 5½. THE CORRELATIONS ARE ALL RAW CORRELATIONS BY THE SHEPPARD FORMULA.

|   | A | V | D | Inf. |
|---|---|---|---|------|
| C | .64 | .75 | .81 | .59 |
| A |   | .52 | .52 | .41 |
| V |   |   | .80 | .81 |
| D |   |   |   | .64 |

The correlation between what is common to C and A and what is common to V and Inf is given by

$$\frac{\sqrt[4]{.75 \times .59 \times .52 \times .41}}{\sqrt{.64 \times .81}}, \text{ or } .77.$$

The correlation between what is common to D and A and what is common to V and Inf is given by

$$\frac{\sqrt[4]{.80 \times .64 \times .52 \times .41}}{\sqrt{.52 \times .81}}, \text{ or } .71.$$

The correlation between what is common to C and D and what is common to A and D is given by

$$\frac{\sqrt[4]{.64 \times .81 \times .52 \times 1.00}}{\sqrt{.81 \times .52}}, \text{ or } 1.11.$$

The average is $.86 \pm .10$ (error is in terms of $\sigma_{t-o}$).

### SUMMARY

We may combine the results from Mr. Tilton's 250 cases and our two groups of 100 and 126 cases roughly, giving equal weight to the last two determinations and as much weight to Mr. Tilton's determination as to the other two together.[11] The weighted average correlations are:

| | |
|---|---|
| Higher with higher | .53 |
| Lower with lower | .64$\frac{1}{5}$ |
| Higher with lower | .57 |
| What is common to two higher with what is common to two lower | .94 |

These facts are almost crucial. They prove that mere association and the higher abilities have in the main the same cause. Almost all of whatever is common to the one sort is common to the other sort. If we are to avoid the conclusion that associative ability is this cause, we must either place the causation of associative ability in the higher ability, or seek a common cause for both which is different from either, such as a general mental energy or vitality. The first of these assumptions is absurd, because associative ability occurs abundantly without any trace of the higher abilities, but these never occur without it. In the lower animals, in idiots, and low imbeciles, and in the young infant, mental connections are formed without the appearance or use of abstraction, generalization, or relational thinking. If either is to be derived from the other, it is surely best to derive the higher abilities from the associative abilities. The second assumption is tolerable, though it

[11] His determination probably deserves even more relative weight than this because his test material was better adapted to bring out any differences between the higher and the lower forms of intellect. If more weight is given, the higher and lower become still less distinguishable.

seems defensive and evasive. It also is entirely empty and meaningless until the "energy" or "vitality" is expressed as some fact known to science. What shall that fact be? Until that fact is chosen, the doctrine that ability in connection-forming, and ability in the higher processes, have a common cause which is not the former, is a mere statement of ignorance. We can think of no fact so suitable as C, the physiological parallel of number of mental connections. The cause must not be a too general vigor or health or energy or sensitivity or conductivity of neurones. For the correlations between intellect and other functions of the nervous system are very far from perfect. Between intellect and mental health or balance, between intellect and sensori-motor skill, between intellect and sensory acuity, between intellect and morality—no one of these correlations would be as close as the correlation between the associative ability and "higher" ability within intellect.

We do not maintain that C is the sole cause of intellect in original nature, so that two persons with identical numbers of C's and identical training will necessarily have identical intellectual achievement. We have already noted, as factors which play a part, strength of curiosity, satisfyingness of thought for thought's sake, and competition from non-intellectual activities and interests. Other thing must be equal, such as health and energy. There is also perhaps a capacity for having the neurones act *with reference one to another,* that is, with *integration,* whose low or negative extreme is pronounced dissociation as in hysteria, and whose high or positive extreme appears as a notable goodsense or adequacy in the use of one's experiences. This capacity may be largely irrespective of C. There is also perhaps a capacity for resisting intellectual panic and confusion, whose low or negative extreme is mania or "flight of ideas" and whose high extreme is a notable steadiness and regulation of each individual connection by the general set or adjustment of the mind at the time. The strength of this capacity may be largely irrespective of C.

These and other possible qualifications do not impair the value of the hypothesis. They amount to making distinctions between basal intellectual capacity and interferences with it or handicaps to it by disassociation as in hysterical lapses, or by irrelevance as in mania. We should have just as much need to make these distinctions if we attributed differences in intellectual capacity to differences in the quality, or in the shape, or in the chemical action of neurones. Nor would two sorts of neural action qualitatively different relieve us from them.

We shall not discuss general arguments pro and con in this report, but will simply note that both the phylogeny and the ontogeny of intellect seems to us to show selection, analysis, abstraction, generalization, and reasoning coming as a direct consequence of increase in the number of connections; and that what little is known of the status of the neurones in very dull individuals is in harmony with the quantitative theory.[12]

[12] See especially Hammarberg, Studier öfver Idiotiens, Klinik och Patologi.

# CHAPTER XVI

## THE MEASUREMENT OF ORIGINAL INTELLECTUAL CAPACITY AND OF ACQUIRED INTELLECTUAL ABILITY

### THE PRESENT STATUS OF OPINION

Psychologists are often credited with the opinion that the intelligence examinations which they have devised, such as the Binet or Army Alpha or Army Beta, measure an individual's original intellectual capacity, irrespective of the opportunities which he has had, or the time he has spent in intellectual activities, or the zeal with which he has engaged in them.

So extreme a view is not, however, held by any of the leaders in this field. The nearest approach to it that we have noted in their statements is that of L. S. Hollingworth, who defines intelligence as "the capacity for learning, the capacity for comprehending and making adaptations to the environment" which "cannot be acquired by any course of training" ['23, p. 192]; and says of the Stanford Binet "It measures intelligence" ['23, p. 67], when discussing means "of singling out intelligence from all the other factors which complicate efficiency in school work" ['23, p. 62].

The following quotations from Colvin, Whipple and Terman are representative:

"There is no reasonable doubt that the present intelligence tests do indicate to a fair degree native ability to learn" [Colvin, '23, p. 336].

Colvin and MacPhail (speaking of Professor Bagley's article, "Educational Determinism or Democracy and the I. Q.") say: "He is right if he means that it is not always easy to determine what this innate learning capacity, this native intelligence is, and that mistakes in individual cases may be made; but he is wrong if he would convey the idea that in general it is not possible to determine within reasonable limits what the native learning capacity of the child is, provided adequate intelligence tests are employed and various common sense precautions taken" ['22a, p. 114].

Terman writes: "As a matter of fact, all the 'intelligence testers' will readily agree with Mr. Lippmann that their tests do not measure simon pure intelligence, but always native ability, plus other things, with no final verdict yet as to exactly how much the other things affect the score. However, nearly all the psychologists believe that native ability counts very heavily" ['22, p. 119]; and elsewhere, "It would, of course, be going too far to deny all possibility of environmental conditions affecting the result of an intelligence test. Certainly no one would expect that a child reared in a cage and denied all intercourse with other human beings could by any system of mental measurement test up to the level of normal children. There is, however, no reason to believe that ordinary differences in social environment (apart from heredity), differences such as those obtaining among unselected children attending approximately the same general type of school in a civilized community, affect to any great extent the validity of the scale" ['16, p. 116].

Whipple writes: "In presenting these results, it ought to be made clear at the outset that no psychologist is foolish enough to suppose that native intelligence is the sole factor in academic success; all that is contended is that it is one factor, and probably the most important single factor, and that it is measurable by wholesale rapid methods with a reasonable degree of precision" ['22, p. 262]; and elsewhere, "We know that the organism arrives at approximate maturity of growth in stature and in many other physical traits in early adolescence; the fact that our test scores indicate the maturing at about the same time of whatever it is we are measuring, like the fact that, regardless of chronological age, the correlation between stature and mental age is high, may very well indicate that our tests are also measuring an intrinsic capacity which matures according to laws of its own and with relatively little influence from the environment" ['23, p. 597].

On the other hand, there are some emphatic assertions that a person's score in a stock intelligence examination is, in very large measure, the product of purely environmental forces. So Cyril Burt writes of the Binet: "Errand boys and paper boys will answer smartly in the money tests. . . . The busy little housewife from an illiterate home, who there carries out the most intricate duties, will yet be unable to put those duties into words. The solitary child of a cultured family—profiting, perhaps, rather by daily intercourse with educated adults than by special inborn gifts— will respond with an information and a phraseology beyond anything he would spontaneously invent or acquire. . . .

"Of these numerous intervening agencies the most potent is, without doubt, educational opportunity. Many of the tests—some of them withdrawn by Binet in his final revision—are sheer tests of school attainments. Reading, writing, dictation are learnt in English lessons; counting and addition and subtraction of money, in arithmetic lessons; drawing from copy and drawing from memory, in drawing lessons; the date is put at the head of every written exercise on every day of the term, and with equal regularity is never heard and never recollected on any day of the vacation. Estimated by the Binet-Simon scale, therefore, a child's apparent intelligence must depend in no small measure upon his class in school" ['21, p. 175].

### GENERAL PRINCIPLES

We have hitherto defined and measured intellect without restrictions as to its origin, and without distinction between sheer ability at thinking and a love of thinking which makes one think oftener, longer, and harder. If, however, either the altitude or the area of Intellect CAVD is entirely due to an original capacity that is entirely independent of the kind or amount of training received and of the intellectual interests inherited or acquired, the fact should be known. If analytic measures are possible whereby certain tasks or symptoms isolate and measure the original capacity, certain others measure the element of interest or zeal, and still others measure the potency of the environments provided, such would be useful in many ways. It might be impossible to measure capacity separately from interest, and still be possible to measure inherited intellectual promise (due to a mixture of capacity and interest) separately from environmental alterations thereof. Or, it might be possible to measure the sheer capacity apart from the interest factor, but not to separate nature's share from nurture's. Either of these last two possibilities would be useful.

We may best begin by certain simple axioms, or, more modestly, truisms. (1) If two men had been subjected to identical circumstances in life, each and every difference between them would be due to original nature; if two were alike originally, all their later differences would be due to the circumstances of life.

(2) In proportion as an intellectual task is one in respect of which all persons have had equally adequate training, so that no conceivable classification by environmental opportunities would correlate at all with success in the task, that task is a measure of original capacity (plus original interest).

(3) In proportion as a *series* of intellectual tasks gives *on the whole* as much advantage to any one set of environmental opportunities as to any other set, that *series* is a measure of original capacity (plus original interest).

(4) Intellectual tasks, success in which requires zero training and is uninfluenced by any kind or amount of training, do not exist and cannot exist, at least not in shape to measure appreciable amounts of intellect.

The first three axioms are self-evident and undisputed, but the fourth may seem to run counter to the beliefs, or at least the hopes, of some psychologists. Indeed, one is tempted to think that children who are set tasks in filling form-boards or tracing mazes, never before having seen one, start at zero and get all the relevant training in the course of the test itself. But that is never the case above the lowest levels. The tracing of a maze rests upon habits of response to location and direction which we once learned; the filling of the simplest form-board depends upon habits of perception of shape and size which we learn as truly as we learn Euclid or shorthand. It is because we have all learned them and learned them early that we tend to forget that they are influenced by training. Because almost everybody has learned them, these tasks are, by axiom 2, more suitable (other things being equal) to measure original capacity than shorthand or Euclid would be. But they cannot be said to require zero training.

It is conceivable that by some direct method of examining the finer anatomy or physiology of the neurones, as by some technique analogous to the X-ray technique, original intellectual power and interest may be separated from acquired ability without any reliance upon axioms 2 and 3. But so long as we measure intellect by the production of intellectual products—success with intellectual tasks—we can never reduce environmental forces to zero; we must always seek to equalize them.

THE USE OF NOVEL TASKS

One common method of obtaining some degree of equalization is to make the tasks novel, so that at least no person will have been taught to do that particular task by environmental forces. This has played a part in the disarranged sentence test, the number-series completions, and the mixed relations or analogies of Army Alpha, in the maze, cube, rhythm, picture-completion, and card-cutting tests of Army Beta, in a majority of the pencil and paper tests for young children unable to read, and in many others. Each year brings forth new selections or adaptations or inventions of tasks where intellect operates with novel data or with old data in new ways.

This method had the further alleged advantage that novelties were supposed to measure ability to analyze and infer and reason—the higher mental processes—better than more customary tasks could. We have seen that this advantage may be of less moment and magnitude than has been supposed, since the "higher" and the "lower" processes measure nearly the same abilities at bottom.

The equalization of environmental influence obtained by novelty in and of itself has one notable practical disadvantage. Special coaching for the tests is likely to produce very great inequalities in favor of those who receive it. For example, the syllogism test of Rogers shown below will be made very much easier for many persons if they are taught to make a diagram representing the given facts by position along a line, as shown below.

Fill in with conclusions which can be correctly drawn from the given facts in each set as shown in the first line.

|  | Given Facts | Conclusions |  |
|---|---|---|---|
|  |  | therefore Y is ............thicker............than............ | V |
| (1) | Z is thicker than X | therefore X is ........................................ | H |
|  | H is as thick as Z | therefore Y is ........................................ | H |
|  | V is thicker than H | therefore X is ........................................ | V |
|  | V is thinner than Y | therefore Z is ........................................ | Y |
|  |  | therefore B is ........................................ | A |
|  | D is greater than B | therefore D is ........................................ | F |
|  | B is equal to E |  |  |
| (2) | E is greater than F | therefore E is ........................................ | A |
|  | C is less than F | therefore B is ........................................ | C |
|  | A is greater than D | therefore A is ........................................ | F |

```
            X        Z
thin _____H_____V_____Y_____ thick
```

```
           E
less   C    F    B        D        A      great
```

## THE USE OF FAMILIAR TASKS

A contrasting method is to use tasks that are so familiar that everybody has had somewhat nearly adequate environmental stimulation to master them, any person's success depending consequently chiefly on his intellectual capacity and interest. Thus, "Are you a boy or a girl?" "Is it morning, afternoon, or evening?" "What month is it?" "Name all the months of the year," tying a bow knot, naming the days of the week, naming six coins, and other elements of the Stanford Binet are tasks which obviously lack novelty. Their merit is not that training has little effect on them, but that training treats all people somewhere nearly alike in respect of them.

The equalization of the environment's influence by choosing tasks where it is adequate for nearly all, is aided by relying on the third rather than the second axiom and using an extensive sampling of things which the world in general stimulates nearly everybody to learn or do. Thus it may be argued that the total number of such words known will be a better index of original intellectual capacity and interest than the knowledge of any particular score of words. The environment may decide that A learns words about things and mechanisms, that B learns words about animals and plants, and that C learns words about people and their actions, but may well have less power over the total number learned.

One method of accentuating the original factors seeks to equalize environmental influence in respect of the data or content involved in the task, by familiarity; and seeks to reduce environmental influence in respect of the operation with the data involved in the task, through novelty. The comprehension of paragraphs whose words singly are all well known, the completion of sentences about familiar facts in familiar words, the solution of unconventional arithmetical problems[1] are typical cases. For example, as-

[1] Such as:
A. If 7 multiplied by some number equals 63, what is the number?

30

sume that a thousand individuals aged 16 have been in attendance upon school in the United States eight years or more (of 150 school days or more) and are measured by a battery of tasks chosen with care (say, from those printed in this volume) to contain only words from the 4,000 known to almost all such individuals, and to require only such arithmetical facts and techniques as are taught in grades three and four.

Differences in the degree of success with such a battery of tasks might reasonably be regarded as largely[2] independent of differences in school environment save in so far as these differences themselves were caused by original differences in capacity and zeal.

### THE USE OF A SERIES GRADED FOR SUSCEPTIBILITY TO ENVIRONMENTAL INFLUENCES

We can then, by one or another of these methods, select or devise a battery of intellectual tasks or tests the score in which (in a group of individuals of the same time, country, and general manner of life) bids fair to be determined

B. What part of 16 equals half of 24?

C. How many quarters of a quarter equal half of a half?

D. In the lines below, each number is gotten in a certain way from the numbers coming before it. Study out what this way is in each line, and then write in the space left for it the number that should come next. The first two lines are already filled in as they should be:

|  |  |  |  |  |  |  |
|---|---|---|---|---|---|---|
| Samples | 2 | 4 | 6 | 8 | 10 | 12 |
|  | 11 | 12 | 14 | 15 | 17 | 18 |
| 1. | 38 | 34 | 30 | 26 |  | ___ |
| 2. | 103 | 95 | 87 | 79 |  | ___ |
| 3. | 1 | 10 | 100 | 1000 |  | ___ |

E. Write the numbers and signs in each line below in the proper order, so that they make a true equation as shown in the two sample lines.

|  |  |  |  |  |  |  |  |  |
|---|---|---|---|---|---|---|---|---|
| Sample lines | 3 | 3 | 6 |  | = | + |  |  |
|  | 4 | 7 | 8 | 20 | = | + | × |  |
| 1. | 2 | 2 | 3 | 5 | 15 | = | − | − | × |
| 2. | 2 | 5 | 6 | 7 | 10 | = | + | + | − |
| 3. | 1 | 4 | 8 | 15 | 20 | = | + | − | − |

[2] How largely will depend upon the disciplinary values of school training and upon the extent to which our novelties are really novel.

to a considerable extent by original nature, another battery the score in which a larger fraction of the score is due to circumstances, and so on. The application of this series of examinations graded from "least subject to environment" to "most subject to environment" would provide a partial analysis of a man's intellectual ability and attribution thereof to his original nature and to his acquisitions. Thus, suppose that the examinations A, B, C, D, and E, when applied to native-born white citizens of the United States, aged 21, depend respectively on nature and nurture in these proportions.

|   | Nature | Nurture |
|---|--------|---------|
| A | 7 | 3 |
| B | 6 | 4 |
| C | 5 | 5 |
| D | 4 | 6 |
| E | 3 | 7 |

Suppose that individuals I and II score as follows:

|    | A | B | C | D | E | Total |
|----|-----|-----|-----|-----|-----|-------|
| I  | 90 | 80 | 70 | 60 | 50 | 350 |
| II | 50 | 60 | 70 | 80 | 90 | 350 |

Then obviously, I and II, who are of equal present status, have it from very different causations. I had much the better original equipment, but has not much improved it. From such measurements, we could infer the relative conditions of individuals at the limit where original nature was 10 and environment 0 in the causation. Thus in the case above, suppose all units to be truly equal and referable to a true zero point. Then by original nature, I would have 120, or six times the original possibility of 20 that II would have. If the environment could have been made as favorable for him as it was for II, he would have had a total score six times as large as II's.

The importance of such analytic measures by a graded series, and of such inferences about the conditions at its limits, depends on (1) the surety with which we can pick tasks to be differently sensitive to original capacity, (2) the extent to which the differential series will extend up and down from the modal condition of sharing of original nature and environment, whatever that may be, (3) the nearness of that mode to the condition where one hundred percent is caused by nature and zero percent by environment, and (4) the restrictions which we have to impose on environmental differences in order to work the plan at all.

Little has been known with surety concerning any of these matters; and we have not had the time or facilities to make more than a beginning at the investigations which are needed. All our work concerns these problems in the case where environmental differences are limited to such as hold for white individuals born and bred in the United States, belonging to the same generation (born say, not over 20 years apart), provided with opportunity to go to school for at least 6 years (or 900 school days) unless they were demonstrably so stupid as to be unable to learn at school, and not deaf, dumb, blind, or insane. If, for example, we state that environmental differences cause only K percent of the differences found in a test in completing sentences or solving arithmetical originals, we do not mean that the percent would not exceed K in a group composed half of present-day Americans and half of their ancestors fifty thousand years ago; or in a group composed half of present-day Americans and half of African pigmies.[3]

In accord with the principles already stated, the tasks which would be chosen as especially indicative of original capacity are sentence-completions, arithmetical problems, and comprehension of paragraphs, especially such as required the use of familiar data in new ways. At the other extreme would be the knowledge of single words and isolated informational items.

When we apply these two extremes, we find that they are really very close together. Either they do not measure

[3] An investigation of tests which may be freed from these limitations in whole or in part is being made by a group of psychologists, with funds supplied by the Spelman Memorial.

two very different things, one the intellect a man has by nature, and the other the intellect which he has acquired by training, or these two are in almost perfect correspondence. For the correlation between whatever is common to the tasks of one extreme and whatever is common to the tasks of the other extreme is almost perfect. The evidence is the same as that brought forward by Mr. Tilton and by us in Chapter XV to prove that associative thinking and analytic, inferential, original thinking have almost identical roots.

As a check, we may contrast, within each form of test, certain elements which home and school advantages would benefit less with certain other elements which they would benefit more. Thus, within the field of sentence-completion, we may divide our elements 65 to 130 into two halves as shown below, as a result of a consensus of expert opinion.

BENEFITED MORE BY HOME AND SCHOOL ADVANTAGES

66. The .............. of the .............. World were kinder than the kings and nobles .............. .............. Old.
68. The .............. of five and ten is fifteen.
70. At .............. time was progress .............. rapid .............. during the last half of the nineteenth .............. .
74. The .............. source .............. wealth in Denmark .............. agriculture.
75. The laws .............. inheritance are for the most .............. unknown.
76. In .............. to maintain .............. health, one should have nourishing .............. .
82. At ancient banquets the .............. of the day seems .............. have .............. the chief .............. of conversation.
84. The Declaration .............. .............. affirms that the Creator .............. all men with certain inalienable .............. .
85. This was done .............. a view .............. causing the .............. of .............. carfares .............. three cents.
93. One of the most difficult problems of representative .............. is that of getting large assemblies to .............. the work of legislation .............. and efficiently.

98. The word virtue is derived from a ............................ ........................ strength.

99. The struggle for ........................ among the lower ........................ has ........................ a commonplace of modern scientific thought.

100. The ........................ World wished to ........................ the New.

101. Saddles and bridles ........................ no unimportant ........................ in the ........................ art.

102. India is rich in ........................ of scenery and climate, ........................ the ........................ mountains to vast ........................ deltas raised ........................ a few ........................ above sea ........................ .

104. Undue consciousness often ........................ the flow of expression ........................ diffuseness is detrimental to a clear and ........................ exposition of our ideas.

106. Throughout the river plains of northern India, two harvests, and, ........................ some provinces, ........................ are ........................ each ........................ .

116. Few historians would ........................ the fact that Marx had a larger and more thorough ........................ on the social ........................ o f h i s time ........................ a n y ........................ living man.

119. Let us very briefly examine the social forces ........................ ........................ at work concentrating or ........................ the ownership ........................ wealth.

123. Modern ........................ inherits ........................ ........................ innate pugnacity and all the love of glory of ........................ ........................ .

124. Let the class that ........................ itself to transportation, for example, ........................ working and the disastrous ........................ to the rest of the ........................ can scarcely ........................ imagined.

125. The monuments of Persepolis ........................ ........................ the use ........................ i n c e n s e ........................ a s ........................ in ancient Persia as ........................ Babylonia.

127. The orderly ........................ peaceful ........................ of our industrial mechanism is a ........................ of public ........................ , and ........................ be secured in ........................ way or ........................ .

128. Ever since the hearing before him ........................ the governor ........................ ........................ giving ........................ spare moment ........................ a ........................ of the case.

129. So far ........................ ........................ the displeasure of the people by ........................ the will of their representatives, a President generally gains ........................ by the bold use of his veto power. It conveys the ........................

............................................ firmness; i t  s h o w s ............................................
............................................ has  a  view  and  does ............................................
............................................ to give effect to it.

### BENEFITED LESS BY HOME AND SCHOOL ADVANTAGES

65. It may ............................................ effort and a long ............................................ but the result is sure.

71. He will come to the meeting ............................................ ............................................ ............................................ the fact ............................................ he ............................................ rather stay quietly at home.

73. No ............................................ what happens wrong is ............................................ right.

77. His friends, ............................................ wished to dissuade him from this undertaking, asserted that ............................................ he followed their advice ............................................ would withdraw their support.

78. It would ............................................ several pages ............................................ to contain the list.

79. Standing beside the grave ............................................ ............................................ great Englishman ............................................ ............................................ enough for us to know ............................................ ............................................ lived and died, and made the ............................................ his heirs.

80. You may safely conclude that you ............................................ in yourself the means of ............................................ at the truth.

81. ............................................ the fact that you disagree with me, I shall continue to aid you.

83. As ............................................ the treasure he had come to seek, probably it existed ............................................ in his own .............................................

86. The ............................................ of a man is to be useful to his .............................................

87. They who are miserable have ............................................ medicine other ............................................ hope.

88. The best is ............................................ too ............................................ ............................................ him.

89. The sublime ............................................ the ridiculous ............................................ often  so  nearly ............................................ ............................................ it is ............................................ to class them separately.  One step above the ............................................ makes the ridiculous, and one step ............................................ t h e ............................................ m a k e s  t h e ............................................ again.

90. ............................................ spite ............................................ many severe ............................................ he is still alive ............................................ the ............................................ of ninety-one.

91. It appears ............................................ whether his debts will be paid.

94. If ............................................ the ............................................ of the year were holidays playing ............................................ be ............................................ tedious ............................................ working.

95. Gratitude ........................ the fairest ........................ that
    s h e d s  ........................  p e r f u m e  ........................
    ........................ heart.
97. Impatience, while it ........................ us to s u r p a s s
    ........................ generations, disposes ........................ to
    overrate their happiness.
103. The American boy ........................ wishes ........................ go
    ........................ college and ........................ to go, has
    only his own weaknesses to thank for it.
104a. ........................ injury nor retaliation nor warding off
    ........................ by evil is ever ........................ .
105. Knighthood and Chivalry are ........................ w o r d s
    ........................ a r e  n e a r l y  ........................ n o t
    ........................ synonymous.
107. ........................ a man ........................ time sufficient for all
    laudable pursuits, and ........................ sufficient for all
    generous purposes, he is free ........................  ........................
    shadow of blame or reproach.
108. Maize contains ........................ small a proportion of nutri-
    tious matter ........................ it ........................ not
    ........................ for horses ........................ which fast
    work is ........................ .
109. The drafting ........................ a measure depends ........................
    the pains ........................ and skill exerted by its
    ........................ .
110. ........................ is natural that being dissatisfied with the
    ........................ , we should form a too ........................
    estimate of the past.
115. Virtue ........................ knowledge, and ........................ is the
    fruit of ignorance.
117. He will do as you request ........................  ........................
    his own feelings.
117a. Where ........................ in nature is ........................ grandeur
    displayed as in the Grand Canyon?
126. He would assign no reason ........................ his action
    ........................ to his ........................  ........................
    to ........................ enemies.

Within the field of arithmetical problems the same consensus lists ten problems as those benefited most by home
and school advantages, and nine as benefited least by them.

We put these "Most" and "Least" tasks into four
groups: Ma, Mb, La, and Lb, Ma and Mb being random
halves of the M's, while La and Lb are random halves of
the L's.

In a group of two hundred normal school students, the correlations are as follows:

| | | | |
|---|---|---|---|
| Ma | with | Mb, | .74 |
| La | with | Lb, | .81 |
| Ma | with | La, | .69 |
| Ma | with | Lb, | .66 |
| Mb | with | La, | .67 |
| Mb | with | Lb, | .72 |

The correlation between the "Most" and the "Least" is thus nearly as high as the correlation within the "Most" or within the "Least," and the correlation between what is common to the "Most" and what is common to the "Least" is .88.

On the whole, the difficulties in the way of analyzing a man's intellect into the contribution of nature and that of nurture by the use of tasks much subject to environmental influences, and tasks little subject to them, are very great. The method is sound, but hardly practicable.

### THE TEST AND RESULTS OF BURT

Burt has sought to measure the relative shares of intelligence, school environment, and age. His work is so important that we quote the report of it in full. In estimating the meaning of his results, we must bear in mind that his "intelligence" is in reality the score in the test (Test 29.—Graded Reasoning Test) quoted below. His final conclusion, that B (the Binet Mental Age) $= .54S + .33I + .11A$, should then be modified to read as follows:

"Of the gross result, then, one-ninth is attributable to age alone, one-third to the ability measured by the Burt Reasoning Tests alone, and over one-half to the ability measured by school attainment alone."

Test 29.—GRADED REASONING TESTS
(Short List)

1.  Tom runs faster than Jim:
    Jack runs slower than Jim.
    Which is the slowest of the three?

## 7 Years.

2.
Kate is cleverer than May.
May is cleverer than Jane.
Who is the cleverest—Jane, Kate, or May?

3. I have bought the following Christmas presents: a pipe, a blouse, some music, a box of cigarettes, a bracelet, a toy engine, a bat, a book, a doll, a walking-stick, and an umbrella.
My brother is eighteen: he does not smoke, nor play cricket, nor play the piano.
I want to give the walking-stick to my father, and the umbrella to my mother.
Which of the above shall I give my brother?

## 8 Years.

4.
I don't like sea voyages:
And I don't like the seaside.
I must spend Easter either in France, or among the Scottish Hills, or on the South Coast.
Which shall it be?

5. The person who stole Brown's purse was neither dark, nor tall, nor clean-shaven.
The only persons in the room at the time were—
1. Jones, who is short, dark, and clean-shaven:
2. Smith, who is fair, short, and bearded:
3. Grant, who is dark, tall, but not clean-shaven.
Who stole Brown's purse?

## 9 Years.

6.
Three boys are sitting in a row:
Harry is to the left of Willie:
George is to the left of Harry.
Which boy is in the middle?

7. In cold, damp climates, root crops, like potatoes and turnips, grow best:
In temperate climates, there are abundant pastures, and oats and barley flourish:
In sub-tropical climates, wheat, olives, and vines flourish:
In tropical climates, date-palms and rice flourish.
The ancient Greeks lived largely on bread, with oil instead of butter: they had wine to drink and raisins for fruit.
Which climate do you think they had?

## 10 Years.

8.    There are four roads here:
I have come from the south and want to go to Melton.
The road to the right leads somewhere else:
Straight ahead it leads only to a farm.
   In which direction is Melton—North, South, East or West?

9.  The doctor thinks Violet has caught some illness.
   If she has a rash, it is probably chicken-pox, measles, or
      scarlet fever:
   If she has been ailing with a cold or cough, she may develop
      whooping-cough, measles, or mumps.
   She has been sneezing and coughing for some days: and now
      spots are appearing on her face and arms.
   What do you think is the matter with Violet?

## 11 Years.

10.  Where the climate is hot, gum-trees and rubber will grow:
   Heather and grass will grow only where it is cold:
      Heather and rubber require plenty of moisture:
      Grass and gum-trees will grow only in fairly dry regions:
   Near the river Amazon it is very hot and very damp.
      Which of the above grows there?

11.  Father has just come home in a brand new overcoat: there is
      clay on his boots and flour on his hat.
   The only places he can have been to are Northgate, Southgate,
      Westgate, or the City; and he has not had time to go to
      more than one of these.
   There is no clay anywhere in the streets except where the
      pavement is up for repair.
   There are tailors' shops only in Southgate, Westgate, and the
      City.
   There are flour mills only in Northgate, Westgate, and the City.
   I know the roads are not being repaired in the City, though
      they may be in the other places.
      Where has father been?

## 12 Years.

12.  Field-mice devour the honey stored by the humble-bees: the
      honey which they store is the chief food of the humble-bees.
   Near towns, there are far more cats than in the open country.
   Cats kill all kinds of mice.
      Where, then, do you think there are most humble-bees—
         in the neighbourhood of towns or in the open country?

13. I started from the church and walked 100 yards:
I turned to the right and walked 50 yards:
I turned to the right again and walked 100 yards.
How far am I from the church?

## 13 Years.

14. A pound of meat should roast for half an hour:
Two pounds of meat should roast for three-quarters of an hour:
Three pounds of meat should roast for one hour:
Eight pounds of meat should roast for two hours and a quarter:
Nine pounds of meat should roast for two hours and a half.

From this can you discover a simple rule by which you can tell from the weight of a joint for how long it should roast?

15. What conclusion can you draw from the following facts?
Iron nails will not float in a pool:
A cup of pure gold dust weighs nearly twenty times as much as a cup of water of the same size:
If you drop a silver sixpence or a copper coin into a puddle, it will sink to the bottom:
A cubic inch (about a tablespoonful) of water weighs less than half an ounce; a cubic inch of brass weighs over two ounces:
A leaden weight will drop to the bottom of the ocean.

Sum up all these observations in one short statement of the following form: "Most ............... are ............... ............... ................."

## 14 Years.

16. John said: "I heard my clock strike yesterday, ten minutes before the first gun fired. I did not count the strokes, but I·am sure it struck more than once, and I think it struck an odd number."
John was out all the morning from the earliest hours: and his clock stopped at five to five the same afternoon.
When do you think the first gun fired?

17. Captain Watts and his son James have been found shot—the father in the chest and the son in the back. Both clearly died instantaneously.
A gun fired close to the person—as, for example, when a man shoots himself—will blacken and even burn the skin or clothes: fired from a greater distance, it will leave no such mark.

The two bodies were found near the middle of a large hall used as a rifle range. Its floor is covered with damp sand, which shows every footprint distinctly. Inside the room there are two pairs of footprints only. A third man standing just outside the door or window could aim at any part of the room: but the pavement outside would show no footmarks.

Under Captain Watts' body was found a gun: no such weapon was found near James.

In each case the coat, where the bullet entered, was blackened with gunpowder, and the cloth a little singed.

Captain Watts was devoted to his son, and would have died sooner than harm him purposely: hence it is impossible to suppose that he killed him deliberately, even in self-defence. But some think that James secretly disliked his father, and hoped to inherit his fortune at his death.

(1) Was Captain Watts' death due to murder, accident, or suicide?

(2) Was James' death due to murder, accident, or suicide?

[Burt, '21, pp. 239–242.]

"For every child in an entire school, comprising just over three hundred pupils aged between seven and fourteen, I have secured the following measurements: first, the child's age; next, his school attainments, measured by an educational examination, the results being revised by the teachers; thirdly, his intelligence measured by special tests of reasoning,[4] the results, again, being checked by the teachers; and, lastly, his mental age, given directly by the present version of the Binet-Simon scale, unchecked and unrevised.

"The first column of figures in Table XX. (our Table 134) shows the six correlations subsisting between these four measurements coupled with one another in every one of the six ways possible.[5]

"From the six 'total' coefficients, taken each in turn, I have first of all eliminated one or other of the four factors operative. From the gross figures I have, by discount, found the net. The resulting 'partial' coefficients are given by the second column of figures in the table. A comparison of these values at once invites several inferences. The resemblance between the Binet-Simon results and the child's school standing seems due more to the common influence of age than to the common influence of intelligence. The resemblance between the Binet-Simon results and the child's intellectual maturity, estimated independently, seems due more to

4 See Appendix IV., pp. 239–242.

5 With a group of nearly 300 children, the probable error for correlations less than .12 ranges between + .038 and + .039. A coefficient under .07, therefore, has little or no significance; one over .11 may be received as trustworthy.

the common influence of school standing than to the common influence of age. The estimates for intellectual maturity owe their correlation with school standing—a correlation by no means high even at the outset—chiefly, but not entirely, to the common influence of age. When the influence of intelligence is excluded, there still remains a correspondence between age and position in school that is unexpectedly—indeed, I apprehend, unwarrantably—close: promotion goes suspiciously with seniority. The negative correlation between school standing and intelligence, obtained when differences in Binet age are eliminated, may seem odd; but even were it larger than it is, it would not be at all inexplicable.[6]  In a group homogeneous in regard to mental age, children who are older chronologically would, in a test measuring inborn intelligence rather than mere mental growth, appear duller; yet, because they are older, the school system elevates them to a somewhat higher class. Hence the paradox of a group whose mental age is uniform: the higher the class, the duller the child.

TABLE 134. (Table XX of Burt).

OBSERVED AND PARTIAL CORRELATIONS BETWEEN AGE, INTELLIGENCE, SCHOOL
ATTAINMENTS, AND THE RESULTS OF THE BINET-SIMON TESTS.

| Factors Correlated | Observed Coefficients | Factor Eliminated | Partial Coefficient (First Order). | Factors Eliminated | Partial Coefficient (Second Order). |
|---|---|---|---|---|---|
| B Tests and School Work | .91 | Intelligence<br>Age | .78<br>.68 | Intelligence and Age | .61 |
| B Tests and Intelligence | .84 | School Work<br>Age | .58<br>.65 | School Work and Age | .56 |
| B Tests and Age | .83 | School Work<br>Intelligence | .19<br>.62 | School Work and Intelligence | .13 |
| School Work and Intelligence | .75 | Tests<br>Age | – .06<br>.40 | Tests and Age | – .07 |
| School Work and Age | .87 | Tests<br>Intelligence | .49<br>.73 | Tests and Intelligence | .49 |
| Intelligence and Age | .70 | Tests<br>School Work | .01<br>.15 | Tests and School Work | .05 |

"Let us now examine the partial coefficients of the second order, coefficients, that is, obtained where two factors have been cancelled in succession (last column of Table XX).

"Intelligence, it may be remembered, was observed to correlate with the Binet tests by .84 and with school attainments by .75. Mediated solely by intelligence, therefore, a correlation between the Binet estimates and school attainments could be predicted amount-

6 The coefficient in question is barely twice its probable error.

ing at least to .75 × .84, that is, .63. The total correlation found, however, was as much as .91. The excess is due, in part at least, to the second common factor of age. But, on eliminating also the effect of age, there is still left a substantial surplus. With both age and intelligence constant, the 'partial' correlation between school attainments and Binet results remains at .61. Of all the partial coefficients of the second order this is the largest. There can, therefore, be little doubt that with the Binet-Simon scale a child's mental age is a measure not only of the amount of intelligence with which he is congenitally endowed, not only of the plane of intelligence at which in the course of life and growth he has eventually arrived; it is also an index, largely if not mainly, of the mass of scholastic information and skill which, in virtue of attendance more or less regular, by dint of instruction more or less effective, he has progressively accumulated in school.

"The correlation of .49 between age and educational attainment, left after the elimination of ability both tested and observed, confirms our previous suspicion of the undue influence of age upon school classification. The only other correlations surviving after the double elimination are those between the Binet tests, on the one hand, and intelligence and age respectively upon the other.

"From the three final correlations thus furnished by the tests, and from the relevant standard deviations, can be calculated the several so-called 'regressions.' The regressions will indicate the relative proportions in which the three factors—age, intelligence, and school attainments—together determine a child's achievements in the Binet-Simon tests. The complete equation is as follows:

$$B = .54 \ S + .33 \ I + .11 \ A,$$

where B = mental age according to the Binet-Simon scale,

S = school attainments expressed in terms of educational age,

I = intellectual development also measured in terms of years, and

A = the chronological age.

"Of the gross result, then, one-ninth is attributable to age, one-third to intellectual development, and over one-half to school attainment. School attainment is thus the preponderant contributor to the Binet-Simon tests. To school the weight assigned is nearly double that of intelligence alone, and distinctly more than that of intelligence and age combined. In determining the child's performance in the Binet-Simon scale, intelligence can bestow but little more than half the share of school, and age but one-third the share of intelligence." [Burt, '21, pp. 181 to 183.]

We are greatly indebted to Burt for this study, especially for the application of the partial-correlation technique to the problem, but we should be very cautious in our use of the facts. Small differences in the observed correlations may make large differences in the partials. These small differences may be in whole or in part due to sampling error, or to differences in the amount of chance error in the original measures producing differences in the attenuation. Suppose, for example, that Burt's Reasoning Tests really measured exactly the same ability as the Binet, but with a greater chance error (the two reliability coefficients being .95 and .80) and that the true correlations for a very large population, each person being perfectly measured, were as shown in Table 135.

If the facts were so, I and B would measure identical abilities and the regression equations, $B = aS + bI + cA$ and $I = dS + eB + fA$ would be identical save that B and I would change places.

Yet all that is required to produce Burt's six coefficients from those of Table 135 is that the self-correlation of Burt's determinations of I be .15 points lower than that of his determination of B (somewhat lower it almost certainly is), and that, by the sampling error of his 300 cases, his correlation of B with I be .03½ too low, his correlation of S with I be .09 too low, and his correlation of I with A be .06½ too low. There is one chance in fifty for the first of the three, one chance in 5,000 for the second, and one chance in seventy for the third. The chance of all three occurring together is very small (though by no means so small as $1/50 \times 1/5000 \times 1/70$, since the same sort of cases that would lower $r_{BI}$ would tend somehat to lower $r_{SI}$ and $r_{AI}$ also), and there is an equal chance that 30,000 cases in place of 300 would strengthen Burt's argument. Indeed, we agree with Burt that score in the Binet series is influenced by school training, and probably to a greater extent than score in Burt's reasoning test series will be. We very much doubt, however, that the amount of influence is so large in the one case or so small in the other as the second-order partials of .61 and — .07 indicate.

It is perhaps worth while to compute what these partials would be if we assume that all of Burt's coefficients are valid, but assume in addition that the self-correlations of his four measures with a second set of independent measures of the same qualities or abilities[7] are .95 for B, .80

TABLE 135.

THE INTERCORRELATIONS OF ONE BINET TEST (B), ONE BURT REASONING TEST (I), ONE MEASURE OF SCHOOL WORK (S), AND AGE (A) BY CERTAIN ASSUMPTIONS CONCERNING THE INTERCORRELATIONS IF AN INFINITE NUMBER OF SUCH TESTS HAD BEEN USED.

| | 1<br>$r_{\infty\infty}$ | 2<br>$r_{II}$ | 3<br>$r_{II}$ by Burt | 4<br>Difference (2–3) |
|---|---|---|---|---|
| BS | .96 | .91 | .91 | 0 |
| BI | 1.00 | .87½ | .84 | .03½ |
| BA | .85 | .83 | .83 | 0 |
| SI | .96 | .84 | .75 | .09 |
| SA | .89 | .87 | .87 | 0 |
| IA | .85 | .76½ | .70 | .06½ |

for I, 1.00 for A, and .95 for S. They will be:
$$r_{BS.IA} = .91 \text{ and } r_{IS.BA} = -.79.$$

Finally, as further evidence of the need of caution in arguments from small differences between correlations, let us apply the well-known attenuation formulae to Burt's six correlations, and obtain their answers to certain questions. The first is: What is the correlation between (a) whatever is common to the ability measured by the Binet and the ability measured by the Burt Test, and (b) whatever is common to School work and Age? The answer is:

$$\frac{\sqrt[4]{.83 \times .91 \times .87 \times .75}}{\sqrt{.84 \times .87}}$$ or .98; that is, almost everything.

The second is: What is the correlation between (a) what-

[7] To prevent possible ambiguity, we add that we mean, not repetitions of the particular Binet and Burt tasks, but a set drawn at random from the same general collection of tasks from which the Binet Tests may be considered a random draft, and a set drawn from the same general collection of tasks from which the Burt Tests may be considered a random draft.

31

ever is common to the ability measured by the Binet and
School work and (b) whatever is common to the ability
measured by the Burt Test and to that measured by Age?
The answer is:

$$\frac{\sqrt[4]{.84 \times .83 \times .75 \times .87}}{\sqrt{.91 \times .70}}$$ or 1.02; that is, everything.

We obtain a similar answer (1.03) to the third question
concerning the correlation between whatever is common to
Binet and Age and whatever is common to Burt and School
work?

These answers are absurd. Not the most passionate
adherent of one general ability as the cause of all possible
excellences would assert that whatever is common to the
ability to score well in Binet and Burt is also common to
Age and School Attainment. Neither Burt nor any other
competent psychologist would entertain the notion that
what is common to success in the Binet and success in
School is the same thing that is common to success in the
Burt and Age.

Such fantastic perfect correlations between common
factors sometimes are due to a statistical fallacy, there
being really *nothing* common in either pair of traits; but
Dr. Burt will be too sagacious to plead this in the present
case.

The fact is that when a number of traits are somewhat
nearly equally intercorrelated, as is the case with B, I, S,
and A in Burt's 300 pupils, partial correlations and inferred correlations between common factors will often show
queer, not to say absurd, results. Both procedures are of
very great value, but they are very sensitive to the influence of the "errors" due to measuring traits in too few persons and with too few tests per person.

The partial correlations computed by Burt for the influence of the separate features of school work seem to us
in better harmony with the view that B and I are two tests
differing moderately in their susceptibility to school train-

ing than with his view that B (for persons alike in I) is very susceptible and I (for persons alike in B) not at all so. They are:

TABLE 136 (XXI of Burt).
OBSERVED AND PARTIAL CORRELATIONS BETWEEN THE BINET-SIMON TESTS AND ATTAINMENTS IN THE SEVERAL SCHOOL SUBJECTS.

|  | Observed Coefficients | Partial Coefficients (Age and Intelligence Eliminated) |
|---|---|---|
| Composition | .63 | .32 |
| Reading | .54 | .26 |
| Dictation | .52 | .21 |
| Arithmetic (Problems) | .55 | .07 |
| Arithmetic (Mechanical) | .41 | .15 |
| Writing | .21 | .01 |
| Drawing | .15 | -.08 |
| Handwork | .18 | -.06 |

It is easy to see how Composition might be a better *symptom* than Dictation and Arithmetic of those parts of intellect which B measured but I failed to measure, but hard to see how training in it could improve B more than training in Dictation and Arithmetic did.

Burt's study, then, though it is by one of the most experienced and able workers in this field and is the most extensive and the most searching study of the problem that we have found, does not convince us either that his Reasoning Tests, when given to a group identical in age and in ability measured by the Binet, will measure original capacity uninfluenced by school advantages, or that the Binet, when given to a group identical in age and in the ability measured by his Reasoning Test score, will measure a composite made up, half or more, of school advantages. If we knew of any test that did the former, we should have repeated his experiments testing out both the Binet and the Burt with the aid of the test of sheer original capacity instead of making this long counter-explanation of his results. But our general study of the problem has not revealed any such test. To this general study we may now return.

## THE USE OF ALTITUDE AND WIDTH OF INTELLECT

According to the orthodox views of what original nature is likely to contribute and what the environment is likely to contribute, it would be reasonable to choose the altitude of intellect and the width W(1C or 1A or 1V or 1D, etc.) as the two extremes, the area A(1C or 1A or 1V or 1D, etc.) being intermediate in its causation. It seems, at least, much easier for a good home or school to increase the number of easy things which a child can do than to enable him to do harder things than he has ever done. Dull men who could never learn to use indirect discourse correctly in Latin can learn the easy features of a score of languages. A favorable opportunity and assiduity seem to be all that are needed to teach anybody twice as many thousand easy accomplishments as he has acquired with meagre opportunity and less study.

This seems almost axiomatic. We were almost convinced of it until we investigated the actual relations between altitude, width, and area of Intellect CAVD and between the higher selective and organizing abilities and the lower or associative. The correlations are such as to cast doubt upon the doctrine that the number of easy intellectual accomplishments which a person learns depends chiefly, or even largely, on the stimulus of the environment. On the contrary, the number which a person can learn seems to be limited by his nature almost as much as is the degree of difficulty which he can master. If, by a miracle, intellectual accomplishments were all of exactly the same difficulty, we have reason to believe that the number which a person had learned at a given age would show the same hereditary relations as are shown now by the altitude which he reaches. As things are, the competent intellects learn approximately all the easy things which the incompetent intellects learn, plus a large balance of harder things. The imbecile probably could not learn twice as many things as he now does, no matter what opportunities were provided for him.

The explanation of the difference between the expectation from general psychology and the results shown in our correlations is to be found in the fact that there are relatively so few easy intellectual accomplishments. In order to increase the number of important things an intellect can do, you soon have to put it to doing harder things, because the easy ones are so soon used up. If there were ten million different single tasks at each level from 25 to 45, it would perhaps be possible to take two intellects of equal original capacity, and by certain deprivations hold one down to three million at level 25, and by certain advantages stimulate the other to reach four or five or six million at that level. And doubtless any wise psychologist would consider this attempt under these conditions much more promising than the attempt by an equal difference in deprivations and advantages, to hold one down to inability to do anything harder than 25, while the other was made able to do tasks at 35 or 40. But the conditions are unreal. To push the second intellect's score up by two or three million would, as things are, mean to have him master tasks above level 25.

Another part of the explanation is found in the fact that altitude as it is used in our correlations is not the same as the altitude meant in the statement that it is much easier for environment to increase the number of easy things an intellect can do than to enable it to do harder things than it has ever done. To do a harder thing means for us to do a *certain percent of the tasks* at a higher altitude, one in forty, or two in forty. Now, if there are twice as many tasks at level 31 as at level 30, the intellect which is stimulated to do 1 in 40 at level 31 has to learn *twice as many tasks* as the intellect which is stimulated to do 16 instead of 15 out of 40 at level 30. This is naturally harder for the environment or for any other force.

A third part of the explanation is to be found in the fact that our correlations represent the status as it is created by such differences in environment as do now act, not the status as it might conceivably be. If the action of the environment is positively and closely correlated with that of original nature, so that the best born are the best bred, and the worst born the worst bred, approximately, the high correlations between altitude and W(1C or 1A or 1V, etc.) which we find, may not be necessary as results of the nature of intellect, and may be alterable, as by giving equally advantageous training to all. Or, if the effect of difference in environment is now very small in comparison to the effect of original nature, so that the high correlations found are chiefly due to original nature, these may be alterable by increasing the differences in environment.

We may then retain in a somewhat tempered form the expectation that environment can extend the area of intellect by adding width somewhat more easily than by adding altitude.

So far as concerns the special question of a differential diagnosis between nature and nurture in the world as it now is, however, we shall receive almost no assistance by using altitude for the symptom of the former, width W(1C or 1A or 1V or 1D, etc.) for the symptom of the latter. Where the width is not 100% or 0%, its correlation with altitude is too near perfection. In the world as it now is, they are due to almost the same causes.

### OTHER METHODS OF SEPARATING ORIGINAL CAPACITY FROM ACQUIRED ABILITY

There are two other ways of approaching the problem, besides that of differential tests. The first is to approximate original nature by measurements early in life before environmental forces have had much opportunity to act on intellect. The second is to measure a man's intellect as we find it and to make the best allowance we can for the favorable or unfavorable action which the environment has had.

The former is not so fantastic as it would have been a few years ago. It would then have been even more absurd to claim to measure original capacity for intellect at three or four or five than to claim to measure at that age the original tendency to adult stature. We now have far better tests of intellect at low levels and in early stages; and the correlations between intellect at three and intellect at thirty, environment being equalized, may be closer than we think, much closer for example than the correlations between stature at three and stature at thirty with equalized environment. The contribution of original nature is all there in the individual at three years, or at three days. How much of it is revealed in external behavior, and how much is hidden in the constitution of the neurones, is a question for investigation.

On the other hand, we have to reckon with the evidence and arguments now being brought forward to prove that the environment of the first three years is very potent. Freud and others contend that the trends of character are much influenced by the environmental forces acting in these years; and we may expect some of them soon to make the same contention with regard to intellect.

The method of measuring original capacity by measuring attainment and making an allowance for the benefits and handicaps of environment, is what has been and is used in many scientific investigations and in practice by wise educators and advisers of youth. For example, of two boys making equal scores in Army Alpha, one from an English-speaking family with four years in an excellent city school, the other from an immigrant family and an inferior school, the second will be rated as the better in natural intellect and future intellectual promise. Its success depends, of course, on the adequacy of one's knowledge of what the environment has been in each individual case, and on the wisdom of one's theories concerning the action of environmental forces on intellect.

In so far as our work improves the measurement of intellect, it will improve this sort of measurement of, or inference about, original capacity for intellect. The balance of the program is to improve measurements of the environmental forces which help or hinder the attainment of intellect.

## SUMMARY

On the whole, the problem of analyzing a person's intellectual ability into an amount due to nature and an amount due to nurture, is unsolved. No task or test has been proved to be a measure of the former alone. The wisest procedure at present is to equalize environmental forces by using a wide variety of data with which all individuals have had adequate experience, and to make as correct allowances as we can for what we cannot equalize. With the progress of science, we may hope for accurate measurements of intellect at earlier and earlier ages, and for truer rules for making allowances for environmental differences.

# CHAPTER XVII

CHANGES IN THE ALTITUDE AND AREA OF INTELLECT WITH AGE

It is not at present possible to distinguish at all accurately within the general gain in intellect with age from 0 to 15 years or later, the share of mere maturity, mere inner growth, from the share of the experience and training which age implies. The reasons for this failure are much the same as for the failure to distinguish the shares of original capacity and environmental circumstances in the determination of intellect. We lack tests which measure maturity by itself, and tests which measure training by itself. We also lack extensive investigations using the partial-correlation technique with such imperfect symptoms of maturity and training as are available. In this chapter, therefore, age means chronological age, *and whatever it involves* under the conditions of present-day life in America.

## ALTITUDE

The curve of altitude of Intellect CAVD with age is of the general parabolic form shown in Fig. 64. There is a rise from 0 to about 30 at $6\frac{1}{2}$, to about $34\frac{1}{2}$ at $10\frac{1}{2}$, and to about $36\frac{1}{2}$ for adults 21 years old.[1]

[1] These estimates are subject to a thorough-going investigation which is being made by Miss Rowell, using our data and additional data obtained by her. They are made from the following facts: The average altitude CAVD of imbeciles of mental age 6–0 to 6–11 is 30.1. Taylor ['23] has shown that ordinary children of chronological age 6–0 to 6–11 do not differ much in such tasks as these, from imbeciles of mental age 6.0 to 7.0. The average altitude CAVD of pupils 10 yr. 0 mo. to 10 yr. 11 mo. in grade 4B of School X, is 33.85. The average altitude CAVD of pupils of the same age in grade 5A of School X is 33.9. The average for pupils of the same age in 5B of School X, is 35.15. (A is the lower half; B is the upper half.) In School X the ordinary pupil 10.0 to 11.0 in age is in grade 5A or 5B. The numbers of ages 9.0 to 10.0 grades 4B, 5A and 5B are 86, 24 and 27; those of age 10.0 to 11.0 are 39, 47 and 88; and those of age 11.0 to 12.0 are 18, 29 and 48. The ordinary pupil of age $10\frac{1}{2}$ may then be expected to score somewhat above

It has been shown that the score in stock intelligence examinations such as the National, Otis, and Haggerty, is substantially a measure of altitude. Consequently, we may take the curves of these scores in relation to age as approximate curves for the altitude of intellect in relation to age, first transposing the scores into terms of equal units.

This has been done for the National A, Otis Advanced, and Haggerty Delta 2, with the results shown in Table 137. The three examinations do not agree at all closely, the Haggerty official norms being especially divergent. Scores in equal units are available for all for the interval from age 10 to age 15. The gain from age 10 to age 11 is 28 percent of the gain from 10 to 15 in the case of the National; 25 percent of it in the Otis, and 20 percent of it in H(I), and 33 percent in H(II). The gain from 11 to 12 is 27, 22, 17½, and 31 percent of the gain from 10 to 15 in the National, Otis, H(I), and H(II), respectively. Corresponding percents for the gain from 12 to 13 are 25, 18, 15, and 35; for the gain from 13 to 14 they are 15, 18, 21, and 6; for the gain from 14 to 15 they are 5, 17, 26½, and − 5.

The discrepancies are about as great if the original scales are used, the percents of the gain from 10 to 15 then being:

| Age | National A | Otis Advanced | Haggerty Delta 2 Official | Haggerty Delta 2 Madsen |
|---|---|---|---|---|
| 10–11 | 28.3 | 23.6 | 18.3 | 33.4 |
| 11–12 | 26.7 | 21.8 | 18.3 | 30.9 |
| 12–13 | 25.0 | 18.2 | 16.7 | 34.3 |
| 13–14 | 15.0 | 18.2 | 21.7 | 5.6 |
| 14–15 | 5.0 | 18.2 | 25.0 | − 4.2 |

the average of 33.9 and 35.15, which is 34.53. As a check on the estimate of 34½ or more for age 10, we have the fact that the 86 nine year olds in grade 4B have a median score of 34.0. In this school the ordinary 9 year old has reached grade 4B or, less often, 4A. The average altitude CAVD of the 44 adult recruits in the United States Army is 36.5. These are enlisted men chosen for training in the Signal Corps, all but one between 18 and 25 years old, whose median amount of schooling is grade 8, and who may therefore be taken to represent the median of the white population, 18 to 24 years old, or a point a little above it in intellect CAVD.

There is evidently need for a careful critical study of these facts. If the three examinations measure the same thing, and if the averages or norms for the ages 10 to 15 are correctly determined, the curves in relation to age should be the same.

TABLE 137.

THE RELATION OF SCORES IN NATIONAL A, OTIS ADVANCED, AND HAGGERTY DELTA 2, TO AGE. H (I) REFERS TO THE OFFICIAL AGE-NORMS; H(II) REFERS TO THE MADSEN RESULTS.

| Age | Scores by the original scale | | | | Scores by a scale of equal units | | | |
| | Nat. | Otis | H(I) | H (II) | Nat. | Otis | H (I) | H (II) |
| --- | --- | --- | --- | --- | --- | --- | --- | --- |
| 8 | 46 | 25 | 25 | 38.8 | 51.2 | | | |
| 9 | 61 | 40 | 43 | 56.6 | 64.5 | 38.6 | | 57.8 |
| 10 | 76 | 55 | 55 | 66.8 | 78.0 | 54.9 | 56.1 | 68.8 |
| 11 | 93 | 68 | 66 | 78.7 | 94.0 | 68.6 | 67.9 | 79.6 |
| 12 | 109 | 80 | 77 | 89.7 | 109.5 | 80.6 | 78.1 | 89.7 |
| 13 | 124 | 90 | 87 | 101.9 | 124.0 | 90.3 | 87.1 | 101.3 |
| 14 | 133 | 100 | 100 | 103.9 | 132.4 | 100.0 | 99.3 | 103.3 |
| 15 | 136 | 110 | 115 | 101.8 | 135.4 | 109.5 | 114.8 | 101.8 |
| 16 | | 120 | | 106.7 | | 119.0 | | 106.9 |
| 17 | | 127 | | | | 125.7 | | |
| 18 | | 130 | | | | 128.6 | | |
| 19 | | 130 | | | | 128.6 | | |

| Gains | By the original scale | | | | By the scale with equal units | | | |
| | Nat. | Otis | H(I) | H (II) | Nat. | Otis | H (I) | H (II) |
| --- | --- | --- | --- | --- | --- | --- | --- | --- |
| 8–9 | 15 | 15 | 18 | 17.8 | 13.3 | | | |
| 9–10 | 15 | 15 | 12 | 10.2 | 13.5 | 16.3 | | 11.0 |
| 10–11 | 17 | 13 | 11 | 11.9 | 16.0 | 13.7 | 11.8 | 10.8 |
| 11–12 | 16 | 12 | 11 | 11.0 | 15.5 | 12.0 | 10.2 | 10.1 |
| 12–13 | 15 | 10 | 10 | 12.2 | 14.5 | 9.7 | 9.0 | 11.6 |
| 13–14 | 9 | 10 | 13 | 2.0 | 8.4 | 9.7 | 12.2 | 2.0 |
| 14–15 | 3 | 10 | 15 | – 2.1ʹ | 3.0 | 9.5 | 15.5 | – 1.5 |
| 15–16 | | 10 | | – 4.9 | | 9.5 | | – 4.9 |
| 16–17 | | 7 | | | | 6.7 | | |
| 17–18 | | 3 | | | | 2.9 | | |
| 18–19 | | 0 | | | | 0.0 | | |

The disagreement between the Haggerty official age-norms and Madsen's results is especially noteworthy because Madsen's selection of 14-year-olds and 15-year-olds is presumably of the superior, the duller ones being more likely to leave school. The average gains from 13 to 14 and from 14 to 15 for all children would consequently tend to be even less than those for his groups.

The general drift of these determinations is toward a parabolic curve of the form of Fig. 64. If the two sets of determinations (by equal-unit scores) of the Haggerty Delta 2 are combined with equal weight, and if the three curves for the three examinations are then combined with equal weight, the rise in the ordinates from 10 to 11, 11 to 12, 12 to 13, 13 to 14, and 14 to 15 are in the proportions: 26.5, 24.4, 22.7, 15.5, and 10.75.

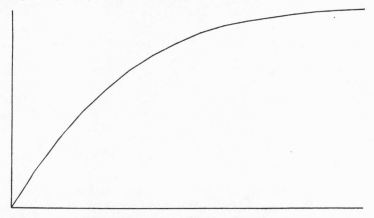

FIG. 64.   The general nature of the relation of altitude of intellect to age in years, 0 to 20.

These results for altitude of intellect in relation to age may be compared with those attained by Brooks ['21], in his careful and extensive experiments. In general our work corroborates his. The gains in what he terms the "higher" functions from 10 to 15 by years according to his final combined table ['21, p. 68], allowing equal weight to the boys and to the girls are in the proportion 24.8, 19.7, 19.4, 18.8, and 17.4. These gains may all be unduly large and the later gains at later ages unduly large in comparison with the gains at earlier ages, because of the practice effect which retesting involves. Data are not available to correct for it.

Probably an allowance of one-twelfth of the gains from age 10 to age 15 would be considered enough by all students of the matter, and too much by a majority of them. If this very large allowance is made, the gains are in the proportions: 28.2, 19.5, 18.9, 17.9, and 15.5. Neither in our CAVD results, nor in the National-Otis-Haggerty estimate, nor in Brooks' results is there any justification for the doctrine that the gain in altitude of intellect of the sort measured by existing intelligence tests is zero after 14, or after 15, or even after 16. It decreases, but it should not become inap-

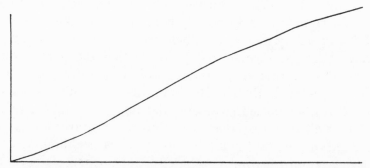

FIG. 65. The relation of area of intellect to age in years 0 to 20, assuming Fig. 64 as correct, with a slight increase in the number of tasks with increase in difficulty.

preciable until 18 or later. According to our results the decrease from 14 to 18 is not an abrupt slowing up of a gain that has been steady hitherto, but is part of a general negative acceleration which began long before the age of $6\frac{1}{2}$.

### AREA

The form of the curve for area of intellect in relation to age is not known even approximately for CAVD or any other specified intellect, since the number of tasks at each altitude is not known. The arguments presented in Chapter XII make it highly improbable that the curve for area is like Fig. 64 with a rapid rise at the lowest ages and decreasing annual increments thereafter. A very moderate increase of the number of tasks with increasing difficulty is sufficient to make the area curve from 0 to 16, one with *increasing* annual increments as in Fig. 65.

### GENERAL CONSIDERATIONS

The limitations of the special tasks used in CAVD, National, Otis, and the like, should be kept in mind in all thought concerning the relation of either altitude or area of intellect to age. The verbal and mathematical tasks which bulk so largely in these examinations may be more like those which occupy the intellects of children from five to fifteen than those which occupy the intellects of young people from fifteen to twenty-five, or those which occupy the intellects of men and women from twenty-five to thirty-five. It is conceivable and probable that the person who ceases to improve in altitude CAVD may continue to improve in altitude Bu, Ch, Ho, So. (Business, Child Management, Household Management, and Social Arrangement).

It is also the case that after a person acquires a certain amount of general linguistic and mathematical ability, and of general information about the sort of things which everybody is ashamed not to know, he usually devotes his mental abilities to the specialized abilities useful in his trade, business, or profession, hobby, and social circle. The correlation between CAVD (or any similar ability) and such specialized abilities is doubtless high, but it is probably not perfect; and these specialized abilities may begin their rapid rise in altitude at an age when CAVD altitude has almost ceased to gain.

# CHAPTER XVIII

## SUMMARY OF RESULTS AND APPLICATIONS TO THE MEASUREMENT OF HUMAN ABILITIES IN GENERAL

### SUMMARY OF RESULTS

All the measurements of intellect which have been made hitherto and which psychologists may expect to make in the future, unless means are found of defining and counting units of connection in the neurones, are inventories. They are records of the degree of success in accomplishing intellectual tasks. If all intellectual tasks are listed and arranged in levels of difficulty, the inventory may be systematized into a record of how many the intellect in question can do at each level and how quickly he can do them. From the record of how many it can do at each level, three useful measures may be abstracted. One is *altitude,* that is, the degree of difficulty at which a given percentage of success is attained. The second is *width,* that is, the percent of successes at any given altitude or the average percent of successes at any given series of altitudes. The third, which may be called *area,* is the total number of tasks done correctly, or the percentage which this total is of the number of tasks in the entire list.

An intellectual task is one, success in which depends upon all of intellect and nothing but intellect. Intellect is definable by a series of tasks, and we have so defined one variety of it, Intellect CAVD, and could so define any other variety of it. A CAVD intellectual task is, then, one success at which depends upon all of Intellect CAVD and nothing but Intellect CAVD. Tasks can be devised which do substantially meet this requirement, success at one of them correlating perfectly (or as closely as its own self-correlation permits) with success in the entire series. CAVD intellect is nearly or quite homogeneous in the sense

469

that the ability which determines success at any one level of difficulty is, to a close approximation, simply a larger or smaller amount of the same ability that determines success at any other level of difficulty. The evidence for this is the very small and uncertain reduction of correlation as more and more remote levels are taken, and the substantially perfect correlation between score at any one level and the sum of the scores at all levels, or any other score representing in any reasonable way ability at the entire series.

No short single task, however, can be measured in respect of its intellectual difficulty, for no short single task can be devised which depends for its success upon all of intellect and nothing but intellect. Even composite tasks made up of forty or more single tasks well selected to represent Intellect CAVD (or any other specified sort of intellect) are not perfectly intellectual and must be treated as measuring intellect plus an error for which allowance must be made in all inferences from measures of their difficulty to measures of their *intellectual* difficulty. With short single tasks, this error becomes so large and so variable amongst different tasks that no trustworthy allowance can be made for it.

The difficulty of a task and the difference in difficulty between one task and another may be measured by the percentages of certain groups which succeed with it. For it has been demonstrated that the form of distribution of a school grade population from 6 to 13 in respect of altitude of intellect is to a very close approximation that of the normal probability surface, defined by $y = \dfrac{1}{\sigma\sqrt{2\pi}}\, e^{-\frac{x^2}{\sigma^2}}$. The difficulty of an intellectual task may also be measured by the percentage of successes among the various trials of the same individual, or by the average of such percentages from any given number of individuals of the same general degree of intellect, since it has been demonstrated that the varying conditions of an individual from time to time (omitting such extreme conditions of sleep, illness, intoxication, and the like, as would obviously unfit him for being tested) are distributed in close approximation to the normal probability surface. We have not made use of this method because it demands, in practical use, a large number of composite intellectual tasks of equal difficulty, and these are not yet available.

The 40-composite tasks A, B, C, etc., were constructed on the basis of measurements of the difficulty of some thousands of single tasks and some hundreds of 10-composites; and were measured in respect of their intellectual difficulty. The result is a series of tasks ranging from A, at which 88 percent of adult imbeciles of mental age 2½ to 5 years suc-

| Composite | Difficulty |
|---|---|
| A | 23 |
| B | 26¼ |
| C | 28¼ |
| D | 29¾ |
| E | 30¾ |
| F | 31¼ |
| G | 32 |
| H | 32¾ |
| I | 34¼ |
| J | 36¼ |
| K | 37¼ |
| L | 38¼ |
| M | 39¼ |
| N | 40 |
| O | 41¼ |
| P | 41¾ |
| Q | 43 |

ceed, to Q, at which only 23 percent of college graduates succeed. The differences in difficulty are determined approximately. They can be determined to any given degree of precision by the methods outlined.

The distance from the difficulty of Task A to the difficulty of Tasks 36 and 37,[1] which are at or near the absolute zero of intellect, has been determined by a consensus of experts as about 4.35 times the difference between Task A and Task C, which is $5.28\sigma_{i9}$. So we have an approximate scale

[1] See Chapter X, page 339.

of intellectual difficulty from an absolute zero in equal units as shown below. This scale is at all points more accurate than the best scales previously available; and is accurate enough for many scientific and practical uses from I to Q, covering the interval from the upper extreme of the feeble-minded to the 98 or 99 percentile adult intellect. It should, however, be improved by more extensive experimentation.

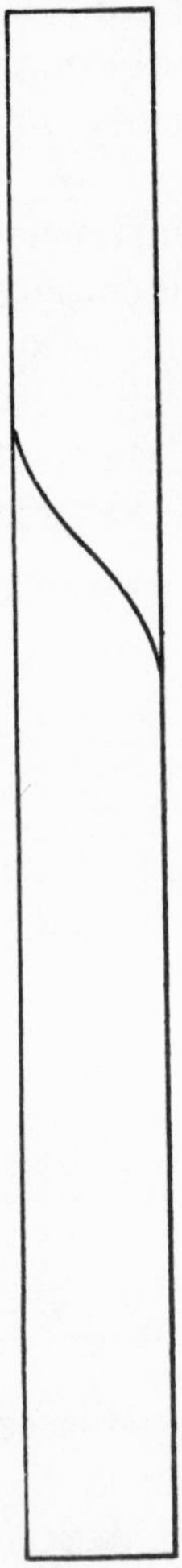

If alternative CAVD composites are constructed to be like A, B, C, etc., respectively, in difficulty, but different from them in content, until all possible CAVD tasks are used, it will be found that the number is not the same at each level. In general, the easier the level, the smaller the number of CAVD tasks that can be made without using the same single task twice.

If the number of tasks possible at level 1 to 5 is a, the number possible at levels 6 to 10 is a + b, the number possible at levels 11 to 15 is a + b + c, and so on. If the tasks of our series are represented by the column of Fig. 66, the total number which could be constructed and which are exemplified or sampled by A, B, C, etc., would be represented by a figure with a top very much wider than its bottom, as in Fig. 67, or Fig. 68, or Fig. 69. When the exact shape of this surface of frequency of intellectual tasks acording to difficulty is determined, the width and area of intellect can be measured. The measurement of an intellect should then be a measurement of its success or failure with each of a series of composite tasks each of which depends for success substantially on all of intellect and nothing but intellect. If the number of these tasks in the scale used to test

FIG. 66. The pattern of area of intellect in a sampling of N tasks, at each level of difficulty.

the intellect in question is proportional at each level to the number of such tasks that the world offers, the width of the intellect in question at each level and its area are given in the record. If the number of tasks in the scale is not proportional to the total existing number in this way, the numbers of the record at each level must be multiplied by suitable factors to obtain widths and area. In either case the total record for a person whence altitude, widths and area

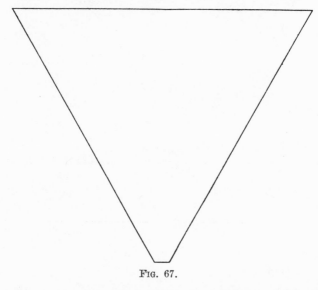

FIG. 67.

are derived may be with high probability inferred from the scores in three 40-composite tasks where the percent of single tasks right is near fifty.

Such a measurement is fundamentally right, and improved varieties of it are all that can be expected on the level of external behavior with voice, paper, and pencil, and the like. The physiological facts in the neurones which produce and, in the deeper sense, are intellect, are not known. When they become known, they may or may not be amenable to observation and measurement.

As a result of the high correlations found between mere associations or connections and the so-called "higher"

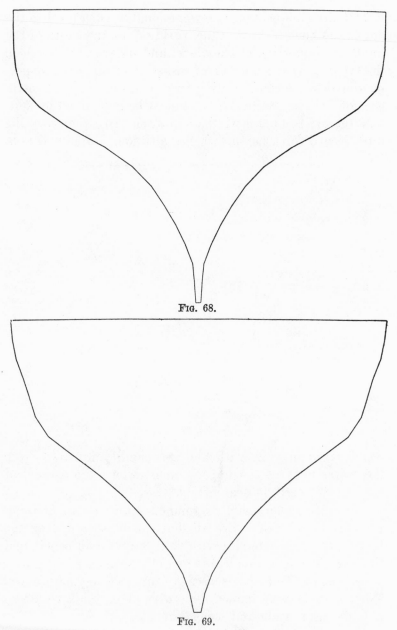

Fig. 68.

Fig. 69.

Figs. 67, 68 and 69.    Samples of probable relations of number of tasks to level of difficulty.

processes of abstraction, generalization, organization and control, inference and reasoning, we have advanced the hypothesis that the original basis for altitude, width, and area of intellect is the mere number of possible connections in the neurones whose connections correspond to having and using ideas. If this hypothesis is verified, it may be possible sometime to discover means of counting the number of possible connections in distinction from the number which actually function, and so of distinguishing original intellectual capacity from acquired intellectual ability. So far as tasks for external behavior are concerned, there are none which measure original capacity for intellect uninfluenced by training. One can only measure intellect, and then make such allowances for advantageous and for disadvantageous training as are shown to be reasonable.

Attaining any specified score in a stock intelligence examination such as the Stanford Binet or Army Alpha or National may best be considered as succeeding with a certain more or less intellectual task. That is, to attain 190 in Army Alpha under standard conditions is to succeed with a certain task; to attain 185 is to succeed with a certain easier task, and so on. With this interpretation of the scores, a scale in equal units can be worked out for any such test over most of its range by suitable experimentation; and this was done for many of these examinations.

Using equal-unit scales, the form of distribution of intellect in a group of the same age was determined for ages 10, 11, 12, 13, and 14, and by inference for younger ages. The results of the determinations for adults were inconclusive, those from Army Alpha and those from Army Examination a being very different.

The change in altitude of intellect with age is obviously characterized by negative acceleration, the curve being roughly as shown in Fig. 64. The change in area of intellect, however, will show a very different course. Even with an extremely conservative estimate of the increase in the number of intellectual tasks as difficulty is increased, the additions to area of Intellect CAVD are larger from 4 to 8 than from 0 to 4, and larger from 8 to 12 than from 4 to 8, in the case of children with ordinary school facilities.

## APPLICATIONS TO THE MEASUREMENT OF HUMAN ABILITIES IN GENERAL

The principles and techniques which we have developed for the measurement of intellect are, with minor modifications, suited to the measurement of a very large proportion of human abilities.

Consider the following list, which is representative of traits which either have been measured in the last twenty years or have been suggested as traits which, for theoretical or practical reasons, it would be desirable to measure, and includes sensory, sensori-motor, academic, moral, social, and economic abilities:

Hearing.
Discrimination of pitch.
General motor skill.
Ability in assembling mechanisms.
Ability in drawing.
Ability in the written use of the vernacular.
Ability in spelling.
Honesty about money.
Honesty about cheating.
Popularity.
Ability in carpentry.
Ability in salesmanship.

A consideration of each case will show that with occasional exceptions the following principles and techniques are applicable:

1. *What is measured is a product produced, a task achieved.* This may seem somewhat far-fetched in the case of hearing, honesty, and popularity. In hearing, the primary product produced is within the nervous system, being evidenced by the person's awareness of sound, but from

the point of view of measurement this is evidenced by the correctness of his "Yes" and "No" products as the trials are made with the sound and with no sound. In honesty, the products produced include acts of *not* doing as well as acts of doing certain things. In popularity the primary products are in the nervous systems of other people, but these are measured by smiles, votes, loans, companionship, and favors of various sorts.

2. *The measurement of any of the products produced involves valuation.* In the case of hearing, discrimination of pitch, and honesty about money and about cheating, the process of valuation is included in the definition of the ability. For hearing, to hear is obviously better than not to hear. For discrimination of pitch, knowing which of two tones is higher is obviously better than not knowing. For honesty about money, not stealing is obviously better than stealing. The question of valuation does exist, but it has been settled by the statement of the kind of product to be produced.

3. *In measuring intellect, we favored the arrangement of tasks so that the score could be success or failure,* though we carefully left room for a scale of credits for various degrees of "goodness" in the accomplishment of an intellectual task. In the cases of drawing, written composition, ability in carpentry, and to a less extent in some of the other abilities, the arrangement of many tasks each for a two-compartment score may not be so effective as the arrangement of fewer tasks each for a score graduated in perhaps fifty or more compartments. How to make full use of such graduated scores and still obtain intelligible measures of difficulty, range and speed then becomes a problem. We may best defer our answer until we have considered the next two principles.

4. *The measurement of the ability is in essence an inventory.* We can satisfactorily define the ability only by a list of the products which it produces—the tasks which it achieves. We measure it only by measuring a sample

which represents this total series. Even the case of hearing is a case of an inventory, though a relatively simple one. A person's hearing is not equally good at all pitches, and there may be other complexities. Discrimination of pitch may vary with the intensity and timbre of the tones.

5. *The tasks in such an inventory (a) vary in difficulty*[2] *and (b) may be usefully considered as varying in difficulty for hearing* (or for discrimination of pitch, or for whatever the ability is) *as a totality, or for such parts of the ability as the task requires,* with more or less intermixture of difficulty due to other factors than hearing (or whatever the ability is). That is, we may usefully entertain the abstract conceptions of difficulty for all of hearing ability and nothing but hearing ability, difficulty for all of ability to discriminate pitches and nothing but that ability, difficulty for all of motor skill and nothing but motor skill, etc.

This should be unquestioned for hearing, discrimination, motor skill, assembling, and spelling. But in the case of the other traits in our list, it is not so clear that the tasks form a graded series in difficulty, and it is much less clear that it will be useful to apply the conception of difficulty for all of a certain ability and nothing but it, and of altitude as a feature of the ability which is measured by the degree of its kind of difficulty at which it can succeed.

For example, we do not often think of increases in ability in English composition as the achievement of harder and harder tasks, but rather as the production of better and better products. This procedure can, however, be put into conformity with the general plan which we have adopted for intellect. All that is needed is to define a certain degree of difficulty as the difficulty of producing a product of a certain excellence. Thus when a person writes a composition on "Fishing" which is scored as 64 on the Hillegas scale, we may regard him as having attempted the following tasks with the stated results.

---

[2] Difficulty being defined for some specified group by the percentage of failures at the task in question.

To write a composition on "Fishing" of quality

|   |   |   |   |   |
|---|---|---|---|---|
| | 40 | or | better | S |
| " | 45 | " | " | S |
| " | 50 | " | " | S |
| " | 55 | " | " | S |
| " | 60 | " | " | S |
| " | 65 | " | " | F |
| " | 70 | " | " | F |
| " | 75 | " | " | F |

This is a part of the answer to the problem raised in connection with the third principle, providing a method of utilizing graded-credit scores and still retaining the advantages of the "success-failure" scoring. It could have been utilized in our completion tasks, scored as 3, 2, 1, or 0, by calling a 3 a success at one level and a 2 a success at a lower level. In using it we should bear in mind that graded-credit scores for one task usually have a considerable subjective element[3] and may need some special provisions to eliminate the errors thereof. We should also bear in mind that nothing is added to the reliability or weight of a determination by re-stating it as a series of successes and failures. To replace "scored 64 by a composition," by "scored 40S, 50S, 60S, 70F, 80F, 90F by a composition," or to replace the latter by "scored 30S, 35S, 40S, 50S, 55S, 60S, 65F, 70F, 75F, 80F, 85F, 90F by a composition," gives no added reliability or weight, so long as it is the same composition scored by the same persons.

We do not have to abandon measurement by the quality of the product measured by a gradation of credits, if we institute measurement by degree of difficulty mastered. The latter may be added without displacing the former.

In the case of drawing, the latter is already in good use. We not only rate products on scales of general and special

[3] This is so unless they are made up by putting together credit points for specified objective features in the product. In that case they are better treated as summations of S's in separate tasks, to wit, the production of those objective features.

merit, but also set series of tasks graded in difficulty. In the case of honesty about money and about cheating, the concept of difficulty is applicable. It is more difficult to be honest in paying a railroad than to be honest in paying a newsboy. Many more men will cheat the government than will cheat their partners. In the case of popularity, the concept is applicable. Indeed, when we say that John is much more popular than James, we usually mean precisely a combination of "altitude" and "width," that, for example, John is more liked than James by the people who like both,[4] and that John is liked by more people than James is at any degree of liking that we may choose to take. In such a case the degrees of difficulty are furnished by the differences in persons and likings, it being "harder" to win much liking than little from the same person, and to win the liking of the least friendly people than that of the most friendly. Carpentry and salesmanship are much like drawing and the written use of the vernacular in respect of the applicability of the concept of difficulty. We can measure variations in the ability either by a graded scale of credits for the quality of the product, or by a series of tasks graded in difficulty; and the second method can be operated with no loss to the first.

Whether in any case it is desirable to operate measurement in terms of the point on a scale consisting of tasks graded for difficulty, where 50%S (or some other assigned percentage of successes) is reached, depends in large measure upon the usefulness of the attempt to abstract out difficulty for, say, ability in carpentry in its entirety and untainted by anything other than ability in carpentry, and measure in terms of it.

In the past, we have not tried to distinguish at all precisely the ability in carpentry from other abilities. If a thousand boys made chairs, we have used the quality of the chairs which they made as a measure of their several abilities in carpentry, despite the fact that John may have

---

4 Or that certain people like John better than any people like James.

succeeded chiefly by general carefulness, and James may have failed by inability to read the instructions, and Tom may have won his standing largely by the artistic excellence of some carving and painting which adorned his chair, and a dozen others may have won their standings, each by a different compound of abilities. In the case of intellect, it is well worth while to seek rigorous measures of intellectual difficulty, because intellect is so important an ability and because altitude of intellect turns out to be a fairly unified, coherent variable properly represented by cardinal numbers. But will this be so with the altitude of ability in carpentry? How many thousands of abilities are we to assign specific difficulties and altitudes to? A girl makes a dress, and we easily thereby have some measurement of her ability to make that sort of a dress. How far shall we go in our use of this task of making a dress as a measure of difficulty for ability in sewing, difficulty for ability in design, difficulty for motor skill, difficulty for executive ability; difficulty for honesty in not obtaining illegitimate help, and so on and on?

The general answer is that it is desirable to settle on the most fundamental and mutually exclusive abilities and learn to measure them first; that many of the thousands of abilities with which the sciences and arts of man deal are doubtless compounds or derivatives of more elemental abilities; that most of them are far from being mutually exclusive; that new professions and trades and topics for study add to the number of these abilities without any alterations in the fundamentals of human nature; and that consequently science may often refuse to measure the altitude of, say, ability in carpentry in its entirety and uninfluenced by anything save ability in carpentry. Ability in carpentry may be left to a looser definition and cruder measurement. If, however, science does undertake to make a true measure of ability in carpentry, it is possible to apply the concept of specific difficulty for ability in carpentry. For the most satisfactory measurement it is necessary to do so. The same will hold of other mental abilities, with few exceptions.

6. *There are usually more tasks than one at each level of difficulty, so that the range or width of the ability at any level may be measured by the percentage correct at that level, and if desired, a measure of surface may be made by summing the widths at all levels.*

This is in a sense a corollary of principle 4. It needs no comment.

7. *Measurements of speed should be of the speed of successful performances. Nothing useful concerning an ability is measured by the time required to fail at a task.*[5]

8. *Width being measured by number and speed by time, the technical problem with any of these abilities is to provide a scale for altitude, that is, for its specific difficulty.* Knowledge of the differences in difficulty (for the ability in question) of a series of tasks, and of their differences from an absolute zero of that difficulty, are the two desiderata in such a scale.

9. *Knowledge of the differences in difficulty (for the ability in question) may be had if (a) the form of distribution of the varying conditions of the ability in an individual is known; or if (b) the form of distribution of the varying abilities of the individuals in a group is known. These*

---

[5] The relative amounts of importance of altitude, width, and speed in the measurement of an ability vary. Consider, for example, drawing, spelling, and typewriting, asking the three questions, "How difficult a task?", "How many tasks at easy levels?", and "How quickly?". In drawing, altitude is of prime importance, since if a person can do the hard tasks, that is, can draw well, he can usually do, or very quickly learn to do, nearly all of the easy tasks, that is, draw identifiable cows, chickens, houses, trees, and the like. In spelling, width is of especial importance, since the ability to spell very difficult words is less valuable for the world's welfare or as a symptom of excellence, whereas failure with an easy word is an annoyance to many; and since the ability to do the hard task does not so often as in drawing presuppose ability with (or quick acquisition of) the easy tasks. In typewriting, speed is obviously relatively more important than it is in drawing or spelling. This is partly because the typist early learns to do all or nearly all of the tasks, and thereafter improves his ability by learning to do them without lapses into error, and more quickly.

*may be ascertained with a high degree of probability by submitting the individual or the group to many graded series of tasks, each series being made with the intent to have tasks spaced at equal intervals of difficulty and to have as many tasks at any one level of difficulty as at any other, by individuals or committees uninfluenced by any preconceptions about the form of distribution. The score to be given is a level score, like those derived and used in Chapters IX, XI, and XIII. Whatever distribution is approximated by the average of these distributions, and more closely when the scores for two or more are averaged than when they are used singly, has a strong probability of being near to the form of distribution which the altitude of that ability would show if measured in truly equal units.*

There may be other useful ways of estimating these amounts of difference. In the case of the beauty of drawings, a consensus of opinion may be preferable, since amount of beauty may be precisely the amount of beauty *as felt.* In the case of ability to discriminate pitch, it may be permissible to forego equality in units of the ability itself and be content with the mere definition of the levels in terms of the physical differences; or the progress of research may justify some method of inference such as that amounts of the ability are inversely proportional to the time required to perceive the difference.

10. Altitude of intellect is distributed approximately in Form A in the case of grade populations from Grade 6 to Grade 13, and of age populations from 11 to 14. There is a substantial likelihood that any one of these grade populations will show a similar form of distribution in the case of the altitude of academic abilities (like ability in reading, or in the use of language, or in academic information) which are bases for promotion and are rather closely correlated with intellect. There is some likelihood that age populations will show a similar form of distribution for altitude of general sensory acuity, or for general sensori-motor capacity, or for general motor skill, or for general mental

health, since variations in these amongst children of like age are probably in large measure due to the same sorts of causes as are variations in intellect in children of like age.

11. An ability is defined by making a series of tasks such that the score in this total series depends on the ability. Thus *an ability is defined by a total series of tasks.* This series may be constituted by assuming that such and such tasks are *as a whole* a measure of the ability, or by assuming that the ranking of individuals in an order for their amounts of the ability by some defined consensus of experts is valid, and selecting a series of tasks success in which correlate perfectly with that order. This is in so far arbitrary. If the ability does correspond to some unified, coherent, fundamental fact in the world, later work with the series of tasks will, to some extent at least, reveal that such is the case. The correlations of parts of the series with other parts will be high; their correlations with abilities outside the series will be lower; the relations to heredity, to age, and to sex will be fairly simple. Some reasonable hypothesis concerning the physiological parallel of the ability is likely to suggest itself. If the ability does not so correspond, but is just a name for some concatenation of aspects which various fundamental abilities take under rather artificial conditions, later work with the series of tasks will probably show it.

12. The ability having been defined by a total series of tasks, *it may be arranged in subseries or composite tasks in an approximate order of difficulty by experiment or consensus or both.*

13. *Each composite task should be representative of the total series qualitatively and should be large enough so that* $r_{at}$ (letting $a$ stand for the total ability) *is 1.00, or as high as the self-correlation of the composite permits.*

14. *Composite tasks will be efficient instruments for measurement in proportion as their single elements are equal in difficulty (not necessarily in specific difficulty for the ability in question) and give a high multiple correlation with ability a.*

15. *These composite tasks should be measured in respect of their differences in difficulty* (for ability a) *one from another.* Even a very inadequate measurement is better than none, so long as its inadequacy is nowise concealed. For we have everything that we had before the measurement was made, undisturbed by it. For example, suppose that in motor skill, composite tasks a, b, c, d, e . . . h are devised and tested with populations at age 2, 4, 6, 8, 10, 12, 14, 16, and 18. Even if we do not know the forms of distribution of altitude of motor skill in these age groups at all accurately, it is better to make a reasonable hypothesis about them and act on it than to remain content with the mere rank order for motor difficulty, that a<b<c<d, etc. Whenever anyone does anything with that rank order in the way of using it in the comparison of any difference or the expression of any relation, he makes some assumption about the amounts of difference b–a, c–b, d–c, etc.[6] There is no workable arithmetic of pure ranks, and cannot be. So long as it is unknown whether c–b is equal to b–a, or ten times b–a or one-tenth of b–a, and the like, we cannot add, subtract, multiply, or divide with rank differences as such.

16. *These composite tasks should also be measured in respect of their differences from an approximate absolute zero of ability a.* Even though the location of zero is hypothetical and has a large margin of possible error, the estimate can do no harm if its unreliability is not concealed. Nothing is distorted by it. It is simply an added feature to be used or neglected as seems wise. Anybody who

---

[6] Thus the Spearman correlation formula

$$r = 2 \cos \frac{\pi}{3} (1 - R) - 1 \text{ where } R = 1 - \frac{6\Sigma g}{n^2 - 1}$$

assumes that the form of distribution of the two traits is Form A, that of the normal probability surface.

Spearman's formula, $r = 2 \sin \left( \frac{\pi}{6} \rho \right)$

$$\text{where } \rho = 1 - \frac{6\Sigma D^2}{n(n^2 - 1)}$$

assumes that the form of distribution of the two traits is Form A. If the form is rectangular, r is taken as equal to ρ wishes to utilize the "times as much" comparison with the facts will have to make some assumption about the location of zero; and the assumption made by the author of the scale is likely to be better than the average of the assumptions of those who use it. He has presumably more knowledge and better judgment about it than the average of them. No one of them is compelled to accept the location which he assigns.

A qualification of "usually" might have been inserted in the paragraph above, because there may be important abilities where any location of the absolute zero is so difficult that any attempt to do so with present knowledge is pretentious and absurd. We doubt this, however. On the contrary, when an ability has been defined by a series of tasks, the extension down from the easiest composite task to a task of the same general sort which requires just a bare trifle of the ability in question is almost a necessary consequence. If a reasonable location of the absolute zero cannot be attained, it is a sign that the ability itself is not an important, unified variable in nature.

There are two important special cases of locating absolute zero which may suitably be considered here. The first is that exemplified by discrimination of pitch, where it is customary to measure down from an upper limit of perfection, using the amount of error made, or the smallest amount of difference discernible, and thinking of its difference down from *zero error* rather than up from *zero ability*. This has its advantages, and it need not be altogether discarded; but it produces numbers which are very ill adapted for quantitative thinking, and may well be supplemented by measures up from a zero, meaning just barely not any ability.

The second is the case where the standard point of reference is the ordinary or modal man. Thus, people commonly measure popularity up and unpopularity down from a condition of average popularity. This procedure has been widely recommended in recent psychological and educational science, and has the very great merits that its point of reference is one near where the measurements are made, is easily definable in reality, and is convenient for studies by correlation and partial correlations. Measures + and — from such a central tendency in units of the variability of the group are also honest, making no pretence at being more than they are. It has the disadvantage of instability, shifting with the group taken. Again science

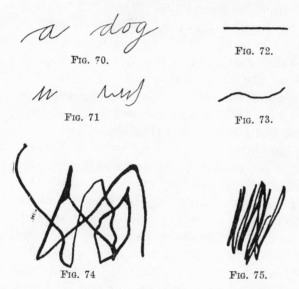

FIG. 70.

FIG. 71

FIG. 72.

FIG. 73.

FIG. 74

FIG. 75.

may retain all these advantages, and still add the different advantages of a true zero.

Finally, attention may be invited to the difference between natural and conventional zero points. In the former, there is a genuine beginning of an important natural phenomenon. In the latter, there is a beginning only from the point of view of some human institution or custom. Thus motor skill in the case of the hand may be said to have its task of zero difficulty somewhere below the point of reaching toward an object and touching it, or of grasping an object touched and bringing it somewhere near the mouth. This is near a natural zero. The tasks of zero difficulty

33

for ability in penmanship and of zero difficulty for ability in drawing would by any reasonable view be tasks which would be much above this zero of manual motor skill. The zero task for penmanship would be to make something which could be identified as writing, though no letter or word could be identified. For example, to copy Fig. 70 with the result shown in Figure 71 may be regarded as near the zero of handwriting. To use pencil or crayon to make a line as "good" as Figure 73 when Fig. 72 is shown as the model may be regarded as near the zero of drawing. To use pencil or crayon to make any kind of a scribble such as Fig. 74 or Fig. 75 may be regarded as zero for the use of a mark-making tool. All three of these zeros are well above the zero of manual motor skill. They come later in life[7] and are impossible for idiots for whom the reaching and grasping are possible.

The number of conventional zeros is legion. We can have tasks of zero difficulty for ability in typewriting, in stringing beads, in shuffling cards, in playing the piano, in playing the violin, in tapping, and scores of other varieties of manual skills; and for certain educational and economic problems each of these zeros may be of value and the reference of measures of ability to it may be desirable.

They will be even more useful if each of them is measured off from the natural zero for manual motor skill, so that reference can be made to it also. This holds as a general principle. Any conventional zero will be made more useful by being itself measured off from some natural zero.

There are two important fields of mental measurement where the principles and techniques which we have developed for intellect do not apply, at least not without radical changes.

The first is the general case of the description and measurement of the connections or bonds whereby any given

[7] The dates may be set roughly as $\frac{1}{2}$ yr. for reaching and grasping, 1 year for making a mark, and 2 years for copying a line. The date for making anything enough distinguishable from general scribbling and mark-making to be called a zero specific to handwriting ability is not known, but is later than 2 years.

condition or state of affairs in a mind leads to another condition or state of affairs in that mind. In such cases we need not and do not use valuation or the concept of difficulty, but simply record that such and such connections exist in such and such degrees of strength from zero up. By the strength of a connection between condition A and condition B, we mean the probability that A will be followed by B. The strength of the connection is measured crudely by the percent which A→B is of A→B + A→C, + A→D, . . . + A → N,[8] and by the length of time that the connection will last without exercise; and somewhat more exactly by this percent and this time in relation to the number and strength of competing tendencies. This is by far the commonest sort of mental measurement.

The second is the measurement of likes and dislikes, interests, desires, "drives," motives, or whatever one chooses to call the facts whereby certain states of affairs are satisfying and others are annoying to the animal. The whole subject of satisfiers and annoyers is in more or less doubt and dispute, but by any view the measurement of how much a man likes the taste of olives or a brisk run up a hill is very different from the measurement of either his intellect or his tendency to contract the pupil in a bright light.

The most striking difference is that the measurement is now up and down from a zero of indifference to A, where the animal neither seems moved to do anything which will change the state of affairs in respect of A, nor seems moved to do anything which will cause A to continue or recur.

Another notable fact is that whereas it is easy to discover whether A or B is more satisfying to any given individual X, it is hard to discover whether A is more satisfying to individual X than to individual Y.

According to our notions, the satisfyingness or annoyingness of any state of affairs to any mind is measurable

[8] The cases where A occurs and apparently leads to nothing are to be included in the count.

by the products produced, including the internal neural products which lead to honest reports of satisfaction and annoyance, welcome and rejection, "for" and "against." We also think that different varieties of satisfyingness such as that of food when hungry and hearing music and being looked at with respectful glances, are intercommensurable; and also susceptible of algebraic computation against amounts of annoyingness. The discussion of any theories of such an hedonic calculus is, however, beyond the scope of this chapter or this book.

# APPENDIX I.

## The Form of Distribution of an Individual's Variations in Intellect

We have elsewhere[1] reported evidence showing that the variations of an individual in separate tests of an ability, each a half hour or so in length, were distributed almost or quite symmetrically about his average or mode, extreme deviations upward being almost or quite as common as extreme deviations downward. It is the purpose of this appendix to present, in a very brief and summary manner, additional evidence to the same effect.

We have confirmed the results in the case of the Army Alpha by using the records of 81 high school students in Milan, Michigan, each with three trials of Alpha, a year apart, given by Superintendent Tape. (Fall of 1919, 1920, 1921.) Fifteen students were at those dates eighth grade, freshmen, and sophomores, respectively; thirty-two were freshmen, sophomores, and juniors; and thirty-four were sophomores, juniors and seniors. The allowances for practice effect and growth were: first group, 15 and 13 points; second group, 16 and 12 points; third group, 13 and 13 points. (The average scores were: first group, 91, 105, and 121; second group, 87, 103, and 115; third group, 104, 117, and 130.) The median of the scores thus corrected was found for each individual, and the two deviations from this median. The distribution of these plus-minus deviations is shown below. The 81 medians themselves are not included.

The average deviation upward is 8.60 points. The average deviation downward is 8.54 points. There are 23 plus deviations and 24 minus deviations which are 10 points or greater.

[1] Jour. of Exp. Psy., vol. 6, pp. 161–167.

| Deviations | 1st Group | Frequencies 2nd Group | 3rd Group | Total | Total Grouping by 9 Points |
|---|---|---|---|---|---|
| − 32, 33, 34 |  | 1 |  | 1 | 1 |
| − 29, 30, 31 |  |  | 1 | 1 |  |
| − 26, 27, 28 |  | 2 |  | 2 | 3 |
| − 23, 24, 25 |  |  |  |  |  |
| − 20, 21, 22 |  | 3 |  | 3 |  |
| − 17, 18, 19 | 1 |  | 2 | 3 | 12 |
| − 14, 15, 16 |  | 2 | 4 | 6 |  |
| − 11, 12, 13 |  | 4 | 3 | 7 |  |
| − 8, 9, 10 | 2 | 7 | 7 | 16 | 40 |
| − 5, 6, 7 | 5 | 5 | 7 | 17 |  |
| − 2, 3, 4 | 6 | 3 | 9 | 18 |  |
| − 1, 0, +1 | 1 | 9 | 6 | 16 | 53 |
| + 2, 3, 4 | 5 | 7 | 7 | 19 |  |
| + 5, 6, 7 | 3 | 9 | 5 | 17 |  |
| + 8, 9, 10 | 3 | 4 | 5 | 12 | 35 |
| +11, 12, 13 | 1 |  | 5 | 6 |  |
| +14, 15, 16 | 1 | 5 | 2 | 8 |  |
| +17, 18, 19 | 1 | 1 | 2 | 4 | 13 |
| +20, 21, 22 |  |  | 1 | 1 |  |
| +23, 24, 25 |  |  | 1 | 1 |  |
| +26, 27, 28 |  | 1 |  | 1 | 4 |
| +29, 30, 31 | 1 | 1 |  | 2 |  |
| +32, 33, 34 |  |  | 1 | 1 | 1 |

39 pupils in Grades 5 and 6 took the Courtis tests in computation four times during the year. The effect of practice was allowed for by adding to the first score the average gain of trial 2 over trial 1, and subtracting from the third score the average gain of trial 3 over trial 2. Trial 4 was treated similarly. The deviations of each individual's scores from his median score were then computed. As the result, we have:

| Deviations | Frequencies |
|---|---|
| − 8 to − 10.5 | 1 |
| − 5 " − 7.5 | 2 |
| − 2 " − 4.5 | 19 |
| − 1.5 " + 1.5 | 107 |
| + 2 " + 4.5 | 20 |
| + 5 " + 7.5 | 4 |
| + 8 " + 10.5 | 0 |

37 pupils in Grades 5 and 6 took the Woody Test, Series A, three times in Oct. (or Nov.), Jan., and May of a school year. The scores were corrected for the practice effect by adding the average gain of trial 2 over trial 1 to the score for trial 1, and subtracting the average gain of trial 3 over trial 2 from the score for trial 3. The deviations of each individual's scores from his median score were then computed. As the result, we have, including the 37 deviations of 0 belonging to the median measures:

| Deviations | Frequencies |
|---|---|
| − 23 to − 31 | 1 |
| − 14 " − 22 | 3 |
| − 5 " − 13 | 16 |
| − 4 " + 4 | 83 |
| + 5 " + 13 | 8 |
| + 14 " + 22 | 2 |
| + 23 " + 31 | 0 |

In records in tests of spelling treated in a similar manner, we have, as the distribution of an individual's deviations from his median, the following:

| Deviations | Frequencies |
|---|---|
| − 32 to − 40 | 0 |
| − 23 " − 31 | 2 |
| − 26 " − 22 | 5 |
| − 5 " − 13 | 24 |
| − 4 " + 4 | 53 |
| + 5 " + 13 | 30 |
| + 19 " + 22 | 4 |
| + 23 " + 31 | 1 |
| + 32 " + 40 | 1 |

Pupils in Grades 4, 5, and 6 were tested with Stanford Binet, National A, National B, Otis Advanced,[2] Myers Mental Measure, Haggerty Delta 2, Illinois, and certain parts of Dearborn. Each score was first turned into a deviation from the median for the group in that test, in terms of the variability of the group in the test in question. Then

[2] Some had the *Otis Primary* instead. For these, estimated scores in the *Otis Advanced* were computed.

it was expressed as a deviation from the average of the eight such deviation-scores for the individual in question. These last deviations represent the variability of an individual around his average ability in intelligence tests. Their distribution is as follows:

| Deviations | Frequencies |
|---|---|
| − 165 to − 194 | 0 |
| − 135 " − 164 | 2 |
| − 105 " − 134 | 1 |
| − 75 " − 104 | 9 |
| − 45 " − 74 | 40 |
| − 15 " − 44 | 124 |
| − 14 " + 14 | 137 |
| + 15 " + 44 | 86 |
| + 45 " + 74 | 41 |
| + 75 " + 104 | 10 |
| + 105 " + 134 | 3 |
| + 135 " + 164 | 2 |
| + 165 " + 194 | 1 |

65 pupils in Grades 8 to 12 were tested with Alpha Form 5, Alpha Form 8, Terman Group Test Form A, Terman Group Test Form B, and half of Part I of the Thorndike Examination for High School Graduates. These five scores for each pupil were treated just as the eight scores described in the previous paragraph, except that the final deviations are deviations from the individual's median instead of from his average.

The resulting distribution was as follows (including the 65 zero deviations of the medians themselves):

| Deviations | Frequencies |
|---|---|
| − 110 to − 129 | 1 |
| − 90 " − 109 | 2 |
| − 70 " − 89 | 10 |
| − 50 " − 69 | 10 |
| − 30 " − 49 | 34 |
| − 10 " − 29 | 47 |
| − 9 " + 9 | 117 |
| + 10 " + 29 | 55 |
| + 30 " + 49 | 27 |
| + 50 " + 69 | 15 |
| + 70 " + 89 | 5 |
| + 90 " + 109 | 2 |
| + 110 " + 129 | 0 |

The variations in I. Q.'s from different Stanford Binet examinations at long intervals are not exactly the sort of evidence that we wish, since variability is complicated with growth and the measure is an indirect ratio, but it is of interest to note the facts.   So we have tabulated the deviations of an individual's separate I. Q.'s from his median I. Q. in all of the cases of Baldwin and Stecher ('22, p. 24) who had at least three separate examinations.   The results are as follows:

| Deviations | Frequencies |
|---|---|
| − 26½ to − 29½ | 1 |
| − 23 " − 26 | 1 |
| − 19½ " − 22½ | 3 |
| − 16 " − 19 | 5 |
| − 12½ " − 15½ | 6 |
| − 9 " − 12 | 19 |
| − 5½ " − 8½ | 28 |
| − 2 " − 5 | 53 |
| − 1½ " + 1½ | 149 |
| + 2 " + 5½ | 60 |
| + 5½ " + 8½ | 27 |
| + 9 " + 12 | 14 |
| + 12½ " + 15½ | 5 |
| + 16 " + 19 | 1 |
| + 19½ " + 22½ | 2 |
| + 23 " + 26 | 1 |
| + 26½ " + 29½ | 0 |

In no one of these six cases is there more than a very slight excess of extreme downward deviations.  On the whole, the balance is about even as shown by the two rough summaries below.

We may expect, in a thousand deviations, about 12 that are $2\frac{3}{4}\sigma$ or more minus to about 7 that are $2\frac{3}{4}\sigma$ or more plus, if we assume that the scoring units in the cases studied are on the average of about the same real value at the lower as at the upper extreme of the ranges studied.  About the real value of the units we know very little, but it seems likely that the tests have more tasks at the lower levels of difficulty than at the upper, rather than the reverse.  So getting equal units would probably reduce the excess of

|  | Courtis | + | Woody | + | Spelling | Total |
|---|---|---|---|---|---|---|
| low | 0 | + | 0 | + | 0 | 0 |
|  | 1 | + | 1 | + | 2 | 4 |
|  | 2 | + | 3 | + | 5 | 10 |
|  | 19 | + | 16 | + | 24 | 59 |
| central | 107 | + | 83 | + | 53 | 243 |
|  | 20 | + | 8 | + | 30 | 58 |
|  | 4 | + | 2 | + | 4 | 10 |
|  | 0 | + | 0 | + | 1 | 1 |
| high | 0 | + | 0 | + | 1 | 1 |

|  | 8 test | + | 5 test | + | repeated I.Q. | Total |
|---|---|---|---|---|---|---|
| low | 0 | + | 0 | + | 1 | 1 |
|  | 2 | + | 3 | + | 9 | 14 |
|  | 50 | + | 54 | + | 53 | 157 |
| central | 347 | + | 219 | + | 262 | 828 |
|  | 54 | + | 47 | + | 46 | 147 |
| high | 3 | + | 2 | + | 4 | 9 |
|  | 0 | + | 0 | + | 0 | 0 |

low deviations rather than increase it. Also, the excess of low deviations will be reduced if we omit the somewhat ambiguous I. Q. data.

These facts with those of the previous report certainly justify the conclusion that the real variations of an individual in a 30-minute test of intellect or school achievement will be found to be approximately symmetrical. This justifies the use of the average in practice, and clears the way for important advances in the theory of mental measurements and the scaling of tasks.

# APPENDIX II.

## The Relation of an Individual's Variability to His Ability in Tests of Intelligence

An individual who takes a number of different trials in a test, using alternative forms arranged to be of equal difficulty, attains varying scores. It is of importance for many purposes to know how the variability of an individual in any ability is related to the amount of the ability which he has, that is, to his average or modal achievement. We have investigated the matter somewhat thoroughly in the case of seventeen tests of intelligence.

It is necessary to distinguish between (a) the apparent, or face-value, relation observed between the variability of an individual's separate *scores* and his average *score,* and (b) the real relation that would be observed if these scores were transmuted into measures such that 1, 2, 3, 4, 5, 6, 7, etc., represented a real arithmetical progression of amounts of the ability. For example, we find that twenty individuals each of whom took (after two preliminary trials, to eliminate the practice effect) from eleven to thirteen forms of Part I of the Thorndike Intelligence Examination for High School Graduates, showed the results of Table 138. If the scores are taken at their face value, it appears that the variability of an individual whose median score is about 105 (from 100 to 113) is very nearly the same as the variability of an individual whose median score is about 128 (125 to 132). If, however, the units of the scoring from 90 to 120 really represent smaller increments of ability than the units from 120 to 145, the real variability of an individual of ability 105 is less than the real variability of an individual of ability 128. The converse is true, if the units of the scoring scale from 90 to 120 really represent larger increments of ability than the units from 120 to 145.

TABLE 138.

VARIATIONS OF THE SCORES OF THIRTEEN (OR FEWER) 30-MINUTE TRIALS WITH PART I OF THE THORNDIKE INTELLIGENCE EXAMINATION FOR HIGH SCHOOL GRADUATES FROM THE MEDIAN SCORE FOR THE INDIVIDUAL IN ALL THIRTEEN TRIALS. 20 GIFTED PUPILS, A, C, D, E, . . . U. 13 DIFFERENT DAYS.

| Individual Median | j 87 | s 95 | d 96 | i 99 | o 99 | j to o 87 to 99 | a, c, e, f, g, h, k, n, q, t 100 to 113 | u 125 | p 125 | l 128 | m 128 | r 132 | u to r 125 to 132 |
|---|---|---|---|---|---|---|---|---|---|---|---|---|---|
| -11, -12, -13 | | | | 1 | | 1 | 1 | | | | 1 | 1 | 2 |
| - 8, - 9, -10 | | 1 | | 2 | 2 | 5 | 8 | 1 | | 2 | 1 | 0 | 4 |
| - 5, - 6, - 7 | 1 | 0 | 2 | 0 | 2 | 5 | 10 | 1 | 3 | 0 | 0 | 1 | 5 |
| - 2, - 3, - 4 | 4 | 4 | 2 | 0 | 1 | 11 | 20 | 2 | 2 | 3 | 2 | 2 | 11 |
| - 1, 0, + 1 | 3 | 3 | 5 | 5 | 2 | 18 | 32 | 3 | 3 | 2 | 3 | 2 | 13 |
| + 2, + 3, + 4 | 0 | 1 | 2 | 2 | 1 | 6 | 9 | 1 | 1 | 2 | 1 | 3 | 8 |
| + 5, + 6, + 7 | 4 | 1 | 2 | 1 | 2 | 10 | 20 | 4 | 1 | 1 | 3 | 2 | 11 |
| + 8, + 9, +10 | 1 | 1 | 0 | 2 | 1 | 5 | 12 | 1 | 2 | 3 | 1 | 1 | 8 |
| +11, +12, +13 | | | | | 2 | 2 | 3 | | 1 | | 1 | | 2 |
| +14, +15, +16 | | | | | | | 4 | | | | | | |
| +17, +18, +19 | | | | | | | 0 | | | | | | |
| +20, +21, +22 | | | | | | | 0 | | | | | | |
| +23, +24, +25 | | | | | | | 1 | | | | | | |
| n | | | | | | 63 | 120 | | | | | | 64 |
| Average Variation | | | | | | 4.2 | 4.8 | | | | | | 4.8 |

Frequency of Variations

The facts concerning the scores taken at their face value are worth knowing and recording, but it is the relation of the "real" variability to the "real" amount of ability that is the essential problem. Our procedure and reasoning are as follows:

We record the face-value score results for many different sorts of tests of the ability in question, and note in each case any facts about the construction of the tests which concern the probability that its units progressively swell or shrink in "real" value over any considerable fraction of the range we are concerned with. We note especially the score results in those cases where there is no reason to expect swelling more than shrinking. The average relation between variability and ability found in these cases may be taken to represent approximately the real relation, until someone produces evidence that, in all or nearly all tests for the ability in question, there are forces leading psychologists, quite without intention, to devise scoring plans which make for progressive swelling or shrinking of units at the same places along the scale of real ability.

The most desirable material for our purpose would be the records of individuals representing a very wide range of ability, there being many of them, and each being measured with many alternative forms of the test in question. Range is desirable to accentuate the relation and measure it throughout. Large populations are desirable to reduce the disturbing effect of individual differences. A large number of trials of the test is desirable to locate exactly the ability to which the variability is related. Unfortunately, there is no such material, and we have to do the best we can by putting together several small ranges, and by using individuals who have been measured by only two trials of the test. Indeed, we use individuals who have been measured by only one trial, by a method which will be described shortly. Whatever the method, however, the result is an estimate of what the relation would be between (a) the variability of an individual in an infinite number of trials or tests or measures of the ability and (*b*) the amount of his ability as measured by the mode or other central tendency of these separate trials or measures.

In general, any material is useful for our purpose by which we can measure the variability of a number of trials or individuals whose central tendency in the ability is low, and also the variability of a number of trials or individuals whose central tendency in the ability is high. The essential difference is that in certain material the relation is very much more liable to blurring and distortion by the inaccuracy of the determinations of average ability itself than it is in other material.

The effect of the inaccuracy of the averages upon our determinations of the relation between average intellect and variation in intellect is somewhat subtle and complicated. We need not discuss it here. After we have gathered and organized the best data we can bearing on the relation, and found, as we shall, that they are best explained by the hypothesis that the variability of an individual neither increases nor decreases according as his average is low or high, we shall have to ask whether the case would be otherwise if the inaccuracies of these averages were reduced.

When we have only two separate trials with a test, it is best to measure an individual's variability by the difference between the two scores, after suitable correction for the practice effect and for differences in the difficulty of the forms used. (Call this difference D.) The average variation of an individual from his average or median (call this A.D.) may be taken as this difference divided by $\sqrt{2}$. The average of the A.D.'s of a group of individuals, all of the same or nearly the same average ability, is the average of their D's divided by $\sqrt{2}$. Table 139 shows the results in the case of a set of scores in the Thorndike Part I, series of 1919 to 1922, so treated.

If we obtained the actual average for each individual and computed his A.D. directly by the formula, $\Sigma$ (devia-

TABLE 139.

THE RELATION BETWEEN AN INDIVIDUAL'S ABILITY AND HIS VARIABILITY. THE VARIABILITY IS THAT OF ONE TRIAL (30 MIN.) OF THE THORNDIKE TEST, PART I, FROM THE AVERAGE OF AN INFINITE NUMBER OF SUCH TRIALS. THE 2 TRIALS WERE TAKEN ON THE SAME DAY.

| | 45 | 50 | 55 | 60 | 65 | 70 | 75 | 105 | 110 | 115 | 120 | 125 | 130 | 135 |
|---|---|---|---|---|---|---|---|---|---|---|---|---|---|---|
| Average score in Th. H.S., Part I, forms I and M | | | | | | | | | | | | | | |
| Average differences (I-M) after allowance for practice and for the difficulty of the two tests. | 10.5 | 12.0 | 9.0 | 8.3 | 9.3 | 8.0 | 10.1 ... | 8.1 | 7.8 | 6.7 | 4.5 | 6.7 | 6.0 | 8.3 |
| Average difference of an individual's score in one trial of 1 form of the test from his average score in the test. (Row 2 ÷ $\sqrt{2}$). | 7.4 | 8.4 | 6.3 | 5.8 | 6.5 | 5.6 | 7.1 ... | 5.7 | 5.5 | 4.7 | 3.2 | 4.7 | 4.2 | 5.8 |
| Number of individuals | 6 | 12 | 9 | 34 | 48 | 61 | 84 ... | 102 | 65 | 50 | 20 | 13 | 3 | 4 |

tions)/2, we should have A.D.'s throughout seven-tenths as large as those of Table 139. This would be because in each case the central tendency had been automatically chosen so as to vary from the true central tendency in the direction of making the A. D. a minimum.

A still more convenient way at times is to estimate the variability of an individual's separate trials around his average indirectly from the variability of $n$ individuals (each measured by a single trial) around the average of the $n$ individuals, using individuals all equal in ability to the individual in question. If $n$ individuals in one trial with Army Alpha all score 165, and in another trial score 168, 160, 171, 159, etc., etc., averaging 165, it may be argued that the deviations of the 168, 160, 171, 159, etc. from 165 are comparable and proportional to the deviations of one individual of ability 165 who took Alpha $n$ times.[3] More exactly, the facts are that any one of $n$ individuals who are all really of ability K in a test does resemble any other of them in variability; and that if there is taken from each of the $n$ distributions representing their separate variabilities, one variation at random, the composite of these selected variations will resemble the distribution of the variations of any one of the $n$ individuals. In the particular matter with which we are concerned, the average of these selected variations will vary only by chance from the average of the averages of the separate individuals' variations, and this will vary only by chance from any one of these averages. The matter of concern to us is that, when $n$ individuals are measured each by only one trial and all score K, they really are not all of ability K, but vary around it. Consequently, when $n$ individuals measured each by one trial are used in place of one individual measured by $n$ trials, the "attenuation" or blurring of the relation is much greater. Using one individual measured by $n$ trials relates the variability to one precisely located amount of ability.

---

[3] Assuming of course that in both cases the effects of practice, interest, and the like are properly allowed for.

Using one trial of each of $n$ similar individuals relates it to an amount which is located with a considerable error. If we keep this attenuation in mind and allow for it, we may use material of this sort when it is desirable.

Even if we have only one trial with a test, it is still possible to estimate the approximate average of the average variations of a group of individuals each from his average, provided the individuals are also measured by some test which correlates fairly closely with the test in question. For example, suppose that ten individuals all score 75 in the score for one trial of the entire Thorndike Intelligence Examination for High School graduates, and score 30, 32, 34, 35, 36, 37, 38, 40, 42, and 48 in Part III of it; and that the general correlation between a one trial score for the entire examination and average ability in a large number of trials of Part III is .90; and that the correlation between the average score in two trials of Part III and the average ability in a large number of trials of Part III is .90 for a similar group. Then we do as well to take the variations in Part III of the ten individuals who all scored 75 in the entire examination as we would do to take the variations of ten individuals who all scored alike in the average of two trials with Part III itself.

We shall make very large use of this indirect method because by its use we can cover wide ranges and have large populations, and also in certain instances because the material available can be treated by no better method.

It should be noted that when the two trials of a test by an individual occur in a single session, the variability measured is that due to the difference of one hour from an adjacent hour, plus, of course, the differences of the content of the two forms of the test that were used. Cases of single-session variability will be so designated wherever they appear in what follows. Except for them, the variability studied is that of a random sampling of different days of an individual (but omitting days when by sickness or other causes he would not be submitted to a test), with a

34

random sampling of alternative forms of the test in question.

Let us first illustrate certain further matters concerning method. Table 138 has already shown the method where we have several trials with the test by an individual on different days. Table 139 has shown the method where we have two trials by an individual.[4] Table 140 below shows the method where we use the array of scores in trial 2 of $n$ individuals scoring alike in trial 1 to represent approximately the $n$ different trials of one individual. The test is still Part I of the Thorndike Examination, as in Tables 138 and 139.

It will be noted that in computing the variability of an array we use as a central tendency, not the actually observed average or median of that array, but the central tendency which seems most probably the true one for it in view of the facts of the entire table, that is, the central tendency given by the total relation line or regression. If the actually observed central tendencies were used, there would result a fallacious diminution of the variability in all arrays, and this would sometimes be a very large error when the number of cases in the array was small.[5] The relation line is determined by plotting the observed medians and drawing a smooth line such as approximately (1) makes the sum of the plus deviations equal to the sum of the minus deviations from it, and (2) distributes these deviations about equally + and — along the course of the line, and (3) has a geometrical form not much variant from the form found in general for the test in question. (That form is, for most of our material, rectilinear). There is thus an element of personal judgment in the decision as to the relation line and consequent placement of the central

---

4 These were on the same day in immediate sequence giving single-session variability.

5 For example, the three cases in Table 140 arrayed under 45 would show an average deviation of 4.5 from the average obtained by considering them alone, whereas they show an average deviation of 8.35 from the average that the whole table indicates as the probably true average for that array.

tendencies from which the variabilities were computed. This, in general, has almost no effect save upon the arrays toward either end, and its effect is greatly reduced so far as our general problem is concerned, by reason of the overlapping of the groups which we have used. Finally, the personal judgment did not, so far as we know, favor any one sort of relation of variability to magnitude more than another; it acted as a chance error.

The midpoint of a class interval of the array which was nearest to the relation line was used as the central tendency from which to compute the variability of the array. The reason for adopting this crude procedure instead of computing the lines of best fit, and computing the variability of each array from the exact point on it that belonged to the array in question, was that we had to choose between spending our time on a few relations computed exactly and on many relations estimated in this rough way. The latter procedure seemed much more instructive per unit of time spent.

Table 141 shows the method where we use the array of scores in one trial in Test X of $n$ individuals scoring alike in some other test closely enough correlated with Test X to serve instead of a trial with Test X itself. The central tendency of an array from which to compute its variability was determined just as in the case of Table 140.

We have four tables of the type of Table 139, and sixteen of the type of Tables 140 and 141, for Part I of the Thorndike Examination. Their summarized results appear as Tables 142 and 143. Our next task is to combine them to give a general estimate of the relation of the variability of an individual to his abiltiy in the case of this test. There are many suitable ways of doing this, each having certain merits. The method which we have adopted is to express each entry of a line of Table 142 as a percent of that line's average[6] entry under abilities 70 to 89 and to average the percents under each ability after weighting them as follows:

[6] This is a roughly weighted average.

| N | Weight |
|---|---|
| 1 or 2 | 1 |
| 3 – 5 | 2 |
| 6 – 12 | 3 |
| 13 – 19 | 4 |
| 20 – 29 | 5 |
| 30 – 39 | 6 |
| 40 – 59 | 7 |
| 60 – 79 | 8 |
| 80 – 99 | 9 |
| 100 – over | 10 |

The use of the percents makes it convenient to compare the relation found for this test with that found for others. The particular weighting used gives some weight to each group studied apart from the number of cases it contains, and adds no weight to size of population over 100 in any one array in any one group, and economizes time. The same procedure was followed with the facts of Table 143.

The relationship shown by the final line of Table 142 and the final line of Table 143 may be seen more clearly if we group the results more coarsely. In combining for the coarse grouping, the average percentages already obtained are weighted each by the sum of the weights attached to it. Thus 133 with a weight of 5 and 50 with a weight of 2 become 109 with a weight of 7; 94 with a weight of 5 and 79 with a weight of 3 become 88 with a weight of 8; 116 with a weight of 9 and 90 with a weight of 8 become 104 with a weight of 17. The relations of Tables 142B and 143 with coarser grouping are shown in Table 144. It should be observed that the grouping carried out in this manner after the variability of groups or arrays has been obtained from the original fine grouping, does not add any new "attenuation." All groupings in what follows were carried out in this manner.

We have, in the case of many tests, material of the sort shown by Tables 142, 143, and 144 for the Thorndike, Part I. In two instances results of different tests have been combined to abbreviate the presentation. The first is where results of the regular Army Beta and the weighted

## TABLE 140.

THORNDIKE INT. EXAM. FOR H. S. GRADUATES, '19–'22 SERIES. PART I, TRIAL 2, ARRAYED UNDER TRIAL 1. TEST OF FEB. '22. 30 = 30 TO 34, 35 = 35 TO 39, ETC.

| Score in Trial 2 \ Score in Trial 1 | 30 | 35 | 40 | 45 | 50 | 55 | 60 | 65 | 70 | 75 | 80 | 85 | 90 | 95 | 100 | 105 | 110 | 115 | 120 | 125 | 130 | 135 |
|---|---|---|---|---|---|---|---|---|---|---|---|---|---|---|---|---|---|---|---|---|---|---|
| 40 | 1 | | | | | | | | | | | | | | | | | | | | | |
| 45 | | | 1 | | | | | | | | | | | | | | | | | | | |
| 50 | | | | 1 | 1 | | | | | | | | | | | | | | | | | |
| 55 | | | 1 | | 1 | 1 | | | | | | | | | | | | | | | | |
| 60 | | | 1 | | | 1 | | | | | | | | | | | | | | | | |
| 65 | | | | 1 | 2 | 2 | | 1 | | | | | | | | | | | | | | |
| 70 | | | 1 | 2 | 3 | | 1 | 2 | 1 | | | | | | | | | | | | | |
| 75 | | | | 2 | 4 | | 4 | 3 | 2 | 2 | | | | | | | | | | | | |
| 80 | | | 1 | 3 | 1 | | 3 | 1 | 4 | 4 | 5 | | | | | | | | | | | |
| 85 | | | | 2 | 5 | | 3 | 4 | 6 | | 2 | 4 | | | | | | | | | | |
| 90 | | | | 1 | 2 | | 2 | 2 | 2 | | 1 | 6 | 5 | | | | | | | | | |
| 95 | | | | 1 | 1 | | 4 | 5 | | | 5 | 8 | 3 | 3 | 1 | 1 | | | 1 | | | |
| 100 | | | | | 1 | 3 | 1 | | | | 1 | 10 | 8 | 2 | 1 | | | 1 | | | | |
| 105 | | | | | 1 | | | | | 2 | | 3 | 7 | 1 | 2 | | 1 | | | | | |
| 110 | | | | | | | | | | | | 2 | 5 | 4 | 6 | 4 | 1 | | 1 | | | |
| 115 | | | | | | | | | | | | | 1 | 2 | 3 | 2 | | 1 | | 2 | | 1 |
| 120 | | | | | | | | | | | | | | | | | | | | | 1 | 1 |
| 125 | | | | | | | | | | | | | | | | | | | | | 2 | 1 |
| 130 | | | | | | | | | | | | | | | 1 | | 2 | | | | 1 | |
| 135 | | | | | | | | | | | | | | | | | | | | | | |
| 140 | | | | | | | | | | | | | | | | | | | | | | |
| 145 | | | | | | | | | | | | | | | | | | | | | | |
| 150 | | | | | | | | | | | | | | | | | | | | | | |
| **n** | 1 | | 1 | 3 | 3 | 1 | 8 | 13 | 15 | 18 | 21 | 27 | 20 | 32 | 27 | 16 | 23 | 10 | 11 | 4 | 4 | 2 |
| **Central Tendency Used** | 50 | | 60 | 65 | 65 | 70 | 75 | 80 | 85 | 90 | 90 | 95 | 100 | 105 | 110 | 110 | 115 | 120 | 125 | 125 | 130 | 135 |
| **Average Deviation** | 10.0 | | 5.0 | 8.35 | 6.65 | 5.00 | 9.40 | 9.60 | 10.35 | 10.0 | 7.85 | 8.50 | 10.5 | 8.30 | 5.95 | 7.5 | 6.75 | 6.5 | 6.80 | 11.25 | 6.25 | 7.5 |

## TABLE 141.

THORNDIKE INT. EX. FOR H. S. GRADUATES, '19–'22 SERIES. PART I, TRIAL 2, ARRAYED UNDER THORNDIKE EXAM., TOTAL SCORE. WOMEN STUDENTS IN HIGH SCHOOL, NORMAL SCHOOL, COLLEGE AND UNIVERSITY. 30 = 30–34; 35 = 35–39, ETC.

Columns: Score in Thorndike Total

| Score in Part I, Trial 2 | 10 | 15 | 20 | 25 | 30 | 35 | 40 | 45 | 50 | 55 | 60 | 65 | 70 | 75 | 80 | 85 | 90 | 95 | 100 | 105 | 110 | N |
|---|---|---|---|---|---|---|---|---|---|---|---|---|---|---|---|---|---|---|---|---|---|---|
| 40 | 1 | | | | | | | | | | | | | | | | | | | | | 1 |
| 45 | | | | | | | | | | | | | | | | | | | | | | 0 |
| 50 | | | 1 | | | | | | | | | | | | | | | | | | | 1 |
| 55 | | 1 | | | | | | | | | | | | | | | | | | | | 1 |
| 60 | | 1 | 4 | | 1 | 2 | | 1 | | | | | | | | | | | | | | 9 |
| 65 | | | 1 | 2 | 2 | 2 | | | | | | | | | | | | | | | | 7 |
| 70 | | | | | 2 | 4 | 2 | 4 | 1 | | | | | | | | | | | | | 13 |
| 75 | | 1 | | | 2 | 6 | 11 | 4 | 2 | 1 | | | | | | | | | | | | 27 |
| 80 | | | | | 1 | 5 | 9 | 2 | 8 | 2 | 2 | | | | | | | | | | | 29 |
| 85 | | | | | | 2 | 7 | 19 | 17 | 6 | 2 | 2 | | | | | | | | | | 55 |
| 90 | | | | | | 1 | 5 | 22 | 11 | 30 | 10 | 8 | | | | | | | | | | 87 |
| 95 | | | | | | | 4 | 6 | 17 | 28 | 22 | 14 | 5 | 1 | | | | | | | | 97 |
| 100 | | | | | | | | 4 | 9 | 20 | 36 | 19 | 10 | 6 | 2 | | | | | | | 106 |
| 105 | | | | | | | | 2 | 9 | 19 | 32 | 30 | 21 | 6 | 5 | 1 | | | | | | 125 |
| 110 | | | | | | | | | | 1 | 18 | 30 | 20 | 19 | 7 | 3 | 6 | | | | | 104 |
| 115 | | | | | | | | | | 2 | 6 | 24 | 23 | 23 | 17 | 7 | 6 | | | | | 108 |
| 120 | | | | | | | | | | | 1 | 5 | 15 | 23 | 14 | 8 | 4 | 2 | 2 | | | 74 |
| 125 | | | | | | | | | | | 1 | 3 | 4 | 9 | 2 | 10 | 5 | 2 | 1 | | | 37 |
| 130 | | | | | | | | | | | | | 2 | 3 | 3 | 8 | 2 | 1 | | | | 19 |
| 135 | | | | | | | | | | | | | 1 | 1 | 2 | 4 | 1 | 5 | 2 | | | 16 |
| 140 | | | | | | | | | | | | | | | | | | | | | 1 | 1 |
| **n** | 1 | 2 | 6 | 2 | 8 | 26 | 38 | 64 | 68 | 124 | 130 | 136 | 95 | 90 | 52 | 41 | 18 | 10 | 5 | 0 | 1 | 917 |
| **Central Tendency Used** | 50 | 55 | 60 | 65 | 70 | 75 | 80 | 85 | 90 | 95 | 100 | 105 | 110 | 115 | 120 | 125 | 130 | 135 | 140 | | 150 | 150 |
| **Average Deviation (in steps of 5 units each)** | 2.00 | 3.00 | 0.50 | 1.00 | 1.50 | 1.54 | 1.16 | 1.25 | 1.25 | 1.54 | 1.15 | 1.39 | 1.58 | 1.14 | 1.31 | 1.24 | 2.17 | 1.10 | 2.00 | | 2.00 | 2.00 |

TABLE 142(A).

THORNDIKE INT. EX. FOR H. S. GRADUATES. PART I AVERAGE DIFFERENCE BETWEEN TWO TRIALS (SINGLE SESSION) IN RELATION TO THE AVERAGE SCORE $\left(\dfrac{\text{SUM OF TRIAL 1 AND TRIAL 2}}{2}\right)$

A = Normal School students.    C = Night school men.
B = Candidates for college entrance.    D = S. A. T. C. candidates.
(The average here is of 3 trials.  The difference is Trial 3 – Trial 2.)

| Average score | 15 | 20 | 25 | 30 | 35 | 40 | 45 | 50 | 55 | 60 | 65 | 70 | 75 | 80 |
|---|---|---|---|---|---|---|---|---|---|---|---|---|---|---|
| Average difference A | | | | | | | 10.5 | 12.0 | 9.0 | 8.3 | 9.3 | 8.0 | 10.1 | 7.9 |
| n | | | | | | | 6 | 12 | 9 | 34 | 48 | 61 | 84 | 103 |
| Average difference B | | | | | | | | | 9.0 | 10.0 | 13.0 | 6.8 | 10.0 | 9.0 |
| n | | | | | | | | | 2 | 3 | 3 | 12 | 12 | 10 |
| Average difference C | 9.75 | 10.5 | 9.0 | 10.0 | 6.0 | 10.2 | 8.1 | 3.8 | 6.0 | 9.8 | 8.1 | 8.0 | 10.1 | 7.0 |
| n | 4 | 2 | 4 | 6 | 7 | 10 | 14 | 18 | 12 | 22 | 26 | 22 | 16 | 24 |
| Average difference D | | | | | | | | | | | 11.5 | 4.9 | | 9.4 |
| n | | | | | | | | | | | 6 | 22 | | 22 |
| Weighted Average percent of the Variability at 70–89 | 117 | 127 | 108 | 120 | 72 | 123 | 107 | 84 | 90 | 108 | 117 | 84 | 118 | 100 |
| Sum of weights | 2 | 1 | 2 | 3 | 3 | 3 | 7 | 7 | 8 | 13 | 17 | 21 | 16 | 23 |

| Average score | 85 | 90 | 95 | 100 | 105 | 110 | 115 | 120 | 125 | 130 | 135 | 140 | 145 |
|---|---|---|---|---|---|---|---|---|---|---|---|---|---|
| Average difference A | 9.2 | 8.1 | 8.4 | 7.8 | 8.1 | 7.8 | 6.7 | 4.5 | 6.7 | 6.0 | 8.3 | | |
| n | 145 | 145 | 115 | 122 | 102 | 65 | 50 | 20 | 13 | 3 | 4 | | |
| Average difference B | 7.6 | 7.5 | 8.5 | 7.9 | 7.6 | 6.2 | 7.1 | 6.6 | 6.8 | 5.4 | 7.4 | 4.2 | 15.0 |
| n | 32 | 30 | 32 | 42 | 49 | 52 | 65 | 43 | 37 | 19 | 15 | 5 | 1 |
| Average difference C | 8.8 | 5.0 | 7.1 | 5.7 | 7.5 | 6.3 | 7.5 | 10.5 | 10.5 | 4.5 | | | |
| n | 18 | 20 | 17 | 9 | 10 | 9 | 2 | 2 | 3 | 2 | | | |
| Average difference D | 8.4 | 7.6 | | 6.1 | 6.0 | 4.9 | | 6.5 | 5.8 | 4.4 | | | |
| n | 48 | 63 | | 113 | 120 | 128 | | 114 | 70 | 23 | | | |
| Weighted Average percent of the Variability at 70–80 | 103 | 88 | 96 | 85 | 87 | 75 | 82 | 78 | 76 | 62 | 92 | 52 | 185 |
| Sum of Weights | 27 | 29 | 20 | 30 | 30 | 28 | 16 | 23 | 20 | 12 | 6 | 2 | 1 |

TABLE 142(B).

SAME AS TABLE 142(A), EXCEPT THAT THE DIFFERENCE IS BETWEEN TRIALS ON DIFFERENT DAY AND THAT THE AVERAGE SCORE IS FROM FOUR TRIALS. NORMAL SCHOOL STUDENTS.

| Average Score | 15 | 20 | 25 | 30 | 35 | 40 | 45 | 50 | 55 | 60 | 65 | 70 | 75 | 80 |
|---|---|---|---|---|---|---|---|---|---|---|---|---|---|---|
| Average Difference | | | | | | | | | | | | 8.0 | 5.2 | 10 |
| n | | | | | | | | | | | | 2 | 10 | 5 |
| Weighted Average Percent of the Variability at 70–89 | | | | | | | | | | | | 102 | 66 | 1 |
| Weight | | | | | | | | | | | | 1 | 3 | |

| Average Score | 85 | 90 | 95 | 100 | 105 | 110 | 115 | 120 | 125 | 130 | 135 | 140 | 14 |
|---|---|---|---|---|---|---|---|---|---|---|---|---|---|
| Average Difference | 8.5 | 6.3 | 8.0 | 7.3 | 8.4 | 7.4 | 6.8 | 6.1 | 1.0 | 9.0 | | | |
| n | 19 | 21 | 17 | 24 | 28 | 18 | 16 | 7 | 1 | 3 | | | |
| Weighted Average Percent of the Variability at 70–80 | 108 | 80 | 102 | 93 | 107 | 94 | 87 | 78 | 13 | 115 | | | |
| Weight | 3 | 5 | 4 | 5 | 5 | 4 | 4 | 3 | 1 | 2 | | | |

Army Beta and a certain picture test[7] have been combined; the second is where the results for the Haggerty Delta 2, the Myers Test, the Kelley Trabue Completion, and the Thorndike Visual Vocabulary are combined. In these combinations each is treated separately up to the point of the *Weighted Average Percents of the Variability at Ability X,* and care is taken to chose Ability X to represent closely the same percentile ability in each of the tests to be combined. Consequently, two variabilities are combined, only if they belong to approximately the same ability. We use the same method of weighting that is used for any one test given to different groups.

[7] Consisting of tests 3, 4 and 5 of the Thorndike, Part II.

TABLE 143.

THORNDIKE INT. EXAM. FOR H. S. GRADUATES.   PART I.   VARIABILITY OF SCORE IN ONE TRIAL ARRAYED UNDER SCORE IN ANOTHER TRIAL OR UNDER TOTAL SCORE IN THE ENTIRE EXAMINATION.   10 = 10 TO 14; 15 = 15 TO 19, ETC.

A, B, C = Night-school men.   D = College entrance candidates.   E, F, G, H = College freshmen plus some others.   I, J = Women in High School, Normal School, and College.   K, L = Men of college grade and below.   M, N = Summer School students at a Normal School.   O, P = Men in High School and College.

| | 10 | 15 | 20 | 25 | 30 | 35 | 40 | 45 | 50 | 55 | 60 | 65 | 70 | 75 |
|---|---|---|---|---|---|---|---|---|---|---|---|---|---|---|
| | | | | | CENTRAL TENDENCY OF THE ARRAY. | | | | | | | | | |
| Group A | 12.5 | | 30.0 | | 22.0 | | 19.0 | | 15.2 | | 16.6 | | 15.6 | |
| n | 4 | | 4 | | 6 | | 16 | | 27 | | 35 | | 50 | |
| Group B | 5.0 | 5.0 | 10.0 | 15.0 | 13.8 | 8.4 | 21.6 | 16.8 | 20.6 | 16.0 | 20.0 | 11.2 | 15.2 | 14.0 |
| n | 2 | 2 | 4 | 2 | 8 | 6 | 13 | 19 | 14 | 15 | 18 | 17 | 19 | 10 |
| Group C | 38.4 | 10.0 | 0 | 10.0 | 20.0 | 12.0 | 12.6 | 10.0 | 16.4 | 22.5 | 17.0 | 14.4 | 17.2 | 9.4 |
| n | 4 | 2 | 1 | 4 | 6 | 5 | 8 | 7 | 11 | 12 | 13 | 18 | 18 | 16 |
| Group D | | | | | | | | | | | | | | 5.0 |
| n | | | | | | | | | | | | | | 2 |
| Group E | | | | | | | | | | | | | 15.0 | 11.8 |
| n | | | | | | | | | | | | | 2 | 11 |
| Group F | | | | | | | | | | | 30.0 | 0 | 13.0 | 10.0 |
| n | | | | | | | | | | | 2 | 1 | 10 | 10 |
| Group G | | | | | | | | 10.0 | | | 17.5 | | 14.1 | |
| n | | | | | | | | 2 | | | 8 | | 27 | |
| Group H | | | | | | | | | | | 20.0 | | 7.8 | |
| n | | | | | | | | | | | 2 | | 9 | |
| Group I | | | | | | | 40.0 | 20.0 | 11.7 | 25.0 | 30.0 | 19.6 | 12.5 | 12.5 |
| n | | | | | | | 1 | 2 | 6 | 2 | 8 | 26 | 40 | 64 |
| Group J | | | | | | | | | 20.0 | 30.0 | 5.0 | 10.0 | 15.0 | 15.4 |
| n | | | | | | | | | 1 | 2 | 6 | 2 | 8 | 26 |
| Group K | | | | | | | | | 20.0 | | 10.0 | 15.0 | 10.0 | 18.8 |
| n | | | | | | | | | 1 | | 1 | 6 | 1 | 8 |
| Group L | | | | | | 10.0 | | 15.0 | 10.0 | 18.0 | 10.0 | 12.9 | 10.8 | 15.8 |
| n | | | | | | 1 | | 2 | 2 | 5 | 1 | 7 | 12 | 31 |
| Group M | | | | | | | 20.0 | 10.0 | 20.0 | 0 | 17.1 | 17.5 | 12.8 | 15.1 |
| n | | | | | | | 1 | 1 | 3 | 1 | 14 | 20 | 18 | 71 |
| Group N | | | | | | 10.0 | 25.0 | 24.0 | 17.5 | 13.8 | 18.2 | 15.6 | 16.5 | 17.9 |
| n | | | | | | 1 | 2 | 5 | 12 | 16 | 22 | 89 | 49 | 67 |
| Group O | | | | | | 40.0 | 5.0 | 11.4 | 14.0 | 19.5 | 15.0 | | 15.9 | 14.7 |
| n | | | | | | 2 | 2 | 7 | 10 | 21 | 36 | | 51 | 71 |
| Group P | | | | | | | | 30.0 | 10.0 | 20.0 | 18.6 | 18.2 | 19.0 | 14.4 |
| n | | | | | | | | 1 | 1 | 2 | 7 | 11 | 21 | 36 |
| eighted Aver- e Percents of e Variability 70 to 89 .........133 | | 50 | 94 | 79 | 116 | 90 | 125 | 106 | 101 | 120 | 114 | 99 | 96 | 96 |
| m of Weights 5 | | 2 | 5 | 3 | 9 | 8 | 15 | 16 | 28 | 22 | 45 | 38 | 64 | 66 |

TABLE 143—(Continued)

*Average Deviation Times 2.*

| | 80 | 85 | 90 | 95 | 100 | 105 | 110 | 115 | 120 | 125 | 130 | 135 | 140 | 145 |
|---|---|---|---|---|---|---|---|---|---|---|---|---|---|---|
| Group A | 12.7 | 18.3 | | 14.0 | | 13.3 | | 15.0 | | 10.0 | | 20.0 | | |
| n | 37 | 41 | | 30 | | 18 | | 6 | | 4 | | 2 | | |
| Group B | 12.9 | 11.8 | 13.0 | 15.6 | 5.0 | 16.6 | 16.6 | 10.0 | | | | | | |
| n | 7 | 11 | 10 | 9 | 4 | 3 | 6 | 2 | | | | | | |
| Group C | 16.7 | 18.8 | 16.4 | 7.2 | 12.6 | 10.0 | | 15.6 | 10.0 | 10.0 | | | | |
| n | 15 | 16 | 11 | 7 | 8 | 6 | | 9 | 2 | 2 | | | | |
| Group D | 11.4 | 50.0 | 11.7 | 16.2 | 13.7 | 16.5 | 11.4 | 12.5 | 9.4 | 11.2 | 13.6 | 12.9 | 10.0 | |
| n | 7 | 2 | 12 | 13 | 41 | 92 | 44 | 112 | 50 | 85 | 25 | 14 | 4 | |
| Group E | 12.0 | 9.2 | 15.2 | 13.7 | 12.9 | 14.8 | 11.9 | 12.5 | 14.5 | 16.0 | 10.0 | 2.5 | 10.0 | |
| n | 10 | 12 | 31 | 38 | 43 | 61 | 59 | 61 | 68 | 16 | 13 | 4 | 2 | |
| Group F | 18.3 | 16.8 | | 13.0 | 14.4 | 13.3 | 16.3 | 13.2 | 11.9 | 14.4 | 13.8 | 10.0 | 15.0 | |
| n | 12 | 31 | | 37 | 45 | 61 | 60 | 106 | 21 | 16 | 13 | 4 | 2 | |
| Group G | 17.5 | | 15.6 | | 15.5 | | 14.6 | | 17.7 | | | 11.1 | | 5.0 |
| n | 71 | | 115 | | 163 | | 118 | | 44 | | | 9 | | 2 |
| Group H | 10.4 | | 16.5 | | 12.7 | | 12.7 | | 13.7 | 10.5 | | 16.0 | | 0 |
| n | 26 | | 68 | | 118 | | 165 | | 110 | 43 | | 10 | | 2 |
| Group I | 15.7 | 15.2 | 16.6 | 15.5 | 15.3 | 11.9 | 11.5 | 15.5 | 11.1 | 13.0 | 16.0 | | | 10.0 |
| n | 70 | 127 | 134 | 139 | 102 | 93 | 53 | 42 | 18 | 10 | 5 | | | 1 |
| Group J | 11.6 | 12.5 | 12.5 | 15.4 | 11.5 | 13.9 | 15.8 | 11.4 | 13.1 | 12.4 | 21.7 | 11.0 | 20.0 | |
| n | 38 | 64 | 68 | 124 | 130 | 136 | 95 | 90 | 52 | 41 | 18 | 10 | 5 | |
| Group K | 19.2 | 20.7 | 17.7 | 17.0 | 21.0 | 16.6 | 13.0 | 13.5 | 13.0 | 16.0 | 12.5 | 15.0 | | |
| n | 13 | 15 | 39 | 27 | 20 | 32 | 43 | 23 | 10 | 15 | 4 | 2 | | |
| Group L | 17.9 | 17.3 | 16.1 | 22.3 | 14.6 | 14.5 | 13.8 | 20.0 | 15.7 | 20.0 | 5.0 | | | |
| n | 19 | 22 | 23 | 22 | 35 | 31 | 32 | 5 | 7 | 1 | 2 | | | |
| Group M | 15.6 | 14.4 | 16.1 | 14.8 | 16.3 | 12.0 | 18.8 | 6.7 | 11.3 | 0 | | | 10.0 | |
| n | 55 | 107 | 38 | 44 | 41 | 10 | 8 | 3 | 8 | 1 | | | 1 | |
| Group N | 14.8 | 13.9 | 16.4 | 16.1 | 21.8 | 8.9 | 20.8 | 15.0 | 10.0 | 20.0 | | | | |
| n | 48 | 33 | 42 | 23 | 11 | 9 | 12 | 2 | 1 | 1 | | | | |
| Group O | 16.7 | 15.4 | 14.9 | 17.3 | 17.6 | 16.6 | 14.4 | 15.2 | 11.5 | 15.6 | 10.8 | 11.4 | | 0 |
| n | 73 | 90 | 89 | 109 | 107 | 87 | 103 | 48 | 39 | 25 | 12 | 7 | | 1 |
| Group P | 14.3 | 13.4 | 14.9 | 14.0 | 15.8 | 14.6 | 13.5 | 14.4 | 12.6 | 12.5 | 13.2 | 12.8 | | 7.1 |
| n | 53 | 70 | 73 | 91 | 90 | 108 | 108 | 85 | 102 | 48 | 41 | 36 | | 7 |
| Weighted Average Percents of the Variability at 70 to 89 | 103 | 102 | 112 | 103 | 103 | 95 | 99 | 91 | 95 | 91 | 92 | 85 | 72 | |
| Sum of Weights | 86 | 84 | 92 | 89 | 106 | 90 | 100 | 77 | 75 | 56 | 34 | 26 | 11 | |

TABLE 144.

THE SUMMARIES OF TABLE 142 AND TABLE 143, WITH COARSER GROUPING.

| Ability | 10 | 20 | 30 | 40 | 50 | 60 | 70 | 80 | 90 | 100 | 110 | 120 | 130 | 140 |
|---|---|---|---|---|---|---|---|---|---|---|---|---|---|---|
| Relative Variability; Table 142 | | | | | | | 75 | 118 | 90 | 100 | 90 | 62 | 115 | 62 |
| Weight | | | | | | | 4 | 6 | 9 | 10 | 8 | 4 | 2 | 14 |
| Relative Variability; Table 143 | 109 | 88 | 104 | 115 | 112 | 107 | 96 | 102 | 108 | 99 | 95 | 93 | 89 | |
| Weight | 7 | 8 | 17 | 31 | 50 | 83 | 130 | 170 | 181 | 196 | 177 | 131 | 60 | |

Our results for all tests are summarized in Table 145. Each pair of lines of entries represents the results from one or more such tables as Table 142 or 143 giving the relative variabilities with increasing amounts of the ability and the weights appertaining thereto. In Table 145 all the entries in one column are for the same amount of ability, to a rough approximation. That is, we arrange the results for any test so that it will fit the general scale from about a 10 percentile fourth-grade intellect to about a 95 percentile college intellect. We have done this only approximately because absolute precision is unattainable with present knowledge and because only a rough approximation is needed for our purpose to discover any general relation between the amount of ability and the variability attached thereto, after allowance for swelling or shrinking of the real values of the units of the scores.

Although all the variabilities in any column pertain to approximately the same amount of ability, they cannot properly be added by columns to show the general drift of Table 145. For the numbers in one row may be percentages on a base very different from that used in some other row. For example, the Army Exam. *a* numbers are on approximately median 9th Grade ability as a base; the Haggerty-Myers-Trabue combination numbers are on approximately median 6A Grade ability as a base; the last seven rows are on approximately median Columbia College Freshmen ability as a base.

We shall later mass the results of Table 145 in a form more suitable to reveal the general relation. Table 145 is to show the relation in each of the different tests or test-amalgamations. It shows no evidence of any tendency for variability to increase with ability. On the contrary, if one had to choose between a law of increase with amount of ability and a law of decrease with amount of ability, he would have to choose the latter. Table 145 also shows, in all but three of its lines, a tendency for the numbers to increase from the lowest extreme for a certain distance, or to decrease toward the highest extreme or to do both. The increase comes in the low range for a test, regardless of whether the ability there is that of a low 4th grade pupil, or a low ninth grade pupil. The decrease also comes in the high range for a test; regardless of what real ability that range covers. This is what would follow from the presumably common tendency of a person or committee devising tests, to provide rather fully tasks along the range of abilities which the test was designed to measure, and to have fewer tasks over an equally long range below or above that. If each task is given an equal credit in the score, the same real variability will of course be represented by a smaller number in the low or in the high than in the middle range, supposing that abundant time is given to exhaust the subjects' abilities. Table 146 gives an illustration of such a case. When the time is limited so that only some, or even none of the individuals do all that they could do, the same effect may be found.

We have studied the facts of Table 145 in connection with the tests themselves in considerable detail and from several points of view. On the whole it seems to us that the most satisfactory explanation is to regard the relation as $y = k$, that is, to consider the variability of an individual as independent of his ability, accounting for the rises and falls in the curves of Table 145 by irregularities in the amount of real ability corresponding to one unit of score in a given test at different ranges of the score. We shall not rehearse the evidence which has impelled us to that conclusion. Some of it is personal. The reader who doubts it should try any alternative relation, using the same criteria of merit for the two.

The general drift of the facts of Table 145 can be studied more easily if they are more coarsely grouped and if the percentages, where possible, are computed on the base of the variability attached to an ability of approximately the median ninth-grade pupil. Table 147 gives such a presentation. In the case of the Modified Thorndike II, the

# TABLE 145.

The Relation of the Variability of an Individual to His Amount of Ability; in Fifteen Tests or Amalgamations of Tests. The upper number is the measure of variability; the lower number (in italics) is the weight attached to it.

| | 4th Grade Median (value / *weight*) | 6th Grade Median (value / *weight*) |
|---|---|---|
| 1. Alpha | 61 / *7*; 73 / *8*; 97 / *8* | 90 / *22*; 104 / *12*; 102; 132 / *3*; 110 / *17*; 109 / *6*; 128 / *10*; 109; 107 / *12*; 84 / *8*; 107 / *12*; 83 / *10* |
| 2. Exam. A | 68 / *18*; 132 / *20*; 88 / *16*; 91 / *34*; 94 / *16*; 107 / *17*; 90 / *22*; 103 / *34* | 102 / *9*; 93 / *45*; 87 / *10*; 104 / *29*; 99 / *8*; 116 / *9*; 125 / *15*; 106 / *16*; 93 / *4*; 109; 104 / *28* |
| 3. Th., Part I. | 94 / *5*; 79 / *3* | 133 / *5*; 97 / *2*; 90 / *8* |
| 4. Otis Adv. | 82 / *3*; 89 / *3*; 54 / *3*; 93 / *4*; 73 / *6*; 99 / *5*; 83 / *6*; 62 / *7* | 97 / *7*; 124 / *8*; 110 / *15*; 56; 80 / *10*; 99 / *9*; 85 / *13*; 111 / *13*; 96 / *5*; 92; 117; 92 / *13* |
| 5. Terman Group | | 96 / *5*; 92 / *3*; 109 / *5* |
| 6. Stanford M. A. | 202 / *3*; 83 / *7* | 91 / *6*; 92 / *14*; 106 / *7*; 107 / *7*; 100 / *8*; 104 / *37*; 108 / *5*; 93 / *8*; 78 / *4*; 73 / *13* |
| 7. National | 94 / *20* | 107 / *14*; 102 / *10*; 90 / *22*; 91 / *23*; 93 / *8*; 86 / *21*; 82 / *13*; 104 / *15*; 80 / *10*; 99 |
| 8. Hag. Myers Composite | 21 / *6*; 71 / *9*; 74 / *10*; 98 / *10*; 106 / *16*; 80 / *18*; 102 / *14*; 92 / *16*; 92 / *27*; 108 / *28* | 116 / *18*; 111 / *16*; 105 / *11*; 92 / *25*; 83 / *26*; 108; 96 / *15*; 100 / *19*; 106; 14 / *118* |
| 9. Beta + Picture Test | 65 / *7*; 73 / *16*; 95 / *10*; 87 / *22* | 89 / *16*; 121 / *5*; 89 / *13*; 112 / *7*; 102; 118 / *20*; 97 / *18*; 115 / *5*; 118 |
| 10. Toops Clerical | | 76 / *6*; 87 / *7*; 92 / *7*; 118 / *6*; 131 / *6*; 161 / *5*; 59 / *6*; 89 / *7*; 5 |
| 11. Th., New, Part I, A | | 63 / *2*; 28 / *2*; 42 / *1*; 59; 49 / *4*; 131 / *3*; 64 / *6*; 118 / *5*; 101 / *5* |
| 12. Th., Part II | | |
| 13. Th., Part II, Mod. | | 95 / *6* |
| 14. Th., Part III | | |
| 15. Th., Part II, New | | |
| 16. Th., New, Pt. I, 45 min. | | 72 / *6* |
| 17. Th., Total | | 119 / *18* |

TABLE 145—(*Continued*).

| | 9th Grade Median | College Freshman Median | | | | | | | | | | | | | | | | |
|---|---|---|---|---|---|---|---|---|---|---|---|---|---|---|---|---|---|---|
| 1. Alpha | 86 / *10* | 114 / *11* | 121 / *11* | 89 / *11* | 129 / *18* | 71 / *10* | 125 / *9* | 117 / *12* | 108 / *8* | 95 / *9* | 69 / *6* | 75 / *4* | 97 / *3* | 95 / *3* | 92 / *34* | 85 / *26* | 72 / *14* | |
| 2. Exam. A. | 102 / *14* | 113 / *18* | 95 / *12* | 111 / *20* | 103 / *12* | 120 / *15* | 91 / *18* | 90 / *14* | | 93 / *10* | 84 / *5* | | | 85 / *3* | | | | |
| 3. Th., Part I. | 120 / *22* | 114 / *45* | 97 / *38* | 96 / *64* | 66 / *12* | 102 / *84* | 86 / *6* | 112 / *92* | 103 / *89* | 95 / *90* | 99 / *100* | 91 / *77* | 91 / *56* | 95 / *75* | 92 / *34* | 67 / *1* | 67 / *2* | 67 / *4* |
| 4. Otis Adv. | 65 / *11* | 127 / *11* | 116 / *13* | 92 / *12* | 80 / *9* | 78 / *9* | 89 / *11* | 100 / *84* | 110 / *6* | 66 / *9* | 87 / *10* | 54 / *4* | 67 / *4* | | | | | |
| 5. Terman Group | 90 / *6* | 11 | 92 / *11* | 93 / *25* | 99 / *7* | 135 / *6* | 98 / *4* | 89 / | | | 83 / *10* | | 85 / *4* | | | | | |
| 6. Stanford M. A. | 99 / *3* | 74 / *3* | 79 / *8* | 100 / *3* | | | 84 / *10* | 110 / *6* | 85 / *11* | | | | | | | | | |
| 7. National | 65 / *13* | 59 / *7* | | | 60 / *2* | | | | | | | | | | | | | |
| 8. Hag. Myers Composite | 80 / *15* | 64 / *6* | | | | | | | | | | | | | | | | |
| 9. Beta + Picture Test | | 78 / *12* | 81 / *12* | 94 / *11* | 90 / *12* | 88 / *4* | | | | | 46 / *3* | | | | | | | |
| 10. Toops Clerical | 98 / *3* | 79 / *3* | | | | | | | | | | | | | | | | |
| 11. Th., New, Part I, A. | 83 / *6* | 100 / *5* | 110 / *5* | 92 / *8* | 122 / *6* | 89 / *4* | 42 / *1* | 104 / *2* | 98 / *2* | 63 / *1* | 184 / *1* | 85 / *14* | 115 / *8* | 93 / *17* | 111 / *14* | 45 / *5* | 50 / *8* | 100 / *5* | 116 / *4* | 65 / *5* | 103 / *4* | 30 / *3* | 69 / *2* |
| 12. Th., Part II. | 86 / *6* | 98 / *14* | 83 / *3* | 100 / *16* | 106 / *3* | 109 / *4* | 100 / *9* | 95 / *6* | 93 / *6* | 107 / *16* | 110 / *17* | 97 / *10* | 88 / *10* | 92 / *7* | 85 / *7* | 89 / *2* | 79 / *6* | 53 / *2* | 67 / *9* | 66 / *9* | 35 / *3* |
| 13. Th., Part II, Mod. | 56 / *2* | 50 / *2* | 100 / *4* | 96 / *4* | 73 / *4* | 103 / *5* | 90 / *7* | 123 / *5* | 69 / *4* | | | | | | | | | |
| 14. Th., Part III. | 60 / *4* | 86 / *8* | 81 / *13* | 93 / *25* | 82 / *23* | 88 / *26* | 109 / *27* | 102 / *30* | 100 / *27* | 102 / *19* | 91 / *26* | 92 / *7* | 79 / *4* | 53 / *2* | 85 / *13* | 77 / *18* | 89 / *3* | 66 / *3* | 67 / *2* |
| 15. Th., Part II, New | | 45 / *2* | 91 / *3* | 70 / *5* | 80 / *5* | 83 / *7* | 87 / *7* | 100 / *7* | 109 / *7* | 91 / *7* | 77 / *6* | 85 / *13* | 65 / *4* | 66 / *9* | 35 / *3* | | | |
| 16. Th., New, Pt. I, 45 min. | | 122 / *2* | 102 / *3* | 67 / *5* | 113 / *5* | 93 / *7* | 125 / *8* | 100 / *7* | 97 / *7* | 117 / *6* | 141 / *6* | 119 / *4* | 115 / *3* | 135 / *3* | | | | |
| 17. Th., Total | 120 / *37* | 117 / *55* | 113 / *69* | 105 / *88* | 104 / *99* | 95 / *78* | 90 / *46* | 81 / *26* | 75 / *12* | 162 / *5* | | | | | | | | |

Thorndike II, new style, and the Thorndike I, new style, with 45 minutes time, the data at or near median ninth grade ability are very scant, so we have combined the results for these three tests giving equal weight to each and report them as an addition to Table 147.

TABLE 146.  THE EFFECT OF SELECTION OF TASKS

| Task. | Real Diffi- culty of Task. | Individual's Real Average Ability. | Individual's Real Average Deviation from his Average. | Credit Given for the Task in the test Score. | Individual's Average Test Score. | Individual's Average Devia- tion in Terms of the test Scores. |
|---|---|---|---|---|---|---|
| a | 101 | | | 1 | | |
| b | 106 | 106 | 5 | 1 | 2 | 1 |
| c | 111 | 111 | 5 | 1 | 3 | 1 |
| d | 116 | 116 | 5 | 1 | 4 | 1 |
| e | 121 | 121 | 5 | 1 | 5 | 1 |
| f | 126 | 126 | 5 | 1 | 6 | 1 + |
| g | 130 | | | 1 | | |
| h | 131 | | | 1 | | |
| i | 132 | | | 1 | | |
| j | 133 | | | 1 | | |
| k | 134 | 134 | 5 | 1 | 11 | 5 − |
| l | 135 | 135 | 5 | 1 | 12 | 5 |
| m | 136 | 136 | 5 | 1 | 13 | 5 |
| n | 137 | 137 | 5 | 1 | 14 | 5 − |
| o | 138 | | | 1 | | |
| p | 139 | | | 1 | | |
| q | 140 | | | 1 | | |
| r | 141 | 141 | 5 | 1 | 18 | 1 + |
| s | 146 | 146 | 5 | 1 | 19 | 1 |
| t | 151 | 151 | 5 | 1 | 20 | 1 |
| u | 156 | 156 | 5 | 1 | 21 | 1 |
| v | 161 | 161 | 5 | 1 | 22 | 1 |
| w | 166 | 166 | 5 | 1 | 23 | 1 |
| x | 171 | | | 1 | | |

There is, in this coarser table, as in Table 145, no evidence that we can detect that the variability either increases or decreases in general with the magnitude.[8]  It

8 Concerning the effect of the error due to inaccuracy of averages mentioned on page 500 we now find that no allowance need be made. The error might have reduced some real tendency, but there is so little evidence of any tendency that we cannot tell whether the reduction has been from a tendency for the variability to increase, or from a tendency for it to decrease. Not knowing in which direction to make the correction, we need not make any.

Eight Levels of Ability.

| | Low Level Fourth or Below Alpha 15–29 | Fourth Grade Alpha 30–49 | Sixth Grade Alpha 50–69 | Seventh Eighth Grades Alpha 70–89 | Ninth Grade Alpha 90–109 | Upper High School Alpha 110–129 | College Freshmen Alpha 130–149 | Upper College Alpha 150 or + |
|---|---|---|---|---|---|---|---|---|
| Alpha Exam. A. | 67  15 | 97  8 | 109  35 | 108  36 | 101  42 | 107  48 | 101  35 | 88  10 |
| Thorndike I | 90  54 | 88  89 | 88  98 | 98  82 | 100  81 | 104  63 | 83  24 | 79  5 |
| Otis Adv. | 85½  6 | 77  31 | 91  15 | 102  48 | 100  144 | 94  399 | 92  382 | 84  266 |
| Terman Group | | | 106½  34 | 98  51 | 100  48 | 85  41 | 86  40 | 62  11 |
| St. Mental Age | 138  10 | 115  13 | 116  8 | 85  8 | 100  21 | 116  17 | 94  43 | 89  4 |
| National | | 139  41 | 153  56 | 117  9 | 100  6 | 116  3 | | |
| Haggerty, Myers, etc. | | | | 119  31 | 100  33 | 109  10 | | |
| Beta + Picture | 81½  23 | 100  99 | 120  141 | 106  113 | 100  46 | 106  23 | 81  7 | |
| Toops | | 103  32 | 103  51 | 118  38 | 100  38 | | | |
| Thorndike, New Ia | | | 98  30 | 110  31 | 100  14 | 107  15 | 129  2 | 87  49 |
| Thorndike, II | | | 66  2 | 53  14 | 100  31 | 105  90 | 96  99 | 114½  42 |
| Thorndike, III, | | | | 87  9 | 100  52 | 111  104 | 123  99 | 75  43 |
| Thorndike Total | | | | 61  6 | 100  110 | 92  157 | 83  223 | |
| Median | 85½ | 100 | 105 | 102 | 100 | 106½ | 93 | 85½ |
| Average (equal weights) | 92 | 103 | 106 | 97 | 100 | 104 | 97 | 85 |
| Average (half weight to entries whose sum of weights <10) | 93 | 103 | 108 | 99 | 100 | 104 | 96 | 85 |
| Combination of Thorndike modified II, New II, and New I | | | | | 100  8 | 121  57 | 143  78 | 123  41 |
| Median (including Thorndike combination with wt. of 2) | 85½ | 100 | 105 | 102 | 100 | 107 | 95 | 87½ |
| Average (including the Thorndike combination with weight of 2) | 92 | 103 | 106 | 97 | 100 | 107 | 104½ | 92½ |

could be argued that it increases a trifle over low levels
of intellect and decreases a trifle over high levels of intellect, but the facts presented in Chapter VII make it much
more probable that the tasks of these tests were too scant,
or the credits too low, or both, at the easy and hard extremes of the tests.

We thus have grounds for replacing cumbrous and ambiguous measures of unreliability of a test in the shape of
its self correlations, by the simple probable error of the
measurement. An adequate determination of this will
suffice anywhere along the range from a dull 10-year-old to
a gifted 20-year-old. We also have validated a new method
of measuring the real differences signified by differences
in arbitrary scores. That transmutation of arbitrary
scores is best (other things being equal) which makes the
variability of an individual the same for all levels from
that of a dull 10-year-old to that of a gifted 20-year-old.
We have further made a step toward using the arrays of
a distribution separately in measuring either the real differences of total scores or the real differences of single
tasks in difficulty. The form of distribution of an array
is determined by three causes, the form of distribution of
the average abilities of individuals in the group in question, the form of distribution of the variations of an individual around his own average, and the relation of the
variability of an individual to his average ability. We
have previously shown that the variability of an individual
is symmetrical and roughly of the form of the normal
probability surface. If it is also of equal magnitude irrespective of the amount of the ability, scaling tasks by what
we may call the array method has many advantages over
the methods hitherto used.

# APPENDIX III

## On the Form of the Distribution of Intellect in the Sixth Grade, the Twelfth Grade, and Among College Freshmen

We have shown elsewhere[1] that the form of distribution of intellect in the ninth grade conforms closely to the so-called normal curve of error. This is the report of a series of similar investigations into the manner in which intellect varies in the sixth grade, the twelfth grade, and among college freshmen.

It has been commonly assumed, whenever tests or tasks have been scaled for difficulty in a group of given educational status, that the form of the distribution of intellect within such a group was truly represented by the normal or Gaussian curve, whose equation is $y = \dfrac{1}{\sigma\sqrt{2\pi}} e^{\frac{-x^2}{2\sigma^2}}$.

It is of practical importance to test the validity of this assumption if the scaling of tasks for difficulty is to be upon a sound basis.

### THE FORM OF DISTRIBUTION OF INTELLECT IN THE SIXTH GRADE

Our data for this grade consist of a series of frequency tables of the scores made by sixth-grade pupils in many different cities of the United States on eleven well-known intelligence examinations. They are listed below with the size of the population for each examination. The sources of the data appear on page 522.

From these data we have plotted the percentage distributions for each test, from the mean as central tendency,

[1] E. L. Thorndike and E. O. Bregman, *Journal of Educational Research*, November, 1924, "On the form of Distribution of Intellect in the Ninth Grade."

| Test | n |
|---|---|
| 1. Otis Advanced Examination | 5952[1] |
| 2. National Intelligence Examination, A | 1668[2] |
| 3. Trabue Completion Exercise A | 1454[3] |
| 4. Pintner Non-Language Examination | 1377[4] |
| 5. Pressey Mental Survey (Cross-out) E | 1057[5] |
| 6. Hagggerty Delta 2 | 916[6] |
| 7. Army Examination A | 742[7] |
| 8. Myers Mental Measure | 724[8] |
| 9. Illinois Examination | 588[9] |
| 10. I. E. R. Tests of Selective and Relational Thinking, Generalization and Organization | 379[10] |
| 11. Army Alpha | 281[11] |

1. Otis, A. S., Manual of Directions.
   Coxe, W. W., Variation in General Intelligence, Jour. Ed. Research, 1921, vol. 4, pp. 188–189.
2. Data of the N. I. T. Committee supplied by Professor Guy M. Whipple.
3. Trabue, M. R., Completion Test Language Scales, p. 8.
4. Unpublished data supplied by Professor Rudolph Pintner.
5. Pressey, S. L., A Brief Group Scale of Intelligence for Use in School Surveys, Jour. Ed. Psy., vol. 11, p. 96, 1920.
6. Madsen, J. N., Intelligence as a Factor in School Progress, School and Society, 1922, vol. 15, p. 285.
7. Memoirs—The National Academy of Sciences, vol. 15, Table 187, p. 537 and Table 20, p. 334.
8. Layton, L. H., Myers, G. C., and Myers, C. E., Group Testing in Altoona, Pa., School and Society, vol. 13, p. 624.
9. Data supplied by Professor W. S. Monroe, Univ. of Illinois.
10. Unpublished data of the Institute of Educational Research, Division of Psychology, Teachers College.
11. Data of the Kansas State Teachers College, Emporia, Kansas.

and in units of one-tenth of the standard deviation of each distribution. The plots appear in Figures 76 to 86.

These individual curves are more or less irregular in outline and of no very constant form. On the whole the curves for the larger populations are the smoothest and most regular.

We are not concerned, however, with the form of distribution based upon any single test or examination. The form of any such single distribution, granting that the sample was both representative and numerically adequate, might not reflect the true form of distribution of intellect

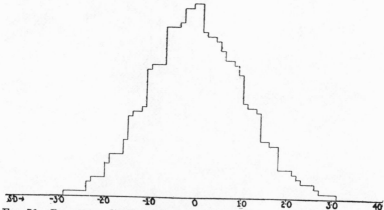

FIG. 76. Percentage distribution of sixth-grade scores in the Otis Advanced Examination. n = 5952.

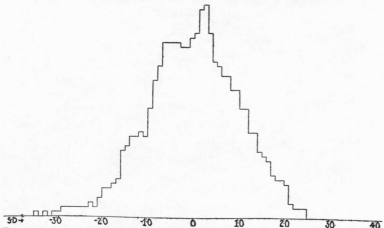

FIG. 77. Percentage distribution of sixth-grade scores in the National Intelligence Examination, Form A. n = 1668.

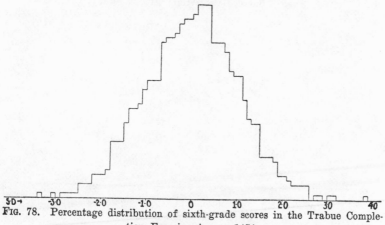

FIG. 78. Percentage distribution of sixth-grade scores in the Trabue Completion Exercise A. n = 1454.

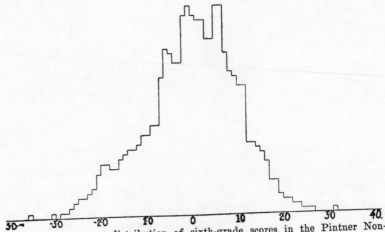

Fig. 79. Percentage distribution of sixth-grade scores in the Pintner Non-Language Examination.   n = 1377.

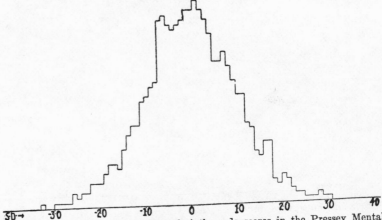

Fig. 80.   Percentage distribution of sixth-grade scores in the Pressey Mental Survey (Cross Out) E.   n = 1057.

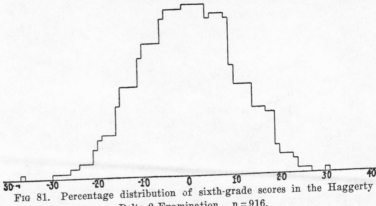

Fig 81.   Percentage distribution of sixth-grade scores in the Haggerty Delta 2 Examination.   n = 916.

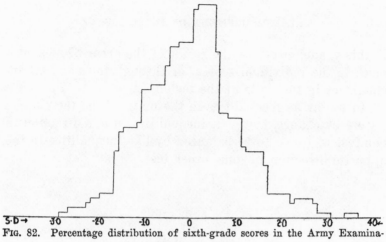

FIG. 82. Percentage distribution of sixth-grade scores in the Army Examination A.   n = 742.

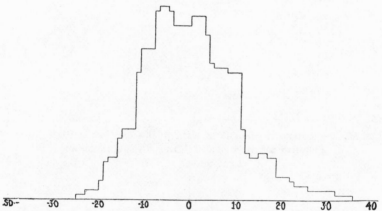

FIG. 83. Percentage distribution of sixth-grade scores in the Myers Mental Measure.   n = 724.

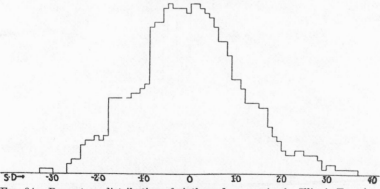

FIG. 84. Percentage distribution of sixth-grade scores in the Illinois Examination.   n = 588.

in this grade, either as the result of the error of measurement in the individual scores, or through the effect of inequalities in the units of the tests.

In so far as inequalities in the units of the tests occur purely by chance, however, inequalities in one direction in one test will tend to be balanced by like inequalities in the opposite direction in some other test.

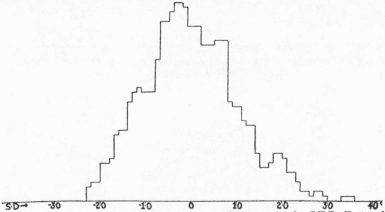

FIG. 85. Percentage distribution of sixth-grade scores in the I.E.R. Tests of Selective and Relational Thinking, Generalization and Organization. n = 379.

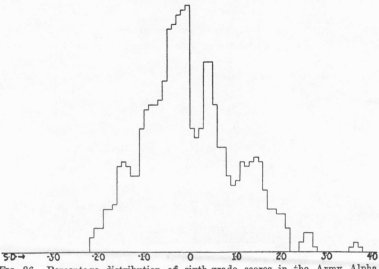

FIG. 86. Percentage distribution of sixth-grade scores in the Army Alpha. n = 281.

We have therefore combined the eleven separate distributions, equal weight being attached to each, into a single composite distribution, by averaging the frequencies for each successive one-tenth sigma, and plotting the resulting curve.

It is shown in Figure 87. For purposes of comparison, the theoretical Gaussian curve has been dotted in.

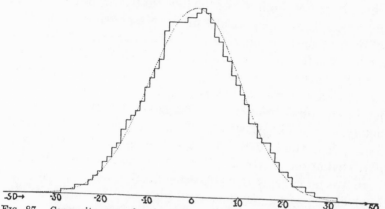

FIG. 87. Composite curve for the sixth grade, based upon eleven single curves. The broken line indicates the theoretical normal curve.

The two conform closely. The fit of the observed curve to the theoretical has been numerically determined by Pearson's Goodness of Fit Method,[2] — $P = .999999$.

In this grade, however, it is possible that inequalities in the units of the tests, although present, do not occur by chance. The sixth grade approximates the middle region of the range of ability for which these tests have been devised. The normal curve bears an excellent reputation in psychological literature. One might conjecture with some show of reason, therefore, that in the construction of these tests there has been a more or less general and conscious effort to adjust the units of the tests so as to distribute pupils according to the normal curve, and that since the sixth grade approximates the mean of the range of ability for which the tests have been generally devised, such

[2] For the method see Tables for Statisticians and Biometricians, edited by Karl Pearson, Intro. pp. XXXI–XXXIII and Table XII.

deliberate inequalities would probably be most effective in and near the sixth grade.

Figure 87 would not then bear evidence as to the intrinsic nature of the distribution of intellect in grade six, but possibly in the psychologists who are responsible for the tests only to the skill in producing a given form of the tests. We should expect such skill to have its limits, however. It seems highly improbable that it would extend to having the same inequalities produce a spurious symmetry not only in the neighborhood of the sixth grade, but throughout the whole range of ability for which the tests are intended. In Grade 9, for instance, it seems reasonable to expect that the potency of any such hypothetical inequalities to produce symmetry would have largely, if not completely, vanished. If we find, then, that the same tests that display a normal curve in Grade 6 display the same form of distribution in Grade 9, we may justly conclude that there are no concerted inequalities in the units of the tests to which the symmetry observed may be attributed.

We have therefore plotted ninth-grade distributions[3]

[3] The ninth-grade population and source for each test are as follows:

| Test | n | Source |
|---|---|---|
| Otis Advanced Examination | 3627 | Otis, A.S., Manual of Directions, '21 |
| National Intel. Ex. A | 494 | Unpublished data of the I.E.R. |
| Trabue Completion Ex. A. | 273 | Trabue, M. R., Completion test Language Scales, p. 10 |
| Pintner Non-Language Ex. | 258 | Unpublished data supplied by Prof. Rudolph Pintner |
| Pressey Mental Survey (Cross Out) E | 303 | Pressey, S. L., Jour. Ed. Psy., vol. XI, p. 96 |
| Haggerty Delta 2 | 2648 | Compiled from unpublished data of the I.E.R. and from records supplied by Dr. W. J. Osburn, Wisconsin Dept. of Ed. |
| Army Examination a | 805 | Memoirs National Academy of Sciences, vol. 15, Table 25, p. 344, Table, 187, p. 537 |
| Myers Mental Measure | 311 | Myers, C. E. and G. C., Measuring Minds, p. 24 |
| Illinois Examination | 380 | Unpublished data of the I.E.R. |
| I.E.R. Tests of Selective and Relational Thinking, Generalization and Organization | 3214 | Unpublished data of the I.E.R. |
| Army Alpha | 1721 | Cobb, M. V., J. Ed. Psy., Nov., '22, Table IV |

for the same series of tests which constitute the sixth-grade data, and have combined these into a composite curve in the same manner as already described. This curve is shown in Figure 88. It is as close a fit to the theóretical curve as Figure 87, the sixth-grade curve. P for Figure 88 is unity.

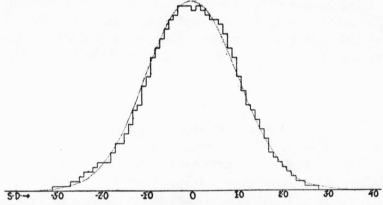

$\overbrace{\text{S·D·→}}$   -30      -20      -10       0       10       20       30       40

FIG. 88. Composite curve for the ninth grade, based upon single curves for the same eleven tests from which the sixth grade composite (Fig. 87) was derived. The broken line indicates the theoretical normal curve.

The symmetry and goodness of fit observed in the distribution of intellect in the sixth grade cannot therefore be due to consistent inequalities in the units of the individual tests.

One factor remains other than the real nature of ability in Grade 6, to which the symmetrical form of Figure 87 may still be due. This is the effect of the error of measurement in the individual scores. The effect of this may be to produce a spurious appearance of symmetry and "normality." For example, if all the pupils in this grade were of absolutely equal ability, measurement of them with fallible instruments would result in a distribution of scores resembling the normal curve of error; and if their real differences were such as to produce a right triangle as the distribution, the error might largely mask this. If these children actually vary in ability according to the normal curve of error, diminishing the errors of measurement should not lessen the symmetry of the group. As a series of measurements of a group grew less fallible, we should expect that the original symmetry, if spurious, would be accordingly diminished, but if intrinsic, would be maintained.

We have attempted to discover the effect of reducing the error of measurement upon the form of distribution of 216 sixth-grade children. Each child had been tested with six different intelligence examinations as follows:[4]

Test

1. Haggerty Delta 2
2. Kelley-Trabue Completion
3. Myers Mental Measure
4. Otis Advanced Examination
5. National Examination B
6. National Examination A

The sum of an individual's scores in two of these tests should give a better measure of that individual's ability than either test alone, and successive summation of the remaining test scores should result in progressive improvement in the measures. The error of measurement presumably grows less and less. If such symmetry as plots from the distribution of scores on the single tests show is spurious and exists solely by virtue of the error of measurement in these single scores, then plots from the summated scores, in which the error is progressively diminished, should grow less and less symmetrical.

Such is not the case. Figures 89 to 94 are plots of the 216 scores in each of the six tests. The fit of each to the theoretical normal distribution is given in Table 148.

Figures 95 to 99 are plots of the distributions obtained by successive addition of the test scores in the order in which the tests are listed in Table 148.

4 We are indebted to Dr. J. L. Stenquist for these unpublished data.

TABLE 148.

THE CLOSENESS OF FIT OF SIX TEST SCORES, TAKEN SINGLY.

| Test | P |
|------|---|
| Haggerty Delta 2 | .570 |
| Myers Mental Measure | .272 |
| Kelley Trabue Completion | .738 |
| Otis Advanced Examination | .496 |
| National B | .543 |
| National A | .067 |

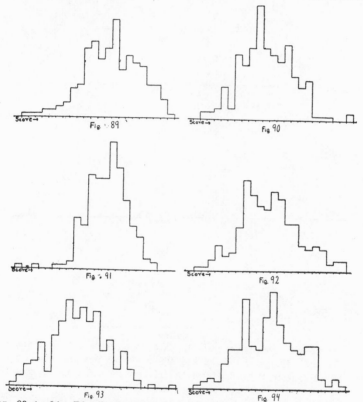

FIGS. 89 to 94.   Distributions of 216 sixth-grade pupils' scores in various
examinations.

FIG. 89.   Haggerty Delta 2.

FIG. 90.   Myers Mental Measure.

FIG. 91.   Kelley-Trabue Completion.

FIG. 92.   Otis Advanced Examination.

FIG. 93.   National Int. Ex. B.

FIG. 94.   National Int. Ex. A.

The fit of each of these to the theoretical is given in Table 149.

There is in these graphs and in these figures no such consistent change, paralleling the change in the error of measurement, as would justify us in attributing such symmetry as the group shows to the error of measurement.

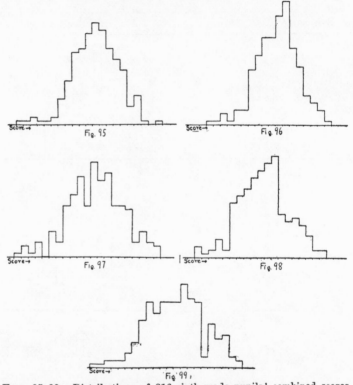

FIGS. 95–99. Distributions of 216 sixth-grade pupils' combined scores.

FIG. 95. Haggerty Delta 2 and Myers Mental Measure combined.

FIG. 96. Haggerty Delta 2, Myers Mental Measure and Kelley-Trabue Completion, combined.

FIG. 97. Haggerty Delta 2, Myers Mental Measure, Kelley-Trabue Completion and Otis Advanced Examination, combined.

FIG. 98. Haggerty Delta 2, Myers Mental Measure, Kelley-Trabue Completion, Otis Advanced Examination, and National Intelligence Examination B, combined.

FIG. 99. Haggerty Delta 2, Myers Mental Measure, Kelley-Trabue Completion, Otis Advanced Examination, National Intelligence Examination B, and National Intelligence Examination A, combined.

When Haggerty and Myers scores are combined the fit is .376 as compared with an average of .421 for them taken separately. When Haggerty, Myers and Kelley-Trabue are combined the fit is .706 as compared with an average of .526 for them taken separately. When Haggerty, Myers, Kelley-Trabue and Otis are combined the fit is .547 as compared with an average of .519 for them taken separately. When Haggerty, Myers, Kelley-Trabue, Otis and National B are combined the fit is .748 as compared with an average of .524 for them taken separately. When all six are combined the fit is .353 as compared with an average of .471 for them taken separately.

TABLE 149.

THE CLOSENESS OF FIT OF SIX TEST SCORES TAKEN TWO OR MORE AT A TIME AND ARRANGED.

| Tests | P |
|-------|---|
| Haggerty and Myers | .376 |
| Haggerty, Myers and Kelley-Trabue | .706 |
| Haggerty, Myers, Kelley-Trabue and Otis | .547 |
| Haggerty, Myers, Kelley-Trabue, Otis and National B | .748 |
| Haggerty, Myers, Kelley-Trabue, Otis, National B and National A | .353 |

We may conclude therefore that intellect in Grade 6, if measured in truly equal units, varies in general accordance with the normal probability curve. Intellectual tasks may therefore be scaled for difficulty in this grade by this hypothesis, with close approximation to the truth.

THE FORM OF THE DISTRIBUTION OF INTELLECT IN THE TWELFTH GRADE

For the twelfth grade we have a series of ten frequency distributions representing the scores made by twelfth-grade pupils in as many different intelligence examinations.

The examinations are listed below, with the number of pupils who took each examination and the sources from which the data were obtained.

| Examination | n | Source |
|---|---|---|
| 1. Terman Group Test of Mental Ability | 4886 | Manual of Directions, page 9. The World Book Co. (The table of percentile scores was converted into a frequency table) |
| 2. Brown University Psychological Examination | 3333 | The Intelligence of Seniors in the High Schools of Massachusetts. Stephen S. Colvin and Andrew H. MacPhail. Bulletin, 1924, No. 9. Department of the Interior, Bureau of Education. Page 14 |
| 3. I.E.R. Tests of Selective and Relational Thinking, Generalization and Organization, Forms A and B | 26385 | Unpublished data of the Institute of Educational Research |
| 4. Thorndike Intelligence Examination for High School Graduates, Part 1, Forms D and N | 1527 | A Mental Educational Survey. G. M. Ruch. University of Iowa Studies in Education, Volume 2, No. 5, page 22 |
| 5. Army Alpha Examination | 1387 | The Limits Set to Educational Achievement by Limited Intelligence. Table VII. M. V. Cobb, Journal of Educational Psychology, November, 1922 |
| 6. Otis Group Intelligence Scale Advanced Examination | 1226 | Manual of Directions, page 60. World Book Co. |
| 7. Strickland Test | 1020 | This is a two-hour examination. The frequency distribution was supplied by the kindness of Professor V. L. Strickland, Kansas State Agricultural College, Manhattan, Kansas |
| 8. Mentimeter Scale | 874 | Monthly Bulletin, Bureau of Educational Research, University of North Carolina, July 21, 1923 |
| 9. Miller Mental Ability Test | 739 | Manual of Directions, page 17. World Book Co. The percentile distribution was converted into a frequency distribution |
| 10. Haggerty Intelligence Examination, Delta 2 | 668 | From data supplied through the courtesy of Dr. W. J. Osburn, State Department of Education, Wisconsin |

[5] 1666 for Form A, 972 for Form B. Plots were made for each form separately and were then combined into a single distribution by averaging.

The frequency distributions of these tests have been converted into percentage distributions, and combined into one composite distribution in the manner already described in Section I. The individual percentage distributions are shown in Figures 100 to 109.

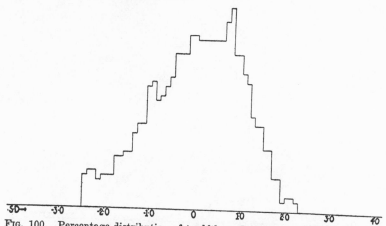

FIG. 100.   Percentage distribution of twelfth-grade scores in the Terman Group Test of Mental Ability.   n = 4886.

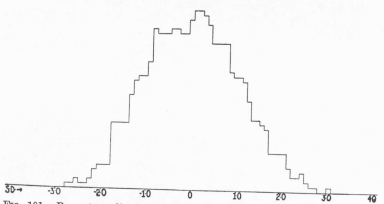

FIG. 101.   Percentage distribution of twelfth-grade scores in the Brown University Psychological Examination.   n = 333.

The composite twelfth-grade distribution appears in Fig. 110.   P for this equals .999911.

Since it is hardly likely, in view of the evidence which has already been presented in connection with the sixth

36

grade and the ninth grade and which will be presented in the next section for college freshmen, that the normality and symmetry of Figure 110 result from the error of measurement, we may conclude that intellect in the twelfth grade is also distributed in conformity to the Gaussian curve.

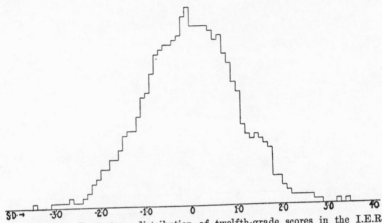

FIG. 102. Percentage distribution of twelfth-grade scores in the I.E.R. Tests of Selective and Relational Thinking, Generalization and Organization. Total n = 2638. (This curve is an average of the separate curves for Forms A and B.)

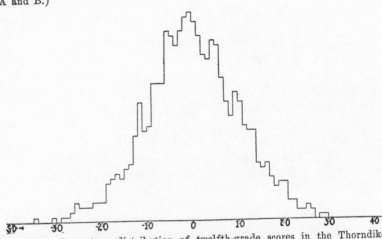

FIG. 103. Percentage distribution of twelfth-grade scores in the Thorndike Examination for High School Graduates, Part I, Forms D and N. N = 1527.

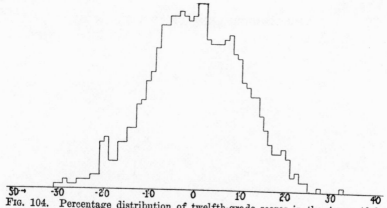

FIG. 104. Percentage distribution of twelfth-grade scores in the Army Alpha Examination. n = 1387.

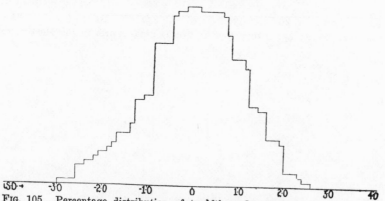

FIG. 105. Percentage distribution of twelfth-grade scores in the Otis Group Intelligence Scale, Advanced Examination. n = 1226.

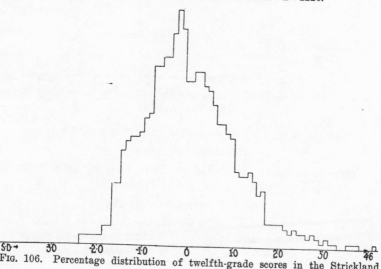

FIG. 106. Percentage distribution of twelfth-grade scores in the Strickland Test. n = 1020.

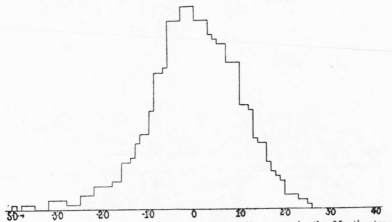

Fig. 107. Percentage distribution of twelfth-grade scores in the Mentimeter
Scale. n = 874.

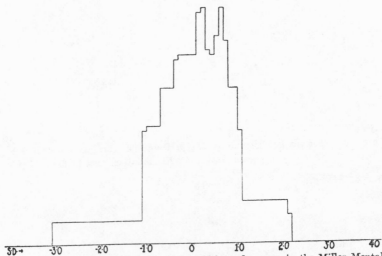

Fig. 108. Percentage distribution of twelfth-grade scores in the Miller Mental
Ability Test. n = 739.

## THE FORM OF THE DISTRIBUTION OF INTELLECT AMONG
### COLLEGE FRESHMEN

The composite distribution for college freshmen is
based upon percentage distributions plotted from frequency tables for the following examinations:[6]

6 Whenever two or more groups, whether for the same or different forms
of the examination, are listed under any examination, separate percentage distributions have been computed for each group so listed. These have then

| Examination | n | Source |
|---|---|---|
| 1. Army Alpha | 2545 | University Students Intelligence Ratings According to the Army Alpha Test. E. L. Noble and George F. Arps. School and Society, Volume 11, page 234. |
| | 400 | Intelligence Tests of Yale Freshmen. J. E. Anderson. School and Society, Volume 11, page 419 |

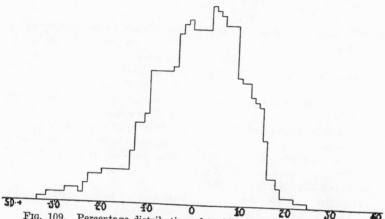

FIG. 109. Percentage distribution of twelfth-grade scores in the Haggerty Intelligence Examination, Delta 2. n = 668. The composite twelfth-grade distribution appears in Figure 110. P for this curve equals .999911.

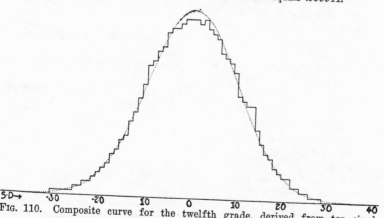

FIG. 110. Composite curve for the twelfth grade, derived from ten single curves. The broken line indicates the theoretical normal curve.

been combined by averaging, equal weight being attached to each group, into a single distribution for each examination. Thus no examination receives greater weight than any other in the final composite distribution.

| Examination | n | Source |
|---|---|---|
| 2. Brown University Psychological Examination | 2118 | Distribution of scores made by six freshmen classes at Brown University. Data supplied by the courtesy of Dr. A. H. MacPhail |
| 3. Army Examination A | 701 | Memoirs of the National Academy of Sciences, Volume 15, page 537, Table 187. |
| 4. Iowa Comprehension Tests | | Data supplied by the courtesy of Dr. |
| B-1 | 1046 | G. M. Ruch |
| D-1 | 1085 | |
| 5. Minnesota Recognition Vocabulary, A-2 | 1208 | Data supplied by the courtesy of Dr. M. E. Haggerty and Dr. D. G. Paterson |
| 6. Morgan Mental Test | 1250 | Data supplied by the courtesy of Dr. J. J. B. Morgan |
| 7. Princeton Examination, Series II | 623 | Data supplied by the courtesy of Dr. C. C. Brigham |
| 8. Smith College Entrance | | Distribution of scores made by four |
| Examination No. 1 | 371 | freshmen classes at Smith College. |
| Examination No. 2 | 486 | Data supplied by the courtesy of |
| Examination No. 3 | 604 | Dr. D. C. Rogers |
| Examination No. 4 | 596 | |
| 9. Thorndike Intelligence Examination for High School Graduates | | Data supplied by the courtesy of Dr. G. M. Ruch |
| Part I, Form B | 1085 | |
| Part I, Forms J and K | 1046 | |
| Part I, Forms E and F and Part II, Form C | 834 | |
| Total score Smith College freshmen | 525 | Data supplied by the courtesy of Dr. Agnes L. Rogers |
| Total score, Columbia freshmen | 356 | Unpublished data of the I.E.R. |
| Part VI, Form C | 272 | Data supplied by the courtesy of Dr. R. M. Smith |
| Thorndike Intelligence Examination for High School Graduates Part I, Forms E and J, Part II, Form C and Part III, Form AA | 241 | Unpublished data of the I.E.R. |
| 10. Thurstone Psychological Examination, Test IV Liberal Arts freshmen | 5495 | A Cycle Omnibus Test for College Freshmen. L. L. Thurstone. Journal of Educational Research, 1921, Volume 4, Table 2 |

| Examination | n | Source |
|---|---|---|
| 11. Yale Examination | | Data supplied by the courtesy of Dr. |
| Preliminary Form | 647 | J. E. Anderson |
| Forms 1 and 2 | 815 | |
| Forms 1 and 2 and 3a | 829 | |
| or 3b | | |
| Forms 1, 2 and 4 | 820 | |

The plots for each examination are shown in Figures 111 to 121.

The composite obtained by averaging Figures 111 to 121 is presented in Figure 122. Its fit to the normal curve is expressed by P = .999988.

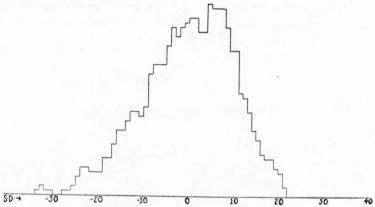

FIG. 111. Percentage distribution of college-freshmen scores in Army Alpha. Composite of separate curves for two groups. Total n = 2945.

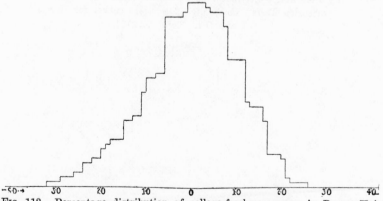

FIG. 112. Percentage distribution of college-freshmen scores in Brown University Psychological Examination. n = 2118.

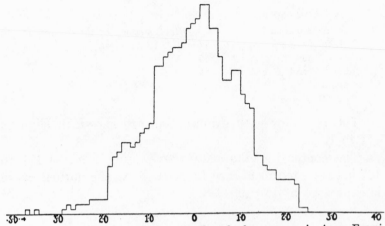

FIG. 113. Percentage distribution of college-freshmen scores in Army Examination A. n = 701.

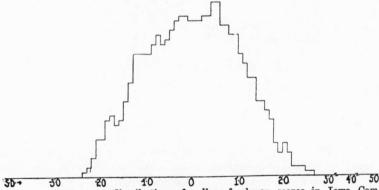

FIG. 114. Percentage distribution of college-freshmen scores in Iowa Comprehension Tests. Composite of separate curves for Forms B-1 and D-1. Total n = 2131.

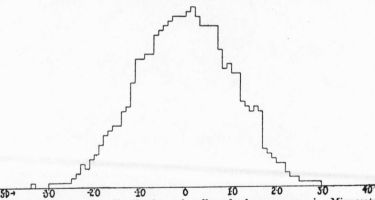

FIG. 115. Percentage distribution of college-freshmen scores in Minnesota Recognition Vocabulary, A-2. n = 1208.

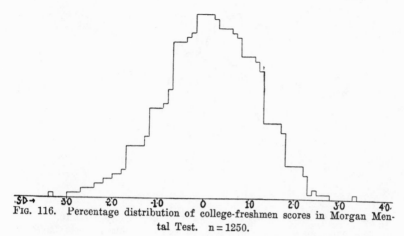

FIG. 116. Percentage distribution of college-freshmen scores in Morgan Mental Test. n = 1250.

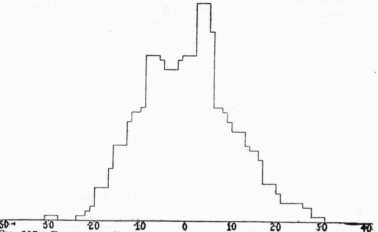

FIG. 117. Percentage distribution of college-freshmen scores in Princeton Examination, Series II. n = 623.

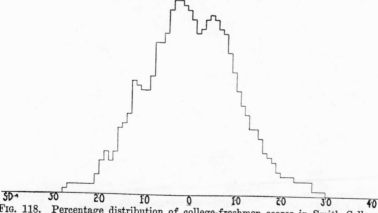

FIG. 118. Percentage distribution of college-freshmen scores in Smith College Entrance Examination. Composite of separate curves for Forms No. 1, 2, 3 and 4. Total n = 2057.

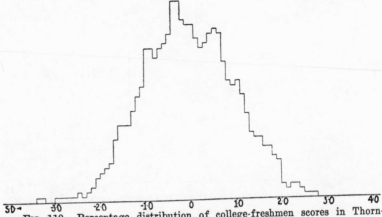

FIG. 119. Percentage distribution of college-freshmen scores in Thorndike Examination for High School Graduates. Composite of separate curves for seven groups, many different forms. (See tabulation, page 540. Total n = 4359.

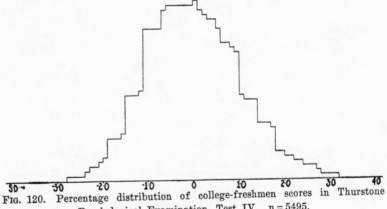

FIG. 120. Percentage distribution of college-freshmen scores in Thurstone Psychological Examination, Test IV. n = 5495.

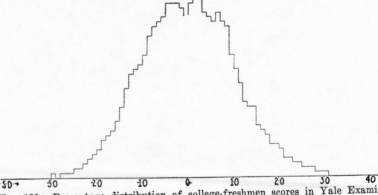

FIG. 121. Percentage distribution of college-freshmen scores in Yale Examination. Composite of separate curves for four groups, several forms. (See tabulation, page 541. Total n = 3111.

## THE EFFECT OF THE ERROR OF MEASUREMENT

We have, for each of six groups of college freshmen, several series of test scores.

For four of these groups, which we have called Groups 1, 2, 3 and 4, we have a series of five scores for each student. Three of the five scores represent each student's record on three major parts of one long examination, or on two parts of one examination, and the total score on a second ex-

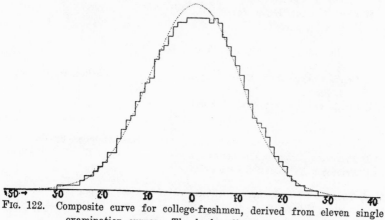

Fig. 122.    Composite curve for college-freshmen, derived from eleven single examination curves.    The broken line indicates the theoretical normal curve.

amination. The fourth and fifth scores represent successive summation of the first two, and all three single scores, respectively.

For the remaining two groups, which we have called Groups 5 and 6, we have, for each student, three sets of scores. The first two represent performance on two major parts of a single examination, or on two separate examinations. The third score is the sum of these two single scores.

The examinations performed by each group, the size of each group and the sources of the data are tabled below.

These data enable us to observe the effect, upon the form of the distribution, of progressively diminishing the error of measurement. If the symmetry and normality

| Examination | Series | Source |
|---|---|---|
| 1. A Thorndike Int. Exam. for H.S.G., Part I, Form J | 1046 | Data supplied by the courtesy of Dr. G. M. Ruch |
| B Thorndike Int. Exam. for H.S.G., Part I, Form K | | |
| C Iowa Comprehension Exam. B–1 | | |
| 2. A Thorndike Int. Exam. for H.S.G., Part I, Form E | 834 | Data supplied by the courtesy of Dr. G. M. Ruch |
| B Thorndike Int. Exam. for H.S.G., Part I, Form F | | |
| C Thorndike Int. Exam. for H.S.G., Part II, Form C | | |
| 3. A Smith College Ent. Exam. Form 3, Part 1 | 633 | Data supplied by the courtesy of Dr. D. C. Rogers |
| B Smith College Ent. Exam. Form 3, Part 2 | | |
| C Smith College Ent. Exam. Form 3, Part 3 | | |
| 4. A Princeton Examination Series V | 629 | Data supplied by the courtesy of Dr. C. C. Brigham |
| B Princeton Examination Series VI | | |
| C Princeton Examination Series VII | | |
| 5. A Thorndike Int. Exam. for H.S.G., Part I, Form B | 1085 | Data supplied by the courtesy of Dr. G. M. Ruch |
| B Iowa Comprehension Exam. D–1 | | |
| 6. A Minnesota Recognition Vocabulary A–2 | 1208 | Data supplied by the courtesy of Dr. M. E. Haggerty and Dr. D. G. Paterson |
| B Minnesota Opposites and Completion of Definitions | 1203 | |

decrease with each successive combination of scores, they are in so far due to the chance error. If they do not decrease with more and more combination, the symmetry and normality are in so far really characteristic of the group itself.

We have examined the effect of squeezing out the error in individual measurements, by successive combination of test scores, upon the form of the distribution of each one of the six groups, and also upon the composite curves obtained by combining the similar series of distributions for each group.

Plots of the series of single and summated scores for each of the six groups are given in Figures 123 to 128.

In each figure the observed frequency distribution is given in solid outline. The broken line gives the frequencies to be expected by the theory of the normal curve wherever they differ from the frequencies of fact.

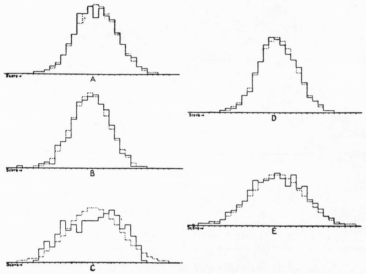

Fig. 123A.  Group 1: Distribution of 1046 Freshmen scores in Thorndike Examination for High-School Graduates, Part I, Form J.

Fig. 123B.  Group 1: Distribution of 1046 Freshmen scores in Thorndike Examination for High-School Graduates, Part I, Form K.

Fig. 123C.  Group 1: Distribution of 1046 Freshmen scores in Iowa Comprehension Examination B-1.

Fig. 123D.  Group 1: Distribution of 1046 Freshmen scores in Thorndike Examination for High-School Graduates, Part I, Form J plus Part I, Form K.

Fig. 123E.  Group 1: Distribution of 1046 Freshmen scores in Thorndike Examination for High-School Graduates, Part I, Form J plus Part I, Form K plus Iowa Comprehension Examination B-1.

The fit of each observed distribution of scores, single and summated, to each series of theoretical normal frequencies has been numerically determined by the Pearson Goodness of Fit Method. The P's are shown in Table 150.

Examination of the figures and the table reveals no consistent and progressive tendency in the individual groups to lessened symmetry and normality with progressive reduction of the error.

In the composite curve the fit to the normal becomes, practically, progressively better.

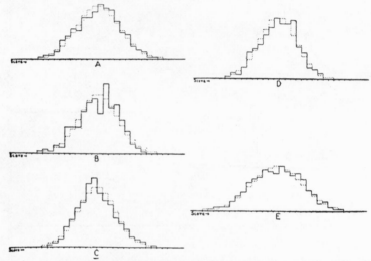

FIG. 124A.  Group 2: Distribution of 834 Freshmen scores in Thorndike Examination for High-School Graduates, Part I, Form E.

FIG. 124B.  Group 2: Distribution of 834 Freshmen scores in Thorndike Examination for High-School Graduates, Part I, Form F.

FIG. 124C.  Group 2: Distribution of 834 Freshmen scores in Thorndike Examination for High-School Graduates, Part II, Form C.

FIG. 124D.  Group 2: Distribution of 834 Freshmen scores in Thorndike Examination for High-School Graduates, Part I, Form E
plus Part I, Form F.

FIG. 124E.  Group 2: Distribution of 834 Freshmen scores in Thorndike Examination for High-School Graduates, Part I, Form E plus
Part I, Form F plus Part II, Form C.

Our data give us two sets of composite distributions, one in which all six groups are represented, and which consists of two curves for the two sets of single scores, and a third distribution of these single scores summated, and a second set of distributions in which only the four groups are represented, for which we have three sets of single scores and the two sets of successively summated scores.

These distributions have been obtained in the same manner as all of our composite distributions, namely, by plotting percentage distributions for each frequency table, and deriving the composite by averaging the percentage fre-

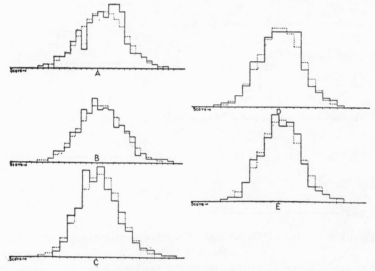

FIG. 125A.   Group 3: Distribution of 633 Freshmen scores in Smith Entrance
Examination, Form 3, Part 1.

FIG. 125B.   Group 3: Distribution of 633 Freshmen scores in Smith Entrance
Examination, Form 3, Part 2.

FIG. 125C.   Group 3: Distribution of 633 Freshmen scores in Smith Entrance
Examination, Form 3, Part 3.

FIG. 125D.   Group 3: Distribution of 633 Freshmen Scores in Smith Entrance
Examination, Form 3, Part 1 plus Form 3, Part 2.

FIG. 125E.   Group 3: Distribution of 633 Freshmen scores in Smith Entrance
Examination, Form 3, Part 1 plus Part 2 plus Part 3.

quencies for each successive $1/10\sigma$ from the mean, equal weight being attached to each distribution.

Figures 129, 130 and 131 present the composite distributions of the single and summated scores of all six groups, Figures 132 to 136 the composite curves of Groups 1 to 4.

The broken lines in Figs. 129 to 136 indicate the "normal" curve.

The fit of each composite curve to the theoretical normal curve is given in Table 151.

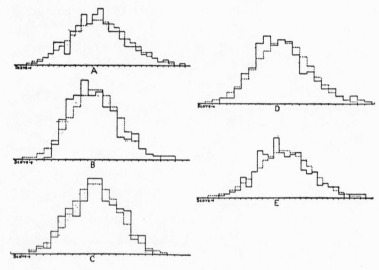

FIG. 126A.   Group 4: Distribution of 629 Freshmen scores in Princeton Examination, Series V.

FIG. 126B.   Group 4: Distribution of 629 Freshmen scores in Princeton Examination, Series VI.

FIG. 126C.   Group 4: Distribution of 629 Freshmen scores in Princeton Examination, Series VII.

FIG. 126D.   Group 4: Distribution of 629 Freshmen scores in Princeton Examination, Series V plus VI.

FIG. 126E.   Group 4: Distribution of 629 Freshmen scores in Princeton Examination, Series V plus VI plus VII.

The error of measurement is therefore not the potent factor in determining the normal symmetrical form of distribution of intellect among college freshmen. We may then conclude that this form of distribution describes the actual variation of intellect in this group.

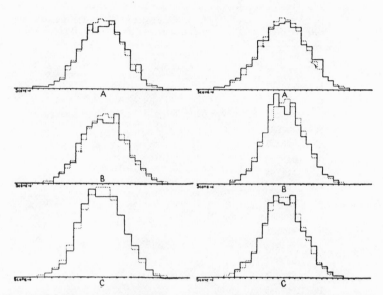

FIG. 127A. Group 5: Distribution of 1,085 Freshmen scores in Thorndike Examination for High-School Graduates, Part I, Form B.

FIG. 127B. Group 5: Distribution of 1,085 Freshmen scores in Iowa Comprehensive Examination D–1.

FIG. 127C. Group 5: Distribution of 1,085 Freshmen scores in Thorndike Examination for High-School Graduates, Part I, Form B plus Iowa Comprehensive Examination D–1.

FIG. 128A. Group 6: Distribution of 1,208 Freshmen scores in Minnesota Vocabulary Examination.

FIG. 128B. Group 5; Distribution of 1,203 Freshmen scores in Minnesota Examinations, Opposites and Definitions.

FIG. 128C. Group 6: Distribution of 1,203 Freshmen scores in Minnesota Examinations, Vocabulary plus Opposites and Definitions.

37

TABLE 150.

GOODNESS OF FIT OF OBSERVED DISTRIBUTIONS—GROUPS 1 TO 6—
TO NORMAL CURVE.

|  |  | P. for dis. of single scores | P. for dis. of sums of A and B scores | P. for dis. of sums of A, B and C scores |
|---|---|---|---|---|
|  | Series |  |  |  |
| Group 1 | A | .863808 | .979015 | .681535 |
|  | B | .340511 |  |  |
|  | C | .000000 |  |  |
| Group 2 | A | .705301 | .108533 | .965324 |
|  | B | .001299 |  |  |
|  | C | .523111 |  |  |
| Group 3 | A | .019390 | .598101 | .279157 |
|  | B | .411783 |  |  |
|  | C | .000717 |  |  |
| Group 4 | A | .028408 | .000038 | .003595 |
|  | B | .000000 |  |  |
|  | C | .006401 |  |  |
| Group 5 | A | .444183 | .486321 |  |
|  | B | .521361 |  |  |
| Group 6 | A | .974138 | .261391 |  |
|  | B | .269385 |  |  |

TABLE 151.

GOODNESS OF FIT OF COMPOSITE DISTRIBUTIONS TO NORMAL CURVE.

|  |  | P. for composite dis. of single scores | P. for composite dis. of sums of A and B scores | P. for composite dis. of sums of A, B and C scores |
|---|---|---|---|---|
|  | Series |  |  |  |
| Groups 1 to 6 | A | .999981 | 1. |  |
|  | B | .999765 |  |  |
| Groups 1 to 4 | A | .986097 | 1. | .999818 |
|  | B | .999713 |  |  |
|  | C | .949824 |  |  |

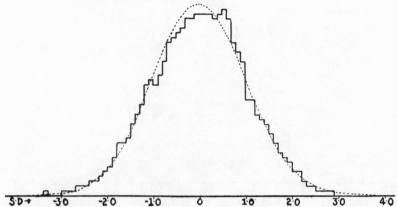

FIG. 129. Composite distribution of college-freshmen scores based on six curves.. Series of A scores.

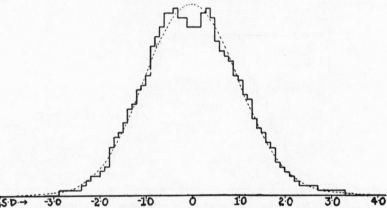

FIG. 130. Composite distribution of college-freshmen scores based on six curves. Series of B scores.

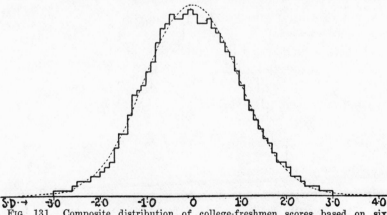

FIG. 131. Composite distribution of college-freshmen scores based on six curves. Sum of the A and B scores.

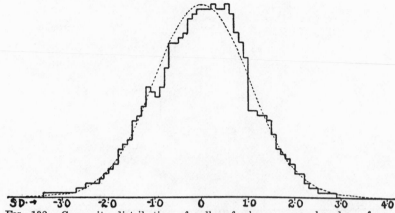

FIG. 132. Composite distribution of college-freshmen scores based on four curves. Series of A scores.

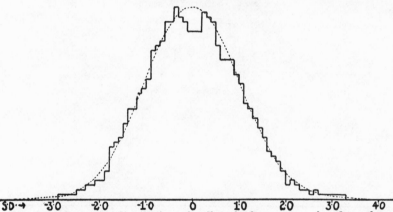

FIG. 133. Composite distribution of college-freshmen scores based on four curves. Series of B scores.

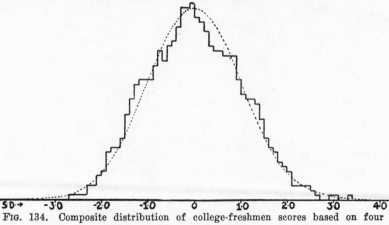

FIG. 134. Composite distribution of college-freshmen scores based on four curves. Series of C scores.

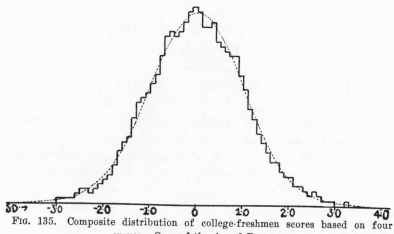

FIG. 135. Composite distribution of college-freshmen scores based on four curves. Sum of the A and B scores.

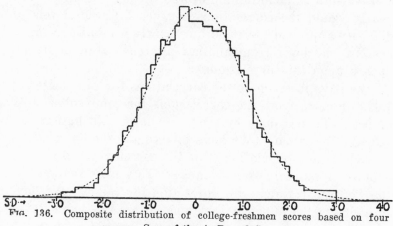

FIG. 136. Composite distribution of college-freshmen scores based on four curves. Sum of the A, B, and C scores.

# APPENDIX IV.

## THE HOMOGENEITY OF INTELLECT CAVD AT ALL LEVELS OF DIFFICULTY

Our question is how far the ability required to succeed with hard CAVD tasks differs from that required to succeed with easy CAVD tasks by being a greater amount of the same kind of thing, and how far, on the contrary, it is qualitatively different. If we had composites at each level of difficulty, made up of, say, a thousand single tasks or enough to measure the ability at each level perfectly, and tested a random million of age twenty with them, how nearly would the correlations between different levels of difficulty approach 1.00; and how nearly would the remoteness of one level from another approach zero in its influence upon the correlations?

We have to estimate the correlations for composites of 1,000 or more from the correlations for composites of 40 or less. This is done by the well-known attenuation formula of Spearman. We have to estimate the correlations in such an age population from the correlations in various groups of more restricted range. This may be done by the Pearson formulae for correction for range. We have to estimate the effect of remoteness over the whole range of difficulty from tasks like those of the 40-Composite A to tasks like those of the 40-Composite Q by the effect of remoteness of two or three steps, since none of our groups was tested over the whole range of difficulty.

We present the facts from four groups. The first is 98 adult imbeciles; the second is 121 candidates for college entrance; the third is 246 pupils of Grade 9; the fourth is 192 pupils of Grade 9.

The 40-Composites A, B, C, and D were divided each into two 20-composites, by taking elements 1, 2, 3, 9, and

556

10 from C, A, V, and D to make AI, BI, etc., and by taking
elements 4, 5, 6, 7, and 8 from C, A, V, and D to make AII,
BII, etc. The correlations between one and another of
these 20-composites AI, AII, BI, BII, CI, CII, DI, and
DII in the case of 98 adults of mental age 30 months
to 60 months, are as shown in Table 152. The self-correlations of AI with AII, BI with BII, CI with CII, and DI
with DII, are also shown there. The correlations between
two composites of infinite length, at various differences of
difficulty, may then by this determination be expected to
be as shown in Table 153.

The average of the correlations of neighboring composites is .94; that of the correlations of composites one
step removed, is .86 (.84 by Pearson, .885 by Sheppard);
that of the A to D correlations is .78 (.71 by Pearson, and
.84 by Sheppard).

TABLE 152.

SELF- AND INTER-CORRELATIONS OF FOUR 40-COMPOSITES OF CAVD, EACH
DIVIDED INTO TWO RANDOM HALVES (I AND II). 98 IMBECILES (P MEANS
PEARSON COEFFICIENT, SH MEANS SHEPPARD COEFFICIENT).

|      | A II<br>P. Sh | B I<br>P  Sh | B II<br>P  Sh | C I<br>P  Sh | C II<br>P  Sh | D I<br>P  Sh | D II<br>P  Sh |
|------|---------|---------|---------|---------|---------|---------|---------|
| A  I | .86 .87 | .78 .80 | .78 .78 | .67 .71 | .73 .78 | .62 .76 | .52 .70 |
| A II |         | .78 .76 | .78 .81 | .68 .71 | .70 .74 | .58 .71 | .49 .67 |
| B  I |         |         | .81 .74 | .74 .83 | .80 .81 | .63 .76 | .59 .72 |
| B II |         |         |         | .76 .78 | .80 .80 | .70 .70 | .62 .77 |
| C  I |         |         |         |         | .81 .91 | .65 .67 | .64 .79 |
| C II |         |         |         |         |         | .73 .70 | .74 .80 |
| D  I |         |         |         |         |         |         | .69 .83 |
| D II |         |         |         |         |         |         |         |

In these and in similar correlations between levels at
different degrees of remoteness, it should be kept in mind
that the range is very restricted, and that if all Americans
of the same chronological ages as these 98 imbeciles had
been measured by A, B, C and D, the correlations would
have been very much higher. The σ of the group of 98
adults was about 8 mental months. That of the group of

"all Americans of comparable chronological ages" would be at least four times as great.[1]

In a group with a variability four times that of the group of 98 imbeciles, the correlations corresponding to the .94, .86, and .78 would be approximately .99½, .99, and .98.

TABLE 153.

THE INTER-CORRELATIONS OF FOUR CAVD COMPOSITE TASKS LIKE A, B, C, AND D IN CONSTITUTION AND DIFFICULTY, BUT EACH CONSISTING OF AN INFINITELY LARGE NUMBER OF SINGLE TASKS. THE INTER-CORRELATIONS OF TABLE 152 CORRECTED FOR ATTENUATION.

|   | B P | B Sh | C P | C Sh | D P | D Sh |
|---|-----|------|-----|------|-----|------|
| A | .93 | .98½ | .83 | .83 | .71 | .84 |
| B |     |      | .96 | .98  | .85 | .94 |
| C |     |      |     |      | .92 | .85 |

TABLE 154.

SELF- AND INTER-CORRELATIONS OF FOUR 40-COMPOSITES OF CAVD, EACH DIVIDED INTO TWO RANDOM HALVES (I AND II) 121 HIGH SCHOOL GRADUATES. (P MEANS PEARSON, SH MEANS SHEPPARD.)

|   | NI P Sh | NII P Sh | OI P Sh | OII P Sh | PI P Sh | PII P Sh | QI P Sh | QII P Sh |
|---|---------|----------|---------|----------|---------|----------|---------|----------|
| NI |  | .57 .46 | .64 .57 | .68 .62 | .55 .57 | .61 .65 | .54 .59 | .47 .37 |
| NII |  |  | .64 .62 | .61 .62 | .58 .62 | .63 .65 | .48 .37 | .52 .41 |
| OI |  |  |  | .66 .71 | .65 .68 | .60 .63 | .60 .65 | .43 .19 |
| OII |  |  |  |  | .60 .68 | .70 .75 | .55 .62 | .53 .39 |
| PI |  |  |  |  |  | .62 .75 | .54 .48 | .50 .48 |
| PII |  |  |  |  |  |  | .46 .39 | .58 .53 |
| QI |  |  |  |  |  |  |  | .49 .47 |
| QII |  |  |  |  |  |  |  |  |

Similar facts for a group of 121 candidates for entrance to college, measured with 20-composites formed by dividing N, O, P, and two 15-composites formed by dividing Q, are shown in Tables 154 and 155. Here the average

[1] The σ of the random sample of 653 men in the draft from 9 camps was 34 mental months. [Memoirs, p. 391.]

correlations are 1.02½ (.995 for P and 1.05½ for Sh), 1.00½ (.96 for P and 1.05 for Sh), and 1.14 (.95 for P and 1.34 for Sh) in order of remoteness.

TABLE 155.

THE INTER-CORRELATIONS OF FOUR CAVD COMPOSITE TASKS LIKE N, O, P AND Q, IN CONSTRUCTION AND DIFFICULTY, BUT EACH CONSISTING OF AN INFINITELY LARGE NUMBER OF SINGLE TASKS.

121 HIGH SCHOOL GRADUATES.

|   | O | | P | | Q | |
|---|---|---|---|---|---|---|
|   | P | Sh | P | Sh | P | Sh |
| N | 1.05 | 1.06½ | .99½ | 1.05 | .95 | 1.34 |
| O |   |   | .99½ | .94 | .92 | 1.05 |
| P |   |   |   |   | .94 | 1.15 |

The 40-composites I, J, K, L, and M, showed the inter-correlations of Table 156 in the case of 246 pupils in Grade 9. The self-correlations when we divide each 40-composite into two 20-composites made of 5C, 5A, 5V, and 5D taken at random were:

|   | P | Sh |
|---|---|---|
| I | .53 | .56 |
| J | .63 | .66 |
| K | .48½ | .59 |
| L | .75 | .75 |
| M | .59 | .53 |

The self-correlations of the respective 40-composites, each with another 40-composite of the same difficulty are then by Spearman's formula $\left( r_2 = \dfrac{2r_1}{1 + r_1} \right)$ as shown below.

|   | P | Sh |
|---|---|---|
| I | .70 | .73 |
| J | .77 | .80 |
| K | .65 | .74 |
| L | .86 | .86 |
| M | .68 | .69 |

The correlations between two composites of infinite length, at various differences of difficulty, derived from Table 156 by using $r_{AB} = \dfrac{r_{A_1B_1}}{\sqrt{r_{A_1A_2}\, r_{B_1B_2}}}$, are as shown in Table 157.

TABLE 156.

THE 'RAW' INTER-CORRELATIONS OF FIVE CAVD 40-COMPOSITES IN 246 PUPILS OF GRADE 9.

|  | J Sh | J P | K Sh | K P | L Sh | L P | M Sh | M P |
|---|---|---|---|---|---|---|---|---|
| I | .59 |  | .53 |  | .62 |  | .49 |  |
| J |  |  | .70 | .66 | .72 | .66 | .72 |  |
| K |  |  |  |  | .67 | .66 | .69 |  |
| L |  |  |  |  |  |  | .63 | .67 |
| M |  |  |  |  |  |  |  |  |

TABLE 157.

THE INTER-CORRELATIONS OF FIVE CAVD COMPOSITE TASKS, LIKE THOSE OF TABLE 156 IN CONSTITUTION AND DIFFICULTY, BUT EACH CONSISTING OF AN INFINITELY LARGE NUMBER OF SINGLE TASKS.

|  | $J_\infty$ Sh | $J_\infty$ P | $K_\infty$ Sh | $K_\infty$ P | $L_\infty$ Sh | $L_\infty$ P | $M_\infty$ Sh | $M_\infty$ P |
|---|---|---|---|---|---|---|---|---|
| $I_\infty$ | .77 |  | .72 |  | .78 |  | .69 |  |
| $J_\infty$ |  |  | .91 | .93 | .87 | .81 | .97 |  |
| $K_\infty$ |  |  |  |  | .84 | .88 | .96½ |  |
| $L_\infty$ |  |  |  |  |  |  | .82 | .87 |

The average of the correlations of neighboring composites in this group is .85; the average of composites one step removed is .84; that of composites two steps removed is .87½; the correlation between the two which are three steps removed is .69.

The composites K, L, M, and N, showed the inter-correlations of Table 158 in the case of 192 pupils in Grade 9. The self-correlations, using 20 with 20, are in order: .67, .76, .57, and .58 using Sheppard's formula, and .58, .80, .64, and .62, using Pearson's formula.

The correlation between a 40-composite and another 40-composite of the same difficulty are then $\left(\text{by } r_2 = \dfrac{2r_1}{1 + r_1}\right)$ as shown below:

|   | Sh | P |
|---|-----|-----|
| K | .80 | .73 |
| L | .86 | .89 |
| M | .73 | .78 |
| N | .73 | .77 |

TABLE 158.

THE "RAW" INTER-CORRELATIONS OF FOUR CAVD COMPOSITES IN 192 PUPILS OF GRADE 9.

|   | L | | M | | N | |
|---|-----|-----|-----|-----|-----|-----|
|   | Sh | P | Sh | P | Sh | P |
| K | .47 | .61 | .59 | .69 | .59 | .61 |
| L |     |     | .77 | .73 | .50 | .57 |
| M |     |     |     |     | .68 | .71 |

TABLE 159.

THE INTER-CORRELATIONS OF FOUR CAVD COMPOSITES LIKE THOSE OF TABLE 158 IN CONSTITUTION AND DIFFICULTY, BUT EACH CONSISTING OF AN INFINITELY LARGE NUMBER OF SINGLE TASKS.

|   | $L_\infty$ | | $M_\infty$ | | $N_\infty$ | |
|---|-----|-----|-----|-----|-----|-----|
|   | Sh | P | Sh | P | Sh | P |
| $K_\infty$ | .56 | .75 | .77 | .91 | .73 | .81 |
| $L_\infty$ |     |     | .97 | .88 | .63 | .69 |
| $M_\infty$ |     |     |     |     | .93 | .92 |

The correlations for composites of infinite length, at the various differences of difficulty, derived from Table 158 by using $r_{AB} = \dfrac{r_{A_1B_1}}{\sqrt{r_{A_1A_2}\, r_{B_1B_2}}}$ are shown in Table 159.

For this group of 192, the average of the correlations of neighboring composites is .83½; that of the composites one step removed is .75; that of the two which are two steps removed is .77.

Table 160 summarizes the facts for all four groups. We correct for restricted range in the groups of high-school graduates and pupils in Grade 9, by taking the variability of age 20 to be twice that of high school graduates or of pupils in Grade 9. The variability of the literates of the draft who took Alpha was $1\frac{2}{3}$ times that of pupils in Grade 9 or of pupils in Grade 12 tested with Alpha. If the illiterates at one extreme and the officers at the other had been included, the variability would have been greater.

TABLE 160.

SUMMARY OF INTER-CORRELATIONS CORRECTED FOR ATTENUATION.

| | Neighboring Composites | Composites One Step Removed | Composites Two Steps Removed | Composites Three Steps Removed |
|---|---|---|---|---|
| 98 imbeciles | .94 | .86 | .78 | |
| 121 H. S. graduates | 1.02½ | 1.00½ | 1.14 | |
| 246 9th grade | .85 | .84 | .87½ | .69 |
| 192 9th grade | .85½ | .75 | .77 | |
| Average | .91 | .86½ | .89 | .85[2] |
| CORRECTED FOR RESTRICTED RANGE | | | | |
| 98 imbeciles | .99½ | .99 | .98 | |
| Average of the other groups | .97½ | .96 | .98[3] | |
| Weighted average of all four groups | .98 | .96¾ | .98[4] | |

The variability of 63,647 enlisted men in four camps in Army Examination $a$ was almost $1\frac{3}{4}$ times that of pupils in Grade 9, and almost 2 times that of college freshmen. Here also the inclusion of the illiterates and officers would have raised the variability of the adult group.

We have in these four determinations, taken together, a proof that the effect of remoteness in difficulty upon the inter-correlations of various CAVD composites is small, and a rough measure of how small it is.

[2] When .69 is averaged with the figures in preceding column.
[3] .96 if the .69 is used in the average.
[4] .96½ if the .69 is used.

The change as we pass from neighboring composites to composites one step removed in difficulty is — .08, — .01, — .08½, and — .02, with an average of — .05 which has a $\sigma_{t-o}$ of ± .034. The change as we pass from neighboring composites to composites two steps removed is — .16, + .02½, — .06½, and + .11½, with an average of — .02, which has a $\sigma_{t-o}$ of ± .102. If we count the three-step case where the change is — .16 (.85 to .69) in with the two-step cases, we have an average of — .05 with a $\sigma_{t-o}$ of ± .107. If the effect of remoteness were large, twice the amount of remoteness would have a greater relative effect, and the effects would all be larger relative to their unreliabilities. One step of remoteness changes the correlation by — .08, — .01, — .08½, — .02, — .08, + .13½, + .03½, + .02, and — .18½. The average of these, — .03, has a $\sigma_{t-o}$ of ± .086. So there is a probability of 36 in a hundred that remoteness *raises* the correlations, and a probability of 64 in 100 that it lowers them.

When the correlations are corrected for the restriction of range, the correlations are around .97 and the average drop for one step of remoteness is .00½.

It is hard to state in any concise fashion how much of a difference in difficulty this obtained drop of .03 corresponds to. We may best simply list the changes in the percent of successes to which the facts which it averages correspond. They are:

| | | | |
|---|---|---|---|
| In the imbeciles, from | 48.3 | to | 12.8 |
| " | 12.8 | to | 6.0 |
| In the college graduates, from | 48.1 | to | 27.5 |
| " | 27.5 | to | 3.7 |
| In the 246 of Grade 9, from | 89.4 | to | 61.4 |
| " | 61.4 | to | 32.9 |
| " | 32.9 | to | 5.3 |
| In the 192 of Grade 9, from | 16.3 | to | 7.2 |
| " | 7.2 | to | 1.1 |

It is somewhat strange that since the drop is so small, the correlation between neighboring composites should not be around .97 and all the obtained correlations nearer to unity than they are. This may be just a matter of chance due to the small populations. Or there may be factors of carelessness and lack of zeal on the part of some of the subjects, and even some undetected cheating, which the correction for attenuation may not properly allow for.

This and other imperfections in the determinations do not, however, impair the essential result that the correlations between composites far apart in difficulty are little, and possibly not at all, lower than the correlations between neighboring composites. The series of CAVD composites from one so easy as the I to one so hard as the Q do measure much the same sort of thing. We do have a right to call it by one name and to measure increases in it by the series of cardinal numbers.

# APPENDIX V.

## THE ADEQUACY OF TASKS OF ANY ONE LEVEL OF DIFFICULTY AS A MEASURE OF ALL OF INTELLECT CAVD

We wish to know how nearly certain CAVD composite tasks would measure all of intellect CAVD and nothing but intellect CAVD, if the number of elements in the tasks were extensive enough to make its own self-correlation 1.00. The answer is given by the correlation corrected for attenuation between any CAVD composite task and any random sampling of all of CAVD. It would, however, be extremely difficult to obtain facilities to test any large group with samples from CAVD at all levels of difficulty. College students, for example, would properly rebel at being given a long list of absurdly easy tasks. It would discourage children in Grade 5 to be asked hundreds of questions none of which they could answer. It is not necessary to sample all of CAVD in the case of any one individual. If our sampling goes down far enough to get near his level of one hundred percent of successes and up far enough to get near his level of zero percent of successes save by chance, our purpose will be served. The correlation between number right in such a sampling and number right in a complete sampling will be almost perfect.

Our data are for such samplings. For example, a group of 246 pupils in Grade 9 were measured in some 200 CAVD tasks, sampling CAVD from level I to level K. This sampling was cut into two halves at random, save that each half had the same number of tasks at each level of difficulty and the same number of C, A, V, and D. The correlation of these two halves was .826 by Sheppard's and .855 by Pearson's formula. The correlation of the score in the 200 with the score in another 200 may then be taken as .90 or .92 according to the formula used.

TABLE 161.

The Correlations between the Number of Single Tasks Responded to Correctly in Various 40-Composites and the Number of Tasks Responded to Correctly in a Long Series of CAVD Tasks, Ranging from Tasks Very Easy for the Group in Question to Tasks Very Hard for the Group in Question: Groups 9I and 9II. (P = Pearson Coefficient; Sh = Sheppard Coefficient.)

| Group | 40-Composite | Raw Correlation with Long Series | | Self-Correlation of 40-Composite | | Self-Correlation of Long Series | | Corrected Correlation with Long Series | |
|---|---|---|---|---|---|---|---|---|---|
| | | Sh | P | Sh | P | Sh | P | Sh | P |
| 246 of Grade 9 | I | .72 | | .73 | .70 | .90 | .92 | .89 | |
| 246 of Grade 9 | J | .89 | .84 | .80 | .77 | | | 1.05 | 1.00 |
| 246 of Grade 9 | K | .82 | .81 | .74 | .65 | | | 1.00 | 1.05 |
| 246 of Grade 9 | L | .93 | .87 | .86 | .86 | | | 1.05 | .98 |
| 246 of Grade 9 | M | .83 | .79 | .69 | .68 | | | 1.05 | 1.00 |
| 192 of Grade 9 | K | .77 | .82 | .80 | .73 | .95 | .93 | .88 | .99 |
| 192 of Grade 9 | L | .93 | .86 | .86 | .89 | | | 1.03 | .95 |
| 192 of Grade 9 | M | .88 | .91 | .73 | .78 | | | 1.06 | 1.07 |
| 192 of Grade 9 | N | .77 | .82 | .73 | .77 | | | .92 | .97 |

The raw correlation between the number right in the 40-composite I and the number right in the entire 200 is .72. The self-correlation of the former is .73. The correlation corrected for attenuation is .89.

The raw correlation between the number right in the 40-composite J and the number right in the entire 200 is .89 by the Sheppard formula and .84 by the Pearson. The self-correlation of J is .80 by the Sheppard and .77 by the Pearson. The correlation corrected for attenuation is 1.05 by the Sheppard and 1.00 by the Pearson.

These and similar facts for tasks of various degrees of difficulty are shown in Tables 161 and 162, which report the results from this group of 246 and from three other groups as follows:—

192 other students in Grade 9 were tested with a somewhat similar long series, including the tasks of the 40-Composites K, L, M and N. 121 candidates for college entrance were measured by a series of 240 completions, 56 arithmetic tasks, 50 vocabulary tasks and 41 paragraph-reading tasks, ranging from such as almost all could do to such as hardly any could do. A summated total score for the number right was computed. The tasks included the 40-Composites N, O, P and Q. 240 first-year students in a Law School, all college graduates, were measured by a series of 53 completion tasks, 56 arithmetic tasks, 100 vocabulary tasks and 41-paragraph-reading tasks, ranging from such as almost all could do to such as hardly any could do. A summated score for CAVD giving equal weight to C, A, V and D was computed. The tasks included the 40-Composites N, O, P and Q.

The self-correlations of the 40-composites for the group of 121 high-school graduates are the averages from determinations, first by $\dfrac{2r_{20,\,20}}{1 + r_{20,\,20}}$ and second by $.03 + r_{40}$, using only nearest neighbors among the composites. Those for the group of 240 college graduates are determined by the second method.

The average of the seventeen corrected coefficients of Table 161 is 1.00 with a mean square error of ± .058.

The average of the eight corrected coefficients of Table 162 is 1.00½ with a mean square error of ± .034.

These results are corroborated by results from a group of 100 university students, from the 240 college graduates of Table 162 but using different 40-composites, and from a group of 147 pupils in Grade 5½.

TABLE 162.

THE CORRELATIONS BETWEEN THE NUMBER OF SINGLE TASKS RESPONDED TO CORRECTLY IN VARIOUS 40-COMPOSITES AND THE NUMBER OF TASKS RESPONDED TO CORRECTLY IN A LONG SERIES OF CAVD TASKS RANGING FROM TASKS VERY EASY FOR THE GROUP IN QUESTION TO TASKS VERY HARD FOR THE GROUP IN QUESTION: GROUPS 13 AND 17.

| Group | 40 Composite | Raw Correlation with Long Series | Self Correlation of 40-Composite | Self Correlation of Long Series | Corrected Correlation with Long Series |
|---|---|---|---|---|---|
| 121 high-school graduates | N | .80 | .69½ | .90 | 1.01 |
| 121 high-school graduates | O | .89 | .78½ | .90 | 1.00 |
| 121 high-school graduates | P | .92 | .78½ | .90 | 1.03 |
| 121 high-school graduates | Q | .77 | .69 | .90 | .98 |
| 240 college graduates | N | .85 | .86 | .95 | .94 |
| 240 college graduates | O | .92 | .86½ | .95 | 1.02 |
| 240 college graduates | P | .89 | .79½ | .95 | 1.02 |
| 240 college graduates | Q | .86 | .72 | .95 | 1.04 |

One hundred students of education, graduates of colleges or normal schools, were measured by 40 sentence-completion tasks, 46 arithmetic tasks, 150 vocabulary tasks, 24 paragraph-reading tasks, 170 information tasks, 180 tasks involving information plus more or less general sagacity, 20 picture-completion tasks, 32 pictorial analogy tasks and 40 geometrical relations tasks. A general summated score, $S_2$, was compiled by combining the results of the 40 C, 150 V and 24 D tasks so as to give a reasonable weight to each sort of task. Two composites (O 75½ and Q 96½), each consisting of 26 single tasks (10 C + 10 V + 6 D, the D scores being multiplied by 1⅔) of approximately equal difficulty within each composite and differing between composites so that 77 percent of the group had 15 or more right in the O 75½ composite while 21 percent had 15 or more right in the Q 96½ composite, showed correlations of .91 and .78½ with the total summation score and a correlation of .66 one with the other.

The self-correlation of the total summation score is almost certainly not over .96 and the average self-correlation of the 40-composites is almost certainly not over .66 + .10 or .76. Using .96 and .75, the corrected correlation between one level and the total score in all levels in this group is $\dfrac{.91 + .78\frac{1}{2}}{2}$ over $\sqrt{.96 \times .76}$ or a little under 1.00.

The 240 college graduates were measured by three composite tasks slightly different from N, O and Q, which we shall denote by 1, 2 and 3. Calling the long total score $s_1$, the correlations are:

$$r_{1_1 2_1} = .73$$
$$r_{1_1 3_1} = .63$$
$$r_{2_1 3_1} = .73$$
$$r_{1_1 s_1} = .85$$
$$r_{2_1 s_1} = .91$$
$$r_{3_1 s_1} = .86$$

The self-correlation of 1, 2 and 3 may be set as about .03 higher than the correlations between 1 and 2 and between 2 and 3, or at .76.[1]

We do not know directly what the self-correlation of the $s_1$ score is, but it can hardly be higher than .95. Using .76 and .95, the corrected correlations between score for a composite of tasks at one degree of difficulty and score in the total CAVD series are 1.00, 1.07 and 1.01, averaging 1.03 with a mean square error of ± .031.

One hundred and forty-four pupils at the very beginning of Grade 6 were tested with a fairly long series of

[1] In the case of the 240 college graduates the correlation between two 40 composites of about equal difficulty was .73½.

570     THE MEASUREMENT OF INTELLIGENCE

CAVD, with time to do all that they could do. A summation score was given with approximately equal weight to C, A, V and D. Included in the series were the 40 tasks of the composite I and the 40 of the composite J. The raw correlation between the number right in level I and the summation score was .91. The raw correlation between the number right in level J and the summation score was .86. The raw correlation between the number right in composite I and the number right in composite J was .75.

We do not know the self-correlations in this group directly, but that for a 40-composite will be near .78 and that for the total score will be near .95. The corrected coefficients will thus here also average close to unity (using .78 and .95, they are 1.00 and 1.06).

We may approach the question of whether one of our 40-composite CAVD tasks measures (except for the chance error due to its having only 40 tasks) all of intellect CAVD and nothing but intellect CAVD by another method. If it does, the average raw correlation $r_{t_1 l_1}$ should in a group of wide range in intellect be little, if any, less than $\sqrt{r_{t_1 t_2}}$.

We have found $r_{t_1 l}$ in groups of the range of a school grade to be, according to the group and the composite, .72, .77, .78$\frac{1}{2}$, .79$\frac{1}{2}$, .79$\frac{1}{2}$, .80, .81, .81$\frac{1}{2}$, .85, .85, .86, .86, .86, .86$\frac{1}{2}$, .87, .89, .89, .89$\frac{1}{2}$, .90, .91, .91, .91, .92 and .92.[2] The median is .86; the average is .853.

The self-correlation $r_{t_1 t_2}$, estimated by the Spearman formula from the two halves, or by taking the correlation with a neighboring composite + .03, is, for the same composites in the same groups,[3] .68$\frac{1}{2}$, .69, .69, .69$\frac{1}{2}$, .69$\frac{1}{2}$, .71$\frac{1}{2}$, .72, .75, .75, .75$\frac{1}{2}$, .76, .76, .76, .76$\frac{1}{2}$, .78, .78, .78$\frac{1}{2}$, .78$\frac{1}{2}$, .79$\frac{1}{2}$, .79$\frac{1}{2}$, .86, .86, .86$\frac{1}{4}$ and .87$\frac{1}{2}$. The median is .76; the average is .765.

2 Where the correlation is determined by both Sheppard and Pearson formulae we use the average of the two results.

3 As before, when both Sheppard and Pearson coefficients were obtained, the average of the two is used.

Within a grade range then $r_{t_1 l_1}$ is .857 and $r_{t_1 t_2}$ is .76$\frac{1}{4}$. $r_{t_1 l_1}$ is $\frac{.857}{.873}$ of $\sqrt{r_{t_1 t_2}}$ or .98 $\sqrt{r_{t_1 t_2}}$. If the range is increased, $r_{t_1 l_1}$ will approach still nearer to $\sqrt{r_{t_1 t_2}}$.

We may then safely conclude that the ability measured by a sufficiently extensive composite of CAVD tasks at a level of difficulty which is appropriate for the group in the sense that the percent of successes in the group will be between 10 and 90, is substantially identical with the ability measured in that group by the total CAVD series. Our CAVD 40-composite tasks measure intellect CAVD as far as their self-correlations permit.

The facts presented here concerning the correlations between 40-composites and long series which approximate to total CAVD series corroborate the conclusion in Appendix IV from the correlations between composites that intellect CAVD is to a high degree homogeneous, the higher levels requiring much the same ability as the lower, but more of it.

There is good reason to believe that, if we had taken intellect GOPI, composed of tasks in observing geometrical relations, giving opposites, completing pictures and answering questions requiring information such as intellectual people acquire, and carried out the same sorts of investigations as we have carried out with intellect CAVD, we should have found that intellect GOPI also was nearly or quite homogeneous at all levels of difficulty, and that a task composed of equal parts of G, O, P and I all of approximately the same difficulty, measured all of intellect GOPI and nothing but intellect GOPI, so far as its own self-correlation permitted. The same would also probably hold for any other selection of tasks in thinking correctly with ideas and symbols. Nothing was done in our selection of CAVD to favor homogeneity. There is no reason to believe that CAVD is any more homogeneous at different levels of difficulty than any other selection of tasks for intellect.

# APPENDIX VI

## THE ESTIMATED FORM OF DISTRIBUTION OF VARIOUS GROUPS

We do not know exactly what the form of distribution of intellect in the 180 adult imbeciles is. They were selected to include the individuals 16 years old or over in two institutions who were from 2½ to 5 years of mental age by the Stanford Binet; and on this basis we should expect the

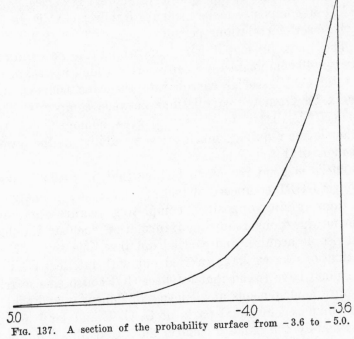

FIG. 137. A section of the probability surface from − 3.6 to − 5.0.

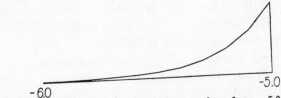

FIG. 138. A section of the probability surface from − 5.0 to − 6.0.

distribution to be a small segment of the low end of the distribution of all persons 16 years old or over, but modified by the error of measurement. Empirically the distribution of the scores in the Stanford Binet is as shown in

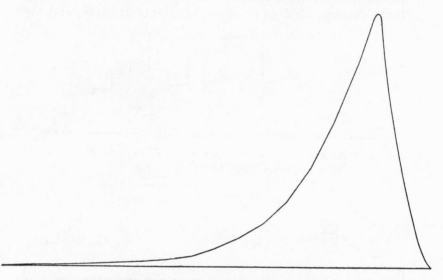

FIG. 139. The result of the application of an error of measurement to the group represented in Fig. 138.

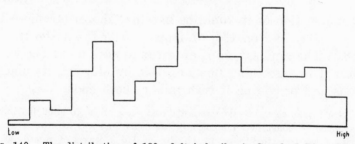

FIG. 140. The distribution of 180 adult imbeciles in Stanford Binet Mental Age.

Fig. 140. By the summation of credits in the 240 CAVDIO tasks, the distribution was that of Fig. 141.

In view of these facts, we have chosen as the probable form of distribution of altitude of intellect in these 180 individuals, if they were measured in equal units, the form shown in Fig. 142.[1] According to it the σ values of the difficulty of the CAVD composites A, B, C, and D are respectively, $-1.68\sigma_A$, $+.05\sigma_B$, $+1.13\sigma_C$ and $+1.83\sigma_D$.

If the low end of the distribution were a fraction of the probability surface undisturbed by the operation of any large factors, such as diseases, accidents at birth, and the

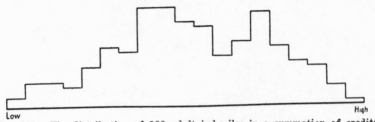

Low                                                                          High

FIG. 141.   The distribution of 180 adult imbeciles in a summation of credits in CAVDIO (I = Inf., O = Opp.)

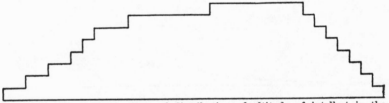

FIG. 142.   The probable form of distribution of altitude of intellect in the group of 180 adult imbeciles.

like, a section of it would be like that shown (from $-3.6\sigma$ to $-5.0\sigma$) in Fig. 137, or from $-5.0\sigma$ to $-6.0\sigma$ in Fig. 138.[2] The application of an error to such a surface would alter it to something like Fig. 139, by blurring its distinctions and providing it with tails at both ends.

[1] We make no claim that this is the best guess at the form of distribution that could be made. On the contrary, we could ourselves improve it by (a) giving other tests to this group, (b) by making a census of records of the mental ages of the inmates (16 years old or older) in institutions for the feeble-minded, and in other ways. We simply have not the time to do so. It is not a matter of much importance except in the case of the estimate of the difficulty of Composite D. In that case the exact determination of the upper tail of the distribution would be very desirable. However, the estimate for Composite D would be hazardous in any case because of the unreliability of the 00.6 as the percent of successes.

[2] The ordinate scale of Fig. 138 is magnified 100 times that of Fig. 137.

We know very little, however, about the forces operating to produce individuals so dull as these; or the form which the extreme low end of the distribution of human intellect takes.

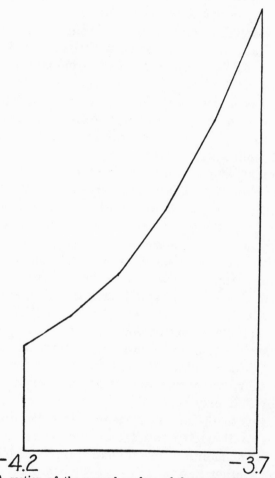

FIG. 143. A section of the normal surface of frequency from −4.2 to −3.7.

We do not know exactly the form of distribution of the 100 feeble-minded of Stanford mental age 6 yr. 0 mo. to 6 yr. 11 mo. If they were a random sampling of all persons sixteen years old or older of mental age 6, the distribution would be approximately that of a segment of the surface of frequency for adult intellect from an I.Q. of $37\frac{1}{2}$ to an I.Q. of 44.4, or from $-6.25\sigma$ to $-5.56\sigma$, if we use Terman's estimate of the variability of intelligence quotients ['16 p. 78]. However, the variability of the intellects of persons chronologically 16 or over is probably much greater than that given by Terman's figures for children, at least from the mode toward the low end; and from $-4.2\sigma$ to $-3.7\sigma$ seems a more probable status by random selection.

As has been stated, we do not know the exact form of the surface of frequency for adult intellect, at its low extreme. It almost certainly is continuous from M.A. 6–11, to M.A. 6–0, and diminishing somewhat in area per unit of abscissa. The low extreme of Form A from $-5.0\sigma$ to $-3.6\sigma$ was shown in Fig. 137. That from $-6.0\sigma$ to $-5.0\sigma$ was shown in Fig. 138. Not much weight should be attached to any estimate from theory of the amount of the diminution in frequency as we go to very dull levels of the total adult population, since we know very little about the causes which are acting to create these levels. Using $-4.2\sigma$ to $-3.7\sigma$ of Form A, we should have the distribution shown in Fig. 143.

However, the selection for commitment is not random, the duller ones being more often committed than the brighter. So the pitch of the curve would be expected to be less sharp than that of the general adult population, whatever that may be.

Turning to the actual measurements, the form of distribution of the 100 imbeciles of mental age 6, if we assume that one month of mental age from 6 to 7 by that scale equals any other month, and that the Stanford Binet measures intellect perfectly, is that shown in Fig. 144.

We do not know what the values of these mental months of the Stanford Binet are in truly equal units, as there have never been any measurements of grade or age groups by the Stanford Binet which are large enough to enable us to apply the procedure which we have used with the National, Otis, Terman group and other examinations. In all probability, the differences in the true values are not great.

We know that the Stanford Binet does not measure intellect perfectly; and we know roughly the amount of the error of a single determination of the Binet as a measurement of the abilities that would be measured by a long series of examinations of the very same sort as the Binet.

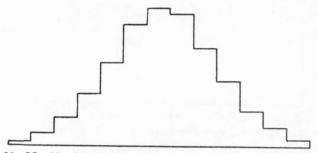

52  56  60  64  68  72  76  80  84  88  92  96  100  104

FIG. 144.  The form of distribution of Group im. 6 in Stanford-Binet Mental Age.

This is a mean $\sigma_{t-o}$ of about 6 mental months, at or near mental age 10. It probably is less around mental age 6, but it will still be large in comparison with the range of 12 months in the measurements themselves. Taking it as 4 mental months, the true intellects of the 100 would range from about 5 yr. 0 mo. of mental age to about 8 years of mental age. However, a long series of examinations of the very same sort as the Binet would probably not measure all of intellect. So that an allowance for the error of the Binet sort of examination, no matter how extensive, must also be made.

It is thus very difficult to make anything like a valid estimate of the probable form of distribution of altitude of intellect measured without error and in equal units.

What we have done is to apply an error of the magnitude shown in Table 163 to the empirically obtained scores grouped as:

25 cases M.A. 6 yr. 0 mo. to 6 yr. 3 mo. inclusive,
33 " " 6 yr. 4 mo. to 6 yr. 7 mo. "
40 " " 6 yr. 8 mo. to 6 yr. 11 mo. "
2 " " 7 yr. 0 mo. to 7 yr. 3 mo. "

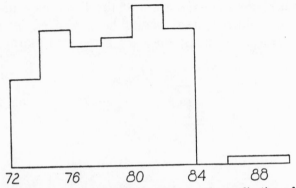

FIG. 145.   The form of distribution resulting by the application of an error of measurement to the Stanford-Binet scores of Group im. 6.

This gives us Fig. 145 as the form of distribution of this group.

Using the form of distribution of Fig. 145, the sigma values for the difficulty of Composites C, D, E, F and G are respectively $-1.90\sigma_C$, $-.45\sigma_D$, $+.29\sigma_E$, $+1.25\sigma_F$, and $+2.08\sigma_G$.

TABLE 163.

DISTRIBUTION OF THE ASSUMED ERROR WHEREBY A STANFORD BINET MENTAL AGE DIFFERS FROM THE MENTAL AGE WHICH WOULD BE FOUND BY A PERFECT MEASUREMENT OF ALTITUDE OF INTELLECT.

| | | | |
|---|---|---|---|
| − 18 mo. to | − 21 mo. | 1 |
| − 14 " " | − 17 " | 2 |
| − 10 " " | − 13 " | 3 |
| − 6 " " | − 9 " | 6 |
| − 2 " " | − 5 " | 8 |
| − 2 " " | + 1 " | 10 |
| + 2 " " | + 5 " | 8 |
| + 6 " " | + 9 " | 6 |
| + 10 " " | + 13 " | 3 |
| + 14 " " | + 17 " | 2 |
| + 18 " " | + 21 " | 1 |

The 50 cases of feeble-minded of Class 3 may be assumed to be of approximately the normal form of distribution in respect of intellect, since they represent those selected by the educational authorities of the institution as belonging in Grade 3 rather than in Grade 2 or Grade 4. We have seen that the process of educational selection for a grade tends in general to produce symmetry and an approximation to Form A. However, there would probably be a curtailment at the upper end and an extension at the lower, since there would be a scarcity of children who were much too bright really to belong to Grade 3, but an abundance of children much too dull to belong there. Whereas, in an ordinary school the forces acting to produce gradation in Grade 3 select from a rectangle, in an institution for feeble-minded they select from a surface which is presumably much higher at the low than at the high end.

In a total CAVD summation score, the distribution was that shown below.

| Quantity | Frequency |
|----------|-----------|
| 60 to 79 | 1 |
| 80 " 99 | 0 |
| 100 " 119 | 1 |
| 120 " 139 | 1 |
| 140 " 159 | 0 |
| 160 " 179 | 3 |
| 180 " 199 | 4 |
| 200 " 219 | 7 |
| 220 " 239 | 13 |
| 240 " 259 | 7 |
| 260 " 279 | 7 |
| 280 " 299 | 4 |
| 300 " 319 | 2 |

In view of these facts we have assumed the form of distribution of this group to be that shown in Table 164. Using this, the difficulty of Composite E is $-1.35\sigma_E$; that of Composite F is $-1.25\sigma_F$; that of G is $-.33\sigma_G$; that of H is $-.41\sigma_H$; that of I is $+1.17\sigma_I$.

It has not been practicable to secure sufficient information outside of our own tests for even the roughest empirical determination of the form of distribution of the Special-Class group. Nor is enough known about the policies of the different schools, principals and teachers, nor about the accuracy of the diagnoses to justify an *a priori* estimate of the selective forces which relegated these pupils to the special classes. There should theoretically be much of negative skewness, since the selection is surely from the dull half and probably from the dullest

TABLE 164.

FORM OF DISTRIBUTION ASSUMED IN OBTAINING MEASURES OF THE DIFFICULTY OF VARIOUS COMPOSITES FOR THE GROUP OF 50 FEEBLE-MINDED.

| Interval | Frequency |
|---|---|
| a        to a +    k | 1 |
| a +    k " a +   2k | 1 |
| a +   2k " a +   3k | 2 |
| a +   3k " a +   4k | 2 |
| a +   4k " a +   5k | 3 |
| a +   5k " a +   6k | 3 |
| a +   6k " a +   7k | 10 |
| a +   7k " a +   8k | 12 |
| a +   8k " a +   9k | 20 |
| a +   9k " a + 10k | 20 |
| a + 10k " a + 11k | 12 |
| a + 11k " a + 12k | 10 |
| a + 12k " a + 13k | 2 |
| a + 13k " a + 14k | 2 |

quarter or eighth rather than from the brighter which results if the effort is to select the fraction of the normal surface between $-1.5$ S.D. and $-2.7$ S.D., but this effort is disturbed by an error distributed as follows, $-.2$ S.D., 1; $-.1$ S.D., 4; 0 S.D., 6; $+.1$ S.D., 4; $+.2$ S.D., 1.

This gives a surface of the form shown in Fig. 146. Using this form of distribution, the differences in difficulty of E, F, G, H, and I, from the median difficulty for the Special Class group are respectively, in units of the $\sigma$ of the group, $-2.61\sigma_E$, $-2.31\sigma_F$, $-1.54\sigma_G$, $-.44\sigma_H$ and $+.36\sigma_I$.

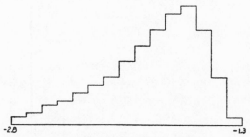

FIG. 146.  The form of distribution assumed in the case of the special class group.

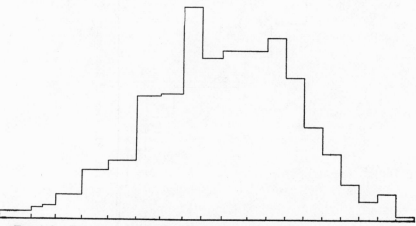

FIG. 147.  The form of distribution of Grade 5 in Army Alpha, in equal units.

FIG. 148.  The form of distribution of Grade 5 in Examination A, in equal units.

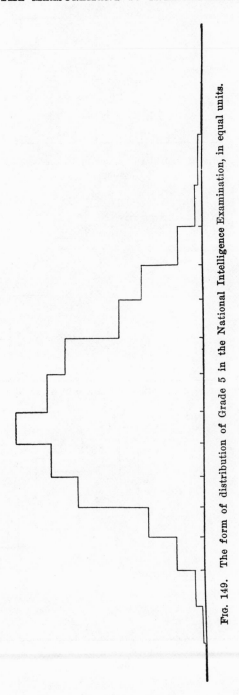

Fig. 149. The form of distribution of Grade 5 in the National Intelligence Examination, in equal units.

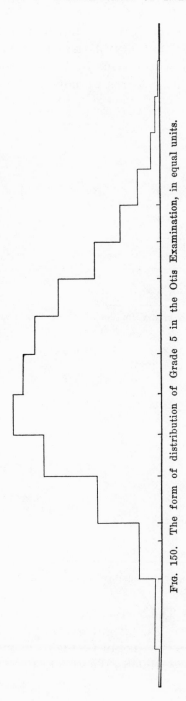

Fig. 150. The form of distribution of Grade 5 in the Otis Examination, in equal units.

To ascertain the form of distribution in Grade 5 and the form of distribution in Grade 4, we have collected the distributions of scores made by these grades in any of the examinations whose scores we have transmuted into scales

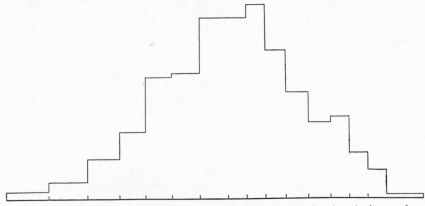

FIG. 151.   The form of distribution of Grade 4 in Examination A, in equal units.

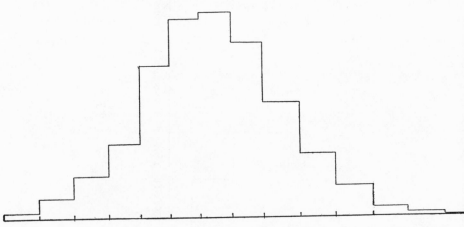

FIG. 152.   The form of distribution of Grade 4 in National A, in equal units.

in equal units.   The surfaces of frequency are drawn, using the equal-unit scales.   Figures 147, 148, 149 and 150 show the essentials in the case of Grade 5; Figures 151, 152, and 153 show the essentials in the case of Grade 4.

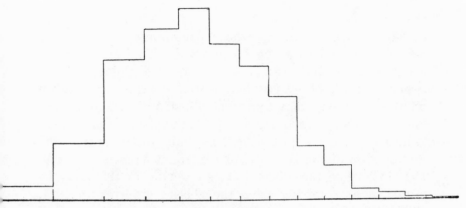

Fig. 153. The form of distribution of Grade 4 in Otis Examination, in equal units.

In view of these curves and the general probabilities of the case, it does not appear that there is justification for assuming any considerable flattening or any considerable skewness. So the form of distribution for Grade 5 and for Grade 4 is taken as that of the normal probability surface.

In order to perfect our measures of the differences in difficulty of levels N, O, P and Q, we need knowledge of

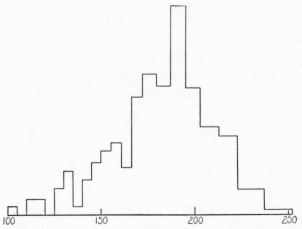

Fig. 154. The form of distribution of first-year law students, '24, in Army Alpha in equal units.

the form of distribution of altitude of intellect in the group of 240 college graduates whose percentage of success at each of these levels we have computed. This group of 240 comprised the first-year class entering the Columbia Law School in 1924. We have their scores in Army Alpha taken on the same day that they took the CAVD examination; and we have learned (in Chapter VII) the approximate values of Army Alpha scores in truly equal units. The distribution of the 240 in Alpha in equal units is shown in Fig. 154. The Law School class entering in 1924 may be regarded as differing from the classes entering in 1921, 1922, and 1923, only by chance in respect of the form of distribution. In the case of each of these classes we have the scores in several intelligence examinations, namely:

CLASS OF 1921

A completion test of about 1 hour.

A paragraph reading test of 1 hour.

A paragraph reading test of 1 hour (selective type).

Thorndike Exam., series 1925–1930, Part I, Form Q.

Thorndike Exam., series 1925–1930, Part I, Form R or S.

An arithmetical composite.

CLASS OF 1922

A paragraph reading test of 1 hour.

A paragraph reading test of 1 hour (selective type).

An examination containing opposites, Briggs's grammatical analogies and a vocabulary test

Thorndike Exam., series 1925–1930, Part I, Form S or V

CLASS OF 1923

An extensive test in sentence completion and arithmetical problems.

An examination containing opposites, Briggs's analogies, and a vocabulary test.

A paragraph reading test of 1 hour.

These records permit the application to "a first-year class in the Columbia Law School" of the same processes of reasoning used in Appendix III in the case of "a grade population." The surfaces of frequency for each separate score are shown in Figs. 155 to 167. They show in

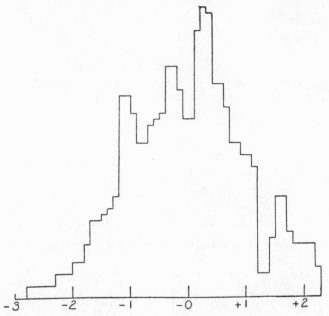

FIG. 155. Form of distribution of first-year law students, '21, Completions.

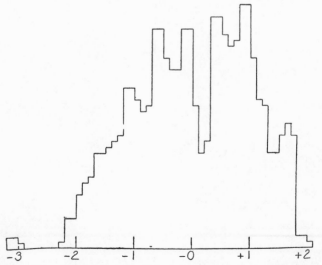

FIG. 156. Form of distribution of first-year law students, '21, Reading I.

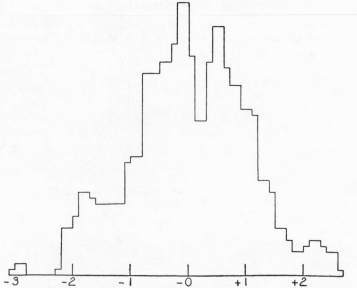

FIG. 157. Form of distribution of first-year law students, '21, Reading II.

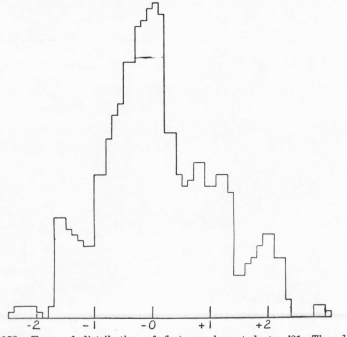

FIG. 158. Form of distribution of first-year law students, '21, Thorndike, Part I–Q.

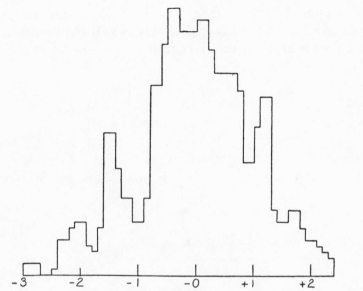

FIG. 159. Form of distribution of first-year law students, '21, Thorndike, Part I, R or S.

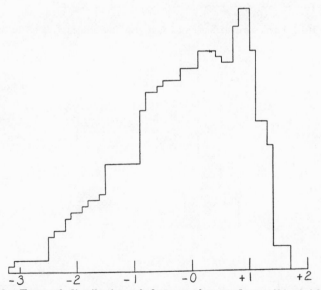

FIG. 160. Form of distribution of first-year law students, '21, Arithmetic.

general a departure from "normality" in the shape of a longer tail at the low end. This is still clearer when we rid the measurements of chance variations by combining

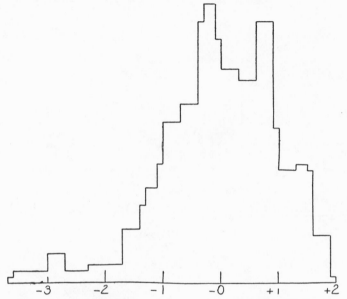

FIG. 161. Form of distribution of first-year law students, '22, Reading I.

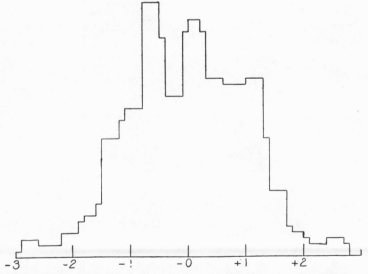

FIG. 162. Form of distribution of first-year law students, '22, Reading II.

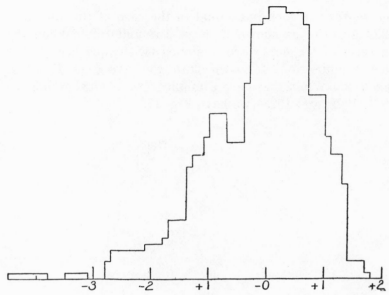

FIG. 163. Form of distribution of first-year law students, '22, Verbal Relations.

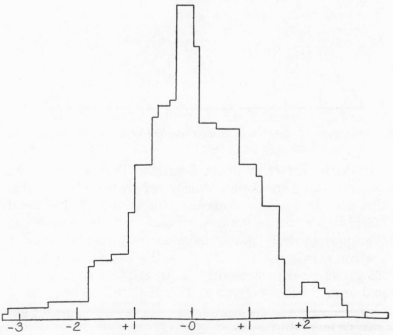

FIG. 164. Form of distribution of first-year law students, '22, Thorndike I, S or U.

the scores for each individual in the case of the 1921 and 1922 groups,[3] as shown in Figs. 168 and 169. When the surfaces of frequency are combined (with equal weight for each examination) for each class, we have Figs. 170, 171, and 172. When these are combined (with equal weight to 1921, 1922, and 1923) we have Fig. 173.

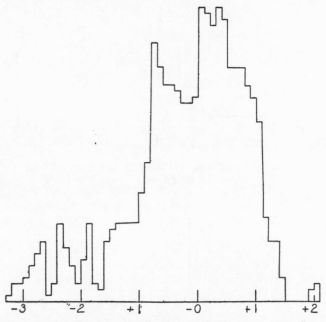

FIG. 165. Form of distribution of first-year law students, '23, Co. and Ar.

Both the direct evidence from the 1924 group itself, when measured by Alpha transposed to a scale of equal units, and the evidence from the groups of 1921, 1922, and 1923 in which the inequalities of units may be assumed to have approximately counterbalanced one another, show a negative skewness. So also does the distribution of the 1923 group when measured by Army Alpha with a scale of equal units. This is shown in Fig. 175. So we have taken

[3] This would be true also with the 1923 group, but we have not had time to make the computations exactly.

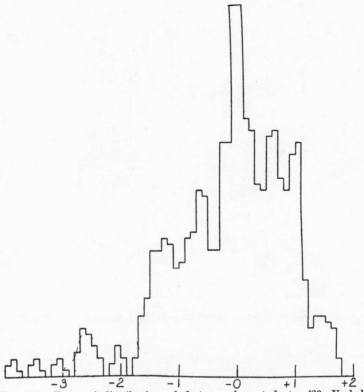

FIG. 166. Form of distribution of first-year law students, '23, Verbal Relations.

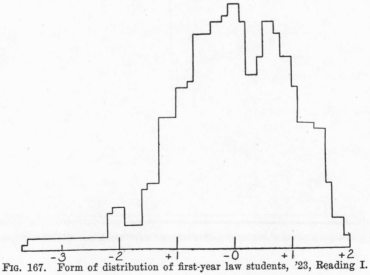

FIG. 167. Form of distribution of first-year law students, '23, Reading I.

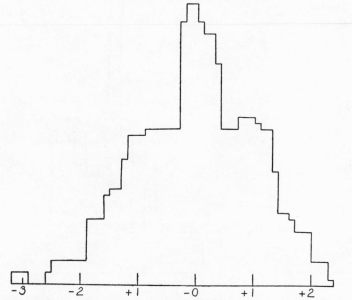

FIG. 168.  Form of distribution of first-year law students, '21, Total Score.

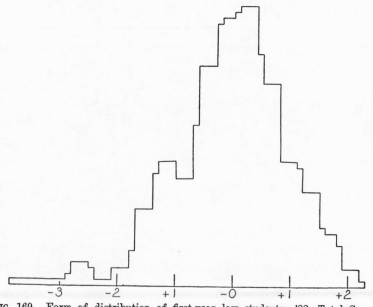

FIG. 169.  Form of distribution of first-year law students, '22, Total Score.

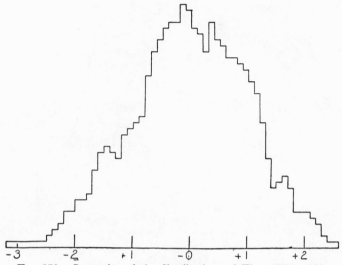

FIG. 170. Composite of the distributions of Figs. 155 to 160.

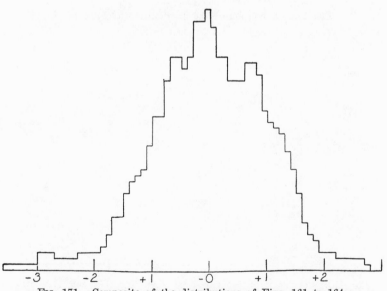

FIG. 171. Composite of the distributions of Figs. 161 to 164.

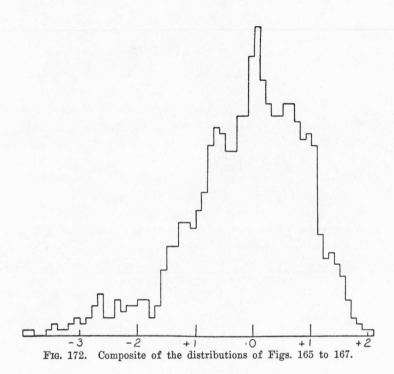

FIG. 172. Composite of the distributions of Figs. 165 to 167.

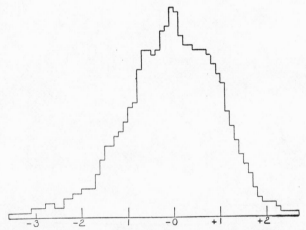

FIG. 173. Composite of the curves of Figs. 170, 171 and 172, with equal weight allowed to each.

the distribution of Table 165, which is that of Fig. 173 with some smoothing, as representing the probable form of distribution of altitude of intellect in the group of 240.

TABLE 165.

THE PROBABLE FORM OF DISTRIBUTION OF ALTITUDE OF INTELLECT IN GROUP 17 (LAW STUDENTS).

| Interval | Frequency permille | Interval | Frequency permille |
|---|---|---|---|
| L to L + 1 | ½ | L + 33 " L + 34 | 37 |
| L + 1 " L + 2 | ½ | L + 34 " L + 35 | 38 |
| L + 2 " L + 3 | ½ | L + 35 " L + 36 | 39 |
| L + 3 " L + 4 | ½ | L + 36 " L + 37 | 39½ |
| L + 4 " L + 5 | 1 | L + 37 " L + 38 | 39½ |
| L + 5 " L + 6 | 1 | L + 38 " L + 39 | 39½ |
| L + 6 " L + 7 | 1½ | L + 39 " L + 40 | 39½ |
| L + 7 " L + 8 | 1½ | L + 40 " L + 41 | 39 |
| L + 8 " L + 9 | 2 | L + 41 " L + 42 | 38 |
| L + 9 " L + 10 | 2 | L + 42 " L + 43 | 37 |
| L + 10 " L + 11 | 2½ | L + 43 " L + 44 | 36 |
| L + 11 " L + 12 | 2½ | L + 44 " L + 45 | 34½ |
| L + 12 " L + 13 | 2½ | L + 45 " L + 46 | 33 |
| L + 13 " L + 14 | 3 | L + 46 " L + 47 | 31 |
| L + 14 " L + 15 | 3½ | L + 47 " L + 48 | 29 |
| L + 15 " L + 16 | 4 | L + 48 " L + 49 | 25½ |
| L + 16 " L + 17 | 4½ | L + 49 " L + 50 | 22 |
| L + 17 " L + 18 | 5½ | L + 50 " L + 51 | 19 |
| L + 18 " L + 19 | 6 | L + 51 " L + 52 | 16 |
| L + 19 " L + 20 | 7 | L + 52 " L + 53 | 13½ |
| L + 20 " L + 21 | 8 | L + 53 " L + 54 | 11 |
| L + 21 " L + 22 | 9 | L + 54 " L + 55 | 8½ |
| L + 22 " L + 23 | 10 | L + 55 " L + 56 | 6 |
| L + 23 " L + 24 | 12 | L + 56 " L + 57 | 4 |
| L + 24 " L + 25 | 14 | L + 57 " L + 58 | 3½ |
| L + 25 " L + 26 | 16 | L + 58 " L + 59 | 3 |
| L + 26 " L + 27 | 18½ | L + 59 " L + 60 | 2½ |
| L + 27 " L + 28 | 21 | L + 60 " L + 61 | 1½ |
| L + 28 " L + 29 | 24 | L + 61 " L + 62 | 1½ |
| L + 29 " L + 30 | 27 | L + 62 " L + 63 | 1 |
| L + 30 " L + 31 | 30 | L + 63 " L + 64 | 1 |
| L + 31 " L + 32 | 33 | L + 64 " L + 65 | ½ |
| L + 32 " L + 33 | 35½ | L + 65 " L + 66 | ½ |

The percents correct for the four levels in question being 95.4, 77.1, 56.7, and 22.9, the values in terms of $\sigma$ distances from the median, are $-1.862$, $-.714$, $-.153$, and $+.738$ in terms of $\sigma_N$, $\sigma_O$, $\sigma_P$ and $\sigma_Q$, respectively.

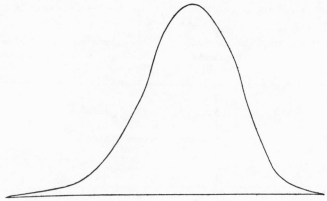

FIG. 174.  The distribution of Fig. 173, with some smoothing.

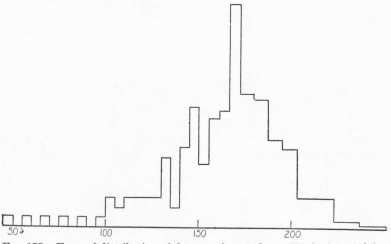

FIG. 175.  Form of distribution of first-year law students, '23, in Army Alpha, in equal units.

In the case of the 44 recruits, a normal form of distribution is assumed because nothing demonstrably better is suggested by the facts available.  These facts are: the reported amount of schooling, the distributions of scores for the group in Otis Intermediate, G.E. Form I (a General Electrical Information test) and the sum of the scores in Composites I, J, and K (but with the arithmetic of K estimated as $\frac{C + V + D}{3}$). They appear in Table 166.

TABLE 166.

DATA FOR ESTIMATING THE FORM OF DISTRIBUTION OF ALTITUDE OF INTELLECT IN THE GROUP AD. (44 RECRUITS).

| Grade Reached | | Otis Int. | | G. E. | | I + J + K | |
|---|---|---|---|---|---|---|---|
| Grade | Freq. | Score | Freq. | Score | Freq. | Score | Freq. |
| 3 or 4 | 1 | 15–19 | 4 | 3– 5 | 3 | 10–29 | 2 |
| 5 or 6 | 10 | 20–34 | 10 | 6– 9 | 6 | 30–49 | 9 |
| 7 or 8 | 18 | 35–49 | 13 | 10–13 | 26 | 50–69 | 9 |
| 9 or 10 | 11 | 50–64 | 12 | 14–17 | 8 | 70–89 | 11 |
| 11 or 12 | 3 | 65–79 | 4 | 18–21 | 2 | 90–109 | 10 |
| | | | | 22–25 | 0 | 110–129 | 3 |
| | | | | 26–29 | 1 | | |
| | | | | 30–33 | 0 | | |
| | | | | 34–37 | 0 | | |
| | | | | 38–41 | 1 | | |

# LIST OF REFERENCES

Anderson, J. E. '20.........Intelligence Tests of Yale Freshmen. School and Society 11: 417–420.

Bailor, E. M. '24.........Content and Form in Tests of Intelligence. Teachers College, Columbia University, Contributions to Education, No. 162, 1924.

Baldwin, B. T., and
Stecher, L. E. '22.........Mental Growth Curve of Normal and Superior Children. University of Iowa Studies 2: No. 1.

Binet, A. '16.........The Development of Intelligence. (English translation by Kite.)

Boas, F., and
Wissler, C. '06.........Statistics of Growth. Report of the U. S. Commissioner of Education for Year ending June 30, 1904, 1: 25–132.

Brooks, F. D. '21.........Changes in Mental Traits with Age, determined by Annual Re-tests. Teachers College, Columbia University, Contributions to Education, No. 116, 1921.

Bulletin, July 21, 1923...Bureau of Educational Research, University of North Carolina.

Burt, C. '21.........Mental and Scholastic Tests.

Carey, G. L., and
Kline, L. W. '23.........The Kline-Carey Measuring Scale for Free-hand Drawing. The Johns Hopkins University Studies in Education, No. 5a, 1923.

Clark, J. R. '25.........The Relation of Speed, Range, and Level to Scores on Intelligence Tests.

Cobb, M. V. '22.........The Limits Set to Educational Achievement by Limited Intelligence. Jour. Educational Psy. 13: 449–464 and 546–555.

Colvin, S. S. '22.........The Present Status of Mental Testing. Educational Review 64: 196–206 and 320–327.

Colvin, S. S., and
MacPhail, A. H. '22a....The Value of Psychological Tests at Brown University. School and Society 16: 113–122.

Colvin, S. S., and
MacPhail, A. H. '24.........The Intelligence of Seniors in the High Schools of Massachusetts. Dept. of the Interior, Bureau of Education, Bulletin No. 9, 1924.

Coxe, W. W. '21.........Variation in General Intelligence. Jour. of Educational Research 4: 187–194.

601

Haggerty, M. E. '23........Haggerty Intelligence Examination; Manual of Directions.

Hammarberg, Carl '93...Studier öfver Idiotiens Klinik och Patologi.

Hillegas, M. B. '12.........Scale for the Measurement of Quality in English Composition by Young People. Teachers College Record 13: 331–384.

Hollingworth, L. S. '23...The Psychology of Subnormal Children.

Kelley, T. L. '19.............The Measurement of Overlapping. Jour. Educational Psy. 10: 458–461.

Kelley, T. L. '21..... .......The Reliability of Test Scores. Jour. Educational Research 3: 370–379.

Kelley, T. L. '23............Statistical Method.

Kelley, T. L. '23a...........The Principles and Technique of Mental Measurement. American Jour. of Psy. 34: 408–432.

Madsen, J. N. '22............Intelligence as a Factor in School Progress. School and Society 15: 285ff.

Memoirs '21....................National Academy of Sciences. Psychological Examining in the U. S. Army, edited by Robert M. Yerkes 15: 1921.

Miller, W. S. '22............Miller Mental Ability Test. Manual of Direction First Revision for Forms A and B.

Myers, C. E., and
Myers, G. C. '21 ...........Measuring Minds.

Myers, C. E.,
Myers, G. C., and
Layton, S. H. '21..... .......Group Mental Testing in Altoona, Pa. School and Society 13: 624–628.

Noble, E. L., and
Arps, G. F. '20................University Students' Intelligence Ratings According to the Army Alpha Test. School and Society 11: 233–237.

Otis, A. S. '21.................Otis Group Intelligence Scale; Manual of Directions, 1921 Revision.

Pearson, K. '14...............Tables for Statisticians and Biometricians.

Pressey, S. L. '20...........A Brief Group Scale of Intelligence for Use in School Surveys. Jour. Educational Psy. 11: 89–100.

Ruch, G. M. '23.... ...........A Mental Educational Survey. Univ. of Iowa Studies in Education 2: No. 5.

Spearman, C. '04...........The Proof and Measurement of Association between Two Things. American Jour. of Psy. 15: 72–101.

Spearman, C. '07............Demonstration of Formulae for True Measurement of Correlation. American Jour. of Psy. 18: 161–169.

Spearman, C. '10............Correlation Calculated from Faulty Data. British Jour. of Psy. 3: 271–295.

Spearman, C. '13............Correlations of Sums and Differences. British Jour. of Psy. 5: 417–426.

Spearman, C. '23............The Nature of Intelligence and the Principles of Cognition.

Taylor, G. A. '23............An Inventory of the Minds of Individuals of Six and Seven Years Mental Age. Teachers College, Columbia University, Contributions to Education, No. 134, 1923.

Terman, L. M. '16............The Measurement of Intelligence.

Terman, L. M. '22............The Great Conspiracy or The Impulse Imperious of Intelligence Tests, Psychoanalyzed and Exposed by Mr. Lippmann. The New Republic 33: 116–120.

Terman, L. M. '23............Terman Group Test of Mental Ability for Grades 7 to 12; Manual of Directions.

Thomson, Godfrey H.
'24 ............................A Formula to Correct for the Effect of Errors of Measurement on the Correlation of Initial Values with Gains. Jour. of Experimental Psy. 3: 321–324.

Thorndike, E. L. '10.....Handwriting. Teachers College Record, II, No. 2.

Thorndike, E. L. '13......The Measurement of Achievement in Drawing. Teachers College Record 14: 1–39.

Thorndike, E. L. '13a...An Introduction to the Theory of Mental and Social Measurements.

Thorndike, E. L. '16.....Tests of Aesthetic Appreciation. Jour. Educational Psy. 7: 509–522.

Thorndike, E. L. '23.....On the Improvement in Intelligence Scores from Fourteen to Eighteen. Jour. Educational Psy. 14: 513–516.

Thorndike, E. L. '24.....The Influence of the Chance Imperfections of Measures upon the Relation of Initial Score to Gain or Loss. Jour. Experimental Psy. 3: 225–232.

Thorndike, E. L.,
Bregman, E. O., and
Cobb, M. V. '24............The Selection of Tasks of Equal Difficulty by a Consensus of Opinion. Jour. Educational Research 9: 133–139.

# 604 LIST OF REFERENCES

Thorndike, E. L., and
Bregman, E. O. '24........On the Form of Distribution of Intellect in the
Ninth Grade. Jour. Educational Research 10:
271–278.

Thurstone, L. L. '21........A Cycle-omnibus Intelligence Test for College
Students. Jour. Educational Research 4: 265–
278.

Trabue, M. R. '16............Completion-Test Language Scales. Teachers College, Columbia University, Contributions to Edu-
cation, No. 77.

Vincent, Leona M. '24...A Study of Intelligence Test Elements. Teachers
College, Columbia University, Contributions to
Education, No. 152, 1924.

Whipple, G. M. '22........Intelligence Tests in Colleges and Universities.
The 21st Yearbook of the National Society for
the Study of Education, Chap. X: 262.

Whipple, G. M. '23........The Intelligence Testing Program and its Objec-
tors—Conscientious and Otherwise. School and
Society 17: 561–568 and 596–604.

Yerkes, R. M. '20............Psychological Examining in the United States
Army. Memoirs, National Academy of Sciences,
15.

# INDEX

Abilities measurable by I. E. R. technique, 476

Ability, defined, 484; to deal with persons, things, ideas, by ideas, 413; to learn as criterion of intelligence, 17; to learn as intelligence test, 408ff.; vs. variability, 43ff., 56, 497ff.

Absolute vs. proportional counts of tasks, 383f.

Absolute zero, 294, 336f., 339ff., 471f., 482, 485f.; and Binet Scale, 403

Acceleration of level with age, negative, 467, 475

Accident, effect on form of distribution of intelligence, 272

Acquired vs. original ability, 95f., 433ff.

Adequacy of one CAVD level for measurement, 565ff.

Advantages from location of zero point, 339

Age changes in altitude and area, 463ff.; in specialized abilities, 468; grouping for intellectual difficulty, 28

Allowance for environmental effect on intelligence, 460ff.

Altitude, as related to width, 376; and nature vs. nurture, 458; and speed of learning, 409; and stock examination score, 403f., 405f.; curve with age, 463; measured without error, 577; of intellect, 24, 33, 104, 469

Ambiguity in content of tests, 1ff.

Analogies test, 9

Analysis of measurement into level, width, speed, 35ff.

Anatomical cause of intellect, 420

ANDERSON, J. E., 539, 541

Annoyers, 489f.

Applications of I. E. R. technique to measurement of human abilities, 476ff.

Arbitrariness in units, 1, 3ff.; in choice of tasks as intellectual, 61

Arbitrary scores transmuted to make variabilities equal, 520

Area of intellect, 24, 339, 378ff., 469; and nature vs. nurture, 458; and stock examination score, 404; as related to altitude and width, 378

Arithmetic problems, as tests, 9; composites, construction of, 193ff.

Army Alpha, 1, 2, 3, 6ff., 10, 15, 22f., 42, 44, 46, 49, 52, 55, 99, 227, 307, 403, 404, 410, 433, 437, 461, 475, 491, 494, 522, 528, 534, 539, 562, 586, 592; form of distribution, 291f.; letter ratings, 7; scores and officers' ratings, 405; scores in equal units, 228ff., 309, 316

Army Beta, 15, 18, 222, 433, 437, 506; form of distribution, 291f.

Army Examination a, 228, 475, 514, 522, 528, 562; form of distribution, 291f.; scores in equal units, 264ff., 309, 313, 316

ARPS, G. F., 539

Array, form of distribution of, to measure difficulty, 40, 54ff.; in correlation table to measure ability vs. variability, 505, 520

Arrays used to measure difficulty, 40

Associative vs. selective and generalizing thought, 414f.

Assumptions in measuring intellectual difficulty, 38, 59

Attenuation, formula, 60, 111, 177, 560f.; formulae used to find common part of tests, 406f., 429f.; corrected for in correlations, 424f.; in composites with few tasks, 556; in variability vs. ability, 500, 502, 506; used on correlations of Burt, 455f.

Average ability of individual, 493f.

Axioms of mental measurement re original and acquired ability, 436

605

# CLASSICS IN PSYCHOLOGY

AN ARNO PRESS COLLECTION

Angell, James Rowland. **Psychology: On Introductory Study of the Structure and Function of Human Consciousness.** 4th edition. 1908

Bain, Alexander. **Mental Science.** 1868

Baldwin, James Mark. **Social and Ethical Interpretations in Mental Development.** 2nd edition. 1899

Bechterev, Vladimir Michailovitch. **General Principles of Human Reflexology.** [1932]

Binet, Alfred and Th[éodore] Simon. **The Development of Intelligence in Children.** 1916

Bogardus, Emory S. **Fundamentals of Social Psychology.** 1924

Buytendijk, F. J. J. **The Mind of the Dog.** 1936

Ebbinghaus, Hermann. **Psychology: An Elementary Text-Book.** 1908

Goddard, Henry Herbert. **The Kallikak Family.** 1931

Hobhouse, L[eonard] T. **Mind in Evolution.** 1915

Holt, Edwin B. **The Concept of Consciousness.** 1914

Külpe, Oswald. **Outlines of Psychology.** 1895

Ladd-Franklin, Christine. **Colour and Colour Theories.** 1929

**Lectures Delivered at the 20th Anniversary Celebration of Clark University.** (Reprinted from *The American Journal of Psychology*, Vol. 21, Nos. 2 and 3). 1910

Lipps, Theodor. **Psychological Studies.** 2nd edition. 1926

Loeb, Jacques. **Comparative Physiology of the Brain and Comparative Psychology.** 1900

Lotze, Hermann. **Outlines of Psychology.** [1885]

McDougall, William. **The Group Mind.** 2nd edition. 1920

Meier, Norman C., editor. **Studies in the Psychology of Art: Volume III.** 1939

Morgan, C. Lloyd. **Habit and Instinct.** 1896

Münsterberg, Hugo. **Psychology and Industrial Efficiency.** 1913

Murchison, Carl, editor. **Psychologies of 1930.** 1930

Piéron, Henri. **Thought and the Brain.** 1927

Pillsbury, W[alter] B[owers]. **Attention.** 1908

[Poffenberger, A. T., editor]. **James McKeen Cattell: Man of Science.** 1947

Preyer, W[illiam] **The Mind of the Child:** Parts I and II. 1890/1889

**The Psychology of Skill:** Three Studies. 1973

Reymert, Martin L., editor. **Feelings and Emotions:** The Wittenberg Symposium. 1928

Ribot, Th[éodule Armand]. **Essay on the Creative Imagination.** 1906

Roback, A[braham] A[aron]. **The Psychology of Character.** 1927

**I. M. Sechenov:** Biographical Sketch and Essays. (Reprinted from *Selected Works* by I. Sechenov). 1935

Sherrington, Charles. **The Integrative Action of the Nervous System.** 2nd edition. 1947

Spearman, C[harles]. **The Nature of 'Intelligence' and the Principles of Cognition.** 1923

Thorndike, Edward L. **Education: A First Book.** 1912

Thorndike, Edward L., E. O. Bregman, M. V. Cobb, et al. **The Measurement of Intelligence.** [1927]

Titchener, Edward Bradford. **Lectures on the Elementary Psychology of Feeling and Attention.** 1908

Titchener, Edward Bradford. **Lectures on the Experimental Psychology of the Thought-Processes.** 1909

Washburn, Margaret Floy. **Movement and Mental Imagery.** 1916

Whipple, Guy Montrose. **Manual of Mental and Physical Tests:** Parts I and II. 2nd edition. 1914/1915

Woodworth, Robert Sessions. **Dynamic Psychology.** 1918

Wundt, Wilhelm. **An Introduction to Psychology.** 1912

Yerkes, Robert M. **The Dancing Mouse** and **The Mind of a Gorilla.** 1907/1926

DATE DUE